LANGUAGE
IN
AMERICA

Charlton Laird

PRENTICE-HALL, INC.
Englewood Cliffs, New Jersey

First PRISM PAPERBACK edition, 1972
Published by arrangement with The World Publishing Company

ISBN: 0–13–522722–4
Library of Congress Catalog Card Number 68–29790

Printed in the United States of America
10   9   8   7   6   5   4   3   2   1

Prentice-Hall International, Inc. (London)
Prentice-Hall of Australia, Pty. Ltd. (Sydney)
Prentice-Hall of Canada, Ltd. (Toronto)
Prentice-Hall of India Private Limited (New Delhi)
Prentice-Hall of Japan, Inc. (Tokyo)

For Robert M. and Johnnie Belle Gorrell

PREFACE

Presumably, no one now living knows enough to write this book. Certainly I do not. Ideally, to write about relationships, one should completely understand the related components, but in this instance no one does. Pierre Teilhard de Chardin, developing brilliantly the story of mankind, insisted that he was overcome by his subject; and the last quarter century has amply demonstrated that even Leonard Bloomfield and Edward Sapir, in spite of their monumental works, had much to learn about language. Yet some subjects cry out for consideration even though no one can consider them well, and surely among these are the interrelations of man and his greatest tool.

Perhaps for this reason—the impossibility of writing an adequate book—few scholars have seriously broached such subjects, and fewer still have written on them in terms that the layman can be expected to understand. Naturally, I am not suggesting that I elected to discuss the impact of language upon man and of man upon language simply because so few others have done so; but if the publisher needs any defense for having brought this book into print, perhaps the paucity of serious studies will exonerate him. I might add, however, that in writing this book I am aware that I join a very large body of sinners, guilty of sins of omission—whatever may have been my sins of commission—and that in an attempt of this sort one writes with all his sins upon him, sins unremitted and unremissible.

Perhaps a word may be in order as to what the book is not, and is not intended to be. It is not mainly original research. I have tried to employ the proved research of others where I knew this to be available, and I can only regret that inevitably I have missed some of it, but I have deliberately done original investigation only when evidence I needed seemed not to have been published—as, for instance, that concerning the influence of Horne Tooke on Noah Webster and the dialectal spread of significant locutions in England and Spain. Likewise, as any scholar will recognize, the book is not mainly a documented survey of existing research. I have endeavored to use the best studies available, and I have intended to document sufficiently to reveal the main lines of my reading and to acknowledge my major indebtednesses, although hundreds of articles from which I have drawn material have gone uncited. Nor have I endeavored to be comprehensive. I have employed comparative approaches to reveal what I hope are fresh insights, and I have tried to propound questions, whether answerable or not, that have seemed to me insufficiently propounded, perhaps even to draw conclusions not frequently dwelt upon, but I have made no attempt to survey all the available material or even to provide a well balanced selection from it. I have tried to reveal, not to review.

Most of my indebtedness is hinted at in the notes, and in a world where justice is seldom done, those hints must suffice. Some help and kindness, however, are of the sorts that do not find their way readily into footnotes. I am grateful to the University of Nevada for a funded leave which made possible my research in Europe and the leisure with which I completed the first draft of the manuscript, and especially to former President Charles J. Armstrong, who convinced me that I should accept this subvention, even though, at my age, the university was not likely to derive much direct benefit. I am indebted to many representatives and former representatives of the publisher during the ten years in which the book was being planned and the manuscript developed, perhaps notably to Benjamin D. Zevin, David Keightley, Richard T. Congdon, Joseph Friend, and David Guralnik, whose generous aid far exceeded the call of duty. Others, colleagues and friends, have assisted in many ways, especially in reading and criticizing earlier drafts of the manuscript; they include Robert M. Gorrell, whose editorial acumen and solid scholarship saved me from many a slip; Helene Laird, who understands among other things her husband's inability to discard outmoded possessions, including inept prose; Donald Fowler and Wayne Suttles, who cannot be held responsible for the mistakes I have made in dealing with Amerindian archaeology and linguistics, but who are responsible for many I did not make in the final draft; and Sven Liljeblad, who not only read the entire manuscript with great perception but also put at my disposal his own unpublished research into the languages of the Great Basin.

CHARLTON LAIRD
University of Nevada

CONTENTS

PART ONE

THE AMERINDIANS: LANGUAGE AT HOME

I

MAN'S MAN-MADE MYSTERY

Man has been variously described as a praying animal, a talking animal, a tool-using animal. He might also be called a mystery moving among mysteries, mysteries mainly not of his making. Man has long seen that he is ignorant of whence he came and why, of where he lives and when; he does not know when time began or where space begins and ends, if it does; and the more he learns about the mind and the emotions, the more he realizes that man does not know what he is. With all these mysteries he has had little to do, except to study them and to be baffled by them, or to accept them and mainly to ignore them. But some mysteries he has devised himself, and the greatest of his inventions is also the greatest of the man-made mysteries. We call it language, and this book is intended to ask questions about it, even though many of the questions appear unanswerable. After all, that is what mysteries are good for, to entertain questions but to provide no answers.

We must assume, if we care to study language, that man made it, because it works as though he had, although thinkers have at times asserted or assumed the contrary. Divines and others have declared, even confidently and vehemently, that God gave man language as a single gift, whole and adequate, and if not immutable, needing no mutation. Among Christian peoples the gift was once believed to have come from the Christian deity, and the principal argument was not about whether or not He gave language, nor about how much He gave, but about where and when He gave it. Among the apologists was Noah Webster, founder of the American lexicographical tradition, who in some ways was a radical about language but not in this, for he introduced his great dictionary by asking where and when the miracle occurred.[1] He concluded that Jehovah gave language to Adam at once, or

---

[1] Noah Webster, *An American Dictionary of the English Language,* 2 vols. (New York: S. Converse, 1828). The books are unpaged, but the passage occurs on the first page of the introduction.

at least before He made Eve. And what of Eve? Did she have to pick up language from her husband by mere human means, while he lorded it over her with his divinely granted power? If so, she was an apt linguist, for she was soon conversing not only with her husband, but also with the Serpent. Or did Jehovah devise a second miracle for her? Was it the old miracle repeated, or did He, perhaps profiting from His experience with Adam's masculine ineptitude with language, provide a different and better miracle for Eve?

Were there, in Eden, in all the time of the world uniquely two people who had exactly the same language and the same use of it because they had it by the same miracle, and did the Almighty here initiate woman's supposed fondness for talk? Webster seems not to have raised the question, and if he did not, he missed an opportunity, for good follower of Genesis that he was, he rather liked to derogate the female of the species. Webster might also have asked when the Lord ceased directing language by miracles. Whenever He did, Webster seems to have trusted that by the eighteenth century the language was no longer God's business but, at least in the United States, Webster's business. This was perhaps Webster's great virtue, as well as his characteristic vice, that he deeply pondered some matters and triumphantly ignored some others.

Rather curiously, earlier thinkers tended to ignore a lack of explanation about the origin of language. Myths account for the making of the world—a maiden gave birth to it, a muskrat dredged it up from the eternal muck, a raven brought it from the skies, or Jehovah laid it bare by separating the waters below from the waters above and creating a firmament to hold up the waters. The myths also account for the making of man—a coyote, or a rattlesnake, or almost anything made him out of dirt and spittle, roots and flowers, ribs, or whatnot. But language is very commonly accepted without much explanation about its origin. Jehovah had no sooner made Adam than He started talking with him; in fact, they progressed so rapidly that they were soon discussing such problems as sex and epistemology. The animals that in many parts of the world were conceived of as preceding man—the coyotes, the ravens, the sea otters—seem to have had no trouble talking with each other or with man, when there were men.

However language got started, man has been remaking it ever since; few gift horses have been so industriously looked in the mouth as has language. All about us is evidence that language is changing every day, and this change is more extensive and more pervasive than most people can understand, probably more pervasive than anyone can understand, even the close students of language. Patterns of speech have been shaping ever since our earliest linguistic records, and these patterns must have been old when our records were new. Furthermore, language seems to respond to the needs and wants of people; that is, man seems to be able, albeit unconsciously, to refashion language, and thus if we are to study speech we must ask questions about man and language, not only questions about each alone.

What questions should we ask? Perhaps some of the best questions are these—best in the sense that the answers would be interesting if available: How, when, and where did man devise language? What has he done to it since he devised it? What has it done to him?

From some points of view these are not the best questions. Many students of language as a science believe—and I respect them for this— that one should ask only those questions that can be answered with scientific accuracy and scientific certainty; all others should be postponed, perhaps indefinitely. Of course there is an opposite view. One can believe, also, that any question that has a simple and certain answer is only a minor question, and that in any subject as vast and varied and baffling as language, any question which has a certain answer is not good enough, at least not good enough to carry us very far. In the end it depends on the kind of questions one likes to ask, those that have easy answers or those that may have no answers at all. For better or for worse, in this book I shall endeavor to ask good questions, and to acknowledge ignorance where we can find no answers.

To our questions, then. The first—how, when, and where did language appear—I shall not consider seriously. Not that it is an unfruitful question, but for reasons that will eventually appear, this is the wrong time to discuss it, and I am the wrong person. During the last century so many ingenious speculators devised so many contradictory guesses and managed to ridicule one another's guesses with such amusing epithets —the bow-wow theory, the moo-moo theory, the whistle and grunt theory—that the whole question became rather a joke, and serious students despaired of talking or even of thinking about the origin of language. Fortunately, this self-imposed deaf-mutism is passing. Fresh thought and new tools are giving us whole new approaches to the study of the origin of language. The nineteenth-century thinkers, realizing that language works on an oral basis, assumed that they should seek the origin of language in sound. The result was babel. Later, more thoughtful people, Vendryes[2] for example, suggested that language has its origin in man's mind, not in his larynx; if this is true, language may be

---

[2] This is mainly intended to be a thoughtful book, rather than a scholarly one, but I shall endeavor to indicate my sources in a general way. I refer here to J. Vendryes, *Language: A Linguistic Introduction to History,* trans. Paul Radin (New York: Alfred A. Knopf, 1951), original, 1921.

so native to man that it grew as he became human, and there may never have been a time or place where anything that could be called language moved through anything that could be called an origin.

More recently still, other avenues have opened, including an approach through art and philosophy—an approach that explains language as having developed by what is sometimes called symbolic transformation.[3] Stemming notably from the late Ernst Cassirer, this approach relies upon the pervading power of symbol. The symbol, Cassirer proposed, is the tool by which man orders the universe; with it he simplifies and makes understandable the enigmatic world in which he moves. With it he transforms the myriad into unity, the ungraspable into art, the imponderable into myth, and the whole into language. Thus language comes into being as the means of the mind, for although it is not the only source of symbol, it provides much the largest and most useful body of symbol that man has ever devised. If this interpretation is valid, then the source of language is to be sought in man's symbol-making power, and language forms as man becomes human.

Another approach is now available to us, an old one that has lately gained new support. A scholar can try to think his way back to origins, as Cassirer and his predecessor Wilhelm Von Humboldt did, or he can try to work his way back, as the philologists have done, going through Latin, Greek, Gothic, and Sanskrit, trying to reconstruct completely extinct languages such as Indo-European or Indo-Hittite, and using these languages as platforms from which to project still farther back. This method has permitted us to describe the growth of language, but thus far it has produced nothing that suggests a language in its early formative stages. Now we have new devices; assuming that language spread from a center or centers, we can examine surviving languages as though they were flotsam scattered by concentric waves. This method has been delayed because it required the accumulation of vast hordes of linguistic detail from all over the world and the sifting and evaluating of that detail. When the detail was assembled, however, the bulk was so vast that no unaided human brain could deal with it. However, computers permit analyses of these facts, analyses which would have been unthinkable twenty years ago. For example, the quantitative evaluation of surviving speech has suggested that languages that have subsequently spread in all directions developed in Central Asia, but the substantiation

---

[3] A good introduction to this approach is provided in Susanne K. Langer, *Philosophy in a New Key* (Cambridge, Mass.: Harvard University Press, 1942); Mentor MD101, 1948, and apparently to be kept in print. A recent development of the traditional approach appears in A. S. Diamond, *The History and Origin of Language* (New York: Philosophical Library, 1959).

of any such guess is many computer-hours away.[4] Meanwhile a layman can notice that, as regards the origins of language, these are exciting times for the experts, but inconclusive times for the observers.

In one sense we seem to have lost the power of making language. In any real sense we probably have not, but nobody any longer initiates language, not at least as I am thinking about language. True, people make up what are called languages, artificial means of speaking and writing; Esperanto is the best known of them, and it seems to be adequate for many purposes, but it is of course quite different from language as a living entity rooted in people's lives, and its inception has nothing to do with the origin of language. Language must somehow have grown from the need of mankind and the nature of man's being. Esperanto was put together from linguistic bits already long-devised and currently in use.

To observe this is to make no adverse comment on Esperanto. As a devised means of communication it should have been constructed from the tested materials of natural languages, as it was, but the devised and the natural are two different sorts of things. Language, in the sense in which I am using the word, seems no longer to come into being unconsciously from native materials. All human beings have language, and none of them feels the need for different or better language sufficiently to start all over again. They rework the language they have. Of course they rework language with symbol, at least in part; all words are symbols. Thus the means with which we remake language, the urge that leads us to remake it, may be the same tools and the same urge with which we made language in the first place, although we now use them differently. Whether or not we do, that is not the problem of this book.

Let us turn, then, to the other two questions I propounded—what has man done to language, and what has language done to man? Presumably, as man fashions and refashions his principal tool, he adapts the tool to his purpose and to his hand. But what of the tool? Does it leave calluses on the hand, different calluses from different uses of the tool, and from different forms of the basic tool, as a hoe and a hammer leave different calluses, and as the calluses differ when the tools are used in different ways? That is, man has shaped his linguistic tools, but have the tools then reshaped man, at least to a degree? These are vague-answer questions, but they may not be impossible questions—not even the second, the answer to which is likely to be the more vague of the two—provided we are prepared to be content with cautious guesses and

---

[4] See, for example, Morris Swadesh, "Linguistic Overview," *Prehistoric Man in the New World,* ed. Jesse J. Jennings and Edward Norbeck (Chicago: William Marsh Rice University and The University of Chicago Press, 1964), pp. 527–56.

tentative answers. And here we might remind ourselves that certainties are rare sorts of birds anyhow, and that an account of the supposed certainties which became uncertainties, which became downright error, would provide a revealing history of scholarship, science, philosophy, and theology, not to mention the most respectable professions, such as law and medicine.

Let us, then, try to consider these questions, aware that our answers may be neither precise nor certain, but that we may see something in language we had not noticed before if we approach it in a new light and from a different angle. To attempt this, I propose that we take one portion of the earth's surface, treat it as a natural laboratory, and ask ourselves what has happened here. In this way we may hope to be as objective and scientific as the material itself permits. I propose, further, that we use the Americas, with attention centered on what has become the United States, although with side glances calculated to assure us that the evidence from within our borders is typical.

Perhaps the obvious reason for choosing the Americas in general and the United States in particular is that I know more about this area than I do about any other, but more objective reasons for the choice could be adduced. As for choosing the United States, it comprises the largest single body of highly cultured individuals in the two continents, and in going from barbarism to automation we are spanning a cultural spread as wide as any we can hope to encounter. Furthermore, the descendants of the aborigines who lived north of the Rio Grande have been studied more, and on the whole more scientifically studied, than have those farther south. They have not endured so well in the flesh, but they have survived better in the monograph. As for treating the Americas as against some portion of Europe or Asia, the New World offers us relatively restricted materials. In time we are dealing mainly with hundreds, not with thousands or even tens of thousands of years. In language we are dealing with two eras and two main movements only, those associated with aborigines, the Indians, and those associated with white men, white men from a restricted area, mainly western Europe, an area showing relatively little linguistic variety. Furthermore, for our restricted time and limited social diversity we have a comparatively large amount of available evidence. About most of the preliterate languages of Europe and Asia we can only conjecture; they are long dead, and if they were studied in their own day, the studies have not survived. In the Americas, on the contrary, preliterate languages still flourish, and languages now extinct or nearly so have been studied with care by learned men using reliable techniques.

Likewise, the societies which have fostered this linguistic evidence provide interesting contrasts. The Indians inhabited the continents for thousands of years, living in varied societies and continuing in them long enough that the resulting cultures may be thought of as stable. These peoples did not invent language; they brought their language or languages with them, but they lived here long enough for the languages to divide into language families and subfamilies, as we believe languages have tended everywhere to divide. On the whole, the aborigines remained relatively primitive, but they included considerable spreads of society—from those who lived mainly on roots, rodents, reptiles, seeds, and insects, to the sophisticated Mayas. Thus the Indians provide us an example of language in a native, stable society.

The white civilization in the Americas, on the other hand, represents society in movement, an invading society, and from our point of view, an invading language or sets of related languages. Furthermore, whereas the Indians were characterized by their poverty of material goods and by their variety of culture, the invading peoples were notable for their material and cultural wealth and their social unity. Unity may seem a strange word to typify Frenchmen, Englishmen, Spaniards, and Portuguese who were industriously shooting one another, but even when they shot they used the same sorts of weapons. They sailed the same types of ships, married by the same rites, read the same books, and worshiped the same God. Even linguistically they were allied; English is closer to French than Eskimo is to Arawak. Furthermore, many a Frenchman could speak both English and Spanish, but it is probably safe to assume that no Eskimo ever learned Arawak.

When we try to think about mankind we have these three essentials— habitable land, people, and language. With land and man, civilization became possible, but only with language did civilization become a reality. With language man could communicate and could preserve what all men had developed; with symbol embodied in language man could order what seemed a world of chaos; with language he could school patterns in his own mind. Let us endeavor to study this essential trinity, then, and let us endeavor to find out what man did to language and language did to man in the Americas, confident that we have here a revealing body of evidence. Our sample will not be entirely typical; no sample ever is; but where would we find another body of evidence at once so typical, so significant, and so handy?

2

LANGUAGE MOVES INTO EMPTY CONTINENTS

In view of the land and the speech involved, the linguistic habitation of the Americas was doubtless the greatest single language movement of all time. Perhaps fifty thousand years ago—to make a relatively safe guess—the Americas provided the greatest unlanguaged land mass in the world. The land area which we think of as Africa, Europe, and Asia had been the home of man from below Rhodesia to beyond Peking for tens of thousands, or hundreds of thousands of years. Man had spawned languages, which had spawned other languages, and languages had been triumphing over each other, borrowing, developing, spreading, and dying, as languages do. Meanwhile, in the Americas there was no language, nor, so far as we know, any creature capable of developing and using language.

Then the inhabitants came. We cannot call their movement a conquest, for no one opposed them, and they probably did not know they were invading. We assume they were hunters and, after the manner of hunters, were pursuing game. As they hunted they brought their language with them, and within the course of some thousands of years the two continents were full of them, or as full as the continents could be, granted the immigrants' rather limited means of finding a living. By the time for which we have extensive linguistic evidence of them, they had developed hundreds of languages in dozens of major language families, and had spread from beyond one arctic circle almost to the other. Such blossoming from one language movement or series of similar movements must have been unprecedented.

Let us examine that blossoming, but first we must notice the land to be inhabited. It consists of two large triangles, rather similar in shape, the base to the north and the tip to the south, the triangles joined by a narrow waist, and the whole lying somewhat above the middle of the earth longitudinally. Thus the broad portion of the northern continent continues roughly from the arctic circle through the temperate zone, and has more land with a temperate climate than has the southern continent, which has its broad area adjacent to the equator. This torrid belt, however, passes over mountain uplands, so that large areas are temperate from altitude if not from latitude. Conversely, wide flatlands of the northern continent are but sparsely habitable because of either cold or drought. Both continents contain portions of two series of mountain ranges which run roughly north and south along the east and west sides with a wide plain between. In both continents the eastern range is much eroded. Some adjacent islands thrust up between the continents to the east; they may be thought of as portions of the old eastern mountain ranges, mostly submerged. At the northwest corner the continents approach the Eurasian land mass, and presumably have been connected to it. To the northeast, connection is not impossible, but would have been remote in time. The continents were well stocked with reptiles, birds, fish, and animals; they had been isolated from the Eurasian land mass long enough for distinct species to develop. Eurasian species inhabiting tropical areas only, hippopotamuses and rhinoceroses for example, are not found in the Americas. This fact would seem to confirm that the last connection of the Americas with Eurasia was to the north; the temperate and cold portions of the southern continent are far from any large mass of land.

Such is the scene of our two "experiments" in living language. Fundamentally, it has not changed much in the thirty to fifty thousand years in which we are interested. The mountain ranges were where they are now, the seacoasts have not varied greatly; most of the major river systems had been developed. Superficially, however, there have been considerable differences, mainly because of changes in climate. At times ice packs developed, so huge that they pushed down across the northern continent, damming rivers, gouging lakes, flattening prairies, and redistributing great areas of the earth's crust. These accumulations of ice absorbed so much of the earth's water that the ocean level was reduced, with corresponding minor but significant shifts in coast lines. At times the climate was so dry that lands now fertile were desert; at other times moisture was so plentiful that lands now fertile were swamps, and areas now desert were capable of supporting considerable populations—in the southwestern United States, for example.

Let us now turn to the time, and here we are in some trouble, because time is often less determinable than space. Or at least our concept of it is less precise, partly because we have several sorts of time, which overlap but do not mesh neatly. We can start with geologic time, which reaches back of anything we need, but as it becomes recent it remains inexact. Then we have archaeologic time, which does not go back far enough and tends to be spotty. It sometimes provides us with tables of sequences, but with few dates to objectify the relationships within the tables. Coupled with chemical time through carbon dating and similar devices, archaeologic time can become relatively exact, but only for certain artifacts discovered under favorable circumstances. Then we have historic time; for some parts of the world it covers thousands of years, but for the Americas never more than a few hundred years, and for many parts of the Americas not more than a few decades. Some parts of South America have, in effect, no history at all; if any civilized men have been there they have left few records. Then there is linguistic time, in some ways the most remarkable of all, but of very uneven worth and difficult to use. If language goes back to the dawn of civilization, then language has been producing evidence for many tens of thousands of years, and some of these early linguistic phenomena must have influenced later developments, and thus can provide derived evidence, but for millennia all this remains very vague. Primitive Group A speaks a language unlike that of Primitive Group B, but curiously similar to the speech of Primitive Group C. We know that Groups A and C share something that neither shares with B, but what they share is often not clear. Linguistic time stretches back into geologic time, down through archaeologic time, and through historic time, but usually not until recently does it become exact. Thus our account of time in the Americas must be something of a jumble, a magpie's nest of snatchings from here and there, but perhaps we can make something of it.

The scene opens less—perhaps much less—than fifty thousand years ago, toward the end of what geologists call the Pleistocene Epoch, during one of the periods of great polar ice caps, when glaciers plowed down into Europe and North America, advancing and receding for millennia, only to advance again. Men were common in the Afro-Eurasian land mass; few if any of them had become anything more sophisticated than hunters and seed-gatherers, mostly nomadic. At the time, world civilization was in what we call the late Old Stone Age; that is, men had developed techniques which permitted the making of useful tools by simple chipping. The bow and arrow had not yet been invented, and sedentary life had not become possible because man had not discovered that shellfish could be food or that seeds could be scattered deliberately on alluvial plains. The most powerful weapon was probably the spear, since in the hands of a strong man it could be lethal, and it permitted the wielder to remain at a distance from his opponent beyond teeth and claws. Presumably the first immigrants to the Americas were not the most sophisticated men of their day; the tundras of northeast Asia would not have supported advanced culture centers, but inventions in one portion of the Afro-Eurasian land mass spread in time to other portions, so that we may assume that those who imported language to the Americas would not have been many thousands or tens of thousands of years behind their fellows to the south.

We cannot date the coming accurately.[1] For a time we had nothing more than rough guesses to date anything early, except that men had filled both continents, and must have been some thousands of years doing it, but dates back of two or three thousand B.C. were commonly dismissed as unrealistic and probably ridiculous. Some geologic evidence suggested earlier dates, but geology is rough with few revealing finds. Then tree-ring dating was developed. This technique rests upon the discovery that trees, especially in areas of sparse and varying precipitation, grow thicker and thinner rings depending upon the variability of available water, and that the patterns of weather, and hence of tree rings, are so numerous and characteristic that a given sequence of thick and thin rings never repeats, at least not within centuries that can be confused with one another, especially when tree-ring sequences are sorted out by data processing machines. Accordingly, if an archaeologist finds a considerable piece of charcoal, he may be able to determine when the tree lived, or if he finds a log imbedded in a building, he can determine the exact year in which the tree was felled and hence the probable date of the building. This discovery provided accurate dates and sequences for many cultures, especially in the southwestern United States, but the technique was useful mainly for sophisticated cultures, for people who constructed something more elaborate than rock shelters, and for climates in which timbers survived rot and termites. Thus tree-ring dating told us little about the primitive American Indians directly; it did give us dates for sedentary cultures in certain areas, and thus allowed us to assume that nomadic America must have existed for

---

[1] For a readable and generally reliable account to its date, see Ruth M. Underhill, *Red Man's America* (Chicago: University of Chicago Press, 1953). More technical are Gordon R. Willey and Philip Phillips, *Method and Theory in American Archaeology* (Chicago: University of Chicago Press, 1958), and Harold Edson Driver, *Indians of North America* (Chicago: University of Chicago Press, 1961). For a popular account, see Frank C. Hibben, *Digging Up America* (New York: Hill and Wang, 1966); for a recent collection of data centered in the valley of Mexico, see *Ancient Oaxaca* (Stanford, Calif.: Stanford University Press, 1966). In what follows, I have relied on these works and somewhat on the most recent summary at this writing, Alex D. Krieger, "Early Man in the New World," *Prehistoric Man in the New World,* ed. Jennings and Norbeck (cited earlier), pp. 23–81, with extensive bibliography. Krieger has a volume in process; he is generally more hospitable to early datings than are most of his fellows.

some thousands of years prior to the first cliffhouse, but did not warrant guesses earlier than about 6000–8000 B.C.

Then came carbon dating. Carbon dissipates at a known rate by radioactivity, and hence any carbon-containing object that is not so old that radioactivity has ceased can be dated roughly, say within a few hundred years. If we find a bit of camel dung, we can discover when the camel defecated, and if we find a mummy wrapped in a blanket made of sagebrush bark and rabbit fur, we can determine roughly when the mummy bones began to deteriorate and when the rabbit had been scurrying among the sagebrush. With this tool, and with greatly increased activity in American archaeology during the last quarter century, our whole understanding of American antiquity has changed. Datings are now so accurate and so numerous that no one can doubt anymore that all parts of North America were inhabited prior to about 10,000 B.C., and not much after that, South America was populated, even to Tierra del Fuego. We are now getting radiocarbon datings at 10,000 B.C. or earlier for Venezuela, the higher portions of Brazil, and at various points in the Andes. Furthermore, by about this time hand grinding stones appear very widely, suggesting—what we know on other grounds—that the big game was becoming scarce, and human beings were turning more to seed-gathering for subsistence. That is, prior to 10,000 B.C. we must account for a considerable period of a hunting culture using projectile points, and a preprojectile period when the spear was the principal weapon.

How much more time must we allow? The question is very lively, being fought out in the journals, and has been since the 1930's, when a campsite in Colorado was dated by competent geologists ca. 25,000 B.C. Subsequently somewhat similar dates were attached to finds in Utah, Arizona, New Mexico, Nevada, and California; one in Texas was dated 30,000 B.C., and another in the Snake River Valley in Idaho, 43,000 B.C. More or less doubt has been cast on most of the earliest dates, however, partly because early supposed human habitations seem to be difficult to distinguish from the nests of various rodents, and because delicate problems of stratification and its disturbance by natural forces are likely to turn apparent evidence into a tissue of *probables* or *possibles*. Thus conservative archaeologists—and one must be conservative in these matters—hesitate to use dates back of about 12,000 B.C. Meanwhile, we might notice that American archaeology is only well begun, that dates have gone mainly in one direction during the past half century, and that we have no reason to suppose that this back-dating is about to stop. Thus we can now think of about a millennium and a half of linguistic growth in the Americas and possibly more—even much more

—especially for small groups, notably in places difficult of access, like much of Alaska. And even the smallest groups would have brought language with them.

For our purposes the date of the earliest Amerindian immigration need not be precise, since for a considerable period prior to 12,000 B.C. the Northwest invited human habitation. The ice cap had absorbed so much moisture that at times the sea level dropped more than 175 feet below its present height; 120 feet would presumably have been enough to expose the sea bottom between what are now Alaska and Siberia, and this land bridge must have been wide enough and must have existed long enough so that any number of men could have passed over, quite un-aware that they were participating in a natural Red Sea miracle. Even if this calculation is wrong, and there was no land bridge, there would presumably have been an ice bridge. Men could have walked from Asia to North America, and we assume they did.

They had reason to come. Presumably they were nomads, accustomed to hunt to the south of the shifting glaciers, killing animals that fed on the lush growth promoted by melting ice. A feast awaited them in Alaska. The climate was then warmer than it is now, and in the interior, at present mainly barren tundra, was a great green bowl protected from the glaciers by a ring of mountains. Here grew great trees whose petri-fied logs have been found associated with the bones of mastodons. Spear points are scattered over the region, and at the foot of a sea cliff at Cape Prince of Wales—the sea cliff was far inland when the sea level was low—such a heap of mastodon ivory survived that carving mastodon tusks has been a major industry with the Eskimo for many years. During the same period, the adjacent Alaskan coast was also ice-free, as was the Mackenzie Valley.

What happened can be reconstructed. Siberian hunters, working east-ward, found themselves in a Pleistocene paradise which provided them with all sorts of game, even with the opportunity to stampede mastodons over cliffs. The word filtered back, and more hunters came. Eventually, they spilled out of the green bowl of Alaska, probably by the Mackenzie River, possibly along the Liard and the route taken today by the Alcan Highway. As the glaciers receded, the hunters spread into the central North American basin and to what is now the southwestern United States, which had an equable climate and at that time adequate mois-ture. Thus before 10,000 B.C., a language with various dialects, or various languages of one or more language families, were scattered over considerable portions of what is now the United States and Canada.

What were these languages? We have no way of knowing, at least not yet, although we are not without guesses. The likeliest place to look, of course, is on either side of the Bering Strait, and here we have evidence. The Chukchian languages on the Asiatic side show strong resemblances to the Eskaleutian languages on the American side, although relationship must have been relatively late, since the languages seem not to have diverged greatly. The Eskimo and Aleut movements are assumed to be the last to the Americas, and these languages are not closely related to stocks farther south. If a Chukchian tongue had come early, we should expect its characteristics to be widespread.

As I write, a more interesting prospect seems to be developing, and even if nothing should come of it, it provides one of those stories that suggest the dramatic and aberrant things that sometimes happen in language study. It involves John P. Harrington, an amazing person, who for more than half a century was likely to pop up wherever something interesting happened in studies of American antiquity. One got letters from him, typed in his inimitable manner, on a long-suffering, seemingly ancient typewriter, and with his characteristic typographical errors. He became interested in the Costanoan languages—part of a larger body of languages known as Penutian—which were spoken by various groups of Indians that in historic times lived to the south of San Francisco Bay, along the coast and in the adjacent mountains, in a belt fifty miles or so wide and perhaps three times as long. The speakers were numerous, but did not survive well; too many were absorbed into the missions along El Camino Real, enslaved on the ranches, or killed with or without the benefit of the white man's plagues. Several early amateur attempts were made to record their languages, attempts on the whole not very valuable because the recorders were untrained and hence knew nothing of linguistic analysis or accurate transcription. One recorder was an Italian priest with a background in Latin; something can be made of his report.

And there was, of course, Harrington. He ferreted out surviving speakers of Penutian and gathered all sorts of information, and Harrington knew his business. Now bundles, bales, boxes, and barrels of his notes are in the Smithsonian Institution, but not only in the Smithsonian. They keep turning up elsewhere, too, even in the dead-letter office. Harrington would write a letter from some out-of-the-way place, with no return address or with a temporary one, and would get the address wrong. Consequently, the letter would land in the dead-letter office. From such improbable places Harrington's effects are being assembled, and used in the reconstruction of Proto-Penutian, the ancestor of several important North American linguistic stocks.

Now an interesting parallel appears. Proto-Penutian seems to resemble Proto-Uralic, an ancestor language of tongues now scatteringly spoken from Hungary and Finland in central and northern Europe to Yukagir in extreme northeast Asia. The closest similarity between the

Costanoan languages in California and the known Uralic languages is that with Proto-Samoyed, now extinct but formerly spoken along the headwaters of the Yenisei River, in what is now southern Siberia. The languages have common bits of vocabulary, seemingly remarkably close, similar consonant systems, similar agglutinative grammars with many suffixes and no prefixes, vowel harmony, tense in the verb, and probably other similarities. That is, at least one large branch of American speech may be descended from a large body of tongues long spoken in northern and central Asia. In fact, Penutian diversity seems to be greater than Uralic diversity, and thus the American survivals may reflect the earlier form of the language—but that is another matter, which need not detain us.

As yet we must emphasize the *may be*. Proto-Penutian itself has not yet been well reconstructed. Of California Penutian languages and related tongues in New Mexico and Canada we know a good bit, but Penutian languages survive also in Mexico, and south of the border the reliable studies are sparse. If there is less knowledge of Indian languages in Mexico, however, there are more Indians, and we may yet have our best evidence from the Mexican Mixe or Zoque or from Mexican Penutian dialects not yet much studied. Even about the Californian Costanoan we can know more; Harrington's vast jumble of notes still has not as yet been worked through.[2]

If a firm relationship could be established between Penutian languages in America and Uralic tongues in Asia, we probably still would not have the original language that came to the Americas—assuming that more than one language did come. The earliest finds in California have been much farther south, but the Penutian phylum is widespread and incorporates many languages; it could not have been recent. Furthermore, if Uralic languages were ever much spoken in northeastern Asia, they have survived but little there; we assume that the language family developed farther west and south. Thus if we postulate that some eastern speakers of Uralic moved into Alaska as one of the middle waves, between the earliest hunters and the latest Eskimo, to become not the first nor yet the last of the bearers of New World speech, we have a plausible hypothesis.

This hypothesis is acquiring collateral support. In the previous chapter we noticed that data processed by computers has revealed relationships that had remained obscure while we worked with bodies of data comprehensible to human minds. Among the new results are suggestions of an apparent relationship between some languages of Central America

---

[2] I am relying heavily upon material as yet unpublished, assembled by my colleague, Otto Sadovszky.

and some in Oceania, among the islands that stretch from Asia down toward Australia. Linguistic materials fed into computers seem to give a correlation of from five to nine per cent between these two areas. These percentages are too high to represent only chance, which should give two or three per cent, at the most four. On the other hand, they are too low to suggest direct descent or migration, which should give much higher percentages. If we postulate, however, that a language developed in the interior of Asia, and that one prong spread southeast down the Malay Peninsula and on to the islands, while another prong moved northeast and across the Bering Strait and thence southward, and if all this took something like ten thousand years or so, these data would be about right. Thus, although we remain vastly ignorant of the relationships between American and Eurasian languages, and of the early spread of languages in the Americas, information is piling up, and it is beginning to suggest something like patterns.[3]

All this has wider implications. Two centuries ago we knew little about the relationships among the languages of the world, except that the Romance languages had sprung up from Latin, that modern Greek had come from ancient Greek, that English had developed from Old English, and the like. Then came the breakthrough provided by the reconstruction of what is now called Proto-Indo-European; scholars demonstrated that most European languages were related genetically and that their relationships could be revealed roughly in a sort of linguistic tree, similar to a genealogical tree. By analogy, Proto-Indo-European suggested that all other languages would have been related genetically within language families, and that most extant languages could be expected to have surviving relatives. Investigation established this theory, so that we now know the relationships of most extant languages, and we can reconstruct their immediate ancestors, and in some instances, their relatively remote ancestors.

Actually, such linguistic trees are not now so much respected as they once were. We are more aware than were our ancestors that a language is never a whole, that a language is always a jumble of dialects, and that languages tend more or less to merge into one another. For example, Spanish, French, and Italian are called separate languages, and certainly native speakers in Madrid, Paris, and Rome are mutually unintelligible, and yet we are told that a traveler can go from southern Spain all around the Mediterranean coast to Italy without ever being in a community whose local dialect is not readily intelligible to the natives of the adjacent communities. That is, in some areas various sorts of Spanish

---

[3] Studying language by data processing is in its infancy, the tentative results as yet available only in learned journals.

fade imperceptibly into various sorts of French that merge with various sorts of Italian. Proto-Indo-European probably was not that much varied within itself or through its relationships to other languages, but it must have been some sort of assemblage of dialects, which, when we reconstruct it, seems to take on a semblance of unity and regularity that it probably never possessed.

Nevertheless, working with these simplified concepts of language, even though our reconstructions do not represent anything that ever existed in such purity, we do have a means of reaching backward in time, and theoretically, if we could continue to shove our linguistic horizon back far enough, we should eventually come to a time when all languages stemmed from one original tongue, or at least from a relatively few centers of linguistic dispersal, even though these centers themselves represented some sort of agglomeration of dialects. We have not been able to do so, and lately we have been encountering enough uncertainty to suggest that we are nearing the limits of the time depth to which time-honored approaches can take us. We can reconstruct a Proto-Indo-European speech that can serve to typify one ancient body of languages, and we can project a Proto-Uralic ancestor for languages to the east and a Proto-Semitic forbear of languages to the southeast and south. But we have not been able to relate these languages into one greater family, or to associate Proto-Indo-European with any other great body of language elsewhere.

With computers we may be able to see new relationships. We may be able, for example, to recreate the ancestor of Asian languages now preserved in America and in other areas of distant dispersal, just as Sanskrit, the language most distant from the homeland of the Indo-Europeans, helped reconstruct Indo-European. Thus we may be on the verge of another great breakthrough in language history; we may be able to push all languages enough farther back so that they will begin to go together. If so, then we can begin to reconstruct the whole history of language, and the bodies of speech native in the Americas may provide part of the essential information.

As to how languages grew on these continents, we can at least present ourselves with handsome alternatives. A body of somewhat homogeneous people may have crossed the land bridge or the arctic ice, established themselves in the Alaskan bowl, and defending this land bridge, allowed no more to come. If such is the case, their descendants spread south until they filled both continents. As they spread, they divided, and as they divided, their language fractured into dialects, which became languages, which became the ancestors of new language families, which have survived until today. Theoretically, this is possible, and something like this would perhaps be the assumption of persons accustomed to think of man as descended from Adam and of the Americas as isolated from the Old World.

Much of the evidence, however, opposes that concept. Presumably, the newcomers have not been in the Americas long enough. We do not know how rapidly languages develop, although we can make plausible guesses—from Proto-Indo-European to modern English is perhaps seven thousand years plus. American archaeologists allow us at least twice that much time for New World inhabitation, but the American Indian languages are much more than twice as diverse as the descendants of Proto-Indo-European. Some new techniques for studying language depth—I shall consider the methods later—have led to guesses of thirty thousand years or more, and that might be plausible, also, on the analogy with known linguistic history. However, as yet only a few reputable archaeologists are willing to admit such dates.

Furthermore, a single migration across what are now the Bering Straits seems unlikely. The original body of hunters would have had no way of realizing that they had come to a new continent, with only one narrow link with the remainder of the world. They would have assumed that if there was one way to get to the new hunting ground, there would be others. Furthermore, they would probably have had no organization with which to delegate part of their members to defend the land or ice bridge, even if they had recognized it for what it was. Thus the point of entry probably was not defended; nobody would have thought of defending it. The hunters may have welcomed population—the more men, the better the chance of driving mastodons over cliffs. The bellies of the hunters were full, and their thoughts concerned tomorrow's mastodon, not geopolitics.

So much for inference; the direct evidence also supports the supposition that America was populated by waves of immigrants, who probably brought with them various dialects or languages, not all of which need have been related in Asia. Excavation at Bering Strait and along the coast of Alaska suggests a succession of peoples. As the glaciers melted the coastal route south opened, so that probably for several thousands of years peoples could have crossed on land or ice or both and wandered south. Even after the land bridge was inundated, crossing would not have been impossible, and as better fishing boats were developed the crossing became easier. A walrus- and seal-hunting culture might well have coasted from Siberia to Alaska; it is not improbable that the Eskimos arrived in this way, and incidentally, Eskimo speech shows considerable unity within itself and sharp diversity from many other languages indigenous on the American continents, as though it belongs to quite a different language family.

The nature and distribution of Indian cultures also suggest repeated immigrations by various sorts of people. Perhaps the obvious evidence of continued connection with Asia is the bow and arrow. They became the characteristic American weapon, but they were presumably invented only once, not in the Americas, and not until after the Americas were populated. Either the bow and arrow were brought by some late arrivals —who can perhaps be called invaders by now, and the arrow may have been their invasion weapon—or the bow and arrow were borrowed from Asia along trade routes that were maintained after the land bridge was closed, and had been for some millennia. Some other divergencies suggest multiple migrations. For example, a rare factor in blood, known as the Diego Factor for the Indian in whom it was discovered, has been found in Asia and in a few groups of American Indians, some in Peru and some on the Caribbean islands. A single migration would argue a greater or lesser spread of a blood factor.

On the contrary, some evidence suggests the unity of the American Indian. Indians of all sizes, shapes, and complexions can be discovered, but they tend to have moderately pigmented skins, rather coarse, straight hair, prominent cheek bones, and dark eyes. They are the only large body of people inhabiting a continuous area where one finds similar blood types and relatively consistent frequencies of these types. All this surely suggests some community, if not unity, of origin, but it can scarcely suggest more than that the bulk of the immigrants came from peoples somewhat related in race. It does not preclude some racial diversity—the so-called almond eyes are characteristic of the Eskimo, for example, but not of most American Indians—and the evidence certainly does not preclude some linguistic diversity among the immigrants; race and language are often associated, but the one does not presume the other.

Apparently, then, people were coming to America in successive waves during many thousand years of the late Pleistocene epoch, and even into historic times. They probably came mainly from one people or from related peoples, but they may have included some people not at all closely related to the others, and they probably brought several, perhaps many, languages or dialects with them. Morris Swadesh, an ingenious but by no means infallible scholar, has estimated that a minimum of 3500 years would have been required for the separation of Eskimo and Aleut tongues in the New World and that some 5000 years more must be allowed to account for the separation of Proto-Eskimo-Aleut from its ancestor in Asia. He believes, further, that by 3000 B.C. all other languages in the two continents would have become sufficiently established to absorb newcomers, and that by roughly 10,000 B.C. most languages would have been well enough defined to resist newcomers.[4] For what these estimates may be worth, they fit well enough into what we know as yet of the archaeology, but they assume some diversity in the languages which came to the New World.

Before we dismiss these early American bodies of speech entirely, however, we should notice a possibility, which embodies what we might call the spreading ripple theory. If a pebble is dropped into a silent pool, ripples will spread in all directions, so that those farthest from the center will be the first or oldest ripples. Presumably, something of this sort happens when culture spreads, although cultural traits do not spread with the uninterrupted regularity of wave motion in water. Generally speaking, however, areas remote from cultural centers tend to preserve older forms and practices, particularly if we define *remoteness* so as to include the impact of such phenomena as cultural backwardness and geographical isolation, as well as distance in space. For example, relatively archaic Scandinavian language has been preserved in Iceland, because its users emigrated there at an early date and did not receive the later developments. During the late Classical period the Celts overran much of western Europe, and throve in areas which are now known as France, northern Italy, the Low Countries, the Balkans, and the like. In these highly civilized areas, Celtic has been obliterated for centuries, but it has clung on in the "Celtic fringe," in remoter Ireland, in the mountains of Scotland and Wales, and on some islands. Speakers of Basque, in the Pyrenees Mountains, presumably preserve remnants of a very early language, because the survivors of some people that throve thousands of years ago—possibly the Ligurians—have resisted change in the mountains.

Similarly, if any survivals of a true dawn-language any longer persist, they should be sought in areas spatially, culturally, and geographically remote from the centers of language dispersal. If we assume, as is likely, the growth of language to have been in Asia, then the best hunting grounds for the most archaic languages would include the less accessible portions of the Himalayas, the mountains and jungles and perhaps some of the deserts of Africa, and the less privileged portions of the Americas, perhaps most likely the mountains and jungles of South America, where peoples must be living today whose ancestors were remote in space, protected by geography, and isolated in culture. Thus, if we ever learn to study language in great depth—and just now we are learning to study it in greater depth than ever before—we may yet find the most archaic evidence somewhere in the obscure corners of the Americas.

---

[4] See "Linguistic Overview," cited above, pp. 529–35.

3

THE LIFE AND TIMES OF AMERINDIA

Amerindians I shall call them henceforth, and their languages, Amerindian. We have no good name for them. They had no name for themselves as a group, most of them being too various to comprehend continental unity and too unsophisticated to grasp geography, to know where they lived or who were their distant cousins. Their immediate neighbors they knew as friends or enemies, and they sometimes had traditions involving remote relatives. The Sauk and Fox, for example, Algonquian inhabitants of the Upper Mississippi, knew that their ancestors had come west and that their eastern relatives were in contact with the white men, but this tribal history covered only a few hundred years, and the legends of most Amerindians were vaguer still. White men who encountered natives had various names for them; the Icelanders called them Skraelings, and thought that at least some of them hopped along on one foot big enough to serve as an umbrella, but the term that triumphed grew out of Columbus' error in supposing that his voyage had ended in India, and hence the inhabitants must be Indians. They had no unity of politics, culture, or language, but for our purposes they had unity. They occupied two continents and they spoke bodies of languages which were uniquely theirs. These languages were about to be overrun and decimated by another body of languages, and this triumph of one body of languages over another lies at the core of our book. Accordingly, by Amerindian I mean whatever native languages have been spoken on the American continents; *Amerindian* so defined has a geographical unity, which limits our study.

What do we know about early Amerindian? From direct evidence, very little, until long after Columbus. Columbus himself barely touched upon the mainland, and he was too much occupied with political, naval, and personal matters to be much concerned with local jargons. As for those who sailed with him, their activities were apparently better calculated to spread the germs of venereal disease than the germs of grammatical study. Even in subsequent centuries, when students with more leisure and more academic curiosity encountered the Amerindians, the results were meager. The frontier was not swarming with linguistic scientists, and although missionaries, traders, travelers, and soldiers sometimes recorded facts concerning the languages they encountered, zealously devoting considerable time to such researches, they were so ignorant of the nature of language and so confident that all languages must be essentially like Latin and their own native tongue that the results are usually curiosa not very useful for close study.

Accordingly, our means of investigation are limited. History helps in the last few hundred years, but we need thousands of years. Archaeology helps for earlier periods, but flint and bone and charcoal speak a most limited idiom. In light of the evidence available today, and insofar as any techniques yet devised give us promise, we shall have to rely mainly upon Amerindian languages still spoken or recently spoken when we endeavor to reconstruct the history of native American speech.

In this we have a well-tried technique, the comparative method. By comparing modern or recent languages like Old English, Gothic, Latin, Greek, and Sanskrit we have been able to describe the relationships of western European languages and to reconstruct their parent, Indo-European. Obviously, the same method can be used for Amerindian, and it has been used. We can demonstrate that languages spoken mainly in North America differed from those spoken mainly in South America; that Shoshone, spoken in Idaho, is related to Aztec, which developed in the Valley of Mexico; that the Sauk legend that their ancestors came from farther east has linguistic support; and the like. For example, here is a sample of common words in some related California languages:

	Head/Hair	Eye	Ear	Tongue	Earth	Fire	Water
1. ENTIMBICH	wo	bus	nak	ego	tübop	kos	paya
2. WOPONUCH	wo	bus	nak	ego	tübop	koso	paya
3. HODOGIDA	wo	pus	nak	ego	tibop	kos	paya
4. TUHUKWADJ	wo	pus	nak	ego	tibop	kos	paya
5. BIG PINE	wo	busi	naka	ego	tibip	koso	paya
6. INDEPENDENCE	wo	busi	naka	ego	tibipa	koso	paya

SOURCE: Adapted from Harold Edson Driver, *Indians of North America* (Chicago: University of Chicago Press, 1961), p. 570.

Obviously, there is too much similarity here to be accidental, and the similarity is greater than appears at a glance. The sound here represented by *ü* is near to the modern American sound [ɨ], a high central vowel close to [i]. Thus *tübop* and *tibop* are not so different as they look, probably not as different as two common American pronunciations of a word which might be suggested by the spellings *milk* and *melk*. Similarly, *p* represents the voiceless form of *b,* and thus the two apparently different sounds represent what a student of language would call free variants of the same phoneme.

Experts can now discuss Proto-Eskimo-Aleut and Proto-Hokan-Siouan, but who spoke the ancestor of the Hokan and Siouan language families, and where, and when? We do not know accurately, and as yet these "proto" languages have not been adequately reconstructed. They are a sort of *x* in an equation; we assume that Proto-Hokan-Siouan must once have been spoken sometime, somewhere, by somebody, or Siouan languages would not now be so similar to Hokan languages as they are, but we are dealing more with a series of relationships than with state-ments which have geographical, chronological, and cultural certainty. And at best, they do not go back far enough. Just as we do not know the relationship of Indo-European to other Eurasian languages, we do not know the relationships of the various Amerindian proto-languages. The comparative method in Amerindian studies has produced notable evi-dence, but as yet no results which reveal the early developments of Amerindian. We shall have to start with recent descriptions of Amer-indian and make what we can of them.

What, then, can we observe Amerindians doing to language? One notices at once that they made an uncommonly large amount of it per capita. They are few, and always have been; although we have no ac-curate census, this much is clear. Early scholars estimated the post-Columbian aborigines at some thirteen million, divided about equally between the continents. The late Professor A. L. Kroeber considered this high, and by re-examining the evidence, reached an estimate of eight and a half million as shown in the table at the top of page 26. Kroeber meant to be conservative, but may have been too conservative. Carl Sapper, a European scholar, went so far as to estimate Central and South America alone at twenty to twenty-five million, and if he has not received much support at this altitude, many scholars would now double Kroeber's figures, especially for South America, so that it would no longer seem safe to estimate the Amerindian population at fewer than ten to fifteen million.

As to their languages, a sort of standard guess has been that the Amerindians produced some two thousand bodies of speech, the re-mainder of the world three thousand, with the Amerindian tongues distributed as follows: north of Mexico, 200; Central America, 350;

North of Rio Grande	900,000
Northwest Mexico	100,000
Northeast Mexico, less than	100,000
Central and Southern Mexico, Guatemala, Salvador	3,000,000
Honduras, Nicaragua	100,000
TOTAL, NORTH AMERICA	4,200,000
Inca Empire	3,000,000
Rest of S. A., including Panama and Costa Rica	1,000,000
West Indies	200,000
TOTAL, SOUTH AMERICA	4,200,000
TOTAL, AMERICAS 1492	8,400,000

SOURCE: *Cultural and Natural Areas of Native North America* (Berkeley: University of California Press, 1939), p. 165.

South America and the West Indies, 1450. This total may be too large; certainly the counts on which it was based included bodies of speech now classed as dialects, not mutually unintelligible languages, but on the other hand some languages disappeared before any counting was started, so that the totals may still be realistic. Considering how few the Amerindians were, and how shallow their time depth when compared with time in the Afro-Eurasian land mass, their linguistic production is staggering. For example, a city like Los Angeles, whose present population would greatly exceed the estimated native population north of Mexico, could go on for decades without altering a single language very much, and this in spite of a Hollywoodian passion for spelling common words in strange ways and promoting the lingo of show-biz. The Amerindians, whose numbers varied from zero to perhaps twenty-five million, during fewer than fifty thousand years, produced thousands of dialects and many linguistic stocks. To put all this in another way, the known native languages of California alone show greater linguistic variety than all the known languages of the continent of Europe.

Obviously, we shall never know how many tongues the Amerindians developed. Many languages were destroyed as their speakers were overwhelmed with gunfire and firewater, with the germs of smallpox and the germs of industrial prosperity. Most bodies of speech must have been relatives of languages which survive or of which we have descriptions; they have been so numerous that they are still being "discovered," discovered in the sense that white scholars have previously been ignorant of them. Recently such a language was identified on the Copper River

Delta in Alaska, having some two hundred surviving speakers, and we do not yet know what languages may be lurking along the Amazon. Others must have been unique remnants. Recently, Beothukan disappeared; it was formerly spoken extensively in Newfoundland, and while it may have been related to Algonquian, it may have been the last survivor of a whole family of Amerindian speech. Languages, like men, are mortal; they are all fated to die, by extinction or by what we might call old age and survival through progeny, but they all pass away. Probably they did not die at more than the normal rate for languages until the white man had begun his rapid advance; then they vanished as though stricken by a strange plague.

Similarly, the geography of Amerindian languages remains uncertain before recent times. We can notice some linguistic patterns, but we are not sure what to make of them. Most surviving languages fall into rather large groups, such groups as those embodied in the great North American linguistic stocks to be mentioned later. They may be fragmented geographically, but usually not much, and some of these inconsistencies can be accounted for by recent migration, some of it partly occasioned by the white invaders. But what does this mean? Does this grouping of related languages mean that a relatively few bodies of Amerindians multiplied and spread so that a single Siouan proto-tribe accounts for most of the descendants who subsequently spoke Sioux, or does it mean that the language of the Proto-Siouan speakers triumphed over other languages and killed them off with political, economic, social, or military weapons? We can observe a few concentrations of minor linguistic stocks, notably in California and in South America east of the Andes and north of what is now northwestern Argentina. Are these relatively undisturbed pockets survivals reflecting a former linguistic scramble that embraced the two continents before the hegemony of such stocks as Algonquian and Na-Dene, or are they the scattered late arrivals that found a diminutive place among the great linguistic families that had been proliferating for ages? The geographical relationships within the welter of languages in central South America does not suggest late arrivals; on the other hand, late arrivals might well have worked down the fertile northwest coast of North America to account for the variety of speech in California. In fact, cultures and bodies of speech are so numerous and so intermingled in California that some scholars have postulated the "fish trap" theory, that groups of Indians who poured in from the north found themselves trapped where the mountains meet the sea toward the southern end of California. This thesis has its obvious flaws; migrating peoples overcome most obstacles, and conversely, white men as well as Amerindians have found many reasons for going to

California and staying there, but the thesis may have validity along with its limitations. In any event, evidence by projections seems not to be conclusive.

The earlier historical evidence is often not very useful. For any body of Indians we are likely to have a number of names, their names for themselves, group names, which were mistaken for tribal names, the nicknames and insults their neighbors heaped on them—some Amerindian groups, for example, were fond of referring to their neighbors as various sorts of offal. Where the Amerindians themselves have survived long enough to become subjects of modern study, these confusions can be eliminated.

Consider the aboriginal inhabitants of what is now southern Idaho. They were called Snakes, Diggers, Skunks, Sheep Eaters, Camas Eaters, and a good many other things. Some of the other titles were revealing, but none of these meant anything much; there was geographical difference among Sheep Eaters, Buffalo Eaters, Fish Eaters, Duck Eaters, Deer Eaters, and Camas Eaters, reflected in their foods. There were also such titles as Ute, Paiute, Gosiute, Shoshone, and Bannock; these titles did mean something socially, but they did not reflect different languages as they were once supposed to, but only dialects of one language. Of these, the people now called Bannock never called themselves that; their name was something like *Neme,* or *Numi* which means "The People," and in the singular, "One Who Speaks Our Native Tongue." The word now attached to them was recorded by various white itinerants as *Ban-at-tees, Panak, Ban-acks, Pannacks, Banax,* and *Bonack,* from original *panaite,* or *panakwi,* which was not a tribal name but a linguistic subdivision, and apparently means *western.* The surviving form, *Bannock,* presumably triumphed by folk etymology, since *bannock* is the name of a Scotch delicacy, which in American speech would be called a cookie. These facts, however, we have only because of modern study, and because the Indians have survived to be studied. Many Amerindians have not survived either physically or culturally, and thus we have little means of assessing the rumors about them. When Swadesh studied the Chitmacha there were some sixty survivors, of whom only one could still speak the language.[1] For many Indian languages even that one last speaker was never completely interviewed.

In spite of this depredation, the Lord's plenty survived, and much of it remains. For a quick survey of language in primitive America we must

---

[1] Morris Swadesh, "Chitmacha," *Linguistic Structures in Native America,* Viking Fund Publications in Anthropology, 6, ed. Harry Hoijer (New York, 1946), p. 313.

remind ourselves of a few terms. A *dialect* is a form of speech used by one linguistic community and understandable in at least one other community, but notably different from the speech used there; different enough, let us say, so that the speakers themselves would be aware of this difference and make formal allowance for it—"This is the way we say it, but over the mountain they say it in another way." A *language* is a set of speech patterns not understandable in other speech communities, and a *family* of languages includes those bodies of speech, including dialects, which are believed to descend from a single, common ancestor.

This terminology is of long standing and common acceptance. It was developed by the philologists, who worked mainly with written languages, notably with dead languages, surviving so meagerly that the multiplicity of dialect did not much confuse the evidence. Sanskrit developed in southern Asia, Old Norse in northern Europe; confusion by contact is likely to have been nil. Gothic survives in effect in the writing of one man; he may have spoken a dialect—probably not even the dialect of a native speaker—but we have no evidence from his contemporaries. Thus the linguistic trees constructed by the philologists are revealing, but deceptively simple. They assume that a reconstructed language must have been one thing and that its descendants are one thing, although a language, so far as we know, is never one thing, but an agglomeration of dialects. Dialects come into being in part by the tendency of the language to fracture, to break up along geographical and social lines, but any dialect will be the result of many influences. Thus the analogy between the descent of languages and the descent of man would be more valid than it is if man inherited acquired characteristics, which we believe he does not. Languages, however, and the various dialects of language, do inherit the acquired characteristics of their ancestors, and thus the whole process of linguistic descent is apparently more complex than the philologists understood.

Modern concepts of language descent are now being somewhat revised, at least in part through American linguistics, and, at least in part, the credit should presumably go both to the Amerindians who created and preserved the linguistic material and to modern scholars who are making use of it. Nineteenth-century philologists, relying mainly upon material concerning Indo-European, and employing relatively few dialects in the form in which these were standardized in written texts, were able to establish what seemed like relatively simple, clear relationships. These simplifications clarified our notions of language, its nature and growth, but when students of Amerindian languages endeavored to apply the conventional linguistic pattern and terminology to the confusion of New World tongues, they found both inadequate.

The classification of Amerindian speech rests upon one of those rare scientific triumphs so broad and sure that they thereafter require only minor revision. Pioneered through the Bureau of American Ethnology and directed by J. W. Powell, the original statement provided the basis of American linguistic study for more than half a century and was accorded such veneration that it became a sort of "dead hand of the past" in American studies, a dead hand so weighty that lifting it required the work of dozens of ethnologists, and it remains one of the scholarly marvels.[2] It determined, at least roughly, the relationships of most languages north of the Rio Grande, but Powell, impelled by the variety of languages with which he had to deal, moved toward a more adequate approach to the problem of language. Finding the concept of language "families" too restricting, he added a broader term, "stock," a somewhat more inclusive designation which became standard among Americanists.

Nor was *stock* sufficient. Involved in the welter of Amerindian linguistic relationships and counter-relationships, scholars invented more terms, until some were endeavoring to recognize seven levels, from the most restricted to the largest groupings, as follows: dialect, language, subfamily, family, superfamily, subphylum, and superphylum. Nor did all scholars use these terms in the same way.

But order seems to be appearing, at least in North America, where new knowledge has revealed new relationships and has permitted reducing the fifty to seventy-five stocks formerly recognized to few stocks and still fewer phyla. Driver[3] recognized nineteen major linguistic groups. Obviously, this was not the last word.

In 1966 Mr. and Mrs. Carl Voegelin's long-awaited map became available (see Map 1).[4] It is not complete and will need revision, as all broad works do, but it emanates from such sane scholarship in a field so plagued with imponderables and rests upon such detailed, reliable information that it will probably be standard for a long time. A few of the Voegelin-supported relationships have already been questioned, and more will be, particularly as to which bodies of speech should be called languages and which dialects, but I shall mainly ignore such differences, assuming that this classification is the best we can hope to have for the present.

---

[2] *Indian Linguistic Families of America North of Mexico,* 7th Annual Report of the Bureau of American Ethnology (Washington, D.C.: U.S. Govt. Printing Office, 1891), pp. 2–142. Powell was assisted by A. S. Gatschet and J. Owen Dorsey.

[3] Harold Edson Driver, *Indians of North America* (previously cited); see pp. 566–80, especially table 5 and map 37.

[4] C. F. and F. M. Voegelin, *Map of North American Indian Languages* (prepared by Rand McNally and Co. for the American Ethnological Society, 1966).

The Voegelins use a relatively simple classification, combining the bulk of North American languages into forty-three families comprising nine phyla, as follows: Arctic-Paleosiberian, consisting in North America of the Eskimo-Aleut family, and extending all along the northern coast and the arctic islands; Na-Dene, comprising the Athapascan family to the northwest, with scattering families to the south and east; Macro-Algonquian, mainly eastern, from Labrador to the Gulf and west to the Mississippi River; Macro-Siouan, strong in the Middle West from southern Canada to Texas with considerable pockets around the Great Lakes (Iroquoian family) and in the southeast; Hokan, scatteringly in California and in northeastern and northwestern Mexico; Penutian, strong in California and in eastern central Mexico; Aztec-Tanoan, dominating the western Great Basin, present in some western plains, much of northern Mexico, and some of central Mexico; Oto-Manguean, mainly in central Mexico; and Macro-Chibchan, from Guatemala south into South America. In addition, the Voegelins have a considerable number of what they call "language isolates" and groups of languages recognized as "families with undetermined phylum affiliations." Some of these groups are extensive; the Salish family in Oregon, Washington, and southwestern Canada includes sixteen languages.

Following is the Voegelin classification. The symbol and number for each language is that used to mark the language on the map; note that within a given phylum each family of languages has its own distinctive symbol. Hyphenated names for individual languages indicate tribal and dialect distinctions. Names followed by an asterisk are thought possibly not to be separate languages and are not located on the map.

AMERICAN ARCTIC-PALEOSIBERIAN
PHYLUM I

Ia ESKIMO-ALEUT FAMILY
- ① Central-Greenlandic Eskimo (Trans-arctic Eskimo)
- ② Alaskan Eskimo (Kuskokwim Eskimo)
- ③ Eastern Aleut (Unalaskan)
- ④ Western Aleut (Atkan, Attuan)

Ib CHUKCHI-KAMCHATKAN FAMILY (in Siberia)

NA-DENE PHYLUM II

IIa ATHAPASCAN FAMILY
- ① Dogrib–Bear Lake–Hare
- ② Chipewyan-Slave-Yellowknife
- ③ Kutchin
- ④ Tanana-Koyukon-Han-Tutchone
- ⑤ Sekani-Beaver-Sarsi
- ⑥ Carrier-Chilcotin

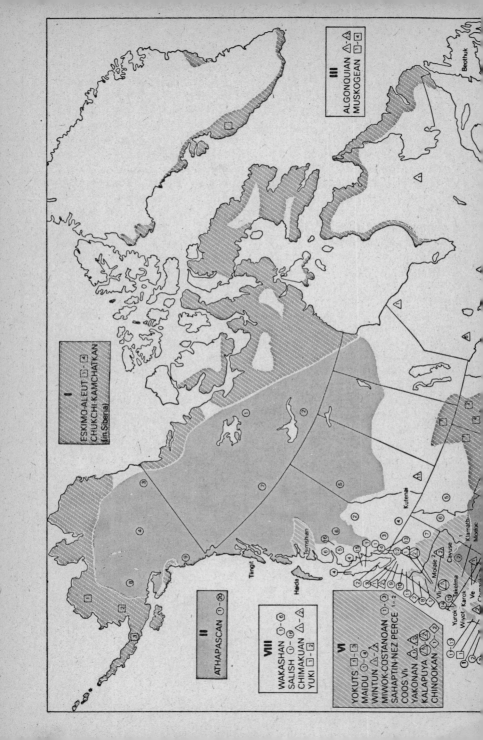

I
ESKIMO-ALEUT ◻-◼
CHUKCHI-KAMCHATKAN
(in Siberia)

III
ALGONQUIAN △-⬭
MUSKOGEAN ⬤-◧

II
ATHAPASCAN ①-⑳

VIII
WAKASHAN ①-⑥
SALISH ①-⑲
CHIMAKUAN △-⬭
YUKI ◻-◨

VI
YOKUTS ◻-⑬
MAIDU ①-④
WINTUN △-⬭
MIWOK-COSTANOAN ①-⑨
SAHAPTIN-NEZ PERCE ¹-²
COOS VII
YAKONAN △-⬭
KALAPUYA ①-④
CHINOOKAN ◇-②

Tingit

Haida

Tsimshian

Kutenai

Moiale

Cayuse

Klamath

Modoc

Beothuk

Yurok Karok
Wiyot
Ye

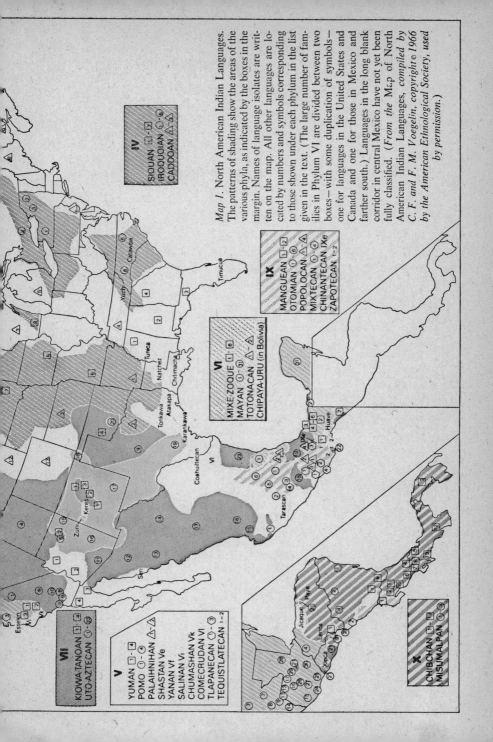

Map 1. North American Indian Languages. The patterns of shading show the areas of the various phyla, as indicated by the boxes in the margin. Names of language isolates are written on the map. All other languages are located by numbers and symbols corresponding to those shown under each phylum in the list given in the text. (The large number of families in Phylum VI are divided between two boxes—with some duplication of symbols—one for languages in the United States and Canada and one for those in Mexico and farther south.) Languages in the long blank corridor in central Mexico have not yet been fully classified. (*From the Map of North American Indian Languages, compiled by C. F. and F. M. Voegelin, copyright© 1966 by the American Ethnological Society, used by permission.*)

IV
SIOUAN □-☒
IROQUOIAN ○-⊘
CADDOAN △-△

IX
MANGUEAN □-12
OTOMIAN ○-6
POPOLOCAN △-△
MIXTECAN ▽-⊽
CHINANTECAN IXe
ZAPOTECAN 1-2

VI
MIXE-ZOQUE □-6
MAYAN ○-17
TOTONACAN △-△
CHIPAYA-URU (in Bolivia)

VI
KIOWA-TANOAN □-4
UTO-AZTECAN ○-69

V
YUMAN □-4
POMO ○-○
PALAIHNIHAN △-△
SHASTAN Ve
YANAN Vf
SALINAN Vi
CHUMASHAN Vk
COMECRUDAN VI
TLAPANECAN ○-3
TEQUISTLATECAN 1-2

X
CHIBCHAN □-12
MISUMALPAN ○-9

③ Tahltan-Kaska
④ Tanaina-Ingalik-Nabesna-Ahtena
⑤ Eyak
⑥ Chasta Costa–Galice–Tututni
⑦ Hupa
⑧ Kato-Wailaki
⑨ Mattole
⑩ Tolowa
⑪ Navaho
⑫ San Carlos Apache
⑬ Chiricahua-Mescalero Apache
⑭ Jicarilla
⑮ Lipan
⑯ Kiowa Apache

IIb Tlingit language isolate
IIc Haida language isolate

MACRO-ALGONQUIAN PHYLUM III

IIIa ALGONQUIAN FAMILY

△1 Cree-Montagnais-Naskapi
△2 Menomini
△3 Fox-Sauk-Kickapoo
△4 Shawnee
△5 Potawatomi
△6 Ojibwa-Ottawa-Algonquin-Salteaux
△7 Delaware
△8 Penobscot-Abnaki
△9 Malecite-Passamaquoddy
△10 Micmac
△11 Blackfoot-Piegan-Blood
△12 Cheyenne
△13 Arapaho-Atsina-Nawathinehena

IIIb Yurok language isolate
IIIc Wiyot language isolate
IIId MUSKOGEAN FAMILY

□1 Choctaw-Chickasaw
□2 Alabama-Koasati
□3 Mikasuki-Hitchiti
□4 Muskogee (Creek)–Seminole

IIIe Natchez language isolate
IIIf Atakapa language isolate
IIIg Chitimacha language isolate
IIIh Tunica language isolate
IIIi Tonkawa language isolate

MACRO-SIOUAN PHYLUM IV

IVa SIOUAN FAMILY

□1 Crow
□2 Hidatsa
□3 Winnebago

    4 Mandan
    5 Iowa-Oto
    6 Omaha-Osage-Ponca-Quapaw-Kansa
    7 Dakota
IVb Catawba language isolate
IVc IROQUOIAN FAMILY
    ① Seneca-Cayuga-Onondaga
    ② Mohawk
    ③ Oneida
    ④ Wyandot (Huron)
    ⑤ Tuscarora
    ⑥ Cherokee
IVd CADDOAN FAMILY
    △ Caddo
    △ Wichita
    △ Pawnee-Arikara
IVe Yuchi language isolate

HOKAN PHYLUM V

Va YUMAN FAMILY
    1 Upland Yuman (Walapai-Havasupai-Yavapai)
    2 Up River Yuman (Mohave-[Maricopa-Kavelchadom-Halchidom]-Yuma)
    3 Delta River Yuman (Cocopa-Kohuana-Halyikwamai)
    4 Southern and Baja California Yuman (Diegueño-Kamia-Akwa'ala-Kiliwa-Nyakipa)
Vb Seri language isolate
Vc POMO FAMILY
    ① Coast Pomo
    ② Northeast Pomo
    ③ Western Clear Lake
    ④ Southeast Clear Lake
Vd PALAIHNIHAN FAMILY
    △ Achumawi
    △ Atsugewi
Ve SHASTAN FAMILY
Vf YANAN FAMILY
Vg Chimariko language isolate
Vh Washo language isolate
Vi SALINAN FAMILY
Vj Karok language isolate
Vk CHUMASHAN FAMILY
Vl COMECRUDAN FAMILY
Vm Coahuiltecan language isolate
Vn Esselen language isolate
Vo Jicaque language isolate
Vp TLAPANECAN FAMILY
    ① Tlapanec
    ② Subtiaba
    ③ Maribichicoa

Vq TEQUISTLATECAN FAMILY
1 Tluamelula
2 Mountain Tlequistlateco

PENUTIAN PHYLUM VI

VIa YOKUTS FAMILY
1. Yokuts, Foothill North
2. Yokuts, Foothill South
3. Yokuts, Valley

VIb MAIDU FAMILY
1. Southern Maidu
2. Northwest Maidu
3. Mountain Maidu
4. Valley Maidu

VIc WINTUN FAMILY
△ Patwin
△ Wintun

VId MIWOK-COSTANOAN FAMILY
1. Sierra Miwok
2. Coast-Lake Miwok
3. Costanoan

VIe Klamath-Modoc language isolate

VIf SAHAPTIN–NEZ PERCE FAMILY
1 Nez Perce
2 Sahaptin

VIg Cayuse language isolate

VIh Molale language isolate

VIi COOS FAMILY

VIj YAKONAN FAMILY
△ Alsea
△ Siuslaw–Lower Umpqua

VIk Takelma language isolate

VIl KALAPUYA FAMILY
△ Santiam-Mackenzie
△ Yonkalla

VIm CHINOOKAN FAMILY
◇ Upper Chinook
◇ Lower Chinook

VIn Tsimshian language isolate

VIo Zuni language isolate

VIp MIXE-ZOQUE (ZOQUEAN) FAMILY
1. Mixe
2. Zoque
3. Sierra Popoluca
4. Texixtepec
5. Sayula
6. Oluta

VIq MAYAN FAMILY
1. Huasteco

② Chontal of Tabasco
③ Chol
④ Chorti
⑤ Punctunc*
⑥ Moianec*
⑦ Tzeltal
⑧ Tzotzil
⑨ Tojolabal
⑩ Chuh
⑪ Jacaltec
⑫ Kanjobal*
⑬ Solomec
⑭ Motozintleco
⑮ Mam
⑯ Aquacatec
⑰ Ixil
⑱ Tacaneco*
⑲ Tlatiman*
⑳ Taquial*
㉑ Tupancal*
㉒ Tutuapa*
㉓ Coyotin*
㉔ Quiche
㉕ Cakchiquel
㉖ Tzutujil
㉗ Rabinal
㉘ Kekchi
㉙ Pokonchi (Pocomchi)
㉚ Pokomam
㉛ Maya

VIr CHIPAYA-URU FAMILY (in Bolivia)
VIs TOTONACAN FAMILY
△ Totonac
△ Tepehua
VIt Huáve language isolate

AZTEC-TANOAN PHYLUM VII

VIIa KIOWA-TANOAN FAMILY
1 Tiwa (Taos-Picuris)-(Isleta-Sandia)
2 Tewa (San Juan–Santa Clara–San Ildefonso–Tesuque–Nambe–Hano)
3 Towa (Jemez)
4 Kiowa
VIIb UTO-AZTECAN FAMILY
① Mono
② Northern Paiute (Paviotso)–Bannock–Snake
③ Shoshone–Gosiute–Wind River–Panamint–Comanche
④ Southern Paiute–Ute–Chemehuevi–Kawaiisu
⑤ Hopi

⑥ Tubatulabal
⑦ Luiseño
⑧ Cahuilla
⑨ Cupeño
⑩ Serrano
⑪ Pima-Papago
⑫ Pima Bajo
⑬ Yaqui-Mayo
⑭ Tarahumara
⑮ Cora
⑯ Huichol
⑰ Tepehuan
⑱ Nahuatl
⑲ Nahuat
⑳ Mecayapan*
㉑ Pipil
㉒ Pochutla
㉓ Tamaulipeco

LANGUAGE ISOLATES AND FAMILIES WITH UNDETERMINED PHYLUM AFFILIATIONS VIII

VIIIa Keres language isolate
VIIIb YUKI FAMILY
    ☐ Yuki
    ② Wappo
VIIIc Beothuk language isolate
VIIId Kutenai language isolate
VIIIe Karankawa language isolate
VIIIf CHIMAKUAN FAMILY
    △ Quileute
    △ Chimakum
VIIIg SALISH FAMILY
    ① Lillooet
    ② Shuswap
    ③ Thompson
    ④ Okanagon-Sanpoil-Coville-Lake
    ⑤ Flathead–Pend d'Oreille–Kalispel–Spokan
    ⑥ Coeur d'Alene
    ⑦ Middle Columbia–Wenatchi
    ⑧ Tillamook
    ⑨ Twana
    ⑩ Upper Chehalis–Cowlitz–Lower Chehalis–Quinault
    ⑪ Snoqualmi-Duamish-Nisqualli
    ⑫ Lummi-Songish-Clallam
    ⑬ Halkomelem
    ⑭ Squamish
    ⑮ Comox-Sishiatl
    ⑯ Bella Coola

VIIIh WAKASHAN FAMILY
- ① Nootka
- ② Nitinat
- ③ Makah
- ④ Kwakiutl
- ⑤ Bella Bella–Heiltsuk
- ⑥ Kitamat-Haisla

VIIIi Timucua language isolate
VIIIj Tarascan language isolate

OTO-MANGUEAN PHYLUM IX

IXa MANGUEAN (CHOROTEGAN) FAMILY
- ① Mangue
- ② Chiapaneco

IXb OTOMIAN (OTOMI-PAME) FAMILY
- ① Otomi
- ② Mazahua
- ③ Ocuiltec
- ④ Matlatzinca
- ⑤ Chichimeca-Jonaz
- ⑥ Pame

IXc POPOLOCAN FAMILY
- △ Popoloc
- △ Chocho
- △ Ixcateco
- △ Mazateco

IXd MIXTECAN FAMILY
- ① Mixtec
- ② Trique
- ③ Cuicateco
- ④ Amuzgo

IXe CHINANTECAN FAMILY
IXf ZAPOTECAN FAMILY
- 1 Zapotec
- 2 Chatino

MACRO-CHIBCHAN PHYLUM X

Xa CHIBCHAN FAMILY
- ① Rama
- ② Guatuso
- ③ Cuna
- ④ Bribri
- ⑤ Terraba
- ⑥ Boruca
- ⑦ Cabecar (Chiripo)–Corrhue
- ⑧ Tucurrike-Orisa
- ⑨ Suerre
- ⑩ Guetar
- ⑪ Voto

　　　　　⑫ Guaymi
　　　　　⑬ Dorasque
　　Xb MISUMALPAN FAMILY
　　　　　① Miskito
　　　　　② Sumo
　　　　　③ Matagalpa
　　Xc Paya language isolate
　　Xd Xinca language isolate
　　Xe Lenca language isolate
　　　　　(N.B. Additional language families in the Macro-Chib-
　　　　　chan phylum, and additional languages in the Chibchan
　　　　　family, are distributed in South America.)

To see a little better how this goes, we might look in more detail at one phylum; and because I expect to use Aztec-Tanoan in the next chapter in another connection, I shall choose that. Linguistically, it shows less variety than some phyla, since it exists in only two families, but geographically and socially it is the medium of extremely diverse speakers, ranging from the northern United States to below the southern tip of Mexico, and its speakers included the sophisticated Aztecs and other Nahuatl speakers and the so-called "Diggers" of northern Nevada, who were among the least privileged of the aborigines.

We have reason to believe that speakers of Proto-Aztec-Tanoan lived somewhere near the present Mexican border, perhaps in Arizona or to the south. Some of them must have moved east, since they occupied much of the area now associated with the Cliff Dwellers and the Basket-makers; their descendants are known to tourists in Taos, Isleta, Santa Clara, San Ildefonso, and other areas now known for crafts. One group moved still farther east; they are represented by the Kiowa in Texas and Oklahoma. Languages of these peoples are grouped into the Kiowa-Tanoan family.

The Uto-Aztecan family is much larger and has its subdivisions. The north-south axis of this family runs through the mountain valleys and the semideserts of the western United States and northern Mexico, although Uto-Aztecan speakers did work west to the Pacific Ocean, east to the Gulf of Mexico, and down into the tropics as far as Salvador. At least two subdivisions have been identified south of the border, one composed of a variety of languages from the Pima-Papago in southern Arizona to the Valley of Mexico along with Nahuat to the northeast, the other notably of Pipil in the jungles to the south. In the Hispanization of central Mexico, many of these languages must have been obliterated, the languages spoken in what are now Aguas Calientes and Zacatecas for example, which the Voegelins prudently omit from their list since we know little of them.

Among the Amerindians who moved north, a number of subdivisions can be observed; the Hopi went east, and other languages appear in southern California—Tubatulabal, Luiseño, Serrano, and others. Other Uto-Aztecan speakers moved farther north; some were found living in the vicinity of Mono Lake and the Owens River Valley, along the borders of what are now Nevada and California; they are to be distinguished from the southern Paiutes in south and central Utah, the Utes, and the Chemehuevi. The Voegelin classification denominates this speech as Mono, and treats it as a language, although more recent research suggests that it is a dialect to be associated with other dialects to the north. The speech of these latter groups, found especially in the valleys of the Snake and Humboldt Rivers, the Voegelins treat as two languages, calling them Northern Paiute or Paviotso, and Shoshone. Actually, these bodies of speech seem to be an extremely complex welter of dialects, spreading east from the Modoc in Oregon and south from the mountainous Primitive Area in central Idaho, some speech communities consisting of no more than a few hundred individuals. For example, the Shoshone speakers who live in the Sawtooth Mountain area were called Sheepeaters because of the mountain sheep that were their specialty; their speech differed from that of their cousins who lived to the southwest on the lava plains and dug camas roots, who differed in turn from the Seedeaters and the Fisheaters along the Snake River. Thus we have one language family, spread out for some fifteen hundred miles north and south, composed of what the Voegelins recognized as twenty-three languages, but embodying hundreds of dialects still spoken and hundreds more that are long dead.

At this point we should remind ourselves that our survey has been limited to North America, that Southern Amerindians were as numerous as Northern Amerindians and may have been as fruitful in language. Unfortunately, the available evidence is sparser south of the isthmus—the evidence, not the phenomena, for South America teems with linguistic data. As yet, however, trained South American scholars have been few, and the impediments of distance, language, politics, and geography have been such that relatively few *nortamericanos* have turned southward. Earlier estimates postulated some seventy-five linguistic stocks, but this estimate was certainly too large, as the earlier estimates for North America were too large. The current guess, so far as I am aware, would reduce Southern Amerindian speech to four phyla and perhaps nineteen or twenty families.[5] This classification suggests less diversity than in North America, and such a conclusion is plausible;

[5] Julian H. Steward and Louis C. Faron, *Native Peoples of South America* (New York: McGraw-Hill, 1959), pp. 16-30.

after all, many sorts of Amerindian speakers probably never got past the isthmus or along the Antilles. Fewer phyla are to be expected south of Central America, but the elaboration of some of these phyla may be very great.

Thus, although many details remain obscure, the salient facts about Amerindian linguistic production are obvious—it is highly varied, and there is a lot of it. The Amerindians developed hundreds of languages and thousands of dialects, and these languages are so diverse that dozens of language families are so remote from each other that intimate grammatical and semantic studies reveal no relationships among them. If relationships existed, if these languages had common ancestors, the connections are so remote and so obscured that they have not yet been detected.

Linguistically, the Amerindians were not only fertile, they were lucky—provided becoming martyrs to the cause of language in a limited and lingering way may be equated with luck. They produced linguistic plenty, and they have been losing their lives and their cultures in a way admirably adapted to the preservation of their linguistic harvest. Had the conquest of the Americas been more rapid—to be specific, if the conquest had been completed and the languages exterminated in three centuries—little linguistic information of much account would have been preserved. Until recently, even the most competent students had few adequate techniques for preserving and studying unwritten languages. Had the Indo-European languages triumphed over the Amerindian tongues in three centuries—and we must think of the conquest as still continuing—we should know little more of Amerindian than we know of the ancient Celtic languages and dialects obliterated by the invading Angles and Saxons in Britain, little more than we know of the Gallic speech overrun by the Romans in what is now France.

This sort of thing did occur, of course; it so happened that many of the Amerindians encountered by the early settlers on the eastern coast were speakers of Algonquian, and thus that phylum has suffered more than have those that were the media of speakers who survived from the military to the social phase of the conquest. Fortunately, however, the Vanishing American has been uncommonly stubborn about not vanishing, and by the late nineteenth century, there was both a will to study the languages of the natives and splendid new techniques which made significant study possible.

The result is that the world is enriched by a wealth of Amerindian linguistic data, partly because the natives declined to die as fast as some of their white brothers wished. In addition, the Amerindians have, on the whole, made the study of their languages not too difficult. True, parts of South America are still dangerous for white men, and many

North American Indians have remained as unreconstructed as have some southern whites. They still consider all white men "the enemy people," but on the whole they have been willing to settle down side by side with their conquerors, and to work with them or to be worked upon.

Accordingly, we have linguistic findings that could not otherwise have been collected; and the more because students of language, also, need time and money, and if they can scurry out to the field over the weekend, it helps. We know as much as we do about the multifarious California Indians because they continued to live within commuting distance of the Department of Anthropology at Berkeley. For example, for a half century, what little we knew of the language of the Washo Indians who live near Carson City, Nevada, we owed to the fact that the late Professor Kroeber caught the train for Reno on a few weekends and spent his spare hours talking with more or less sober Washos on the local skid row. This was fly-by-night linguistics which Kroeber was the first to deprecate—one should add that he worked through an educated Washo, saving what he could in the brief time at his disposal—and a lesser scholar could have made nothing of it at all, but until recently Kroeber's interim report contained most of what we knew linguistically of a very interesting people.[6] By such narrow margins has some Amerindian wealth been preserved.

So much for the quantity of linguistic evidence that the Amerindians produced and helped to preserve. Was their product distinctive? Does it contribute anything different to language? Does insight into Amerindian languages alter or improve our insight into language as a phenomenon? The answers to all these questions must be yes, yet the evidence is so complicated and the nature of language so evasive and obscure that the answers cannot be simply yes. Students of American languages have on the whole been understandably reluctant to attempt answers, and thus I do not have many precedents to follow or many authorities on whom to lean. But something must be attempted.[7]

---

[6] A. L. Kroeber, "The Washo Language of East Central California and Nevada," *University of California Publications in American Archaeology and Ethnology,* IV (1907), 251–317.

[7] Franz Boas dared to make some generalizations in the introduction to the *Handbook of American Indian Languages,* Bureau of American Ethnology *Bulletin 40,* 2 vols. (Washington, D.C., 1911–22), but he lacked much material later made available. Edward Sapir readily attempted informed guesses, but most of his studies were essays in research, and his excellent *Language* (New York: Harcourt, Brace and Co., 1921) was too general to warrant speculation on one body of languages; something similar can be said of the writings of Leonard Bloomfield. Benjamin Lee Whorf never hesitated to get in over his linguistic depth, and he has done most suggestive work, of which I shall take advantage in another connection. A number of younger linguists such as Dorothy

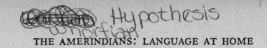

Part of the difficulty discouraging any popular statement grows from the necessity of dealing with concepts not readily comprehensible to most minds shaped in an Indo-European language community. Language is slippery and subtle stuff, but most people assume they know how it works because they believe they know how their own language works. This last assumption may be unfounded, but even if valid, it is likely only to impede a grasp of how languages work that are essentially different. Anyone who has grown to maturity using an Indo-European language is likely to assume that any grammar must work through parts of speech: nouns and verbs, some modifiers, and other particles like prepositions, conjunctions, and pronouns. He assumes that a language is made up of words, that these words combine into sentences, of which the cores are subjects and predicates, particularly subjects and verbs, often with various sorts of complements. He accepts without question the supposition that all verbs involve tense, that gender is associated with sex, that modifiers can be divided into adverbs and adjectives, and that the core of every complete thought will be a predication, beginning with a subject and continuing with a verb. He assumes that only with these linguistic units can communication, even thinking, take place.

None of these assumptions is reliable. True, expression by means of subject, verb, and complement is widespread in language, but it is not the only means of thinking or communicating, and many languages manage very well without much of it, and are more terse for avoiding it. Words in our sense are common, but they are by no means the only linguistic units, and they often do not provide a good basis for linguistic analysis. Parts of speech exist everywhere in the sense that all languages have classes of linguistic forms, and both nouns and verbs are widespread, but in many languages these distinctions are not sharp, and sequences of parts of speech, although they may be much more extensive and complicated than in English, do not in most instances closely resemble any grammatical statement likely to be taught in an American school. Tense is not a universal property of verbs, for it may be the property of nouns or of neither; sex is not usually the basis of gender, in the sense that gender is the classification of nouns; modifiers may be, but usually are not, divided into those which do or do not modify nouns— and not only because a language may have no nouns in our sense of the word.

Thus, language does not necessarily follow the restricted patterns which characterize western European tongues, and we are fortunate

Lee and the late Clyde Kluckhohn have been interested in this problem, but as yet, and for good reasons, a well-chastened caution is the fashion among students of Amerindian. One of the best brief surveys is that in Driver, cited earlier.

that the hundreds of Amerindian types of speech offer us highly varied sorts of linguistic structure. We did not need knowledge of Amerindian to convince us that not all bodies of speech are like Indo-European languages; evidence from Asia, Africa, and the Pacific Islands would demonstrate that, but Amerindian languages, by the wealth of their forms and of their philosophic concepts, and by the care with which some of them have been studied, do greatly enhance our significant linguistic material and provide us with dramatic concepts.

But what, specifically, did these linguistically inventive Amerindians produce? In any final way, the question is unanswerable, but we can seek revealing samples.

4

THE AMERINDIAN GIFT OF TONGUES

If we are to ask ourselves how the Amerindian languages and minds interacted, we must first inquire what the Amerindians produced in language. What was the character of their linguistic genius? So far as I know, no competent student of American languages has recently attempted thoroughgoing answers to these questions, and a number have suggested that the questions are premature and should not be asked. But the questions are inevitably there, whether or not we presume to phrase them, and partial answers are surely better than none, provided we recognize that they are partial.

We might start by seeing what a passage of Amerindian prose looks like. It cannot be typical; the Amerindians had rhetorical traditions, as have all peoples with any cultural pretensions, but they had no one rhetoric. Amerindian prose can be highly poetic, highly generalized, notable for almost any quality we might care to name, and we can scarcely, in a book addressed to general readers, approach it directly. We must examine it in translation or through the medium of a bilingual speaker. The following may serve as a passable sample. It is from an account by Mrs. Oregon Jim, a Yurok living along the Klamath River in northern California, who was explaining why she would not speak to another old woman or her relatives or to anyone who spoke to them.

It seems that a certain woman abandoned various husbands, but when she took up with a Hupa, that was too much—and they called her *kimolin,* dirty, partly because none of the husbands had paid anything for her, although she came of a good family. Among her bastard sons one grew up in a Presbyterian mission; he was stupid, and "had even less sense than the Presbyterians have." In fact, he had so little sense that he came down from the mission school to see the Fish Dance and was all dressed up, showing off his straw hat with a ribbon on it, and insulting people, especially Tuley-Creek Jim, who because of the insults tried later to collect from the bastard's relatives. The family had no money, not even the fifteen dollars Tuley-Creek Jim asked, but the young bastard kept saying, "Look at my pants. Look at my shirt. I am just like a white man. I can say anything I please." Tuley-Creek Jim got pretty mad, and when a brother-in-law of his was in a canoe passing a corpse-place where people were making crying-songs for somebody dead at the home of the boastful bastard's family, he refused to stop. People on the shore endeavored to prevent this insult by detaining the canoe, and among these was Billy Brooks, a relative of Mrs. Oregon Jim.

"Hey! You fellow-living-with-a-woman-you-haven't-paid-for!" he [the brother-in-law] said to Billy Brooks, "make these fellows let go of my canoe."
Billy was surprised. He hadn't been holding the canoe. And anyway, he did not expect to be addressed that way. *Las-son* is what he had heard addressed to him. That means "half-married, or improperly married to a woman in the house by the trail." Brooks had had no money to pay for a wife, so he went to live with his woman instead of taking her home to him. That is what we call being half-married. Everybody called Billy that way, behind his back. "Half-married-into-the-house-by-the-trail" was his name.
When Billy got over being surprised at this form of address, he got mad. He pointed at the fellow in the canoe. He swore the worst way a person can swear. What he said was awful. He pointed at him. He was mad clear through. He didn't care what he said. "Your deceased relatives," is what he said to Coyote-Jim's brother-in-law, in the canoe. [*Coyote-Jim* seems to be an alternative name for Tuley-Creek Jim.] He said it right out loud. He pointed at the canoe. That's the time he said "Your deceased relatives." "All your deceased relatives," he said to those in the canoe. [The meaning is apparently "the deceased relatives of all of you."]

The attack was devastating. The brother-in-law sat down in the canoe aghast, and Billy's friends let go the canoe, which floated off down the river. Now Billy was in serious trouble because he had used words that referred to the dead relatives of the people in the canoe, and the family of the boastful bastard was in trouble, too, because Billy blamed them for the affair.

"I've got to pay money," Billy Brooks said to them then. "I got mad and swore something terrible at Coyote-Jim's brother-in-law. That was on account of you people. If you had paid what you owed to Coyote-Jim, Coyote-Jim's brother-in-law would not have gone past your house while you were crying, and you wouldn't have held his canoe, and he wouldn't have addressed me as he did, and I wouldn't have said what I did. Moreover, Wokel Dave was in the canoe, and when I said that which I said, it applied to him, too. I feel terrible mean about what I said. I've got to have trouble with both those men. There were others in the canoe, too, but they are poor people, and don't amount to anything. But Dave is a rich man. Now all this trouble is on your account, and you've got to pay me two dollars and a half."

The old man at Wahsek was in trouble. "First my mouse says to Coyote-Jim what should not in any case have been said," the old man complained. (We call illegitimate children "mice" because they eat, and stay around, and nobody has paid for them.) "Now on account of what my mouse said, all this other trouble has happened."

But Billy could get no money out of the relatives of the "mouse," and he had none of his own, and accordingly he had to take a job as scout with some soldiers trying to chase some Yurok horse thieves; one of the soldiers got into a fight trying to steal a woman, and they were all so bloodied in the fight that when the soldier fired his pistol he hit another Yurok, who died, and who happened to be a relative of the old woman with whom Mrs. Oregon Jim had been feuding ever since.[1]

This is an instructive tale; it reveals a good bit about the commercial, sexual, and social practices of the Yurok, along with some of their intellectual processes, and it suggests something of the role that language played in the lives of these people. Yurok had pleasant figurative inventions like calling illegitimate children "mice," and a few hastily used words could foment feuds that involved whole families for generations. Not only was reference to dead relatives taboo; apparently the very words were so horrible that Billy could not repeat them in his confession, and could come no closer than "I wouldn't have said what I did." We are involved here with magic and religion, with law, government, and mores, but these appear through cruxes in the use of language. Some qualities of Yurok diction and rhetoric doubtless color the Amerindian English; we notice that related ideas become involved with locutions which in English would probably appear as a word with modifiers, or in some subordinate construction, but in Yurok seem to cluster as interreliant units, expressed in *fellow-living-with-a-woman-you-haven't-paid-for* and *half-married-into-the-house-by-the-trail*. We notice a heavy reliance upon brief utterances, *Look at my pants, Look at my shirt,* which in English come out as abrupt simple sentences, but may have been any sort of terse labeling in Yurok.

Going beyond this sample, we need to ask if Amerindian languages themselves can be characterized, as a whole, or in groups. Here we should remind ourselves that Amerindia was culturally diverse, that probably few generalizations apply to all Amerindia, in language or in anything else. Continent-wide traits are scarce, and detailed description

---

[1] T. T. Waterman, "All Is Trouble along the Klamath," in *American Indian Life,* ed. Elsie Clews Parsons (New York: B. W. Huebsch, 1925), pp. 289–96.

has revealed languages of the greatest diversity, in phonetics, vocabulary, and structure.[2]

We might begin where we can be fairly sure of ourselves, with Amerindian *onomastics*—onomastics is the study of names, and the giving of names. The Amerindians gave names to all prominent aspects of the continents they filled, in most instances many names, in what may have been the most extensive onomastic orgy of all time. We are not sure what we should make of the Biblical account of the manner in which Jehovah called up all the animals before Adam and accepted as their names whatever Adam called them. The more one contemplates the multiplicity of fauna and flora upon the earth, and the manner in which languages seem to have grown, the more difficulty one encounters in imagining a time in which any human being, even an Adam, could have encountered and designated all visible beings, not to mention the miscroscopic creatures and those beings which seem to be plants, but which can be shown to be animals. In fact, even the best students in the Hebraic tradition are inclined to feel that this event must have its largest implications in art and philosophy.[3] But if the Lord never called up all the animals one sunny afternoon for Adam to name, He did call up many of them, over considerable periods of time and in many places, to be named by the Amerindians.

Here was a naming day, indeed. When the Amerindians broke into the Americas, millions of square miles were before them, stuffed with running, flying, swimming, creeping, and crawling things, not to mention the stationary ones, and all nameless. Through the centuries these creatures and objects were named, some many times and in many tongues, in hundreds of languages and in thousands of dialects. Furthermore, selected objects were named in great detail, particularly those that entered intimately into the lives of the aborigines. In the dialects of northern South America, for example, where the potato is a staple, local

---

[2] I shall rely on widely scattered materials, but notably on *Linguistic Structures in Native America* and Boas, *Handbook of American Indian Languages,* both cited earlier. Some of Sapir's work is summarized in his *Language,* cited earlier, and reprinted in *Selected Writings of Edward Sapir,* ed. David G. Mandelbaum (Berkeley and Los Angeles: University of California Press, 1949). Ethnological and linguistic series are many and indispensable; the most extensive and readily available are the *Bulletins* and *Reports* of the Bureau of American Ethnology. Many of the most important studies now appear in journals like *Language, American Anthropologist,* and *International Journal of American Linguistics.* A good selection is collected in *Language in Culture and Society,* ed. Dell Hymes (New York: Harper & Row, 1964); it contains 69 pieces by 59 authors, with bibliography and "reference notes."

[3] Note, for example, that charming volume by Noah Jonathan Jacobs, *Naming Day in Eden* (New York: The Macmillan Co., 1958).

Indians may have more than two hundred different names for different sorts of potatoes, and these may differ from potato terms in neighboring dialects, names conceived on other classifications. Similarly, the Amerindians who lived by snaring ducks had a great variety of names for waterfowl, names which describe the bird, its plumage, its edibility, its habits—particularly those which made it amenable to capture.

Most of this body of terminology has vanished; white men did not bother to preserve it and Amerindians could not. Not even place names have survived; true, Indian names have been used as place names by white men—Multnomah, Klackamas, Penobscot, Ojibway, Illinois, thousands of them in whatever spelling—but on the whole these have been prominent Amerindian personal names, supposed tribal names, or other words which have been attached by the white man to something in the vicinity. White men have not normally preserved the Amerindian names for the Amerindian places, nor have white men normally been aware that the continent was already well named when they arrived. There have been exceptions, some of them notable; most stream names preserve local Indian words in western Washington, where an occasional *North River* or *Otter Creek* contrasts strangely with *Hoquiam, Humptulups, Queniult, Hoh, Chalat, Soleduck,* and *Pysht*. Elsewhere, *Mississippi* is the Sauk word for "big water," and *Chicago* presumably means something like "stinking place," wild onions having formerly grown there. Such survivals are rather more common in Canada and in Latin America than within the United States, presumably because the name-givers survived better. Place names like *Popocatepetl* and *Titicaca* presumably preserve old designations, but at least within the United States genuine survivals are the exceptions, and even outside the United States the great bulk from all the name-giving has vanished. Some names for things have survived. A number of Nahuatl names for distinctively American objects have become part of world terminology—*atlatl, chicle, chocolate, copal, tomato*—and many more. Similarly, Arawak words have been picked up among the Caribbean Islands, *barbecue, cacique, cannibal, canoe,* and on through the alphabet. Scattering words memorialize objects in the northern hemisphere—*kinnikinik, poganip, kiva, menhaden*.

Now we must ask ourselves what impact this need for names had upon the Amerindians themselves. Here, surely, is a hazardous question, one not very amenable to any documentable answer. The need for names must have had some impact, social and psychological, with at least indirect linguistic results. Later we shall need to observe that the white invaders were very much aware of the unnamed nature of the new world, at least unnamed for them. This awareness must have done things to them and for them which we must later consider in some detail, but their situation was not that of the Amerindians. The white men had come from a well-named world into a nameless one. They knew—all but the earliest and more ignorant of them—that names have legal status, that they are collected into books, that they have wide and common currency. Presumably the Amerindians may have had no such insights; most of them had no books, no written statutes, no conception of wide currency.

At the very least, the possession of place names must have encouraged the worldwide tendency to ethnocentrism. The Jews are not the only group that have felt they are God's chosen ones. Some such denomination, in whatever dialect, seems to have been the almost universal name that man has given himself; thus, terms of *mankind, man, the people*—such as *Na-Dene* for peoples sometimes called Athapascans —were common designations for Amerindian groups. Native place names must have helped. Having one's own set of names for all things and places must have encouraged a conviction of belonging to a natural trinity made up of God, our people, and the world.

Some of these new names were presumably outright coinages. Birds with distinctive calls were no doubt named in imitation of what these sounds suggested in various Amerindian languages, as the white men later named the bobwhite and the whippoorwill. Most of the names, however, would have grown somehow out of Asian words, and many of these were no doubt compounds suited to animals and objects in the new world. An Amerindian who saw a strange duck would be in no doubt as to what it was; ducks are readily identifiable almost everywhere. He would be most likely to call the thing a "duck," using the word for such a bird that his language had inherited from an Asian language, and he would then add anything more that he conceived to be appropriate, probably from the same Asian language. This was, of course, the device used later by the white men when they named *bufflehead ducks, canvasback ducks, sharp-tailed ducks, Labrador ducks,* and the like. Something of this sort the Amerindian name-givers must have done, but just what is now obscure and must be mostly lost, although we shall know something more when we can relate Amerindian tongues to their reconstructed ancestors or their surviving relatives in Asia.

Some Amerindians were much concerned with personal names; the Iroquois possessed only a limited stock of names, and a child might have to wait for years for the possessor of a name to die so that he could inherit it. Certain California Indians progressed through a sequence of names, through infancy, puberty, matrimony, and the like. Other Amerindians, notably in the plains, were allowed to assume names to celebrate their triumphs. Many tribes had elaborate taboos against the use or nonuse of names, particularly as they involved the dead or certain family relationships. The lore of this sort is extensive, but it probably had only limited impact on language. More pertinent may be the fact that many students of Amerindian languages have noticed that the tongues they were studying were nominally rich, that is, they contained a high proportion of what we call nouns. Furthermore, a not uncommon structure among the Amerindians provided "sentences"—we must call them this although they do not fit the Indo-European pattern—which are composed of a name plus various modifiers and classifiers. For example: "A dark man is standing over there" can become *man* plus a sequence of affixes, *dark, vertical position, distant.* Boas was of the opinion that the prevalence among Amerindian languages of descriptive nouns led the natives to make up descriptive words for phenomena introduced by the white man instead of borrowing the English; the Tsimshian of British Columbia call rice *looking like maggots* and dozens of Amerindian groups must have called the steamboat some equivalent of *walking on water, fire on his back.*

Did the need for naming move at least some Amerindian languages toward a preference for nouns and for structures centered upon nouns? At first blush the suggestion seems implausible on a number of grounds. Most Amerindians probably lived without much notion of the need for names; the salient features of their limited worlds—few of them traveled far, even the nomadic hunters—were all named, as were the more notable of the fauna and flora of their areas, and they were not much interested, anyhow, in plants or animals that did not enter into their struggles for food, shelter, and safety. Furthermore, granted the Amerindians had a penchant for names—and this is by no means certain—we do not know what this means or what caused it; logically, nominalization in language may have resulted from linguistic structure as well as the structure having resulted from the place names. *Post hoc* need not imply *propter hoc.*

Obviously, these are potent arguments, but some rebuttal is possible. Granted that in recent millennia most Amerindians lived most of the time in an Amerindian-named world, this was not always true. We know that although languages are constantly changing, they sometimes go through formative stages which set up patterns which thereafter may prove relatively resistant to change. This tendency toward patterning is most obvious, perhaps, in sound, where one need no more than mention developments like those described in Grimm's Law and the Great English Vowel Shift, but the principle must pertain in grammatical and semantic patterns as well. If a language went through a great period of name-giving, this phenomenon may have altered the pattern of the language sufficiently to persist, particularly if name-giving continued, as it might with a nomadic people. Some Amerindians could have been nomadic for long periods—for example, the Folsom hunters that preyed upon the game south of the glaciers, even though they did not travel fast or far. Many Amerindians must have encountered various complexes of flora and fauna. Speakers of Na-Dene, for example, are today found in the lush Pacific Northwest, in California, in the semidesert Southwest, in the intervening mountains, and along the seacoasts. Presumably the speakers of no one of the Na-Dene languages encountered all the natural phenomena of these highly diverse areas, but since they came by way of Alaska all of them must have encountered at least two, and presumably most of them would have experienced more.

Of course, if Amerindian languages run to names for things, this is an interesting fact, however the languages developed this characteristic. The tendency would do something to structure the minds of the users of the language, perhaps instilling a tendency to respect objective reality, for example, which some competent students believe to be characteristic of many Amerindian tongues.

Now to grammar, and here we should agree upon some principles and some terminology, since *grammar* and terms associated with it are incendiary. They promote fights among people who have not determined what they are fighting about. *Grammar* is often used to indicate fashion in language; is it now fashionable to say *he don't* or *he doesn't, like I said* or *as I said?* For such questions, students of language use the word *usage,* and I shall consider usage problems later, but when I use the word *grammar* I shall mean the way language works. All languages have working units; whatever else they may do, these units usually involve meaning. In English, units of language are often called *words; the, small,* and *boy* are formative units, and the way they work together is grammar.

This statement, simple enough, becomes complex if we examine it. Not all symbols in a dictionary are so clearly working units as are *the, small,* and *boy. Boy* may be one working unit, but *boys* would seem to be two, *boy* plus the letter *s* or the sound /z/, since *s* or /z/ attached to all sorts of words like *boy* will form plurals, as in *girls, houses,* and *cars.* (Symbols like /z/, placed within slant lines, are what are now called *phonemes,* working units of sound.) Furthermore, identical forms having various uses may be difficult to distinguish as words. Is *man* one word or four or more? Presumably an English-speaking Martian might say, "Man! Did that man man the man craft!" Is *space craft* one word or two, and will it become one if we spell it *spacecraft?* That is, words as they are conventionally defined in dictionaries are determined by meaning, spelling, function, etymology, or all of them, but meanings are not exact and spelling is whimsical. Since students of language try to be scientific, they are skeptical of terms which seem not to designate real things and cannot be exactly defined. They like to approach language as sound, which is measurable; thus the spelled word *boys* is made up of two working units of language /bɔɪ/ and /z/. These units are called *morphemes,* and we shall need the term in thinking about Amerindian languages, partly because students of language work with these concepts, and partly because, since Amerindian tongues were not much written, they profited from no tradition of words crystallized in dictionaries.

With working units, two treatments are possible, putting them together or keeping them apart. Consider the first: granted that a language includes units for *duck, man,* and *many,* they can be combined into *duck-many,* and *man-many.* That is, the unit for *many,* or some corruption of it, can become a classifier, an indication of the plural, as *s* or /z/ indicates the plural in *boys.* This device has been very common in language, and it can become elaborate; most languages have made some use of it, hundreds or thousands have relied mainly upon it, and many have developed paradigms that order hundreds of sound-combinations to designate and delineate cases, tenses, moods, directions of modification, and the like. This grammatical device, bringing units together, is called *synthesis;* in the form familiar in classical Latin and in Indo-European it is commonly called *inflection,* since it seems to rely on a change in word form.

Now let us notice the second possibility, that linguistic units can be kept apart. Their order may reveal relationship: for example, *I do* has an impact different from *Do I?,* although the difference relies upon the order of the units. *The Executives Club* differs from *Club the executives!* This sort of grammar is called *analytic*—since *analysis* contrasts with *synthesis*—and also *isolating* or *distributive.* It can employ devices other than word order, notably individual words which reveal relationship—in English, words like *of* and *and.*

The languages of the world provide examples of many sorts of devices for bringing grammatical units together or keeping them apart, but one synthetic device, incorporation, is so common in Amerindian speech that we should mention it particularly. To understand how this works we might observe the English command, "Get out!" This is composed only of a verb, or of a verb with a kind of postpositive—some people would call it an adverb or a preposition—but we understand that there is an implied subject something like *you,* and there is probably an implied complement, something like *the door, of here, of my presence,* or, *of this group.* In English, these ideas need not be expressed, but if they were expressed, and expressed in such a way that they could be used only by attaching them to the verb, we should have an incorporating structure. That is, incorporation is the grammatical device by which the subject or the complement or both can be incorporated within the verb.

As an example we might use a Yana phrasal cluster cited by Sapir—Yana was one of the many tongues spoken in north central California: *yabanauma—wildjigummaha'nigi,* which means "let each one of us by all means move west across the creek." Sapir breaks it into what would be called morphemes and analyzes it as follows:

It consists of elements of three types—a nuclear element or "stem" (ya- "several people move"); formal elements of mode (-ha, hortatory) and person (-nigi "we"); and elements of a modifying sort which cannot occur independently but which nevertheless express ideas that would ordinarily be rendered by independent words (-banauma- "everybody," -wil- "across," -dji- "to the west," -gumma- "indeed.")[4]

Since the incorporation of the subject within the verb is familiar from traditional grammar—it is common in many Indo-European languages, in Latin, Russian, some Romance languages, and many others—the characteristic quality here is the incorporation of the object. In fact, a good many students of Amerindian have noticed that the tongues they have had under study tended to hinge sentences on the object rather than upon the subject. An English sentence, or at least many an English sentence, can be thought of as a subject modified by everything else in the sentence, and these modifiers include the verb. In *The girls are powdering,* the construction *are powdering* is normally thought of as predication, but it certainly modifies, also, in the sense that it describes the girls at the moment. Such sentences can be found in most Amerindian tongues, but scholar after scholar has been impressed with the dominance of the verb in Amerindian sentences, and the fact that the verb may be more oriented to the object than to the subject, as though the Amerindian were interested in the result more than the cause. Has a sense for incorporation led the Amerindians toward this preference for thinking from the object, or has the sense for the result encouraged the development of incorporating structures? Here, as so frequently in the study of language, the relative antiquity of hens and eggs seems difficult to determine, but we might notice that such a change could be deeply significant. What, for example, would be the impact upon science if our language induced us to think from results, not from immediate causes? To this question we must return, although in a larger context.

To put this in another way, many Amerindian languages are what is

---

[4] *Selected Writings,* cited above, pp. 173–74.

called *inferentially marked*. Many languages are what is called *paradigmatically marked*, that is, words tend to fall into paradigms as a salient part of the grammatical description. Latin provides an example. Other languages are *syntactically marked;* of this sort English, with its relatively rigid word order, may serve as a type. Other languages, including many Amerindian tongues, are inferentially marked; in some of these languages, for example, the subject and verb, or the subject and verb and another noun cannot be identified, but must be inferred by other means, if what we would call the subject and verb need to be identified.

Among the other devices often associated with incorporation is *polysynthesis,* bringing together morphemes which cannot be used independently as words, but which have known uses in combination with other morphemes. In our word *indirectness,* for example, the morpheme *direct* can work alone, but the morphemes *in-* and *-ness* must work with something else in a polysynthetic combination. In English, a combination like *indirectness* always includes at least one morpheme which can work by itself, but this is not necessarily true of polysynthetic languages. Theoretically, three affixes, none of which could be used alone, might work together in one subject-verb-complement cluster.

Neither incorporation nor polysynthesis dominates central structure among Amerindian languages, but they are common enough to be significant. Languages which rely heavily upon such devices seem not to be very common throughout the earth, nowhere near so common as grammars that use what we would call words, and combine these into subjects, verbs and complements as relatively separate entities. Hence, the extensive occurrence of these devices probably means something, although we may not know what.

The Eskimo-Aleut languages, for example, which spread all along the arctic coast of North America, are highly polysynthetic, as are the Algonquian languages spoken in central and eastern Canada and down into New England. The Amerindians who used these tongues were all relatively unsophisticated. Did they represent the backward survivals of an early, widespread, but very simple culture, clinging on in the inhospitable climes of the north? Or were they late arrivals who took over the icy shores and the frigid tundras because their predecessors had abandoned them? We can answer only that as yet we have no adequate basis for decision.

Some other peculiarities serve to characterize language families, but not to distinguish Amerindian languages. The Na-Dene languages, mentioned earlier, not only favor constructions hinging upon what we would call nouns, but they distinguish words by pitch. In Navaho, for example, *yāzīd* means "You pour it down" if the first syllable is low and the second high, but "I have poured it down" if both syllables are low. Some Amerindian languages have very few consonants, and these appear in orderly sequences; the voiceless stops /p, t, k/ will have their voiced equivalents /b, d, g/. Others may not have these sequences complete, and some may have individual sounds variously complicated. A sound like /p/ may appear with variations, which a linguist calls *allophones,* that is, variant sounds in the language which may serve for /p/. In Paiute, for example, what we would call /p/, a voiceless sound, may appear in certain circumstances as a voiced sound, which we would call /b/, or it may appear with more or less breath, sounds which have been transcribed /'p/ and /''p/. These sounds are about what a speaker of English would be likely to produce if he tried to pronounce *h-p,* an *h* sound moving into a *p* sound. Furthermore, these sounds can be what is called geminated, that is, pronounced twice, an effect which can be produced in English by pronouncing *hippo* as though it were two words *hip-po* and *habit* as though it were *hab-bit.* Also, these sounds interchange depending upon their occurrence within words, and these differences vary by dialect. In Bannock, a northern Paiute language spoken in southeastern Idaho, the sound may be a voiced stop /b/ or /bh/, contrasting with /p/ or /'p/ as a free variant, but in the Walker River dialect in central Nevada a fricative can contrast with a voiced stop, a geminate voiceless stop, and a geminate voiced stop, but only medially. That is, these changes cannot take place at the beginning of a sequence of sound, only within the sequence, and the variant that is used will depend upon the nature of the preceding sound.[5] Iroquois, on the other hand, is said not to have a single consonant made with the lips. Other Amerindian languages are heavily consonanted, including voiceless *l*'s, variously vocalized *r*'s, and the relatively rare sounds known as glottalized stops and affricates, made by closing the windpipe or the back of the throat. In fact there are even supposed to be instances in which narrators have transposed a whole series of lateral clicks into vertical clicks for humorous stylistic purposes, as a writer in English might make a certain character lisp or substitute the nasal /n/ for the nasal /ŋ/, often spelled *ng.*

Voicing in Amerindian languages is in some ways so peculiar that scholars have had trouble recording voice. In English, as in most Indo-European languages, voicing is relatively clear and regular; the consonants in *bid* are voiced; the corresponding consonants in *pit* are not. Partly the uncertainty is involved in differences in stress and in aspiration

---

[5] For the material concerning Paiute dialects, as yet unpublished, I am indebted to Drs. Sven Liljeblad and Wayne Suttles.

(breath), but many Amerindians either ignore voicing or use it in ways difficult for speakers of English to hear. All vowels in Indo-European are presumably voiced, except when the speaker whispers, but some Amerindian languages include whisper vowels without voice. Among some Eskimos the men pronounce /p, t, k, g/ in the manner which seems to be traditional, but the women transform these sounds into /m, n, ṇ, ŋ/ (the corresponding nasals, that is, sounds made through the nose), and lately some of the men have taken to imitating the women.

Pitch patterns within sentences are varied, but they can be expected to be unlike those in Modern English. A modern American sentence, for example, is likely to have relatively level stress with few variations until near the end, when, in one frequent pattern, the voice rises slightly and then drops sharply. The Takelma of southwest Oregon, on the other hand, have several sound patterns within the sentence and a sharp rise at the end. Many of the Great Basin Indians use a pitch sequence which rises slowly to about a third of the way through a clause or sentence and then fades gradually down, so that the whole gives the effect of lazy waves. This pattern appears especially in public addresses, as though the speaker were trying to lull his audience into sleep, and since much Indian oratory is highly repetitious, this is often the effect.

A few languages have had one set of terms to be used among or to females, another among males, and these dual systems can be much more extensive than the Eskimo fad mentioned above. In at least one case a whole language was used by the men, another by the women and children, but there were reasons other than linguistic for that; the cannibalistic Caribs in northern South America defeated a group of Arawaks, devoured the Arawak men and enslaved the women. Thus for a time Carib remained the language of the men, Arawak the language of the women and children. But sex differentiation in languages can occur without cannibalism. Among the Kosati of southwestern Louisiana, who speak a Muscogian language, the women use terms which differ from those in use among the men, and teach their children the appropriate forms. Apparently the forms considered suitable for females are more archaic than those used by males—for what reason, no one knows. Something similar has been observed in California, for example among the Yana, but here the forms used by women seem to have been cut down from the form used by men. For deer the men say ba-na, the women ba'. The men call the grizzly bear t'en'-an but the women say t'et'. The male form is used among men exclusively, the female form among women or for mixed conversations. These distinctions in language on the basis of sex were presumably more widely distributed than they are now, and similar distinctions have been observed in Asia.

Whistled language had a limited use, and was apparently restricted to males, as among the Mazateco in northern Oaxaca, Mexico. The women could understand the whistled medium, and at least some of them could use it, although a woman who communicated by whistling was embarrassed if anyone heard her. It was mainly employed for communication at a distance, and seems to have had a simple vocabulary and grammar, but all males could translate anything out of it and could translate into it anything that their society was likely to prompt them to say. Recorded samples of speech are usually something like "What," or "Come here, friend," but whistling sufficed also for "Is it your own coffee that you are picking there?" and "Three pesos are given me where I am going with it." Apparently whistled communication depended in part on the auditor being able to guess the subject of the conversation and upon the whistled sounds imitating the tone patterns of verbal speech. For example, all Spanish names were borrowed into Mazateco with similar tone patterns, and thus if two persons were present with three-syllable names like *Modesto* or *Ricardo* they could not be distinguished in whistled speech.

The degree to which familiar concepts like tense, mode, and case occur in Amerindian languages varies greatly. Some languages make little or no use of these; others have them developed far more precisely than has English. Takelma has eight different forms for the first person singular, but they are not case forms in our sense, for they must all be translated *I.* They are to be used, not in different relationships to the verb, but with different sorts of verbs, one with the timeless form, one with the future transitive, another with the future intransitive, and the like. Not uncommon in Amerindia, as among the Siuslaw of western Oregon, is the device whereby plurality is indicated in the subject for intransitive verbs, in the object for transitive verbs.

To see how some of these linguistic devices work with one another, we might notice a pleasant sequence of changes that Franz Boas has rung on the sentence *He is sick,* which with us means that a specific individual is ill at the moment. Eskimo would have to say something like *single man is being sick,* and the idea of sickness would be involved in the verb, but this verb would not imply anything about time, whether the man is now sick, has been sick, or is likely to become so. Of course Eskimo could say these things, but not in the verb. In Kwakiutl, a northwestern language, the sickness would of necessity be more definitely identified, both as to place and as to the reliability of the information as provided by an informant. That is, the grammar must make clear where the sick man and the informant were, whether or not the informant saw the sick man and the speaker the informant. Thus the sentence might be translated as "definite man near to informant and visible to him sick; informant near speaker and visible to him." Of course *invisible* could be substituted for *visible* if occasion warranted, and positions could be otherwise indicated. Furthermore, the speaker would have to indicate whether this was a new subject being brought up, or one that had been discussed before; to use Boas' words, "in case the speaker had not seen the sick person himself, he would have to express whether he knows by hearsay or by evidence that the person is sick, or whether he has dreamed it." In Ponca, a Siouan tongue, the speaker would have to indicate whether the sick man was moving or stationary.[6]

A specialized linguistic device appears in Nootka, a language represented by various dialects in southwestern Canada and in Washington. Partly by the use of additional suffixes and partly by what Sapir calls "consonantal play," that is, "altering certain consonants . . . to other consonants that are phonetically related to them, or by inserting meaningless consonants or consonant clusters. . . . It is possible and often customary in Nootka to imply in speech some physical characteristic of the person addressed or spoken of. . . ." The physical classes of people which can be so identified are apparently "children, unusually fat or heavy people, unusually short adults, those suffering from some defect of the eye, hunchbacks, those that are lame, left-handed persons, and circumcised males." Similarly diminutives permitted special effects; the result of using a diminutive when referring to a full-grown muscular male named Sam would be to call him "little cross-eyed Sammy," an epithet which Sam could be expected to resent, one which would be employed only in teasing or as an insult if used to his face. The Nootka even have a name for this sort of speech, "to talk in sore-eyed fashion." Otherwise meaningless syllables may be added to the diminutive to indicate whether the person is lame or left-handed, and for a hunchback light sounds which we would associate with s are changed to heavier sounds which we would associate with *k, ch,* or *g.* For circumcised males a syllable *-ct-* was inserted; thus a famous man who was born circumcised and whose name was Toxmis was referred to as Toctxmis to emphasize what was felt to be his deformity. Some mental characteristics may be similarly satirized; cowards are referred to "by making the voice small," and for greedy persons the syllable *-tcx-* is inserted, since it refers to ravens—Raven is a mythological creature famous among the Nootka for his greed. Similarly, among the nearby Takelma, a voiceless

[6] Here, as elsewhere, details are collected from widely dispersed sources; some material is surveyed in Boas, *Handbook of American Indian Languages,* cited above, I, 1–83. The example of the sick man occurs on p. 43.

l identifies the speech of the clumsy bear, and *s* sounds are freely inserted to suggest the sneezing of the coyote.[7]

Among the minor matters worthy of note in Amerindia are onomatopoeia and reduplication. The first, an echoic or imitative device for making words and structures, gives us such words as English *choo-choo* and *murmur* and many terms in Amerindian. This development is of course to be expected, since the Amerindians lived mainly in contact with sound-making creatures. What more natural than that the Labrador Algonkins call an owl an *uhu* and that the call which sounds to us like *whip-poor-will* sounded to the Sauk like *muck-a-wiss*. Most Amerindian groups made more or less use of this device. Reduplication, also, is a common practice, once prevalent in most Indo-European languages, although now mainly sporadic in English. We say, "Run! Run!" not only to express our excitement but to urge that the runner keep running. Similarly, we say "You run. You run, too," and these could be reduced in speech to "Run! Run!" one command directed to one runner, and the other to a second. Thus the repetition of a word or a syllable is a common device to indicate either the plural of an action or the continuation to some foreseen result. Among the Tsimshian of the Northwest, *haos* is one dog, *hashaos*[8] a pack of dogs; *heits* is to send, but *heisheits* to send repeatedly; *hanx* is thin, *hanhanx* is to be downright skinny. Among the Takelma *hel-* is to sing and *helel-* to go on singing. Reduplicated syllables may undergo changes, of course; among the Coos of western Oregon *qaic* is small, but *qeqaicu la witin* means something like "His blood is clubbed into small pieces." Among the Siuslaw the suffix *-ax* indicates that a word refers to people; applied to the word for "long ago," *wanwits,* it identifies old-timers, and doubled it suggests people of very ancient or mythological times. In some exuberant languages syllables may be reduplicated several times.

And so on. This sort of thing, noticing peculiarities of certain bodies of Amerindian speech which have at least degrees of commonality, could be continued indefinitely. Such material evidences the linguistic fecundity of the Amerindians, but it does less than one could wish to

---

[7] Edward Sapir, "Abnormal Types of Speech in Nootka," *Canada, Geological Survey Memoir,* 62, *Anthropological Series,* 5 (Ottawa: Government Printing Bureau, 1915); reprinted in *Selected Writings,* cited above, pp. 179–96.

[8] Here and elsewhere I have silently normalized the phonetic transcriptions, but I trust not to alter the aspects of language involved in the discussion. Transcriptions into the International Phonetic Alphabet or any of the more recent phonemic systems are too specific to be considered in a volume of this sort, and any locution may involve the working of a number of linguistic principles. Elucidating all of them would become cumbersome. For example, the word I have rendered *hashaos* Boas transcribed *hasha'°s.* The curious will find some description of phonemics in Chapter 22.

typify Amerindian generally. As we have noticed earlier, Americanists have on the whole been cautious; if they have sometimes inferred less from their material than they might have, they have at least not deluged us with hasty generalizations. Perhaps as near to a summary as I know is that by Sapir, who in the course of characterizing Takelma, wrote as follows:

> Some of the more important of these typical or at any rate widespread American traits, that are found in Takelma, are: the incorporation of the pronominal (and nominal) object in the verb; the incorporation of the possessive pronouns in the noun; the closer association with the verb-form of the object than the subject; the inclusion of a considerable number of instrumental and local modifications in the verb-complex; the weak development of differences of tense in the verb and of number in the verb and noun; and the impossibility of drawing a sharp line between mode and tense.[9]

He could have added a tendency toward reduplication, and if he had not been dealing with Takelma he would probably have noticed a secondary tendency to employ nominal structures, along with a primary tendency to center upon the verb. He surely would have agreed that different languages can be expected to assort ideas differently, and that although we may not have good generalizations as to the manner in which ideas are assorted in Amerindia, differences and probably tendencies are to be expected. In fact, Sapir elsewhere evinced great interest in this subject, though caution in dealing with it.

Thus far, our sketching and sampling have produced no very startling or sweeping results, but at least one other method remains to be tried: relatively close examination of a more limited but carefully selected body of material, and in a book of this sort we must emphasize the *relatively* as a qualifier of the *close examination*. No close examination is possible without special background and technical discussion, but we might limit our field and examine it somewhat consistently. Here I propose Hopi, as studied by Benjamin Lee Whorf. Frankly, I am not here endeavoring to be typical, but to produce the most favorable and revealing case I know of, particularly for what language may have done. Whether the seeming significance of this case reflects the excellence of Hopi as a language or the acuity of Whorf as an observer, I shall not attempt to guess. Whorf became convinced that Hopi was a remarkable language, and modern students have become convinced that Whorf was a remarkable scholar. Whether or not all languages would be as revealing as Whorf made Hopi if all scholars were as perceptive as Whorf is an interesting if idle question. One might notice, however, that Whorf

---

[9] In Boas, *Handbook of American Indian Languages,* cited above, II, 282.

was of the Boas-Sapir school of language study, that he learned his linguistics from them, insofar as he did not learn it from the Indians he studied, and that although Boas and Sapir believed in careful, scientific work, they never lost sight of the fact that the end of knowledge is understanding, not just more knowledge.

Whorf was apparently an engaging and stimulating man, with a penetrating mind and a zestful curiosity. He had no formal training in linguistics, did not become interested in it until he was mature, and never pursued it except as an avocation, but by the time of his death at forty-four (July 26, 1941), he was the author of highly revealing studies and the principal exponent of what has become known as the Whorfian Thesis, which is surely one of the interesting ideas of our time.[10] I am not aware that it has ever been phrased succinctly, but it might be approximated as follows: Apparent reality is not actual reality, but a relatively consistent conception, related to reality but growing from language and consequently structured by concepts within the language or languages of those who do the conceiving. All bodies of supposed knowledge are thus reflections of language, even knowledge as theoretically objective as is science. That is, since minds work through language, we have no objective reality but only the various reflections of an ideal reality prompted by the various patternings of ideas in languages.

Before we discuss this thesis we should turn to Whorf's work. He did not live to finish his studies nor to systematize his findings, but many of his conclusions are clear enough; he made subsidiary use of many languages, notably Nootka and Eskimo, using mainly the research of other men, but his most extensive evidence comes from Hopi and his own researches into it.

Except for particles, in Whorf's view, Hopi contains only nouns and verbs, nothing that we would call modifiers. Hopi is even more strongly inflected than are Latin and Greek, but it is also incorporating and thus suggests the pattern of many other Amerindian tongues. Again like

---

[10] The principle is often called the Sapir-Whorf Thesis, since Sapir's name is normally associated with its inception and development, but see Herbert Landar, *Language and Culture* (New York: Oxford University Press, 1966), pp. 217–224 for vigorous reservations. Whorf published no volume, but his most significant writings have been intelligently collected in *Language, Thought, and Reality: Selected Writings of Benjamin Lee Whorf*, ed. John B. Carroll (Cambridge, Mass.: Technology Press of Massachusetts Institute of Technology, 1956) with a bibliography of the remainder. The Whorfian Thesis was made the subject of a learned conference reported in *Language in Culture: Conference on the Interrelations of Language and Other Aspects of Culture*, ed. Harry Hoijer (Chicago: University of Chicago Press, 1954), which consists of seven papers by the editor and others, along with excerpts from discussions that grew out of these papers. The whole is required reading for anyone interested in Whorf.

many Amerindian languages, predication tends to center in the verb, the relationship of the verb with the object, or sometimes in what we would call the object itself, because the lines between what seem to be the verb and the object are obscured. Also, as in many Amerindian languages, the inflection is not much concerned with tense and number in our sense, but involves reality and potentiality. In fact, Whorf went so far as to say that time is not involved in the grammatical system, and that the Hopi concept of the universe does not involve time as a continuum flowing upon man.[11]

We might notice instances. If a Hopi is considering the fact of a man running, the important aspect of the act is not that it happens while he speaks, or that it has happened, or that it is anticipated. Time, if it is important, he can indicate in another way, very much as we say "I go tomorrow," leaving ourselves uncommitted as to time in the verb, including it in what we call an adverbial noun—but one should note that Hopi construction does not involve a modifier as does English. The Hopi, instead of saying "It is hot in the summer," say something like "Heat exists summering." Hopi verbs distinguish among what Whorf calls *manifest, manifesting,* and *nomic. Manifest* is suggestive of the English indicative; Whorf explains it as objective, that is, a report by an eyewitness or reliable reporter. *Manifesting* is subjective, but since the language is dynamic, everything which has not happened is conceived of as potentially capable of coming about. That is, the difference seems to be—although Whorf did not draw this analogy—about that between a tray of ice cubes visible to the speaker and an ice-cube tray full of water which is at the moment, or may soon be, in the freezing compartment. That is, *manifesting* is either in process of becoming manifest or it is in such state that it may become manifest. Naturally, all statements that we would put into the conditional, subjunctive, or future would appear as manifesting in Hopi, but with a different emphasis.

We, too, have been aware of the uncertainty of the future, and have embodied this uncertainty in a great variety of forms, but—theoretically at least—we keep the idea of futurity central, while elaborating it with various devices suggesting uncertainty; such as "I shall go," "I ought to go," "I've got to go," "I may go," "I will go if I can," "I'll try to go," "I expect to go," "I usually go," "I shall consider going," "I ought to be able to go," "I may be able to go," "I am in a position to go," "I shall take into account the possibility of going," "Assuming that I go," "As-

---

[11] "The Psychological Reality of Phonemes," *Language, Thought, and Reality,* cited earlier, p. 58; trans. from the original in French, "La Réalité psychologique des phonèmes," *Journal de Psychologie Normale et Pathologique,* XXX (1933), 247–65.

suming that I am able to go," and "Assuming that I still want to go."
These sequences of words tend to lose their character of qualified states
of uncertainty and to become simple futures; "I am going to mail a
letter" may still mean that the speaker is walking toward a mailbox, but
it now usually means future only. The letter need not be written. Similarly, our auxiliaries *shall* and *will* have not always been marks of the
future; a thousand years ago they meant *ought* and *wish* respectively.

The Hopi, on the other hand, keep the emphasis upon uncertainty of
statement, and make time secondary. This uncertainty they qualify again
with some ten modal forms that permit—and even require—them to be
still more exact in their statements about reality and the degree and
nature of manifesting. Whorf felt that the central notion here was a hope
of potentialities coming to be, but whether or not he is right about that,
apparently the Hopi can distinguish in a sentence like "He can make
trouble" between the ideas that he as an individual is capable of making
trouble and the similar but different idea that the conditions are such
that a person in his position would be able to make trouble. Many
concepts can be expressed through these modes, which become much
more cumbersome in English. The Hopi impotential implies that an
intention came to nothing; in the impotential, "The man ran away"
implies also that the man was later caught, and "I went hunting" suggests "but I didn't get anything."

Every Hopi sentence centers upon an assertion, but it need not have a
subject, and even the verbal portion of the predication may be expressed
in something other than what we would call a verb. The assertion may
grow, for example, with what Whorf called an "ambivalent," which can
be either what we should call a noun or a verb, but of course Hopi does
not need this distinction in our sense. Rather, Hopi apparently has a
classification of words by duration; "events of necessary brief duration
cannot be anything but verbs," as Whorf phrases it. Thus *lightning,
wave, flame, meteor, puff of smoke, pulsation* are verbs, "whereas
'cloud' or 'storm' are at about the lower limit of duration for nouns."
Changes in the nature of movement may be embodied in changes in the
stem of a syllable cluster; for example, Hopi seems to be uncommonly
sensitive to any wavelike or pulsing motion, and thus the Hopi by the
necessities of language have become at least as sensitive to wave-motion
as we have become by the necessities of studying waves in such activities
as broadcasting. Wavelike motion, furthermore, in what Whorf calls the
"segmentative" becomes different in different substances; for example,
in something liquid *wa'la* means *makes one wave, gives a splash* and with
reduplication *wala'lata* means *it tosses in waves, it is kicking up a sea*.
Whorf continues as follows:

But suppose again that the phenomenon denoted by the stem is one resulting from the type of force known in physics as torque (tendency to produce rotation), which in order for any effect to be apparent requires that the substance be a body with at least a certain degree of rigidity and yet capable of certain degrees of motion relative to other bodies. In this case a single deformation or displacement as denoted by the punctual will be either a single oscillation or a single turning of this body according to the degree of freedom implied in the root-meaning; while, if the effect continues, it will continue as a train of oscillatings or a continued rotation and may or may not involve an advance through space at the same time: this, then, will be the meaning of the segmentative. Examples of this type of meaning are:

wa'ya	makes a waving shake (like a small tree shaken)
na'ya	makes a sway from one side to another
pi'ya	makes a flap like a pair of wings
ta'ya	makes a racking shake
no'ya	makes a circuit (axial turning combined with advance in an arc)
ro'ya	makes a turn or twist
ri'ya	makes a quick spin[12]

Similarly, what Whorf finds he must class as nouns have three genders; these do not involve sex, but are animate, inanimate, and vegetative. These, in turn, have seven different cases—although of course not the cases of Latin and Greek—and can have what he calls voice as well. For example, "the eventive voice" produces "manifestations of characteristic visual outlines and figure arrangements, occurring as moving outlines . . . ," that is, "one break occurs, one slit into an edge occurs, one drop englobes and drips off." Working out statements with the elaborate Hopi system for inflections can become complicated. For instance, Whorf cites the simple sentence "The girl who lived in yonder house came running," and then pluralizes this. In our view all that has happened is that more than one girl is running possibly from more than one house, so that *girl* becomes *girls* and *house* may become *houses*. In Hopi, however, the whole event has altered so that each of the seven units must undergo inflectional change. The important thing in Hopi is not that the number has been changed but that the action has been intensified, and this revision of concept moves throughout the expression; as Whorf puts it, "a number of punctual situations have become tensive." The two sentences would be transcribed something like the following:[13]

---

[12] From "The Punctual and Segmentative Aspects of Verbs in Hopi," first printed *Language*, XI (1936), 127–31; reprinted in *Language, Thought, and Reality*, ed. John B. Carroll (cited earlier), where the quotation occurs p. 53.

[13] I have normalized Whorf's transcription in order that it will look like one sentence instead of several, mainly by removing diacritical signs and by using an apostrophe for Whorf's /?/, which is an indication of glottalization.

| ma.na | 'ayam | ki.v qa | teqa | | 'ank | warikiwta |
| namaNT | 'ay x | ki. kihet | 'an | y sqam | 'ah | yetekiwyenwa |

The significant matter here is not that Hopi is or is not more succinct than modern English, that it makes less or more use of inflectional change than do Latin and Greek, that it encourages more or less exact observation of natural phenomena than do French and German, or that its system of centering predication in an uncommonly subtle incorporating sequence does or does not provide for a sensitivity to shading in ideas which Whorf found unparalleled in his experience. He apparently thought it was a better language with which to record scientific data than is any Indo-European language he knew, including English and Greek, and one should recall here that Whorf was an applied scientist, and apparently a good one.[14] His opinion, even though it is an opinion, cannot be taken lightly. He finds that a number of Amerindian languages, including Hopi, "abound in finely wrought, beautifully logical discriminations about causation, action, result, dynamic or energic quality, directness of experience," and the like. "In this respect they far outdistance the European languages. . . . It takes but little real scientific study of the preliterate languages, especially those in America, to show how much more precise and finely elaborated is the system of relationships in many such tongues than is ours. By comparison with American [Amerindian] languages, the formal systemization of ideas in English, German, French, or Italian seems poor and jejune."[15]

But this still is not the point. All languages have strengths; they all have soft spots. Perhaps the easiest sorts of linguistic legerdemain—they cannot be called trickery because the intent is honest, however unreliable the results—are those by which a language is extolled because it excels another language in a given construction. We are sometimes told that Russian is more picturesque than English because a given Russian phrase loses some of its color when translated into English, or that

---

[14] He was a heating engineer who became a legend. On one occasion he is said to have been refused admission to a factory building; he remonstrated, adding that they need not fear he would discover the secret formula for their product, since he knew it already. When they were skeptical, he wrote it out, and when they were aghast and asked him how he had gotten it, he answered that, their product being what it was and the chemical possibilities being what they are, they could not possibly use any other formula. He got in. He refused professorships in linguistics at the best universities on the principle that his study of language on a pure basis might suffer if he made a living by it.

[15] The Hopi material is in the articles by Whorf collected in volumes cited above edited by Carroll and Hoijer. The generalization is from "Linguistic Considerations of Thinking in Primitive Communities," printed in Carroll, pp. 65–86; the quotation, pp. 83–84.

Greek is better than Russian because for a given idea Russian requires three words and Greek only one. The evidence is usually sound, but the conclusions are not, because in other constructions one would find just the reverse, or at least, a different virtue. Thus the point is not that Hopi has great virtues, even when compared with the most admired languages, but that Hopi works with concepts so foreign to those in the familiar Indo-European languages that with it we can see more clearly the role of language in society and culture.

This concept Whorf was not slow to grasp or to exploit. "In this Hopi view," he writes, "time disappears and space is altered, so that it is no longer the homogeneous and instantaneous timeless space of our supposed intuition or of classical Newtonian mechanics." In their place, vitalistic and animistic concepts provide a basis for a description of the world, and these concepts are implicit "in the very structure and grammar" of Hopi language. "Whether such a civilization as ours would be possible with widely different linguistic handling of time is a large question," Whorf concedes, but he observes that we have been a long time coming to the concept of relativity, and he suggests that we have taken so long because we have assumed that Newtonian concepts of space and time "are sensed by everyone intuitively" and are hence objectively and exclusively true. "The offhand answer," he continues, "laying the blame on intuition for our slowness in discovering mysteries of the Cosmos, such as relativity, is the wrong one. The right answer is: Newtonian space, time, and matter are no intuitions. They are recepts from culture and language. That is where Newton got them." He notices that "science is beginning to find that there is something in the Cosmos that is not in accord with the concepts we have formed," and he suggests that Hopi, if it will not help scientists find the new language they need, may at least help them see what is wrong with the old one.[16]

Presumably, similar fresh approaches would appear in any large body of Amerindian languages, provided the evidence was studied in sufficient detail and with insight. Navaho, for example, has an interesting verb system. It consists of what are called bound forms, that is, forms that cannot appear alone but must always be linked to something else. They are either active or neuter; thus they give great attention to movement, and to what has been described as "eventing," so that even a construction meaning "to be busy" becomes something like "to move about continually in reference to it." Papago has a revealing concept of number. Nouns either concern individuals, or involve all members of a

(margin annotation: bound forms)

---

[16] "The Relation of Habitual Thought and Behavior to Language," *Language, Culture, and Personality*, ed. Leslie Spier (Menasha, Wis.: Sapir Memorial Publication Fund, 1941), pp. 75–93; Carroll, pp. 134–59, the quotations, pp. 152–53.

group, and thus plural is something between these. Trees are individuals, because they grow up separately from the ground, but shrubs are included within an aggregate because they grow together as brush. Yokuts relies heavily upon suffixes, and since these are mostly generalization, Yokuts narrative style is simple, straightforward, and, to a speaker of English, flat and lacking in detail. To a Yokuts speaker, on the other hand, English is jerky and lacking in dignity.

Zuni has three levels of speech—sacred speech used in a *kiva* or for religious purposes, standard speech used for most purposes, and slang, which is tolerated but looked upon as an indiscretion in which the young can be expected to indulge. Slang and sacred speech are defined in accordance with Zuni concepts; for example, "to breathe in" may be sacred, since the concepts of wind blowing and breathing are felt to have religious significance. On the other hand, to call a woman a "well" is slang, since the Zuni associate thirst and sexual desire. A Zuni explained that to use slang in the *kiva* would be no more appropriate than to bring in a radio, which is apparently about as sacrilegious as one can get. Geography naturally affects vocabulary; for example, in the semidesert West most watercourses are marked with one or more of several native cottonwoods, so that the word for *cottonwood* also becomes the word for "wood," "a tree," "a stick," and the like. When the word is borrowed into another language, as into Kiowa, the speaker must say something like *real cottonwood* if he means *cottonwood tree*.

Some Amerindian languages may be instructive for language learning and language transmission. In a modern society based upon urban living, children learn language extensively through other children. In the sparsely settled areas of the Americas, however—and most American areas were sparsely settled most of the time—children spent much of their time working with the adult members of the family, and thus learned from adults. In antiquity all language must have been learned in this way, and hence the present-day dwellers in the desert West may throw light on the language learning of our ancestors as well as their own. Isolation produces interesting side effects; for example, since the boys would work with men, the girls with the women, language habits on the basis of sex were encouraged. Similarly, the Comanche, long a seminomadic desert people, taught their children baby talk, which was felt to be appropriate to their age, and which they would later learn not to use.

Here we might remind ourselves of Boas' observation that language may provide the best means of studying the essential ideas of a people, because whereas the ideas expressed formally in philosophical terms are consciously constructed, those that are embodied in the language have grown unconsciously. However that may be, the Amerindian's greatest contribution to civilization may yet prove to be that he jarred the speakers of Indo-European languages from their intellectual complacency, and that he did it with language. Study of Amerindian languages is helping us to see how language cultures minds, and hence helping us to pose the proposition that no set of concepts can be objective, that no science or any other body of knowledge built upon concepts which have grown within any single body of language can escape linguistic orientation, and thus that language and not reality may be at the center of man's life. Presumably we could have reached these conclusions with any other body of language; if the thesis is valid, it should appear—as apparently it does—in a comparison of Indo-European languages with any other varied bodies of speech, those native in Africa or Asia as well as those in America. But the fact remains that the Amerindians did produce a rich body of linguistic detail, and they preserved it in a time and place in which it could be studied and is being studied.

Earlier we noted that one achievement of the Amerindians grew from their having produced so much language, linguistic phenomena that have provided modern scholars material with which to develop new means of study. As a sample we might consider *glottochronology*, a technique mentioned above in connection with the wanderings of Uto-Aztecan, but not there identified. The term is sufficiently recent so that your dictionary may not help you much; it refers to a technique for dating linguistic events by the replacement of basic words in the vocabulary.[17]

The procedure rests upon the theory that over long periods all languages change at a relatively constant rate. Over short periods as periods go in slow-moving language, even some hundreds of years, this is obviously not true. We have no difficulty reading the works of our Puritan ancestors, written three hundred years ago, but Geoffrey Chaucer, if he had encountered as a child the late Old English written three hundred years before his birth, would have found most of it incomprehensible. As the same time, the Anglo-French that he heard spoken had changed very much more rapidly than had the French of the Continent, which he learned to read. In like manner, an educated modern Frisian can read *Beowulf* almost at sight because Old Frisian, closely related to Old English, has changed relatively little in the last fifteen hundred years. But the theory is that such differences in rate of change are unusual—languages seldom compete in a culture as extensively bilingual as that of England after the Conquest even for short periods—and that over long periods the differences in rate of change level out.

---

[17] I take it that some practitioners would prefer the term *lexicostatistics* for the technique as I am describing it, but the differences between the terms seem not to be great, and *glottochronology* has the wider currency.

Accordingly, scholars have tried to isolate the relatively durable portions of language and to use only these for temporal measurement. Sound is usually rather durable; the Indo-European vowel system has survived to a remarkable degree in most European languages, and many consonants have remained unchanged for millennia. But there are exceptions—too many exceptions. More than half the vowels in English changed markedly within a few centuries, and the Romance consonants, all from Latin, have notably diverged. Grammar usually changes slowly, but grammar is hard to measure. Words are the most measurable parts of language, particularly if the observer contents himself with noticing whether a word is there or not there. Accordingly, the glottochronologists use words, and they try to select the most durable words—for simplicity, I am here using the term *word* for any recognized symbol for a working semantic unit, even though a language may not be made up of units which closely resemble the "words" in an English dictionary.

Obviously, some words are not very durable. Hundreds of words, perhaps thousands, involved in nineteenth-century religious sects have vanished. Meanwhile thousands of new words used for automobile parts, in space travel, for the so-called wonder drugs, have entered the language in the last quarter century. But this is highly specialized vocabulary, words for new things, many of them concocted to fill a need that had not been known before. Some words, on the other hand, refer to no new things. Without man there is no language. All men die, and they are born with fathers and mothers. Thus we can trust that words like *man, die, father, mother, drink* and *eat* will change relatively slowly, and as a matter of fact all these words were in Indo-European thousands of years ago, meaning essentially what they do now in their basic use.

Many glottochronologists have worked with no more than two hundred carefully selected words, and for limited purposes one hundred are thought to suffice. Presumably words in the following list will decline at about fifteen per cent per thousand years:

I, thou, we, this, that, who, what, not, all, many, one, two, big, long, small, woman, man, person, fish, bird, dog, louse, tree, seed, leaf, root, bark, skin, flesh, blood, bone, grease, egg, horn, tail, feather, hair, head, ear, eye, nose, mouth, tooth, tongue, claw, foot, knee, hand, belly, neck, breasts, heart, liver, drink, eat, bite, see, hear, know, sleep, die, kill, swim, fly, walk, come, lie, sit, stand, give, say, sun, moon, star, water, rain, stone, sand, earth, cloud, smoke, fire, ash, burn, path, mountain, red, green, yellow, white, black, night, hot, cold, full, new, good, round, dry, name.

If this technique is reliable, it provides us with a measurement of time depth somewhat commensurate with carbon dating for archaeology. The student has only to study a modern language, reconstruct its ancestor by triangulating from the known relatives of the language—most languages have known relatives—and the parent language can be dated.

The method has weaknesses. It is not so readily employable as is carbon dating; one little bit of offal is enough for a carbon sample, but collecting samples of language and reconstructing a proto-language can be an arduous task. Even so, the key words quickly become too few. If a vocabulary loses fifteen percent per thousand years, only relatively shallow time depths can be measured. Furthermore, the sample is so small that even a modest probable error can be disruptive; if the word list loses an average of fifteen words per thousand years, a consistent variation of a half dozen words either way would soon render the results less than fifty percent reliable. Furthermore, some tests run on languages whose history is known—we have records for Latin, Greek, Sanskrit, Hebrew, Chinese, and some others extending beyond two thousand years—do not entirely confirm the reliability of the method.

After all, that any part of all languages changes at a fixed rate is only an assumption. Even if steady change does characterize selected vocabulary in most languages, what would happen in a society having taboos against using words for parts of the body, for bodily functions, for family relationships? Such taboos could change, and these areas include much of the supposedly "stable" vocabulary. Furthermore, the method assumes one sharp break; that is, speakers of Proto-language X are assumed to have split into speakers of X^1 and X^2. But suppose that the two drifted apart slowly, with much borrowing back and forth—as British and American speech borrow today—or suppose that X^1 and X^2 separated, but centuries later recombined? Much can happen during the millennia. And we seem to have evidence that movement in space and conflict between cultures stimulate linguistic growth. How do we know that the language under study has not experienced an aberrant background, or that even our control cases have not been abnormally nomadic or unusually sedentary?

Accordingly, some scholars have rejected glottochronology completely. Many others—perhaps most of those who have used the method—believe it has some validity, especially if used with caution and in conjunction with other approaches. Morris Swadesh, inventor of the technique, has written recently that he believes it to be reliable up to about 5000 years, and that it can be refined so that it will be reliable up to 15,000.[18]

---

[18] "Linguistics as an Instrument of Prehistory," *Southwest Journal of Anthropology*, XV (1959), 20–35; reprinted in *Language in Culture and Society*, cited earlier, pp. 575–84. See also D. W. Hymes, "Lexicostatistics So Far," *Current Anthropology*, 1 (1960), 3–44. For a study of probabilities and more recent bibliography, see C. Douglas Chretien, "The Mathematical Models of Glottochronology," *Language*, XXXVIII (1962), 11–37.

With this reservation, then, that the findings of glottochronology can be accepted only with caution, we might see how it works in a given instance, and since I have already made some use of it in the previous chapter when we were considering the wanderings of the Uto-Aztecans, we may as well return to that subject and add some detail. As we have seen, in addition to minor isolated groups, speakers of Uto-Aztecan today or in historic times have occupied a broad belt of land from central Idaho to central Mexico. The resulting linguistic map is somewhat broken up by speakers of other languages, but we assume that these bodies of speech represent pockets of earlier languages, or later intrusions, mainly the latter.

Before glottochronology can be brought to bear, preliminary studies are required. For Uto-Aztecan these are available and were summarized in an earlier chapter—I am ignoring Tanoan, since, so far as I know, it has not been subject to research revealing time depth. As we have seen, studies of modern speakers of Uto-Aztecan suggest that the language spread south into Mexico and north into the United States; side branches from the northern group of languages moved east into New Mexico and west into California; Uto-Aztecan speakers continued to move north, occupying most of the Great Basin, and even moved east once more to spill over the Rocky Mountains into the western plains.

What can glottochronology add to this picture? It provides us with supposed time depths for each of these subdivisions. It gives us about forty-five to fifty centuries from the time Aztec broke off from the languages which moved north, the differences in dates depending upon the varieties of Aztec used for statistics. It gives us about thirty centuries for Hopi, which moved east, nearly forty for the languages that moved west into California, and about thirty for the break of Numic to the north. The next great movement would have been relatively rapid, north and east through the Great Basin, beginning about a thousand years ago.

We now have the materials of something like an account of one of those tremendous migrations, suggestive of the population explosion of the Indo-Europeans, if less significant. An important group of people built up in the Southwest, perhaps along the Gila River, ca. 3000 B.C.; possibly they profited from a period of greater rainfall, or they may have learned about irrigation. They may have acquired the bow and arrow; when the Aztecs got as far as the Valley of Mexico they had become a warlike lot, but the northern groups seem to have been, and remain to this day, a remarkably peaceful spread of people. At any rate, some of these Amerindians moved south through the mountain valleys of northwest Mexico, and considerable time elapsed before population pressures in the homeland encouraged more emigration. Then, somewhat before the Christian era these Gila River People, if they may be so called, spilled over into the Upper Colorado basin, where the Hopi still live; a little later some moved into southern California, and some shoved north. These last groups encountered the inhospitable Mojave Desert, and another millennium or so elapsed before they got very far. Then suddenly —suddenly as these things go—they surged north and east until they had filled most of the Great Basin between the Rockies and the Sierra Nevada, north of the Colorado and south of the headwaters of the Snake.

Why? It is unlikely that they were conquering; they are not now the conquering sort, and they probably have not been. They prefer to live peacefully, even though they have to pay for their peace with long hours of labor and patient endurance—the labor that some of these Amerindians expend for mere existence is fantastic. More likely, something had killed or drawn off the previous inhabitants of the Great Basin so that the "Peaceful People," as some of them called themselves, could move in quietly. Perhaps the acquisition of the horse by the Plains Indians made hunting buffalo so profitable that the Great Basin Indians, who probably had been accustomed to working both sides of the Rockies anyhow, heard about the new hunting grounds and abandoned their old hard life in the semidesert. This guess is rendered somewhat more probable because one of the branches of the Shoshone went all the way; they were apparently pulled up into the Snake River valley, crossed over into Wyoming, and then drifted south and east to become the Comanche of the far western prairies, desert Indians whom the whites found hunting buffalo on horseback. Thus one of the curious side effects of the acquisition of the horse by the Plains Indians may have been a sudden efflorescence of dialects among the Numic peoples, who industriously went along creating variant linguistic forms all the way from western Oregon to Wyoming, from Utah and Nevada, north to Montana. A horse explosion led to a food explosion, which provided a population explosion and a population shift, which led to a language explosion, and to one of the richest bodies of dialectal variants that modern scholars have at their disposal.

At least one other Amerindian linguistic contribution must detain us briefly—writing. When Columbus landed, most of the inhabitants of the two hemispheres were without any script. All Amerindians could, of course, make some sort of picture representations, pecking at rocks, painting on surfaces, but if most of the Amerindians had anything resembling a system of writing the evidence is lost—and we doubt that it would have been. Amerindians provided one exception, however, the hieroglyphic writing of the Mayas and the Aztecs.

As every literate person knows, the Mayas developed a remarkable culture, to a considerable degree indigenous. At a time when much of Europe north of the Mediterranean coastal areas was inhabited by relatively unsophisticated hunters and fishers—the earliest known Mayan carving is presumably dated A.D. 320—Amerindians of Mezo-America had developed corbel architecture, highly stylized carving, and a knowledge of mathematics which permitted them to make the most exact astronomical predictions of which any people were then capable. Some of this culture may have come from Africa; presumably men could have floated across the South Atlantic, and similarities between South American and some African cultures suggest that somebody may have done this and that the migration may have had some effect. The Maya calendar, for example, shows some resemblance to the zodiac, but the resemblances are not precise enough to be very convincing.

The strongest evidence against the Maya culture having been borrowed is that there was no place from which to borrow it; the Maya could not have borrowed the concept of zero, because when they were first using it, no one in the Eurasian land mass seems to have understood zero, and if the Mayans could conceive zero why should we doubt that they developed the remainder of their mathematics? As for the writing, that shows no detailed resemblance to any other known script; of course the idea of writing could have been borrowed, but rebus writing is not an advanced concept, and if the Mayas did borrow the notion of writing, one wonders why they did not get the concept of an alphabet, which had been known for at least two thousand years when Mayan culture was young.[19] If the influence was early, however, say during the second millennium B.C., explorers or occupants of a wind-blown derelict might have brought the idea of a rebus from Africa but not that of an alphabet, since hieroglyphic writing made little use of letters. While an earlier edition of this book was in press, Thor Heyerdahl, who had already crossed the Pacific Ocean on a balsa raft, endeavored to float across the Atlantic in a papyrus boat, hoping thereby to demonstrate that Egyptian ideas and culture could have been so introduced into the New World. He did not achieve landfall, but with an inexperienced crew and a vessel that probably only approximated the ancient papyrus boats, he came so close that no one need any longer doubt that north Africans could have floated across the Atlantic Ocean several times. A few Egyptians, blown off course, would not have influenced Amerindian tongues much, but they could have introduced writing for religious and governmental uses. Ques-

---

[19] About Maya writing I am relying particularly upon J. Eric S. Thompson, *Maya Hieroglyphic Writing,* rev. ed. (Norman, Okla.: University of Oklahoma Press, 1960).

tions remain, of course, such as why, if writing was introduced, it did not spread farther—to the Andean cultures, for example. But Yucatan, home of the Mayas, was itself one of the likely landing points, and sophisticated stuff like writing had few places to spread in Amerindia; to the north it would have encountered provinciality and to the south vast reaches of jungle. Thus we must recognize that the idea of writing *could* have been imported, without being sure what, if anything, came in, or where, when, or how it arrived.[20]

The Aztec numerical system, which presumably reflects the Mayan, was relatively simple. A dot represented one, presumably one finger or toe, since dots were repeated through nineteen. Twenty was a flag, and twenty times twenty, or four hundred, was a sign supposed to denote hairs; twenty times four hundred, or eight thousand, was represented by a bag of cacao beans, these being used as a unit of trade. This system sufficed for rebus writing; that is, the keeper of records could draw a bale of cotton or a blanket along with the appropriate number. Thus, if a town's tax were 8,421 jars of honey, the tax roll would include a jar plus a bag of beans, the hair sign, a flag, and a dot.

As writing, the Maya hieroglyphs are imperfectly understood, so imperfectly that the noncalendric glyphs are as yet in the main unread. For the calendric glyphs scholars have had the help of the relationships in mathematics along with modern knowledge of astronomy, and Mayan observations were so accurate that a modern scholar often knows how a mathematical glyph should read before he has read it. In fact, in the mathematical portions scholars can catch the typographical errors, if a slip of the chisel in carving can be called a typographical error. Little except the mathematical portions of the writing has been deciphered, however, although survivals are tolerably extensive.[21]

A start was made by a sixteenth-century bishop, Diego de Landa, who worked with native informants, learned the names of the days and the twenty-day months, and supposed he had recorded the Maya alphabet. The difficulty is that apparently the Mayas had no alphabet; Landa made the mistake, common to many amateur students of language, of

---

20 For a popular account of the crossings, see Thor Heyerdahl, *The RA Expeditions* (New York: Doubleday, 1971). At this writing, no more scientific account has appeared, and in any event the documented details of navigation would be unlikely to have much bearing on the linguistic importance of the voyages.
21 Whorf was interested in the hieroglyphs and believed he had solved their mystery, but his solution has not found general acceptance. Russian authorities have claimed that Y. V. Knorozov solved the puzzle by what he called a Marxist-Leninist approach, but his discovery does not seem to have led to the reading of the glyphs. Thompson has printed a partial glossary and index, with illustrations, and is said to be preparing an exhaustive one; for bibliography, see Thompson, pp. vi–vii, 329–47.

assuming that the tongue they are endeavoring to study must be essentially like a language they know. Landa started with the Spanish alphabet, which he pronounced letter by letter, and asked his informant to write it down in Maya. Unfortunately, the native had no concept of an alphabet, and accordingly he drew a stylized picture of the native word for whatever sound he guessed the bishop had emitted. When the bishop said *b,* which was pronounced in earlier Spanish about like English *bay,* the native drew a picture of a foot, which is presumably the Maya rebus for travel. Thus Landa produced a work that modern scholars characterize as "of some use," but not the Rosetta Stone he hoped he was providing, and as yet most of the glyphs are so far from being read that we do not even know whether they are charms, religious doctrine, historical chronicles, or what. Repetitions are numerous, in spite of the varied sources from which glyphs come—three brief codexes, numerous stelae, walls of religious and governmental buildings, stone lintels, and the like—but as yet we are not even certain in what language the symbols are written, perhaps an ancestor of Yucatec or Chol-Chorti-Mopan.

The development of a system of writing must inevitably figure prominently in our estimate of the Mayan intelligence and cultural capacity. For these purposes the testimony of Mayan writing is not likely to be exaggerated, but its social importance can be overestimated. Considering the great value we attach, and rightly, to the development of writing in the east Mediterranean area, we should remind ourselves that the impact of Mayan writing was strictly limited. We may assume that it promoted the development of Mayan astronomy and mathematics, that these subjects could not have existed in their exactness and complexity without it. We may perhaps assume, also, that it was crucial in the development of what seems to have been a rather elaborate theocracy, where it would have been used to codify both the governmental and theological statements. It must have had other uses; the architects, for example, understood numbers and used them.

But all this was limited, except in its indirect application. We assume that writing, and probably reading, was the exclusive possession of the priestly class, and quite possibly only of the more learned of them. Ability to use Mayan writing was perhaps no more common than the ability to use the quantum theory is with us—or perhaps relativity might provide a better analogy. All Americans of any sophistication know of the theory of relativity; they assume that its truth has been demonstrated; they venerate its discoverer; they believe it is of great importance for modern man; and they are enough aware of it so that they are encouraged to think in a relativistic way about all sorts of subjects. Few men living, however, could demonstrate its truth or understand the demonstration if it were worked out for them. Similarly, all cultured Mayas must have seen the glyphic writing; they probably knew that knowledge important for church and state, for their lives and their futures, was recorded there. But only relatively few would have known what sort of information was hidden in the glyphs, and fewer still could have worked comfortably with the glyphs themselves. The impact of Amerindian tongues upon man, except as it promoted studies or fields of activity which themselves had side effects, was almost exclusively the impact of oral language.

PART TWO

INDO-EUROPEAN INVADES: LANGUAGES IN MOTION

5

THE RESTLESS ONES: WRITERS OF LANGUAGE

The second wave of language into the Americas becomes part of recorded history because the invaders could record, moving within historic time, say roughly the second half of the second millennium, A.D. 1500–2000. The first of these dates ignores exploration that came to nothing permanent. After about the year A.D. 1000 Greenlanders, Icelanders, and Norwegians repeatedly coasted Labrador and lands to the south, may have penetrated inland to the Great Lakes, and maintained settlements of sufficient permanence so that their presence in lands to the west was known in the capitals of Europe at least as early as the beginning of the twelfth century.[1]

The second date presumes that the subjugation and even the extinction of Amerindian languages will continue, and that extinction will accelerate so much during the next half century that Amerindian languages will be reduced in Latin America to something like their present state farther north. By that time even pockets like the languages in the Upper Amazon drainage, which are in effect not yet in contact with English, Spanish, or Portuguese, will probably have been reduced to secondary languages in areas dominated by Indo-European speech. In much of South America, native tongues will have become moribund if not extinct; that is, no body of children will be learning Amerindian tongues over large areas as their unique natural linguistic medium.

---

[1] Such claims have long been advanced by the Scandinavians and their supporters, long ridiculed by Hispanists and some others, but with the publication of R. A. Skelton, Thomas E. Marston, and George D. Painter, *The Vinland Map and the Tartar Relation* (New Haven and London: Yale University Press, 1965), the case for Leif Ericson and his countrymen seems fairly clear. The differences in the results from the two movements stemmed, apparently, not from inadequacies in exploration. The Norsemen were skilled seamen and they could move by relatively short voyages over open water, but they had no wealthy culture behind them. Sixteenth-century Spain could afford ventures in the New World; eleventh-century Norway could not.

In retrospect, this second great movement of language into the Americas can be thought of as an invasion, although arriving white men did not usually come as invaders, and established Amerindians did not usually act like defenders. The newcomers thought of themselves as explorers, missionaries, merchants, and eventually settlers; in their eyes they were not invaders because they did not concede that the home of roaming savages was inhabited in any real sense. Spatially most of the American continents were inhabited by peoples of no very advanced culture; the highly civilized areas—the Incan highlands, the Valley of Mexico, and the like—were also the heavily populated areas, so that although the urbanized centers accounted for large portions of the entire population, not many of the newcomers encountered such Amerindians, nor recognized culture when they blundered upon it. Cortes was probably unaware that he was killing better astronomers than he or any of his men. What he knew was that he had gunpowder and the natives did not. Thus a Spaniard, fighting a Frenchman, was aware that the Frenchman was part of the human race; the same Spaniard might be only vaguely aware that an Amerindian also had the inherent rights of a human being.

This contempt of the supposedly civilized for the inhabitants of undeveloped areas is not unusual; pygmies were hunted and skinned on the theory that they were some sort of monkey, and the Tasmanians seem to have been exterminated—as were the American passenger pigeons—for sport. At certain times and places the Amerindians were hunted by their civilized guest, but this was not generally the practice, whether from humanity or fear. But many newcomers thought of the natives as nonhuman creatures or, at best, as some sort of lower human beings, with inferior morals, punier brains, more bestial feelings, and less consequential rights than could be presumed in a European.

Although exceptions were conspicuous, they were few and usually were thwarted. A William Penn might endeavor to treat the red men as brothers; Roger Williams might insist that the white men had no legal right to deprive the aborigines of their lands; Puritans who encouraged emigration may have tried to arrange that only men and women of good character and good intent be allowed to go to New England, lest the natives be corrupted. Such lofty sentiments were rare, and humanitarian conduct that sprouted from lofty sentiments was rarer still. The Amerindians concluded that the peace-loving Quakers were deceitful cowards; most of the settlements were commercial ventures where "men not much given to religion" debauched the native women and angered the native men. The Puritans often suspected that their red neighbors were minions of the Devil whom good Christians should either convert or dispatch.

William Bradford, notably pious and not notably vengeful, could gloat over the butchering of some four hundred Pequots in the following terms:

It was a fearful sight to see them thus frying in the fire, and the streams of blood quenching the same, and horrible was the stink and scent thereof. But the victory seemed a sweet sacrifice, and they gave the praise thereof to God who had wrought so wonderfully for them, thus to enclose their enemies in their hands, and give them so speedy a victory over so proud and insulting an enemy.[2]

One may have difficulty unscrambling the Reverend Bradford's pronoun antecedents, but no one can miss the suggestion that however the broiling Pequots stank in the noses of men, this burnt offering was sweet in the nostrils of the Old Testament Jehovah. Interracial etiquette was perhaps not better farther west; the backwoodsmen who defeated Tecumseh skinned their victims and displayed the hides. If we may believe Washington Irving's third-hand account, early Californians delighted in

. . . hunting the poor Indian like wild beasts, killing them without mercy. The Mexicans excelled at this savage sport; chasing their unfortunate victims at full speed, noosing them around the neck with their lassos, and then dragging them to death![3]

Thus, however the humanitarian theorists may have philosophized that the Amerindians were human, with the rights of human beings, those who dealt with the natives were seldom trammeled by high principles. Whether from bigotry, brutality, or the animosities that grew from friction bred by fear and contempt, the newcomers seldom thought of the Amerindians as sufficiently human to warrant human consideration.

The Amerindians, for different reasons, did not see the coming of the paler-complexioned men as an invasion. They were not much aware of the concept of invasion; they had their feuds and rivalries, even their wars, but wars did not usually result in invasions, conquests, and unconditional surrender. A raiding party might kill a few men, capture a few women, steal what they could find, and vanish as rapidly as possible to repel a retaliatory raid. The Inca sought prisoners because their

---

[2] *History of Plymouth Plantation, 1620–47* (Boston: Houghton Mifflin Co. for The Massachusetts Historical Society, 1912), II, 252. I owe the reference, along with much that concerns the Colonial period, to Louis B. Wright, *The Colonial Civilization of North America, 1607–1763* (London: Eyre & Spottiswoode, 1949). Here and in subsequent colonial material, spelling and punctuation have been somewhat normalized.

[3] I owe the reference to James D. Hart, *American Images of Spanish California* (Berkeley: Friends of the Bancroft Library, University of California, 1960), p. 5.

religion required human sacrifice; among some Woods Indians—that is, Amerindians of the northern hemisphere living east of the great prairie —prisoners were tortured to provide a Roman holiday, but on the whole, war in the Americas was not an instrument of conquest. In fact, the Americas were relatively peaceful, as the sketchiest comparison of American and European history will suggest. Most Amerindians did not think in terms of conquest.

Nor did their backgrounds encourage the concept of invasion. Having no navigation of any consequence, only scanty communication beyond their immediate neighbors, they had little notion of geography. The ancestors of the modern Peruvians may have floated to the Easter Islands, but they probably never floated back to tell the ancient Peruvians about their discoveries. The Amerindians did not know that they inhabited two continents, that these continents might have been conceived as a sort of unity, or that there were other and more densely populated continents, whose inhabitants might want to flow into the Amerindian lands.

A few natives had the vision to understand the new danger at least vaguely. Black Hawk, a Sauk war chief, saw the whites moving into the Upper Mississippi Valley, seizing the Amerindians' fields, plowing up their crops, and commanding their waterways. He tried to organize a general uprising to drive the invaders out and to hold the land for its traditional owners. He was too late; the whites were by now well established. All but a few hotheads among the Amerindians were too timid or too prudent to rise, and after a few skirmishes and random killings the Black Hawk War ended as did most Amerindian uprisings, with the indiscriminate slaughter of native men, women, and children. Tecumseh and a few others attempted organized resistance, taking advantage of international differences among the whites themselves, but most of the native malcontents resembled Geronimo, who caused recurrent inconvenience, but mainly as a leader of marauding bands.

Actually, the Amerindians succumbed from a failure of language as much as from anything else. Had they recognized the coming of the speakers of Indo-European for what it was, an invasion, they could have resisted. They were well equipped to defend the Americas. True, they were horribly outnumbered, and perhaps three quarters of their scanty defenders were in vulnerable concentration in central Mexico and Peru, but the fight is not necessarily to the numerous. In deserts and deep forests numbers may contribute mainly to starvation, and the Amerindians were so placed and so trained that they could have resisted for centuries had they possessed the government and the communications to make concerted resistance possible. The war was lost, not for the loss of a horseshoe nail, but from the lack of a *lingua franca*.

Both position and terrain favored the Amerindians. The northern coast was defended by ice; no attack there was possible. The Argentinian pampas would have provided a foothold, but it was isolated from the remainder of the continent by lofty mountains and jungles that are yet to be consistently penetrated. The long west coast was protected by its very length; vessels did find their way "around the Horn," but the passage was stormy and long, especially in the days of slow transportation. The voyage trebled or quadrupled the length of already burdensome lines of communication to Europe. Thus the Amerindians were, in effect, safe from every direction but the east, and here they could deploy in such depth that they could have defended themselves against anything that the sixteenth, seventeenth, eighteenth, and probably the nineteenth century could have sent against them. Not the least of their assets was that they already knew how to fight a mobile war. Most of the attackers did not, and even those few who did would have been restrained by the Colonel Blimps of the day from practicing their native martial arts.

The very military prowess and the grasp of what has been called military science would have prevented Europeans from any adequate assault. Military fashions, which developed from the charges of medieval knights and flourished with the conquests of Napoleon, worked well enough in parklike Europe, studded with well-cleared fields to gallop over and great cities to be defended or taken as prizes. That these heavy-footed maneuvers were not suited to the American wilderness, General Edward Braddock could have attested, had he not been shot down along with his British regulars by a few French and Indians.

The American continents were won mainly by bacilli, enzymes, and their epidemic kind, by the decimation of the native food supplies—notably the bison—and by various sorts of irregulars. Some of these latter were military men who had thrown their books away, but most of them were militia, operating more or less officially, or they were opportunists, pioneers from the white man's point of view, freebooters as the Amerindians saw them. In any event, they were colonials or native-born white men who had learned their martial techniques directly or indirectly from the Amerindians themselves, not from the pages of Jomini or Clausewitz, or from the classrooms of Sandhurst or St. Cyr. In some areas the white men found their way easy because they were welcomed, as in Mexico and Peru; elsewhere they were not much molested until they could build up in numbers and could learn from the natives the means of destroying their hosts. Once the invaders had learned tactics from the natives, their superior weapons triumphed.

How did the two groups differ? Superficially, the differences were obvious, and most contemporary observations were superficial. The peoples differed in race; they looked different. Actually, this difference need not have mattered much. Amerindians presumably have as much aptitude for European culture as have Europeans; the Mexican princes showed much more understanding of Christian charity than did the *conquistadores,* but the distinction had its importance. It permitted the Amerindians to recognize the invaders, to receive them as gods or guests, or to fear them as strangers; it permitted the invaders to identify their victims, and it permitted them to indulge a sense of self-righteousness while treating human beings inhumanely.

They differed in religion. The Amerindians had nothing approaching a common religion. Cults might develop and spread from tribe to tribe, from area to area, as the peyote cult and the Ghost Dance have done in recent times, but tribe differed from tribe, and within tribes religion often followed clan and phratry distinctions. Medicine men were common, but medicine men are not one thing, any more than priests are one thing, and even a widespread devotion like the Plains and Woods belief in a mystical experience, of which the medicine bundle became the talisman, was local and highly varied.

Ostensibly, the invaders had a common religion; they were all Christians, all readers of the same Bible, all destined for the same Heaven or Hell. True, they husbanded sect-born rivalries, and they imported old religious wars. The English and the Dutch fought the French and the Spanish as much because the former were Protestants and the latter were Catholics as because they were subjects of rival crowns. If New England was well endowed with bigots, the Catholics were not immune to prejudice; Jesuit missionaries to Canada often viewed the slaughtering of English settlers with less than Christian compassion. The settlers were *"ces perfides ennemis de Dieu et de l'Eglise"* (these perfidious enemies of God and the Church), and when an English ship foundered, Father Joseph Germain saw in this disaster the hand of God. Observing the shore covered with hundreds of corpses, his only recorded regret is that since they "were all dead in heresy," their souls must have gone to Hell.[4] Jesuits were given to insisting that the loyalty of the Indians to the French was in reality the loyalty of the Indians to the Catholic Church, and that Dutch brandy was bad both for the Indians and for French trade, but in spite of these sectarian differences, Christianity did provide the invaders some semblance of unity that the Amerindians lacked.

Most obviously, the invaders and the invaded differed in worldly goods. The invaders had much, the invaded relatively little. The in-

---

[4] See, for example, the numerous accounts in *Voyageurs, robes noires, et coureurs de bois,* Publications of the Institute of French Studies, Inc., Columbia University, ed. Charles Upson Clark (New York, 1934). Father Germain's letter, pp. 90–98, is unusually revealing; the quoted passages are pp. 95, 97.

vaders themselves to a degree redressed this imbalance; for furs they traded essentials like knives and blankets, and to gain allies they supplied guns and ammunition. They also supplied guns for hunting, which guns served as well for fighting, even for fighting the man who had supplied the guns; many a white man died on the frontier that his fellow might wear a beaver hat in London or Paris, but the Amerindian never approached in worldly opulence the invader from Europe. The invaders had ships, and could arrive where and when they pleased; the defenders were restricted to inland waterways, to small vessels, mainly canoes and dugouts, and few of these. The invaders had guns and ammunition, clothing and food—or they had them whenever they took the trouble to import them. The defenders often starved and had to fight mainly with hand weapons. Even when they acquired guns, often poor ones, the Amerindians were usually impoverished for ammunition, and the white men had the advantage of every new improvement. The repeating rifle was more deadly than the musket, as the musket had been more deadly than the bow and arrow.

The ostensibly significant differences concerned communications and administration. The Europeans knew little enough about the Americas and their inhabitants, but they acquired and disseminated information; early maps are replete with sea serpents and men whose heads, as Othello put it, "do grow beneath their shoulders," but geographical, biological, and even anthropological information accumulated. Although the newcomers had no grand plan, their social commonality, based upon written language, gave them inevitably a sort of community. In North America, they fought with one another; Georgia was developed more to provide a buffer against the Spanish in St. Augustine than against the Seminoles, but at least the invaders operated in large groups, with a consciousness of the group and with some plans for the whole group. As a rule they fought one another only if their respective nations were formally at war. In South and Central America the conquest attained a semblance of order because it was conducted by the two great empires of the Hispanic peninsula; Cuban Spaniards did not war upon Mexican Spaniards, nor did Catholic Cubans molest Catholic Brazilian Portuguese.

The Amerindians, on the other hand, knew almost nothing of their invaders—who they were, whence they had come, where they were going, or why they were here. Had they known as much of the white men as the white men knew of them, and had they possessed anything like extensive government, they would never have allowed the white men to move in, to rob, to debauch, to enslave, and eventually to exterminate.

The invaders' knowledge and organization, furthermore, were parts of the whole complex of European culture, which again was an aspect of the culture that earlier had centered upon the eastern Mediterranean. Hence we must ask ourselves: what was the essential difference between the European and Amerindian cultures? And here the question brings us back once more to language, for the fundamental difference seems to have been this: the invaders had written language, but the defenders did not. The difference has superficial importance; the invaders could communicate at a distance; the defenders could not. The invaders could know what had happened last year, a hundred years ago, and could see broad patterns; except by hearsay, the defenders could not. The real difference, however, grew from the possession of the kind of culture which can be built with written language. The invaders had written for several thousand years; the defenders were just moving into the era of writing, and because their ancestors had not been able to read and write, they lost two continents.

Here we must distinguish between writing and reading as acquired skills and writing and reading as social forces. Writing of a sort, of course, the Amerindians had; who cannot peck a picture on a rock if he has two rocks and the idea? Some rock painting was developed enough to be stylized; several protected rock surfaces in the Snake River valley have preserved what seems to be a highly stylized sort of picture writing, involving symbols which were probably linguistic as well as pictorial, and since these works have survived in areas remote from one another and are at once recognizable by style, they must represent the survivals of a formally taught school. We have already seen that the Aztecs and some other Central Americans had a punning sort of rebus writing. Such evidence is interesting archaeologically and historically; it even preserves bits of information, but as we have seen, it was nothing to live with, nothing that could have had much impact on the Amerindians.

Similarly, the Eurasians a few millennia B.C. had writing, somewhat more advanced than the Amerindian, but still not culturally very significant. That the Sumerians and Akkads in the Tigris-Euphrates valley had writing of a sort, which they used in limited ways, doubtless accounts in part for the brilliance of that culture; that the Egyptians carved on stone and later wrote on papyrus probably made their far-flung empire possible. The Hittites, the Chinese, and the Tocharians were writing peoples, all. Important early empires came from writing peoples, and this coincidence is too striking to be without significance.

Nonwriting peoples could mount conquests, but they could not build great civilizations. By our standards, not even the early empires wrote much, and by our standards, also, they were not far-flung societies, nor did they enjoy very advanced culture. High and complex culture, extensive bodies of relatively unified peoples, require much writing, writing as a part of the culture, not merely writing as a possession of the savants, the priestly class, and the leading bureaucrats. In effect, complex culture seems to require an extensive writing system and all that goes with it in the hands of a considerable proportion of the population: for European culture this system was provided by an alphabet.

The alphabet was presumably invented only once, by some Semitic peoples, perhaps as early as 2000 B.C.[5] They probably acquired the idea of a letter, although perhaps not of an alphabet, from the Egyptians, along with some Egyptian symbols for letters. The Phoenicians spread the alphabet, and they or their ancestors may have developed it, but during these early times we are not dealing with a social force. For several centuries, perhaps for a millennium after it was devised, the alphabet was still an esoteric possession, a somewhat handier way of doing what could be done as well with a syllabary. After all, carving on stone is not rapid even if the carver uses an alphabet.

With the alphabet, however, empires grew. The alphabet helped the Phoenicians to expand into a Mediterranean empire; it helped the miraculous growth of Greece; it was involved in the flowering of the Hellenic cities in the early centuries B.C. It came into its own with the Latin alphabet, and we observe no accident when we notice that the father of most modern alphabets spread with the empire that is the father of most European nations. The early history of western and northern Europe could be written quite revealingly as the record of the manner in which one group of barbarians after another grew up to be able to make intelligent use of the Latin alphabet. And when the invaders of the Americas, whether they were Italian, French, Spanish, Portuguese, Dutch, Scandinavian, or English arrived on strange shores, they came, armed not only with blunderbusses and muskets, with broadaxes and flint and steel, but also with the Latin alphabet and all that it had made possible.

Thus the fundamental advantage of the invaders was that they could write, and that they had inherited the culture that had grown through a millennium or two among people to whom writing was common enough to be a social phenomenon. Naturally, nobody noticed this basic advan-

---

[5] The standard work is David Diringer, *The Alphabet: A Key to the History of Mankind* (New York: Philosophical Library, 1948). For a more popular summary, see Diringer, *Writing* (London: Thames and Hudson, 1962). Ernest Doblhofer, *Voices in Stone,* trans. Mervyn Savill (New York: The Viking Press, 1961), essentially follows Diringer. For the theory that the Greeks developed the first true alphabet, see Ignace J. Gelb, *A Study of Writing* (Chicago: University of Chicago Press, 1952).

tage. Captain John Smith, captured by the Indians, was able to send his compatriots written messages, and he seems to feel that his safety arose, in part, from the fact that his savage captor "so amazedly admired as he suffered me to proceed in a discourse of the roundness of the earth, the course of the sun, moon, stars, and planets."[6] What the Amerindian made of this harangue we do not know, but even Smith relied mainly on his own prowess, his ships, and his weapons, which in turn rested upon written language—Smith had not himself deduced the forms and movements of the planets. He had read all this in books.

Other permeating cleavages went equally unremarked, among them a difference in fundamental philosophy. People can be dichotomized in many ways, of course, including this: they assume either that their world is one of change or that it is not. Inevitably culture changes, but in many parts of the world and at many times—probably at most times and places—this change is so slow and so various, so accompanied with and confused by surface drifts in all directions, by birth and death, by youth and age, by fortune and misfortune, that the broad drift of a culture passes quite unnoticed. In most societies most people assume that things will be pretty much what they have been, that they will go pretty much as they have gone. Such people want themselves and their surroundings to be stable.

The European and Amerindian cultures were essentially alike in their reliance upon stability. In Europe, throughout the Middle Ages and centuries following, notably until the population movements that accompanied the industrial revolution, most people lived where their parents had lived and did what these parents had done. Their society was static, and they wanted it to remain so, or perhaps become a bit more prosperous for them personally. Similarly, the Amerindians, although as individuals they lived in highly varied cultures, lived in societies not characterized by change as to place, mores, or way of life. Naturally, if offered an immediate advantage they grasped at it; they welcomed a better way to trap and kill game, a better price for their pelts, brighter beads for their moccasins, and an iron pot instead of fragile native jugs. They welcomed horses—and here was one exception, for the horses did change the plains society and change it rapidly. They even welcomed the chance to get drunk with firewater, and firewater, too, changed their society by decaying it. In the main, however, when the whites altered native lives, the Amerindians wanted no such change, and they wanted if possible to go back to the unchangeable world of their ancestors.

Thus a longing for stability was characteristic of both the European

---

[6] *General History of Virginia* (1624), many times reprinted.

and the Amerindian cultures, but in the Americas a subtle change permeated the white colonists. They grew to expect change, even to welcome it. They included adventurers and opportunists of many sorts, and they were tumbled into a world that had to change and be changed if they were to survive. They expected to change things and to prosper by the change. This attitude has continued and has probably become an aspect of the American temper. The American knows that the city in which he lives will look different in a few years; the car he buys next year will be different from the one he bought last year—presumably better. He expects new building materials, new fabrics, new designs, new architecture, new organizations, new everything. He not only expects it, he rather welcomes it. The whites had come from a static society, but they moved into a new land being pulled from barbarism to high culture in a few generations, and these generations corresponded with the decades which saw the transformation of Western culture from reliance upon the individual to reliance upon society, in which horsepower became more a measure than a means.

The two groups differed, also, in degree of hospitality to the languages of others, and the whites—albeit with understandable reason—were purblind and bigoted when compared with the natives. Considering the levels of their culture, the Amerindians evinced a lively interest in learning the languages of their guests and conquerors. Amerindians taken to Europe picked up languages quickly, and many a white man in this country was relieved to find that the Indians he encountered could talk a little of his language. What were the mathematical probabilities of encountering in 1620, say in Somerset or Kent, a couple of cottagers who could converse in Pequot? But when the Mayflower landed on the "bleak New England shore," there were Samoset and Squanto, ready to welcome the newcomers in English. The white man could often make nothing more than grunts of what he heard, and usually he did not try—the prevalent notion that Amerindians had a universal vocabulary consisting of "Ugh" probably attests more to the insensitivity of the white man's hearing than it does to the inadequacy of Amerindian speech.

Of course, the Amerindians had some advantage; the invaders spoke few languages, the invaded, many. Along the St. Lawrence waterway, Amerindians would have heard both French and English; in the middle colonial states, English and Dutch, in the Southwest and in Florida, English and Spanish. In Latin America, some Indians must have heard both Spanish and Portuguese, along with other strays, including German in the late years. On the other hand, the white man would have had to learn hundreds of languages if he had bothered. On the whole he did not bother. The Amerindians were intrigued by the strange speech of these creatures who obviously had so much and could do so much; a few of the invaders, mainly merchants and divines, endeavored to learn the native speech as part of their jobs, but most of the invaders assumed— and many of their descendants assume today—that Amerindian languages were crude assemblages of grunts and mumblings, not worthy of civilized attention. Leonard Bloomfield, perhaps more than any other the founder of the American school of modern linguistics, recounts an instructive anecdote. To appreciate its flavor the reader should know that Bloomfield studied the Chippewa language and that he may have known more about it than any other white person ever has or ever will. The following is Bloomfield's account:

A physician, of good general background and education, who had been hunting in the north woods, told me that the Chippewa language contains only a few hundred words. Upon question, he said that he got this information from his guide, a Chippewa Indian. When I tried to state the diagnostic setting, the physician, our host, briefly and with signs of displeasure repeated his statement and then turned his back to me. A third person, observing this discourtesy, explained that I had some experience of the language in question. This information had no effect.[7]

And this, of course, was the reaction of one who had profited from scientific training.

Thus the white speakers moved swaddled in smug isolation. They partook of a common provincialism where strange languages are involved; almost all unlettered people, along with many who consider themselves literate, incline to be contemptuous of alien speech. I recall the remark of a mestiza servant of a friend of mine in Mexico. She was irked by my persistently running a typewriter during the hours which she felt should be sacred to the siesta, and reported my malfeasance to her mistress. My hostess explained that I deserved special consideration because I was a guest, and because I was a learned man who wrote books. The mestiza was not impressed. "How can he be so smart as you say he is," she asked, "when he cannot even talk Spanish well, which is so easy, and the most beautiful language in the world?" The white men were insulated, also, by their certainty that they were civilized men dealing with savages, and they held the local languages in the same contempt they felt for the local dress, warfare, table manners, and sexual practices. But in addition they brought with them two complex sets of pride and belief which helped to blind even the learned among the invaders.

---

[7] "Secondary and Tertiary Responses to Language," *Language*, XX (1944), p. 52, n. 9.

The better known was the classical tradition, embodied in the Latin and Greek languages. Everybody knew that European civilization was the inheritor of the great Roman Empire, which had encompassed in its day the known world and most of the world that remained much known until long after 1492. A European claimed a noble heritage, bequeathed to him in the literatures of the past, the basis of learning, and in the language of Cicero, which was generally felt to be also the language of God. One had only to look in any Bible to find Jehovah and Christ both talking Latin, or to attend church and hear the Lord speaking Latin through the mouth of the priest. Of course, the scholars of the day knew better; they were quite aware that no scrap of the Bible, or even of the Apocrypha or the epigrapha was written in Latin, and that the generally accepted version, at least in western Europe, was that translated into Latin by Jerome in the fourth century A.D. Most Christians, however, had never heard of Jerome; they never questioned either the antiquity or the divinity of Latin, and the thinking habits of the invaders were the thinking habits of most people.

In addition, the role of Latin as the universal language—universal in the literal sense of encompassing the universe, including Hell and Heaven along with the earth—was given at least tolerance in the highest places. Even devils were exorcised in Latin, and only in Latin. After all, "the Court of Heaven" was more than a figure of speech, and justice would be done there. A busy and devious imp might be able to plead ignorance of a vernacular tongue, that he did not know he had been exorcised. He could pretend he had not had time to learn all the gibberish of the world, and that he did not understand the rigmarole being pronounced in an obscure and outrageous dialect like English, but not even a minor devil could pretend he did not know Latin.

This veneration for Latin had practical use for the invaders, particularly when it was linked with another common linguistic inheritance, of which the newcomers were mainly ignorant, although ignorance did not prevent their profiting thereby. The invaders had no common language; a Portuguese could make nothing of what a Dutchman said, any more than an Aleut could understand Quechua. On the other hand—whereas probably no single word has been borrowed from Quechua into Aleut, and if the languages are genealogically related, the connection is so remote that grammatical similarity is not observable—all of the invaders had a notable community in language. As we have just seen, except for the Russians, who in the end did not account for much, they all had the Latin alphabet. Anyone who knew the letters in one language knew them for all the languages, albeit with somewhat varying pronunciations. When they endeavored to learn another European language, they had a good start. French, Italian, Spanish, and Portuguese—all prominently involved in the New World—had derived from Latin and had strong sororal affinities with one another. English had borrowed extensively from Latin, and from descendants of it, like French and Spanish.

Furthermore, all these languages were Indo-European languages; they had descended from a common ancestor, and however the grammar of these languages might be changing—English had changed markedly— they preserved evidences of the parent grammar. They all relied upon what we call sentences, made up of subjects and predicates, and they all retained at least vestiges of the Indo-European inflectional system. As the Romance languages were related through their common ancestor, Latin, so the northern languages—English, Dutch, along with German and Scandinavian languages, which became important later—had a common ancestor in Proto-Germanic, which was cognate with Latin. And of course the northern languages had borrowed from one another— sea terms, for example, since ships' crews tend to be international, and through Scandinavian, and Dutch, and other settlements in England. Thus the invaders, if they had no common language, had common bases for language, and incidentally, if any of them needed any bolstering for their convictions that the local grammar reflected grammar itself, they had it in their common Indo-European grammatical heritage. But to consider how this insulating prejudice developed we must look at the concept of "Universal Grammar."

In its purity, the concept is deeply philosophical; it may help in man's quest to reveal himself to himself. As it was corrupted, it suggests the humor of the bright, ironical gods. It became the tool of bigots and the delight of pedants, for it gave play to man's love of easy solutions, to his love of resolving mysteries by attributing them to the Deity, and it relied upon man's gullibility in the presence of sliding middle terms. Here the slippery middle term was *grammar,* which can, and is, used at once to indicate either the working of language or the policing of language. In the hands of eighteenth-century thinkers, many of whom had a strong ecclesiastical cast, it shifted gently from an inquiry into the nature of man and mind to a body of dicta hurled by the wrathful gods from some linguistic Sinai.

As Noam Chomsky has lately shown,[8] a man like Descartes understood that, since all men have language, there must be something in man that leads him to build language, something that directs his building of language. Thus our problem is to find out how much universality there is

---

[8] *Cartesian Linguistics: A Chapter in the History of Rationalist Thought,* Studies in Language, ed. Noam Chomsky and Morris Halle (New York and London: Harper & Row, 1966). Descartes was followed by others, notably Wilhelm von Humboldt; Chomsky provides bibliography.

in language, and how this reflects or reveals the nature of man. Of course Descartes, living when he did (1596–1650), had no way of knowing how diverse are the languages of the world, but even so, he must have been right; if we can get deep enough into language and into man, we must inevitably find universals. Descartes died without much pursuing this idea; he had followers who have not been much studied, and hence we do not know as yet very clearly what happened.

But if Descartes was misunderstood, his students cannot be much blamed—Descartes is scarcely bedtime reading. Furthermore, an easier explanation was ready at hand; once one had the term *Universal Grammar,* its meaning would have been, to most speculators, implicit. Had not God given man language? Everyone knew He had, and since He had, the universality of language would reflect the universality of God. And where would He have revealed this universal grammar? Obviously, in His universal language, which was Latin—or if not Latin, it was Greek in which He had seen fit to record the New Testament. If any corroboration were needed, grammarians had it in the similarity of Latin and Greek grammars, a similarity which permitted them to assume that these languages were both fairly close indicators of Universal Grammar, not much corrupted from God's own Universal Grammar, in any event the best that could be expected in a latterday world.

The change was fundamental and its impact profound. Although Descartes' Universal Grammar rests upon philosophical logic, the new concept replaced it with what amounted to a doctrine of Universal Usage, which has no foundation, philosophical, theological, linguistic, or any other. If by *usage* we mean correctness of idiom at a given time and place, then *Universal Grammar* in the sense of Universal Usage is a contradiction in terms. None of the three thousand or so languages of which we have record in the world closely resembles any other language, and thus no particular locution could be universally correct.

This illogicality did not discourage self-righteous polemics. What was right and what was wrong—rightness being determined by resemblance to Latin usage and wrongness by divergence from Latin—became the burden of many a volume in which pedants belabored a solecistic public, along with one another, for indulging in supposed barbarisms. That is another story, to which we must return later, but for the moment we can notice that all colonials from Europe would have believed they brought with them, in their Classical heritage, an approximation of linguistic truth. If their own grammar, whether it was Spanish, French, English, or whatnot, was more corrupted from the perfect original than was Latin, it would be nowhere near as corrupt as the grammar—if, indeed, it could be called grammar at all—that had, in effect, been corrupted out of existence in the mumbles and grunts which was all the colonials heard in native speech.

Thus the idea of Universal Grammar, although it was conceived in pure thought, provided the most blundering bigot with justification for his self-righteous pride.

6

THE BEACHHEADS OF INVADING LANGUAGE

So now the second phase of language in America begins. The Amerindians had developed mainly static cultures in which languages served as the natural monopolies they are, the unique and relatively unconscious medium for a linguistic community. Now we must deal with language in motion, with languages in conflict with other languages, with speech no longer rooted in a stable economy. The new languages came as part of the baggage of the newcomers, and though for our purposes the luggage is more interesting than the luggage bearers, we should perhaps sketch the actions of these bringers of language.

A modern strategist, looking at a map of the Americas, would mark the utility of the islands which we call the West Indies. Sufficiently offshore to be free from short-range attack, and adequate for staging bases, they occupy the center of a half circle which permits an invader to move north, south, or west. Columbus, sailing west, drifted somewhat south and blundered into them; they thus became the staging bases for the Spanish empire only, but as such they influenced, even directed, the course of American colonization.

One might speculate on the complexion of the modern world if, instead of drifting south, Columbus had held due west from the Azores and had found his way into Chesapeake Bay. He did not, and once the great power of Spain was firmly set in the West Indies, however Drake might raid and the French might probe, the northern European nations gained no extensive dominion south of the Indies—bits like British Guiana and French Martinique were exceptions that have become anachronisms. The Spanish, having their bases, could move south into Venezuela, west into Mexico, north into Florida, and eventually into Texas and the Southwest. Portugal, blocked off from the staging islands, moved south, and partly because it had to rely mainly on the sparse

Brazilian harbors, Portuguese became a poor second among Latin-American varieties of speech.

Meanwhile, northern European nations were moving toward North America. Had Columbus held west or drifted a bit north, the Spanish might have become entrenched in the Chesapeake area and in the Hudson and St. Lawrence estuaries, forcing the French, and probably the English, to shift south. But Columbus drifted south as well as west, and thus, with minor exceptions—Spain held Florida and New Orleans for a time, and Mexicans founded San Francisco—a line drawn roughly west from the northern West Indies has become the boundary between the varieties of American speech, English with some French to the north, Spanish with some Portuguese to the south.

For the moment we might ignore the Portuguese and the French. Theirs were potent empires in the great colonial centuries, and no contemporary would have belittled their probable futures. To the north, the French, not the English, appeared dominant; to the south the Papacy presumably endeavored to divide the New World evenly between the great maritime Catholic powers, Portugal and Spain. In retrospect, however, the movements of the Spanish and the English become central, and we may appropriately center our attention upon them. That the hegemony of Spanish over Portuguese in Latin America may not continue is another question, to be raised later. As for Portuguese in North America, some place names suggest a Portuguese origin, but if Portuguese-speaking colonists came, they did not spread far or stay long.

The Spanish and English colonizations contrast sharply. The Spanish occupation started early and developed rapidly. Based on discovery and aimed at quick riches, it relied on armed power and sustained itself by pillage. It struck rapidly at concentrations of population in modern Mexico and Peru; although the conquistadors were drawn more by the inhabitants' wealth than by the inhabitants themselves, in seizing these centers, the invaders paralyzed major resistance and promoted an influx of European culture. Almost all the "firsts" in the Americas are Latin-American firsts—the first printing press, the first university, the first church. On the other hand, language spread slowly. Spanish dominated the cities, but its use in the back country spread very slowly; even today, although the population is mainly Spanish-speaking, we might plausibly guess that native languages are spoken over more square miles than are Spanish and Portuguese.

The English occupation, although it started late and developed slowly, pervaded as it moved. It was not much based on conquest, possibly because the Indians north of Mexico had little worth stealing, but one might observe that traditionally the English had thriven through settlement. When the Angles and Saxons overran the island of Britain, they moved slowly, appropriating land and developing it. Again, when the Danes and Norwegians came, although they pillaged and sacked, they eventually settled down. In America, Englishmen took most of two centuries to occupy the narrow eastern seaboard and to spill much over the Appalachians; but when they did move, they surged so overwhelmingly that it is difficult today to find natives of the continental United States who are ignorant of English.

Of the land areas, the northern proved the more accessible. Although Mexico was ripe for conquest, and fell quickly, South America was really less open to invasion than a first glance might indicate. To the west the mountains are precipitous, the rivers short and not very useful; landings are contained at or near the coast. The continent is open to the east, but not readily. To the north the great Orinoco and Amazon rivers lead into the rich interior, but they lead also into inhospitable jungles. To the south are fine harbors, but Bahia de Todos Santos and Rio de Janeiro do not give access to great river systems. Only far to the south did the Rio de la Plata become the center of important developments at Buenos Aires and Montevideo, but even so, growth was limited. The Paraná River leads into difficult country.

The northern continent was enveloped in three movements suggestive of grand strategy. There was no strategy, of course; the incoming speakers of Indo-European languages were rivals, often openly at war, but the configuration of the land and climate encouraged movements which broadly resembled strategic campaigns. The northern coast was shielded by ice, but the eastern coast, conveniently broken by bays, was generally temperate. What would now be called beachheads were established, based upon the gulfs, most of which were important estuaries: the St. Lawrence, Boston Harbor, the mouth of the Hudson, the Delaware Bay and River, the Chesapeake with its various river systems, the bays at Charleston, Savannah, and St. Augustine. Mostly these were English settlements, or they became so with the decline of Dutch and Swedish settlements, with French on the northern fringe, Spanish on the south. The buildup was slow during the seventeenth century and quickened during the eighteenth, by which time the second movement had begun, a giant pincers moving along the St. Lawrence–Great Lakes waterway to the north, and up the Mississippi Valley from the south. This movement, started by the French, was completed by the British and Americans, who split the pincers into two, using the Ohio River.

The early nineteenth century witnessed a third great movement, another pincers. The Mexican Spaniards worked up into the southwest of what is now the United States and along the Pacific Coast. The Russians and British moved south along the same coast, and the central pocket was split by minor pincer movements, drives west from the American states, mainly one to the north following the Missouri, Snake, Humboldt, and Columbia rivers, and one to the south around the mountains to link—however inharmoniously—with the Mexican advance. This final movement culminated soon after 1850, and what we must, from a linguistic point of view, call pockets of resistance in the mountains and deserts were subsequently mopped up.

Since I expect to focus major attention on what happened in the United States, we should examine the beachheads of Indo-European speech from Canada to Florida. All the early important settlements that survived were started in the seventeenth century; none flourished much before the eighteenth, even Quebec only moderately. For our purposes, minor chronology is not very important; Jamestown, Virginia, was settled before Plymouth, Massachusetts, but we are concerned with the growth of language, not with whose foot first hit which rock. Language works slowly, even in boom times for language, albeit the American Colonial period was most certainly a boom time. Accordingly, we may as well start at the north and work south.

To the north, the French spoke language of two sorts, dialectically distinct. Quebec was founded by Champlain in 1608, but Breton and Norman fishermen coasted these waters at least somewhat earlier. Consider the little island of Arichat, off the southern shore of Cape Breton Island. Small colonies of Norman fishermen have survived there for centuries, speaking a jumbled dialect of English words out of Boston and Scandinavianized French out of the Middle Ages, which is the despair of the good nuns trained in Quebec, who try to teach them to speak Parisian French properly. Similar agglomerations occur throughout the maritime provinces in the back country. I recall that, driving late, I camped in what I supposed to be a deserted clearing in provincial Quebec. In the morning, an irate swarthy gentleman accosted me, demanding "un piastre per compy," by which he meant that I owed him a dollar. No suggestion of nasalization appeared in his *un,* as there had not been in any French dialect prior to the Renaissance. *Piastre* is the corruption of the name of an ancient coin, the Italian *piastra,* a term not generally used in French for the dollar. I have spelled his word for *pour* like English *per,* but actually his pronunciation was more like American *purr,* which is often pronounced somewhat lower in the mouth than is *per* and much lower than the French *pour.* The final syllable of his *comper,* a verbal concocted out of English *camp,* lacked the stress one would expect in a French infinitive. In short, he was probably talking very much as did Chaucer's Nun, and for the same reason, she having picked up her patois, directly or indirectly, from the fisher folk of Stratford-atte-Bowe, who had it from Normandy. Canadian provincial French has been host to strays from various French dialects, particularly those of Normandy and Brittany.

These imported provincial dialects had their imports. As every reader of *Evangeline* knows, the British, who had occasionally captured Port Royal from the French and had consistently lost it, fell upon the peaceful Acadians and dispersed several thousand of them. Most of those who were scattered along the eastern coast returned after the British hysteria had subsided, but a group in Louisiana, centered upon St. Martinville, remained, the so-called Cajuns. A professorial friend of mine, a native of Montreal, was lately visiting in the area with his French wife. Since he knew Canadian French, he found that he and the waitress could chat familiarly, and he told her that his wife also was French. But the two women could scarcely understand one another. "What kind of French do you speak?" the Cajun asked. "I speak the kind of French we speak in France. What kind do you speak?" The Cajun replied proudly, "I speak the real French." Linguistic islands like Cajun are the flotsam of accident, but the vast network of French which spread thickly through much of the continent was no accident, although it is now noticeable mainly in place names transplanted by the Canadian trappers, traders, and missionaries. The priests, of course, spoke mainly cultured French, but the bulk of those who carried French west were the sons of men who had brought to the new country the provincial dialects of the old.

Meanwhile, Canada also supported aristocratic, even courtly French. Men like Champlain and La Salle were courtly gentlemen, and they were accompanied by men and women who were the more scrupulous in their cultivation of all things elegant because they lived in the wilds of the New World, where culture, if it was to be preserved at all, must be preserved sedulously. Again and again this phenomenon appears; cultured settlers on the frontier will cling so fiercely to the customs of the homeland as they remember it that they quickly become pedantic and old-fashioned. Thus the provincials in the New World, particularly the governmental set in Quebec, the ecclesiastics, and the more important merchants and professional families who were associated with them, cultivated French assiduously, and their descendants today proudly believe that they have preserved French in a purity that has been lost in mercantilized Paris, and they may be right.

This devotion to French is reflected sensitively in Willa Cather's *Shadows on the Rock,* a semi-novelistic series of sketches set in seventeenth-century Quebec, fictional, of course, but grounded solidly on documents. Miss Cather makes little point of language differences; she is concerned with the whole social climate, but in mirroring the time she reveals language in Quebec as something more than a handy means of communication.

Consider the apothecary, Euclide Auclair. He cannot divert his eyes from the ships streaming away down the St. Lawrence in October, for they assure him that "the world" still exists, although he will have no news of it for eight months, including a long winter. He tries to surround himself with French order, with French wine, with the herbarium he is collecting, destined for France. A timid little man from Paris, he has his daughter read La Fontaine to him in the evening, while he corrects her pronunciation, against the time when she will be sent to France to school. French is part of his life, and he would have agreed with the nun who wrote back to France, "Tout y est sauvage, les fleurs aussi bien que les hommes (everything here is wild and uncontrolled, the flowers as well as the men)." Cultured French was the language high up on the "rock," where lived the Count Frontenac and the bishops. Down in the lower town were the bordellos for the sailors and the trappers, the wholesale houses where the nondescript refugees from pre-Revolutionary poverty in France mingled with the native Canadians, and all sorts of Canuck blendings of whites and Indians. From them, mainly, came the spoken French that later diffused through the continent.

To the south the colonies were mainly Germanic—especially English —and Protestant, and whether or not for these reasons, on the whole the Indians fared worse there. Roy Harvey Pearce has suggested that philosophically the Indians were an affront to Europeans. The Renaissance Englishman, with his sense for order, could find in disordered America no basis for a microcosm of God's universe.[1] More particularly, social, political, commercial, and religious differences impeded understanding between the colonists and the natives. In New England the Reverend Solomon Stoddard observed that the Puritan at war with the Indians "harrows them, and saws them, and puts them to the sword, and the most terrible death that can be," and he justifies such actions, explaining, "We had sufficient light from the word of God for our

[1] *The Savages of America: A Study of the Indian and the Idea of Civilization* (Baltimore: Johns Hopkins Press, 1953). In carefully documented research, Pearce surveys the various colonies; see pp. 6–42, perhaps especially pp. 8, 15, 19–20, 23, 35. I shall rely upon him without further citation. I have acknowledged elsewhere my debt to Louis B. Wright, *The Colonial Civilization of North America, 1607–1763;* he has bibliographies for all colonies and reprints significant passages. For more extensive bibliographies, see *A History of American Life,* ed. Arthur M. Schlesinger and Dixon Ryan Fox, 12 vols. (New York: The Macmillan Co., 1927–1944).

proceedings." The aborigines, being children of Satan, were to be converted, and if they resisted conversion, destroyed. John Winthrop rejoiced that the Lord had sent a "wonderful plague" which opened land for occupation, since the natives "are neere all dead of the small Poxe, so as the Lord hathe cleared our title to what we possess." Pearce further notes that farther south "The Indian became for the seventeenth-century Virginians a symbol not of a man in the grip of devilish ignorance but of a man standing fiercely and grimly in the path of civilization." God would be glorified by a rich and prosperous Virginia, and thus it was God's will that the Indian be put out of the way.

With variations, attitudes like these determined patterns of conduct in most English-speaking colonies, but since we shall need later to consider the dialectal areas of the east coast, the variations have some significance. For the settlements centered upon Massachusetts Bay, we shall need few of the conventional details. Every American child knows 1620, if he knows few other dates; he knows about turkeys and Pilgrim Fathers giving thanks, whether or not he has an inkling of how and why his country was settled. In fact, these are among the socially accepted bits of information about ourselves. A grade school teacher in the Orient reported to me that she had told her charges the story of American settlement as she conceived it, and of course included the account of the landing of the *Mayflower* on Plymouth Rock, and of the *Speedwell,* which proved to be an unseaworthy craft, and had to turn back. A little Oriental girl was much moved by this account, as she understood it, and wrote a poem:

> Abandoned Speedwell!
> She was unworthy sea crab,
> And she sit upon a rock.

Not all misinterpretations of Colonial history have been so fruitful.

The newcomers suffered horribly from disease and hunger, from cold and the mental terrors of a strange and often hostile land, but less than they might have expected. Most of the neighboring Indians had been decimated by disease—perhaps smallpox or influenza acquired from white fishermen—and those who remained were relatively friendly. When they were not, the newly arrived guests did not hesitate to deal with intransigence, after they were strong enough. Emanuel Downing, urging vigorous action upon John Winthrop, a key figure among the Puritan magistrates, could write as follows:

A war with the Narragansett is very considerable to this plantation, for I doubt whether it be a sin in us, having power in our hands, to suffer them to maintain the worship of the devil which their paw-waws [pow-wows] often do. Secondly, if upon a just war the Lord should deliver them into our hands, we might easily have men, women, and children enough to exchange for Moors [presumably Negroes], which will be more gainful pillage for us than we conceive, for I do not see how we can thrive until we get a stock of slaves. . . .[2]

These are lesser known aspects of a settlement that a learned son of a great Boston family, James Truslow Adams, has characterized as follows: "In fact, the Bible and the beaver were the two mainstays of the young colony. The former saved its morale and the latter paid its bills; and the rodent's share was a large one."[3] Even some frivolity has come to light. No less an authority than William Bradford reported that one Thomas Morton, gentleman, onetime lawyer of Clifford's Inn, pioneered a community at what he called Merry Mount, where he

. . . became lord of misrule and maintained, as it were, a school of atheism . . . After they had got much by trading with the Indians, they spent it as vainly, in quaffing and drinking both wine and strong waters in excess, as some reported, ten in a morning. They also set up a May-pole, drinking and dancing about it many days together, inviting the Indian women for their consorts, dancing and frisking together (like so many fairies or furies rather) and worse practices, as if they had anew revived and celebrated the feasts of the Roman goddess Flora, or the beastly practices of the mad Bacchanalians.[4]

We are here less concerned, however, with the friskings at Merry Mount or the dunkings at Salem than with two other characteristics of the colony. The Bay community, along with its offshoots north and west from Maine, New Hampshire, and Vermont, and down through Massachusetts to Connecticut and Rhode Island, became a center for democracy and a learned interest in letters and language, insofar as there were such centers in the New World. Claiming democratic leanings for the tight little theocracy run by the Puritan divines may seem an inordinate boast, particularly since the majority of the population was disenfranchised—few could qualify for church members, which required solid evidence of conviction of salvation. The fathers of New England had little better than contempt for what they called "a mere democracy." But we should remember that Protestantism harbored seeds of democracy in its theory, however the Puritan theocrats may have diverged

---

[2] Most of the cited passages that follow are conveniently reprinted in Wright; see Wright's index for pages. This particular passage, pp. 91–92.
[3] *Provincial Society, 1690–1763* (*History of American Life,* Vol. 3 [New York: The Macmillan Co., 1927]); I owe the reference to Wright, pp. 77–78.
[4] See Wright, p. 79.

from democracy in politics. Protestantism rested salvation in one way or another upon the individual, upon his conviction of sin and his faith in salvation, not upon participation in sacerdotal rituals. Thus Protestantism shifted religious faith away from a supreme power and toward human decision, and as religious thinking shifted, so in good time shifted political theory.

That the sons of Boston Bay fostered books and learning, no one can doubt. The early Puritan leaders tended to be divines, with sound classical educations—one notes the readiness with which Bradford turned to the classics in condemning the doings at Merry Mount. These divines were always composing sermons, memorializing the government, penning epistles home to England, or describing the wonders of the New World. If I may distort a recent witticism, there was more writing per square head around Massachusetts Bay than among most other populations of which we have record. True, culture slacked off somewhat in the eighteenth century; the learned immigrants were eventually gathered to the celestial bosom, and tilling the Lord's inhospitable vineyard among the field stones of New England absorbed so much time that local schools were few, poor, and sporadically attended. But the tradition survived; Harvard University is so named because John Harvard gave two hundred books, and Yale has a similar bequest behind it. New England could mount the first notable school of letters in the New World and develop the first considerable body of scholarly and professional writers; all the early American lexicographers of note were New Englanders— Webster, Worcester, Whitney—as were most of the important early textbook writers. Even the Franklins, the Philadelphia printers, brought the black art from Boston.

Throughout much of the Atlantic seaboard we shall observe that the influence of the learned is readily exaggerated, that the numerous common people, not the notable but notably few aristocrats, were usually the molders of linguistic forces. The teachers, writers, and sermonizers of New England, however, wielded linguistic power far beyond their numbers. As for schooling, Ezechial Cheever was exemplary. He was Master, first of Ipswich Grammar School and later of Boston Public Latin School, where he taught Latin and some Greek. Louis B. Wright describes him as follows:

Stroking his long white beard, he was a figure as venerable as Moses, but when he snatched his birch rod, his wrath blazed like Jehovah's rage. Cheever, the author of a Latin *Accidence,* turned out a long line of pupils well drilled in correct grammar, good manners, and sound principles of religion.[5]

---

[5] See Wright, p. 113.

In contrast, to the south and west, a community developed with a sharp eye for business, a tongue for languages, and a taste for tippling, but with little devotion to piety, letters, or learning. The official British explorers somehow missed one of the gems of the east coast, New York harbor and its estuary, but an Englishman in the service of the Dutch, Henry Hudson, opened the way to fur trading, and in the 1620's to settlement. The Dutch dominated the Hudson Valley for a half century before the British were able to make a pretext, through the then Duke of York, to seize the place.

The colony endured the usual vicissitudes, dogged by disease, hunger, and administrative incompetence, by inadequate support from the mother country, and by a paternalism more fascistic than fatherly, all spiced with international intrigue. As a band of merchants, the West India Company was established ostensibly for trade, but as an adjunct of the government, it was intended to promote the Protestant war in the New World against the encroachment of Catholic Spain. Indian troubles appeared early. Under the orders of Governor Willem Kieft, soldiers attacked a band of sleeping Indians—innocent refugees fleeing another tribe—about eighty of them, by David de Vries' reckoning:

. . . infants were torn from their mothers' breasts and hacked to pieces in the presence of their parents, and the pieces thrown into the fire and in the water, and other sucklings, being bound to small boards, were cut, stuck, pierced, and miserably massacred in a manner to move a heart of stone.[6]

The Indians retaliated, burning, killing, and pillaging, until they were stockaded out by what has become Wall Street. Another governor shocked the solid citizens by flouncing in petticoats in the tap houses. Dictatorial government led to grumblings and revolt, and to the eventual execution of a popular leader, one Jacob Leisler—an incident of the British regime, but one which serves to remind us that the character of New Amsterdam continued to become the character of early New York.

Commercially, the colony throve. The Dutch traded with the Chesapeake and Virginia settlers, throughout the West Indies, and on the European continent. Meanwhile these ventures prompted competition from Swedish settlements along the Delaware; practically, the Swedes were often rivals, but officially they were friendly, too. Gustavus Adolphus hoped to grow in Delaware "the brightest gem in his crown," and the Dutch were not entirely averse—after all, one more Protestant buffer against the Catholics to the south might not be amiss. Actually, few

---

[6] *Korte Historiael* (1655), trans. in part in *Narratives of New Netherland*, ed. J. F. Jameson (New York: Barnes & Noble, 1909), and reprinted in Wright, p. 135, although omitted from the index.

Swedes came; Sweden itself was an undeveloped wooded country, which was encouraging immigration from Finland, and the Swedes became "just numerous enough to annoy the Dutch." In the end, the great development of any American colony depended upon a tide of immigration from the homeland; for New Amsterdam or New Sweden no such tide ever set in, and the colony was eventually overrun by the sweep of English settlers from Connecticut, a sweep legitimized in 1664 by the official privateering of the Duke of York. Thus, historically, the settlement on the island of the Manhattoes may have had its principal influence through its impact on the British colonies; the Dutch kept the French out of the vital Hudson River valley until the New Englanders were strong enough to defend, after a fashion, their western frontier.

Linguistically, New Amsterdam bequeathed to the new continent an important heritage, but culturally it was a desert. Even moderately learned divines sent out to minister to the spiritual needs of the colony went home in disgust. Libraries were almost nonexistent, whereas in New England and Virginia early book collections surprise us by their extent. Even old Peter Stuyvesant, who was no dandified esthete by anybody's reckoning, was shocked by the seventeen taprooms, the absence of a school, and the one unfinished church—a handful of the devout were meeting in an attic. He proposed a school and offered to help finance it himself, but the local tipplers were not much interested, and Peter had to import a tutor for his children. The colony was more than a century old before it had an institution of higher learning, King's College, the ancestor of Columbia University, and even then all schools were private. But they were polyglot, ten English, two Dutch, one French, and one Hebrew.

Almost from the beginning, the colony centering upon New Amsterdam spoke a babel of tongues; Dutch predominated, of course, until English overwhelmed it, but Dutch was not necessarily the native tongue of the Dutchmen, since many of the early settlers had been refugees in Holland, Walloons and French Huguenots. New Rochelle became a center of Huguenot culture; Palatinate Germans settled along the Hudson. The infiltrating British included Welsh, Irish, and Scots, and from the beginning, traders included Jews, Italians, and Portuguese, albeit in face of an official provision that all immigrants to the colony must be Protestants. The Swedish governor, Johan (Big Guts) Printz, had to write home for a Latin secretary who could carry on official correspondence with his neighbors; of the first three patents issued in New Amsterdam, one went to a Dutchman, one to an Englishman, and one to a Dane. We shall later see that the area south and west of the Hudson became crucial for the character of American speech; we must doubtless assume that the polyglot nature of the settlements centered upon the island of Manhattan had something to do with the eventual character of North American speech.

Still farther south and west, the settlements associated with the City of Brotherly Love were at once suggestive of and sharply contrasted to those that sprouted from New Amsterdam. Philadelphia was founded for principles, not profit. True, idealism had its limits; jealous Virginians could charge that the pious Quakers were far too hospitable to pirates, and the founder, William Penn, obviously loved his self-portrait as a great patron, sweeping down to Philadelphia from his rural estate, enthroned on his six-oared barge. Scotch-Irish Presbyterians, attracted to the fat lands of Pennsylvania, insisted on starting wars by butchering inconveniently domiciled savages and justifying their slaughters with innumerable Biblical texts. Even the Quakers themselves, generally devoted to the love of man and learning, tended to discourage the reading of "plays, romances, novels, and other pernicious books."

Nonetheless, Penn was a man of parts and principles, and his career in the New World gives comfort to those who believe in the rewards of virtue. A complex figure, he was always in and out of trouble, even in and out of jail, and he was capable of both great foresight and great gullibility—a common cheat by the name of Philip Ford, whom Penn had trusted like a son, bilked him out of the Pennsylvania colony, and Penn had to raise £7,600 to buy it back. But he was obviously sincere in his effort to set up in the New World a haven for man and a monument to God; the peaceful prosperity of Philadelphia was due to something more than the richness of the surrounding farm lands, the acumen of the Philadelphia merchants, and Penn's dexterity as a real estate agent—his advertising brochures brought immigrants from many a distressed area of Europe. Philadelphia rapidly outstripped its rivals to the north and south, and became both a financial and an intellectual capital of the colonies, with a lively book trade, both foreign and domestic, before it became the governmental capital of a new nation.

As a medley of languages, Philadelphia and its environs rivaled polyglot New Amsterdam. The base was English, but English of all sorts, and when the counties to the southeast of Pennsylvania wished to separate, the Philadelphians were not averse; after all, the area that eventually became Delaware was what one Quaker called "that Frenchified, Scotchified, Dutchified place." From the first, the City of Brotherly Love welcomed abused brethren from wherever they came. Welshmen and Ulstermen were numerous enough among the early settlers to color the settlements of both eastern Pennsylvania and western New Jersey. Penn's publicity, disseminated on the continent, brought floods of

Palatinate Germans, who were suffering oppression in the seventeenth century, along with Huguenots from France, and various Scandinavians, who joined remnants of Gustavus Adolphus' Swedes. The Germans of Germantown, and to the west toward Lancaster (Manheim, Lititz, Strasburg, Petersburg, Schoeneck, and many more), maintained one of the few bodies of non-English speech within the United States that was stable enough to develop a dialect, the so-called Pennsylvania Dutch.

Thus Philadelphia was polyglot, as well as hospitable and cultured, perhaps polyglot because hospitable, but for whatever reason, it shared this quality with settlements to the north and east. If polyglotism means anything—and in language it surely must—then we have here an extensive polyglot stretch, the seaboard all the way from western Connecticut to Chesapeake Bay, and we shall see later that it is upon just this segment that the great central North American dialect has its foundation.

The colonies from Chesapeake Bay to Florida can best be considered as growing from a single movement, which started in what is now Virginia and fanned out. As was usual, early years were troubled. The first settlement on Roanoke Island in 1585 vanished completely; and some later groups survived only by eating rodents, and one man wintered on his pickled wife, whom he had murdered and salted away. As in other colonies, the natives were often hostile and frequently abused; there was sporadic killing as the whites edged west along the waterways. The colony throve unevenly, with tobacco the cash crop—not the only crop, but dominant enough so that the glut of a volatile market could and did bring recurrent disaster. Even so, the richness of the tidal plains and the plenitude of cheap slave labor encouraged prosperity, even wealth. The pattern set in Virginia was repeated with minor variations in Maryland, and later in the Carolinas and Georgia. Maryland was feudal and to a degree Catholic; Georgia was encouraged as a buffer against the Spanish in Florida, and supported as a program for the relief of debtors, but common manners of life ran through most of these settlements.

Two social complexes, with linguistic habits overlaid upon the social, appeared early and continued. The dominant people grabbed land and became great planters; although they were not aristocrats in the British sense, they aped aristocrats. Many became wealthy; they sent their sons to Europe to be educated, imported books and fine furniture, built pillared mansions along the rivers, and maintained town houses in the coastal cities for the social season. A man like Captain Samuel Matthews could direct a small village from which he victualed ships:

he sowes yeerly store of Hempe and Flax, and causes it to be spun; he keeps Weavers, and hath a Tan-house, causes Leather to be dressed, hath eight Shoemakers employed in their trade, hath forty Negroe servants, brings them up to Trades in the house.[7]

He had whole sections in grain, barns swarming with domestic animals, and was sufficiently established to marry the daughter of a London knight. There were hundreds like him, thousands greater or lesser, but great enough and numerous enough to culture a way of life unlike that in the middle states or in New England. The area differed, also, in the degree to which the people maintained connections with the mother country; the southern cities spoke middle-class English from London. Echoes of Vauxhall and Pall Mall—or at least of Fleet Street—might be heard in Baltimore, Charleston, and Savannah, and on many a plantation, before they were heard in provincial English towns like Leeds and Hull.

These self-grown aristocrats, however potent they may have been as individuals, were of course relatively few. The men and women who were doing the work were the many, and they, also, fall roughly into two classes. One group felt the pressure of the great landowners who were able to seize the flat, rich coastal lands, the ports, and the navigable portions of rivers. These lesser men—often indentured servants who had worked themselves free—migrated west, where hillier land and thinner soil above the escarpment known as the Fall Line discouraged farming on a grand scale. They became the "poor white" population of the back country and the uplands, different in origin from the planters, and even more different in culture. They had no aristocratic tradition, and no means with which to ape one. Their manners they had from the hut or the jail—many a Tory judge could think of no reward more befitting a rascal or a bad debtor than to send him to the New World—and their skimpy formal learning, such as it was, suffered under the rigors of pioneering.

We have noticed a similar cultural decline farther north, although with a difference. In New England, learned composition declined from the seventeenth century into the eighteenth, as the well-read Puritan divines died and were replaced by the products of the local schools. In the North, however, although the competency of the community declined, it declined only to revive; the decline of culture represented mainly a dip in the cutural level of the whole community, and when

---

[7] I owe the reference to Wright, cited previously, p. 45; he refers to "an account of 1649." For a similar case, see Marcus Wilson Jernegan, *Laboring and Dependent Classes in Colonial America, 1607–1783*, Social Service Monographs, 17 (Chicago: University of Chicago Press, 1931), pp. 225–26, n. 49.

books and learning were restored, the community was no more divided than before.

In the South, on the other hand, cultural decline intensified community boundaries. The planter class suffered no permanent decline; an eighteenth-century planter was at least as likely to have been educated formally in England as was a seventeenth-century planter; even an eighteenth-century planter who was himself an immigrant was much more likely to own a library, to live in a city, and to be surrounded by some evidences of culture. But sons of the indentured servants participated in no such resurgence; the people who had come to the New World because they had failed in the Old did little better with changed surroundings. Those who moved into the back country gained independence with their new lands and became hardy, self-reliant folk, but with a low level of literacy. Other underprivileged whites stayed in the society dominated by the great planters and merchants. They tended to become overseers, tradesmen, small businessmen, practitioners with modest professional pretensions. Negro slaves took over the common labor, even much of the skilled labor. Education without wealth was not easy; schools and colleges, even for the middle class, were not much encouraged. When the Reverend James Blair urged the idea of a college because education promoted the saving of souls, a treasury official snorted, "Souls! Damn your souls! Make tobacco!" Blair was a tough-minded Scot, and he finally got his college, William and Mary, but he obtained the money from the Crown, not from the planters. Meanwhile, lower-class and lower middle-class Southerners lived in sight of the glamorous plantation-house, glimpsed the social-seaport culture, and might eventually work into it, but for generations they were not much of it.

Elsewhere along the southern coast, time, the men, and the land produced variations upon what we might call the Virginia pattern, but the variations were relatively inconsequential when compared with those farther north. Maryland was ostensibly Catholic, but only ostensibly so, since for whatever reason—there are suggestions that the reasons were more rooted in the leanness of Lord Baltimore's purse than in the breadth of his Lordship's vision—all sects were welcomed, and the government took pains that Protestants should not be persecuted as were Catholics in England. Maryland was no less patrician than Virginia; in theory the Calverts owned all the land. George Calvert was Lord Baltimore, whose charter made him "Absolute Lord and Proprietary of Maryland and Avalon." His charter passed to his son, Cecilius, so that tenants held leaseholds only, and the practices of leasing produced results similar to those in Virginia. The rich lands along the

Chesapeake tended to fall into the hands of great English landholders, while the back country sufficed for tough but indigent Scotch and Irish.

Similarly, to the south, various colonies developed various embroideries upon the pattern without altering it much. In the Carolinas agriculture rested upon a broader base, and generally escaped the boom-or-bust prosperity of Virginia. Turpentine, tar, spars, and other forest products useful in shipping provided ready cash crops, so that Charles Town, modern Charleston, rivaled New York as a center of the Indian trade. The traders were tough fellows; they included renegade Scots, as determined as the Reverend Blair but of a different stamp, escaped jailbirds or malefactors who had never been apprehended. When they rendezvoused in Charles Town, as they did once a year, decent ladies kept to their boudoirs, and the constabulary found another way to look. The cobblestones rang to their hobnailed boots; they submitted their annual contracts to the merchants who supplied them with trading goods, while the sailors' dives prospered. Then the backwoodsmen disappeared for another year, to send back bales of furs and lines of captive Amerindians to be sold as slaves. Of course, this abuse of the natives brought reprisals in the form of uprisings—the traders were proud of their skulduggery, especially of their prowess in debauching the native women. One of the most notable of the participants in shenanigans with the local Indians, Captain Thomas Nairne, was broiled for several days over a slow fire. Picturesque variations like these work themselves out in time, and in the Carolinas as well as in Virginia and Maryland, patrician societies centered upon the cities and were spread out through the fat lands. The two sorts of less privileged classes occupied lesser stations in the coastal culture or became modest landholders in the back country, what would have been called yeomen in England.

Least characteristic, perhaps, was the most southerly of the British colonies, Georgia, for which the theory, as Wright notices, "was a curious medley of Utopian idealism, hard-headed mercantilism, and resurgent imperialism." To take these in reverse order, the imperialism involved both the growing power of France, based upon the Mississippi River and the gulf ports like those at Mobile and Biloxi, and the growing power of Spain in Florida. A buffer was welcome. As to the second, Georgia had forests as did the Carolinas; it had access to the southern plains as did the Carolinas, and could reasonably be expected to thrive from the fur trade as had Charles Town; it had plantation land and back-country land. By the time Englishmen became interested in Georgia, enough fortunes had been made and lost in America so that risk money was available, but risk money likes big profits, which in Georgia were avidly pursued and sometimes realized. Meanwhile, idealism, also, permeated Georgia. To a considerable degree, the trustees of the colony conceived of it as a land of promise where the debt-oppressed of the Old World could find salvation in the New. They were reflecting, of course, one of the pervading eighteenth-century notions, associated with the name of Jean-Jacques Rousseau, that civilization had become root-bound because culture is in essence stultifying, that if man is to attain his natural stature he must attune his living to nature.

Actually, the noble experiment led to only secondary variations. Debtors who prospered in Georgia tended to return—though in freedom —to England, but the fame of Georgia as a home for the homeless brought the persecuted from various parts of the world. Georgia's reputation contributed to the remarkable career of Gottlieb Priber, for example, who endeavored to develop an ideal community among the Cherokee; unfortunately for the future of Priber's noble venture, his idealistic community stubbornly blocked off British expansion to the west and seriously hampered the prosperous fur trade. Priber was disposed of, the more readily because compromising documents were found in his possession, a Cherokee dictionary and an "extremely wicked" work entitled *Kingdom of Paradise*. We can infer the content of this manuscript only from its detractors; they pointed out that Priber "enumerates many whimsical privileges and natural rights, as he calls them, which his citizens are to be entitled to." This all sounds very much like eighteenth-century Rousseauism, and when his detractors accused him also of advocating "dissolving of marriage and allowing community of women, and all kinds of licentiousness," one suspects they were making the most of a good opening, and that Priber's concern for freedom inclined more to the political than the sexual. However that may be, Georgia developed in general in accordance with the pattern; if there were rather more of the common people in Georgia than in Virginia, if the wool hat has a long ancestry among the crackers, there was also Savannah.

Farther south the Spaniards held Florida. We can, in effect, ignore them, although their contemporaries did not. They were the northern spearhead of the great Spanish power, a constant threat, but no more than that. The Spaniards were occluded to the west by the Gulf of Mexico, and hemmed in to the north by the growth of Georgia. A minor pawn in the international chess of the eighteenth century, they were eventually withdrawn while their linguistic impact was still negligible. The northward thrustings of Spanish as a language will concern us again and again, at New Orleans, in Texas, in New Mexico and Arizona, and in California, but the potentially very great Spanish foothold in Florida, however portentous it may have appeared in 1660, seems three hundred years later to have been inconsequential.

Thus, with some picturesque variations, five patterns of culture developed along the eastern coast of North America. We can discount at once the Spanish colony in Florida to the south; it might have developed, but did not, and eventually it fell into the southern pattern, a pattern violently disrupted by twentieth-century population shifts—but that is another story. At the northern end a French colony prospered, which had continuing influence, but an influence tempered by a shift from French to English; the British capture of Quebec led to a flood of English immigrants into Canada, particularly after the American Revolution. All this had linguistic consequences which we must consider later. Within what was to become the United States, three areas developed. To the north, the New England culture centered upon Boston, flourished from Maine to Connecticut and west to the Hudson, relatively democratic and relatively literate. To the south, the midland areas stretched from about the mouth of the Hudson River to Chesapeake Bay; still farther south, from Chesapeake Bay to Florida—and eventually including Florida—the derivatives of the Virginia culture supported an aristocratic planter-merchant society, balanced by the underprivileged class made up of the lower classes along the littoral and the small farmers in the back country.

These were the men and women who apparently brought skilled hands to a new world. The hands were the visible contributions; the owners of the hands also brought invisible contributions, craft skills, bodies of knowledge, and tricks of mental training. In the end these invisible assets often proved the more enduring and the more creative; among them were language habits.

7

THE CASE OF THE LINGUISTIC LUGGAGE

We can now refine our question: What language came from where in America, and how did it grow? Superficially the answer is easy. Everybody brought the language of his native land, along with whatever other languages he had acquired. These languages can be known; the learned language, for example, was usually Latin. When a body of Moravians had to leave Georgia, the Methodist missionary George Whitefield welcomed them in Pennsylvania, which was known as the Barony of Nazareth. Whitefield spoke no German, and the Moravians spoke no English; but he and the Reverend Peter Boehler managed, in Latin, to fight so fiercely about Predestination that the Methodist ordered the Moravians off his property.[1] Such dealings in strange tongues are conspicuous, being activities of the learned, who are inclined to write about themselves and one another. Similarly, the main languages can be known. To the north and west, in a great crescent from the St. Lawrence estuary to New Orleans was French. The language persisted, giving way gradually to English, leaving remnants behind it; *Orleans* is generally pronounced in the northern part of the United States so that the word comprises two syllables, but many Southern speakers use three syllables, /or li ənz/, an obvious corruption of the French pronunciation. On the other hand, what is now *Nova Scotia,* one of the earliest areas of French settlement, did not enjoy its Latinized form of *New Scotland* until after the passing of La Nouvelle France. To the south was Spanish, triumphant south of about the thirtieth parallel, moribund to the north. In between, as well as to the north and west, English was to triumph everywhere, although it was confused and was to continue confused by various other

---

[1] Frederic Klees, *The Pennsylvania Dutch* (New York: The Macmillan Co., 1958), pp. 96–97. I shall have occasion to refer to Klees again; he provides a select but extensive bibliography in "notes," pp. 445–51.

tongues, at first by Dutch, Swedish, and German, later by other speech as well.

In a broad way, then, we know who spoke what and where. But Spanish is not one thing, as any gringo tourist speaking *the-theo* Spanish has discovered as soon as he has entered Mexico. Nor is French one thing; until shortly before the first French settlers came to the Americas, the speech of that country was thought of as two languages, the *langue d'oïl* and the *langue d'oc*—a name preserved, of course, in Languedoc— and even as Champlain was cruising the St. Lawrence, his compatriots in Paris were developing the nasals characteristic of Parisian speech, nasals which are not as yet part of many of the French dialects, including dialects prominent in the baggage of the settlers of New France.

Nor is English one thing. Any American who has traveled the more rural parts of England must have found himself surrounded by speech so foreign to him that he could not even follow the subject of the con- versation. The voyager among British dialects is forced to recognize that a sound which we might spell *bairn* and pronounce /beə˞n/ may refer to either a barn or a child; he can hear *old* pronounced so that it rhymes with American *told, called, clawed, bowed, hod, had,* and a number of others. What speech, then, did these newcomers bring with them? They brought their own languages, but they also brought their own dialects of those languages. Hence, we must know whence they came, and what dialects were spoken there. Neither is easy to know, for the language of migrants can be readily determined, but not the dialect.

Just at the start we get some help. We might suppose that the most important distinctions and the most difficult information to acquire would concern the dialects of what are now called the foreign speakers, the speakers of languages other than English. But not so; let us consider an example. The so-called Pennsylvania Dutch—and they often prefer to be called Dutch, from *Deutsch,* than German—include a variety of refugees to this country in the seventeenth and eighteenth centuries, Reformed Lutherans from Württemberg and Alsace, Moravians from the Palatinate, Schwenkfelders and Amish and Mennonites, all some- what mixed up with refugees from Poland, Bohemia, and elsewhere, but still relatively identifiable both in Europe and America. "Pennsylvania Dutch differs slightly from county to county according to the origin of the original settlers," Frederic Klees writes, but there is "a remarkable degree of standardization." The language is

. . . merely the eighteenth-century dialect of the Palatinate . . . with some borrowings from Württemberg and Switzerland. If the particular brand of Pennsylvania Dutch is that of Lancaster County or upper Montgomery or

Bucks, there are more Swiss additions, since the early settlers of these places were frequently from Switzerland; but if the Pennsylvania Dutch is that of Berks County or Lehigh, it is almost pure Pfalz.

This last term, not much known in English, refers to an area in the eastern Palatinate. The dialect has apparently been preserved with sufficient accuracy to have saved the lives of Americans during the late war; at least one body of Pennsylvania Dutch on skirmish were not machine-gunned, presumably because the Nazis who heard them talking assumed they were Palatinate German.

However much such tales embody the folklore of a polyglot war, the fact seems to be that Pennsylvania Dutch has preserved dialects of the mother country, with considerable purity, but the fact has little importance. True, some words borrowed from Pennsylvania Dutch into English probably assume their present form because of the peculiarities of dialects; *strubbly* (disheveled), *putz* (crèche), *wunnerfitisch* (inquisitive), and *toot* (paper sack), probably take their form in Modern English because of their roots in a particular German dialect. But for any broad view of American English we are not here talking about much. The contribution of Pennsylvania Dutch to modern American speech is small, if picturesque; the percentage of this contribution that has been materially altered by the fact that some speakers came from Mannheim or Heidelberg rather than rural Pfalz is a minor influence within a minor influence.

The whole impact of these speakers of German dialects, however, may not be minor. The fact that a large body of people was speaking German, any kind of German, over a long period of time is probably more significant than the kind of German they spoke. According to recent estimates, some 300,000 Americans feel more comfortable speaking Pennsylvania Dutch than speaking English, and a considerably larger number use the language readily.[2]

At this point we should recall that bilingual speakers in sufficient numbers do strange things to language, one of which may be that they speed up language change, and to apply this principle we may need a fine distinction. Broadly speaking, two groups of language were brought to the New World, two sorts when looked at from the point of view of the eventual impact of these languages. One was the language that was to triumph, English north of the Gulf of Mexico, Spanish in most areas to the south, Portuguese in some others, notably Brazil. I shall call these tongues dominant languages. The other comprised the various sorts of

---

[2] See Klees, cited earlier, *passim,* perhaps especially for specific use of the dialect, pp. 273–82.

speech that were to succumb to a dominant language; I shall call them moribund colonial languages. For example, in the Americas, tongues like Chinese and Welsh have persisted only in very restricted groups; German (as Pennsylvania Dutch), Spanish, and Yiddish are extensively spoken but are declining as second languages. Various African tongues brought by slaves were crushed so soon and finally that we scarcely know the linguistic families from which they descend, much less the languages and dialects—speech in Brazil provides an exception, and a variety of Yoruba, a language of the Niger-Dahomey area, seems to have become a sort of general Negro language, known as *Nago*. The state of French can be determined less arbitrarily, since we deal here with both linguistic extent and social vehemence; I shall consider it later. Roughly, however, dominant and moribund colonial languages can be distinguished, and the distinction concerns us because of the differing roles played by dialect in the two linguistic groups.

Of course, all languages are more or less characterized by dialects and by dialectal differences. With languages that play a secondary role, however, dialectal differences may have only minor impact. The notable fact of early New York linguistic history is that whole languages were in conflict. When an Alsatian Huguenot encountered an Amsterdam Dutchman, the important facts were not that one spoke Alsatian French and the other Amsterdam Dutch, but that they spoke two different languages, neither of which was to survive in New York. True, the words we inherit in American speech from Dutch are not quite what they might have been had these inheritances come from a different Dutch dialect, but the inheritances are few and the differences minor. Speech would not be much altered in this country if *cruller* were spelled or pronounced differently.

These moribund evidences of language, though they have been picturesque and have given us interesting linguistic bits, have not changed the main course of language in this country. They have not much influenced the pronunciation; an immigrant will speak with an accent, but his American-born children on the whole do not, to say nothing of their English accent being much influenced by the dialectal differences in their ancestral Dutch. The moribund speech did not much affect grammar, although a foreign phrase has occasionally been picked up, usually for humorous purposes. For example, "Wat you tank?" probably did not give us "What you think?" or the whole series of questions in which we dispense with *do*. The moribund languages did not much influence basic vocabulary. For example, the Dutch borrowings are said to be relatively unusual in that they have entered into common speech more extensively than have the French and Spanish—although the French were common during the heyday of fur trade in the North, and although Spanish throve during early mining and ranching in the Southwest. The following is Albert H. Marckwardt's classification by groups of the twenty-seven supposed Dutch borrowings:[3]

Food	Transportation	Farm and Building
cole slaw	caboose	hay barrack
cookie	scow	stoop ("porch")
cruller	sleigh	saw buck
pit ("stone" or "seed")	span (of horses)	
pot cheese		
waffle		

Toponymics	Social Classification	Miscellaneous
bush (back country)	boss	boodle
hook (of land)	patroon	dingus
	Yankee	dope
		dumb ("stupid")
		logy
		poppycock
		Santa Claus
		snoop
		spook

A Dutch etymology for all these (e.g., *Yankee*) is not certain, and probably *knickerbockers* and *knickers* and perhaps a few others could be added, but none of these words comes very close to those that most of us have to live with most of the time. Historians have noticed that for a time words like *blicksen* for lightning, *bosch* for forest, *bouwriji* for farm, *brief* for letter, *handschoen* for gloves, and some others were common on Long Island and to the north of Manhattan, but these words were few and short-lived.[4] Dialect is not the most important characteristic of moribund colonial languages.

In dominant languages, however, dialects matter. In a moribund language the dialects can frequently be ignored because the language declines too soon and plays a role too minor to permit anything as subtle as dialect to have much impact. A dominant language, on the other hand, tends to survive extensively, and since it lives as dialect, it tends to survive as dialect.

---

[3] See p. 48 of Marckwardt's revealing little book, *American English* (New York: Oxford University Press, 1958), on which I shall rely frequently.
[4] Thomas Jefferson Wertenbaker, *The Founding of American Civilization* (New York: Cooper Square Publishers, 1938), p. 109.

Now, before we ask ourselves who brought which British dialects, we must survey dialects in England to discover what language was available to be brought. Anyone who knows anything of earlier forms of English and who travels in Britain today, will become aware that the speech of a thousand years ago has been preserved differently in different parts of the country. When he hears in the north, "gannin' doon the wye," and compares it with "going da-oon the stray-it," heard in London, he assumes that a variety of linguistic forces have been at work; if he knows the history of his native language, he may observe that prominent among them is a strong tendency to preserve Old English forms in the north. He will recognize *gannin'* as more closely related to Old English *gan* than to modern *going,* which shows normal southern English development and an *-ing* present participle ending which developed relatively late. The *doon* is simply the Old English pronunciation of our word *down,* unchanged in a thousand years and more. My spelling *wye* is an attempt to suggest a pronunciation somewhat closer to the Old English *weg* than are the more conventional pronunciations of *way,* and the word itself was more popular a thousand years ago than it is now, being partially superseded by the Latin *street* and the Old English word that has become *road.*

This sort of thing is pervasive. It permeates all British dialects, which reflect variously the preservation of older forms, along with more recent influences. Standard Modern English has derived mainly from the dialect of London and its environs, but mathematically, an immigrant to America was likely to bring with him a dialect of some other area, since only recently has London acquired anything like its present proportion of the English population. That is, English speech from York in the north, from Oxford toward the west, or from Canterbury in the southeast would have passed as current in the seventeenth century, but would now be notably dialectal in Britain. If it came to this country, and thus avoided the leveling effect of London, it would become standard American English while remaining dialectal British English. We must consider the background of British dialects.

All languages of any extent have dialects, but dialects have been notably characteristic of English from the time when there was anything that could be called English. The island of Britain had been inhabited by Celts during early historic time; the Romans subdued these Celts, and in turn Germanic-speaking peoples overran the Romano-Celtic culture, bringing at least three Germanic dialects. The first Germanic speakers occupied the southeast point of the island, in what is now Kent. We know little of them, except that they enjoyed adaptable international manners; they were probably professional soldiers, freebooters, pirates

—one can use more or less polite terms. Whether they spoke a fifth-century equivalent of Damon Runyon's gangster cant we do not know, but their language differed from other Old English dialects, and the speech of their descendants has differed from other English speech ever since.

The Angles, from the vicinity of the present Danish peninsula, settled along the east coast. They eventually held the land from the Thames estuary to the mountainous north, where the Celtic Scots and Picts clung to the rough country. Either these Angles represented two minor linguistic groups or the inhabitants developed in different ways after they arrived; dialects centering upon present-day Lincoln differ from those centering upon present-day York. These speakers differed also from those who settled along the southern coast, the continental Saxons, and these people, also, either brought or developed dialectal subdivisions. That is, by the seventh century when political differences had settled down in Britain to minor bickerings suggestive of tribal warfare, a small dialect survived in southeast England, and two large dialects, both with subdivisions, dominated the remaining more habitable portions of the island, Anglian-Mercian to the northeast, various sorts of Saxon to the southwest.

This basic pattern underwent various embroideries. In the ninth century the Danes and the Norwegians moved in; their arrival signaled a half century or so of raids and uprisings, internecine war of the bloodiest sort, but when it was all over the same old lines had been accentuated. The newly-arrived Scandinavians, bringing with them another sort of Germanic speech, had taken over roughly the area previously occupied by descendants of the Angles, the reason being, of course, that the Saxons, not the speakers of Anglian and Mercian, had subdued the invaders.

Linguistic peace did not last long. In 1066 the Normans moved in, bringing a Scandinavianized dialect of French with them, Norman French being the dialect acquired by Danish-Norwegian invaders in France, relatives of those same Danes and Norwegians who had overrun England some two centuries earlier. The impact of this invasion upon vocabulary has often been exaggerated, but from our point of view it was of the greatest importance. The old Saxon capital had been Winchester, which now declined into a county town. London grew as the capital; it grew as the principal port bringing in continental ideas and goods, and those came in French form. Thus London was the center of the growing French influence. This French influence produced both obvious and obscure effects. The obvious ones concern vocabulary; people in London used more words borrowed from French than did those in the back country. The writings of Chaucer and Gower, for example, both Londoners, are seeded with French words; contemporary works by outlanders, the authors of *Gawayne and the Greene Knight* and *Piers Ploughman,* for example, lean more heavily on Old English. But the obscure effects may be more important. London was much more polyglot than York to the north, which would have been more polyglot than the Malvern Hills, a rural area close to Wales. If we are right in guessing that polyglotism promotes linguistic change, then the dialect of London, the dialect from which modern standard English has sprung, would likely have been the most rapidly changing dialect.

Apparently it was. Of course, all dialects were changing, and in part London English only seems to have changed faster because it was changing toward Modern English, whereas some dialects were producing changes that have not become standard. English changed with remarkable rapidity for three or four hundred years after 1200, much more rapidly than related dialects on the continent, and partly because the London dialect is the measuring stick. In London occurred the sharpest, most prolonged contest between English and French; here also was a strong smattering of other speech, Flemish, Italian, Dutch, sprinklings of Scandinavian and Hebrew. And here all dialects of England mingled because lords from all over the realm brought their retinues. The speech of London had reason to be unstable, especially in the fourteenth, fifteenth, and sixteenth centuries. We must assume that the earlier Scandinavian influx in the north had encouraged linguistic change also; apparently it did, for northern verb forms changed rapidly, but the total effect of this polyglotism of the north was blunted by another fact. Old Norse was conservative when compared with Old English, although related to it; for example, *k* sounds in Old English generally changed in the south to the sound we spell *ch,* but this change did not take place in Old Norse, a fact which apparently discouraged this change in the north of England. In any event, *church* in the south is *kirk* in Scotland; and southern *chester* from Latin *castrum,* as in *Chester, Dorchester,* and *Chichester,* remains *caster* in the north, as in *Doncaster* and *Lancaster.*

Whatever the reason, this seems to have been the result: The dialect of London moved more rapidly from Old English than did the dialects of the north, west, and south. This drift was so marked that a century after Chaucer died his language had become strange to Londoners, and editors of Chaucer were regularly Scotsmen, whose language had changed so little that it still approximated Middle English. Similarly, in the south, many dialects contained voiced consonants that were voiceless farther north, and some of the pronunciations persist only in the outlying dialects in Britain, *zin* for *sin, zoul* for *soul, vox* for *fox*—

though the female form *vixen,* with the voiced initial consonant, has become standard—and the like. That is, beginning well before the American immigrations, a trend had developed in British speech that was to have profound effects upon the importation of English into the New World. The dialect of London was developing; this dialect was to become the ancestor of cultivated English speech, both in and out of the capital.

Furthermore, and just at this time, dialects were apparently diverging more along social lines than previously. Such divergence is, of course, not unusual, and most speakers of English know the phenomenon. In England, British Received Standard is taught in schools and becomes the mark of well-bred people; in the United States and elsewhere, English exists on various levels, but notably on two: standard cultured speech as against nonstandard vulgate. If you call the home of a professional person and are told, "Naw, he ain't t' hum," you would assume you were not speaking to a member of the family, and this assumption would be made even by many of those who would themselves say, "He ain't t' hum."

Such distinctions must have been maintained in Middle English, also, but the surviving evidence suggests that social levels of language were not delineated with anything like the prescriptive care that characterizes them today. Early Middle English was a socially limited speech. For some hundreds of years after the Norman conquest, English was not an official language in England. Cultured people spoke French and no doubt cultivated it, but for centuries English was not an official, literary, or learned medium. By the fourteenth century this state of affairs was changing; long before Shakespeare's time, English of the court was looked upon as correct speech, and well-bred young people were taught it. By 1530, John Palgrave, in the course of instructing his readers on the proper pronunciation of French, says that the French *a* has a sound "suche we use with us, where the best englysshe is spoken." A tutor reporting to Thomas Cromwell, "chief Secretary vnto the Kings Maiestie," declares that young Gregory is being taught by "dailie heringe hime to read sumwhat in thenglishe tongue, and advertisenge hime of the naturell and true kynde of pronuntiacon thereof."[5] Sir Thomas Elyot wrote in his *Boke named the Governour* (1531),

Hit shall be expedient that a nobelmanes sonne in his infancie, haue with hym continually onely suche as may accustome hym by litle and litle to

---

[5] Henry Cecil Wyld, *A History of Modern Colloquial English,* 3d. ed. (Oxford: Basil Blackwell, 1936), p. 103. I shall rely heavily on Wyld for the development of British colloquial English.

speake pure and elegant latin. Semblably the nourishes [nurses] and other women aboute hym, if it be possible, to do the same; or, at the leste way that they speke none englisshe but that which is cleane, polite, perfectly and articulately pronounced, omittinge no lettre or sillable, as folisshe women oftentimes do of a wantonnesse, wherby diuers noble men and gentilmennes chyldren, (as I do at this daye knowe) haue attained corrupte and foule pronuntiation.

All this suggests standards of English usage and careful cultivation of these standards. The speech of the court became a regional dialect, and by imitation a social dialect, cultivated by those at court and those who had courtly ambitions.

Many had such ambitions and the English Renaissance court had literary and intellectual pretensions. Even Henry VIII, in spite of his interests in matrimony and affairs of state, had been trained to be a scholar; the daughters of Sir Thomas More and Henry's daughter Elizabeth were not the only young women who could astound the learned by conversing in Greek. Raleigh, Sidney, Wyatt, Surrey, Bacon, and many others were men of letters as well as court officials, and if Lyly and Spenser were not court officials it was for no lack of trying. Nor were professors a rarity at court; Roger Ascham, don at Cambridge, held various governmental posts, as did Sir John Cheke and Sir Thomas Smith of the same university. All wrote on learned subjects.

Some distinguished figures brought local speech to court; a contemporary reported of Sir Walter Raleigh, "notwithstanding his so great mastership in style, and his conversation with the learnedest and politest persons, yet he spoke broad Devonshire to his dyeing day." John Lyly was born in Kent, and in spite of his literary affectations may never have entirely outgrown his native Kentish. Bishop Hugh Latimer, frequently chosen to preach before Edward VI, was the son of a "yeoman father who had no landes of his name" and his mother "mylked kyne." He, too, must have learned the approved speech, although he retained "a copious flow of invective, and a ready if a rude and coarse eloquence." As he puts it, his father "kept me to schole, or elles I had not bene able to haue preached before the kinges maiestie nowe."[6]

Fortunately, these important people wrote so many books that we know something of their language. Letters have survived also, which reveal that their literary usage was nothing esoteric, but a refinement of their working speech. But how can we say, other than by guessing, that this cultured speech of the court, which was in process of becoming

---

[6] Wyld studies the styles of Raleigh, Lyly, and some of their contemporaries in detail; see pp. 99–147, especially 109–10, 131–32.

the cultured class speech of the nation, was to be contrasted to the speech of the men in the London street? The common man is not notably eloquent, and we have less information about ordinary Londoners than we might have had if the city had not suffered the great fire of 1666. Some bits remain, however, among them the diary of Henry Machyn,[7] a merchant tailor who, although he seems to have been a Yorkshireman, was living in London somewhat before Shakespeare's time. He exemplifies many of the characteristics that we associate with folk speech of the day, including what is learnedly called "misplacement of an initial aspirate," more commonly, dropping and adding *h*'s. He wrote *alffe* and *alff* for *half*, *alfpenny* for *halfpenny*, *Anton courte* for *Hampton Court*, *elmet* for *helmet*, *arnesse* for *harness*, *alters* for *halters*, *ard* for *hard*, *yt* for the verb *hit*, *ade* for *head*, and *Allallows* for *All Hallows*. On the other hand, with him *answered* became *hanswered*, *asked* became *haskyd*, *ear* became *here*, *every* became *hevere*, *arms* became *harmes*, *Ambrose* became *Hambrose*, and *Alexander* became *Halesander*.[8] One never finds a court person writing this way, particularly those individuals whose English was not tinged heavily with Anglo-Norman.

Now we should add, what has been implied above in the writings of people like Elyot, that this concern for "correct" English is involved in Latinity. Latin, and to a degree Greek, was the basis of formal education. The upper cultural levels were strongly Latinate, the middle levels somewhat Latinate, and the lower levels—lower, that is, in financial and social station—were but little touched by classical traditions or the Latin language. To see how this went, let us consider the activities of Edgar, legitimate son of the Earl of Gloucester, as he appears in Shakespeare's *King Lear*.

Edgar is a splendid young man, scion of a noble house. Falsely accused by Gloucester's illegitimate son, Edmund, of being a traitor, he is forced to flee. Alone on the heath, he communes as follows:

> I heard myself proclaimed;
> And by the happy hollow of a tree
> Escaped the hunt. No port is free; no place

---

[7] *The Diary of H. Machyn, Citizen and Merchant Taylor of London, 1550–1563,* The Camden Society Publications, 42 (London, 1848). It has been studied by Axel Wijk, *The Orthography and Pronunciation of Henry Machyn, the London Diarist: A Study of the Southeast Yorkshire Dialect in the Early Sixteenth Century,* Stockholm Studies in English, 1 (Uppsala: Appleberg, 1937), and somewhat more conveniently in Wyld, cited earlier, pp. 141–47, where the quotations I shall employ will be found.

[8] For further examples see Wijk, pp. 219–21 and entries under *h* in the Appendix.

> That guard, and most unusual vigilance,
> Does not attend my taking. Whiles I may 'scape,
> I will preserve myself; and am bethought
> To take the barest and most poorest shape
> That ever penury, in contempt of man,
> Brought near to beast: my face I'll grime with filth;
> Blanket my loins; elf all my hair in knots;
> And with presented nakedness out-face
> The winds and persecutions of the sky.

We need not, of course, accept this as a transcript of cultured upper-teenage speech in Miles Standish's time. It is poetry; not every young man, mussing his hair, would say he "elfed" it, implying that sprites had been at work, but the Latinate cast of the whole passage may well reflect the cultivated speech of the day. Notice, "No port is free; no place / That guard, and most unusual vigilance, / Does not attend my taking." The lines have a classical march as well as a sprinkling of Latinate terminology. "Persecutions of the sky" is Latinate as well as poetic.

Now we might remind ourselves that Edgar was no learned man, no scholar, or orator, no mouther of legal phrases. He had been educated to be a gentleman, not to be a student. He may have known Latin, but probably not much. He certainly had had a tutor who knew Latin well, and the structures in which the young man was tutored, the vocabulary in which he was encouraged, had a Latinate tinge. His Latinity shows, not only in his formal speeches to his father and others, but even in his private thoughts.

Now let us return to his adventures. Having disguised himself as an insane beggar who need not say much but "Tom's a-cold," he encounters Lear on the heath and is eventually accosted by his own father, from whom he must conceal his identity. Probably aware that his imitation of uneducated diction would not have been very convincing, he mentions that he has known a better station, "A serving-man, proud in heart and mind; that curled my hair; wore gloves in my cap," one who "hath had three suits to his back, six shirts to his body, horse to ride, and weapon to wear. . . ." This description suggests an upper middle-class person now fallen on evil days, and when Gloucester asks who he is, he replies,

Poor Tom; that eats the swimming frog, the toad, the tadpole, the wall-newt and the water; that in the fury of his heart, when the foul fiend rages, eats cow-dung for sallets; swallows the old rat and the ditch-dog; drinks the green mantle of the standing pool; who is whipped from tithing to tithing, and imprisoned and imprisoned . . .

> But mice and rats, and such small deer
> Have been Tom's food for seven long year.

This verbal disguise, along with Edgar's elfed hair, is sufficient to deceive old Gloucester, who is much excited, and with good reason, for his kindness to Lear is discovered, and he is to be paid for this supposed treachery by being blinded and turned out.

Edgar becomes his guide to Dover, still pretending only to be Poor Tom, and during the course of the journey they are discovered by an unprincipled scamp named Oswald, who endeavors to kill the old man, "a proclaimed prize," to claim the reward. Edgar now adopts another disguise. He and Gloucester are approaching Dover and thus must be in Kent, an area whose dialect descends from that of the Jutes, the earliest of the Germanic freebooters. Accordingly, he conceals his identity from Oswald by trying to talk like a local bumpkin; he has some kind of club which he calls a ballow, supposedly a corruption of the word *baton,* and with it he confronts Oswald, who is a coward but armed with a sword.

OSWALD:. . . . Hence,
      Lest that the infection of his fortune take
      Like hold on thee. Let go his arme.
  EDGAR: Chill not let go, zir, without vurther 'casion.
OSWALD: Let go, Slaue, or thou dy'st.
  EDGAR: Good Gentleman goe your gate, and let poore volke pass: and 'chud ha' bin zwaggered out of my life, 'twould not ha' bin zo long as 'tis, by a vortnight. Nay, come not neere th'old man: keepe out che vor' ye, or ice try whither your Costard, or my Ballow be the harder; chill be plaine with you.[9]

The dramatics of the scene require that Edgar beat Oswald to the ground with his cudgel, which Edgar does, but if we are interested in his speech we might notice some details. The spelling indicates that Shakespeare is here trying to suggest a heavy burr in the speech, even heavier than the spelling indicates, for a good artist merely suggests dialect without trying to reproduce it. For example, *'twould* is spelled as we would spell it, but it may have been pronounced more like *two-old,* with the *w* and *l* sounded. Some other words are historically interesting; *chill* is what remains of Anglo-Saxon *ic wille; 'chud* is probably the remains of *ic sholde,* and *vor'* means "warm." *Gate* has the obsolete meaning *way,* and probably was pronounced, as it still is in many dialects, to rhyme with *mite.* All of the sounds represented by *f* in other dialects are here represented by *v* and that of *s* by *z.* This was a common character-

[9] IV, 6, 228–38. The passage is here reproduced in the spelling of the First Folio, perhaps most readily available in the following facsimile: *Mr. William Shakespeares Comedies, Histories, & Tragedies,* ed. Helge Kökeritz (New Haven: Yale University Press, 1954).

istic of many southern dialects, a tendency to voice fricative vowels that
are voiceless farther north.

These are, of course, artistic efforts to reflect the speech of the late
sixteenth century, but we have abundant other evidence that Shakespeare was a keen observer of the speech of his day, and while his plays
do not contain accurate representations of it, we are entitled to assume
that they are suggestive of dialectal differences, both geographical and
social. Unfortunately, Shakespeare gives us no picture of great deprav-
ity; he wrote no *Lower Depths* or *Tobacco Road*. Servingmen and "prat-
tling nurses," country yokels, soldiers and sailors, rabble from the
streets, even a few "rude mechanicals," play minor roles, but they mostly
say little or are involved in various sorts of clowning. Extended transcripts of what seems to be genuine uncultured speech are hard to come
by, partly because the uncultured could not record themselves if they
wished, and they probably did not much wish.

Contemporary journalists have preserved samples, however. The following is an imaginary underworld conversation printed in Thomas
Harman, *A Caueat or Warening, for Common Cvrsetors Vulgarely
Called Vagabones* (London, 1567).[10] Doubtless it was concocted to
display Harman's favorite bits of underworld cant, but we may probably
accept it as at least revealing. It represents uncultured speech, probably
exaggerated to be deliberately mystifying to law-abiding eavesdroppers.
The speeches in cant are translated by Harman into sixteenth-century
conventional English. The person called a Roge is a small-time thief; the
term for Vprightman might be deceiving without some definition such as
the following, taken from a contemporary description also printed in
Harman:

An Vpright Man. An Vpright man is one that goeth wyth the trunchion
. . . [and] is of so much authority, that meeting with any of his profession,
he may cal them to accompt, & commaund a share or snap vnto him selfe,
of al that they haue gained by their trade in one moneth. And if he doo
them wrong, they haue no remedy agaynst hym, no though he beate them,
as he vseth commonly to do. He may also commaund any of their women,
which they cal Doxies, to serue his turne.

The following is the conversation—the cant first, the contemporary
translation (in italic) below it:[11]

---

[10] Printed, with some other similar pieces, in the publications of the Early English
Text Society, Extra Series, 9, ed. Edward Viles and F. J. Furnivall (London,
1869).

[11] To promote easier reading, the style, i.e., capitalization, paragraphing, and use
of italics, has been modernized; but since the spelling presumably suggests the
pronunciation, Harman's orthography has been preserved.

VPRIGHTMAN: Bene Lightmans to they quarromes, in what lipkin has thou lypped in this darkemans, whether in lybbege or in the strummell?

Good morrowe to thy body, in what house hast thou lyne in all night, whether in a bed, or in the strawe?

ROGE: I couched a hogshead in a Skypper this darkemans.

I layd me downe to sleep in a barne this night.

VPRIGHTMAN: I towre the strummel trine vpon thy nabchet and Togman.

I see the strawe hang vpon thy cap and coate.

ROGE: I say by the Salomon I will lage it of with a gage of bene bouse; then cut to my nose watch.

I sweare by the masse, I wull washe it of with a quart of good drynke; then saye to me what thou wylt.

MAN: Why, hast thou any lowre in thy bonge to bouse?

Why, hast thou any money in thy purse to drinke?

ROGE: But a flagge, a wyn, and a make.

But a groat, a penny, and a halfe penny.

MAN: Why, where is the kene that hat the bene bouse?

Where is the house that hath good drinke?

ROGE: A bene mort hereby at the signe of the prauncer.

A good wyfe here by at the signe of the hors.

MAN: I cutt it is quyer bouse, I boused a flagge the last dark mans.

I saye it is small and naughtye drynke. I dranke a groate there the last night.

ROGE: But bouse there a bord, and thou shalt haue beneship.

But drinke there a shyllinge, and thou shalt haue very good.

Tower ye yander is the kene, dup the gygger, and maund that is bene shyp.

Se you, yonder is the house, open the doore, and aske for the best.

MAN: This bouse is as benshyp as rome bouse.

This drinke is as good as wyne.

Now I tower that bene bouse makes nase nabes.

Now I see that good drinke makes a dronken heade.

Mande of this morte what bene pecke is in her ken.

Ask of this wyfe what good meate she hath in her house.

ROGE: She hath a Cacling chete, a grunting chete, ruff Pecke, cassan, and popplarr of yarum.

She hath a hen, a pyg, baken, chese, and mylke porrage.

MAN: That is beneshyp to our watche.

That is very good for vs.

Now we haue well bousd, let vs strike some chete.

Nowe we haue well dronke, let vs steale some thinge.

Yonder dwelleth a quyere cuffen, it were beneship to myll him.

Yonder dwelleth a hoggeshe and chroylyshe man, it were very well donne to robbe him.

ROGE: Now bynge we a waste to hygh pad, the ruffmanes is by.
Naye, let vs go hence to the hygh waye, the wodes is at hand.

MAN: So may we happen on the Harmanes, and cly the Iarke, or to the quyerken and skower quyaer cramprings, and so to tryning on a chates.
So we may chaunce to set in the stockes, eyther be whypped, eyther had to prison house, and there be shackled with boltes and fetters, and then to hange on the gallowes.

ROGE: Gerry gan, the ruffian clye thee.
A torde in thy mouth, the dewyll take thee.

MAN: What, stowe your bene, cofe, and cut benat whydds, and byng we to rome vyle, to nyp a bong; so shall we haue lowre for the bousing ken, and when we byng back to the deuseauyel, we wylll fylche some duddes of the Ruffemans, or myll the ken for a lagge of dudes.
What, holde your peace, good fellowe, and speake better wordes, and go we to London, to cut a purse; then shal we haue money for the ale house, and when wee come backe agaiyne into the country, wee wyll steale some lynnen clothes of one [off'n, that is, off of?] hedges, or robbe some house of a bucke of clothes.

How much speech of this sort got to the New World is hard to say, but some did. For example, *bene* is not generally recorded as a general term for good, but Maitland knew it in this sense, along with *Upright Man,* and attributed them both to Gypsy origins.[12] Worcester and Webster[13] both knew *doxy,* which they recognized as British cant for "a beggar's trull," but they seem to have been unaware of the American usage, probably from homely origins, which Maitland said was "applied to little girls as a term of endearment." Similarly, *bouse,* which never attained a degree of respectability in England, has enjoyed considerable popularity on this side of the Atlantic as *booze,* of which the spelling and the modern pronunciation suggest that the medieval pronunciation was brought to this country, while surviving in Britain only dialectally. Likewise, *dud,* rag, or *duds,* clothes, never attained anything like respectability in Britain, but Robert Burns in eighteenth-century Scotland did not hesitate to use it; in *Tam O'Shanter,* Tam is understandably amazed to observe a witches' dance in which

> . . . ilka carlin swat and reekit,
> And coost her duddies to the wark
> And linket at it in her sark!

[12] James Maitland, *The American Slang Dictionary* (Chicago, 1891). An adequate dictionary of American slang is yet to be prepared, but Harold Wentworth and Stuart Berg Flexner's *Dictionary of American Slang* (New York: T. Y. Crowell, 1960) represents a great step forward.

[13] Joseph E. Worcester, *A Dictionary of the English Language* (Boston: Hickling, Swan, and Brewer, 1860). Webster has been cited earlier.

(Every old crone threw off her clothes to the work and went at it in her undershirt.) The word must have been current in the colonies in the eighteenth century; Hugh Henry Brackenridge was of Scotch extraction, but he had been graduated from Princeton and had lived in this country most of his life when he wrote in a novel published in 1792, "There might not have been time to have washed his duds."[14] Webster thought *dud* came from Scottish, and branded it "a vulgar word," but Worcester gives no indication that he considered the word disreputable, and comments that it is "commonly used in the plural in the sense of rags, or tattered garments." One can scarcely escape the suggestion that some words which had only vulgate or even vulgar standing in England found their way to the colonies and to something like respectability in a new land.

Many a human derelict, many a convicted felon became an honorable and respected man in the New World; many an indentured servant became the mother of a respectable family. Similarly, many a cant, vulgar, or provincial locution in the Old World acquired respectability in the New, passed current in dignified speech, even in fashionable boudoirs, and became the progenitor of a whole new family of words in the Land of Linguistic Promise.

---

[14] Cited under *dud* in *A Dictionary of American English on Historical Principles,* ed. Sir William A. Craigie and James R. Hulbert (Chicago: University of Chicago Press, 1938–44). The novel, *Modern Chivalry, or the Adventures of Captain Farrago and Teague O'Regan* (Philadelphia, 1846), has been reprinted under various titles.

8

LINGUISTIC CUSTOMS INSPECTION

All immigrants are smugglers, albeit innocently. However pitifully meager the belongings they have salvaged from the wreck of previous lives, they bring with them possessions that no inspector can identify and no quarantine can stop—language. Even the babes are beginning to develop language habits, and, concerning dialects, we should now ask ourselves what linguistic luggage poured ashore when ships docked in the New World.

For speakers of the moribund colonial languages, speech that was to vanish or to survive only in linguistic pockets, the answer is easy because we need not inquire with much particularity. We have already seen that the dialects in moribund languages had only minor impact as dialects, and we can usually find out that a German is a German and a Swede a Swede. We may not be sure how many Swedes came and just when, but even this information we can estimate. This we need to do, since a foreign language is an irritant, a stimulant, a catalyst, an unsettling agent, and even though we may not be sure how it unsettles, we can be fairly sure that the more numerous the irritants, the greater the irritation.

Linguistic change, whether one calls it growth or corruption, can go so far that the surviving language becomes what we call *creolized*. Something of this sort must have happened, for example, in the making of Modern French. Both French and Italian come from Vulgar Latin, but Italian has grown with relatively normal development in the Italian peninsula, with only moderate mingling of other tongues, for the past two millennia or so. Vulgar Latin in what was called Gaul, however, was first in conflict with Celtic and then with Germanic speech—the Franks were Germans. Presumably in part as a result of this conflict, French is now so different from Latin that only a close student of language can trace many of the relationships in vocabulary, grammar, and pronunciation.

Rather similar creolizing has taken place on American continents, notably at the expense of French, and to a lesser degree of Spanish, Portuguese, and English. The breakdown has gone so far that Jew-Tongo, spoken in Guiana, seems to have derived from both English and Portuguese, and scholars debate as to whether Papimentu, spoken and even written on the island of Curaçao, stems more from Portuguese or Spanish. There are other instances: Haitian Creole, Negro French in Louisiana, and French Cajun (but not the French of New Orleans), Caribbean Creole based on French and spoken on Dominica and other islands, Taki-taki, a Negro English in Surinam, Jamaican English, Gullah based on American English along the coasts of Georgia and the Carolinas, along with pidgins, including the Chinook jargon of the Northwest.

This whole problem of the mingling and creolizing of languages has been notably neglected, probably in part because the speakers of such languages are mostly socially underprivileged, and many writers have been interested in what was called the purity of language, not in its life. Language mingling has been thought of as miscegenation, and the offspring have suffered the ostracism not unknown to halfbreeds and bastards in other areas than language. Now, however, we have careful studies of the whole problem, and of certain creolized languages, especially of Haitian.[1]

At this writing, French remains the official language of Haiti, but it may not continue so with the decline of the French empire and the rise of color and of native speech. The bulk of the inhabitants, more than three million, speak a language which was formerly described as "an amalgam of French, English, African, Spanish, and Indian dialects," but more recent studies, particularly those of Robert A. Hall, make clear—I am quoting Hall—that:

The basic features of Haitian grammatical structure are those which are common to both French and West African languages, with some which are

---

[1] For a survey of problems and for a bibliography see Einar Haugen, "Bilingualism in the Americas: A Bibliography and Research Guide," *Publications of the American Dialect Society,* 26 (1956), which relies heavily on Uriel Weinreich, *Languages in Contact: Findings and Problems,* Linguistic Circle of New York, 1 (1953). Haitian has attracted a number of scholars, including Robert A. Hall, Jr.; see his *Haitian Creole: Grammar, Texts, Vocabulary,* Memoirs of the American Folklore Society, 43 (1953). On Jamaican, see Frederic G. Cassidy, *Jamaica Talk: Three Hundred Years of the English Language in Jamaica* (London: Macmillan; New York: St. Martin's, 1961); Beryl Loftman Bailey, *Jamaican Creole Syntax: A Transformational Approach* (New York: Cambridge University Press, 1968).

peculiar to French and some peculiar to West African speech. . . . What took place in the reshaping of French linguistic structure in the formation of Creole was simply a process of loan-translation, whereby French elements were joined together in accordance with the semantic patterns of African morphology.

The results are words like *lavil-la* for "the town." The basis is, of course, French *la ville,* but since the Africans who learned the word did not recognize *la* as the article, they followed the African pattern and they added *la* at the end. The French *après* (presumably here an adverb meaning *after, next*) was cut down to *ape-* and became an indication that something was to happen, and *causer* (*to induce*) was spelled *koze.* When these were put together with the remains of a pronoun you have *l-ape-koze,* which seems to mean something like "I have the impression this will be done." That is, French verbs have been combined with non-verbal elements to create new verb forms which reflect aspect, the manner in which a speaker views an action.

No comparable creolizing has taken place elsewhere in the Americas, if in *comparable* we include both the number of speakers and the extent of linguistic change. The millions of Africans and the dwindling number of Amerindians within the borders of the United States have had their impact, but most of this amalgamation has been too scattered to have more than minor effects on language, by processes we have yet to discuss, and Gullah, which probably cannot be considered more than a striking dialect, involves relatively few speakers. Canadian French, on the other hand, does affect large numbers of people, some four million in Canada, by current estimates, and perhaps a million more that have emigrated to the United States, notably to the factory towns of New England. The French speech thus imported to the States, although it has set up bilingual communities which inevitably have their impact, can scarcely survive, but French in Canada has been anything but creolized, and in the face of some handicaps it has shown astounding vigor.

We should note, first, that we have here the reverse of creolizing. French was the established language when English moved in, and within certain areas has remained so, although many of its speakers are bilingual. Not an official language, although it is the medium of much official material, including street signs, it is an established language, resisting another established language, and endeavoring to keep itself pure. Few embattled minorities defend themselves with more devotion— not to say at times ferocity—or rely more upon language in their devotion. The French tongue, the French culture, and the French Catholic faith constitute a trinity that has maintained to a remarkable degree a body essentially alien to British Canada. I am told that, even as I write this, English street signs in Quebec are being torn down, and a tourist reports that she was unable to order a meal in English. "This is a French restaurant," the waitress said, enunciating with careful precision, "I do not speak English." A Scotch Presbyterian friend of mine reports that as a boy in Quebec he was beaten by gangs of children, partly because he was not Catholic, but even more because he spoke English.

In language, pride and the womb may be mightier than the sword; so has it been with the Canadian French and their speech. Considering the circumstances, they have mingled with the English and the Amerindians remarkably little; some 10,000 emigrating French men and women have become 5,000,000 French Canadians, multiplying 500 times in 350 years. Thus the supposedly French portion of the population has remained relatively stable in relation to the whole—and this in spite of extensive immigration of non-French speakers and extensive emigration of French speakers—roughly thirty percent of the total for generations. Meanwhile, speakers of French have remained cohesive, vocal, and self-conscious about their language. The nineteenth-century brochure by J. P. Tardivel, *L'Anglicisme; voilà l'ennemi* (Anglicization: There's the Enemy), has supplied a slogan for more than the Société du Parler Français au Canada: many a French speaker agrees with Victor Barbeau that "Considerée du point de vue purement linguistique, cette corruption est à fois curieuse et amusante. Considerée du point de vue social, elle est tragique." (Considered from a purely linguistic point of view, this corruption [of French by English] seems at times engaging and amusing. Considered from the social point of view, it is tragic.)[2]

The preservation of linguistic purity is deemed an essential force in preserving Gallic culture, and French is thus more durable as a language than the number of its speakers would suggest. It is less subject to Anglicization than it might be were its speakers dispersed in English-speaking areas, but it is not strategically located. The maritime and St. Lawrence provinces are not the liveliest centers of population growth, and Quebec itself has slipped from first to ninth place in a land not notable for its cities.

French speakers in Canada are not of one sort, there being two main dialects, the maritime or Acadian, and the dialect of the St. Lawrence valley, the former smaller and markedly aberrant from standard French, the latter larger and differing from European French less than do the maritime dialects. Individual French speakers, also, are more or less French. Many, particularly in the older rural areas, speak only local French. Many—probably rather more—are bilingual. Others, particularly those of French extraction who have moved out of the old French

<hr>

[2] Haugen, cited earlier, p. 22. For a general survey, see William Wood, "The French Canadians," *Immigrant Backgrounds*, ed. Henry Pratt Fairchild (New York: J. Wiley and Sons; London: Chapman & Hall, 1927).

core-land, retain some French, but in an English-speaking area they lose it rapidly.

Thus, linguistically, Canada presents us with an anomaly, anything but a pattern that can be accepted for the American continents. Speakers of Canadian French did not become a base from which the language moved into the interior by dialects. Neither is it clearly moribund, like Dutch in New York or Mexican Spanish in the Southwest. It has survived, vigorously, and may continue to survive, but it is occluded. It has not gone anywhere, and seems to have nowhere to go. The Canadian English dialects—about which we know too little—developed from bases that were established relatively late and farther west, and these were, in part, the northern prong of developments in the United States to the south.

South of the Canadian border, British dialects are obviously important. At first glance, finding out about these dialects would seem to be relatively easy and the results reliable. Britain is rather notable for the distinctness of its dialects; these continue until today, and dialectology has been pursued in Britain with sufficient success so that, as any reader of George Bernard Shaw's *Pygmalion* will have surmised, we have rough descriptions of all British speech. Furthermore, the history of these dialects can be reconstructed with some confidence. We know where persons like William Penn came from, and in what social strata they lived. We can make a good guess as to how they talked.

Now a difficulty arises. The dialect of Philadelphia will not have been much influenced by William Penn. He was neither permanent enough nor numerous enough. Similarly the dialect of Boston was not much influenced by William Bradford, who lived out his life in the Massachusetts Bay colony, and as governor for more than twenty years had great social and political influence; but he was only one speaker, and as such, his impact would not have been great. He did not have even the impact of an author; his *History of Plymouth Plantation,* for which he is mainly remembered, was not discovered and published until 1856. Even Anne Bradstreet, supposedly our first poet, author of *The Tenth Muse Lately Sprung Up in America,* did not have much impact; she was alone, whereas Richard Devon was many. His name appears in the following complete quotation of a document:

I, John Williams of Boston, Butcher, doe binde myself, to Tho. Brattle, Treasurer of Said Towne, in Some of forty pounds, that Richard Deven shall not be chargeable to the Towne, 29th Sept. 1679.

His
John   x   Williams
Marke

That is, Richard Deven was an indentured servant; we know his name, and we know that his name was legion, but we do not know whence he came or in what dialect he talked with his illiterate master.[3] We can learn that on July 10, 1726, one Benjamin Colman delivered *A Sermon Preached to Some Miserable Pirates* (Boston, 1726), but in what British dialect the reverend exhorted or in what dialects the pirates endeavored to understand him, is harder to know. The underprivileged usually remained, in early times, the unidentified.

Popular conceptions of American colonial history have grossly under-estimated the numbers and importance of the indigents, debtors, indentured servants, even the criminals—human flotsam generally—who found their way to colonial America. Understandably, we have fostered the comforting aspects of our ancestry; we have preferred to venerate the Roger Williamses, to dwell upon those who came to new shores seeking social justice, political and religious liberty, and to ignore the plethora of Manhattan pothouse keepers. This human preference gained natural support, for the literate tended to be the leaders, and the literate could perpetuate their own memories by writing. They did so, often unintentionally. Meanwhile the illiterate have tended to become also the inconspicuous, and even those who could and did write a little usually ignored what we should like to know. An immigrant may record where he took ship, in which foul holds he suffered what privations, what goods he brought with him—how much cash and other worldy effects— where he landed, and what happened to him there. He usually does not tell us what dialect his mother spoke nor with what children he learned what speech. Of his linguistic gear he is unaware, and he leaves us little information with which to guess.

Thus, only for the very few do we have the information with which to reconstruct their backgrounds. Of the many we are ignorant, and for a considerable number we are deliberately made ignorant. A woman of easy virtue, apprehended and shipped to the colonies, is not likely to reveal her origin. A confirmed pickpocket may conceal both his name and his nativity. A man slugged and shanghaied in Liverpool and shipped to be sold as an indentured servant may or may not have lived in Liverpool; in fact, the chances are he did not. The pickpocket apprehended in London may or may not have talked Cockney, and the London debtor need not have been a London native.

---

[3] See Jernegan, *Laboring and Dependent Classes in Colonial America, 1607–1783*, cited earlier, p. 193; see also Stanley C. Johnson, *A History of Emigration from the United Kingdom to North America, 1763–1912* (London: S. Routledge & Sons, 1913).

Knowing who was who in the colonies is relatively easy, but discovering who was not who, what he was, and whence—that can be baffling. Even the numbers of these people are difficult to determine, although they must have been considerable. On the whole, immigrants are people in trouble; if they were not in trouble, they would presumably not have migrated. The trouble may not be to their discredit, and the troubles tend more toward bank trouble than girl trouble, but trouble can be assumed in a large percentage of cases. Emigration to the American colonies was perhaps to a remarkable extent idealistic—"idealistic" subsumes religious ideals, although this definition does some of our ancestors too much honor—but the presence of idealism and love of adventure among the emigrational motives can scarcely alter the basic fact that most emigrants are fleeing something; and that those bound for the American colonies were selected at the source as are emigrants everywhere. Most of them had debts or delinquencies; they melted quietly away from their old homes, and grew inconspicuously in the new lands.

If there was such a thing as a typical American immigrant, he was probably lower middle class, having trouble making a living. The most abject did not usually come, except as they might be deported; they lacked either the ambition or the means to move. They became public charges or corpses buried at the public expense; of these latter there were tens of thousands—during the Irish potato famine, for example. Of course, the indigent might fall foul of the law, indigence leading them to crime or debtor's prison, from whence they might be shipped abroad to save public expense, but we may probably assume that most of the emigrants were ordinary, law-abiding people, not destitute but in trouble.

Their numbers are not easy to estimate,[4] but one finds bits of evidence. Poverty in Scotland and Ireland in the late eighteenth century and in the early nineteenth century led to emigration from those areas—earlier emigration had been English, but by 1800 the new English factories were absorbing the famished farm laborers, and no doubt semi-starvation in Huddersfield, old England, seemed preferable to massacre in Deerfield, New England. But Scotland and Ireland knew no such relief. Estimates in the *Gentleman's Magazine,* 1774, suggest that in the five years prior to the American Revolution some 43,720 emigrants left five Irish ports. Emigration from Scotland was presumably even more lively. Edinburgh newspapers mention groups of fifty to a hundred, banded together and headed for any port that would harbor a ship to

---

[4] Some material is brought together in Jernegan. I shall rely heavily upon it, and upon Wertenbaker, *The Founding of American Civilization,* cited earlier.

take them to America, with the explanation: "The cause of this emigration they assign to be want of the means of livelihood." As famines increased, so did the flood of migrants. During the Irish famine of 1840, which must have been abnormally severe, perhaps a quarter of Ireland's eight million died in one year; in subsequent years the annual emigration rose to more than a hundred thousand.

If the bulk of the emigrants to America were voluntary fugitives, many were involuntary, for servants, particularly indentured servants, early became welcome. In 1619, John Porey (or Pory), secretary of the colony of Virginia, wrote as follows:

All our riches for the present doe consiste in Tobacco, wherein one man . . . by the meanes of six servants hath cleared at one crop a thousand pound English . . . our principal wealth consisteth in servants.[5]

In the South, slaves tended to replace these white servants, but not entirely, since the servants multiplied, even out of wedlock. Apparently male indentured servants were encouraged by their masters to have relations with slaves, because any child born to a woman in servitude usually became the property of the master. In the North the prevalence of freed indentured women servants accounts in part for the large number of "orphans," who were so numerous as to occasion special "Orphans' Courts." Lists of these derelicts described them in such terms as "Child apprenticed, born of a single free white woman." Most of these orphans must have passed unnoticed, but they came to the attention of the court if the foster parent did not support them or "neglected his or her education, or instruction in the principles of Christianity."[6] Although the number of indentured servants must remain uncertain, observers agreed that at any one time the percentage of such servants was remarkably large in comparison with the total population—and of course, many in the population who were not in servitude were children of parents who had been.

Not all indentured servants were ignorant, of course, even though they tended not to come from the wealthier sort. An observer complaining of the lack of education in the colonies wrote as follows:

What is still less credible is that at least two thirds of the little education we receive are derived from instructors, who are either indented servants or transported felons. Not a ship arrives with redemptioners or convicts, in which schoolmasters are not as regularly advertised for sale, as weavers,

---

[5] Jernegan reprints the passage, pp. 225–26.
[6] Jernegan has reviewed this material, *passim;* for a revealing table, see p. 156.

tailors, or any other trade; with little other difference, that I can hear of, excepting perhaps that the former do not usually fetch so good a price as the latter.[7]

Not all debtors became servants. Some were imported by benefactors and maintained in part at the public charge. Among these were Palatinate debtors, of whom several shiploads arrived in New York alone after the bad winter of 1708, including eight hundred families who were receiving charity, one to eight to the family, several thousand in all, and in this hospitality New York was not alone.

Inevitably, the transported felons occasioned the liveliest angers, and hence the most numerous editorial references. The *American Weekly Mercury* (Pennsylvania) of February 14, 1721, commenting upon the influx of transported criminals, regretted that

. . . these plantations cannot be ordered to be better populated than by such absolute villains and loose women, as these proved to be by their wretched lives and criminal actions, and if they settle anywhere in these parts can only by a natural consequence leave bad seeds amongst us.

No more hospitable was the *Virginia Gazette* of May 24, 1751:

When we see our papers filled continually with accounts of the most audacious Robberies, the most cruel Murders, and infinite other Villainies perpetuated [sic] by convicts transported from Europe, what melancholy and what terrible Reflections must it occasion. . . . These are some of thy Favours Britain. Thou art called Mother Country; but what good Mother ever sent thieves and villains to accompany her children; to corrupt with their infectious vices and to murder the rest.

These outbursts savor of the familiar editorial propensity to "view with alarm" but no such leaning could have prompted one Narcissus Luttrell to record in his diary for November 17, 1692, that a ship at Leith, Scotland, had aboard her fifty lewd women out of houses of correction and thirty more "that walked the streets at night." The *London Magazine* sometimes listed transported people; for May, 1747, it supplied 887 names. Plausible estimates suggest that during the years 1717–75, some 10,000 felons were shipped to the American colonies from the Old Bailey alone, and if the Old Bailey was the most populous British jail, it was one of many. The total number of felons shipped to what is now the United States must have been at least twice that, a not inconsiderable proportion in a land whose population might have aver-

---

[7] J. Boucher, *A View of the Causes and Consequences of the American Revolution* (London, 1797), pp. 183–84; cited Jernegan, p. 225, n. 41.

aged something like two million during that period. Something of this sort may have been in the mind of Dr. Samuel Johnson when he re- marked of the colonials, "Sir, they are a race of convicts, and ought to be content with anything we allow them short of hanging."[8]

The practice of dumping convicts on the American colonies stirred Benjamin Franklin to repeated protests, and Franklin was an eminently sensible gentleman whom no one can accuse of wild-eyed radicalism. Writing to a friend in 1753 he declared that "shipmasters were taking felons from German jails for the sake of profits," and of the British, he wrote in the London *Chronicle* in 1769: "Their emptying their jails into our settlements, is an insult and a contempt, the cruelest that ever one people offered another." When this practice was defended to him on the ground that in order to maintain order, the British authorities had to get rid of the convicts they could not execute, he countered by asking if the Americans would be justified in sending unwanted rattlesnakes to England.

Thus the nature, if not the details, of the evidence is clear. We usually cannot say that John Smith and his family, a farm laborer from the vicinity of Tunbridge Wells, speaking a rural Sussex dialect, established himself on a farm near Hartford, Connecticut, and that John Doe, con- victed pickpocket, speaking London Cockney, was deported to New York and disappeared into the underworld of that place, where he pre- sumably remained, since his new habitat was convenient for his old profession. We can say, however, that on the whole the language im- ported to the new world would have been the language of the poorer classes, if not many of the poorest, including at least a smattering of convicts. It would not have included any considerable proportion of the speakers of the growing dialect founded on court speech, the ancestor of modern British Received Standard. An immigrant from London, for example, was more likely to speak Cockney, even the thieves' jargon we have already noticed, than he was to speak the growing social dialect based upon polite conversation at the Court of St. James.

Early immigration tended to be British, and to establish British dialects as the basis of American speech. Among the earlier immigrants, both north and south, were a preponderant number from the south and southeast of England and from the London area—however and when- ever they or their ancestors got to the London area. The speech of these groups was supplemented by Scottish; by 1775 Highlanders are said to have numbered twenty thousand in North Carolina alone, and as Pro-

---

[8] I owe most of these references to Jernegan, cited earlier; see especially pp. 48–49; 224–25.

fessor Wertenbaker has pointed out, "In the period from 1680 to 1765, the so-called Golden Age of Virginia history, the three most prominent figures in this English colony were Scots—the Reverend James Blair, Governor Alexander Spotswood, and Governor Robert Dinwiddie."[9] With the industrial revolution in England, British immigration declined, giving way to Scottish and eventually to Irish migration, but in their various ways all these groups brought relatively archaic speech, that of the middle and lower classes in England and of the more peripheral areas where Celtic languages had given way to English. The earlier colonies, both north and south, seem to have been pioneered by settlers from southern and southeastern England. Later, other English areas, along with Scotland, Ireland, and Wales, provided floods of immigrants, but by this time the middle American colonies were popular. The Dutch, Swedes, and other non-British impediments had been removed, and the colonies of the Baltimores and the Penns offered special inducements, in climate, in land, and in official hospitality.

Can we not be more accurate? A few decades back the answer would have been *no,* but since about 1930 a technique for the study of language in relation to populations has begun to produce evidence. Developed in Europe in the preceding century and now commonly called *linguistic geography* or *dialect geography,* it is being pursued in many parts of the United States, a circumstance which encourages us to direct our study to North America, since linguistic geography has been only sparsely pursued in most Spanish-speaking and Portuguese-speaking countries. Fortunately, for the most significant North American areas, the results are mostly in and published. This is one reason that the study of language is so exciting right now; new techniques and new concepts are producing new insights. This particular insight warrants a chapter by itself.

---

[9] Thomas Jefferson Wertenbaker, *Early Scotch Contributions to the United States* (Glasgow: Jackson, Son, and Co., 1945), p. 15.

9

LINGUISTIC GEOGRAPHY: MICROSCOPE FOR LANGUAGE SLEUTHS

Once when I was addressing a body of English teachers, and the question of the precise determination of usage arose, I said that we had a new technique for this, and pretended that I could not remember a common word.

"You know," I said, "what do you call it? You put a plank on a saw-horse or something, with a youngster on either end, and they bounce up and down."

Almost everbody said, "Seesaw," or "Teeter-totter." Reminding myself that this could not have happened on the east coast, I ignored the teeter-totter speakers.

"Oh, yes, *seesaw!* And what was the other one?"

I got a chorus of *teeter-totters*.

"Isn't there any other?"

There was a silence for a time. Then a man raised his hand and said, "We used to call it a *tippity-bounce.*"

"If you recall *tippity-bounce,*" I said, "you may have forgotten *tilt, tilting board,* and *dandle.*"

Immediately he became excited. "That's right," he said. "Some of the kids called them that, but we never did, and I had forgotten."

"And you or your parents," I said, "come from southern Rhode Island, or had some connection with Block Island."

"Yes, Providence," he replied. "And we went to Block Island summers. Had an aunt there."

How could I do this? Mainly because I was lucky—lucky in that my informant happened to know a word having very restricted currency, and lucky also in that I happened to be able to remember what I had read about it. But if I had known enough of the findings of linguistic

143

geography in this country, I need not have been lucky. If he had said *cock horse* or *cocky-horse,* I should have been able to tell him that he came from eastern North Carolina, in the lower Pamlico River area, or from southern Delaware or Maryland. If he had said *tinter,* I should have known that the chances favored the Connecticut Valley, but that he might have come from somewhere to the west, down along the coast or even up into southern Vermont. Even if he had said *teetering board,* I should have known that the chances were strong for New England, but that he might have come from upstate New York or areas to the west.

Anyone who will read the literature can do something similar with other words.[1] We might look at a form that describes coasting face downward. Naturally, it appears only where snow is plentiful, but from Chesapeake Bay north it occurs in bewildering variety. Virginia knows mainly *belly-buster,* with an occasional *belly-gut, belly-gutter, belly-wop* or *belly-wopper(s)* as we get up into Maryland, where the latter terms are especially popular. Pennsylvania runs heavily to *belly-bump* and *belly-bumper(s),* along with a few *belly-womper(s),* and the relatively rare *belly-grinder* to the southwest. In New York State, *belly-wop* and its relatives are common, along with *belly-gut* and *belly-gutter,* and especially in the Mohawk Valley, *belly-whacker.* In the Hudson Valley and down into New Jersey, *belly-flop* and *belly-flopper* are common. The largest body of *belly-wop* speakers is outside Maryland and centered on New York City. In New England *belly-bump* is commonest, with *belly-bunt* a common variant, along with *belly-gut* in western Connecticut and Massachusetts, plus some occurrences of *belly-flop.* There is even an occasional *belly-whacker,* and the exotic *belly-flouncer,* which presumably occurs only on Nantucket Island.

In the South, euphemisms for *bull* are interesting. As Professor Hans Kurath puts it:

The plain term bull is current everywhere, and in the North Midland and New York State other expressions are rare. In New England, the South and the South Midland, however, the plain term is not used by older folk of one sex in the presence of the other. Even many of the younger generation prefer the veiled expressions of the Victorian era.[2]

Beginning in the Carolinas, *beast, male beast,* and *stock beast* are common in the tidewater, with occasional occurrences of *steer* and *male cow.* Toward the mountains *ox, brute, male brute,* and *stock brute*

---

[1] I am relying mainly upon Hans Kurath, *A Word Geography of the Eastern United States,* Studies in American English, 1 (Ann Arbor: University of Michigan Press, 1949).

[2] Kurath, p. 62.

appear. These continue into Virginia, where *steer, ox,* and *male cow* become common. Lower West Virginia contributes the relatively rare *masculine* (rhymes with *pine*), which, curiously enough, occurs also in Nantucket, south of Cape Cod. West Virginia also has *sire,* which occurs sporadically in Pennsylvania and throughout much of New England. Vermont and New Hampshire indulge in the Latinate *toro,* along with the graphic *top cow. Critter* occurs sporadically.

This sort of thing can be fun, but linguistic geography is more serious than the juggling of curiosa. It attempts to describe and plot dialects, and to trace the movement of peoples by tracing the movement of their locutions. With it we can study with something approaching scientific objectivity the state of the language at any time or place; we can speak with confidence about usage, and can determine, if we wish, who says *he don't* and *you-all,* and in what circumstances.

For such purposes the most picturesque results may not be the most revealing. Something must lie behind the occurrence of *belly-flouncer* on the island of Nantucket, and there only; one would link this dialect with *masculine* as a noun occurring on Nantucket and also in far-off West Virginia. We should probably assume that Nantucket folk tended to go to sea more than to the west, but that somebody from Nantucket took *masculine* with him to West Virginia. If so, this is worth knowing, but linguistic geography aims at broader generalizations, and for these purposes the most varied and picturesque words are not always the most useful.

To understand this, we should see how a linguistic geographer works. First he must know what sort of information he wants, since surveys can be made for special purposes, but as yet specializing is mostly for the future; basic surveys for the country have not as yet been completed. Let us assume, then, that no survey has been made for an area in question, and that a survey is intended to reveal major dialect areas, major linguistic movements, and principal trends in vocabulary, pronunciation, and usage. Next the director of the survey prepares his questionnaire. This is a key part of the operation, for once the survey is started it cannot be fundamentally changed, and an inadequate sampling will inevitably produce inadequate results, however knowingly the data are interpreted.

The most successful surveys in this country have made use of some eight hundred subjects for questions, some calculated to elicit such material as I have already used, to discover whether the informant uses *belly-bunt, belly-womper, belly-slam,* or whatever, and how many such words he knows. Other questions are intended to reveal pronunciation; does the informant pronounce the medial consonant in *greasy* with the sound of *s* or of *z,* the medial consonants of *without* like the initial consonant in *thin, thine, tine,* or *dine?* Some questions will involve grammar and usage; does he say *he don't* or *he doesn't, all the boys* or *all of the boys?* Naturally, such a list of questions must be prepared on the basis of careful study of the language area, and then it must be tested in the field before it becomes the basis of actual field work, which will consume hundreds of thousands of man-hours. How much weight should be given to children's counting-out games and the words in them? Farmers call animals in various ways, but do these ways fall into sharp patterns, and are they durable enough to be revealing? What about the balance between geographical and social dialect levels?

Once a suitable list of locutions is determined, field work can be planned, and here alternatives must be considered. The conventional means are interviews and questionnaires. Questionnaires are the cheaper. Several thousand can be printed or mimeographed at modest cost, and local people can always be found to distribute them. They are also inflexible and even of uncertain value. Will the questionnaires come into the appropriate hands? Will all informants use the questionnaire in the same way? Even ages may be falsified; and informants may get other people to help them. Linguistic geographers have tended to distrust questionnaires, but some use can be made of them if they are handled carefully. Gordon R. Wood, in a study I shall cite later, apparently obtained good results for the interior South, but he was admittedly making only a preliminary survey against the time when the job could be done properly, and even so he felt he had to throw out two thousand of the three thousand sets of answers returned. Some investigators have retested with questionnaires when the original survey raised questions but did not answer them. Many careful students, however, feel there is no substitute for the interview.

Interviewing is costly. In the first place, the interviewers must be trained people grounded in phonemics and phonetics, sensitive to differences in sound. They must be students of language, so that they know what they are doing. Granted that a field staff has been recruited and trained, more time elapses sifting prospective informants. Not everyone is more than sixty, has not been graduated from high school, has lived all his life in one community, is intelligent enough to be a good informant, and is willing to sacrifice two hours a day for a week or so and without pay. Even after an informant has been located and talked into cooperating, he may at any moment become temperamental, ill, timid, or tired, especially since many of the potentially best informants are advanced in years. Since each interviewee consumes so much precious time, informants must be chosen with care, for geographical spread, social status, age, sex, race, religion, and anything else that may produce significant variables. All this becomes so complicated that anything like an ideal set of informants is not even to be dreamed of, but at a minimum, geographical spread is supplemented with spread in age and in cultural or educational background.

Once the field data are taken, the job is only well under way. The evidence must be assembled, assorted, and interpreted. The older method was to transcribe everything onto maps—eight hundred items, eight hundred maps. These maps can eventually be published; in this country the first atlas of this sort may be the last. *The Linguistic Atlas of New England,*[3] a beautiful set, bound in six volumes and containing 734 maps, was printed with a subsidy at sixty dollars. It has come into such demand that never again is any copy likely to sell for as little as two hundred dollars. Faced with the mounting costs of printing, many linguistic geographers are turning to the printing of variants in lists; this method is cheaper, if not so graphic or so satisfying to get one's hands on, but the cost of printing on plates the "atlas" for the whole country would run into more millions than most scholars see in their future. Many dialect atlases may be published only on magnetic tapes.

However the information is assembled and ordered, it must be put on maps for working purposes. For example, let us assume that we have decided to study the occurrence of *worm fence.* Since we have no record of this word very far south or very far north, it is apparently a Midland expression, occurring with high frequency and almost exclusively in New Jersey, Pennsylvania, Delaware, Maryland, and West Virginia. Scatterings of evidence occur in Virginia west of Chesapeake Bay, in western Connecticut and Massachusetts, and again in southern Virginia and North Carolina. These occurrences suggest random accidents or evidences of minor dialect areas. Our main job is to plot the northern and southern limits of *worm fence* as the dominant term, or at least as a very common term. Consequently, we determine the most northerly evidence of the term that seems to be within the area of common occurrence, and we trace this line west, connecting all these northernmost occurrences. The resulting line is what is called an *isogloss.*

To see how this works out, compare Map 2 with Map 3. Map 2 gives the actual occurrence of *worm fence* as opposed to *snake fence* and *zigzag fence*—*rail fence* is assumed to be common—and Map 3 gives you the *worm fence* isogloss, here shown as a dotted line. Map 3 shows, also, how isoglosses from various locutions can be superimposed so that we can determine roughly the boundaries between the main dialect areas.

---

[3] Hans Kurath and others (Providence, R.I.: Brown University, 1939–43).

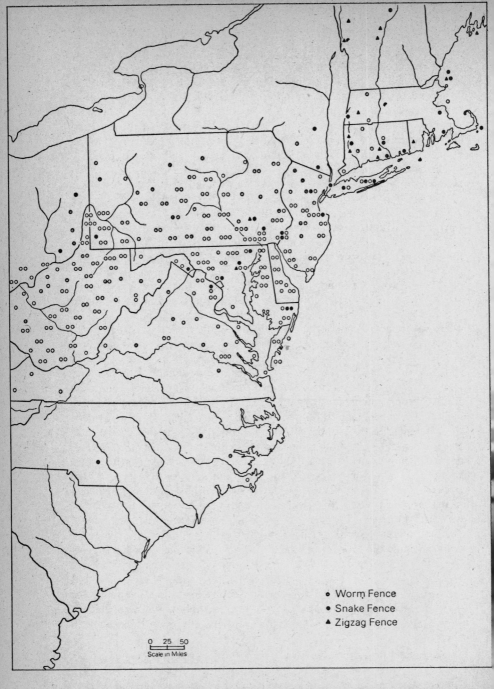

Map 2. The Occurrence of Variants for *Rail Fence*. (From Hans Kurath, A Word Geography of the Eastern United States [*Ann Arbor: University of Michigan Press, 1949*], fig. 64, copyright 1949 by the University of Michigan, used by permission.)

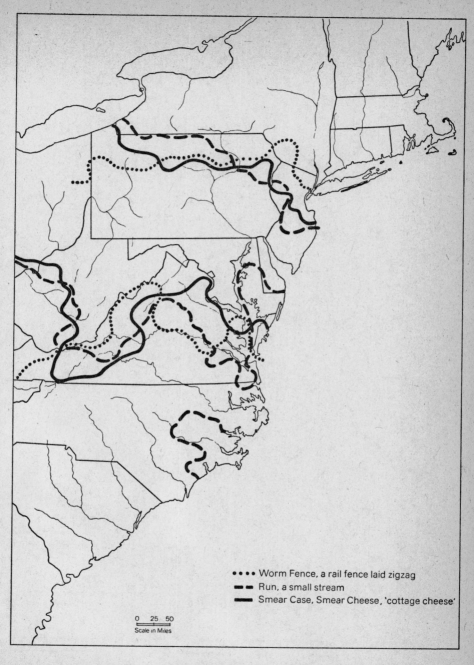

Map 3. Some Isoglosses of the North Midland. *(From Kurath, op. cit., fig. 18, copyright 1949 by the University of Michigan, used by permission.)*

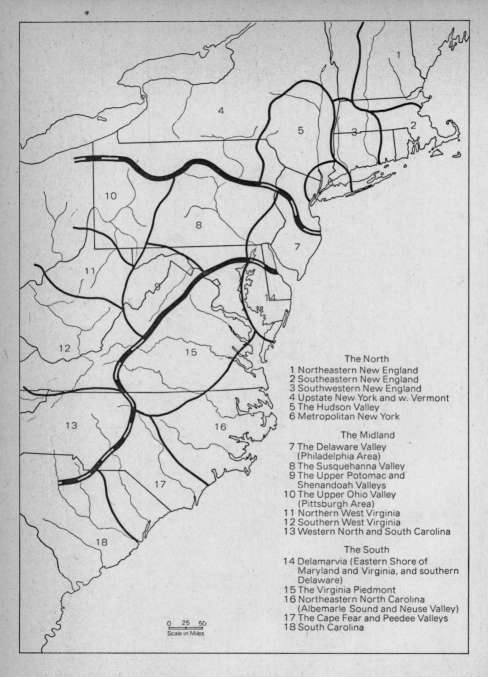

The North
1 Northeastern New England
2 Southeastern New England
3 Southwestern New England
4 Upstate New York and w. Vermont
5 The Hudson Valley
6 Metropolitan New York

The Midland
7 The Delaware Valley
  (Philadelphia Area)
8 The Susquehanna Valley
9 The Upper Potomac and
  Shenandoah Valleys
10 The Upper Ohio Valley
  (Pittsburgh Area)
11 Northern West Virginia
12 Southern West Virginia
13 Western North and South Carolina

The South
14 Delamarvia (Eastern Shore of
  Maryland and Virginia, and southern
  Delaware)
15 The Virginia Piedmont
16 Northeastern North Carolina
  (Albemarle Sound and Neuse Valley)
17 The Cape Fear and Peedee Valleys
18 South Carolina

0 25 50
Scale in Miles

Map 4. The Speech Areas of the Eastern States. *(From Kurath, op. cit., fig. 3, copy-right 1949 by the University of Michigan, used by permission.)*

Here the isoglosses for *worm fence,* both north and south, are super-imposed upon those for *run* (as against words like *branch, creek,* and the like) and those for *smear case,* or *smear cheese* (as against *cottage cheese* or *pot cheese*).

Map 3, then, brings together part of the evidence for the main dialectal divisions along the east coast, as follows: Northern, from about the Hudson estuary north to Canada; North Midland, from Delaware to just south of the Hudson estuary; Southern, from Chesapeake Bay south. Such lines would not be reliable with so little evidence as these three sets of isoglosses, of course, but they can be supported with many more. Nor are they sharp; minor dialect areas appear within them, and other minor dialect areas overlap them; the New York area, for ex-ample, has its own dialectal peculiarities that break into both Northern and North Midland, and the Charleston dialect appears within a sub-division of Southern. Map 4 shows Kurath's main divisions and main subdivisions along the Atlantic seaboard and the area immediately to the west.

These results check roughly with what history tells us about popula-tion movements, although the linguistic results are more detailed, more consistent than anything history provides. For example, we might notice what happened to Pennsylvanians. In our earlier survey of settlements, we observed that once the settlements north and west of Delaware Bay were well started, they grew rapidly, encouraged by good land, good climate, and relatively benevolent provisions for immigration and gov-ernment. Movement was westward, so that even before the Revolution-ary War and all through it, population edged west along the Ohio and the old Wilderness Road, but the British were pressing from the north, and augmenting the intermittent Indian troubles. Western migrants tended to swing south, enticed by valleys like the Shenandoah and Ap-palachian, which bear to the southwest. Thus, settlers drawn toward Kentucky and Tennessee joined with migrants from another population center in western North Carolina, which spilled through outlets like Moccasin Gap in southwestern Virginia. All this is more precise in the dialect maps than in the scattered historical records.

Thus in a broad way, American dialects are coming into focus. Three bodies of speech that build up in the eastern coastal states were well established by the time the way for westward movement had been opened with the termination of the War of 1812, the resulting decline of danger from Indians, the elimination of French political activity, and the restriction of British activity to the area north of the Great Lakes. These bodies of speech stemmed from the British dialects that had arrived during the seventeenth and eighteenth centuries, mainly dialects of un-tutored Britons whose speech represented English patterns current by the time of the first Queen Elizabeth or before. They were composite in origin; although we may have yet to raise the question in any detail as to whence in England these early speakers came, we may assume that no British dialect would have been transported undiluted and re-established in the colonies, but that emigrants would have tended to group themselves geographically and to continue their groupings as they became immigrants. Thus the seventeenth-century and eighteenth-century immigrants were extremely important—perhaps, in the light of subsequent developments, among the most important people linguistically in all time.

We might examine this guess, and to do so, we must anticipate a bit. We shall later observe that English is developing as a world language, at least as a world second language, a language which all people of any cultural pretensions will learn in addition to their native language, whether that is Swahili, Italian, or whatever. But English is not one thing. Which English will this world language be? If this world development of English had taken place in the first half of the twentieth century, the favored dialect would have been British Received Standard. It did not take place then, and if it takes place in the second half of the twentieth century, the controlling dialect will be central North American. Thus the people who, by settling in the British American coastal colonies, determined in a broad way the basic American speech patterns, set the direction for what is not only the largest single body of spoken and written English; they may have set, also, the direction of the first world language, for although Latin has been called a world language, it was the language only of the world inhabited by Europeans, and only the western half of that.

To understand this varying linguistic potential, let us imagine twin sisters, whom we may as well call Britannia and Columbia, living in Southampton, in southern England. Britannia marries John Bull, eldest son of a small crofter who has just lost his bit of land in the squeezes by which the great British landlords were swallowing the little ones. Britannia has a small dowry; they use this money to start a shop, which they promote by good management and long hours. Britannia helps run the shop and rears five children who become solid citizens. She considerably influences the speech of these citizens and their families, and has some impact upon patrons of the shop, people she meets at church, and her immediate neighbors. If we were to devise a measuring concept which we might call a linguistic index, a numerical scale to evaluate the degree of impact a person has upon the future of language, with average impact called one, we might give Britannia something like two or three, as against her husband, who might get one or two, and a bachelor farm laborer, who would be below average at a quarter or a half.

Meanwhile, Columbia has married John's younger brother, Samuel, less practical than his brother, more visionary, a smooth talker, rather engaging, but not very stable. He tries to become a barrister, but he has neither the friends nor the money, perhaps not even the intelligence for it. He takes to drink, dabbles in various business ventures, fritters away Columbia's bit of dowry, even goes to debtor's prison. He is generally a disgrace to John, who hopes to become a wealthy merchant. Columbia has been occupied with pregnancy and subsequent nursing, but she raises a little money, partly through the death of an aunt, partly through John, who would willingly see his scapegrace brother well out of the country—beyond further embroilments with the law, liquor, and appeals for cash. Columbia and her family sail for the American colonies.

Samuel's imagination is fired by the prospects of the New World, and he can read. He hears of a new community to the west, takes his little family there, and finds that he has become a great man. He sets himself up as a lawyer, even becomes justice of the peace when the town grows into the county seat, and is soon a power in state politics. He has laid out what was left of Aunt Hester's bequest in wild land, which soon becomes valuable. People call him "squire"; had he gone south it would have been "colonel." Meanwhile, Columbia has borne more children, who become various important people in the community, carrying Columbia's dialect with them. She educates her own children, starts a school and a Sunday school, and when her husband grows too important for her to continue as a schoolmarm, she becomes the local social leader, a walking linguistic model. As the community grows from fifty, to a hundred and fifty, to two thousand, to fifty thousand, the newcomers are always fewer than the old settlers, and they always tend to adopt the pattern of the established citizens. The "Johnnie-come-lately" is always out of fashion, and in Columbiatown, Columbia's dialect is always in fashion.

Thus as the community grows, it tends to continue the speech that was set up by the first settlers, speech determined more by Columbia than by any other one person. What would her linguistic index be? Obviously much higher than her sister's back in Southampton, perhaps twenty, fifty, or five hundred. Even if we could estimate her impact upon American speech, we should still have to guess whether to double or quadruple or further augment it as American English spreads abroad. Suppose, for example, that her great-great-great-grandson, Sammy, still speaking with the flavor of Columbia's dialect, sets up the whole English-teaching program for a new African nation, trains its teachers, and writes its textbooks. In some ways, young Sammy and his sister are now doing in Africa and Latin America, at least as far as the spread of English is concerned, what Samuel and Columbia did in North America two centuries ago. In language the itinerant becomes either more or less potent than the stay-at-home, depending upon circumstances of which he is mainly unaware, and to which he would be indifferent.

To put all this in another way, imagine you had been standing on the wharf of a colonial American port, and had been attracted to an unusually woebegone indentured servant put up for sale. Shanghaied out of a London pub, he was now dirty, destitute, half-starved, emaciated from weeks of fever in the stinking hold of a ship fit only for its most numerous inhabitants, rats and other vermin. Imagine, further, that you had been endowed with a foresight no man could then be expected to have, and accordingly you say to this involuntary immigrant, "Tough luck, Old Man, but you can solace yourself with the thought that you are influencing the future of mankind. By getting yourself shanghaied you have helped determine the course of the eventual world language." "What, Sir?" he might ask, assuming plausibly that you were one of those creatures out of his fevered dreams, or at best one of the completely crazy colonials he has heard of. You try to make him see: "The fact is, my good man," you continue, "by coming here you will inevitably influence the English which will be learned, in a couple of centuries, in—say, Quito or Tanzania." All this would have sounded like insanity; actually, it would have been prophecy.

Let us now return to our major east-coast dialects. They were to have vast impact upon the future of American English and indirectly upon other English as well. They were hybrids, since they represented at once some mingling of British dialects and some maintaining of Old World dialect distinctions, but once they were established they tended, as they moved west, to flow as entities, preserving most of their characteristics, while blending somewhat as they mingled with other dialects.

For example, the inland and gulf southeastern states were settled by two main movements, representing different Southern dialects—the speech of the two southern groups we have noticed earlier, the city and plantation dwellers along the estuaries and the fat lands of the coast, and the less privileged folk in the hill and mountain country above the Fall Line. The coastal people from the Carolinas and Georgia angled with *fish bait, earthworms,* or *fishworms,* displayed knickknacks on *mantels* or *mantel boards,* and put produce in *gunny sacks* or *guano sacks.* The people from the back country were likely to fish with *red worms* or *fishworms,* to keep knickknacks on a *fireboard,* to put produce in *tow sacks* or *croker sacks,* and to call a paper bag a *poke.* These two bodies of speakers sent migrants west, but at different times and by different routes.

The back country people moved first, spilling over the mountains into

Kentucky and Tennessee, fanned out north to the Indian barrier, that is, into the lower portion of the states north of the Ohio River, and south to the Gulf of Mexico, although only sparsely into Alabama and Mississippi, skirted the older French and Spanish settlements in Louisiana, followed up the Arkansas River into Arkansas and on into Colorado in time for the silver rush, and then turned south again to Texas after the war with Mexico. They can be traced along these sinuous wanderings because wherever they went they left behind them speakers who fished with red worms, had fireboards, and used tow sacks, croker sacks, and pokes.

The people in the lowlands were later to start moving. With burgeoning plantations, booming cities, and thriving ports they saw no reason to leave. Besides, any swing along the Gulf was blocked by the Choctaw and the Cherokee. Eventually, however, the flat lands filled up; the Indians were moved out; and the plantation culture surged west, overran the back country people who filtered into Alabama and Mississippi, and swept on into Texas, fishing with earthworms, fishworms, or fish bait as they went, putting their produce in guano sacks and gunny sacks, and building houses having mantels and mantel boards. About that time the War Between the States overtook them, and their dialect never got much past the Rocky Mountains.

Thus modern Texas is a criss-cross of dialects. Eastern, southern, and central Texas abound with terms from the plantation area of the Old South in the Carolinas and Georgia, and from this stream as it had developed in Alabama and Mississippi. To the north are the "red-worm" speakers from the back country, with pokes and croker sacks. Coming up from the southwest is a sort of backlash associated with Mexicans and the cattle industry. Now, of course, new centers are growing with cities like Houston and Dallas, but even so, once dialects are established they tend to preserve themselves, so that the linguistic map of Texas reflects much more of the old coastal division between the "red-worm" speakers and the "fishworm" speakers than the intervening thousand miles might lead one to expect.[4]

Not all routes by which American English has moved west have as yet been traced, but the main lines of movement are fairly well established.

---

[4] For the Louisiana and Texas material I am relying on E. Bagby Atwood, *The Regional Vocabulary of Texas* (Austin: University of Texas Press, 1963). It is essentially a word geography; the late Professor Atwood had expected to continue it with studies of the sounds and the grammar. For Louisiana some further material is available in Mima Babington and E. Bagby Atwood, "Lexical Usage in Southern Louisiana," *Publications of the American Dialect Society*, 36 (Nov., 1961), 1–24.

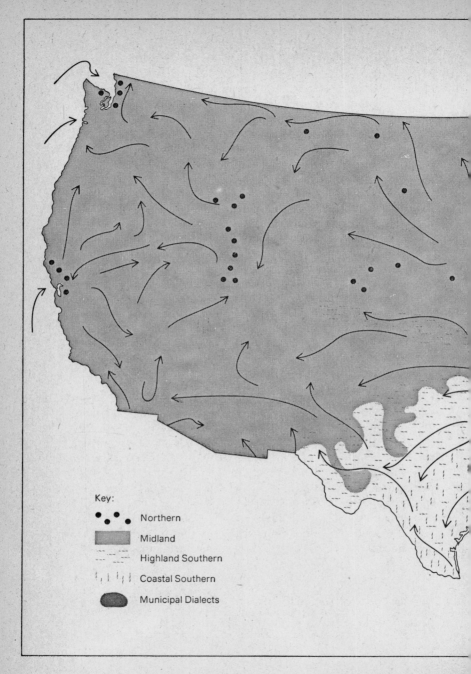

Map 5. The Westward Sweep

Key:
- Northern
- Midland
- Highland Southern
- Coastal Southern
- Municipal Dialects

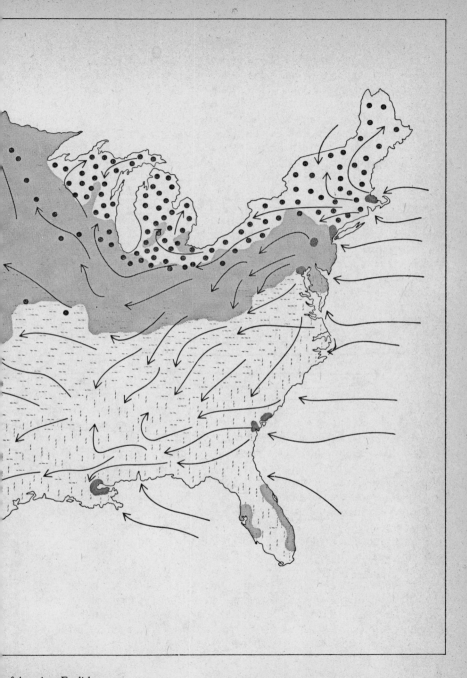

The westward movement of American English is suggested by Map 5. Linguistically, we are all Hansels and Gretels, leaving bits behind as we move, bits that can be interpreted once we have the key. Thus words like the synonyms for *angle worm* (*fishworm, fishing worm, fish bait, eel worm, red worm, ground worm, rain worm, eace worm,* and *angle dog*), which help to mark off dialects on the east coast, take different configurations as they move west, but the patterns remain generally distinguishable. Similarly, to the north, the dialects of the Midland and the North moved from the Atlantic coast. Only preliminary reports are as yet available for this area, but apparently a line can be drawn roughly west from Pittsburgh, cutting across Ohio, Indiana, and Illinois, veering somewhat northwesterly. North of this line are influences from New England and New York, along with the Midland; south of it the Midland is purer, except as Highland Southern works north.

Of course, dialects develop as they go, and their patterns tend to become confused. Whereas the main dialect lines in the United States, following the westward immigration, tend to run east and west, some north and south lines develop, also. One such line cuts down through the Dakotas, where the farming terms from Iowa and Minnesota encountered the backlash of mountain terms from Montana and Wyoming. Similarly, in Colorado, the basic dialects were set up by two early gold rushes, one from the southeast along the Arkansas River, bringing Southernisms, and one from the northeast along the South Platte River, bringing locutions from North Midland, which had become the dominant dialect in the upper Middle West. In all this welter, rare localisms of the east coast tended to dwindle; neither *tippity-bounce* nor *dandle* survived the gold rush to Colorado, but new words were developed for new concepts, many of them working back from the southwest. A mountain meadow became a *park,* and Colorado adopted the general Great Basin word for the man who drifts from mining boom to mining boom. Fittingly he is called a *boomer.*

The far western movements followed two main lines, one south of the Rocky Mountains, along routes like the Santa Fe Trail, one up the Platte and Missouri rivers. This second movement forked, some immigrants following the Oregon Trail through what is now Idaho, down the Snake and Columbia rivers, to Oregon and Washington, the other branching southwest, past Great Salt Lake, down the Humboldt River, and thence to California by such gaps as Donner Pass. On the west coast some immigrants, notably from the Northern speech areas, arrived in ports like San Francisco, and their dialects radiated from there, eventually seeping back across the Sierra Nevada into the Great Basin. A dialect associated with the Latter-Day Saints has fanned out from the valley of Great Salt Lake.

Thus dialect geography is providing an increasingly clear picture of how American speech developed.[5] We know with some certainty and in some detail what happened on the east coast. Much material has been collected for the remainder of the country, and enough of it is published so that major outlines and some details can be made out. Unfortunately, the Canadian portion of the linguistic atlas has not thriven, and consequently we know less of what has happened north of the Canadian-American border.

Something can be inferred, particularly since we now have an excellent dictionary of Canadianisms,[6] which reveals a wealth of terms not previously accessible: *Boston name* (any non-Amerindian word), *Calgary redeye* (tomato juice and beer), *French pony* (a small, stout horse used in the Quebec area), *gritty* (characteristic of the now-obsolete Grit Party), *homer* (not a home run, but a person who supports the home team), *honey bucket* (an outside toilet), *longline skinner* (driver capable of handling several teams of horses or mules), *seat-of-the-pants flier* (a bush pilot), *tuckamore* (low-growing intertwined evergreens; somewhat similar to American English chaparral). Clearly, the vocabulary is rich in terms related to the Indians and to subarctic living, but a dictionary cannot replace linguistic geography for dialect study. Meanwhile, we can infer that dialects or subdialects will appear for the Maritime Provinces, for what used to be called Lower and Upper Canada —the Quebec and Ontario areas respectively—for Vancouver and the west coast, for the central prairies, and probably for the tundra north, but the picture will remain fuzzy until we have systematic sampling.

We are now ready to return to an earlier question: What can dialect geography tell us of the language brought to this country, and where it landed?

---

[5] The material I have been citing is mainly available as yet only in articles and brief monographs, published in periodicals and series, notably in *PADS (Publications of the American Dialect Society)*. Some of it is well surveyed in two recent works, Joseph H. Friend, *An Introduction to English Linguistics* (Cleveland: The World Publishing Company, 1967), and Carroll E. Reed, *Dialects of American English* (Cleveland: The World Publishing Company, 1967). Both contain maps, especially the latter, which includes previously unpublished research.

[6] Walter S. Avis et al., eds., *A Dictionary of Canadianisms* (Toronto: W. J. Gage, Ltd., 1967). This volume was missed in an earlier edition of *Language in America,* which was in press at the time.

10

INTERNATIONAL LINGUISTICS: WHY WE TALK LIKE AMERICANS

Britons, at times not averse to twitting their transatlantic cousins for being intellectually and culturally backward, do not base jibes on linguistic geography. The technique was not developed by English-speaking peoples, and was already well promoted in the United States before British scholars did much about it. Accordingly, although we have relatively satisfactory descriptions of the dialects that developed along the eastern coast of North America, we have most unsatisfactory records of the motherland from which this speech was brought. Linguistic geography is now actively pursued in England, but the records for only the northern counties are as yet coming into print, and these happen not to be the counties in which we are most interested. We shall have to make what we can of available material.

Immediately, we are in difficulties. Locutions most used to study population movements within the United States cannot be traced across the Atlantic. Their trails stop at the shore, and the reason for this would seem to be, as Lear's fool would have said, "a pretty reason." In marking off American dialects and their westward courses, a rather curious assemblage of words has been the most revealing. When you serenade a bride and groom with tin pans, do you call it a *shivaree* or a *calithumpian band*? Do you cook in a *skillet, spider,* or *creeper*? Do you keep cows in a *cuppin, cow pound, cow break, milk lot, milking break,* or a *pightle*? With what euphemisms do you designate bulls? Do you identify a dragonfly as a *snake feeder, snake doctor, darning needle, devil's darning needle, mosquito hawk, spindle, snake servant, snake garder, snake heeder,* or *snake waiter*? Is a bastard a *Sunday Baby,* a *ketchcold,* or a *come-by-chance*? With what combinations of *sookie, sooie, vootie, coo-chickie, cootie, whookie,* and *co-boss* do you call barnyard creatures?

We notice at once a characteristic common to these words—they have a strong native flavor. The charivari (or however you like to pronounce and spell it), was probably an American institution; similarly, although Britons eat plenty of fish, for good reasons these are mostly fish from the sea, whereas in early days the river fish was a staple in American diet and the angleworm accordingly a key item in domestic economy. Bulls and bastards must have abounded in England, but at least the bulls were more characteristic of colonial farms than of London streets; and in all likelihood the prudery that prompted our handsome terms intended to promote modesty of expression, and to obscure a reference to bovine virility, was characteristic of a colonial culture. Dragonflies are common throughout the eastern half of the United States, much rarer in England. As for terms like *belly-bump* and *belly-whomp,* snow deep enough for coasting is rare or unknown in the more populous parts of Britain. Similarly, calling farm birds and animals was highly characteristic of the American side of the water, mainly rural, generally well stocked with domestic beasts and fowls, profligate in wild acres where stock roamed at will. Calling wandering beasts was not characteristic of a tight little island which was well stone-walled and hedged, even when it was still extensively rural.

That is, the most revealing words for American linguistic geography have been words which grew from the character of native American life—and let me add here that although I have selected picturesque examples, I have not deliberately distorted the evidence. Do you call a paper bag a *poke* or a *toot?* There were no paper bags in the eighteenth century. What is your name for a corn husk? There were no corn husks because, practically speaking, there was no maize in eighteenth-century Britain. That is, my examples are, I believe, fair examples. The question, then, is this: Why do American uses of words reveal American dialects better than do the old British words which the colonists imported? The answer must be a guess, but a plausible guess, and in the light of other evidence to appear later I do not see how it can be wrong. Some native words delineate local dialects and local population movements because their most revealing uses had local origins and thus local distribution. Words already well established in England do not make good words for dialect study on this side of the water because the immigrants had become so mingled in the simple process of getting here that their native dialects became confounded and blunted in the process.

If this guess is reliable, it has implications. It means that although we may expect that most of the phenomena of early American speech will be familiar British phenomena transplanted to the New World, these phenomena will not be so sharply isolated that we can ever say that the dialect of Roanoke, Virginia, or Portland, Maine, is a clear offshoot from the dialect of Devonshire or Sussex. The guess suggests that although many British dialects were brought to this country—perhaps most British dialects or even all British dialects—none of them is likely to have been preserved here in its purity. We must expect to find a paisley of British speech in America, not a checkerboard of it.

That is, dialects of the American eastern seaboard may be linguistic mavericks, especially in vocabulary. They seem to break most of the rules. Usually, in language as in society, a local phenomenon is more likely to reflect a local borrowing than to reflect a local growth. As we have seen, this was true of the westward movement of American dialects. Thus the most revealing words for linguistic study have been those that moved in patterns. But apparently in crossing the ocean, patterns were obscured, so that the most revealing words are those of native origin or distinctive native growth. Of course these locutions may not be so native as they seem; they may appear as native only because we know so little of linguistic geography in England, but at this date, words seem not to help us much in tracing language across the Atlantic.

That is, characteristically local American uses reflect American dialectal practices, and being local they were native. At this point we have to guess when we assume that few uses except native locutions were local, because most British words were confounded in the multiplicity of the origins and destinations of immigrants. We may know more in the future; no one can say that tomorrow a new technique, or a new use of an old technique, may not reveal new truth. We may some day have dialect studies in Britain that will reveal which words had local and only local currency in the England of the eighteenth century. We can then restudy the speech of the American eastern seaboard—if it has not changed too much by that date—and learn where these locutions became current in the United States. But as of this writing, that knowledge is at least two jumps away; the British have not completed their dialect studies, and we cannot study the colonial areas to test such words until we can identify the words.

At this writing, the transference of sound provides us the most revealing evidence. I am relying mainly on the excellent study done by Hans Kurath and Raven I. McDavid, Jr.; they have put together the findings of American dialect geography, preliminary dialect studies in England, and historical observations available in old dictionaries.[1] I have been

---

[1] *The Pronunciation of English in the Atlantic States* (Ann Arbor: University of Michigan Press, 1961). The authors survey American pronunciation and make British comparisons where they are available; for England they had the preliminary studies of the late Guy S. Lowman, Jr., who had worked in the

able to supplement their findings with some field study in key areas and for key locutions. Following is a digest of the evidence; I have omitted sounds for which no interesting material from Britain is available, and since we are here concerned with the growth of dialects on the eastern coast of the United States, I have ignored for the present the westward spread of seaboard speech. Even so, the evidence inevitably becomes detailed; anyone who prefers to take the details on faith will find a summary at the end.[2]

VARIANTS OF SO-CALLED SHORT i, THAT IS, /I/.

rinse   The eighteenth-century British lexicographer Walker wrote, "This word is often corruptly pronounced as if written *rense . . .* but this impropriety is daily losing ground." It is losing ground in this country, too, although both pronunciations were imported; in England it can still be heard in the south.

VARIANTS OF SO-CALLED SHORT e, /ɛ/

again   The pronunciation that rhymes with *pen* has become standard American; it is characteristic of much folk speech in central England. The pronunciation which rhymes with *pin,*

American dialect survey. The survey for England is appearing as follows: *Survey of English Dialects,* ed. Harold Orton and Eugene Dieth (Leeds, England: University of Leeds, 1962 . . .). Some ten volumes are projected. For a more detailed study of American phonology, but with little on British, see Hans Kurath, *A Phonology and Prosody of Modern English* (Ann Arbor: University of Michigan Press, 1964). For British, Joseph Wright's *The English Dialect Dictionary,* 6 vols. (London: H. Frowde; New York: G. P. Putnam's Sons, 1898–1905), and his *The English Dialect Grammar* (Oxford and New York: H. Frowde, 1905) are still useful, as is Thomas Sheridan's *A Complete Dictionary of the English Language,* 2d ed. (London: Charles Dilly, in the Poultry, 1789). On British English dialects G. L. Brook, *English Dialects* (London: Andre Deutsch, 1963) is excellent within its purposes, but it lacks the detail necessary for the present study.

[2] Several lexicographers are referred to on later pages without further identification. John A. Walker edited the first dictionary of English giving extensive attention to pronunciation, *A Critical Pronouncing Dictionary,* of which the expanded second edition (1797) is the most useful. Noah Webster's *American Dictionary of the English Language* (1828), cited earlier, is likewise more useful in its second edition, by Chauncey A. Goodrich (Springfield, Mass.: George and Charles Merriam, 1848). Joseph E. Worcester, *A Dictionary of the English Language* (1860), cited earlier, stems from Webster but is independent in its judgments. In the descriptions above, I have placed some symbols within slant lines. That is, I am here making use of what is called *phonemics.* I have tried to write the passages so that they will be understandable without these symbols, and anyone who has trouble will find an approximation of them in the International Phonetic Alphabet, which appears in the introduction of most good dictionaries. The curious will find some discussion of phonemics in Chapter 21.

widely current in folk speech in the United States, is common in eastern England. The pronunciation which rhymes with *pain*, though now common in British Received Standard, was late and but sporadically imported.

deaf   Chaucer apparently pronounced this word to rhyme with *leaf*, but for half a millennium the pronunciation has been more associated with northern than with southern England, a fact which probably accounts for its being restricted to folk speech in the United States. The rare pronunciations that rhyme with *skiff* and *safe* occur on both sides of the Atlantic.

egg   The standard pronunciation in both British and American English rhymes with *leg*, but American folk speech has a form that rhymes with *Haig* and a number of diphthongs approaching this sound /ɛᴵ, ɛə, eᴵ/. These seem to have their ancestors in similar southeastern British diphthongs from Kent and Surrey and north to Norfolk.

keg   Standard pronunciation on both sides of the Atlantic rhymes with *leg*, but a widespread folk pronunciation rhymes with *hag*. This is apparently the British pronunciation recorded from the fifteenth century, in Sheridan as *kag*, and later in the spelling *cag*, which is recommended in the 1848 Webster and included in Worcester.

kettle   The evidence is not very sharp, but a pronunciation suggested by the spelling *kittle* is common in British folk speech, especially in the south, and in American folk speech, especially in northern New England and North Carolina.

yellow   The Middle Atlantic and Northern states have a pronunciation suggestive of the spelling, but in the South scholars have found "an almost bewildering variety of other pronunciations." The most common of these variants are a pronunciation suggested by the spelling *yalluh* /jælə/ and one suggested by *yulluh* /jʌlə/. Sheridan enters the word as *yallow*. The main difference is thus one that goes back to Anglo-Saxon times, more than a thousand years, when a sound about like the vowel in *bet* was common, but showed some variation with a sound like that in *bat* to the west and *bot*, later *but*, in the southeast. Thus the American standard form reflects the common Old English form, the American folk forms the British dialectic forms. Even the rare American pronunciation suggested by a spelling *yilluh* also has rare occurrence in the southeast of Britain. I have heard it in Surrey.

yesterday   Besides the standard pronunciation, one suggested by the spelling *yisterday* is current in folk speech, mainly in New England and parts of the South. This pronunciation was recorded but disapproved by Walker in England in the eighteenth century, and it is still current in folk speech in southeast England, from East Anglia, north of the Thames, through the southern counties as far west as Gloucestershire.

VARIANTS OF SO-CALLED SHORT *a*, THAT IS, /æ/

aunt

The common American pronunciation does not distinguish *aunt* and *ant;* this pronunciation of *aunt* seems to have been the common one in England during the eighteenth century and is still heard both north and south of the mouth of the Thames from Norfolk to Essex and Kent; it seems to be standard in many communities. Sounds further back in the mouth, more commonly associated with words like *car* and *garden* /a, ɑ, ʁ/,[3] are later British developments which have been introduced, partly for purposes of prestige, in parts of New England and the South. Kurath and McDavid add, "It is also significant that Eastern New England, which demonstrably derives other dialect features from East Anglia and the London area, is the area in which this split into /æ/ and /a/ has become most fully established."[4]

can't

We have here to deal with three sorts of pronunciation, those which rhyme with *pant* and *paint,* and the various sounds associated with words like *car* and *garden*. All three sounds occur on both sides of the Atlantic. The first, with the sound of *pant,* is most common in America; it seems to have been characteristic eighteenth-century British pronunciation, and is still common in the southeast. The pronunciation that rhymes with *paint* is common in folk speech in the southern American states and in the southern British counties, usually with a diphthongal glide. The mid and back vowels associated with *car* and *garden* are now standard in British speech and in folk speech in most areas, especially in the North Midland. They occur in America in odd patterns, in much of New England, in scattered areas as a prestige pronunciation, and in coastal South Carolina and Georgia as an evidence of uncultured speech.

pasture

Something similar seems to have happened here, with the front sound of the vowel of *pant* now extremely rare in England, preserved only patchily in the southeast, but standard in most American speech—the word itself in the American sense is now rare in British speech. The sound associated with *car* and *garden*, standard in British English, occurs commonly in Virginia and some other parts of the South and scatteringly in New England.

rather

We have here to do with five pronunciations, which rhyme with *gather, father, feather, brother,* and *bather.* The first

---

[3] The limitation of type fonts makes accurate transcription difficult. I am using /ʁ/ for a sound somewhat higher and farther forward than /ɔ/.

[4] Kurath and McDavid, p. 136.

four have all been imported from England, but, significantly, not the last. As in many other words, the first of these vowels was common in England in the eighteenth century and has become the usual American pronunciation. The later British pronunciation rhyming with *father* was introduced as a cultivated pronunciation, especially in the cities. Pronunciations rhyming with *feather* and *brother*, characteristic respectively of East Anglia and of the Midlands in England, occur scatteringly in this country, again notably in the South and the North. The sound rhyming with *bather*, common in Britain from Lincolnshire north, seems not to have survived on the west side of the Atlantic. Kurath and McDavid observe: "This confirms the general impression that distinctive features of the dialects of the northern counties of England, of Scotland, and of Northern Ireland rarely survive in American English."

stamp   Here the standard American and British Received Standard pronunciation rhymes with *lamp,* a pronunciation which we assume to be old since it is preserved as folk pronunciation in most of the southeastern counties except Middlesex, counties which agree repeatedly with American standard speech. Both speech areas have sounds which appear in the various pronunciations of *lawn* and *calm,* but the distribution on both sides of the water is too patchy to be very revealing. Obviously, however, all these pronunciations were imported. One rare American pronunciation, which rhymes with *lump,* if it had a British origin, has now apparently disappeared there.

catch   Rhymes with *match, fetch,* or *pitch* occur on both sides of the Atlantic, with the latter pronunciation rare. The *match* pronunciation is now standard in both areas, but dialect surveys show the *fetch* pronunciation usual east of the Appalachians both north and south; exceptions center in Pennsylvania and the New York City area. In England this pronunciation persists in folk speech in the southeastern counties, and W. Nelson Francis reports that it is common also to the northwest, in an area "corresponding precisely to the West Midland area or Middle English."[5] Walker tells us that in his day it was pronounced "like the noun *ketch,*" which he called "a deviation from the true sound." The standard British pronunciation apparently comes from the western counties, perhaps supported by northern speech.

radish   Walker said this word in his day was "commonly, but corruptly, pronounced as if written *reddish,*" and this pronun-

---

[5] See "Some Dialect Verb Forms in England," *Orbis,* tome 10, no. 1 (1961), p. 8. For further details on the American distribution, see Raven I. McDavid, Jr., "Notes on the Pronunciation of 'Catch,'" *College English,* XIV (1952–53), 290–91.

ciation seems still to be common north of the Thames. It is common in American South and South Midland. Pronunciations with the sound of *had* occur south of the Thames in England, and in the United States in North and North Midland Speech.

VARIANTS OF SO-CALLED BROAD *a*, /ɑ/

calm A considerable variety of pronunciations from those rhyming with *ham* to those using the vowel of *dawn* are found on both sides of the Atlantic, although a pronunciation rhyming with *Tom* is standard. The *ham* sound characteristic of folk speech in the American South and scatteringly in New England, survives in Britain only patchily except in the extreme southeast, although Sheridan recorded the word as *kam*. The folk speech of some of the American Midlands, rhyming with *gaum*, suggests Northern Scotch, and Irish speech on the British side of the water.

hearth Pronunciations vary on both sides of the water, rhyming with sounds like those in *forth*, *Garth*, *earth*, and *path*. The *forth*-pronunciation, standard for British English, did not become so until the eighteenth century, and the American Standard, more frequently like *Garth* than *forth*, is common in England only in the folk speech of the Midlands, but can be heard in the south.

VARIANTS OF THE CENTRAL VOWEL /ʌ/, OFTEN CALLED SHORT *u*

nothing Two main pronunciations have the vowels of *hot* or *hut*, the latter being standard in both England and the United States. The *hot*-pronunciation is common in rural speech in New England and in southeast England; it is the regular development of Middle English shortened *o*, whereas the standard forms are aberrant.

VARIANTS OF SO-CALLED SHORT DOUBLE *o* OR SHORT *u*, /ʊ/

butcher The pronunciation with the sound of *foot* is common on both sides of the water, a pronunciation with the sound of *boot* survives in the coastal areas of both countries. A southern British rural pronunciation with the vowel of *hut* has not survived in America.

VARIANTS OF SO-CALLED LONG *e*, /i/

bleat Standard on both sides of the water is the vowel of *heat*, but this seems to be uncommon in American folk speech on the east coast, where the vowel of *bait* occurs in the South and sounds associated with *bat* and *car* occur most commonly in the North. All these pronunciations are known in England, and the *car* type is associated with south central England.

either
neither

American folk pronunciations suggested by the spellings *ither, ether,* and *uther* apparently stem from British folk pronunciations rhyming with *heather.* Pronunciations with the vowels of *eel* and *aisle* have long been common in English speech, but the *aisle* form, which seems not to have survived on the American side of the Atlantic, became popular in Britain in the nineteenth century, and was imported as a prestige form. As a result, both pronunciations are now common in the United States, evincing both geographical and social distributions.

VARIANTS OF SO-CALLED LONG *a,* /e/

drain

The word rhymes with either *rain* or *bean,* both of which are still current in the eastern British counties and in the folk speech of both the northern and southern sections of the American Atlantic seaboard. Spellings indicate that both pronunciations were in cultivated use when the colonies were settled. The pronunciation rhyming with *rain* is characteristic of rustic speech in the United States only in the Midlands, from Pennsylvania into southern New England.

VARIANTS OF SO-CALLED LONG DOUBLE *o* OR LONG *u,* /u/

broom

Pronunciations with the vowels of *two* and *pull* must have existed in folk and even cultured speech in England for centuries, although the pronunciation with the vowel of *two* is now standard. The two forms have become standard in the United States, and the patterns in folk speech are varied, but the *two*-vowel predominates in the Midlands, the *pull*-form to the north and south. The vowel in *room* follows similar patterns.

root

Pronunciations rhyming with *boot* and *foot* occur on both sides of the water, with the *foot* sound characteristic only of a few southern counties in England and in northeastern New England outside the metropolitan areas.

food

The relatively rare pronunciation in Pennsylvania and some other areas which rhymes with *good* is presumably from Ulster Scots influence.

ewe

The varied pronunciations of this word can be roughly reflected by the spellings *you, yo, eeoo* /ju, jo, iu/ and the like. They appear scatteringly in both countries, but the pronunciation suggested by *yo* is the most widely spread

English folk pronunciation, and is also the most widely spread in rural America, especially in the South and North.

VARIANTS OF SO-CALLED LONG *o*, /o/

loam

A pronunciation which rhymes with *home* is standard in both British and American speech, but a pronunciation rhyming with *tomb* is common in the midland and southern counties of England and has been imported from thence into a broad area extending from parts of New England south and west to West Virginia. A pronunciation having the checked vowel of *book* /ʊ/ appears in Suffolk, England, and the northernmost portion of New England. The pronunciation rhyming with *tomb* has apparently been borrowed from British standard speech and is said to be much more common among the folk in the United States than in the homeland.

home

Standard pronunciation on both sides of the Atlantic employs the free vowel of *know*, but folk speech in both areas has a wide variety of diphthongs and vowels, some rhyming with the various pronunciations of *room* and *broom*, others suggested by the spelling *hum*, especially in *at home* /təhʌm/, notably in the northern and southern American states.

won't

Kurath and McDavid[6] identify five vowels used in the word in American speech, those of *stone, sun, moon, bull,* and *lawn*. All of these sounds occur scatteringly in the British southern and eastern counties so that they "point to a wider currency of these types at the time when the American colonies were peopled." The vowel of *stonę* in British Standard is more characteristic of Britain's north and west, and of the American Midlands.

yolk

The standard British pronunciation is sufficiently common in the United States to make Adlai Stevenson's pun possible, "Eggheads of the world arise; you have nothing to lose but your yolks." Along with this pronunciation is a bewildering variety in which the *l* is pronounced, of which the most common are suggested by spellings like *yolk* and *yelk*. Most of these pronunciations can be paralleled in Britain, but the spread is varied in both countries. Walker recommended *yelk* and so did Webster. Sheridan recorded both *yelk* and *yolk* as spellings, but pronounced both *yoke*. The pronunciation suggestive of *yoke* was apparently notably northern, and the predominance of this pronunciation, even on a folk basis, in Pennsylvania and adjacent areas can presumably be attributed to the Ulster Scots.

---

[6] Kurath and McDavid, p. 159.

VARIANTS OF THE BACK VOWEL OF *law,* /ɔ/

daughter   British Standard speech has the vowel of *law,* apparently based upon the dialect of London and the counties to the north, and this is the common cultured pronunciation in the United States as well. A pronunciation suggested by the spelling *dotter* in Pennsylvania and adjacent areas may reflect Scotch Ulster influences, and a pronunciation rhyming with *carter,* in its various pronunciations is common both north and south on the Atlantic coast and in the southern and southwestern British counties.

haunted   The most common pronunciation with the vowel of *law* was apparently an innovation in eighteenth-century England; Walker disapproved of it, and in America neither Webster nor Worcester included it. The pronunciation with the vowel of *car,* in its various sounds, is common in New England and the North Midlands; it is widespread in Britain, and presumably came from the southeastern British counties. A pronunciation rhyming with *panted,* common in southern America, is now heard mainly in the southwestern British counties.

sausage   In addition to the common pronunciation with the vowel of *law,* pronunciations suggested by the spelling *sossidge* occur along the eastern seaboard of the United States and in the southern counties of England. A pronunciation with the vowel of *hat* in northeastern New England, which seems to have fallen out in modern Britain, seems indicated in eighteenth-century letters in central England as *sassage* by the spelling.

VARIANTS OF DIPHTHONGS

drought   Pronunciations are current on both sides of the Atlantic rhyming with the following words: *out, bought, mouth, moth,* and *tooth,* but only the latter is interesting from our point of view. A Scotch import, it is current in Pennsylvania. For the variation of the fricative /θ/ and the plosive /t/ see also *without* below.

joint   Vagaries of this diphthong defy brief summary, but the pronunciation suggested by the spelling *jernt* is probably an Americanism and the pronunciation with the vowel of *five* is commonest in England, from East Anglia north, in America in the North and in the South.

VARIANTS OF UNSTRESSED VOWELS

sofa   The final vowel is commonly schwa /ə/ on both sides of the ocean, but a pronunciation rhyming with *trophy* occurs in New England, the Upper South, and some other places, and in England from Lincolnshire east. A pronunciation approximately rhyming with *loafer* occurs in British southern coastal counties, and sporadically in America.

borrow

In addition to the standard pronunciation with an *o* sound in the final syllable, schwa /ə/ is common in the northern American states and in the central eastern counties in England. A pronunciation rhyming with *hurry* is common in the southern American states and in the south coastal counties of England, with remnant pronunciations farther north.

tomato

The final vowel having the sound of *o* in British Received Standard is common in America, but a final schwa /ə/, common at most levels in American speech, is characteristic of British folk speech over a wide area. Pronunciations suggested by the spelling *tomater* are common in the southern American states and the southern English counties.

VARIANTS OF /r/ AND A PRECEDING VOWEL

care

Pronunciations of /r/ and a preceding vowel vary so bewilderingly that they can be no more than suggested here. For *care*, Kurath and McDavid recognize the following (the swung dashes indicate spreads of sound): /keə~ker~kær~ kæə~kɪr~kiə~kjɜ/. They add that local variants have vowels as far back in the mouth as /ɑ/, observing that Standard British English has /kɛə/, with /keə/ more common to the south, but that "the precise historical connections of the American variants is a problem for future investigation." This British pronunciation, often without any *r* sound, is heard extensively in cultured speech in the United States, both North and South, whereas Midland American speech inclines to a vowel like that in *head,* with a retroflex after the vowel. Pronunciations with /ə/ and /ɑ/, along with many of those having /æ/ and the Southern /kjɛ/, seem to be American developments.

poor

Kurath and McDavid record the spread of sound as /pur~ puə~pʊr~pʊə~por~poə/, and in some Southern speech the word can be heard with almost no perceptible glide, /po/. In some of these dialects the same sound serves for *sure,* /šo/, like the common pronunciation of *show,* but not for *pure,* which rhymes with *sure* in many other dialects. As is frequently the case with such words, variants with the retroflex are characteristic of American Midland, whereas Northern and some Southern speech agrees with Standard British English in the extensive use of /puə/, with a diphthong like that of *shoe a* in *to shoe a horse.* The pronunciations with /o/, especially noticeable in Virginia and in parts of Kentucky and Tennessee, are apparently American developments.

Somewhat similar spreads of sound characterize other words in which *r* follows a vowel, such as *flower, barn, for, orange, park, wire, merry,* and the like; see also *rather* and *hearth* above.

CONSONANTS

door

Post-vocalic *r* in words like *door, poor, care,* and *ear* was apparently pronounced as part of a retroflex diphthong /ɔɚ/ in the south and west of England during the period of American settlement; it has become characteristic of the American Midlands. An unsyllabic unstressed vowel without qualities associated with *r* was characteristic of the area north and east of the Thames; it is common in both northern and southern American speech. This apparently became a prestige pronunciation, at least partly on the basis of British Received Standard, and spread from cities like Boston, New York, and Charleston. The loss of *r* or a retroflex vowel in parts of the South, such that *door* rhymes essentially with *go,* /lɔɚ/ seems to have been a American development.

law and order

An intrusive *r* used to link words is not uncommon in New England and in parts of Old England, notably the section north of the Thames known as East Anglia. By this development *law* is pronounced as though spelled *lawr* /lɔɚ/.

swallow it

A "linking" *r* or retroflex vowel /ɚ/, by which *swallow it* is pronounced as though spelled *swaller-it* /swalɚɪt/, is common in many phrases in British folk speech in the eastern and southern counties, and must at one time have been common all along the American Atlantic seaboard, but it is now more characteristic of American folk speech in the North and the South, is rare in the Midlands, and avoided in cultivated speech.

library

Pronunciations suggested by the following three spellings were apparently introduced variously along the American seaboard from the English eastern and southern counties: *library, libary, libry.*

garden
car

From the Potomac to the Savannah rivers, and in some areas to the west, the initial consonant is followed by a glide, in a pronunciation which might be suggested by spelling *giyadin, kiya* /gjadɪn, kja/. The intrusive glide apparently develops from a palatalized stop in eastern and southern British folk speech.

nephew

In the common American pronunciation the middle consonant has the sound of /f/ with scattering survivals of a pronunciation /v/, which is common in Britain, although both pronunciations survive there. The form with /v/ perpetuates the French *neveu,* borrowed probably in the late thirteenth century, whereas the /f/ pronunciation reflects a pseudo-learned correction, embodied in the spelling, from the sixteenth century. The fact is curious, and probably significant, that the pronunciation based upon traditional speech has triumphed in Britain, the supposedly "correct" form based on spelling in the United States.

without This word has both the voiced fricative /ð/ and the voiceless fricative /θ/ on both sides of the Atlantic, the former standard, although less regularly so in the United States than in England where the voiceless form is apparently more common toward the north. The prevalence of this form in Pennsylvania and adjacent areas is probably in part attributable to the Scots and other Northerners. The plosive forms /t/ and /d/ occur in folk speech in both England and the United States; see *drought,* above.

greasy Pronunciations with /s/ and /z/ exist on both sides of the ocean, with lines of demarcation rather distinct in both areas. In England, /z/ predominates in the east counties, /s/ in the central and western counties. This tendency to voice /s/ and some other consonants is continuous from Old English—it will be recalled that Shakespeare makes Edgar voice fricatives when he is trying to talk like a Kentish yokel. In the United States both pronunciations must once have been well mingled, but now the North has /s/, the South /z/, with a belt of mingling which includes a number of metropolitan areas like New York and Philadelphia. New England, which often follows East Anglia, here diverges from it.

vase Pronunciations with the terminal consonant /s/ or /z/ exist on both sides of the Atlantic, the former common in the United States, the latter in Britain. The differences here seem to be chronological rather than geographic. The pronunciation with /s/ is older, reflecting voiceless fricatives of French and Latin; that with /z/ is a British development late enough so that it was not much brought to colonial America. The prestige pronunciation with /z/ was apparently a relatively late importation.

wheelbarrow In this and a number of words having similar initial consonants the /hw/ has been reduced to /w/, scatteringly in the United States, much more extensively in Britain. Here, as elsewhere, the northern and southern states have been more conservative, preserving the older British pronunciation, whereas the midland states tend to the reduced /w/, characteristic of later English pronunciation. This pronunciation has been introduced from Britain also into the coastal cities, but being a late eighteenth-century change in England, it never became firmly established on the American coast and arrived too late to move west much.

mushroom   Dissyllabic and trisyllabic forms, with terminal /n/ or /m/, are so widely scattered on both sides of the Atlantic that one must assume that this variety in pronunciation was common during the American colonial period. The pronunciation with /n/, based on the Old French *musseron,* was for a time the prestige pronunciation but is declining everywhere, probably partly on the basis of the modern spelling that developed on the basis of folk etymology, the basis of the word being *mousse,* moss.

This survey, sketchy though it is, makes some conclusions obvious and permits some guesses. Notable as a conclusion is this: American speech, including American dialects, rests upon British dialects. Presumably American English has developed; language is always changing, and some locutions should have sprouted, west of the Atlantic during the past three centuries, speech sounds independent of developments on the eastern side during the same period, but if so, the evidence is scanty. British pronunciations that have not been recorded in America are few, and these pronunciations are rare in the homeland. American pronunciations with no recorded British counterpart are also few and generally rare. Of course, some of these American oddities may represent Old English pronunciations which have fallen out in England, but even if we assume that every pronunciation unique in the United States and Canada is a vagary of the New World, we still have rather fewer innovations than would have been expected in three centuries of oral use, and we can account for this remarkable stability of early American English only by reminding ourselves that colonies usually tend to be conservative.

Correspondingly, the American pronunciations are overwhelmingly reflected in British pronunciations current over wide areas, and they form observable, if not very sharp, patterns. American colonial speech suggests seventeenth-century and eighteenth-century British speech, notably of southeastern England from somewhat north of the Thames, especially from East Anglia and the London area, down to Kent and as far west as Devonshire, although with somewhat abating influences as one goes west. These characteristics of southeastern folk speech have been generously preserved in New England, upper New York State, and the South. Midland speech from the mouth of the Hudson to Chesapeake Bay (although not usually in Delmarva on the coastal side of the Bay) is often distinct from that of the North and the South, tending to preserve more pronunciations from central and western England, especially when these reflect cultivated middle-class and upper-class speech, and notably when such sounds are reinforced by northern British speech. Immigration from northern England was not heavy enough to transplant many exclusively northern pronunciations, the exceptions involving the Scotch and Scotch-Irish, who arrived in Pennsylvania in sufficient numbers to establish a smattering of sounds.

No American folk dialect derives exclusively from one local British dialect. Dialects of New England tend to reflect dialects of East Anglia, with admixtures from the southern British counties. Southern dialects in the United States show rather more variety, and tend to reflect London and the lower Thames and the southern British counties, with the eastern counties represented rather less. The American Midlands, centered upon Pennsylvania, sometimes differ from both the North and the South, and when Midland forms are distinct they tend to reflect central, western, and northern Britain, along with cultivated seventeenth-century and eighteenth-century British speech. Often this American coastal area, however, breaks into North Midland and South Midland, the North Midland inclining to New England and New York State, the South Midland inclining to various southern dialects.

Pronunciations widespread in the United States generally arrived early, say roughly before 1750. Later imports, whether from later immigration —the Irish, and much of the Scotch, for instance—or from developments in the late eighteenth century in England, tended not to survive, or to be restricted locally. Thus the loss of aspiration in the /hw/ pronunciation —so that *wheat* is pronounced as though spelled *weet,* and *which* as though it were spelled *witch*—tends to appear spottily in the New World and mainly in pockets along the eastern seacoast.

The importation of British sounds thus tends to confirm the evidence for American dialects as we discerned it in the testimony of vocabulary, and tends to provide some evidence for the origin of these dialects in eighteenth-century Britain, but not very sharp evidence. We must assume that a great variety of dialects were brought to the New World, that immigrants were sufficiently scattered along the coast so that no clear reflections of individual British dialects ever existed on the American Atlantic seaboard. Such patterns as were preserved in the New World were somewhat further obscured by local developments; for example, East Anglian forms tend to triumph in New England, but occasionally just the reverse is true. As W. Nelson Francis puts it, most regions on the Atlantic seaboard were probably "dialectal melting pots."[7]

So much for what linguistic geography tells us about the American importation of British pronunciations. Thus far the technique has provided information in at least one other area, verb forms. Referring to

---

[7] "Some Dialect Verb Forms," cited earlier, p. 8.

yesterday, do you say, *I ate my dinner, I et my dinner,* or *I eat my dinner?* On a folk basis all forms are current on both sides of the Atlantic. Do you say *I rose, I rised,* or *I riz?* Is the past of *take* something like *taked, took, tooked, taken,* or *tuck?* Is one *dogbit* or *bitten by a dog?* In place of *saw* do you use *seed, seen* or *see?*

As usually with dialect we must here deal with seeming vagary, but these variants also display a pattern, and behind the pattern looms a principle. To understand the broader implications, we should remind ourselves of a bit of linguistic history. Indo-European, the ancestor of most European and some non-European languages, was highly inflected, notably in the verb. A major fact—or the major fact—in the grammar of most descendants of Indo-European is that they have been losing these inflections and replacing them with some other grammatical devices. This change—whether you call it decay or growth, and it certainly is both—went farther in the Germanic branch of the family than in most other branches, a fact that accounts in part for the guess that Proto-Germanic was the speech of a subject people, learning the parent language corruptly. However that may be, the loss of inflection in the Germanic tongues contrasts with the similar but lesser loss of inflection in Latin, Greek, and most Slavic languages. Furthermore, this leveling of the old inflections has gone farthest in English, so far that no case inflections at all survive in the adjectival systems, and relatively few in nouns and verbs.

The decay in the verb forms, however, accounts for many dialectal variants. The process had already begun in prehistoric times, but the English preserved many old verbs which formed their principal parts by change in an internal vowel; we still have some of these verbs, somewhat simplified, but suggestive of the older forms: *sing, sang, sung; write, wrote, written; eat, ate, eaten.* Beside these old verbs were relatively younger verbs, which had been converted from another verb form or from a word other than a verb. That is, we say *live, lived*—instead of something like *live, lav, loven*—because *live* was formerly not a verb. It comes from an Indo-European base something like **-leip-*,[8] which meant to stick or remain, which became the word for the body remaining after death, from which a verb developed for what the body does before it dies. Being a made verb it followed a simplified pattern, composed of only two basic parts, the first person present singular or the infinitive, *live,* and a combined present and past participle formed

---

[8] An asterisk before a linguistic unit means that the form is reconstructed, not recorded. Indo-European was presumably not written, and thus it has been entirely reconstructed, mainly through triangulation from modern languages and dead languages which were written.

merely by adding /d/ or /t/ preceded by a neutral vowel if necessary, in this case spelled *lived*. Most verbs in English made during recorded time have followed this pattern; some were relatively early verbs like *answered*, which comes from the Old English *andswaru*, a noun meaning *an oath against;* others are later, even current formations and borrowings (*orbited, jeeped*). Some few have been left uninflected (*broadcast*).

The unsettling of the verb system has given us variant verb forms in shifting states of respectability. On the whole the new verbs, the so-called weak or regular verbs like *live, lived*, show little diversity; by analogy an occasional form like *proven* may develop beside historical *proved*, but instances are rare. But among the old verbs, sometimes called strong verbs and sometimes irregular verbs, confusion is a fact of life. Many of these verbs have been lost entirely; verbs like *miltsian*, to pity, and *elnian*, to encourage, have gone, leaving no more than a scattering of dialectal traces. None of the older verbs that have survived have done so without scars. We say *help, helped*, but the Old English principal parts were *helpan, healp, hulpen, holpen*, and the preterit *holp* is still used in both England and America and was quite respectable until recently; it is now characteristic only of folk speech, although Shakespeare makes a nobleman say of King Lear weeping in the storm, "Poor old man, he holpe the Heauens to raine."[9]

Such instances are legion. The old verbs, by Shakespeare's time relatively few, were being made over by analogy into the pattern of the new verbs, which were by then relatively many, but this process was not simple. Notably, it included the reducing of the three basic Old English past and past participial forms to one, as when *healp, hulpen*, and *holpen* became *helped*, and it included a change of form. The Old English past participle ended in /n/, and the vowels of the past forms always differed somewhat from the vowel of the infinitive, but the new form ended with /d/ or /t/, and the vowel of the present tense became the vowel of all tenses. Of course, these changes did not take place at once; actors in one of Shakespeare's plays did not say *holpen* in 1607 and *helped* in 1608. The old forms would be preserved in some areas among some speakers, and new ones would develop among others. Children would learn to say *growed* and *climbed*, while their elders were still saying *grew* and *clomb*, while in another community or at another social level everybody had learned to say *growed*, while elsewhere everybody was still saying *grew*.

Examples would involve both sorts of changes; in the process of making Old English *slepan* into a regular verb, both *sleeped* and *slept*

---

[9] III, 7, 61. So in the Folio, cited earlier; many modern editions have *rage*.

become common preterits; in reducing Old English *seon* in the direction of a regular verb, the past participle *seen* was used for all past forms, *I seen him* as well as *I have seen him*. That is, the difference between the "correct" or accepted forms and the "incorrect" or dialectal or vulgar forms has been determined by the degree of conversion of an old verb to the form of a new verb at the time speakers happened to become self-conscious about their language and to determine that the then fashionable form was correct. *Growed* had not developed enough to be fashionable, and consequently *growed* is now dialectal or vulgar; so is *seed* for *saw*. Similarly, *drinked* developed enough to survive in southwestern England, *drunked* enough to survive scatteringly in the northwest, the old form *drunken* survived only as a modifier, and the old past *drank* never quite killed off what remained of *drunken* as a past participle, which became *drunk*.

The survival and non-survival of the old and new forms illustrate a bewildering variety of trends, but although the details are complicated, the patterns are relatively simple. The result is rather like one of those children's games, in which the players must stop in whatever position they may have been caught when the magic word was shouted. As children's movements go, this freezing of verb forms was not abrupt; standardization is still continuing, but the changes were abrupt as developments in language go, for language develops over centuries and millennia. When speakers of English in the nineteenth century settled upon whatever forms were then fashionable, they made them respectable and made all others suspect. If a growing new form like *growed* had not yet become fashionable enough, it was out of fashion, it remained out of fashion, and probably now always will be. If old forms like *saw* and *seen* were still fashionable, they were saved and never jettisoned for the new combined preterit-participle form *seed,* which might have driven them both out had it enjoyed a century or two more of relatively unpoliced speech. *Graven,* as a perfect standard form, managed to survive beside *graved,* but *holp* went under, as did *heern, clum,* and *tuck,* along with hundreds more.

So much for the origin and nature of the variant verb forms. They confirm what we have already concluded on other grounds, that the wealth of aberrant American verb forms reflects primarily the wealth of forms in British dialects. American verb forms are uncommonly numerous and hence uncommonly interesting as language phenomena, because when English was exported to America, the English language was in process of shifting from one type of verb to another, and the confusion resulting from this shift was exported to the colonies.

We should now examine the distribution of these forms on both sides of the Atlantic. Verb forms can be selected that are remarkably sharp in

reflecting the American basic dialects. The following are characteristically Northern: *won't* pronounced to rhyme with *hunt, be* for *am* and
other forms of *to be, hadn't ought, dove, et* and *see* as preterits. The
following are almost exclusively Midland, with some spilling over into
the South: *boilt* for *boiled, clum, dogbit,* and *seen* as preterits. The
following are almost solidly Midland and Southern: *heered, sweated, eat*
as preterits. The following are basically Southern except that many
forms appear in western North Carolina and Virginia that otherwise
incline to Midland: *he do, what make, belongs to be, freezed, Is I?
hearn, gwine, div, riz* (these last two are heard in northeast New England
also), *holp, seed, mought, taken* as a preterit, *tuck* and *might could.*
The following are much more common in the North and South than in
the Midlands: *clim, waked,* and *wan't* (wasn't).

The difficulty is that these most revealing verb forms on the western
side of the Atlantic have either not been studied on the eastern side, or
they show no very distinctive distribution there. Apparently they are
British forms that were subject to unusual local development in their
new home. On the other hand, the verbs that have thus far been shown
to have geographic distribution in Britain appear, like other common
words in the motherland, to have become rather jumbled when they
suffered transportation. Among the verbs under considerable pressure is
drink, drank, drunk, which in standard speech has maintained forms not
much different from those in Old English. The past participle shows
wide variation in folk speech, however, with *drucken* in northern England, *drank* and an occasional *drinked* in central, eastern, and southeastern England, and *drinked* and *adrinked* in the southwest. Characteristically, northern English *drucken* seems not to have been imported
sufficiently to survive. The American southern states have preserved
drunken, the Old English past participle, although it seems to have
disappeared in England. Negro speakers have completed the leveling
process with "Is you drink?" but the forms that seem to reveal areas in
Britain, *drinked* and *drank,* although they are widely prevalent through
many of the coastal states, are too evenly distributed to be revealing.
Webster gives *drank* as the standard form, listing *drunken* and even
drunk as obsolete; here then, as frequently, New England in the late
eighteenth and early nineteenth centuries must have reflected the English
midland and southeastern counties. Thus the verb forms tend to support
what we have already tentatively concluded, but the support is not very
precise.

One detail of these British verb forms is at least curious. Students of
language have long been puzzled why we say *he does,* not *he doth,* that
is, why the third person singular present indicative ends in /z/. The

Old English form ending in /θ/, which we should spell *th,* persisted long in southern speech; it was brought to the New World along with many other southern locutions. All such verb forms were tending to weaken or fall off entirely in England, and thus it is not surprising that a northern form developed in /z/, spelled *s;* what is surprising is that the northern British /z/ form has become standard in both British and American speech. In Shakespeare's time, the people like Ben Jonson and William Camden, who wrote books, apparently preferred the form spelled *-th,* and *-th* forms are plentiful in the writings of the divines who tell us about New England. Of course, ordinary people do not write many books, and hence their speech is not usually preserved, but for London we have a remarkable exception in Henry Machyn (flourished 1550), mentioned in Chapter 7. He uses endings in *-s,* as in "she was carried to her tomb [where] she leys with a herse-cloth of gold the wych lyys [over her]." We shall probably have to assume that common people like Machyn were using /z/ endings when educated people were still using /θ/ endings, and this guess gains confirmation many places. For example, consider the rogue's talk produced earlier; when Harman writes himself, he uses *canteth* and *speaketh,* but he makes the rogue say *makes.*[10]

Now here is the problem: how did these northern forms reach London and the southern counties in sufficient force to triumph, and more particularly, why do they simultaneously triumph in America, where both forms must have been introduced, but where northern forms did not usually survive? A possible answer involves both history and linguistic geography. As for the history, in the late ninth century Scandinavians, mainly Danes and Norwegians, overran the island of Britain and eventually made peace, but only after they had been given the northeastern part of what is now England, as far south as East Anglia, which was subsequently inhabited by the surviving Angles and the invading Danes and Norwegians. Linguistic geography is revealing, a bundle of isoglosses that run along the border of this old Danish settlement, including the northeast counties, and curving down to encompass the eastern portion of East Anglia, along a Scandinavian stronghold. But East Anglia and the uncultured people of the London area demonstrably stand behind many Americanisms.

Thus it would seem that while the /θ/ forms remained popular among the more cultured people well down into the eighteenth century, as early as the sixteenth century, common people in the East Anglian and Lon-

---

[10] Examples are scarce, since Machyn used mainly first-person or plural verbs, but for some further instances see Wyld, cited earlier, pp. 146–47, 333.

don areas—and probably elsewhere, as well as in the north—were learning to use the verb forms influenced by Scandinavian speech, including the third person singular in /z/. Meanwhile, educated New Englanders had brought with them the fashionable /θ/ pronunciations, but the common people from East Anglia and the London area greatly outnumbered them, and thus the /z/ pronunciations triumphed in the New World, too. Webster in 1828 gives -*es* and -*eth* as alternate forms, but one suspects he includes the -*eth* endings mainly because they were enshrined in the King James version of the Bible—it would have been less than decent to have the Lord talking like Henry Machyn—and Webster was nothing if not a professing Christian. In his own writing he always used the -*s* endings.

Thus part of the chart of the importation of the English language into the New World seems moderately clear, if not very precise in detail. Most American locutions were British locutions transplanted. On the whole these locutions have come from midland, southern, and eastern England, with considerable leaning toward the southeast, toward the London and East Anglian areas, the latter notably in its connection with New England, the London speech perhaps more noticeable in the American South. In this the North Atlantic and Southern American states tend to agree with each other against the Midland states, especially Pennsylvania and adjacent areas, where some Scotch-Irish influences can be observed, but this Midland American area is not distinctly northern British, even though it contrasts with the areas to the north and south of it, which clearly rely upon southern and eastern British dialects. Although many American locutions stem from the British, the imported dialects became somewhat confused in the New World, where new centers of emphasis and dissemination developed such that the popularity and growth of individual locutions vary considerably. Many British linguistic habits, particularly although not exclusively northern ones, have had little or no development in this country; others, notably those from the London area, from East Anglia and parts of the southern and southeastern counties, have gained a spread and respectability never acquired in the land of their origin.

11

ENGLISH ON TWO CONTINENTS: WHAT IT
MEANS TO BE FOOTLOOSE

Having a sampling of the available evidence, what can we make of it? First, how adequate is the sample? In some ways it is quite good. We can know, in surprising detail and with convincing objectivity, where American vocabulary came from, and within limits this vocabulary reveals sound. We have been able to account for distinctively American pronunciations as survivals of British pronunciations not now accepted in British Received Standard, but still more or less common in both folk and relatively cultured speech. Thus we can observe that the British pronunciation of *can't* /kɔnt/, which is popularly represented by the spelling *cawn't,* and which rhymes with the common American pronunciation of *haunt,* is a late development that did not become widely established in the American colonies because it developed in the mother country mainly after the colonial patterns were set. The American pronunciations that rhyme with *pant* or *font,* that is /kænt/ and /kɑnt/ respectively, are merely older pronunciations, relatively close to Middle English, pronunciations that even yet are heard more widely in England, at least so far as geographical distribution is concerned, than is the more approved form /kɔnt/ or /kʌnt/.

Similarly, other sounds often supposed to be characteristically American can be traced to widespread English pronunciations now out of fashion. These include a number of sounds associated with *r*-spellings. Here we should note that the *r* spelling has a number of uses in English. Initially it is an /r/ as in *rough* and *rate,* and it is sometimes an /r/ medially, as in *irate,* but terminally, as in *letter* and *bear,* it usually does not represent an *r* sound. That is, in neither British nor American speech are the last sounds in *letter* the sound of a vowel plus the sound of an *r.* The *r* merely indicates that the preceding vowel is retroflex, that is, that it ends with the tip of the tongue curled back. Thus, when a Briton pronounces *clerk* to rhyme with *hark* and an American pronounces it to rhyme with *jerk,* they may only be using different retroflex vowels, each different from, but about equally close to, the Middle English vowel. Similarly, when some Englishmen and some Americans pronounce *car* so that it might be written *cah* /kɑə/, they are reducing a diphthong including a retroflex vowel to a diphthong without retroflex.

Likewise, we might notice what happened to the Middle English *oo* sound, transcribed /u/. This remained unchanged in Scottish and a number of northern English dialects, where *house* is pronounced so that it rhymes with *goose,* that is, /hus/. In most other dialects this became a diphthong; in British Received Standard and in most Northern and Midland American dialects it developed into a sound like that in *wow,* that is, /hɑus/. In southeastern British dialects, however, the first element of this diphthong is pronounced a little farther forward in the mouth; that is, the vowel starts with the common American sound in *cant, man, have.* The resulting diphthong might be suggested by the spelling *hey-oos,* in phonemics /hæus/ or /hɛus/. These pronunciations are widespread in the area from which American dialects stemmed, and thus we need not be surprised to find them in New England, and characteristically from Chesapeake Bay south and southwest. They flourish in several variations; even in the single state of Texas you can hear at least three different degrees to which this first part of the diphthong is moved forward, and some have a nasal added, but the American dialectal pronunciations are merely slight variations upon the southern British developments from Middle English.

For example, notice the words *know* and *cup* as these are pronounced in British Received Standard and in cultivated American English. The first contained a back vowel in Middle English, so that it would have rhymed with modern *gnaw,* that is, /knɔ/. In accordance with the general English pattern for stressed vowels, this one has moved forward in both British and American speech, but whereas it has remained a relatively simple vowel in standard American, so that *know* is pronounced something like /no/,' in British Received Standard this vowel becomes a diphthong, as in /nɑu/. Actually, the initial sound is farther back than /ɑ/, and the whole is not unlike the vowel in *house* and *out* as it can be heard in Baltimore. The second word, *cup,* is pronounced in British Received Standard about like the American word *cop,* a slang term for a policeman, although the British sound is slightly higher than the vowel in American *cop.* Here both the British and the American pronunciations of the vowel in *cup* represent a lowering of the Middle English sound— that is, of /ʊ/, about the sound in *hood, full,* except that the British sound has dropped more and is lower.

Thus, if we start from the American end and ask where American sounds come from, the answer is simple and consistent. On the whole, American sounds come from British sounds, some of them altered slightly—language everywhere is always changing—but altered rather less, on the whole, than these same sounds have changed in England. If we start from the other end, however, from the British end, the answer is not quite so orderly. A considerable number of British sounds seem not to have survived much in America, and since they must have been brought here, one cannot avoid wondering why.

Take, for example, words like *day, rain,* and *maid.* These contained a diphthong in Middle English, the sound now common in words like *aisle, pile, mile.* This is the same diphthong with which the lyricist of *My Fair Lady* is having fun. The flower girl is supposed to say, *The rain in Spain stays mainly in the plain,* which is faulty climatology but sound linguistics. Being a Cockney, she pronounces this in a way that might be roughly rendered in conventional spelling as follows: *The rine in spine styes minely in the pline.* This pronunciation is illustrated also by the story of the American aviator who was wounded and taken to an English hospital. He woke the next day, rather better off than he felt, and moaned, "Have I come here t' die?" The English nurse said cheerfully, "Oh, no; yi cime yistadie." This pronunciation is characteristic not only of Cockney but of most of the southern and southeastern British dialects, those of the areas from which most American dialects developed, but curiously enough, this pronunciation is almost unknown for these words in the United States. Why? It surely did not die out and then redevelop in the southeastern English dialects, but if not, why is it so scarce in America? It was, of course, disapproved; seventeenth-century and eighteenth-century writers inveighed against the pronunciation, but inveighing did not eradicate other pronunciations.

Whatever the reason, two other peculiarities of the dialects of southeastern England did not much survive transference to the New World. Loss of initial aspiration—commonly called dropping an *h*—appeared as early as the fourteenth century in a spelling like *alf* for *half;* this is well attested for London and other southeastern areas by the time of the early American settlements with *elmet* for *helmet, owsold* for *household, astely* for *hastily,* and the like. This pronunciation has persisted in southeastern England; one frequently hears /æv/ for *have,* /æd/ for *had,* /æus/ *house* and the like, with no initial aspiration. In the same areas, aspiration is added to words that historically did not have it; from the fourteenth century and later we find spellings like *herthe* for *earth, hour* for *our, howlde* for *old, hat* for *at,* and *hobblegaschons* for *obligations.* This practice is now less common in England than the loss of aspiration, but it can still be heard, and both tendencies would have been imported into the New World, where they survived but little. In the United States /æv/ can be heard for *have* in an unstressed position, and many speakers pronounce *when* and *wen* alike, but such pronunciations tend to be sparse except in combination with /w/.

One other peculiarity of southeastern British speech has been but patchily established in the New World. All through southern and southeastern England one can hear terminal and medial stops replaced by glottal stops—a statement which takes a bit of explanation. A word like *hot* ends in an alveolar stop; that is, the air is stopped by putting the tongue against the ridge back of the upper front teeth. In a glottal stop the air is stopped by closing the channel for air at the back of the throat. This sound is hard to detect in a sentence like *The room is hot,* because the last word comes out about like *ha,* and to the average ear the word sounds as though the *t* has been dropped. The true sound, however, appears in a sentence like *He bought it* /hi bɔ' ɪ'/. (In the transcription I am using the apostrophe (') to indicate a sharp break in the flow of air, accompanied by little sound.) These glottal stops work in this way; I heard a Londoner advise a driver to move his car by saying /pʊl ɪ' ap ə bɪ' gɑvnə jul æv ðə bæ' tʊ' ɔf ɪ'/, that is, *"Pull it up a bit, Governor. You'll have the back took off it,"* in which both *back* and *took* come out, not with a final /k/, but with a glottal stop. Similarly, the /t/ can be replaced by a glottal stop, so that *bottle* is pronounced /ba'l/, and *beautiful* comes out /bju'ɪfəl/. These same pronunciations can be heard commonly in Connecticut and in some other parts of New England and New York City.

We could cite a modest number of such scattered importations if this book aimed at completeness, but one difference is too extensive to be ignored and too complicated to be well classified. I refer to what is often called the dropping of final *g* in American speech, in pronunciations indicated by spellings like *goin'* and *seein'*. Of course, this does not really represent the dropping of a /g/. The final sound of *going* is not a combination of /n/ plus /g/. The *ng* is only a spelling. The actual difference between *going* and *goin'*—except that there may also be an intrusive /w/—is that *going* ends in a nasal formed by stopping air with the tongue raised to the roof of the mouth, a sound represented in phonetics and phonemics by /ŋ/, whereas *goin'* ends in a nasal formed by stopping the air at the base of the teeth. That is, the difference is that *going* uses a nasal /ŋ/, made rather far from the vowel, whereas *goin'* uses a nasal /n/, conveniently close to the vowel.

But curiously, this substitution of one nasal for another does not represent the difference between the American and British pronunciations. In this they are much the same, and lest I here be accused of listening with an American ear, I shall quote the standard British authority on the subject, Henry Cecil Wyld:

Such pronunciations as *huntin'*, *shillin'*, etc., which for some reason are considered as a subject of jest in certain circles, while in others they are censured, are of considerable antiquity, as the examples which follow will show. The substitution of '*n*' for '*ng*' /ŋ/ in Present Participles and Verbal Nouns was at one time apparently almost universal in every type of English speech. At the present time this habit obtains in practically all Regional dialects of the South and South Midlands, and among large sections of speakers of Received Standard English. Apparently in the twenties of the last century a strong reaction set in in favour of the more "correct" pronunciation, as it was considered, and what was in reality an innovation, based upon the spelling, was so far successful that the [ŋ] pronunciation ('with -*ng*') has now a vogue among the educated at least as wide as the more conservative one with -*n*.[1]

As Wyld indicates, he supports his contention with examples, which include *besichen* (*beseeching*) in a letter from Queen Elizabeth to James VI, which is surely as near to the King's and Queen's English as one can get.

As would be expected, this form with /n/ rather than /ŋ/ was imported into America and must have been the standard form here, as it was in the homeland; but the same reform on the basis of spelling swept through the United States, albeit later than the 1820's, so that many careful American speakers now use the /ŋ/ for *going,* and the /n/ nasal is considered evidence of slovenly speech. So far as my own rough check is valid, the percentage of /n/ and /ŋ/ is much the same on the two sides of the Atlantic. But in the pronunciation with /n/, different vowels are used—/ə/ in the United States and /ɪ/ in England—and it is the vowel I suspect, rather than the nasal, that offends sensitive British ears.

To understand this variety in development, we should recall that all languages reveal a tendency to reduce a vowel when stress moves from it. Stress has done a good bit of moving in English, English of all persuasions; for example, when the endings fell off English words, the vowels tended to become neutral before they disappeared; they became what is often called *schwa* /ə/ before they became nothing. This tendency, to reduce an unaccented vowel to schwa, strongly characteristic of American speech, is less characteristic of British speech, and thus the real difference between what an American and a Briton is likely to do to a present participle is not that one is more likely to drop the

---

[1] *Colloquial English,* cited earlier, p. 289.

g—that is, use the nasal /n/ rather than the nasal /ŋ/—but that the Briton is likely to preserve the quality of the vowel and say *goin'* /gɔɪn/ (rhymes with *show in*), whereas the American is likely to reduce the unaccented vowel to schwa and say /goən/ or even /gon/.

So much for sound. What of grammar? We have already seen that verb forms which have become established in the United States have mainly been imported from Britain, although fashion has not always chosen the same forms on both sides of the water. But verb forms are only a minor part of grammar; the language works understandably if not very elegantly however the user juggles *did* and *done, take* and *took.* The more pervasive and subtle aspects of grammar, however, have been too little studied on either side of the water, and still less comparatively. For example, many Britons accuse Americans of barbarously putting prepositions at the ends of sentences, that is, of using what are more properly called verb-adverb combinations, merged verbs, verb sets, or verbs with separable suffixes, verbs like *blow up, turn on,* and *find out.* These verbal forms appear as early as Old English and have been increasing ever since; I have a private theory that they have grown faster in the United States than in Britain, but they have never been adequately studied. Certainly they were common in England when the speech patterns that were to become American dialects embarked from the mother country. For example, an eighteenth-century innkeeper advertised as follows:

All favors will be strictly attended to, and gratefully acknowledged by,

> The Public's much obliged
> And very humble servant
> W. WEEKS

Presumably Mr. Weeks was proud of his advertisement; he could have been, for *attend to* is a good verb, different in use from *attend,* but obviously this construction needed no devising from an illiterate Yankee bumpkin. It was in use among reputable Britons. W. Weeks operated what was probably the best inn in Salisbury, and such a person would have been a man of substance.[2]

Whatever the differences between British and American grammar, however, they are not great. Superficial observation will confirm this fact. Both types of English use sentences, and the patterns within these sentences do not differ fundamentally. In all forms of English one says *by the curb,* not *curb by the,* even though the British prefer the spelling *kerb* and use *by* somewhat differently from the way Americans use it.

---

[2] When I was last in Salisbury, the notice was still exposed in the modern descendant of W. Weeks' inn, but I assume not for its rhetorical implications.

When an American tourist and a British countryman find that they cannot understand each other, the difficulty is usually in pronunciation and vocabulary, not in grammar. And here we might remind ourselves that grammar changes relatively slowly, much more slowly than does vocabulary, and that the great shift in English grammar had taken place long enough before 1605 so that all Englishmen by that time used a grammar common in its broad aspects. English had formerly employed a grammar based upon inflection, but by the seventeenth century all English dialects used grammars based upon analytic devices; that is, they used word order and relationship words, such as prepositions. Doubtless research could reveal that these distributive devices varied from dialect to dialect and that some were brought to the colonies more than were some others, but research is so inadequate here that I had best not try to guess which locutions, where, when, and how much.

We should consider another aspect of language, pitch and tone, language as a sequence of sound, and here we must notice a curious inconsistency. Tone and speech rhythm provide the most noticeable quality of language; we can listen to tone and pitch even in a language we cannot understand, yet pitch rhythms have been but little studied, especially on a comparative basis. Presumably this curious gap in our knowledge remains because of the inadequacy of our linguistic tools. The philologists could not study tone much; they worked on written language mainly, and most alphabets and syllabaries do not record pitch. With the growth of modern linguistics, students still neglected pitch perhaps partly because the International Phonetic Alphabet, although it does permit recording pitch, does not treat pitch as part of a pattern. This inadequcy of IPA suggests one reason for the current shift away from phonetics and toward phonemics, which does provide a ready means of studying pitch. We now have machines with which we can study pitch scientifically, and we have, in phonemics, a working means of studying pitch, but as yet research in pitch has mainly been subsidiary to the study of the physical properties of sound or to grammar. I know of no comprehensive study, geographical and social, of pitch patterns in either the United States or Britain, and without both we can do no more than sample and guess.

Some facts about pitch patterns seem obvious. More patterns are current in Britain than in the United States, and British patterns tend to have more variety than have American patterns, that is, more changes of pitch within a sentence. How old are these patterns? Old enough so that they were mostly brought to the New World, but leveled by the mingling of dialects there? Do pitch patterns have a probability of survival different from the probability of survival in pronunciation and vocabulary? Is relatively toneless speech a notable characteristic of those areas of Britain from which American sounds and vocabulary seem to have derived? Quite possibly. Personally, I believe I hear patterns closer to the American in Surrey and London than I do in Oxford and Shropshire, but all this is guessing. So far as I am aware no one has seriously attempted to collect the current speech patterns of the counties from which American dialects have mainly flowed; nor has anyone then put them beside the speech patterns that can still be heard on the American eastern seaboard, although this could be an exciting piece of research.

Some speech patterns are used on both sides of the Atlantic; some are not. Presumably, the commonest American declarative pattern is something like the following:

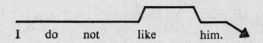

This pattern can be heard in England, also, but along with it a pattern something like the following, especially frequent in cultivated speech:

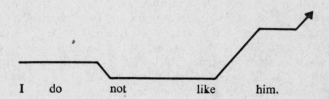

That is, the declarative sentence rises instead of falling. This has many variants. I heard an Oxfordshire mother saying to her daughter

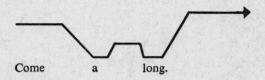

One interesting detail is that some rising declarative patterns occur in the United States, especially in the South, where some speakers will close each sentence with a rising tone. Personally, I have no doubt that

this southern rising pitch was imported from England just as was the southern diphthong in *house* beginning with an /æ/, but my guess is far too impressionistic. Another intriguing sentence pattern, common in the southern British counties, appears only in rather long sentences, so far as I have observed, in which the highest and most sharply rising tone comes at an important break within the sentence, at the point that might be marked in punctuation with a semicolon or a comma and coordinating conjunction.

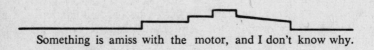

Something is amiss with the motor, and I don't know why.

I suspect that this pattern can be heard also in the American South and in New England, although, theoretically, American speech has a holding pitch at this point. My guess is that British tonal patterns have been borrowed less extensively than British pronunciations and vocabulary, that the tonal patterns suffered more than most other aspects of speech in the mingling that accompanied migrating, but that British patterns most common in the States can be observed sporadically. That is, American tones are probably British tones, with some development and a great deal of loss, but this is a guess where research is inadequate.

Theoretically, we should also compare American with other varieties of English on the basis of stress and what the phonemists call *juncture,* a word which we can approximate for lay purposes with *pause.* Stress has been noticed as an aspect of vocabulary; the differences between the pronunciations of *laboratory* and *dictionary* on the two sides of water are in part variations of stress. We have had little comparative study of international differences in stress as linguistic pattern, however, and even less study of juncture. Accordingly, I shall ignore these intriguing fields.

What can we say by way of summary? The broad outlines are not in doubt. Early immigration was mainly from England, with pockets of speech like Dutch, German, and Welsh sufficient to encourage linguistic change, notably from the Hudson estuary to Chesapeake Bay, but not enough to negate the fundamental statement that American dialects rest upon British dialects. Through much of the seventeenth century settlements grew slowly, partly because England endured a civil war, which set in soon after the first Puritan settlements and was followed by what we should now call a "cold war," with relatively republican England at odds with monarchical Europe. For various reasons this immigration came mainly from the south and east. Ventures like those of the Virginia Company and the Baltimores had to be approved in London and tended to center there. The Puritans, who settled New England, were strong in East Anglia, in the South, and in the Midlands; northern England tended to be Presbyterian in religion and provincial in outlook.

With the late seventeenth century, immigration increased so much that the eighteenth became the definitive century for American dialects. In England this time was characterized by the French wars, the growth in wealth and station of the great landed families, the beginning of London as a national center, and turmoil among the lower and middle classes. The last two factors are of particular interest to us; London became a great processor and exporter of human beings, which human beings carried their London language with them. As for the common people, the professional and trading groups were growing in importance, but the old basis of English life centered in the manor; its relatively self-contained farms and crofts were being disrupted, notably by the Corn Laws, the Enclosure Acts, and the industrial revolution. To see how these affected American dialects we must glance at them separately.

The Corn Laws were essentially a tariff on wheat, a tariff which made agriculture profitable, highly profitable if one could control sufficient fat land. The wealthy people, especially the great landed families, grabbed land, and here their principal instruments were the Enclosure Acts. To understand the impact of these acts we must remember that strip agri-

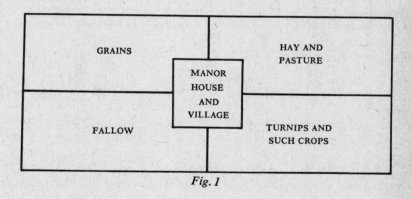

Fig. 1

culture had been common in England during the Middle Ages. For example, a stylized sort of manor might look like Figure 1. The land is divided into four parts, the use of the land rotated so that after one section raises grain for a time it can be allowed to recuperate by lying fallow or serving as pasture. In order that crops will be distributed among all farm families, the people live in the village in the center and a family farms a strip in each quarter of the whole lot of land. That is, assuming that the manor supports ten families, a plan of the area would look like Figure 2. Now let us assume that each of these families has five sons, so that on the death of the fathers each strip is divided into five strips, each with a furrow or a strip of sod to separate it from the next strip. The strips are now quite narrow, but the process continues, with the strips getting narrower every time a father dies; obviously, if a system like this continues long, the land will become mostly useless boundaries between strips, and by the eighteenth century much land was badly cut up in this manner.

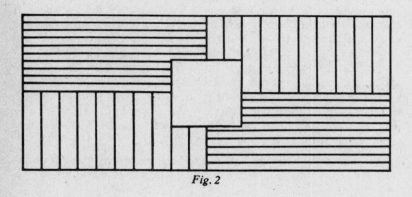

Fig. 2

Now came the Enclosure Acts. These required that every property owner show title to his property and enclose it. Most of these small landholders had no evidence of title; their families had always lived there, and everybody knew it, but nobody could prove it in writing. In fact, most of these people could not read or write. Furthermore, these narrow strips defied enclosure; the strips would have been mostly fence, and there were no cheap fences—stone in some areas, hawthorn hedges in others, both expensive in labor and consumptive of space; barbed wire was a nineteenth-century American development. The result was that many small farmers were forced off the land, to migrate or starve.

Before we consider where they might go, let us observe the industrial revolution. This started as a different means of spinning and weaving fibers into cloth—at first, wool. The great body of English yeomen, from before the time that Chaucer was policing the wool trade in London, worked on manors and profited from wool. A yeoman's family expected to raise most of its food, along with some wool that could be clipped, spun, and woven by the family into cloth and sold as a cash crop. Now a series of inventions made hand spinning and weaving unprofitable. By 1830 mills had been developed so that one twelve-year-old girl, working suicidal hours in a mill, could produce as much cloth as a village of 250 would have produced a century earlier. This development also drove the crofters from their crofts. The kind of agriculture they knew was no longer wanted, but the resulting industries provided homes for some displaced persons in the new cities that sprang up around the mills—at first woolen mills, later cotton mills that processed the cotton from Egypt, the Orient, and the Americas.

Now geography becomes important. Southern England tends to be rather flat, with some downs—what are called in American English, rolling hills—and rather sluggish streams. To the north and west the land becomes more mountainous, with dashing streams and exposed strata of coal. Naturally, the rich farming areas with the relatively heavy rural populations were mainly among the flat lands of the Midlands and the South. Here people were forced from their lands. In the North factories appeared where coal provided steam power and where the swift rivers provided water power. If a northern farmer lost his land, he could move to one of the nearby mill towns. Thus the northerners tended not to take northern speech to the New World; they took it to Leeds or Huddersfield. Some of the southerners moved there, too, although not in sufficient numbers to make northern speech over into southern speech. Generally speaking, displaced southerners had two possible havens: they could move to London, which might prove to be only the first step toward the New World, perhaps after a hitch in the Old Bailey for debt, or they might leave directly for the colonies, and for eighteenth-century speakers of English the colonies were mainly the colonies along the North American Atlantic seaboard.

Thus, although the reasons for emigration changed, the sources of American dialects remained pretty much the same. Southern and southeastern England was seafaring England, so that names associated with both early Virginia and Massachusetts Bay, whether for religious or merchant-adventuring reasons, were midland and southern names, and presumably those voyagers whose names we do not know, those who accompanied the known persons in sufficient numbers to carry bodies of language, were midland and southern, also. Later, when the Enclosure Acts and the industrial revolution encouraged emigration, the emigrants tended to leave from the same areas although now for different reasons.

Emigrants tended to come from the less privileged classes, displaced farm workers, moderately skilled artisans, small businessmen, servants, and the like. Usually the most destitute did not leave because they could not, except as indentured servants or condemned criminals. Accordingly, we need to ask ourselves, not why American dialects differ from the most fashionable English dialects, but why they do not differ more sharply than they do. We have noticed repeatedly that an accepted American locution was identical with that of good middle-class English speech in the eighteenth century.

We must now observe that both the similarities and the differences in modern speech rest upon a curious coincidence. London, the center of the dialects which sired American speech, was also the social and governmental capital and thus the center of the most fashionable British speech. For example, the author of the *Arte of English Poesie* (1589)— he was presumably either George or Richard Puttenham, both reputable rhetoricians—recommended as follows:

Our maker [that is] poet therefore at these days shall not follow Piers Plowman, nor Gower, nor Lydgate, not yet Chaucer, for their language is now out of use with us; neither shall he take the terms of Northern-men, such as they use in daily talk, whether they be noblemen, or gentlemen, or their best clerks, all is a matter; nor in effect any speech used beyond the river of Trent. [That is, not north of Lincolnshire.] Though no man can deny but that theirs is the purer English-Saxon at this day, yet it is not so courtly nor so current as our Southern English is; no more is the far Western man's speech. Ye shall therefore take the usual speech of the Court, and that of London and the shires lying about London within sixty miles, and not much above.[3]

A divider with one point set at London and the other set for sixty miles on a scale map will inscribe a circle that will take in most of the areas which retain today strong resemblances to American speech.

American speech, then, comes from the area of fashionable English speech, but from the middle- and lower middle-classes of this area, and hence preserved relatively older forms because English speech was changing rapidly in the Middle Ages and the Renaissance, notably in the London area. Meanwhile, people of the rural areas, and the lower classes of the urban areas, provided the conservative elements, always a

[3] The passage has been noticed frequently, and is conveniently reprinted in Richard Foster Jones, *The Triumph of the English Language* (Stanford, Calif.: Stanford University Press, 1965), p. 138. The *Arte* was several times reprinted; the modern edition is that by Gladys D. Wilcock and Alice Walker (Cambridge: Cambridge University Press, 1936).

century or two behind the more sophisticated speakers. This was the language, the speech of the unfashionable people in the fashionable area, which became the basis of American English in Massachusetts Bay and the Chesapeake-Virginia area in the seventeenth century. It continued to be the basis of the dialects of the northern and southern American seaboard during the buildup of the eighteenth century. Thus the likeness between Northern and Southern American speech is accounted for, and the similarity between American and British cultured English; had American immigration come mainly from Westmorland, for example, British and American English might now be as different as Danish and Norwegian.

A problem remains, however. How do we account for New Jersey, Pennsylvania, and adjacent areas, where the speech differs from the dialects both to the north and the south? Vocabulary of the regions, as revealed by linguistic geography, leaves the fact of difference beyond dispute. Other sorts of evidence confirm roughly the lines laid out by vocabulary. But why this difference?

What are the characteristics of this midland dialect? It occasionally preserves northern British forms, not usually exclusively northern forms except a few Scotticisms, but it alone does this. It is inclined to agree more frequently with central and even western British speech than do the other American areas. Neither of these trends is sharp; they must be considered, but they seem not enough. The area more frequently agrees with prevailing American speech, if there is such a thing; in fact, while linguistic geography was in its infancy in this country, many observers concluded—I confess that I was one of them—that most middle-western and all western American speech grew from midland dialects as these fanned out, going west; the current theory is that midland speech diminished as it went west, was encroached upon from both the North and South, until some rather complicated blending was achieved west of the Mississippi River.

Are there other plausible guesses about Pennsylvania and the remainder of the coastal American midlands? First we might ask how Pennsylvania and the adjacent country differed from other areas in settlement. Relatively speaking, Pennsylvania started late; early sporadic ventures into what is now Pennsylvania and New Jersey did not amount to much until after William Penn's concern with the colony, which began in the 1680's.

In contrast, by that time New England and the plantation areas of Virginia and North Carolina were well established, and their linguistic patterns were taking shape. The Puritans were strong in East Anglia, of course, and in many southern British counties; the reasons for setting sail from Plymouth were presumably not entirely navigational. Similarly, Virginia was closely tied to business ventures centered in London, and southern plantations were extensively manned with colonists, voluntary or involuntary, from the London area. Between 1635 and 1680 the number of white indentured servants sent to Virginia alone averaged more than a thousand a year, and toward the end of this period their numbers were greatly augmented by prisoners banished to the colonies to work out their servitude. The London jails supplied the greater number. After the collapse of the Cromwellian revolution their numbers were augmented by tens of thousands of political prisoners; as one writer put it, after the Restoration "Royalists could think of no punishment more fitting for recalcitrant dissenters than transportation to the plantations." The Roundheads, of course, were strong in London.[4]

Pennsylvania and New Jersey missed these sources of population, and the movement to the Delaware and Susquehanna valleys was delayed until the eighteenth century. By then, however, the temperate climate, the fat lands, the general benevolence of Quaker government encouraged rapid growth and responsible immigrants. On the whole the arrivals in Pennsylvania were probably linguistically later and financially more competent than the bulk of immigrants either north or south. In England the Quakers were strong in the central counties; they attracted Welshmen from the west and Presbyterians from the north, who often did not feel very welcome in Puritan New England or Church of England Virginia. They would have brought with them dialects somewhat more suggestive of accepted middle-class speech than had the dissenters who went to Massachusetts or the jailbirds who were dispatched to Virginia.

We might recall, also, that the midland settlements were the great polyglot communities, and whatever polyglotism does to language, it certainly does something, and it probably encourages linguistic change. No doubt the results vary with the native speakers with whom the foreign speakers associate. In the South the slaves learned anything but cultured English; what could they be expected to learn from a deported London felon who was brought up on thieves' cant? But the Palatinate Germans, the Jewish merchants, the French Huguenots, and the Dutch patroons were neither intellectually nor financially underprivileged, and when they endeavored to learn English they would have sought to learn it from people of competence. We may here have the explanation for the

---

[4] Jernegan, cited earlier, p. 49, suggests that Virginians seeking genealogies scan the records of Newgate prison rather than the British peerage. For estimates of the number of indentured servants, see Thomas J. Wertenbaker, *Patrician and Plebian in Virginia* (New York: Russell & Russell, 1959), p. 159.

fact—one of the solider we have observed—that Midland verb forms tend to approach the verbs of cultivated speech more nearly than do those of either the Northern or the Southern states.

Thus we might propose several reasons for the linguistic distinction between the American midlands and the areas to the north and the south. The immigrants probably included more speakers from northern, western, and central counties, smaller percentages from the southeast. The immigrants probably came from somewhat higher social strata, and they probably came later; thus they reflected more of eighteenth-century middle-class speech, less of seventeenth-century folk speech. They lived in the most polyglot American colonial communities south of Canada and north of Florida.

We have then, three basic American dialects, with variations, but the dialects of the New World are not so numerous, so varied, or so sharply delineated as the English dialects in the Old World. British dialects have never undergone the blending and blunting that occurred when immigrants were shuffled during the crossing; for a time nobody went to Pennsylvania because there were no settlements there, but when Pennsylvania became the most attractive of the American colonies, immigrants from many areas could be expected to converge upon it. Similarly, there was a time when the plantation area of Virginia and the Carolinas was attractive and another time when the best land had all been taken up and when immigrants could be expected to strike farther inland or turn south to the newer colonies in Georgia. Thus the shifting of settlement patterns probably accounts in part for the subdialects. The difference in the cultural level of those who came and those who stayed at home must have made a difference; no doubt part of the deep revulsion that early British travelers felt for American speech grew from their having heard cultured Americans using locutions which at home characterized the speech of servants and farm laborers.

Another blending influence grew from a colonial desire to imitate the mother country. The evidence is overwhelming that the eighteenth century in England saw a great reform movement in language, a reform which accepted the speech of the court as a standard for cultivated English usage. This usage changed with the changing fortunes of the royal families, with the rise and fall of various great lords and ladies from various portions of the island, but it continued and grew, and by the eighteenth century had been accelerated by a lively concern to reform and purify the language. Presumably, Dr. Samuel Johnson would not have received enough subscriptions to print his great dictionary had he not innocently encouraged his subscribers to trust that his work would "refine" and forever "fix" a language which was felt to be insufficiently polished. The leveling that has grown from this movement has given us what is now recognized as British Received Standard, and if it was not universally received in the eighteenth century, it was growing rapidly into acceptance.

Of course the locutions to be fixed were old folk expressions, with an ancestry shared by the different but related expressions growing in the colonies, but the eighteenth-century dictators of usage could not know that. We have, among others, the testimony on this point of the British philologist Wyld, who writes,

> It must be reiterated that all the "reforms" in pronunciation and grammar which have passed into general currency in colloquial English during the last century and a half, have come from below, not from above, in the first instance, so far as we can discover.[5]

One should add that by *colloquial English,* Wyld means what might be called the speech of literate people. Of course, not everyone approved these developments. Jonathan Swift attributed them to a "licentiousness which entered with the restoration, and from infecting our religion and morals fell to corrupt our language." So far as language was concerned he considered "that the court, which used to be the standard of propriety and correctness of speech, was then and I think hath ever since continued, the worst school in England." But he was largely ignored, and the model of the day was "correctness," although what was correct was not always apparent. Doubtless most important persons would have accepted the dictum of the learned Dr. Johnson that, "For pronunciation the best general rule is, to consider those the most elegant speakers who deviate least from the written words." The evidence is clear that during the eighteenth century efforts to police language became common in England, and within limits effective.[6]

England was coming of age; in the eighteenth century she was growing into a world power, and by the nineteenth century she had become one, the center of an empire. Meanwhile, the landed gentry, many of them prosperous rustics, were metamorphosing into gentlemen; the new great merchants were growing from the old little merchants. Englishmen were cultivating sophistication, and London was becoming one of the capitals of Europe, not merely the port nearest to Europe on a backward, offshore island. At this time, also, printing was growing in potency. For a time mechanical reproduction had been merely a cheaper sort of handwriting. Even in the seventeenth century, books were few

---

[5] Wyld, *Colloquial English,* cited earlier, p. 184.
[6] This material has been canvassed several times, perhaps best by Wyld, pp. 157–88, and Albert C. Baugh, *A History of the English Language,* 2nd ed. (New York: Appleton-Century-Crofts, Inc., 1957), pp. 306–55, where these and other quotations will be found.

and printings small, and these were mainly the classics, textbooks, books of practical instruction, religious works, and the like; periodicals were, until the last years, nonexistent. By the eighteenth century, however, all sorts of works were burgeoning, including dictionaries, grammars, rhetorics, and volumes calculated to tell everybody how he ought and ought not to speak, write, spell, and punctuate.

Accordingly, at this time many Briticisms were developed, roughly standardized, and even popularized. On the whole these changes were not imported to America. They were developments of the eighteenth century in England, but developments among people who were not abandoning their sophisticated life in cultured Britain for a wild land infested with tomahawk-bearing Iroquois and colonials addicted to low language—even the British stage boor Tony Lumpkin could not endure anything "low." The new language habits did not seep down to the middle or lower classes in England until much later—in fact, they are still seeping. Meanwhile, when eighteenth-century Britons came to Pennsylvania, to the southern uplands, even to the growing cities of the coast, they brought with them the eighteenth-century version of the same dialects that had already been imported in seventeenth-century versions. The fashionable speech of the British eighteenth century did not get much imported during the formative eighteenth-century years in the English colonies in America.

Later some speech was imported enough to further confuse the American dialects. Students sent to the mother country for schooling— American colleges and even good preparatory schools were scarce and generally poor until well into the nineteenth century—would bring back British pronunciations, and admiring hangers-on would imitate them. Travelers from the crude colonies would acquire, either deliberately or by genuine admiration, the accent of the cultured mother country. Thus the coastal American cities—Boston, New York, Philadelphia, Baltimore, Charleston, Savannah, along with inland capitals like Richmond —became secondary centers for the spread of language, the language of the growing British Received Standard. Accordingly, the so-called broad *a*'s in Boston exceed those in Chicago, but these imports were generally too little and too late to become more than minor influences in the speech of the New World. Once the basic dialects developed on the Atlantic seaboard, they moved west as dialects, following the patterns of western settlement, occasionally diverted by secondary dispersal centers like New Orleans, becoming further blunted and blended as they interwove with one another but maintaining enough integrity so that dialects can still be observed even to the Pacific Coast and the backward mountainous areas, in fact, throughout the phantasmagoria of American English.

12

A CONTROL CASE: SPANISH AND
THE NEW WORLD

I have assumed, for purposes of discussion, that in studying the importation of English into the United States and Canada, we have been examining something more than an event in the history of one language, that
we have been studying the phenomenon of language in migration. In this
I may be wrong. Perhaps all languages move differently, and perhaps I
have no right to generalize by observing the manner in which British
English became American English. Ideally, I should study all languages
known to have moved. Since this is inexpedient, I shall check our findings against at least one other example, and in the Americas the obvious
second choice is Spanish.

Already one of the great languages of the world, it is potentially even
greater, since it is the native tongue of much of a continent and of
important adjuncts like Central America and the West Indies. If it can
avoid fragmentation into Mexican, Cuban, Argentinian, and the like,
and should something halt the rapid development of English—an atomic
war, for example—it might become the best candidate for a world
language. And if we know less of Spanish than we do of English, if
modern techniques have been but inadequately applied to it, we know
more of it, much more, than we know of Portuguese, its only rival in
Latin America.

For the future, I may be choosing the wrong language. Many Brazil-
ians will doubtless think I am, for Brazil is the largest Latin American
country and probably potentially the greatest, with vast resources,
mainly only sampled, and the principal sources of today may not be the
most important sources of tomorrow. Industry needs water, quantities of
it, and the world's largest body of little used fresh water controlled by
one political entity flows through Brazil. On the other hand, desaliniza-
tion may render fresh water commercially obsolete. One deals always

with these imponderables; the future of Portuguese against Spanish may be settled by the scientists now working to change the sea into fresh water, but we can scarcely hope to ponder that imponderable to any linguistic purpose. For our needs, Spanish is the obvious choice because we know more of it than we know of Portuguese, partly because, historically, Portuguese is a Spanish dialect.

Accordingly, let us turn to Spain, the source of American Spanish, as England is the source of American English. At once we are struck by engaging parallels, both historical and geographic. As the waves of barbarism sweeping west through northern Europe broke on the shores of England, the waves of civilization, sweeping west along the shores of the Mediterranean, broke on the shores of Spain.

Various persuasions of more or less barbaric Celts and Germans, working west mainly north of the Alps, finally landed in the British Isles, which were so near to the European continent that England was almost a peninsula in historic times, as it had been in actuality during prehistoric times. English as a language rests upon this absorption of one barbaric people after another, the sequence interrupted only by a few centuries of Roman occupation. Land's End, for these peoples, was the southwestern tip of England.

Similarly, every great Mediterranean culture, beginning with the Phoenician, swept west along the Mediterranean and had nowhere to go beyond Spain. As for geography, when these westward-moving cultures came to the Cape of Finisterre, the northwest tip of Spain, they had reached the Romanic version of Land's End in both geography and place-naming. The German word for peninsula is *Halbinsul, half island,* and the English islands were near enough to the French coast to function almost as a peninsula, where migrants, faced with the sea, had to make a stand. Similarly, the Spanish peninsula has functioned pretty much as an offshore island, since the Pyrenees run all along its northern edge and plunge into the sea at both ends; invasion has come by sea from Africa—there were no cannons at Gibraltar then—or by sea from islands like the Balearics, as well as by land from what is now France.

Language everywhere is linked to culture, but to an unusual degree the dialectal history of Spanish is understandable only in the light of these successive invasions. We do not know who painted the caves of Santillana along the precipitous northern coast—perhaps the Ligurians or the ancestors of the Iberians, who were in Spain when history starts in the West. These Iberians, like the men who raised Stonehenge, were capable of handling huge, rather roughly hewn stones, which can still be seen in the foundation of the towering fortress in Tarragona, the Roman capital of Iberia, on the eastern coast. Long before there was any Rome, the Phoenicians were at Tarragona and elsewhere; rows of their graves yet adorn the necropolis there, with the amphora, lamps, and other trappings associated with East Mediterranean cultures. Of course, the Greeks followed the Phoenicians, and the Carthaginians took over from the Greeks and then clashed with the Romans. In fact, the Romans became worried when the Carthaginians threw them out of Spain, and it was through Spain that Hannibal mounted his conquest of the Italian peninsula. Some Celts were there also, but apparently few enough so that they left no linguistic evidence beyond scattered place names, names of fortresses ending in -*briga* or -*dunum,* or victories celebrated with *sega-*.

With the collapse of the Roman Empire, after about the fourth century A.D., the peninsula was overrun by Germanic barbarians, of whom the Goths remained in control, except that they never did much to subjugate various mountain peoples along the northern coast. Were these the remnants of the ancient Iberians who are supposed to have been early invaders from Africa? We know little of them. Or were they descendants of still earlier Ligurians? We know little of them, either. Whoever these northerners were, they made the mountains unhealthy for anyone else, as Charlemagne learned when his rear guard was slaughtered in a minor action which became the basis of the *Chanson de Roland.*

The Goths were only nicely established when the Mohammedan Moors arrived. Theirs was a long history in Spain. They occupied much of the country and made a sortie into the land of the Franks, where they were stopped at the battle of Tours, after which they settled down in the more hospitable portions of southern Spain and made it part of the highly civilized Mohammedan world. The Goths and various other peoples stayed in the high, rather barren central plateaus, nominally overrun by the Moors, but often in a prudently restrained state of revolt.

The Muslim empire was notably diverse, and what is now southern Spain participated in culture after culture, dominated at times by the sophisticated merchants of Bagdad, at other times by Berbers from the Sahara Desert, and by all sorts of peoples between them, both geographically and culturally. These rivalries led to bickering, and whenever internecine war diverted the Moors in southern Spain, the Goths would sortie from their hilltop castles in the north, and occasionally make some headway in pushing the infidels toward the sea. More frequently the Goths were soundly thrashed and sent back to the mountains, and if one goes to the Alhambra and studies there the wealth of art, architecture, science, and civilized thinking that is still represented in that amazing and seemingly impregnable fortress, one can understand that the relatively barbaric Goths, hibernating in their bleakness, could not embarrass the Moors much if the Moors were inclined to fight. Even more revealing, perhaps, is the ancient mosque of the Caliphs of Cordova, where a forest of some 850 Moorish arches and double arches housed for centuries one of the two centers of the Mohammedan religious world. Pilgrims could go to either Mecca or Cordova, known as Fecca. Accordingly the proverbial Andalusian expression today for a fool's errand is to go "from Fecca to Mecca," since making the pilgrimage to the Arabian peninsula was silly if one had already been to Cordova. Here was a sacred copy of the Koran, and the visitor can still trace with his feet the trough in the marble made by the sandals of worshipers passing seven times around the holy book. Southern Spain was one of the anchors of an empire which lasted as long as did the Roman Empire, some eight centuries, and stretched from the Tigris-Euphrates valley to the Pillars of Hercules.

Thus for nearly a thousand years the peninsula of what is now Spain was a curiously divided area. To the south and southeast were the Moors with their Alhambras and their mosques, with their expert agriculture, prospering in the rich valleys like that of the Guadalquivir, with the plains and harbors that had attracted the Greeks and the Phoenicians.

To the north was the relatively barren central plateau of Spain, where the Godos, including descendants of the Goths, in kingdoms like those of old Castile and Leon, with capitals like Burgos, ruled in a manner not far from barbarism. The annals of these old north central kingdoms are not very edifying; they are replete with fratricides, but are not for some time notable for the arts, learning, or letters.

Still farther to the north, in the mountains and against the sea, were the descendants of ancient peoples. To the northwest, the Galicians became a sort of medieval Switzerland. Too stubborn, too poor, and too well defended by mountains to be very attractive to conquerors, they inhabited—and still inhabit—a lush country of precipitous green mountains and narrow, fertile valleys that lead into fjord-like estuaries, swarming with sea food. It is a pleasant retreat for a few people with rural and maritime inclinations, but it happened, also, to become an international center. Whatever the facts, the legend is that one Santiago —Sant Yague in the older spelling—the Apostle James, came to convert Spain, but returned to Jerusalem in disappointment, to be martyred by Herod. His followers brought his body back to Spain and buried it secretly, where it rested in peace until the year 844, when a battler against the Moors needed help; this he received from a knight mounted on a white steed with a red cross in his hands, who was readily recognized as Sant Yague. Thereafter, the saint had a few more centuries in peace, until a star appeared to some shepherds in a field (by a little juggling, *Compostela* can be made into *campo stella,* star in the field) and guided these shepherds to the saint's grave.

In more skeptical times, this tale might have been discredited by its similarity to the Christ story, but the eleventh century was not noted for skepticism of this sort, and in any event, if a miraculous star had brought shepherds to Christ, a fact which all devout Christians emphatically believed, why should not a star lead shepherds to Sant Yague, who also had been martyred by Herod? Whatever the reason, Santiago de Compostela became one of the great shrines of the Middle Ages, to which it is said a half million pilgrims came annually. Many of these pilgrims were mendicants, of course, but many were not; Santiago throve as a community and is a jewel city today with an ancient university, although it ceased to burgeon after pilgrimages went out of fashion with the growth of the Renaissance.

To the east, on the Mediterranean coastal plain, were the Catalans, who centered on ancient Phoenician and Roman cities like Tarragona and Barcelona. Their affiliations and their geography directed them toward France and the Mediterranean countries, while they tended to turn their prosperous commercial backs on the remainder of the peninsula, whether Moorish or Christian.

In the mountains to the west of Cataluña, near what is now the Spanish-French border, on the Bay of Biscay side, were the Basques. Linguistically, they are the most interesting people on the peninsula because they are eccentric, but they are so eccentric that they need not concern us much. Their language has not been related to any other known tongue, living or dead, and has not been very successfully analyzed, especially the verb, which is exceedingly complex. Humboldt thought he discovered 216 conjugations, and a more recent scholar studied 50,000 forms with only partial results. A verbal construction apparently tends to comprise a patient-verb-agent sequence, in which the patient is the recipient, and in which the agent is closer to what we should call a subject. That is, a standard sentence resembles a passive sentence in English, with many auxiliaries used in distinctively idiomatic ways. It is said to be a very forthright, positive language, inclined to elaborate on things rather than ideas. It probably had little impact upon Hispanic languages as a whole, for the Basques were few in number, and did not get much embroiled in revolutionary or dynastic conflicts. However, they did have close ethnic links with the Cantabrians, their neighbors to the west, and through them Basque had some impact. For example, sounds associated with *f* were either nonexistent or very rare in Basque, but the sound is common in Latin words. Presumably the

Basques could not pronounce *f* readily, and hence Latin *fabulare* became Spanish *hablar* (to speak) and Latin *facere* became Spanish *hacer* (to make). The *f* sound became a heavy breath and then disappeared; presumably the Cantabrians acquired this pronunciation from the Basques, and in Castilian, Spanish based upon Cantabrian, it later spread widely.[1]

In the light of later developments we should notice these Cantabrians, who, along with the Asturians and Leonese, held some of the northern mountains. A tough lot in a rough part of the world, they threw the Romans out repeatedly, and although pacified under Caesar, they were subdued by neither the Romans nor the Visigoths. Eventually, they developed a sort of cultural center at Oña with the monastery of Castilla Vieja (Old Castle). As Moorish pressure lessened, all these northern peoples tended to expand to the south; the Cantabrians came to the Godos and to Burgos, and eventually beyond to Toledo. Their north central dialect became Castilian, the basis of fashionable modern peninsular Spanish.

As the Middle Ages waned, so did the Mohammedan empire, until it broke up. Christian forays into Mohammedan territory had never ceased; now sizable conquests became feasible, and one by one the ancient Moorish strongholds fell—Cordova, Seville, even Granada; the peninsula was once more theoretically united, and Columbus, fortified with the Queen's jewels, set out to discover a new route to the Orient and found a New World which was to become the new home of Spanish. The old central kingdoms, variously mingled of Goths, Cantabrians, Leonese, and what not, if they were not notably learned, continued belligerent, and it was they who directed the conquest of the peninsula and emerged as the masters of Spain, with all the power and prestige that go with royalty and a royal court. Furthermore, by the ramifications of European politics, the central European Hapsburgs, fortified with the wealth of the Low Countries, became rulers of Spain. Thus the capitals of the onetime Gothic barbarians and mountain-bred descendants of various dawn peoples became, with the Holy Roman Empire, the capital of Europe, insofar as it had a capital.

We must now ask ourselves what all this means for the dialects of the peninsula, and for answers we must return to the northern peoples moving south out of their mountain-girt coast and the Pyrenees. To the west the Galicians swept south in a belt along the Atlantic, but dynastic considerations turned the southern part of this movement into a separate country, Portugal; its one-time Galician dialect is now known as Portu-

---

[1] This development has been the subject of controversy; for a discussion, see William J. Entwistle, *The Spanish Language*, 2nd ed. (London: Faber & Faber, 1962), pp. 160–63.

guese. To the east, the Basques stayed home, while the Catalans bulged south along the Mediterranean shore, enveloping Valencia, but as a kingdom developed with its center in Barcelona, Catalan interest turned toward southern France, the Mediterranean islands, and even northern Africa, where the Catalans made considerable conquests. The dialect of these people, close to French Provençal, is perhaps not sufficiently distinctive to be called a separate language, but Barcelonans will tell you it is, and Catalans today speak it in defiance of the government in Madrid, which has tried to exterminate it. At Montserrat works are still published in it,[2] but it never got far south of Valencia nor spread inland.

In the center Castilian—so-called, presumably, from Castilla Vieja— fanned out as it spread south. During the centuries of this expansion, the kings of the Cantabrian-Gothic central highlands sometimes combined with Aragon to the east or Leon to the west, sometimes overran one or the other. The upshot, however, was that by the time the Christian movement had reached the Guadalquivir River, which runs across southern Spain, Aragon and Leon both had been pretty much occluded, although Leonese-Asturian had strong influences in what is called Estremadura, the southwestern area of modern Spain. To the south was Andalusia and its bordering dialects; it centers on the rich Guadalquivir valley, but it includes also the southern coast and some intervening mountains, both rather barren and now sparsely populated. Dialects deriving from Latin survived here in spite of Arabic, which was the language of the conquerors, very much as English survived in England, despite the French-speaking Normans. Arabic was the language of the rulers, but Andalusians who did not have to deal with rulers did not bother with it much, and the basis of the population remained non-Arabic. Even in Granada, the last great Arabic stronghold, it is said that of 200,000 only 500 were not the children or grandchildren of Christians. There were bilinguals, of course, but even their reputation was such that *ladino,* from the term for the Latinized Moors, implies deceitful, untrustworthy. Many Arabic words were borrowed, and Andalusia abounds in Arabic place names, but the basis of the language, the grammatical and sound systems, along with most of the vocabulary, remained what they had become through natural growth from Vulgar Latin. Thus, linguistically, the main conflict in the Spanish peninsula was that between the Castilians, coming down from the north, and the Andalusians, who occupied the old strongholds of the Moors.

A high plateau, somewhat cut by mountains, comprises central Spain,

---

[2] They are published by the Abadia de Montserrat; they include a series of studies, *Biblioteca Monastica,* local history, *Analecta Montserratensia,* and a religious periodical, *Vida Cristiana.*

generally rather dry and barren. This is the area that Washington Irving describes in the early pages of *The Alhambra*.

In the interior provinces the traveler occasionally traverses great tracts cultivated with grain as far as the eye can reach, waving at times with verdure, at other times naked and sunburnt, but he looks round in vain for the hand that has tilled the soil. At length he perceives some village on a steep hill or rugged crag, with mouldering battlements and ruined watch-tower—a stronghold, in old times, against civil war or Moorish inroad; for the custom among the peasantry of congregating together for mutual protection is kept up in most parts of Spain, in consequence of the marauding of roving freebooters.

But though a great part of Spain is deficient in the garniture of groves and forests, and the softer charms of ornamental cultivation, yet its scenery is noble in its severity and in unison with the attributes of its people; and I think that I better understand the proud, hardy, frugal, and abstemious Spaniard, his manly defiance of hardships and contempt of effeminate indulgences, since I have seen the country he inhabits.

There is something too, in the sternly simple features of the Spanish landscape, that impresses on the soul a feeling of sublimity. The immense plains of the Castiles and of La Mancha, extending as far as the eye can reach, derive an interest from their very nakedness and immensity, and possess, in some degree, the solemn grandeur of the ocean.

These central plateaus will not support much population. At least they never have, and do not now, except that they contain Madrid, the capital city, which has grown as capital cities tend to. The old capital cities of the north had been mountain centers like Burgos and Leon, then Valladolid as the Christians crept south, then Toledo, an ideal medieval capital for a monarch who needed a natural castle, since it is almost completely surrounded by the Tagus River. The cramped little hill of Toledo, however, was no place for a world capital, and Madrid became a place of importance when, in 1561, Philip II selected it as his seat of government, and the city acquired distinction during the eighteenth century, when Charles III poured wealth into it. It had formerly been a village and then a small fort guarding a ford; it was best known for a supposed miracle involving a statue of the Virgin found in a measure of grain.

When Ferdinand and Isabella of Castile and Leon united Spain as a Christian country, the old dialects took on a dramatic new alignment. All Spanish dialects go back to Latin—except, of course, Basque. Only the Romans apparently dominated the country enough, and long enough, to spread their language throughout it. Prudentius, one of the adornments of late classical Latin, was a Spaniard, and Isadore of Seville, the author of a work standard for centuries, betrays his origin in his name. Even the long Moorish occupation, although it seeded Spanish with words beginning *al-* and spattered the southern landscape with place names like *Algeciras* and *Alicante,* never did more than influence the established Latin. Thus for centuries Spanish grew as various sorts of Latinized dialects, as the speech of areas like Seville, as the language that spread with the conquerors from Cataluña, as the tongues of backward areas like Galicia, all sorts of Spanish. But with the aggrandizement of the court of the Catholic Kings, two sorts of Spanish became conspicuous, the fashionable dialect of the court, and all the others, the unfashionable remainder. Thus Castilian Spanish became the "best" Spanish, the "purest" Spanish, cultivated for international use, taught in the schools in Spain and abroad—I recall the outraged horror of an American university department head when a young instructor suggested that he teach Mexican rather than Castilian Spanish—and cultivated by many educated Spaniards to whom the dialect is not native, the *español correcto.* It seems to be spreading, but is still not much heard outside central Spain and parts of the north.

Castilian is a good dialect; there is nothing wrong with it, but to praise it as the "pure" Spanish is nonsense. In fact, the word "pure" does not mean much when applied to language, except that it gives one body of speakers the opportunity to become smug at the expense of another body of speakers. Why is one corruption of Latin purer than another corruption of Latin? And of course the differences between the Spanish dialects are mainly the results of the different ways in which Latin had changed as it developed among Gallegos, Basques, Iberians, Jews, Moors, Cantabrians, and many others. It grew with the different speech rhythms of the volatile Sevillanos in the sunny south and dour Goths on their desolate plateaus. If a pure dialect is one that has not changed, there is no such thing; if a pure dialect is one that has not borrowed, it is likely to be a relatively backward dialect. Certainly English is not the worse for its multitudinous borrowings from French, Italian, Latin, Greek, and dozens of other languages. If the most nearly pure dialect is the one that has changed least, Catalan, although disapproved by the government in Castilian Madrid, should be a good candidate. It seems to be to Spanish what Provençal is to French, an older form of the language, closer to the mother tongue. Galician, also, might be called the purest. As the speech of relatively backward people isolated in their mountains, one would expect it to be conservative, and apparently it is.

Times change slowly in Galicia; even beasts of burden are few. The roads there serve for stout-haunched Galician women carrying huge burdens on their heads, *camiones gallegos* (Galician trucks), as one tourist denominated them. Similarly, Latin sounds, lost in much of the peninsula, can still be heard in Galicia. One of the workhorse words in Spanish is *hacer,* meaning to do or to make. The *h* indicates that it was presumably formerly aspirated, but that sound has been lost, and in most Spanish dialects one is likely to hear it pronounced /aθer/, /asea˞/, or /asɛə/, with no initial consonant sound. This is all that is left of Latin *facere,* but in Galicia you can still hear something like /fakɛrɛ/, /faχɛrɛ/, or /faɣɛrɛ/, which is perhaps not much different from the Vulgar Latin that Roman merchants, soldiers, and workmen brought from Rome, with the Latin initial /f/ still intact and the Latin sound /k/ not much altered.[3]

In short, if Castilian is the purest dialect, one wonders how Washington Irving's illiterate peasants and muleteers managed to purify it. The answer, of course, is that they did not. Languages do not survive by purity; they prosper by the power of their users, and to a degree by their adequacy, which in turn grows from the demands made upon the language. Castilian may well be the most adequate Spanish dialect, because the most has been demanded of it by the most zealous speakers.

Far from being conservative, Castilian seems to have been an inventive dialect, notable for its changes and for the consistency with which these changes moved through the language. In this, circumstances provided some help. During the half millennium of Moorish decline after about the year one thousand, central Spain became the non-Mohammedan center of the peninsula. Cistercians came from France, and many of the important monasteries grew in central and north central Spain. Chanceries like that at Toledo exerted a regulating influence, and literary works like the *Cid*—in spite of a smattering of Judaic and Mozarabic—set standards for Castilian. The late Middle Ages even witnessed a considerable effort to make Castilian an adequate language by deliberately borrowing from Latin, as the cultivators of English did during the Renaissance.[4] All this was not continuous or uniform; for a time Catalan throve, and Galician was preferred for love poetry, since it was thought to be more mellifluous than Castilian, but for centuries the speech that developed from the mountain-dwelling Cantabrians was schooled and developed by the learned, the literary, and the governmental.

We have then, Castilian, the language of the rulers, to a degree a

---

[3] The symbol /ɣ/ is intended to represent the voiced equivalent of /χ/, that is, a voiced velar fricative, about what might be suggested by the sequence *ghghgh,* a *g* sound but continuing instead of stopped.

[4] See Entwistle, *The Spanish Language,* pp. 159–77. The linguistic impact of literary works can easily be overestimated and often has been, but the fourteenth-century and fifteenth-century production in Castilian is impressive.

polite language, noticeably different from other sorts of speech on the peninsula, occupying the center. To the south is Andalusian, from laughing Seville to the lonesome Sierra Nevada, where Moorish influence was longest and strongest, again with its own strong characteristics. The remainder of the periphery of the peninsula was occupied by various dialects, generally more conservative than either Castilian or Andalusian, some of them—Galician and Catalan—so much more conservative that they are sometimes called separate languages.

Which Spanish dialects moved to the New World? Here we encounter some trouble, at both ends of the journey. Linguistic geography, which was our best tool for English, has been insufficiently developed for Spanish.[5] The technique spread early south from France, but publication has been impeded, notably by the civil war and by political differences associated with it—linguistic geography takes time and money. In Latin America projects are apparently only beginning, and accordingly, we must use philological studies. For Spain, these are excellent, especially some recent ones. For Latin America, glossaries of local usages are plentiful, although many of them have been prepared in an amateurish manner by zealous reformers who assumed that Castilian Spanish is Spanish, and that any deviation from it in Latin America must represent corruption, not the survival of a genuine but different dialect. Thus, we cannot hope to speak of American Spanish in the detail possible for American English, but the outlines should be evident.

In a broad way the history of Spanish is strikingly like that of English. English is a descendant of Indo-European through one of the IE daughter languages, Germanic, a language which underwent numerous vicissitudes at the ends of the known earth and changed rather rapidly from a heavily inflected or synthetic language to a strongly distributive or analytic language—that is, it lost such signaling devices as inflectional endings and developed in their stead such instruments as sentence patterns and relationship words. Spanish descends from another daughter of Indo-European, Italic, through Latin, and it too has moved from inflection toward analysis and rather more than have some of its sister Romance languages. That is, the dialects of English can be thought of as mainly the results of several sorts of decay and rebuilding of the primitive language, as these took place in the various British areas, geographical and cultural. Similarly, the Spanish dialects can be thought of as stages and movements in the decay of Latin and the regrowth that accompanied decay.

---

[5] See Novarro Tomas, "The Linguistic Atlas of Spain and the Spanish of America," *Bulletin of the American Council of Learned Societies,* XXXIV (1942), 68–74.

These changes can be pervasive as well as varied. For example, classical Latin had a pitch accent, which sometimes did and sometimes did not become a stress accent, so that the same word may have different accents in various dialects. In language, change of accent can change all sorts of other things. Accordingly, as Scottish and London dialects differed in part because the older grammar decayed in one way in Scotland and another way in southeast England, so Barcelona speech differs from Madrid speech partly because Barcelona is situated in the strongly Romanized Catalan area of Spain whereas Madrid speech grows from the Latin of the isolated Cantabrians and the immigrant Goths. Barcelona is not far from the ancient Roman capital of Tarragona; it faces east upon the same seas upon which Naples and Genoa face west. It was in the Roman corridor along the east coast of the peninsula, and a Roman city grew there—even as I write, parts of it are being excavated under the Christian cathedral. During the long millennium of Moorish occupation, the Barcelonans and their fellow Catalans turned from the Jews and Moors in the south toward the Roman Christians to the north and east. The Latin language changed among them, but we should scarcely expect it to change among these relatively sophisticated, relatively Romanized people as it changed among the somewhat barbarous Godos, hiding in the more barren mountains of the central plateau, harboring whatever they had learned from the Cantabrians and from their own Germanic dialects.

Thus we may expect that, as the North American dialects reflect the various degrees of change from primitive Germanic that developed in the areas from which North American colonization stems, the Latin American dialects will be colored by the nature and rate of decay from Latin—and the corresponding growth that can be expected in a living language—among the Spaniards who were the first to move when the New World was open to immigration.

The qualities of these changes in English and Spanish are remarkably suggestive of each other. English has lost most of the Old English endings; Spanish has simplified the elaborate Latin conjugation of the verb and has cashiered most of the Latin endings revealing case, thus continuing a process already well begun in Vulgar Latin. To replace these case endings, English has developed relationship words like *of* and *under,* developing them from earlier meanings; similarly, Spanish has taken meaningful words and turned them into relationship words. It has greatly increased the use of the prepositions like *ad* and *de,* which were already creeping into Vulgar Latin and building new ones. For example, *adonde,* meaning where, or whither, has been made out of *ad-, -de-,* and *unde,* the latter meaning *place.* Even the new, elaborate verbs are similar. English has made a new future recently by recognizing that verbs of motion imply a future as a result of the motion. "We are going to see about that" presumably can mean that various persons are in motion and that when they arrive at a certain point they will occupy a position from which they can observe. But usually the words would not now mean that at all. "I am going to get married," does not usually mean that the bride is in motion toward the church; she can say this sitting down, or over the telephone. Interestingly enough, Spanish has developed the same future, so that the Spanish word meaning *to go* can be used as *go* is used in English; *vamos a verlo* means literally "We are going to see it," but as in English this would usually indicate simple future. Similarly, the verbs *have, do, make,* and *be* have become auxiliaries in Spanish, and are crowding out the inflected forms where these survive. Even the words for hope, *esperar,* and wish, *querer,* are becoming auxiliaries, as are their English counterparts; when we say "I want to go," we do not express an actual want, and when we say "I hope to go," we are usually doing no more than to indicate that a future is uncertain. I shall suggest later that such verbs may show a livelier growth in American than in British speech. Hispanists find them unusually prevalent in Latin American Spanish.

Similarly, another characteristic of modern English grammar, perhaps notably of American English grammar, may be developing in modern Spanish. I refer to a growing fluidity within predicates, so that words often called verbs, complements, adverbs, and prepositions become so interreliant that the meaning of one determines the use of another. For example, in the sentence *Mary took a tramp in the woods,* Mary may be either an outdoor enthusiast or a juvenile delinquent, depending upon what *took* and *tramp* are doing in the sentence. If *to take a tramp* is thought of as a verb phrase, Mary has been walking, but if *took* is the verb with the complement *tramp,* the sentence reports Mary's sexual vagaries. This confusion of adverbial, verbal, and nominal elements in the predicate is even clearer in a favorite sentence of mine, which I fear I have used elsewhere: *Preparing the barbecue, the host turned on the spit.* If *turned on* is the verb, the host is engaging in routine poolside hospitality, but if *on the spit* is what is called an adverbial phrase of place, then the host is revolving in a gruesome spectacle, rather over-doing his hospitality. Locutions of this sort have been insufficiently studied in both Spanish and English, and in Spanish they are often included among the *numerosas locuciones adverbiales* which are said to be notably characteristic of Latin American speech. For example, *no mas,* which literally means *no more*—a meaning commonly covered by *nada mas*—appears in many Latin American locutions strongly suggestive of verbs, adverbs, and complements. Many of these involve particles like *de, la, al,* and *en.*[6] The whole drift in English will be considered again in Chapter 23.

In the extent of dialectal fragmentation, also, English and Spanish are similar on the two sides of the Atlantic. North American English, as we have seen, is remarkable among the language areas of the earth for its approach to uniformity. Similarly, all students accustomed to the numerous and varied dialects of the Spanish peninsula have been struck by the relative uniformity of Latin American speech. The following is the conclusion of Professor Alonso Zamora Vicente:

> Spanish American presents . . . a consistent homogeneity. Within the vast American territory, the differences are minor, when considered within the whole structure of the language. There are many fewer differences between any two regions in the vast stretches of America, so far as the distinctions one might encounter are concerned, than, for example, between two neighboring valleys of Asturia. Phonetic phenomena repeat throughout the new world, from New Mexico to Tierra del Fuego. Certain regions will evince a preference for this or that phenomenon, but all appear in all parts, and, in addition, all are known in the Spanish peninsula.[7]

For a somewhat similar homogeneity in the dialects of American English, we were able to identify at least three causes. First, some blending had taken place as an incident of migration, so that immigrants who came to Philadelphia, for example, had come from many places in England. We may perhaps assume such blending of Spanish peninsular tongues, as Basques rubbed elbows with Catalans and with speakers of Mozarabic dialects—those that resulted from Moorish influence— whether blending was more or less potent in the southern than in the northward migration. Second, we noticed that some homogeneity resulted from a restricted area of origin, southeastern England; whether

---

[6] For numerous examples of verbal, adverbial, and prepositional uses in Latin America, see Charles E. Kany, *American-Spanish Syntax* (Chicago: University of Chicago Press, 1945), a capable book, although the late Professor Kany was more concerned with recording forms and tracing their origins than with analyzing their functions. See also references in Entwistle, pp. 231–32.

[7] *Dialectologia española,* 2nd ed. (Madrid: Biblioteca Romanica Hispanica, Editorial Gredos, 1960), pp. 306–07. I know no comparable work in English; Kany is cited above. Vicente Garcia de Diego, *Manual de dialectologia española,* 2nd ed. (Madrid: Ediciones Cultura Hispanica, 1959), is also useful and excellent for Galician and Catalan, but is not much concerned with Latin America. The best general treatment in English is that mentioned earlier, Entwistle's *The Spanish Language.* Max Leopold Wagner, *Lingua e dialetti dell' America spagnola* (Florence: Le Lingue Estere, 1949), is more detailed for American Spanish; for current bibliography and scholarly study, files of *Biblioteca de dialectologia hispanoamericana* are indispensable.

emigration from Spain came from a restricted area we must consider. Third, key movements of speakers of English, so far as language in North America was concerned, took place early enough so that American speakers did not participate in sweeping changes that have permeated fashionable modern British speech. These phenomena, also, we must investigate for Latin American speakers of Spanish.

That is, granted that we know something of the European Spanish dialects, the key questions are: who came to the New World, and when? The financial backers of the early explorations, by Columbus and others, were the so-called Christian Kings, Ferdinand and Isabella, and their supporters from the high central plateau, notably Castile and Leon. The emigrants, however, were probably not mainly their supporters. Some of the Spanish treasure-hunters may have come from these groups, but they had just won the riches of southern Spain; they had no occasion to emigrate. Columbus himself was presumably a Genoese who had lately been living in Portugal, and although the Barcelonans claim him as a Catalan, no one supposes he was Castilian. In any event, he and later captains would not have influenced the language much. His pilot, Juan de la Cosa, was a Basque. His crew, apparently, came from the little town of Huelva, the seaport for Seville. They presumably spoke 'Andalusian, with some admixture from Estremadura, which has a somewhat similar dialect, and is in some ways conservative—the Latin *f* long survived there.

This first, conspicuous example might well be exceptional, but there is collateral evidence. Cortes and Pizzaro came from Estremadura, and earlier chroniclers asserted that almost all colonists were Andalusians and Estremadurans. Rural Andalusia was apparently ready to move in the sixteenth century; Arabic agriculture had declined when the Arabs left, and the country people departed for the New World in such numbers as to depopulate the more barren areas. Available documents suggest that of the 124 first settlers in the Argentine, 60 were Andalusians and 20 Estremadurans. Other estimates place the Andalusians as low as 35 to 40 per cent, not more than the combined colonists from Castile and Leon. Later sailing lists show central and southern Spain more nearly equal. Seville, however, had been and continued to be the center of colonial administration, and the southern cities, cities which had flourished with an international flavor since the days of the Moors, continued to dominate the American trade. As Plymouth and Portsmouth on the southern coast of England had been staging centers for North America, cities like Seville, Granada, Malaga, Almeria, Murcia, and Cartagena— along with Lisbon in Portugal—were staging centers for the Americas. Furthermore, as those who could not make a living in the wilder parts of

England came to London, and from London went to the colonies, so Basques and Galicians, who were perpetually overpopulating their mountains, came to Granada, Cordova, and Seville, and from thence went to the New World. Some came from the populous east coast, also, from the vicinities of cities like Alicante, Valencia, Tarragona, and Barcelona.

Thus, although immigration to Latin America cannot at this time be pinpointed, the general distribution seems clear. The Andalusians and their immediate neighbors in the south were the most numerous, so that we need not be surprised if Latin American dialects are dominantly Andalusian. Modern Spaniards will tell you that Andalusians swallow their words, by hiatus, syncope, and apocope—that is, they clip the ends of words, elide syllables within words, and use only a break in sound where there has formerly been a consonant. Farther north children count *uno, dos, tres,* but in much of the south they count *un, do, tre. Veinte-dos* becomes *vent-o,* a sound which can be approximated in English by *bent-toe,* since an initial sound with a *v* is often a stop. Vulgar Latin for a horse, *caballus,* which became French *cheval,* is well preserved in Castilian as *caballo,* but is likely to come out something like *k'vazhuh* /kvaʒʊ/ in middle-class Andalusian. Characteristically, in Mexico, where the word was associated with the ruling "men on horseback," one can hear pronunciations with *l,* /kəvaljo/, /kvalo/, but in the Plata and the Argentine, where horses were more involved in working, one gets the *zh* or so-called soft-*g* sounds, / kvadʒə/, kvaʒə/. Andalusians use what is called the *se-seo* as against the *the-theo;* that is, *c* and *z* are pronounced about like English *s* rather than like English *th* /θ/ as in *think.* They also pronounce *d* about as speakers of English do, whereas the approved, but not universal pronunciation in Castilian is like English *th* in *those* /ð/. Thus an Andalusian pronounces *ciudad* (city) something like *see-o-dahd* /siədad/, but the approved pronunciation in Madrid is *thee-o-thath* /θɪəðað/, with the latter two *th* sounds voiced. Andalusia also uses what is called the *yeismo;* that is, the sound spelled *ll* is pronounced like *y,* as in French. Intervocalic *d* tends to become absorbed in adjacent vowels, so that *cansado* /kansado/ becomes /kansao/, another phenomenon common outside Castilian, although this one appears even in Castilian folk speech.

The next largest group were Castilians, who spoke the ancestor of the present fashionable Spanish, the basis of *español correcto.* These two dialects, Andalusian and Castilian, can be contrasted, although as a matter of fact they are not so far from each other as either is from some other sorts of Hispanic speech, Asturian to the far north, for example, or either of the dialects, Catalan and Galician, that are often called separate languages. Here we should remind ourselves, however, that all varieties of speech in the Hispanic peninsula except Basque have descended from Vulgar Latin, and they differ because of the different dialects of Vulgar Latin and because of the different ways in which Latin has developed under various influences, including the impact of Arabic and Hebrew in the south, of Germanic dialects in the north, of the conservatism of mountainous Galicia and Romanized Cataluña. Thus Latinisms preserved in Andalusia may receive support in the New World by the same Latinisms preserved in other dialects. For example, in Barcelona, and in a good many other areas, *ciudad* is pronounced *see-o-dahd,* as it is in Seville and Granada, not as it is in Madrid, and as we have seen, this is the common Latin American pronunciation. The Aragonians, east of Castile, agreed with the Leonese to the west in preserving the Latin *f* and other peculiarities that the descendants of the Cantabrians in the center had lost. In general, the dialects of Barcelona to the east and of Salamanca to the west, although they are geographically remote from Granada and Seville in the south, are linguistically closer to the speech of those cities than to the dialects of Madrid in the center.

Thus, linguistically, we may divide the Spanish colonists into three large groups, as follows: the Andalusians, especially western Andalusians, the most numerous; the Castilians, less numerous but as a single entity a strong second; all other geographically peripheral groups, who tend to be rather southern than northern. Thus the Andalusians were not only the largest linguistic group, but they got more support from the other dialects than did the central Castilians. Even the northeastern and northwestern groups tended to give more support to Andalusia than to Castile, since the speech of these northern areas is conservative. For example, a speaker of English who knows some Spanish and some Vulgar Latin can blunder through Catalan rather easily; anything that does not look like Spanish to him is likely to look like Latin.

Of course these dialects of old Spain survived variously in the New World. For example, Basques journeyed widely wherever there were sheep to herd; they came in considerable numbers even to the United States, notably to Idaho and Nevada, but they scattered so widely in the mountains that they must be thought of as a moribund linguistic pocket whose dialects do not count for much, whether they speak Basque, Vasco-Spanish, Vasco-French, or all three. Galicians also spread throughout Latin America; they have been exceedingly coherent—the Gallegos are the Scotch of the Spanish peninsula for clannishness—and I am told that Galician societies can be found in Latin-American cities everywhere, but they are dominant over no extensive areas.

Most linguistic groups, however, are not so well defined; apparently the same sort of mixing and mingling that characterizes English-speaking emigrants can be observed among the speakers of Spanish who left for the New World. Nevertheless, as in English-speaking North America, there are differences, and we may expect these to reflect at least three sets of influences: those associated with the source of the immigration, geographically and culturally; those associated with the time of the immigration; and those associated with the reception of the immigrants and of the migrating language.

Five Latin-American Spanish dialects have been identified with some certainty.[8] The Caribbean zone started with Columbus in 1492 and spread through the Antilles to Venezuela and Colombia on a native substratum of Carib and Arawak. Its domination of the islands was extensive. The Mexican zone started in 1519, spread south into Central America, and north into what are now parts of the United States, notably in New Mexico, Arizona, and California; it mingled with a substratum of Maya-Quiche and Nahuatl. Spanish was the language of a relatively sophisticated ruling class, but it penetrated slowly among the Indians. Thus, Mexican Spanish is relatively more conservative than Caribbean Spanish or Spanish of the Plata estuary or of the Argentine, to be mentioned below. The Andean zone started in Ecuador and Peru in 1527 and spread northeast into Bolivia, much of Colombia and Venezuela, and southeast into Argentina, with a substratum of Quechua and Aimara. The role of Spanish here was similar to that in Mexico; it meant wealth and power, and was conservative. The Plata River zone, starting in 1536, based upon the Plata estuary, included Uruguay and Paraguay, with much of Argentina, on a substratum of Mapuche and Tupi-Guarani. Once more, Spanish is associated with wealth and power, but since wealth in the Plata area was more agricultural than mineral, diffusion of the invading language was somewhat more extensive. The fifth zone, the Chilean, from 1541 on, stretches along the western slope of the southern Andes, with a substratum of Mapuche. Diffusion of Spanish here was restricted.

So far as I know, no reliable study has linked any one of these areas overwhelmingly with a specific dialect of the Spanish peninsula. This is not, of course, to suggest that no individual area of the homeland is not more extensively reflected in some parts of the New World than in others. Several studies of Spanish in the Antilles have revealed marked

---

[8] The pioneer work here was that of Juan Ignacio de Armas, *Origenes del lenguaje criollo*, 2d. ed. (Havana: Viuda de Soler, 1882), somewhat elaborated by Henriquez Urena. These results can no doubt be greatly refined, and linguistic atlases have been proposed, but not at this date produced.

survival of West Andalusian, a phenomenon that might have been postulated from the apparently West Andalusian cast of the crews of Columbus and some other early explorers. On the other hand, the Castilian *the-theo* has survived sporadically in the Argentine and in upland Peru, and some areas have preserved archaic evidence of Moorish and Jewish Spanish, but no one European Hispanic dialect has become the unique forbear of a sharply defined South American dialect area.[9]

Thus the geographical sources of Latin American dialects are somewhat obscured, but the time involved can be readily determined. Few Spanish speakers settled in the New World before 1500, and all main dialect areas had Spanish speakers before 1550. We may probably assume that all major dialects would have been well established during the subsequent century, say by 1650, particularly since this was a period of great Spanish expansion.

Fortunately, we need be in no great doubt as to the general characteristics of southern Spanish dialects at the time of colonization. They can be inferred with some confidence from sixteenth-century writings, and many of these characteristics survive today, particularly in the less sophisticated speech. Many Castilians and others from central Spain moved into the conquered areas, and their speech became the fashion, but probably only in the cities, and there only among the select few. Seville and Cordova became Castilian centers, as the most casual visitor to the Alcazar must observe, but the dialects spoken there today are notably not Castilian although they reveal evidence of Castilian influences. Even these northernisms probably did not influence the southern dialects much until after the key emigration to the New World, although many old Castilian forms found their way across the Atlantic, probably because many Castilians did. The basic fact, for Latin-American dialects, is that, whether the immigrants brought with them Andalusian from the south, Aragonian from the northeast, Estremaduran from the southwest, or even Castilian itself, they would have brought these dialects before the distinctive characteristics of modern Castilian had developed.

The dominant inhabitants of north central Spain during the Moorish days, as we have seen, were Cantabrians, Aragonese, Leonese, and those Goths who had elected to stay in Spain, along with some Swabians and others whom they had absorbed. These Spanish Goths were Ger-

---

[9] This material is as yet mainly available in scholarly journals, but much has been digested in the notes to Vicente's survey of Latin American Spanish; see his *Dialectologia española,* cited earlier, pp. 355–61. So far as I know, a proposed study by Peter Boyd-Bowman, *La Procedencia regional de los primitivos colonzadores de América* has not as yet appeared.

manic-speaking peoples. One of their ancient capitals was named Burgos, which is merely the Spanish form of the same Proto-Germanic word that became Old English *burh,* "an enclosed place," which gives us such place names as Edin*burgh,* Canter*bury,* and Peter*borough* along with the American slang term *burg* and the terminal portion of many an American manufactured place name, *Pittsburgh, Newburg, Emmetsburg,* and the like. The Moors pushed many of these Germanic invaders out of the rich southern valleys, but the Goths proved very durable in the rough, semi-arid central plateau and, with the mountain people who pushed south, became the core of those who completed the reconquest of the peninsula. Their regime did not, however, play any large part in world affairs until after the Spanish and Portuguese adventurers in the New World had brought gold and silver pouring into the motherland of Latin-American culture, and in the process of the pillaging, these adventurers had already determined the characteristics of American dialects, basing these dialects upon predynastic Spain. Latin America paid a good price for the blessings of colonialism; European culture and the Spanish language may have been worth it, but it is at least ironical that the language and culture of the Castilian Christian Kings were going out of fashion even as Latin America borrowed them.

To see dramatically what happened, one should visit the Royal Palace (Palacio Real) in Madrid and the Escorial, the royal court, in the nearby mountains. In 1559 the Treaty of Cateau-Cambrésis had left Spain the most powerful country in Europe; Philip II, with the rape of the New World and the pillage of the Low Countries, moved his residence from the medieval hill of Toledo to Madrid, which he and his successors adorned with a nouveau-riche zeal for colossal stone work and a bad taste remarkable even in an era notable for the triumph of pomposity. The Louvre and Versailles, in spite of the art treasures they house, may suggest the overblown self-importance of a statue on horseback, but they have some Gallic lightness, too. The Spanish regal piles are similarly colossal—perhaps they only seem bigger because they are so much heavier—and they are even more lushly ornate. Gold, silver, jewels, statuary, ceramics, paintings, slabs of semiprecious stones, ornate stuffs, and inlaid woods riot with little judgment and no modesty. Gilded cupids flap from the ceilings and dribble all down the walls; rooms gleam in porcelain, florid silk, and polished slabs of stone, and are smothered in lapis lazuli tables and tortured gilt furniture. Tapestry must be measured in acres or hectares, and hangings parade with pompous figures, bulbous cupids, and porcelain-complexioned shepherdesses. They are monuments, these buildings, to too much wealth, too much power, too much pomposity and self-love, too much subservient labor, too little taste, and no restraint at all. One is reminded that a little sense of humor would have saved the Spanish people from these monstrosities and from the Inquisition; they are part of the same mentality, the same divorcement from mankind. Philip II has been called many sorts of criminal, but few observers have accused him of having a sense of humor.

These changes in court life, of course, need not have fashioned language. A fondness for convoluted gilt furniture in the bedroom and Torquemadaism in the torture chamber need not alter the way one pronounces a z; but violent changes in life, isolation, and blending of tongues apparently encourage linguistic change. In France, the nasal vowels and the clipping of terminal consonants grew with the burgeoning of the court. Even in England, as we have seen, where the court was relatively homey and provincial as great courts went in the eighteenth century, a new dialect developed that has changed the complexion of British Received Standard. The Spanish court was a polyglot world to itself as even Hanoverian Britain never became, and that the language developed rapidly is to be expected. The new Castilian became the *español correcto*.

Actually, the developments were nothing unusual as linguistic changes go. Consider for example, the *the-theo,* a pronunciation whereby words spelled with z or c before a front vowel like e are pronounced with the initial sound of English *thin* or *think.* A tale popular among devotees of Spanish in this country ostensibly accounts for the phenomenon. It seems that Philip II lisped—or perhaps it was Charles III, since people who tell this yarn tend to be hazy about detail—and to flatter him his courtiers lisped also. Eventually the habit infected all Castilian speakers. Crimes enough have been laid at Philip's door, but we probably need not convict him of this one, since the tale is improbable on the face of it. Even if he did lisp, and even if his courtiers imitated him, they would have had to corrupt their wives, their wives would have had to corrupt the children's nurses, and the children would have needed time to grow up and have more children before a fad like this could become established, by which time Philip would have gone to his rest and nonlisping kings would have been setting new fashions. The whole tale ignores the fact that favorite words and tricks of phrase can become popular and be picked up quickly, but language-wide changes in pronunciation are much slower and tend to come from broad movements, not from individual limitations.

If this tale is current in Spain, I did not find it there, and we need no special circumstance to account for the shift in pronunciation. Languages are always changing; they drift by dialect, and this change is just the sort that a student of language expects. Furthermore, it was well started long before either Philip II or Charles III. We do not fully understand the etiology of such sound-changes—they are called *drift* in language—but we can describe them. Apparently, in pronunciation, they always take place on the basis of slight changes in the way a sound is made. For example, in English a stressed vowel like that in *hate* has become a vowel like that in *heat;* we can describe this by saying that the sound has moved forward in the mouth. Similarly, in Old English the word for *mother* was spelled something like *modor* and the word for *father* was something like *fader.* That is, in phonetic terms, the voiced Old English stop /d/ become the corresponding fricative /ð/, spelled *th.*

The Castilian change, whereby sounds associated with *z* and *c* in some positions became /θ/, a sound which we spell *th,* can be similarly described. These *c* and *z* spellings in much of Spain and in Latin America represent the sound we associate with *s,* and phonetically the difference between /s/ and /θ/ is very slight. Each sound can be made in different ways, but all require that a flow of air be directed at the upper front teeth. In some pronunciations the voiceless *th* sound, /θ/, is accompanied by a rising of the tip of the tongue, but the essential difference is that for the /s/ the tongue is contoured into a groove so that a narrow jet of air strikes the teeth whereas for /θ/ the tongue spreads the flow of air. For an agile muscle like the tongue, the necessary movement is minor indeed. Especially is this true in Andalusian and in Latin American speech, where the *s* sound is made in conjunction with either the upper or lower teeth and the *th* sound is made in the same area. The confusion is more difficult in Castilian, which uses what is called the *cachuminal s,* made with the tongue on the roof of the mouth, where a *th* sound becomes difficult.

Other characteristics of Castilian represent common phonetic developments, and they are not unusual in character or amount for a dialect undergoing relatively rapid drift. One of these changes is the same as that which took place in English when *modor* became *mother.* The stop /d/ became the corresponding fricative /ð/, that is, the speaker instead of stopping the flow of air completely as in /d/, lets it go rather slowly, making a buzzing sound. We have already observed the working of this difference in the pronunciations of *ciudad,* both *see-o-dahd* in Latin America and much of Spain, *thee-o-thath* /θiəðɑð/ in *español correcto.* Similarly the *español correcto* of double *l* as against the so-called *yeismo* represents a slight difference in the use of the tongue. In English such a spelling has an *l* sound, sometimes a prolonged *l,* as in *spelling.* In French this spelling represents a semivowel, as in *oreille* (ear), roughly a *y* sound, the *yeismo.* Castilian combines the two sounds by the simple device of relaxing the tongue before the *l* sound has quite finished and turning the sound into a vowel. The New World preserves occasional curious survivals of Castilian, especially in areas where the aristocrats were strong; for example, the Castilian cachuminal *s,* mentioned above, which survives sporadically in the New World, as in the sound implied by the spelling *Mexico* as against *Mejico.*

There are, of course, other characteristics of modern Castilian, but these will perhaps suffice. *Yeismo* is presumably declining in modern Spain but is widely heard; it is common if not universal in Latin America. The voiced fricative pronunciation of *d,* /ð/, can be heard outside Madrid, but sparsely; even cultured Barcelonans, for example, do not much use it; it is extremely rare in Latin America. The *the-theo* is somewhat more common in Spain, as against the older *se-seo,* but is restricted to geographical areas and social strata; in Latin America it is rare and often ridiculed as an affectation—as the British and eastern American broad *a* may be ridiculed north of the Rio Grande. Likewise Latin America still scatteringly preserves the old aspirated *h* from Latin *f,* which early disappeared from Castilian but lived on in Andalusian and other geographically peripheral Spanish dialects.

Thus the differences between Latin-American Spanish and peninsular Spanish are rooted in the same causes that have stimulated differences between North American and British dialects. The American dialects, in each case, stem from an earlier form of the language, Spanish of the sixteenth and seventeenth centuries, English of the seventeenth and eighteenth centuries. Languages live and move by dialect, and the dialects of the New World rested only in part upon the dialects that eventually became fashionable in the mother country; the reasons were both geographical and social, since thriving areas do not usually export people, and emigrants are likely to come from middle and lower income groups. Standard speech in the mother country underwent a change based upon the fashions of an emergent court; these new fashions were only sparsely imported into the New World. Thus the movement of English to North America and of Spanish to Latin America can be described in almost identical terms.

Of course, there are differences. On the whole, the highlands of South and Central America, for example Peru and central Mexico, attracted the Castilians; these were rich areas, attractive to the ruling caste, and the climate was not unlike that of the Spanish Meseta. The hot lower countries were not as repulsive to Andalusians as they were to the northerners, notably not to the poorer Andalusians, who no doubt had little choice. Accordingly, Andean Spanish can be distinguished from the more tropical Spanish. Some locutions now thought of as vulgarisms in Spain are characteristic of *gaucho;* some others have been most clearly retained in mountainous Chile. Latin America has sired linguistic developments; languages always do, and rather unusual developments should be expected in an invading language that lives for centuries beside a native language. In many Latin-American communities—and these include considerable cities—Spanish or Portuguese is the language of the formally educated people, but local Indian languages remain the speech of the common people. Some of these local languages have spread; I am told that Quechua has become a lingua franca, a sort of trade language, for vast areas of the Andean highlands where it was never native.

What can we say of these native languages? Did they affect Spanish? Among English-speaking invaders, the native languages affected only vocabulary, and that sparsely, but in Latin America the native languages had a better chance. They lived longer, and in many areas are still thriving. Yet the answer is the same. Amerindians may have provided a body of imperfect speakers who promoted linguistic change, but Spanish did not acquire Amerindian sounds. Spanish did not shift its grammar to account for Amerindian grammar, with a few possible exceptions such as the limited influence of the Quechuan suffix *y,* although many Amerindian languages in Latin-American areas have grammars markedly different from Spanish. Spanish is becoming more analytic, and Otomi is highly analytic, but Otomi has apparently not induced any analytic developments in Mexican Spanish. Some vocabulary has come from native languages, mainly for native objects or practices, and again as in English-speaking America, these words have come from relatively few Amerindian languages. The newcomers encountered one body of flora and fauna in the Antilles, another in the Valley of Mexico, a third in the Andes, and a fourth in what is now Brazil. Accordingly, borrowed words are mainly from Caribbean speech, from the various dialects spoken in the Valley of Mexico—especially Nahuatl—from Quechua, and from Tupi-Guarani. These local words were picked up by the missionaries and spread, so that words which were native in Nahuatl and Quechua now appear to be native in other sorts of tribal speech. Sometimes the Amerindian word will linger on for particular purposes. For example, cattle kept for milk and tended in a traditional manner in the Argentine are known by Amerindian terms, *tambo* or *tambillo,* but a modern dairy with electric milkers requires the Spanish word, *lecheria.*

All this has led to some borrowing of Amerindian vocabulary into Latin American Spanish, probably more than into North American English, but the native portion of the common word stock is not large. Similarly, the impact of aboriginal grammar and phonetics is probably more noticeable south of the Rio Grande than north of it, perhaps because to the south bilingual speakers have been more numerous over longer periods, but the influence of native grammar and pronunciation has been minor. In Yucatan the indigenous glottal stop is supposed to have had some effect on local Spanish, and the Nahuatl suffix -*ecatl* has provided the Castilian suffix -*eca*, -*eco*, as in *Azteca*, and seems to have led to coinages like *bireco* and *chapaneco*, but the demonstrable examples are few. Even the variant pronunciations of *Mexico*, popularly attributed to native influences, one involving an *x* sound /ks/ and one a palatal fricative /χ/, presumably stem from dialectal difference in Spain, not from the Amerindians. All careful studies of Latin American Spanish lead to the same conclusion, that all sounds and all widely used grammatical practices which characterize the speech of the New World can be found in the Old and presumably come from the Hispanic peninsula.[10]

In toto, then, cultivated Latin American speech resembles cultivated Spanish or Portuguese speech, except that it includes more archaisms, reveals more blending of dialects, and contains more survivals from dialects no longer fashionable in official circles, especially from the dialects of Andalusia. American Spanish has grown naturally from sixteenth-century Spanish dialects, although it differs noticeably from Castilian, as indeed do most dialects in modern Spain. Inevitably, the speech of an educated Latin American includes more of what are now "vulgarisms" than does the language of a comparable speaker in the homeland, but this is only another way of saying that the speech of the sixteenth-century folk has survived more in the New World than it did in the Old, south as well as north of the Rio Grande.

To return, then, to our original question: How does an invading language behave? We were able to describe the British dialects in the United States with some particularity. The dialects brought older middle-class and lower-class forms; they mingled forms somewhat, they added to them, but they tended to preserve them and to distribute them in accordance with describable patterns. Linguistically, almost everything in the New World can be traced from the Old. For the conduct of Spanish dialects in Latin America our evidence is not so sharp, but insofar as we have the evidence it corroborates the conclusions for North America, corroborates them so closely that a common general description would serve equally well for either invading language.[11]

---

[10] For an excellent survey, see Vicente, cited earlier, pp. 314–19, 355–61.

[11] In order that Portuguese will not be completely ignored, I might add that apparently similar remarks could be made. See Entwistle, cited above, pp. 278–323, especially 316–23.

We might attempt such a general description on the assumption that, although two bodies of language provide an insufficient sample for generalization, they may be suggestive. Both bodies of language were conservative; their speakers were colonials, looking to the mother country and preserving much of what they had known in the Old World. The bodies of speech tended to standardization; new dialects developed, of course, but the dialects were fewer than in the mother country and revealed some blending of speech through the mingling of emigrants. New language centers were established in the New World, from which new dialects spread. These dialects tended to be made of ingredients from the Old World, and since speakers of the dialects were recruited on the basis of geographical and class distinctions, the speech of the New World represented a great growth of some dialects in the mother country, a neglect of some others. In the bodies of languages considered—although these evidences must be assumed to be in part coincidences—the new dialects emphasized middle-class and lower middle-class speech, especially the speech of selected maritime centers and adjacent areas, and not the fashionable speech of the court. Once a dialect was established in the New World, it tended to resist further influences, even from the homeland. The new dialects increased greatly in vocabulary, in part as a response to the needs of a new life and to new surroundings, but in part by borrowing from the native tongues. In some instances change seems to have been accelerated, but probably from polyglotism that resulted from languages in motion, not from the movement itself. The new dialects, once they had become established, started behaving like any sedentary bodies of speech, although they were vigorously condemned in the mother country, and by some speakers of these dialects, as "corruptions" of the supposedly pure language of fashionable speakers in the mother country.

13

NAME-GIVING, OR HOW TO PLAY GOD BUT STAY IN EDEN

According to the older theology, still variously adhered to, Adam and Eve were evicted from Eden because they had eaten of the fruit of the tree of the knowledge of good and evil, and had thus presumed to be God—as the King James version puts it, quoting the Lord God, "Man has become one of us." But man has found a way to become godlike in a small way, and escape retribution. In fact, if we may credit another Genesiacal account, Jehovah himself initiated Adam into an exploit savoring of the divine.

According to Genesis, Jehovah called all the animals before Adam and let him name them. It may have been so, although giving names is a godlike act. It partakes of the eternal, creating what was not before, for although the word, or the sound, or the concept, or whatever lies back of a name may have been long in existence, the sound had not become a part of this creation until it became also a name. Adam was playing at being God when he called out names for creatures, and it is quite in the spirit of the Old Testament Father in His gentler moods that He was pleased at Adam's childish gestures toward creation.

Men like to play at being God, as children like to play at being men and women. Naming goes deep in us. The Iroquois had a body of names, owned by older members of the group; since no new ones could be created, a baby went nameless until a name fell vacant by death. Heroes in many lands have boasted that they refused their name to no man—though possession of an opponent's name might provide a rascal with magical powers. Parents indulge their godlike powers in having created by giving the child a name, and the name may be second in importance only to the child itself. So, also, with children—"And what is dolly's name?" Even the naming of a boat requires a ceremony, a woman, and a bottle of champagne. When a girl marries, she signifies the new status by changing her name, taking her husband's name as she takes his bed.

A world of difference stands between a land named and one un-named, and just here the New World was different from the Old. In Europe everything was already named, and only new arrivals like babies and boats could be named afresh. A European lived in a land of names. Everything was named, and with names had come order. A named river flowed from named mountains to a named sea, past named villages, with named streets, named houses, named occupants whose named ancestors had lived there time out of mind. Even the babies born there might be named of necessity, Will's son or Lavransdatter, or might of necessity or custom take the name of the saint on whose day they were born. The chirping, yapping, or braying creatures, even the silent fish, were named. Man lived under the hand of God's law, made manifest by the names He had either given or sanctioned.

All this appeared different in the New World. It was not, of course. Everything was named there, too, at least everything within the Amer-indian ken, for hunters, fishers, even pickers of berries, who live at the mercy of terrain and weather, know nature well. The Amerindians had named all salient physical features on the American continents, often many times, for the so-called lands of various tribes were always more or less in dispute, and most portions of the continents must have been swept over again and again by one wave of Amerindians or another. Even in historic times the Sauk and the Fox fought their way from the Eastern seaboard to the Mississippi, the Blackfoot all the way to the Rockies. The lane between the Sierras and the sea, the pathway along which many Indians worked their way south from Bering Strait, saw many peoples. Similarly, most of the prominent living things in the Americas had names, dozens of names. Inedible plants might be pretty much ignored, but anything that served for food—and most living objects, animal or vegetable, served for food, raiment, weapons, or something—had names, usually many names. A duck might be known among one people for its red head, among others for the quality of the meat, the season at which it was taken, its call, the downy quality of the feathers, or their ceremonial use. The Americas were scattered thick with names when the European came here, but of this great name stock the invaders were mainly ignorant, and their descendants are still rela-tively ignorant of it, and likely to remain so.

This seemingly wholesale need for naming, although it had no foun-dation in fact and grew from the ignorance of the invaders, had very real effects among the newcomers. The effects may be difficult to identify, but they must have been there. At least some residue must remain, and it must be widespread. Allen Walker Read has estimated that in the United States alone more than a million names could be traced, and George R. Stewart has raised the guess to three million. Millions more must have gone unrecorded. Whatever the specific effects of this name-giving, it helped make Americans what they are, and presumably had something to do with making them different from their ancestors.

To the invading European, the Americas were disordered, and if the newcomers needed evidence of this disorder, they had it in a world seemingly unnamed. A man could not describe where he was going or report where he had been; no names pinned down mountains, lakes, and swamps. In this new land a man could play God in earnest if he wished. He could look up at the mountain with which he had charted his course, and ask, "What's she called, thet peak." "Cain't rightly say. Don't know as I ever heerd." "Well, I'm goin' ta name her Rose, for my daughter Rose," and the name might stick. This particular name did. An old lady told me how she named a pass through the mountains near the family ranch. Her people had discovered the pass, or so she supposed, and she named it La Paz, a phrase which she found in *Leslie's Magazine,* and which she supposed meant *the pass.* It does not, but naming the pass for peace certainly does no harm, and the event was one of the great experiences of her life, along with being married and having children. American pioneers are supposed to have been a self-reliant lot, who transmitted some of their peculiarities to the national character; they are supposed at times to have been a bumptious lot. If so, they may have cultured the characteristic, playing Adam from coast to coast.

The New World was new, not only in the sense that it was another one; a new dress or a new car may be very much like its predecessor, but the New World was different. The immigrant who came from the flat, wooded lands of East Anglia might know the sea—a considerable number of immigrants came from Norwich, for instance—but the interminable forests of Maine or Michigan, the treeless prairies of the Missouri Valley, the playas and the sage plateaus of the Great Basin, the peaks of the Rockies and the Sierras, the deserts of the Southwest—these were as another world, or another series of worlds. To Britons, especially those from southeastern and central England, even the more mountainous areas of western Massachusetts or the relatively cozy irregularities of the Appalachians would have been unreal, and the waters themselves were inhabited by strangers—the quahog and the muskrat are not known in the British Isles. As for the creatures that flew or crawled or ran, they were an almost entirely new set of earth inhabitants, even those with European relatives being often unrecognizable in their American manifestation. But they had to be lived with, and so they were reduced to something manageable with language—new names, new categories, new ways of conceiving life.

The first names given by European explorers, presumably, were those applied by the Norwegians and Icelanders during the early centuries of our millennium. Even though some early accounts warrant discounting, they seem to attest that the Norwegians called the place Vineland, dubbed the inhabitants Skraelingers, and thought they saw what they called an Einpeddiger, a one-footed man. He popped up out of the brush, shot an arrow into one of the men in a coasting boat, and disappeared so rapidly that the Scandinavians, who have never been famed as sprinters, identified him as one of the legendary unipeds. These supposed creatures, reported by classical writers, were said to have only one foot, so big and flat that when one of them was tired or hot he could lie down on his back and use the foot for a sunshade. He could also leap rapidly on his one foot, and this bobbing speed identified him for the Norwegians; they did not actually see the one foot, but were convinced no normal human could run so fast.

On the whole, the newcomers provided names of two sorts, those attached to the land and those given to the inhabitants. This duality has its interest, because the processes of the two sorts of naming differed somewhat, but an even more important duality affects not only the land and the language, but the namer himself. The first is knowable, although detailed, interesting, and sometimes difficult—who named what, when, and why? But the second, if it must in the end remain unknowable, is even more significant.[1]

Some naming was official and formal, although it did not always remain permanent, and thus many features already well named were rebaptized by successive newcomers. For example, Newfoundland, the "newe-found-land" of Cabot, was not at first so named by the supposed discoverer.[2] The geographer Hakluyt reported,

---

[1] Not always is the standard general work highly readable, but for American names it is: George R. Stewart, *Names on the Land,* 2nd ed. (Boston: Houghton Mifflin, 1958). Mencken includes a good treatment, best consulted in the one-volume edition; see H. L. Mencken, *The American Language,* rev. Raven I. McDavid, Jr. (New York: Alfred A. Knopf, 1963). The standard bibliography is that of Pauline A. Seeley and Richard B. Sealock, *Bibliography of Place Name Literature* (Chicago: American Library Association, 1948), continued in *Names,* the official journal of the American Name Society. For many states scholarly dictionaries of place names are available, of which perhaps the most ambitious is that of Erwin Gudde, *California Place Names,* 2nd ed. (Berkeley: University of California Press, 1960). Superb, also, is Donald J. Orth, *Dictionary of Alaska Place Names,* United States Geological Survey Professional Paper 567 (Washington, D.C.: United States Government Printing Office, 1967). For a general dictionary of American onomastics, see George F. Stewart, *American Place-Names: A Concise and Selective Dictionary for the Continental United States of America* (New York: Oxford University Press, 1970).

[2] For the materials in this paragraph I am indebted to E. R. Seary, "The Anatomy of Newfoundland Place-Names," *Names,* VI (1958), 193–207.

In the yere of our Lord 1497 John Cabot . . . discovered that which no man before that time had attempted, on the 24 of June, about five of the clocke early in the morning. This land he called Prima Vista, that is to say, First seene, because as I suppose it was that part whereof they had the first sight from the sea.

Apparently Basque fishermen were already there; not only did Montreal record a Port aux Basques, but the modern Port au Port, which seems to mean nothing, derives from *Apphorportu,* which apparently includes the word *port,* for harbor, but also apparently includes an old Basque word for a bowl, the latter perhaps suggested by the shape of the harbor or the milk-bowl calmness of the bay. The Portuguese named the island for their king, *Terra del Rey de Portugall.* The French scattered the island with names, and misunderstood the English ones; thus Tickle Harbor became *Havre chatouilleux. Tickle,* in older English, meant a strait difficult to negotiate, but *chatouilleux,* as the Larousse puts it, is to be "susceptible to repeated light touches which ordinarily provoke laughter." In their turn the English misunderstood the French; Sebastian Cabot, presented with the French form of the Eleven Thousand Virgins, *Onze mille virgines,* produced a handsome, Indian-like name, *Onsemilyogines.* Thus almost everybody associated with the island in exploration or settlement misunderstood everybody else and corrupted the others' names; even more frequently, one body of national name-givers ignored the others, probably because they never heard of them.

Official names often complimented official persons—*Virginia* for the Virgin Queen, the *Carolinas* for the Latinized form of King Charles's name, *Georgia* similarly for King George, and *Maryland* for Queen Mary. Among the French, La Salle named the regal west for his sovereign, Louis, calling it *Louisiane,* and Cartier named for the saint of the day, St. Lawrence, the river whose estuary gave him harbor. The Spanish were even more zealous in spreading the names of saints (*San Diego, San Francisco, Santa Barbara, Santa Catalina, Santiago*), honor to pious objects and practices (*Santa Cruz, Vera Cruz, Sacramento*), and salutes to their sovereigns (*Monterey, Point Reyes,* the *Philippines*). Explorers and immigrants everywhere tended to name the new land for the old: *New England, Nouvelle France, Nieu Amsterdam, Nueva España,* including *Nueva Galicia, Nuevo Leon,* and hundreds more. Even Sir Francis Drake, not to be outdone by the Spaniards who scattered the names of saints from Santa Ines in Tierra del Fuego north to beyond San Mateo, named a cape in Alaska for a pious Briton, the Venerable Bede. Various salient features were named, sooner or later, for the explorers themselves, *Hudson, Champlain, Magellan,* and even for cartographers, *America.*

With time, formal naming became organized. In New England, the General Court determined names, tending to prefer former homes of the immigrants. "Whereas it hath been a commendable practice of the inhabitants of all the Colonies of these parts," the Court observed, "that as this country hath its denomination from our dear native Country of England, and thence is called New England, so the planters, in their first settling of most new plantations have given names to those plantations of some Cities and Towns in England, thereby intending to keep up and leave to posterity the memorial of several places of note there, as Boston, Hartford, Windsor, York, Ipswich, Braintree, and Exeter. . . ." The Court concluded that, in view of the recent triumphs over the Pequots, the Jurisdiction of Connecticut had a harbor to name, and in order that they might "thereby leave to posterity the memory of that renowned city of London, from whence we had our transportation, [they, the Court] have thought fit, in honor to that famous City, to call the said plantation, New London."[3]

This official determining of important names was continued after confederation, with Congress designating the names of territories when they were formed and of states when they were admitted. By this time a predilection for Indian names had developed, sometimes supposedly genuine Indian names like *Tennessee, Oklahoma, Illinois, Iowa, Utah,* and *Dakota,* sometimes trumped-up names like *Indiana,* or words of dubious ancestry like *Oregon* and *Idaho. Texas* was presumably a word of greeting, but it was mistaken for the name of a people. Some words underwent odd journeys and curious transmogrifications. A west Pennsylvania valley, which the Delawares named something like Mecheweam-ing, meaning "place of the big flats," was the scene of an Indian massacre, celebrated in a sentimental poem, *Gertrude of Wyoming,* the Indian name having been cut down by natural erosion to something that could be spelled. The piece became popular, and *Wyoming* was borrowed into sundry novels and poetic effusions, turned up as the name of counties in three states, and was rapidly picking up post offices when it was commandeered by Congressman James M. Ashley on the theory that it was a "beautiful name," however unsuited it might be to a mountainous Western state in the short-grass country.

This whole question of Indian names and what they mean has been an amusing and baffling one. That words are folk-etymologized from strange languages is widely known; a burned area was called in French *Bois Brulé,* burned woods, and has become Bob Ruly. A band of contentious fellows died unshriven after brawling, and since, at best, they

---

[3] I owe the citations to Stewart, cited earlier; see pp. 52–53.

would go to a Spanish purgatory, a stream where their bones were discovered was called El Rio de las Animas Perdidas en Purgatorio, "River of the Lost Souls in Purgatory." French trappers understood the sequence well enough and translated the last word into *Purgatoire,* but subsequent cowboys had no feeling for the words, and made it *Picketwire.* Pleasant vagaries of this sort are to be expected in folk speech, but what might be called the "Old Indian Fallacy" permeates American onomastics, even among well-educated solid citizens—onomastics, or onomatology, is the serious study of naming.

Apparently, something about an ancient Amerindian inspires confidence. Anyone even noddingly acquainted with the ways of the human mind in the presence of a fact knows that uneducated doddering white men—or doddering white women, for that matter—cannot be trusted to cackle out reliable history or etymology, especially the etymology of an ancient form of the language. But for the same reason, "old Indians" are supposed to know; if you want to discover what an Amerindian place name means, all you need do is ask an old Indian, almost any old Indian. Whatever his native speech may be, anything he replies will be the true etymology, even though the next old Indian may toss you a quite different answer.

With all respect to Amerindian integrity, such childlike faith is peculiarly inappropriate when one is dealing etymologically with aged aborigines. In the first place, most old Indians do not and did not know English very well, especially those old Indians who were alive when Amerindian names were being widely adopted. Nor did the interrogators know native languages very well. Usually both the informant and the interlocutor were incapable of discussing a linguistic question in any language that the two had in common, and the problem is more difficult than either speaker was likely to assume. We have already seen that Amerindian languages are basically different from Indo-European languages, and thus when a white man asks for a word he is likely to get a syllable, or some sort of phrasal combination that is not at all what he requested. Neither he nor the Amerindian knows that they are completely and fundamentally misunderstanding each other. Furthermore, the average Amerindian is no more likely to be able to tell you what Minnesota means than the average dweller in New York is likely to be able to explain how the name of his city is related to a word for a yew tree. Furthermore, some of these Indian names can be what Mencken conservatively calls "very formidable." He cited *Quohquinapassakessamamagnog* and *Chargoggagaugmanchaugagoggchaubunagungamaugg.*[4]

---

[4] In the Mencken/McDavid volume, cited earlier, p. 646.

Thus, the old Indian is likely to be entirely unreliable, even if he is laboring to be informative. Many Amerindians did not so labor. Even well-disposed aborigines were likely to become so wearied with what they considered the silly questions of white men that they were inclined to agree to anything, just to get rid of a bore. Or, as Mencken has pointed out, they might answer the request for a name with the equivalent of "Go to Hell!" Furthermore, not all Amerindians were well intentioned. Many have hated white men with cold fury and good reasons; if they could no longer tomahawk a white man, they could indulge a delicate revenge by telling their white brothers preposterous fibs, which any local red man could detect, but which a gullible white man could not. Behind almost any Amerindian's stolid exterior, a lively sense of humor may play, and he may indulge a peculiar delight in making a fool of the lordly conqueror.

But let us take an example, and *Idaho* will serve as well as another.[5] Various etymologizers have traced it to Comanche and Shoshone—although the Shoshone I have talked to say they never heard it. Here, however, we are in no great difficulty because the languages are closely related, and the word may well occur in both, if it occurred in either. Apparently it was first recorded in 1859, when gold discoveries in the "Pikes Peak area" spurred agitation for a new territory. The first permanent white settlement in the vicinity had been called Idahoe Springs, and when the Senate committee considered the problem, the gossip was that of the various proposed names, including *Yampa,* "a bear," and *Lula,* "mountain fairy," the choice was likely to go to *Idahoe,* supposed to mean "Gem of the Mountains." Suddenly the name was dropped. It had been proposed by the territorial delegate, but as Professor George Stewart suggests, "Possibly he feared that like many other Indian names it meant something better not translated."[6] After all, *Chicago* meant some kind of big stink; it had been innocently adopted by the citizens of what was formerly Fort Dearborn, and now they were saddled with it, although the local boosters had no desire to learn just what kind of stink was intended. As for *Idaho,* this is not an implausible guess; after all, the word had apparently come from *Idahi,* a Kiowa-Apache epithet for the Comanche, and the nicknames of one tribe for another notably involved insults, being homely terms that might be delicately rendered as "sources of foul odors," "eaters of feces," "performers of unnatural acts," and the like. Whatever the reason, the Senate committee suddenly dropped *Idahoe;* a Democrat proposed *Jefferson,* but a Republican

---

[5] Much of the information is surveyed in an anonymous article [H. J. Swinney?], "New Notes on the Word 'Idaho,'" *Idaho Yesterdays,* II, no. 1 (1958), 26–28.
[6] In *Names on the Land,* cited earlier, p. 303.

demurred, and they agreed on a sonorous Spanish word whose translation could be known, *Colorado*—the senators, orators all, tended to like sonorous words that could be rolled off the tongue.

Idaho, however, was not finished. It had become known as a possible name for something, and it cropped up on a steamboat associated with a man from the Snake River valley, as a mining name when there were silver strikes in the area, and as a county name given by the Washington legislature—the Snake River valley was at that time part of Washington. When the Snake River country was about to become a territory itself, the name of *Idaho* was again proposed, but that great name-giver James M. Ashley was opposed. He had a new candidate, *Montana.* After a lively exchange *Idaho* won, apparently because legislators were convinced that it meant "Gem of the Mountains"—and what could be at once more flattering and more appropriate? *Montana* had to be kept in reserve until another mountainous area appeared as a candidate for territorial admission.

For a time, apparently, no one pointed out that "Gem of the Mountains" was palpably an implausible translation—the Indians had no gems. Nor could anyone devise an interpretation by which this concatenation of syllables could mean *Gem of the Mountains* anyhow. But the interpretation persisted. It was too good to lose.

Now a man by the name of John H. Reese enters the story. Idaho in the early 1900's was not a highly sophisticated area, and Reese was, for his time and place, an unusual person. He was a high-school teacher, and hence relatively learned, and his family had operated a trading post, so that he had a working knowledge of the local Shoshone dialect. He was a scholar at heart, and contemptuous of other local historians, whom he considered amateurish; he produced a book called *Idaho: Chronology, Nomenclature, Bibliography* (Chicago, 1918), which was widely accepted.

Reese asserted that *Idaho* was a corruption of *Ed-dah-ho,* the first syllable meaning *down,* the second either *sun* or *mountain,* and the final syllable an exclamative. The relatively conservative *Idaho Guide* accepted this to the extent of assuming that the word meant something like "the sun is up," roughly the equivalent of "Good Morning," but not all writers were conservative. Since *dah* could be either *sun* or *mountain,* they assumed that it was both and asserted that *Idaho* meant, "Behold! The sun is coming down the mountain!" Furthermore, this new interpretation was linked with the earlier one, and one local historian wrote that the Indians "beheld a lustrous rim of light shining from the mountain top. The radiant mountain crown or diadem was likened to a gem glittering from a snowy peak."

We should now ask ourselves how Reese knew that *Idaho* was a corruption of *Ed-dah-ho,* syllables of which he thought he could make some sense. If they were corruptions, why not corruptions of something else, of which he could not make sense, or made unreliable sense? Here we might fruitfully look at a dictionary of American Indian terms. We shall notice at once that all Indian names of any consequence appear in dozens of forms, only one or two of which have become common, usually by accident. For example, a group of Indians may be called either *Chippewa* or *Ojibway;* actually, these terms resemble each other phonetically, but some are so remote that we wonder how two human sets of ears could have produced such variant results from a common original until we recall that sounds are elusive, that the ears were not trained ears, and that many sounds in Amerindian languages have no equivalents in Indo-European languages. Untrained people, some of them not very bright, were recording, after a lapse of time that would have dulled memory, sounds that they had no way of writing, even if they had any precise way of hearing. For example, a city in this same Idaho is called *Pocatello,* presumably named for an old chief of the vicinity; I have talked with the chief's surviving relatives, who pronounce his name in a way that I cannot represent accurately in English spelling, but it would be suggested by something like Puckendarryuh /pʌkəndaʀjə/.

Now we should notice another source of uncertainty. Since we do not know exactly what was recorded, we do not know how to interpret it. We might take an analogy from English. We might take two syllables, any two syllables, but let us assume that a Negrito thinks he has heard me say something which could be written *Ma's horse.* He interprets this as best he can, but suppose I have actually said *Ma's hoarse,* since she has a cold, which would provide quite a different place name with a very different meaning. Now suppose I happen to have a Southern accent— and of course all Amerindians, like everybody else, spoke in dialectal accents—so that I pronounce *my* rather like *mah,* and what I really mean to say is *my source* (mah source). Only slight inaccuracies in recording—much less than the difference between *purgatorio* and *picketwire*—would produce *Ma's worse, mice wars, muss haws, mah* (my) *sores, my saws* (horse being pronounced *haws*), and dozens of others with hundreds of possible "meanings." Thus the only reputable students of Shoshonean dialects that I know insist flatly that they have no way of knowing with any certainty what *Idaho* means, if, indeed, it means anything and is not merely an inexplicable blunder.

So much for the Old Indian Fallacy, which started to work at least as early as Captain John Smith, who recorded *Patowomek* (also recorded as *Potowanmeak*), now spelled *Potomac,* and *Saquesahanock,* now spelled *Susquehanna.* Smith had the impression that these were names of some local Indians, but he knew relatively little about the Indians of Virginia, to say nothing of those to the north—Indians called the Suquehanoughs seem also to have been called the Andastes and the Wighcocomocoes. The process of bestowing and misinterpreting Indian names continues, and is likely to augment notably in Latin America, as the back country, well seeded with Indian names, fosters more and more population centers. One result of all this has been that sound students of onomastics have tended to shun Amerindian place names, understandably preferring to say nothing rather than talk nonsense. The state of native American linguistics was such that they felt they could not work with confidence. Now, however, all this is changing; every year additional studies of Amerindian languages see the light of print, and this development has now gone so far that the appropriately conservative American Name Society has reversed its position and has celebrated its active search for studies of native place names with a "Special Issue on Indian Names."[7]

The process of bestowing official names, begun by the explorers, continued by institutions like the General Court of New England, and inherited by Congress for territories and states, has more recently been absorbed for the lesser communities by other bodies. Railroads have been great givers of names. In the eastern states, railroads tended to link existing communities and to produce few new names; farther west, although a railroad might run from one named place to another, it would give rise to stations which became communities, taking their names from the station named by the railroad. In the Far West, when a railroad opened up hundreds of miles of relatively uninhabited country, a railroad official might write out names by the dozens, turning to some list or other when his ingenuity failed. One division superintendent apparently fancied Romantic poets—*Goethe, Schiller, Ossian*—and one preferred composers, *Wagner* and *Verdi,* the latter now pronounced *vurdie.* In the more remote areas the Park Service and the Forest Service have given names; particularly, they have endeavored to discover and preserve little-known names, but they have also hesitated to give official sanction, by writing them on government maps, to names preserving an analogy with the more private parts of an Amerindian woman's anatomy and to the male genitals. One, however, has notably survived; *Trois Tetons,* a name given by early trappers to three prominent peaks in what

---

[7] *Names: Journal of the American Name Society,* XV (1967), 157–242. See particularly the "Introduction" by the special editor for the issue, Hamill Kᵉnny.

is now Teton National Park, was too well established to be tampered with, and the words being French, the mammary implications are lost on many speakers of English.

In recent times the great giver of official names has been the postal department in Washington. It could not name communities, of course, but it could refuse to handle mail except to post offices which had been approved, and it could refuse to sanction names already pre-empted by another community in the state or an adjacent state. Thus communities ambitious to honor George Washington, or to advertise themselves with *London* or *Bellevue,* found that name after proposed name was vetoed by the postal authorities. In desperation—after all, one must get the mail—many a local official has written to Washington asking for a name that would be approved. Thus one postal official admitted naming towns after all his relatives and "all the kids in the block."

Perhaps the most common names in the Americas as elsewhere—at least in English-speaking America, which has fewer religious names than Latin America—are those that have arisen from the land itself, from people living on the land, with relatively little name-giving by any specific individual. A sandy hook is so designated because it is one, and in course of using the description the sandy hook becomes Sandy Hook. The inlet nearby, where the natives found oysters, became the oyster bay, and then Oyster Bay. Of two streams, one became Big Creek, which can be traversed either at Salt Lick Ford or Oxbow Crossing. Maps of the West wriggle with stream beds named Dry Creek, a term apt in most seasons. And so it went; necessary descriptions of terrain in an unnamed land became place names. Sometimes, of course, individuals were involved, especially in the presence of death. When a man was killed, his companions would name the spot for him; so a stream was named for Pere Marquette, and once a name becomes attached to a stream it may name a county, a city, a university. Even unidentified bones are enough to name a stream Deadman's Run. A spot may be named conveniently for its inhabitants; the intersections where the Joneses live is called Jones Corners, and the island where hogs are left for safekeeping, Hog Island.

Natural salt is responsible for a pattern of names in the Ohio River valley, where salt water trapped in geologic times worked up through noncomformities and on reaching the surface left deposits of sodium chloride, which account for salt rivers, salt springs, and areas where the dirt is so impregnated with salt that animals would lick it. These local saline deposits have long since lost both their economic and their sporting importance, but the valley is now scattered (see Map 6) with place names like *Lick, Licking, Salt, Saline,* and *Mahoning,* the latter ap-

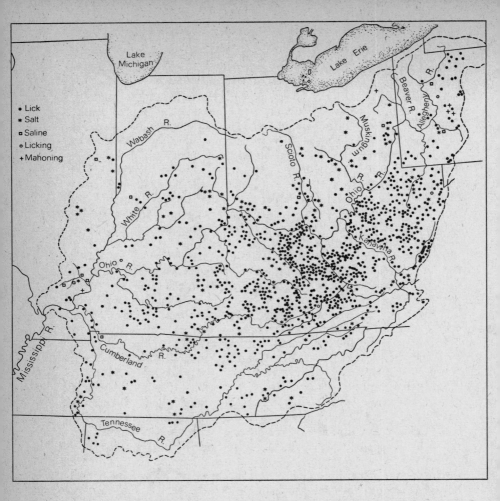

Map 6. Salt-Derived Place Names in the Ohio Valley. *(Adapted by John A. Jakle from his map first appearing in* Names, *XVI [March 1968], drawn by James A. Bier; used by permission of Professor Jakle.)*

parently from Delaware *m'hoani,* "salt lick," since hunting-minded Amerindians would have known the likely places to lie in wait for game. Names like *Blue Water* and *White Water* may also derive from the presence of salt.[8]

Closely related are the names that celebrate good hunting or fishing— *Raccoon Creek, Bear Valley, Buck Canyon, Pickerel Point, Catfish Slough;* such names were scattered everywhere by men who had to live wholly or in part from the land. A place might be named for its notable denizens, *Rattlesnake Hill* and *Pigeon Roost,* whether or not for a specific event. Captain John Smith named Stingray Isle for the strange fish that stung him there—and eventually provided his dinner—and one Anthony Parkhurst reported to Hakluyt that in the New World there were "many other kinds of birdes store, too long to write, especially at one Island named Penguin, where wee may driue them on a planke into our ship as many as shall lade her. These birds are also called Penguins, and cannot flie."[9] As a matter of fact we do not know, in this instance, whether or not *penguin* means "white head," and if so whether the white head refers to the top of the bird or the top of a white headland, but it all illustrates a widespread principle, that the names of places and their habitants play back and forth in name-giving.

This sort of thing has presumably happened all over the world. Many Amerindian names seem to be the simplest sorts of description of terrain: *Mississippi* is presumably Big Water, and even *Tia Juana* is not Aunt Jane in Spanish, but only what folk etymology did to Amerindian *tiwana,* which apparently means something like "by the sea." In many parts of the world these words are old enough to be difficult to decode— as are the Amerindian words—but words given by the newcomers are usually in known languages, although these are not always recognizable to everyone. Take, for example, the older names in New York City. The *Bowery* is from De Bouwerji, "the farm," since there was a farm there in the days of the Dutch. Farther up the island, the *Bronx* is where the Broncs lived, and since Colen Donck was an important man, a Jonk-heer, his place was known as the Jonkheer's, *Yonkers. Vlacht-bosch* did not have to change much to become *Flatbush,* nor *Brede Weigh* to become *Broadway.* Wall Street is named for any number of uses of the word *waal,* including the equivalent of *wall* and a Dutch term for an anchorage. *Krum Marisje,* "the little crooked marsh," became the *Crummashie,* which looked strange enough to be an Indian name, and by folk etymology became *Gramercy Park.*

Some names record supposed, or at least desired manifestations. In

[8] John A. Jakle, "Salt-Derived Place Names in the Ohio Valley," *Names,* XVI (March 1968), 1–5.
[9] Quoted in Seary, cited earlier, 196–97.

Latin American areas ecclesiastical and political virtues are honored—
La Libertad, Esperanza, and *Progreso* (liberty, hope, and progress) are
within a few miles of one another—but the English-speaking immigrants, with a strong Protestant bias, produced *Fort Patience, Hope-in-
Faith,* and best known of all, *Concord.* The fad, however, never grew
strong; even *Philadelphia,* "The City of Brotherly Love," set no great
fashion among the Quakers, and a name like *Liberty* became a bit
ridiculous when it spawned *North Liberty* and *West Liberty. What
Cheer,* Iowa, and *Why Not,* North Carolina, are difficult to take seriously, but the practice continues with *Truth and Consequences,* New
Mexico, one of the more recent.

One place-naming pattern is apparently a North American growth,
sired by William Penn. Here we should notice the older machinery for
identifying an address, a means that is now so foreign to American ways
of thinking that it requires explanation. Addresses in England and on
the Continent did not formerly include numbers, or streets in the sense
in which they are now conceived in this country, as thoroughfares
treated as wholes. A designation like King's Parade or Bishop's Gate did
not indicate a continuous road-like access to addresses, which would
have one name however far it might extend. It was an area, an area that
comprised the land fronting upon a road or street, usually only a few
blocks of this frontage. If one had an address to seek, in Cheapside at
the Sign of the Elephant and Castle, he had only to go to Cheapside—
and in a community of moderate size all natives would know where this
area was to be found—and look about for the proper sign. This worked
very well if the community was not large; it would work for people who
could not read and write or even count.

To see how this worked—and in some areas still works—we might
look at a thoroughfare in London, which would be recognized as one
street in the United States. Running through the heart of the city, it
begins at the west margin of my map as Goldhawk Road, but soon
becomes Holland Park Avenue and then Notting Hill Gate. For some
distance it is Bayswater Road, then Hyde Park Terrace and Hyde Park
Place, and approaching the city center, Oxford Street. Oxford Street
gives way to New Oxford Street, which becomes Holborn, sometimes
called High Holborn, then Holborn Viaduct, then Newgate Street, which
is momentarily Martin's le Grand before it becomes Cheapside. At some
of these intersections a thoroughfare cannot be identified with certainty,
but this street seems to continue as Cornhill Leadenhall Street, Aldgate
High Street, Whitechapel High Street, White Chapel Road, Mile End
Road, Bow Road, and High Street before it gets off the other side of the
map.

This concept of a street as more an area than an endless thoroughfare presumably accounts for the British idiom, "He lives *in* High Street," whereas an American would say "He lives *on* Fifth Avenue." In the United States to live *in* the street is to live between the gutters, whereas in England to live *on* a street is to murder the Queen's English.

The cities of the Old World were not planned, of course, and even the earlier American cities were not laid out, as the narrow meanderings in older Boston still attest, but when Penn planned Philadelphia he did it with a chart. Being a Quaker and no respecter of veneration to persons, he began at one edge of the plat and called the first street First Street, followed by Second Street, and so on to the other edge of the chart. To avoid involving human individuals, he named cross streets for "things that spontaneously grow in the country," Vine, Walnut, Chestnut, and the like. The scheme was practical, sensible, well adapted to promoters laying out cities in the wilderness, convenient in a society notable for the high proportion of its strangers, handy for a nation of travelers and people who had recently moved, or were about to. As other eastern cities grew, they adopted it, and it spread west everywhere. For example, at the extreme northwest the last considerable community is Bellingham, Washington; it is somewhat cut up by a bay, a creek, and an estuary, but it has numbered streets crossed by Holly, Chestnut, Maple, Laurel, and Myrtle. Some towns have used letters for cross streets, or names like those of the states in alphabetical order, or the presidents in the order of their succession. Palo Alto, California, a university community, made its salute to learning by naming streets for colleges—Bowdoin, Hanover—and for poets—Chaucer, Longfellow, Tennyson, all in convenient alphabetical order, and the same practices have appeared in St. Louis and Cleveland.

In the South, and in some other areas, Penn's system was somewhat altered to permit a central square with a park and a bandstand, but in general, North American communities built after the Colonial days were squared off into rectangles with some kind of number system, usually with a hundred numbers to a block. The system was improved; thoroughfares going one way were called streets and those at right angles were called avenues, with designations like *boulevard, road,* and *lane* reserved for thoroughfares going in odd directions, and *alleys* used for thoroughfares between the more important designations. This system permitted the use of numbers in both directions. With a sure point from which to start, such as the rectangular intersection of two rivers, this system permitted immediate and certain identification of any point within the city, although an occasional town would lose First Street and Second Street when a river undercut a bank, or acquire Front Street, Commercial Row, and the Embarcadero when land was reclaimed from a lake or the ocean.

Most communities have not had guaranteed rectangular boundaries, and accordingly have not pushed the system to its logical conclusion by starting with a central point and using a sequence of numbers, letters, and points of the compass, working in all directions from this central point. Some have; they can number all streets one way and all avenues the other, and add designations like NE and SW. Or they can use numbers in one direction and letters in the opposite direction and use only names like North First Street and East A Avenue. Even older communities like Cedar Rapids, Iowa, and Salt Lake City have been able to apply a four-way system to a city not originally so denominated. Now all this order is succumbing to a new confusion, since popular real estate developments, and even those only pretending to be popular, incline to have neither streets nor avenues, but *drives, courts, circles, places, terraces,* and *parkways.*

Some peculiarities, including the development of generic terms, grew from the nature of the land and the way it was explored. The Amerindians had named rivers by segments, very much as the British named streets as areas, but as Professor Stewart has pointed out,[10] American practices differed. An explorer like La Salle, sailing down a river, called all of it by whatever name seemed appropriate when he first encountered it. On the other hand, settlers working up a stream tended to think of it as though it were treelike and to designate its tributaries as branches, and produce the North Fork of the West Branch of the Yuba River. A smaller stream might become a *run* above tidewater where the water always ran in one direction. The peculiarities of a new land, unlike the more parklike British Isles, led to the twisting of old terms to new uses and the adoption or adaptation of words from other tongues—*bayou, canyon, bluff, arroyo, slough, hollow, coolie, swamp, neck, knob, hogback, mesa, pond, beck, bald, park* (in the sense of mountain meadow), *bottom, plaja, barren, hole* (in the sense of a mountain valley), *notch, gap, swale,* and many more.

Various movements scattered names locally. The Latter-Day Saints named Nauvoo, Illinois, and then spattered Utah with names out of the *Book of Mormon,* the *Pearl of Great Price,* and other of their sacred books—*Moroni, Nephi, Manti,* and *Lehi*—along with *Deseret,* the name of the new Promised Land, and words in its praise like *Vernal* and *Bountiful,* and the names of the leaders: *Logan, Ogden, Brigham,* and *Smith.*

Among the name-giving phenomena of the Far West is a folkloristic figure, a sort of onomastic Johnny Appleseed of the mining camps, asso-

---

10 See *Names on the Land,* cited earlier, pp. 94–95, 131.

ciated with the prospectors and "boomers," those who followed the
latest mining boom. Among the equipment of his trade was a stock
of names appropriate for mines. In any occupation where fortune or
poverty could shift with the turn of a spade—either on the card table
or in the new "diggings"—superstition could be expected to thrive, and in
naming mines it did. Some prospectors and boomers had favorite names;
they had once "struck it rich," and had subsequently lost it all on wine,
women, and stud poker, but they continued to encourage good luck by
giving every new-staked claim the name that had once brought wealth.
Others used hopeful names—*Lucky Boy, Bullion, Gold Nugget, Bo-
nanza,* and *Solid Silver*—or names associated with famous mines or
mining areas, such as *Golconda, Potosi, Ophir, Empire, Mother Lode,
Monterey, Comstock,* and *Gold Hill.* Sometimes legends fostered these
names; perhaps the most widespread is that, while a prospector was
making camp, his donkey indulged in ore-producing antics. She was
most likely to aim a hoof at her owner, and be awkward enough to hit a
nearby rock ledge, knocking off a hunk of pure silver. If one can believe
the legends, the West was raining with debris from the hooves of non-
dexterous asses. As a matter of fact, there were no clumsy mules or
donkeys in the mountainous and desert West; clumsy quadrupeds could
not survive there, but they have lived in legend, and they scattered the
West with variants upon *Jackass,* which gave rise to *Jackass Flats,
Jackass Well, Jackass Pass, Jackass Diggings,* and the like.

Of course, any number of these tendencies might have worked together; we do not know why mines are named *Burning Moscow,*
whether somehow from the burning of Moscow in the Napoleonic Wars
or from folk etymology involving *mosca,* Spanish for "fly," whether
horse flies, jackass flies, or fireflies. One of the most persistent names
was *Yellow Jacket.* Whether the name originated from a nest of stinging
insects, a piece of raiment used as a flag, or some as yet unguessed folk
etymology, it is scattered on the pages of western claim books and on
hundreds of desert hills. I once found some mining stakes, on which the
details of the claim had been painted with some substance that had
preserved the wood long enough to leave the writing in relief. So far as I
could learn, nobody had ever found anything on the barren hump on
which these stakes stood, but the area had once enjoyed a mild boom.
As I half expected, the raised letters read *Yellow Jacket.* Often mining
stakes were less evidence of mineral than of the omnipresent boomer
with his Autolycus' pack of names.

Humor has perhaps not been a notable characteristic of American
name-givers, but the New World offered opportunities for onomastics
that are probably unique. Never before had a great continent been over-

run so quickly and so completely as was North America. All this came to a climax in the West, where hundreds of thousands of miles were roamed by a relatively few thousand whites, mostly men, and mostly without much to amuse them but cards and salacious talk.

This sort of thing must have happened from the dawn of time. It is inconceivable that the hordes of Genghis Khan did not laugh and taunt as well as rape, that the marauding Vikings did not adorn the island of Britain with Scandinavian humor; but if so, most of the evidence has vanished. In the Americas the Amerindians had numerous names both erotic and scatological, but whether these represented humor or an indifference to the taboos common among the whites is hard to say. This sort of thing must have started early; such terms have been largely eliminated along the East Coast; even the relatively innocuous *Hungry Harbor* and *Ruin Point* disappeared only recently. E. R. Seary,[11] recording such names as *Blow-me-down* and *Come-by-chance,* adds that there are others "which would correct any impression that Newfoundland has been named by young ladies." From the Middle West some evidence of humor survives in designations like *Hog Eye, Rat Lake,* and *Shake Rag Under the Hill*—a name like *Intercourse* was not of the stuff that could endure—but the land of the miner and the cowhand has preserved the greatest wealth of picturesque names.

The more salacious names have gone, partly because they were usually attached to stage stations which have vanished, to landmarks no longer of consequence, or to some other notability in a land where *sic transit gloria* was a jig-time operation. Some were applauded with guffaws but never dignified with print. Some less salty remain. A volume in my library carries on the flyleaf, "A. H. Hart's Book / Bought in Whiskey Diggings / May 22, 1862 / California." How many places were named *Hangtown, Gallows-Gulch, Boozeville, Razzle-Dazzle, Undershirt Hill, Poker City, Horsethief Hollow, Jump Off, Gomorrah, Gouge Eye, Humbug Flat, Red Light,* and *Shirt Tail* can now never be known. Curiously, a few innocent titles have become suspect; *Skid Row* was presumably named from the fact that logs were "skidded," a technical term in lumbering, since to skid is to drag a log. *Skid Road* became *Skid Row,* and a *skid row* is now either a noun or a modifier referring to the rendezvous of bums, winos, and transients on their uppers.

Not only the land, but the inhabitants of the land and of the adjacent air and water required naming. European explorers and immigrants found themselves surrounded by rooted, running, creeping, crawling,

---

11 "The Anatomy of Newfoundland Place-Names," cited earlier, p. 207; a much more extensive study is in process.

flying, and swimming things, most of which were strange to them, some so strange that white men had never encountered their like before. In Europe were no armadillos or anteaters, no potatoes or peanuts, and in the eyes of the newcomers all these creations were nude of names. To compound the confusion, the theory of evolution had not yet been propounded. In fact, faith provided no room for such a theory, since the official notion throughout most of the eighteenth century and earlier, described as the Great Chain of Being, postulated a series of individual creations stretching in a great chain from God to inert matter. Thus the newcomers lacked the key that would have permitted them to explain similarities between the species in the New World and their related species in the Old. Insofar as the explorers and immigrants were looking for any order in the creatures of the New World, they were looking for "missing links" in the chain of being, phenomena that would provide the link between plants and animals, for example, or between lower animals and man.

Some denizens of the New World were enough like their European cousins to be named with the old name and a new modifier. Antlers identified deer as deer; the shambling gait, along with strength, fur, and hibernation identified bears; quacks and broad bills identified ducks. *A Dictionary of Americanisms*[12] lists dozens of ducks, *army ducks, black ducks, bufflehead ducks, butter ducks, canvas ducks, canvasback ducks, Carolina ducks, confederate ducks, cornfield ducks, creek ducks, crow ducks,* and on through the alphabet to *water, western, wheat,* and *wood ducks.* The American robin looked enough like the English robin to be so named, however inappropriately. The bison suggested a buffalo enough to be called a buffalo, and to give rise to compounds like *buffalo gals, buffalo cider, buffalo fever, buffalo horse, buffalo pecker, buffalo pound, buffalo wallow,* and dozens more, along with nicknames. A North Carolina sympathizer with the Damyankees was called a *buffalo.*

Sometimes the category of recognizable creatures was stretched a bit; a prairie dog was obviously not a dog, but he was so named by analogy. Some animals were named for notable conduct, among them the shitepokes, heron-like creatures of several varieties, who, when frightened, behave like the soldiers in *The Naked and the Dead;* they have difficulty maintaining what Norman Mailer calls a tight cincture. According to

---

[12] In the following discussions, when I do not specifically mention an early dictionary, it may be assumed that I am relying mainly on one or both of two excellent modern dictionaries of Americanisms, *A Dictionary of American English on Historical Principles,* ed. William A. Craigie and James R. Hulbert, 4 vols. (Chicago: University of Chicago Press, 1938); *A Dictionary of Americanisms,* ed. Mitford M. Mathews, 2 vols. (Chicago: University of Chicago Press, 1951).

legend, a fleeing shitepoke could evacuate for half a mile; the latter part of his name means *bag*.

If the new creature did not fit readily into a familiar class, the handiest source for a name was an Indian word. Here the favorite languages were Algonquian in North America and Nahuatl in Mexico, apparently because these were the languages with which the newcomers had the most early, literate contact. *Raccoon,* cut down to *coon,* and *opossum,* cut down to *possum*, were among the early borrowings. Peter Force, in a compilation of 1610 called *A True Declaration of the Estate of the Colonie in Virginia,* reports that "There are Arocouns, and Apossouns, in shape like to piggies." The marsupial powers of the opossum intrigued the newcomers; Robert Rogers wrote, "The Opposum is a remarkable animal in this country, having under its belly a bag or false belly, in which they breed their young." Captain John Smith reports that Powhatan made him presents of what he called *raugrough-cuns,* raccoons; the word apparently comes from an Algonquian term something like *arakun,* "scratcher," from the animal's habit of scratching for crawfish and similar food. The animal fascinated the newcomers because it was supposed to be able to transform itself into a snake and, at an appropriate time, reverse the process. As late as 1799, Col. James Smith reported that "It is a received opinion among the Indians that the snakes and racoons are transmutable; and that a great many of the snakes turn racoons every fall, and racoons snakes every spring."

Creatures like the moose, chipmunk, and menhaden were remarkable enough in one way or another to encourage the borrowing of Amerindian names. *Moose* is apparently from some Algonquian word like *mus,* meaning "to tear away," the big beasts being herbivores and fond of tender bark. Almost any powerful, gangling creature with a nose resembling a boxing glove can be ridiculed as a moose, but curiously enough the animal has served also for a political party, the Bull Moose party of Theodore Roosevelt, and a fraternal order, along with compounds like *moose-cat,* which has been defined as "anyone possessing great strength, ability, and what not." Furthermore, "a poor but handsome young girl who marries an old, wrinkled, ill-looking rich man, is said to have married a moose-face." The chipmunk, ubiquitous in wooded parts of the country, agile beyond belief and saucy beyond description, apparently gets his name from an Algonquian word something like *atchitamon,* meaning "headfirst," for the creature's method of traveling down trees. By folk etymology the word became *chitmonk* and then *chipmunk,* probably on the theory that it is a monkey-like beast that says "chip." The menhaden, an oily but not very edible fish, kept the early Massachusetts Bay settlers from starving; the local Amerindians had cautioned the white men to put a menhaden in each hill of corn, and any unwary Middle Westerner who has tried to raise corn in New England without fertilizer will know why. The word, also spelled *Munnawhatteaug,* apparently means "Fertilizer."

Of course, all these naming processes can be combined. Consider the various small marmots, found from coast to coast; the eastern examples, living in burrows and having a generally porcine contour, were called *ground hogs.* The Algonquian name *wejack* also was applied, a term which seems to mean "a fisher," perhaps because these marmots were confused with animals like the otter, which is aquatic. These beasts were soon called *woodshocks,* probably because the consonant in *wejack* represented by the *j* had a *d-zh* sound, a version which made no sense to a speaker of English, and accordingly the word was changed and a suitable etymology provided, as follows: "The woodchuck . . . when eating makes a noise like a hog, whence he is named Woodchuck, or chuck of the wood." So far as we know, the word *chuck* has never meant *hog,* but it sounds rather as though it ought to.

Some of the more famous plant names were borrowed in Latin America, words like *cocoa, maize, tomato,* and their relatives. *Cocoa* comes from Spanish and Portuguese *cacao,* a rendering of the native word *cacauatl;* combined with the native word for water, *latl,* it gives us *chocolate.* West Indian *mahiz* became Spanish *maiz* and British *maize,* a term known in the United States, but not much used there. *Corn* was a generic term for grain in English, used as a specialized name for the most extensively eaten grain, wheat, but in the United States *Indian corn* has been cut down to *corn.* Similarly, Nahuatl *tomatl* provided Spanish *tomate* and English *tomato.* Some vegetables grown in both English-speaking and Spanish-speaking America have gone different ways; the peanut, ground pea, or goober is still called by the Nahuatl name in Mexico, variously spelled *cacahuate, cacahuete, cacahuey,* and the like.

An extensive confusion surrounds the most popular American vegetable,[13] the salvation of the poor of Europe, the basis of strong waters like *aqua vit,* and a stimulant for Hiberno-American politics—for without potato famines in Ireland, would we have had our Kennedys and Sullivans, our various O'Briens and O'Connells? If we may believe Francisco Lopez de Gomara, it all started with Christopher Columbus, who in 1493 brought back with him forty parrots, ten Indians, ten turkeys, "maize from which they make bread," various rabbits and rodents, and "patatas." These latter were apparently some variety of tuberous root of the sort now called sweet potatoes or yams. The word

---

[13] The basic study here is that of Pedro Henriquez Ureña, "Papa y batata," in *Para la historia de los indigenismos* (Buenos Aires: Universidad de Buenos Aires, 1938).

soon starts cropping up in the reports of other explorers and in Spanish writers, for the *batata*—soon with the initial consonant unvoiced to *patata*—became a delicacy prized for its sweetness. One must remember, of course, that sweets were relished more before human taste buds were cloyed with beet and cane products; the *patata* was made into confections and preserves. The word worked its way north, and it was presumably for the connotations of sweetness that Falstaff, supposing he is about to seduce Mistress Page, shouts out, "Let the skie raine Potatoes!" *Batata* was a Spanish pronunciation of a Haitian word; meanwhile, the Spaniards had taken the Valley of Mexico, where they again encountered the sweet vegetable, but now with a Nahuatl name, which in the form *camotes* has become the common Latin-American word.

Meanwhile, other Spaniards were pressing toward the Inca kingdom in the Andes, where they discovered another edible root known as *papa.* This was not so much valued; it was not sweet at all. The tuber went from South America to Virginia, however, and thence to England and Ireland, where it accounted for the great increase in Irish population in the eighteenth century. How *potatoes* replaced *papas* is not quite clear, but perhaps because a catalogue of plants as early as 1599 listed papas as *patatas bastardas.* Whatever the reason, these "bastard potatoes" grew in popularity, probably because they were *not* sweet and would grow in temperate climates where tropical *batatas* could not endure. They became *Irish potatoes,* and finally just *potatoes,* although in Spain and some other countries they are still called *papas.* Accordingly, in the United States, the original *batatas,* must be called *sweet potatoes* to distinguish them from the *papas,* which became *potatoes.*

Meanwhile, the so-called Irish potato had been confused with a North American tuberous root, the Jerusalem artichoke, sometimes called in Spanish *cotufa* or *chufa;* curiously, the word means a sweet. An old proverb warns against expecting to "find *chufas* in the sea"—and the word became the basis of the German word for potatoes, *Kartoffeln.* Quite early another term appeared in English, *yam,* probably from the Portuguese *inhame,* which could have derived from Senegalese *nyami,* "to eat," or from some other unknown source—a number of spellings like *igname, nname,* and *inany* appear in early manuscripts. This term was applied to what may have been *batatas* taken to the East Indies and then reimported, or it may have represented a similar but unrelated plant (of the genus *Dioscorea* rather than the genus *Ipomoea* of Latin America); the wanderings of these sweetish tropical tubers cannot now be certainly traced. In the United States the word *yam* is now used to designate certain sweet potatoes thought to be superior, and ironically, in Ireland and parts of Scotland it is the name for the so-called Irish potato. Ironically, also, in the old home of the *batata* the *norteamericano* word is now translated into *papa dulce,* sweet potato. I omit some dozens of other words and combinations based upon various Amerindian languages and Hispanic dialects, not to mention spontaneous terms like the French *pomme de terre,* translated into German *Erdapfel.*

Perhaps the most fruitful orgy of plant and animal naming of all time was incidental to the exploration of the Louisiana Territory by Lewis and Clark, although its onomastic importance resulted from no accident. Thomas Jefferson had been interested in the problem of an unknown, unexplored, unnamed continent, and had planned a western expedition. When he became President, he appointed his private secretary, Captain Meriwether Lewis, to lead an exploring party, and Lewis invited his friend William Clark. Both were military men, but they represented the relatively learned military tradition, and Lewis, especially, endeavored to study natural history as part of his preparation for the trip. By now, 1803–6, the Linnaeian classification was available so that, although Lewis was no scientist, he had learned help in allocating names sensibly, and the godlike function of name-giving was apparently taken very seriously by both leaders of the expedition.

"Every page of their journals," Professor Elijah Harry Crisswell writes,

offers eloquent testimony to the diligence with which the explorers approached this task. Voluminous descriptions carefully set down under trying conditions after long hours of acute hardship on land and water, earnest cogitations of new plants or animals, selection of seemingly correct names with later abandonment after more mature thought—all these things show that the task of naming was undertaken with no less enthusiasm than other duties that might seem to the casual eye of more importance.[14]

Many names survived several versions before Lewis was content with them. Usually the explorers avoided French and Indian names, possibly because they did not know how to pronounce them, but they recorded the terms. They made an exception for the *camas* (*Camassia quamash*), which was a staple of many mountain Indians—one of the tribes of Shoshone are known in their own speech as Camas-eaters—perhaps out of respect to a plant that provided them food when game and their own supplies failed them. Clark on his first acquaintance with it called it *pah-see-goo,* which he later recorded *Pasheco quarmash,* which was apparently the basis of Lewis' *squawmash,* later *quamash,* which gave the name to the *Quamas Plains* in the Snake River valley and provided the

---

[14] *Lewis and Clark: Linguistic Pioneers, The University of Missouri Studies,* XV, 2 (April, 1940), cxix.

modern form of the word. The grizzly bears gave Lewis trouble, also, linguistically as well as physically. He had ready names for them—*brown bear, yellow bear, white bear, silver-gray bear, variegated bear, grizzly bear,* and *hoh-host*—but were they one variety or two? He finally called in the Indians; they were in no doubt. Presented with skins, they distinguished the mountain bears from the coastal bears, and had names for both of them. Nor did Lewis always triumph among his confreres; Clark seems to have named the prairie dogs, which Lewis had called *barking squirrels,* probably a more nearly accurate name.

The result of all this was some 1,528 named objects, and most of the names have endured. When Crisswell made his study he did not have the advantage of modern dictionaries of Americanisms, but nearly half the forms were previously unrecorded in any dictionary, and many that had been recorded were known to be Americanisms. We may plausibly estimate that Lewis and Clark added more than a thousand terms to the wordstock of English, which must stand as some sort of record in vocabulary making.

Not only the geographical features and the dumb beasts were involved in nomenclature; hundreds of millions of Americans also have needed names. On the whole, the patterns here have been neither complex nor original. Traditions of personal naming in England continued in the new country, and other groups of immigrants conformed. Scandinavians abandoned their patterns of naming with -*son,* -*sen,* and -*datter.* Once a name got to this country as *Pederson* it stayed *Pederson,* even though the son of *Nels Pederson* might have become *Peder Nelson* had the family stayed in Denmark. The Spaniards dropped their hyphenations with the wife's name, eliminating most cognomens like *Salazar y Zaragoza;* even orientals started writing their surnames last. Practices among Roman Catholics of including the name of at least one saint were already well established in Britain, as well as in lands where Catholicism was more common. Many non-English-speaking immigrants changed their names voluntarily to avoid embarrassment, or enforcedly because recording officials were not much blessed with either tolerance or orthography. German *Bauer,* meaning workman, became *Bower;* *Schmidt* became *Smith,* and *Pwyll Gruffydd* became *Bill Griffith.* Not infrequently names were translated; Swedish *Sjostrand* became English *Seashore* and German *Schneider* became *Taylor.* Some were appropriated in exuberance; Herbert Gold says his immigrant father adopted the name of what he had expected to pick up in the streets. Minority groups tried to escape radical prejudice by sloughing off names like *Goldfarb* and *Dubinsky,* making them look like English, or simply by adopting any English name they liked. Amerindians and Negroes sometimes appropriated the names of white men they admired, or took as a name words they associated with good things. Thus names like *Johnny Corn-bread, Mustache Jimmie, Coffee Charlie, Annie Doughnuts,* and *Suzy Calico* are not uncommon. Apparently this espousing of names stopped in time to forestall such potential denominations as *President Spark Plug, Coke Roosevelt,* and *Hi Octane Gas.*

In effect, in the United States, naming of human beings has been restricted to given names, since patronymics were inevitable and automatic. Even people whose names were *Dam*—probably from highly respectable German *Dahm*—and *Hell,* which means "bright" in German, have often done nothing about it. According to one account a patriotic Adam Dam read in the newspaper that the Hells had just had a reunion and had had a hell of a time. He decided his own family should invite all the Dam relatives and have a Dam reunion, which they did. Respectable names that have vulgar sounds in another language have caused some embarrassments; I remember a garrulous old hag confiding to me as a child that she knew a family "whose name is Schütz —isn't that awful?" but usually such difficulties disappear when the umlaut is lost.

Even given names have on the whole followed conventional patterns. Cognomens like *Grant* and *Bruce,* religious appellations like *John* and *James,* have mingled with heroic heirlooms, like *Charles* and *Edward.* Some have followed occasional fads; the Puritans favored virtues like *Faith* and *Prudence;* some Biblical names like *Ezekiel, Hephzibah,* and *Jeremiah* have fallen out of fashion. Sects, like the Latter-Day Saints, have favored their leaders so that names like *Heber* and *Hyrum* have lingered on. Southern belles are likely to accumulate combinations like *Sarajane, Lucypearl,* and *Maryannette.* At this writing we have a flock of *-bird* names, deriving from the family of a Texas President, *Ladybird, Lynda Bird,* and the like.

Perhaps the most engaging is a middle-western and southern penchant for humorous names, many of which have been collected by Professor Thomas Pyles,[15] who associates the fad with nonbaptismal naming. "It is highly unlikely," he writes, "that any man of God . . . would consent in the course of his sacerdotal duties to confer upon hapless infants such names as Buzz Buzz, Coeta, Merdine, Aslean, La Void, Arsie, Phalla, and Paz—all legal names borne by Bible Belters of repute." Such names are not the exclusive property of the uneducated underprivileged; Ima Hogg was important in Houston society, and her father was governor of Texas. Her sister's name, Ura Hogg, is scarcely more refined. The following are given names: Dawn Robin, Kitty Bit,

---

[15] "Bible Belt Onomastics or Some Curiosities of Anti-Pedobaptist Nomenclature," *Names,* VII (1959), 84–100.

Lance Amorus, Charm, Dimple, Pixianne, Orchid Favia, Satire, Fairy, Acid, Tyty, Kas Ray, Delyte, Dovey, and Mary Sunshine. Some of the most engaging results follow from combinations of otherwise innocuous names; the following attracted Professor Pyles' attention: Oleander Lafayette Fitzgerald III, Ed Ek, Shellie Swilley, Early Hawaiian McKinnon, Sandy Candy, Earl Curl, Percy Nursery, Lovie Slappy, Esperanza Le Socke, Pamela Gay Day, Girlie Burns, Fawn Grey, Trawick Dunkle, Martha Magdalene Toot, Okla Bobo, Melody Clinkenbeard, Pleasant Weathers, Honey Combs, French Crown, Golden Gamble, Royal Child, Goode Carr, Early Priest, Robin Starling, Paris Singer, Etta Turnipseed, Summer Robbins, Shari Class, Love Snow, Rocky Mountain, Alto Hooten, Early Wages, Drew Swords, English Piper, Candy Barr, Minor Peeples, Bunker Hill, Charming Fox, Diamond Queen, France Paris, Jack Frost, Merry English, Erie Lake, Fannie Bottom, Pinkie Bottom, Virgin Muse, Fairy Guy, and Dill L. Pickle, who grew up to be a pickle salesman. I can add Christ Seraphim.

Something should be said about naming in Latin America, where patterns similar to those in North America appear with variations.[16] Places are named for rulers and other people at home, though perhaps rather less; they are named for explorers and early settlers. As we have already seen, they are named for cities and states in Spain and Portugal —*Guadalajara, Lerida, Zaragoza, Sevilla, Segovia, Almeria, Cartagena, Cordova, Valladolid*—many of them repeated in country after country, but the fashion of naming towns for all the cities of the world, for Berlin, Moscow, and Peking, for cities with which the inhabitants had no connection, seems not to have become popular south of the Rio Grande. Places were named, also, because of characteristics, *Piedra Negra,* Black Rock, *Agua Caliente,* Hot Water, and *Ojo Frio,* Cold Pool, since *ojo,* the word for eye, is used for a small, clear body of water.

Triumphantly, Latin Americans have named places for saints and sacred manifestations, for the patron saint of a settler, for the saint on whose day a discovery was made. The actual process may be uncertain; *Santiago* in Cuba could have been named for Santiago de Compostela in Spain or from the saint for whom the Spanish town is named. Mountains like the Sierra Madre and Sierra Nevada in the New World could have been named for the ranges in the Old or for the sacred personages honored by such mountains. Saints' names could even be given because they were borne by explorers or notable personages; was *Cristobal* named for Cristobal Colon (known to speakers of English as Christopher Columbus) or for the saint, without any assistance from Colum-

[16] I am here relying heavily on an excellent study by Nils M. Holmer, "Indian Place Names in South America and the Antilles," *Names,* VIII (1960), 133–49, 197–219; IX (1961), 37–52.

bus? However these namings came about, they are found everywhere. The Spanish and Portuguese have been devout peoples, and much of the exploration and early settlement took place during the centuries when Catholicism was most vigorous in the Hispanic peninsula. Men in danger feel uncommon need for religious aid and solace, and neither exploration nor pioneering is likely to contribute to peace of mind. Furthermore, to the Spanish and Portuguese explorers, as to the English and French to the north, the new continents could be considered, for all practical purposes, unnamed. The result was that religious names were scattered thick and almost everywhere; quite probably more religious names were given in Latin America during three centuries after 1492 than were ever given elsewhere in a commensurate period.

Latin American place-naming was complicated by confusion in heavenly onomastics—various divine personages participated variously in a number of names. According to a tale more or less vouched for by an Argentinian engineer, a construction worker fell from the eighth floor but could not collect his breath and his presence of mind until he was passing the fifth floor. "San Antonio," he shouted in desperation. Instantaneously he was stopped in midair and remained suspended while a sepulchral voice asked, "Which San Antonio?" The workman wracked his confused wits and blurted, "San Antonio de Padua!" "That's not me," the voice answered, and the workman splashed. Under such handicaps, statistics become unreliable, but H. Ned Sellye,[17] using appropriate caution, has produced plausible summaries. He totaled 233 saints honored with place names of which the leaders are as follows: San Jose, 429 place names; San Juan, 365; San Antonio, 337. Rather surprisingly, Santa Maria (the Blessed Virgin Mary) is tied for fifth with San Francisco at 275, just behind San Pedro with 276, but the totals are confused by the fact that Guadalupe, 200 names, along with La Virgen and Magdalene may also be tributes to the Virgin, and if she were given any large part of these, she would lead handsomely with more than 500. We may be surprised, however, at the relative neglect of female saints generally. They account for only about one-fifth of the saint-names prominent enough to get into the United States Board of Geographic Names, *Gazetteer No. 15*. According to the same list, about one in six of the important Mexican place names derives from saints, and this calculation excludes ecclesiastical terms like Vera Cruz, of which there are 170, Sacramento, El Santo Cristo, Jesus, and Santo Niño.

Notable, also, are the Amerindian names, both for their number and their patterns of appearance. The interior, especially, is thick with them, especially for streams and bodies of water, more than in English-speak-

---

[17] I saw the study in manuscript; it will presumably be published in *Names*.

ing America, apparently because the aborigines have been less molested. Inevitably, the natives tended to live along water courses; in the more barren areas, water supplied life, and in the jungles it supplied a highway. These Amerindians, like people universally, tended to call rivers merely "water," or added some simple designative. For example, the eastern half of the continent is generally well watered—except for some highlands of Brazil—and the local languages here tend to be varieties of Tupi-Guarani, in which syllable clusters for water are something like *Parana, Para,* and *Paragua.* As elsewhere in Amerindian, forms and exact translations are difficult, but whether these combinations mean water washing as waves, water still in a lake, water flowing in a stream, or water falling as rain, syllables like these appear so consistently in connection with liquid phenomena that the patterns are clear. The results include the name for a country, *Paraguay,* along with many words meaning Big Water—*Paraguacu* and *Paranayuba,* and *Iguassu.* Unnumbered rivers are named *Parana* or *Para;* there are further developments like *Parahyba, Paraíba, Paragua, Paranaguá, Piraparaná, Paramaraibo, Parnahyba, Paratari, Paranatinga,* with interminable variations in spelling and possibly in meaning.

Further variations could be pursued. With Arawak to the north, syllables for "water" produce different forms, as do Araucanian terms to the south. To the west, beyond the Andes, a suffix *-yacu* may mean "water" or "river," and hence we have *Pumayacu,* Puma River, *Sarayacu,* Maize River, and combined with a Spanish word, *Burrayacu,* Donkey River. But there are no Big Rivers here nor conventional translations of Amerindian names for them; although streams called Rio Grande abound to the east, the Andes crowd the sea, leaving no room for "big rivers" there. Other minor variations might be noticed. Latin-American Indians, like relatively primitive peoples in many lands, are likely to call themselves merely "the people," and thus the Quechua call themselves *Runa* or *Runacuna,* the word for human beings, and language becomes *Runasimi,* "the speech of the people." Parts of the body, on the other hand, are used figuratively in ways unfamiliar to Indo-European speakers; the "mouth" of a river is not the point at which it empties into another body of water, but the banks of the stream, as though the land were thought of as biting into the water.

Thus place-naming has had its peculiarities in the Americas, but these differences suggest the characteristics of place-naming everywhere, except that here new languages were overrunning old languages, doing the conquering at different rates of speed and in different patterns. Accordingly, the impact of men on names and of names on men was somewhat varied from the relationships known in lands long and permanently settled.

PART THREE

AMERICAN ENGLISH IS BORN

14

WESTWARD THE COURSE OF LANGUAGE

English required about a century to work west. Presumably the first English was spoken on the North American continent shortly after 1600; not until about 1800 did the language push much west of the Appalachians, while most of the continent north of the Valley of Mexico still lived by means of aboriginal tongues, with only trickles of English, French, and Spanish along the waterways, fresh or salt. By 1900 the movement was mainly over. English was the current speech everywhere except in sparsely settled scatterings of mountain, desert, and tundra—except where it was in effect restricted by law, as in parts of what is now Oklahoma. The United States, from having been a colony of Europe, had become a modern nation, with sophisticated cities, learned societies, cultural centers, and world congresses. It had turned from pioneering to international affairs sufficiently to fight a dynastic war, the Spanish-American War of 1898.

Quite probably no language ever grew so fast in numbers of speakers and area involved. During the nineteenth century, the official census mounted from a little over 5,000,000 to more than 75,000,000, almost 1500 per cent. During the same time the area dominated by English rose from less than half a million square miles—this allows generously for the scattering of speakers of English who had spilled over the Appalachians—to well above three million, an increase of perhaps seven times. This expansion probably accounts in large measure for the relative uniformity of American English, but within millions of square miles and among tens of millions of obstreperous individuals, uniformity has its limits.

First, we might notice that the American colonies, approaching the maturity of statehood, experienced a sort of linguistic adolescence. The whole analogy of the new United States as a kind of teen-age culture can be revealing, for the nineteenth century in English-speaking North

America was enthusiastic, exuberant, relatively illiterate, and given to fads, bad judgment, bad taste, and indifference to the rights and feelings of others. The analogy is peculiarly apt in language.

Much as very young people tend to ignore sex, very young peoples tend to ignore language—but only while they are very young. A time comes during the growth of any normal boy, when, after having tolerated girls as one of the obvious mistakes of an otherwise omniscient supreme being, he discovers that a girl is the most exciting, most desirable, most beautiful of all creations. Similarly, at the approach of maturity, societies become conscious of language. Prior to that time, they have been speaking it furiously, but they have not been much likely to talk about it. They have not told one another what a glorious gift language is, or that their language is better than other languages, nor have they asked themselves what they should do to make it better, or to preserve its purity, or to support it in the exalted stage it has reached as the most beautiful, the most eloquent, the most refined language in the world. Then, sometimes rather suddenly, as national trends go, they do start asking such questions and indulging the corresponding enthusiasms.

In the United States, the two periods became curiously commingled. American English was but moving into its natural period of adolescent exuberance, developing from the sixteenth- and seventeenth-century English that had been imported into the New World, when more sophisticated—if not more tempered—fashions were introduced from the mother country.

Here we should recall Universal Grammar, sketched in Chapter 5, which provided the invading Europeans with philosophical justification for overweening pride in their language. Transformed into what might better have been called the Doctrine of Universal Usage, it supplied learned eighteenth-century reformers with weapons to batter down both ignorance and the opposition. They asserted that "there is ONE TRUTH, like one Sun, that has enlightened human intelligence through every age, and saved it from the darkness of both Sophistry and Error."[1] Armed with such an all-conquering tool, writers on language

---

[1] For a brief survey of the discussion of usage in the eighteenth century, see Sterling Andrus Leonard, *The Doctrine of Correctness in English Usage 1700–1800,* University of Wisconsin Studies in Language and Literature, 25 (Madison: University of Wisconsin Press, 1929). This passage, p. 47; Leonard is quoting James Harris, *Hermes: or A Philosophical Inquiry Concerning Philosophical Grammar,* 4th ed. (London: C. Nourse, 1786), p. x; first edition, 1751. The passage is perhaps most readily available in *English as Language,* ed. Charlton Laird and Robert M. Gorrell (New York: Harcourt, Brace & World, 1961), p. 185.

evinced a confidence, even an arrogance, more characteristic of neophytes in newly founded religions than of scholars skeptical of fledgling truth. As a matter of fact, many so-called grammarians were divines turned part-time savants, who were more concerned with regulating linguistic traffic than with pursuing the nature and habits of language. Patronizingly, they conceded that the benighted past may have provided occasion for error, but they smugly asserted that error in the future was inexcusable, now that Universal Grammar had been discovered.

Had eighteenth-century policers of usage enjoyed any considerable acquaintance with the multitudinous languages that have spawned throughout the globe, or with the wealth of grammatical evidence that has burgeoned on the human tongue, and had they seriously entertained the question of whether unwritten languages might not be worthy of serious consideration, worthy equally with European languages, they would have had reason to question the universality of Universal Usage. They might have asked how they were to recognize, out of all grammars, "that grammar, which without regarding the several Idioms of particular languages, only respects those principles, that are essential to them all."[2] Even granted that all languages were comprised within the seventy-two that were supposed to have sprung up after Babel, they might have wondered how any one man was to know all these seventy-two and to indefatigably determine what were the essentials of each. Some eighteenth-century thinkers did raise serious questions about language, but most writers who were heard most did not probe very deeply.[3] With God and the Classics behind them, they were confident they had the answers, and they were more interested in old-fashioned enforcement than in any newfangled understanding.

Most grammarians apparently agreed with James Harris, author of *Hermes,* the most widely admired work on the subject, that "the Greek language is of all the most elegant and complete." Even Latin, long the foundation of English learning and the source of previously accepted grammars like those of Ben Jonson, was considered only "a Species of Greek somewhat debased." Romance languages were obviously even more corrupt, and as for tongues like German, Dutch, and English, which were supposed to be corruptions of Gothic, "modern languages, particularly those of Gothic extraction, . . . [are] not near so accurate, and the sound of them . . . [is] much more unpleasant than that

---

[2] Harris, cited earlier, p. 11; reprinted in *English as Language,* cited earlier, p. 200.

[3] A young scholar, Allen Curtis, is restudying eighteenth-century linguistic thought. He tells me he is finding much more substance in it than is revealed in Leonard's study cited above. Leonard died without an opportunity to revise his work, but the fact remains that the widely read people who set the patterns were not very philosophic. Curtis expects to publish something soon.

of the Greek."⁴ Of course, Harris had never heard an ancient Greek speak what was assumed to be the most mellifluous of all languages, but this limitation did not deter him or many of his contemporaries. To study classical Greek was, they trusted, to study Universal Grammar, and to rebuke and police a juvenile delinquent tongue like upstart English, the authoritarians had only to ascertain the rules of Greek and apply them.

In effect, the solution was even simpler. Few people were sufficiently philosophic to concern themselves with universals, but many were zealous to correct the usage of others. Furthermore, not many people, even learned people, knew Greek well, but all educated persons commanded the elements of classical Latin. Thus most writers on grammar settled for Latin grammar, and only classical Latin grammar; the grammar of Vulgar Latin, which more nearly resembles the grammar of English, was largely unknown, and it would probably have been ignored as corrupt had it been known. Accordingly, "grammar" was mainly the Latin grammar that happened to have been taught in the British schools, and thus Universal Grammar incidentally licensed all pedants to become bigots. Only a smattering of Latin grammar sufficed for pedantry, and accordingly almost everybody that wrote seriously on language could correct almost everybody else. Pedants made up long lists of improprieties in Shakespeare and his contemporaries, declaring that this was "vile," that was "barbarous," and much more was "bad English." They even censured the authorized version of the Bible, condemning "Whom do men say that I am?" Some objected to Touchstone's "Who Time ambles withal," turning it into "With whom Time ambles withal," which may be good grammar, but is scarcely good poetry or good theater.⁵

The same century witnessed concern over vocabulary, as dictionaries came into their own. Theoretically, dictionaries had existed for some time; the first work conceded to be a dictionary in English is Robert Cawdrey's *Table Alphabetical* (1604), but it is a poor thing, and the nature of seventeenth-century English dictionaries can be inferred from the title of a work by Elisha Coles, *An English Dictionary, explaining*

---

⁴ *Hermes*, cited earlier, *passim*, especially pp. 147–48.
⁵ The material is well surveyed in Leonard, cited earlier, perhaps especially pp. 179–96. Passages are reprinted in *English as Language*, cited earlier, pp. 190–97. One of the most self-righteous revisers of standard prose was James Buchanan, author of *Regular English Syntax* (London: J. Wren, 1767), and presumably of *The British Grammar: or an Essay in Four Parts on Speaking and Writing in the English Language Grammatically and Inditing Elegantly* (London: J. Buchanan, 1762); a second edition appeared with the title *An Essay . . .* (London: E. & C. Dilly, 1766). Other prescriptionists who provided rules for what Buchanan called "inditing elegantly" include Robert Baker, John Hornsey, William Ward, George Campbell, and Zachary Grey; Leonard provides documentation for these and many more.

Difficult Terms . . . containing Many thousand hard Words (1676).
That is, a dictionary was supposed to explain hard words for relatively
ignorant people who could not be expected to know much; it neither
was, nor was intended to be, an objective description of the language.
During that century, however, lexicography was being developed on
the Continent; the new principles and practices were imported into
England, notably by Nathaniel Bailey, who provided for English in
An Universal Etymological Dictionary (1728) much of that lexicographical insight for which Samuel Johnson is given popular credit.
Furthermore, the Académie Française was endeavoring to turn its
dictionary to the service of the French language, the French Empire,
and civilization itself. Gallic savants believed that the great French
language had attained such excellence that henceforth it could do
nothing but decline, and accordingly, relying upon conviction well
surveyed today in Voltaire's *Philosophical Dictionary,* they determined
to preserve it by embodying it in a monumental work. All languages,
Voltaire explained, are imperfect because men have made them, and not
by any logical processes. Language has been somewhat pruned of its
barbarisms by good breeding, but meanwhile it has been corrupted by
trade, by the blunders of the ignorant, and by the fopperies of the
foolish, especially through "the affectation of mediocre authors." He
then concludes, "Albeit all languages are imperfect, we need not there-
for alter them. On the contrary, one must adhere very particularly to the
manner in which the good authors have employed them. When one has a
sufficient number of approved authors, a language is fixed."

Of course, no modern student of language will concede that any
language ever has been rendered unchangeable or is ever likely to be so,
but in a well-ordered, eighteenth-century world this thesis seemed
plausible. Accordingly, as he admits in his preface, Dr. Johnson set out
to "purify" English and then to "fix" it. During the process of making a
dictionary he became convinced that purifying was imperfect and fixing
was impossible, and he apologized to his subscribers for having taken
their money on false pretenses, however innocently these pretenses had
been entertained. He continued to act, however, as though he thought a
language could and should be absolute, and most other English lexicographers apparently imitated his manner more than they followed his
professions. George Campbell, for example, very sensibly observed
that decisions as to correctness should depend upon "reputable, national,
and present usage," and the pronouncement was given some lip service
but very little tongue service; editors applauded the dictum and ignored
it. The eighteenth century saw dozens of dictionaries in England, and
most of them relied upon usage by fiat.

Thus the concern for language, both words and grammar, that flared

up in the New World after the Revolutionary War, was in part only the
sort of laggard echo from the mother country that can be expected in
any colony—and the American settlements remained culturally colonies
of the British Isles long after they refused to admit any political al-
legiance. In other ways, however, the American manifestations were
different, perhaps because the natural curiosity about language and a
concern for it, prompted by the linguistic skirmishing in the mother
country, were accentuated by the hate and chauvinism fostered by eight
years of war. Suggestive of this development and its impact upon
American English and the speakers of it are two names, Noah Webster
and Goold Brown, the first so familiar that *webster,* still usually capitalized, is commonly used in the United States as a synonym for *dictionary* and but little as an obsolete form of *weaver,* while Goold Brown is
known only to grammarians, and to but few of them.

First, to Webster.

15

NOAH WEBSTER: CRACKER-BARREL LEXICOGRAPHY

In Webster, America produced what might have been expected from the New World, the preeminent cracker-barrel lexicographer, who knew all the answers. More a hack of all intellectual trades than a scholar, he was passably schooled but not learned, not even in the subject for which he is now best known. He was intelligent, but he had neither wit nor profundity, and he probably never felt the lack of either quality. He was alert, devout, industrious, patriotic, persistent, public-spirited, conceited, and perverse. Ignorance never dampened his fire, nor did a sense of humor temper his finality.

He never hesitated to espouse any profession or to assay any problem; he discussed anything from the demon rum to "fripperies of the head," by which he meant his wife's hats. He dispatched problems of epidemiology, although he was no doctor; he argued theology, although he was neither philosopher nor divine; he read law, but was never able to practice successfully, and he did little better as an editor. For a time he was an obscure schoolteacher, and he was an itinerant lecturer for as long as he could live from the take at the door. In the end he triumphed more by ingenuity, longevity, and one-track-mindedness than by any of the lovelier virtues, but he was a great man, and his memory should be able to endure more of the truth about him than some members of his family have wished to allow, and more than publishers who acquired his name have cared to recognize.[1]

---

[1] Two recent, generally competent studies of Webster are available, Erwin C. Shoemaker, *Noah Webster: Pioneer of Learning* (New York: Columbia University Press, 1936), and Harry R. Warfel, *Noah Webster, Schoolmaster to America* (New York: The Macmillan Co., 1936). The scholarly and conservative study of Webster by Horace E. Scudder for the American Men of Letters series, *Noah Webster* (Boston and New York: Houghton Mifflin, 1882), so infuriated some of Webster's descendants that they endeavored to restore their progenitor's image

He had the proper breeding to typify homespun linguistics. He was born in 1758 on the outskirts of Hartford, Connecticut, of a father who was a farmer, justice of the peace, and son of a former governor of the state, and of a mother descended from William Bradford, second governor of Plymouth Colony. Webster attended Yale, where he neither distinguished nor disgraced himself; he was not expelled as was a fellow student epitomized as "profane Butler"—who seems also to have been involved in a riot—and he was among those who President Ezra Stiles said "disputed inimitably well" in a senior forensic demonstration. The Revolutionary War was in progress: Webster drilled with a student defense group, and when fighting was expected at Lake Champlain and in the Hudson Valley, he joined groups of volunteers but did not reach either battlefield in time for combat. Along with other students he was sent home, when the college larder was empty, to bring food from the farm. Graduated in 1778, he read law and endeavored to practice in his home community, but he did not attract paying clients; times were hard, and many of Webster's contemporaries did not find him personally charming. No doubt he was more bumptious at twenty than at eighty, when his grandchildren adored him. He opened a local school, which attracted few scholars; disappointed in love, he started west, and happened upon Goshen, New York, then as now a rural community west of the Hudson, where he opened a grammar school for the children of refugees from New York City, headquarters of the British forces.

Webster was not long to be detained by Goshen. He had the imagination of a Walter Mitty and the drive of a bulldozer. He readily saw great vistas with himself at the center of them; he never gave up anything readily, and he was no rural schoolteacher by temperament. He found himself teaching an ancient text, Thomas Dilworth's *New Guide to the English Tongue* (1740), which for its inadequate pedagogy was offen-

---

by publishing a two-volume running commentary with documents, *Notes on the Life of Noah Webster,* compiled by Emily Ellsworth Fowler Ford, ed. Emily Ellsworth Ford Skeel, 2 vols. (New York: privately printed, 1912). It contains Webster's journal and other records, including letters not previously published. Selected correspondence appears in *Letters of Noah Webster,* ed. Harry R. Warfel (New York: Library Publishers, 1953); and there is an excellent bibliography: Emily Ellsworth Skeel, *A Bibliography of the Writings of Noah Webster,* ed. Edwin H. Carpenter, Jr. (New York: New York Public Library, 1958). Many works, like Robert Keith Leavitt, *Noah's Ark: New England Yankees and the Endless Quest* (Springfield, Mass.: G & C. Merriam Co., 1947) are too much influenced by the exigencies of publishing to be used without great caution, less for inaccuracies than for significant omissions. Webster has been well treated in some standard works, perhaps notably in Mencken/McDavid, *The American Language,* cited earlier, and in George Philip Krapp, *The English Language in America,* 2 vols. (New York: The Century Co. for the Modern Language Association of America, 1925).

sive to a Yale-trained teacher and which by lauding kings, queens, and parliaments was offensive to any man who hated the British kings, their taxes, their women, and their works. He decided to write a great *Grammatical Institute* which would purify the American language and promote American patriotism. Characteristically, he set to work at once.

If Webster was a visionary, he was also a worthy son of the Wooden Nutmeg State, with an eye to income. Although he projected a speller, a grammar, and a book of readings, he ignored the more ambitious works for a time and concentrated on the speller. By the time he was ready to print in 1783, the war was over, and the country was crying for textbooks. Before the Revolution most textbooks had been imported from England, although a few had been pirated and printed in the City of Brotherly Love. By now they were worn into dust; an untutored crop of children was ready for school, although few but Webster had books ready to print. His speller became immediately popular, and during his lifetime sold nearly 40,000,000 copies; revised, it sold nearly as many more, and celebrated its hundredth anniversary as Appleton's best-selling book. It supported Webster and his family modestly for the remainder of his days, for his other ventures produced only sporadic money; even the great dictionary of 1828 on which his fame rests never brought him much income.

We should perhaps notice that in Webster's day spelling books were fundamental in the elementary curriculum, more ambitious works than are modern spellers. "Spelling" comprised pronunciation, elocution, usage, even literary taste in various and modest ways, and it implied religion, morality, and etiquette. The embracing nature of Webster's little book is partly reflected in its title, which for the revised version of 1804—dated in the copyright "the twenty-eighth year of the Independence of the United States of America"—reads, *The American Spelling Book: Containing the Rudiments of the English Language*. In my copies[2] the running head throughout is "An Easy Standard of Pronunciation," and the book opens with a definition of language and an analysis of sounds. Along with graded lessons in spelling and collections of words intended to illustrate phonetic principles, the book contains verses to be learned and passages to be read, surveys of common

---

[2] (Brattleborough, Vt.: William Fessenden, 1815; New Brunswick, N.J.: Terhune & Letson, 1831.) The book underwent hundreds of small printings from dozens of small presses, but in copies I have examined the content varies but little, mostly in details of printing. Woodcuts were copies of a common original, although doubtless many times removed, and are occasionally reversed. On what is often unnumbered page iii, someone, presumably Webster, puffs the book, praises its system of teaching pronunciation, and with the passing years, increases the claimed circulation.

phenomena, fables, a moral catechism, and discussions of "Domestic Economy," including a "History of the Grog-Drinker." The "Fable of the Boy That Stole Apples" leads to the "MORAL: If good words and gentle means will not reclaim the wicked, they must be dealt with in a more severe manner." Webster points out in his preface that "in the familiar lessons for reading, care has been taken to express ideas in plain, but not in vulgar language; and to combine, with the familiarity of objects, useful truth and practical principles."

Webster admitted that his speller, "when first published, encountered an opposition." He might have been more accurate had he said it encountered several sorts of opposition, including that from the adherents of certain sects who felt that he was "teaching the children agenst the Christian religion." The objection was that the Psalms of David could not be sung except with the pronunciation *sal-va-ci-on,* whereas "he's making all the children say sal-va-shun." No doubt he also had in mind such attacks as those from an anonymous writer of letters to the press, who signed himself "Dilworth's Ghost," and who accused Webster of having stolen his book from old Dilworth. He was also accused of undermining right thinking and sound pedagogy by introducing new methods, in such attacks as that of the influential New York *Aurora:*

> His spelling-book has done more injury in the common schools of the country than the genius of ignorance herself could have conceived a hope of, by his ridiculous attempts to alter the *syllable* division of words and to *new model* the spelling, by a capricious but utterly incompetent attempt of his own weak conception.[3]

Eventually, however, he had some reason to boast that "it has become the principal elementary book in the United States."

This eminence was not easily won. Publishing houses as we know them did not then exist. Even the "art of printing" was a rare skill; presses and fonts of type, since they had to be imported, were not easily come by, and even acquiring a stock of paper adequate for the printing of a book presented problems. Worse, the existing transportation system did not permit central printing and distribution. Even ocean travel was expensive, limited to a few coastal vessels which linked the major cities between Boston and Charleston, from whence some goods could move inland, especially by river, but overland transport of heavy goods was impractical. In effect, textbooks had to be printed in and distributed from the larger communities. Webster's speller was advertised in the

---

[3] This and other adverse notices have been assembled in Bergen Evans, "Noah Webster Had the Same Troubles," *The New York Times Magazine,* May 13, 1962, pp. 11, 77, 79–80.

Hartford *Courant* at fourteen pence a copy, ten shillings for a dozen, a price which would account for little cartage. In effect, Webster had to sell rights of his book to local printers, hoping to collect a fee for the privilege of printing. But why should printers pay a fee? No law prevented them from buying a copy for fourteen pence and printing as many duplicates as they pleased. Accordingly, Webster had copyright laws drawn and toured the country, urging the various states to adopt them.

His next years were busy ones. Back in Hartford, an attempted rhetorical school did not attract the invited ladies and gentlemen who were to have learned the most refined pronunciation, but Webster brought out his second part of the *Grammatical Institute,* and with a double interest in copyright laws he redoubled his activities. When his spelling innovations were attacked, he developed theories of spelling reform, and when he could not afford to travel to places like Georgia, he lectured. He was becoming a bit of a figure, if a somewhat startling figure, inclined to deprecate "the little regard that is paid to the literary improvement of females," and to call Dilworth "a mere Latin grammar indifferently translated," which was "tolerably harmless" only because it was "very little used and still less understood."

The state of his grammatical thinking is probably revealed in an outline of his lectures, read before thirty auditors at "Mr. Hunt's School House in Boston." According to Webster's advertisement,[4] the first lecture was to include the following:

Introduction. Origin of the English Language, Derivation of the European Languages from the ancient Celtic. General History of the English Language. Its copiousness. Effect of this Irregularity of Orthography. Causes of this.

These lectures must have shed fresh if uncertain light in the Boston of 1786 for any ladies and gentlemen interested in language, in spite of Webster's inadequacy and the impossibility of treating these subjects in two hours. European languages have not derived from "the ancient Celtic," and there is no evidence that Webster knew much about ancient or any other Celtic. He did not at this time know Old English, and he never attached much importance to Middle English, so that his "General History of the English Language" must have been general indeed. Without intimate knowledge of Middle English he could not have discussed with much penetration the causes of irregularity in English spelling. Still,

---

[4] *Massachusetts Sentinel,* July 12, 1786; reprinted in *Notes on the Life of Noah Webster,* cited earlier, I, 160–61.

most public addresses were no nearer the truth and were much less daring.

Subsequent lectures were to treat the "Dialects of the Eastern, the Middle, and the Southern States"—Webster was far ahead of his day in recognizing the importance of dialects—the "Differences between English and Americans" along with the "Corruption of Language in England," which led to "Reasons why the English should not be our Standard, either in Language or Manners," "Prevailing Errors in the use of Words," "Errors of Grammarians in the Arrangement of Verbs," and eventually, "Defects in our mode of Education," including "Female Education." The whole, if it does not inspire us to believe that Webster was abreast of the best eighteenth-century scholarship, suggests that in his own colonial way, Noah was doing some original thinking.

As a matter of fact, Webster was not a happy man when he was delivering those lectures in Boston. His *Grammatical Institute,* completed in 1785, had not swept the country; except for the spelling book, it was doing badly. True, he projected revisions of the grammar and the reader, but at twenty-seven he felt the press of old age upon him. On his birthday he wrote, "a few revolutions more . . . will turn me off the stage," and every birthday he celebrated with some such remark. He could no longer live by his lectures; in smaller places like Salem they often did well enough, but when he tried to establish himself in the great capitals, he was successful with neither the ladies nor the literati.

He tried Philadelphia first, where he recorded, "the ladies will not dance with strangers, if they can help it—polite indeed!" Some event had apparently rankled, for he recorded the affront, also, in his *Lesser Journal:*[5] "People in high life suppose they have a right to dispense with the rules of civility." His second lecture "drew only a small audience, the weather is bad." He derived some comfort from his last lecture read "to 150 with great applause," and the series closed with an anthem, but he had to recognize that a previous series had drawn a thousand auditors. Writing to his printers, he consoled himself, "Even the Philadelphians, who are much inclined to find fault, acknowledge that my remarks are new and my design laudable." Later he complained that, although his books were used in Charleston and New York, they were neither printed nor adopted in Philadelphia. He made some friends, but not even all of these were without reservations; one of the most cordial of them, Timothy Pickering, commented as follows:

With respect to Mr. Webster, you must have noticed that with a competent share of good sense, he possessed a quantum sufficit of vanity, so that he really overrated his own talents. He imagined he was a good reader, but I

---

[5] Excerpts are published in *Notes on the Life of Noah Webster.*

had so much friendship for him as to point out his defects. . . . He was particularly defective in reading poetry, and this perhaps as much as anything disgusted his audience. In truth, there was so much of egotism, especially in a young man, apparent in his communications, as to prevent his hearers receiving the satisfaction which might otherwise have been derived from many ingenious observations . . . Dr. Shippen told me that his son attended one evening and was very much disgusted, but added that his son had not given him a fair chance. I have taken the liberty in a letter since his departure to tell him that diffidence in a public lecturer, especially in a young man, was essential to the art of pleasing. As to the encouragement he met with, I do not think it was to be boasted of; at the same time bating the truly displeasing marks of vanity, I think the encouragement received was less than he deserved.[6]

Pickering also said that he admired Webster for "his ingenuity, learning and industry."

As for the remainder of his attempt, only sixteen students attended his lecture at Princeton, although Yale did a little better. He reported that his audience in New York was "about as numerous as that in Philadelphia," which, with Webster's generosity in totals, probably means that it was smaller. Webster complained to Pickering that "the people in Boston did not attend my lectures," and that, in his home town of Hartford, "I read my lectures to a few friends . . . but most people paid no attention to them."

Just at this moment, however, Webster's genius came to his rescue. He was always bristling with ideas and projects; if one failed another might unexpectedly succeed, and fortuitously, one did. He had, among other ventures, devised a simplified means of spelling, and had written a little in it, to the almost universal horror of his readers. The following is one of his sentences:

During the course of ten or twelv years, I have been laboring to correct popular errors, and to assist my yung brethren in the road to truth and virtue; my publications for theze purposes have been numerous; much time haz been spent, which I do not regret, and much censure incurred, which my hart tells me I do not deserv.[7]

At least one American, however, could be expected to be hospitable to a new idea—Benjamin Franklin, now eighty, back from his long assignment abroad. An international gentleman, Franklin had become aware

---

[6] *Notes on the Life of Noah Webster,* I, 102–3.

[7] He composed several brief pieces illustrating his spelling system, some of which are printed in *A Collection of Essays and Fugitive Writings* (Boston, 1790). For his principles, see "An Essay on the Necessity, Advantages and Practicability of Reforming the Mode of Spelling," in *Dissertations on the English Language* (Boston, 1789); reprinted in Scholars' Facsimiles and Reprints, ed. Harry R. Warfel (Gainesville, Fla., 1951).

that archaic spelling constituted the great weakness of the English language, and he recognized that a new country can reform spelling much more easily than can an old one, with interests heavily vested in trained people and printed works. Zealous that his country become a world leader and reformer, he offered Webster the use of his private printing press to develop and disseminate a new alphabet.

Webster replied with alacrity. Here, he felt, was his opening. He had been coolly received, if not positively affronted, in the nation's political, social, and economic capital, but "the great Dr. Franklin" would open all doors. Surely, the great doctor would recommend legislation to the federal government, and Webster would be put in charge of a national movement for spelling reform—as for Webster, had he not already assisted General George Washington to find a secretary? Webster wrote, "If your Excellency can furnish me with any prospects. . . ."

Franklin probably anticipated nothing like the active patronship that Webster envisaged, but he found some teaching for the young enthusiast, and by late autumn of 1786, Webster was in Philadelphia again, hoping to publish his lectures—if no one would any longer hear them, perhaps a puff from Franklin would sell them—revising his grammar, and borrowing books from Dr. Franklin's private library, especially those that concerned language and spelling reform. He felt he was on the threshold of great things, and he was. He was about to be beset by love and an idea, and he was never to recover from the effects of either, for the lady was to involve him in matrimony, and the idea was to color books of which he had not as yet dreamed.

The idea hit him first. His journal for January 1, 1787, reads as follows: "Read Horne's Diversions of Purley, a new & useful Theory of Language." This sounds innocuous enough, but it records a revolution in Webster which changed his life and had wide implications for the study and growth of English in America. As for the lady, Miss Rebecca Greenleaf, she soon appears as both the "sweet" and the "agreeable Miss Greenleaf," and it is apparently to her he writes as "the best," but more than two years were to elapse before Noah could record in his journal, July 26, 1789, that he was "much better" after a touch of influenza, and that "this day I became a husband." Matrimony brought him a dowry, with which he once more set up as a lawyer in Hartford and was once more unsuccessful, so that he returned eventually to the writing of textbooks. Thus he resolved his matrimony as most men do; he became the head of a household with which he lived as most husbands do; but from the reading of *The Diversions of Purley* he found no ready cure.

Now we must observe one of those curious quirks in history, by which a relatively obscure book by a renegade cleric, a disbarred barrister, and a radical accused of treason changed the course of the study of language, and to a degree language itself, in the New World, although the book was fundamentally unsound, honeycombed with error, and ignored by all the better students of language in its day.

John Horne, better known as John Horne Tooke, had a good university education which led naturally to the ministry, but his conscience would not sanction the requirements of the cloth. He abandoned his living and read law, but he became involved in radical movements that the very conservative government of his day considered dangerous, and he was prevented from practicing. He lived precariously, while giving his support to any cause he believed just and underprivileged. One, curiously, was that of a country gentleman by the name of Tooke, who seemed about to lose his patrimony; Horne wrote him, apologizing for being in no position to defend abused persons in court, but outlining a defense that would win the case. It did, and in gratitude Tooke, a bachelor without heirs, willed his property, a place called Purley, to Horne on condition that he become John Horne Tooke.[8]

Another incident more directly concerns us. Horne—not yet Tooke— a believer in the rights of man, ardently supported the American colonies against the British government, and held a mass meeting to raise money for the widows and orphans of the Americans killed at Lexington and Concord, who, Horne insisted, had been murdered. To the British government, these men had been killed in process of an armed rebellion against law and order; the government did not welcome Horne's interpretation, and when war was declared they jailed him for treason. Of course the "treason," if there was any, was ex post facto, and Horne was eventually released, but during the year he spent in jail he may have written a draft of *Epea Pteronta* (Winged Words) *or The Diversions of Purley,* which purported to be a transcript of weekend conversations of Horne and his friends from nearby London. The book was attracting attention when Franklin was in London, on his way home from France; the money Horne had collected was to be paid to the American ambassador, and considering Franklin's interest in language and in all new ideas, we may assume he acquired a copy of the book, by this loyal friend of all Americans, quite possibly from Horne's hand. However he obtained it, we may probably assume, also, that he called it

---

8 On Tooke see Minnie Clare Yarborough, *John Horne Tooke* (New York: Columbia University Press, 1926). Hans Aarsleff, *The Study of Language in England, 1780–1860* (Princeton: Princeton University Press, 1967), includes an excellent study of Tooke, but does not treat the influence of the *Diversions* abroad.

to Webster's attention; Webster had dined with him December 30, 1786, the evening but one before he recorded his reading of the book.[9]

However Webster acquired Tooke long enough to study and excerpt the volume, the result was immediate and ineradicable. He does not frequently mention his reading in his diary. He will record with what ladies he danced, with whom he took tea, upon what important gentleman he waited, when he delivered lectures and how many people heard him and whether they applauded, when he writes and at what, how he travels and what weather he encounters; he even records when he started taking morning baths and what was the effect upon his health, but he seldom mentions a book. But for Webster, Tooke was heady waters. He quotes with approval Erasmus Darwin's comment that Tooke had "unfolded by a single flash of light, the whole theory of language," and he acts thereafter as though, once illumined, he needed Tooke no more. From Tooke he derived a revelation that must have approached a psychiatric insight; he saw language and himself anew, and even came to feel that he had progressed far beyond the master, but if he never felt the occasion to consult Tooke again, such self-immurement is not inconsistent with what we know of him as a man and as a student of language.

He became fond of offering a suit of clothes to anybody who could answer a question on language which he would propound—the question, of course, was only one of Tooke's ingeniously wild diversions, diverted even more wildly by Webster. He dropped his project to revise his lectures, and did not print them until more than two years later, when they had apparently been revised according to Tooke. Webster had previously been much concerned with fixing the language, with purifying it, standardizing it, and purging it of dialects and improprieties. As late as April, 1786, he had written "there is no longer any doubt that I shall be able to effect a uniformity of language and education throughout this continent."[10] That was Webster the lecturer to ladies and gentlemen, but lecturer Webster was quite different when he became author Webster, publishing the *Dissertations on the English Language* in 1789.

Of the five *Dissertations* that constitute the volume, the first three and

---

[9] This would have been the first edition of 1784. Revised, it became the first volume of an eventual two-volume work. The first American edition (Philadelphia, 1806–07) was based on the second English edition (1798–1805), but I have found no evidence that Webster ever saw the expanded work or ever saw any copy of Tooke again. He bequeathed his more important books to Yale and Amherst, with which he had connections; no copy of Tooke appears in any of his known bequests; see Charlton Laird, "Etymology, Anglo-Saxon, and Noah Webster," *American Speech*, X, no. 15 (1946), 13–15.

[10] *Notes on the Life of Noah Webster*, I, 114; Webster's zeal for policing the language is well summarized in Shoemaker, *Noah Webster*, pp. 243–301.

the fifth contain pretty much what Webster had promised to tell his audiences, except that the lectures seem to have been hastily revised to bring them in line with Tooke, and they are provided with "Notes Historical and Critical." Webster is still concerned with improprieties and the errors of other grammarians, but he is now not so sure that all dialects can be reduced to one by proper instruction in the schools, and his notes provide the history for his notion that all modern European languages derive from the Celtic. He now declares himself "an advocate for the opinion" of those "who suppose the Celts and Goths to be descended from the same original stock. The separation however must have been very early, and probably as early as the first age after the flood."

Dissertation IV, however, seems to be entirely new, little more than a digest of Tooke, and a digest, furthermore, which contains the details that were to supply Webster with disquisitions for the remainder of his long life. "The discovery of the time theory of the construction of language seems to have been reserved for Mr. Horne Tooke," Webster writes, and he goes on to explain that nouns were invented first, then verbs, and finally particles. He includes, also, his favorite examples, that *if* came from *give* (spelled *gif* in what Webster called Saxon), that *by* came from *beon,* and that *with* came from Icelandic *wiþan*. It is perhaps unnecessary to observe that no reputable student of language would today tolerate the notion that anyone has been able to determine which parts of speech were first invented, if indeed, language was devised as parts of speech, and that these Tooke-Webster derivations cannot be characterized as anything more serious than whimsical howlers. If, however, Webster inherited from Tooke a plenitude of unsound theory and factual blunder, he acquired, also, a fresh and broader, and in some ways sounder, outlook upon language than he had ever been able to entertain before.

Though an amateur, Tooke was an inspired amateur. He had studied Latin and Greek at the university, and although he knew little of the history of English or of its relationships with other languages, he saw that language resulted from some sort of growth, that this growth was rooted in the human mind, and that to understand a language one must study that language and its background. From Tooke, Webster acquired some notion of the importance of change in language, and the idea that the study of English etymology should be based upon a study of the older forms of the language.

Even the learned in Tooke's day might have read him with profit; at Cambridge and Oxford were good scholars who could edit ancient texts and write dictionaries and grammars of Old English,[11] but they had nothing but contempt for Tooke, who was an amateur in language, a heretic in theology, and an anti-Tory, a hater of the crown. Which of these sins blackened him most in the eyes of the scholar-divines of the universities might be hard to say, but the fact remains that they could have learned something, had they tried, from this heretic in language and theology. Doubtless they laughed at Tooke's blunders and never asked themselves seriously whether ingenious ideas might yet lurk in this tissue of error.

Webster, however, was not handicapped by learning. As yet he knew no Old English and quite probably had never seen any, except in excerpts that were part of the stock in trade of introductions to dictionaries, but he continued to write on language, combining his zeal for a simplified spelling with his new insights from Tooke. In "An Enquiry into the Origins of the Words Domesday, Parish, Parliament, Peer, and Bacon: With Remarks New and Interesting," he derived all words but the first, quite erroneously, from a word which "in the Gothic or ancient German was spelt *bar.*" He cites a Saxon law, but only in Latin and at second hand. Meanwhile, he was busy revising his old works in light of his new vision.[12]

The first volume to feel the impact of Tooke in the New World was Webster's grammar, Part II of his *Grammatical Institute.* Webster had made no secret of the source of this work; he claimed only that he had taken the grammar of "the great Dr. Lowth" and had made it understandable to less advanced pupils. Robert Lowth (1710–87), a bishop and a Hebrew scholar, was the author of the most widely admired grammar of English, *Short Introduction to English Grammar* (1762), which Webster had used for his grammar as he had used Dilworth for his speller and as he was later to use Entick as the basis of his dictionaries,[13] but even by 1785 he apparently felt he had progressed beyond Lowth. "Every English grammar I have seen," he wrote, "even the great Dr. Lowth's, is extremely erroneous and defective," and he added that his own grammar was used "as far as Portsmouth in New Hampshire." With the reading of Tooke, however, he apparently saw that his book, also, was "erroneous and defective."

At any rate, he changed it. He was revising when he read the *Diversions,* and apparently feeling he could not then rewrite entirely, he

[11] See Eleanor M. Adams, *The Study of Anglo-Saxon in the Eighteenth Century,* Yale Studies in English, 15 (New Haven: Yale University Press, 1917), 85–113.
[12] In *A Collection of Essays and Fugitive Writings,* cited earlier, pp. 249–303.
[13] The Reverend John Entick was a minor figure in eighteenth-century lexicography, but his was a well known name in the New World by virtue of the widespread piracy of his works, especially of his abridged *Spelling Dictionary;* see p. 298, n. 4.

started adorning the text with prefaces and footnotes. New editions were likely to call attention to "new remarks and examples," and to concede, "I acknowledge I have changed my opinion, since the first edition." He says he has formed his new outlook by "laborious and critical investigations of the language, particularly in ancient authors," but whose hand is behind these new researches is apparent. "Into how many classes may words be distributed?" Webster asks, and replies, "Six: Nouns, Articles, Pronouns, Adjectives, Verbs, Abbreviations or Particles," and a footnote explains, "This distribution is new. . . . See Horne's *Diversions of Purley.*" The discussion of interjections leads to a footnote which runs eight pages, beginning,

> The theory of adverbs, conjunctions and prepositions, which I call *abbreviations* is novel. I shall therefore introduce an abstract from Mr. Horne's explanations, as I find them in his *Diversions of Purley.*[14]

Webster then provides what was to become a familiar digest in many of his works, that *if* comes from *give, unless* from *onlesan, yet* from *get, but* from *be-out, since* from *seen thence, of* from *afora, by* from *beon,* and other derivations found in the *Diversions* along with some of his own. These etymologies are of course all unfounded, but in fairness to Tooke and Webster we should note that not all their guesses were wrong and that many English relationship words do come from earlier modifiers, verbs, and particles.

Webster continued to publish this second part of his *Institute* for twenty years, but after initial popularity it declined. Webster's success had brought numerous younger American competitors into the field, and Lindley Murray's *English Grammar* (1795) simplified Lowth even more than Webster had, and if Murray ever read Tooke he did not make the mistake of taking him seriously, at least not in his textbooks. Murray soon dominated the market. Webster later asserted that he withdrew his grammar because he had become convinced that all grammars of English were wrong, that he felt it "immoral to publish what appeared to be false rules and principles," and that he withdrew the old volume while preparing a correct one, but his motives were probably more practical and less idealistic than he later recalled. After about 1800, printers complained that they could no longer sell his grammar except as an adjunct to his spelling book, and that accordingly they could pay him no royalties.[15]

---

[14] I am quoting from the Fifth Connecticut Edition (Hartford: Hudson & Goodwin, 1796), pp. 6–7; many printings had something of the sort.

[15] Webster did not announce these reasons for withdrawing the grammar until 1828, and as with many people, time often colored his perspective in his favor.

After Webster's disappointment in Philadelphia, he determined to change his way of life—the project with Franklin had come to nothing, partly no doubt because the aging minister was now in ill health, but mainly, we may suppose, because Franklin had never expected to promote Webster as Webster had hoped. On October 16, 1788, the prospective spelling reformer wrote, "My birth-Day. 30 years of my life gone. A large portion of the ordinary age of man! I have read much, written much, & tried to do much good, but with little advantage to myself. I will now leave writing & do more lucrative business." He added that he was a lonely bachelor. As we have seen, Miss Greenleaf took care of his bachelor state, and her money helped him toward more "lucrative business," but his expenses grew with his family, and some fifteen years later we find him back in semirural Connecticut, this time in New Haven, hoping once more to live by writing. He revised his speller to keep alive, and embarked on two new projects, both of which grew out of that New Year's Day in Philadelphia when he read the *Diversions of Purley*.

The first of these two Tooke-inspired volumes submitted for publication was *A Philosophical and Practical Grammar of the English Language* (New Haven, 1807). As early as 1785 Webster had considered Lowth "susceptible of improvement," and as for other grammars, they had "introduced more errors than they correct. Neither Lowth nor Johnson understood the Saxon or Primitive English, without which no man can compile a real English Grammar." Spurred on by Tooke, Webster had now learned to read Old English, which he called *Saxon*. "For the outline of the system here offered," he wrote, "I am indebted to the *Diversions of Purley*." He had fleshed out Tooke with his own "researches into the ancient English, or Saxon language," and had constructed his grammar on what these researches "have proved; to my full satisfaction, to be its only legitimate principles and established usages."

He had hoped to publish the book in England, but it was a strange

His correspondence suggests that he did not refuse to let anyone print his book, though he did try to substitute for it a new edition to be mentioned below. He wrote his friend Joel Barlow, "My *Grammar* had its run and has been succeeded by Murray." See *Letters,* ed. Warfel, cited earlier, p. 292. His printers in Boston declared "we should not be willing to pay anything for them"—that is, parts II and III of the *Institute*—and printers in Wilmington reported that in Maryland, Pennsylvania, and Delaware, "there has been very little demand, indeed we may say none." See unpublished correspondence excerpted in Shoemaker, cited earlier, pp. 125–26. As late as June, 1805, however, with a new book almost ready for the press, Webster wrote a prospective printer that he had "declined to permit further impressions of my Grammar on the ground of its imperfection," but after suggesting that the customer wait for the revised volume, he cannily added, "At the same time, I know grammars will be used; and mine is probably not worse than others; in some particulars I think it better." See *Letters,* pp. 262–63.

brew to a public conditioned to Lowth and Lindley Murray, embodying Webster's discontent with the rigidity of Latin grammar and with the inapplicability of that grammar to English, along with evidence of his faith in the *Diversions of Purley*. No British publisher would touch it. Webster tried American publishers. They refused, and he had to print it privately. It did not sell. He revised. Still it did not sell. It never survived for a reprinting, never became a pupil's grammar, but it did grow into a grammarian's grammar.

Webster's rivals read it with some skepticism, but with some awe, also, and quoted it so much with and without acknowledgment that Tooke's name echoed all down through the nineteenth-century writing of grammar and even turned up in England. Murray quoted it in a new edition of his grammar, but Webster accused him of plagiarism, and was so furious that twenty years later he inserted an attack on Murray, using conspicuously large type for the purpose. "Now the fact is," he wrote, "the passages borrowed amount to thirty or more, and they are so incorporated into his work, that no person except myself would detect the plagiarisms, without a particular view to this object."[16] Webster included a digest of his grammar in the first edition of his dictionary, assuring his "fellow citizens" that "it is the last effort I shall make to arrest the progress of error, on this subject. It needs the club of Hercules, wielded by the arm of a giant, to destroy the hydra of educational prejudice. The club and the arm, I pretend not to possess. . . ."

The second venture, also, relied in part upon Tooke, who had characterized all of Samuel Johnson's work on language, including his dictionary, which had by now become standard, as "contemptible performances." Webster now produced an American dictionary for American users. He was as much patriot as pedagogue; as Bergen Evans has put it, though Webster came back with the militia from Saratoga, "in a sense he never took off his uniform. He continued to fight the British all his life."[17] He believed in the new American nation; he believed that its government, its home life, its religion, its language, and its genius were right before God and Horne Tooke, and he proposed to strengthen them all by strengthening its language. He produced *A Compendious Dictionary of the English Language* (Hartford and New Haven, 1806) in which, according to the title page, "FIVE THOUSAND Words are added to the number found in the BEST ENGLISH COMPENDS: The

---

16 *An American Dictionary of the English Language,* 2 vols. (New York: S. Converse, 1828); about midway in the introduction; the volume is unpaged. Murray was a highly successful lawyer, and seems to have been a kindly gentleman. In general he appears to have been uncommonly considerate of Webster; by 1828 he was two years in his grave. The charge, along with the grammar, was omitted from the 1841 and subsequent editions of the dictionary.

17 Evans, cited earlier, p. 11.

PRONUNCIATION marked . . . and the DEFINITIONS OF many words amended and improved."

Since Webster seldom suffered from false modesty, and material that is today reserved for publishers' blurbs was formerly written into title pages, some exaggeration is to be expected, and we may be surprised there is so little. Most of Webster's claims here have foundation, and he has even omitted a few that he might have advanced. He did augment all British dictionaries then in print, and although he wisely avoided mentioning the fact—albeit his restraint did not save him from censure, as will appear later—he excised rare concoctions like *jackalent, foutra,* and *jiggumbob.* When he claimed to have improved definitions, he was stating a simple fact; he had great powers of definition, and he simplified and clarified the work of the best British lexicographers. When he claimed to have "corrected" spelling, he was using inappropriate language, but even here he had a point.

For example, British *labour* Webster spelled *labor.* The British spelling had come down from the Middle Ages, and was an invention of Norman scribes, although Webster apparently did not know this. In French spelling, then as now, *ou* represented /u/, the sound of *oo* in *hoot* and *toot;* it was used in *labour* because the word had been borrowed from French, carried an accent on the last syllable, and was pronounced something like *la-boor,* /læbuɚ/. In later English the pronunciation approached the modern one, which might be spelled *lay-br,* /lebɚ/, or *lay-buh,* /lebə/, and by 1600 this pronunciation was recognized sufficiently so that some printers used *labor* as a spelling, others *labour.* The British spelling was standardized in the eighteenth century, but one is entitled to wonder why such lovers of Latin as Lowth and Johnson preferred the Old French and Middle English *labour* to the classical *labor.* Thus Webster could scarcely claim that his *labor* was correct and Johnson's *labour* was wrong, but he could have said that his spelling had an ancestry as good as any that could be claimed for the British spelling and that it was supported by pronunciation and good sense. His spelling triumphed in American usage, at least in many words ending in *-our* in British usage, along with *theater* as against *theatre, center* as against *centre;* he cut *musick* and *publick* down to *music* and *public,* although he failed in his equally sensible *imagin, primitiv,* and *thum.*

Perhaps his greatest achievement was this, that he had collected and incorporated into his dictionary thousands of words that had been missed by Johnson and his followers, many of them new American terms for new American objects like *banjo, possum,* and *hominy,* but some of them British terms that lexicographers like William Kendrick, Thomas Sheridan, Frederick Barlow, and John Walker had missed.

Webster no doubt trusted that his countrymen would applaud his labors. They did not. He reckoned without the bigotry of the colonial mind and the blind fury of pedagogues, in and out of editorial chairs, when anybody tampers with their prejudices in spelling or usage. In their view, Webster had meddled with both. That he had not presumed to introduce projected spellings like *pleze* and *waz* did not save him; his *Fugitiv Essays* (1790), if never widely read, were known in editorial offices. His book was condemned before it was read. The mere announcement of the volume was occasion, as Bergen Evans has pointed out, "to let slip the dogs of merriment," along with thunders of insult and abuse.[18]

Publication after publication attacked him. The *Boston Palladium* declared that if the book were to include only "pure English" it would be "superfluous," but since the editor had proposed that "the vulgar provincialisms of uneducated Americans are to be quoted as authorities for language," the result would be a "volume of *foul* and *unclean* things" which might appropriately be called "NOAH'S ARK." Others called the author "coxcomb general of the United States," "a pusillanimous, half-begotten, self-dubbed patriot," and a "literary puppy." The Philadelphia *Aurora* deemed "preposterous" the assertion that new words had been introduced and old meanings changed in the two centuries of American habitation, and dismissed the volume as the work of "the genius of ignorance," the author of "pseudo-political and pseudo-philosophical nonsense." Webster's book was called a "silly project" which could lead only to confusion. The *Gazette of the United States* trusted that it would "meet with the contempt it deserves from all friends of literature." The *Palladium* explained that any language "arrived at its zenith, like ours, . . . requires no introduction of new words." That new words had been introduced, and that the introduction was no fault of Webster's, did not concern them. So far as they were concerned, "Colloquial barbarisms abound in all countries, but among no civilized people are they admitted with impunity into books." That creatures like raccoons and opossums did exist in the New World and not in the Old, and that the poor things needed some sort of names was not the *Palladium*'s affair. That "the Connecticut lexicographer" was proposing to include the words of African slaves into Back Bay English would have been laughable to the *Boston Palladium* had it not been tragic.

No doubt Webster's being a Yale man did not enhance the cordiality

---

[18] Cited earlier; Evans also collected editorial observations on Webster, some of them excerpted in the next paragraph.

of his reception in Cambridge, but one must concede that his own manner of dealing with his fellow men did not always enhance his welcome. When Webster was visiting the Harvard campus in an effort to promote his dictionary, a young Yale graduate doing advanced study there found himself embarrassed for his fellow alumnus and wrote of him as follows:

> But the great and capital defect is the unbounded vanity of the man, (Perhaps I use a hard expression, but I use such as I hear, and such as I am inclined to think is proper from his publications and conversations which I have heard related) which is so great as to excite ridicule. Many of the principal characters here have visited or corresponded with men in England, and when they hear Webster say that he has more knowledge than any European they are rather disposed to laugh than to admire.[19]

Apparently the young man was not exaggerating, since Webster frequently implied in print and asserted in his letters that he had surpassed all others in at least some areas of lexicographical study. Shortly after he had completed his 1806 dictionary he wrote:

> In philology I have made some progress and many discoveries that throw light on language and history. I feel able to say with confidence that I have penetrated into this branch of literature beyond any European. . . ."[20]

After surveying his study of Oriental languages he wrote in 1810,

> This examination has been attended with much advantage and will produce results wholly new and, I believe, unknown even in Europe.

Returned from Europe in 1826, his conviction was confirmed; he wrote to DeWitt Clinton,

> Philology, I find, in England is in a very low state: the ablest scholars frankly acknowledge they have not given it much attention; and I found no man who had explored the field which I have been examining and no person who could give me any aid in the most interesting part of my undertaking.[21]

Even toward the end of his life, in 1837, he defended himself from a slur by the British lexicographer, Charles Richardson, by suggesting his own supremacy in etymology. He wrote, "neither Tooke, nor 'the elders of lexicography' nor the modern etymologists—not even the Germans,

---

[19] Quoted in Harry R. Warfel, *Schoolmaster to America* (New York: The Macmillan Co., 1936), p. 322.
[20] *Letters,* cited earlier, p. 279.
[21] *Letters,* pp. 333, 416; see also 291–92.

whose works I have seen—have reached the most important part of etymology, the original significance of the radix of the word, from which all other significations flow." Tooke had laid down "the first principle," that all usages must spring from an original meaning of the word; but, Webster adds, "he has in most cases failed to find that meaning, and you [Richardson] have rarely or never advanced a step beyond him." Obviously, Webster felt that he had taken those crucial steps.

Thus Webster's most ambitious and original works to their date, both published within the years 1806–07, were failures when compared with his expectations. His reaction was characteristic. He fought back against his critics, he attacked those who were not his enemies, and he projected a still greater dictionary, to be "The Dictionary," as he called it, the greatest dictionary on either side of the water. In 1812, being short of money, he moved his family to the rural community of Amherst, where he helped found a college.

Webster was now nearly fifty and needy;[22] most of his contemporaries were dead or soon would be, but praying to the Lord—with whom he maintained an intimate relationship—that he would be spared for his great work, he had embarked upon a project that was to occupy him for twenty years. Characteristically, he turned once more to the Word of God and of Horne Tooke. For fact he relied on the Bible, for method on the *Diversions of Purley*. He accepted Genesis literally, although he recognized that it required explication, and he seemed not to doubt his own competence as an explicator. The Word said that Jehovah talked with Adam; therefore, the power of speech and at least the working rudiments of a language were the immediate gift of God. This language was uniquely preserved by Noah and his sons, after the flood, and Webster named all European and many Asiatic languages Shemitic, on the theory that they were developed by the descendants of Shem, and he believed that this language is now preserved in a form most archaic and hence most pure in what he called Chaldee.

Now Horne Tooke enters. Tooke had propounded the theory that all meanings of a word must flow from the original word; to study etymology one had to determine the original word and its meaning, and observe how this meaning comprised all subsequent, derived meanings. This is obvious nonsense, though the fallacies in it are now more readily detected than in Tooke's day. For example, the basic idea in *foot* is movement, since the Indo-European base **ped-,* or **pod-,* apparently meant *go,* but *pedestal,* from the same root word, presumably refers to

---

22 He was trying to raise money by subscriptions to his proposed dictionary, apparently unsuccessfully; see *Letters,* pp. 275, 280, 281, and *passim*.

something immovable; it ceases to serve as a pedestal if it moves. This sort of thing can be observed in the history of most common words, and any body of people is likely to so use its language that a large percentage of the named meanings will have been developed or altered within relatively few centuries, altered without respect to the original word. Of course one meaning is likely to lead to another; *ped- or *pod- was involved in moving, and the foot of a creature was the instrument of movement, but the foot of a pillar remained stationary. This, however, was not what Tooke meant or what Webster understood.

Although Webster had admired Tooke for twenty years, he apparently appreciated the full impact of Tooke's theory only after he had embarked upon his great work. He tells us that he became aware of the importance of the origin of language, that his volume was then under way, but that he laid it aside for ten years while he made a "synopsis" of twenty languages—the manuscript, unprinted, is still in the New York Public Library, and must now be considered no more than a curiosity. Of particular interest to him, of course, were what he called Oriental languages, particularly those close to Chaldee; he even owned a Coptic dictionary, although he used it little. Preserved in the Amherst College library, it contains a few Webster marginalia, but nobody has ever used it much for anything. Perhaps he found few likely leads in it, since most Asiatic and African languages are not closely related to English. Whatever the reason, his practice was more random than his theory; he mounted all the dictionaries he could acquire on a semicircular desk built for the purpose, and walked around it, looking for words that began with the letter of the modern English word. In this he relied solely on consonants, since he believed that vowels change and are unreliable; he worked, furthermore, with letters rather than with sounds, another principle which would be rejected by any modern student. Incidentally, just at this time, of course, the evidence was coming to light which has led to our understanding of language relationships. Webster even encountered some of this evidence, probably during his stay at Oxford, but he rejected Sir William Jones' findings out of hand.[23]

Having completed his great study, Webster believed he had surpassed all other lexicographers. He says so repeatedly, and continued to say so in some of the last words we have from him. He admits that

Junius, Skinner, . . . Bailey, and Johnson are sufficiently correct in referring English words to the language from which they are immediately derived, especially when the orthography is too plain to be mistaken. All this is well,

---

[23] See the introduction to the 1828 edition, unpaged, under "Change of Vowels."

but it can hardly be called etymology, or the deduction of words from their originals.

He dismisses other etymologists, some with faint praise; he even abandons Tooke, "whose researches were very limited," and who had "fallen into material errors." From his own study, "The result has been to open what are to me new views of language, and to unfold what appear to be the genuine principles on which these languages are constructed." In no language, he says, have the original significations of words been found. To do so is not easy, and Webster declared that others had failed because they were not persistent or had not the keys; "even I," he adds, "have sometimes been in doubt," but "I have compared most of the radical words, in more than twenty languages twice, and some of them three times. . . . I have sometimes had a word under consideration *two* or *three* years." As late as 1839 he wrote,

The process of tracing words to their primary sense, and from that sense deducing the secondary significations and terms to express them is probably *new*. I know of no author who has attempted it with any success. In this branch of etymology, even the German scholars, the most accurate philologists in Europe, appear to be wholly deficient. To this investigation I devoted about ten years, and my reward is ample.[24]

In one of his last published writings, advertising the 1841 edition of his dictionary, he declared:

But to trace words to their origin, and show their primary or radical signification; to ascertain the origin of a great number of English words derived from other languages, and explain the physical actions or properties from which abstract and moral ideas have received their names: *hic labor, hoc opus est.* In this department of etymology, all European books which I have seen are most miserably deficient.[25]

As might have been expected the results were fantastic. The following may serve as an example:

CHUK, *n.* A word used in calling swine. It is the original name of that animal, which our ancestors brought with them from Persia, where it is still in use, Pers. *chuk,* Zend, *chuk,* a hog; Sans., *sugara.* Our ancestors, while in England adopted the Welsh *hwc,* hog, but *chuck* is retained in our popular

---

[24] *Observations on Language, and on the Errors of Classbooks* (New Haven: S. Babcock, 1839), pp. 5–6.
[25] From "State of English Philology," in *Commendations of Dr. N. Webster's Books* (Springfield? 1841?), unpaged; curiously, when the essay was reprinted in the year of Webster's death, the passage was excised. See *A Collection of Papers on Political, Literary and Moral Subjects* (New York: Webster & Clark, 1843), pp. 338–73.

name of *woodchuck,* that is, wood hog. This is a remarkable proof of the original seat of the Teutonic nations.

This blunder was one of Webster's triumphs; he referred to it again and again, in the introduction to his dictionary, in lectures, and in essays. He presumably did not know that Old English *hogg* is related to *heawian,* and probably comes through Old Norse, meaning castrated. Had he known that *woodchuck* comes from a local Indian word, he would not have been impressed; that would only have confirmed his theory. Had anyone asked how this lonesome word managed to survive for thousands of years unrecorded, only to crop up in the New England backwoods, and there not for any kind of pig, he would not have been interested. He had no concern with tracing words and boasted of it. Accused of being ignorant of the older English authors, he replied, "This is untrue; I had been for forty years acquainted with some of the best of the old authors; but I never found any use in consulting them, except in illustrating three or four words." Meanwhile, he was speculating whether Minerva was to be derived from English *man* or German *Arbeit,* and whether the *Dodanim* of Genesis is not an error for *Rhodanim,* "evidently the Hebrew plural of *Rhodan,* the original name, whence *Rhone,* in France."

Thus Webster's favorite etymologies deserved the learned laughter with which they were received. They survived several editions, probably because Webster's successor, son-in-law Chauncey A. Goodrich, did not dare face the family furor that would have followed his revising them. In the first edition after Noah's death the son-in-law phrased the matter delicately as follows: "In respect to the *Etymologies,* the Editor has not considered it as lying within his province, to make any material altera-tions."[26] Goodrich, a Yale professor who had the understanding to engage competent specialists, must have known better; one can only wonder what scholarly twitting he endured from his colleagues. Later editors, not in danger of family henpecking, silently jettisoned many of the master's etymologies.

Nor did Webster fare much better in other portions of his dictionary, although most scholars today would say that he deserved high praise, recognition which did not come to him in his lifetime. A modern critic may wince at his prudery; he rebuked Johnson for having used Shake-speare as an authority, since "play-writers in describing low scenes and vulgar characters, use low language." He had expunged such words, and he boasted "that there is not a vocabulary of the English language extant, so free from *local, vulgar,* and *obscene* words as mine!" In most departments of lexicography, however, Webster did well, and in some

---

[26] *An American Dictionary of the English Language* (Springfield, Mass.: George and Charles Merriam, 1848), p. iv.

superbly. In pronunciation and spelling his work compares favorably with that of the British editors. He is to be applauded for having made use of the best American writers, men like Washington, Adams, Jefferson, and Franklin. In his word list and in his definitions he excelled his contemporaries on either side of the water, both in the number and in the selection of his entries.

Webster very rightly observed that Johnson and his followers in England had been too belletristic. Concerned with purifying the language, they had relied upon great literary figures. Within limits this procedure is sound, but however refined the language of an Addison may be, the Addisons of the world do not much discuss some subjects, and Webster, with his background in law and his interest in science, knew it. He greatly augmented the words from such specialized fields. Nor did he stop with specialized words; his critics, by rebuking him for endeavoring to improve upon Johnson, have made themselves, not Noah, look ridiculous. He could well be proud of being able to list improvements like the following:

Words of common use, many of which are as important as any in the language. Of these, the following may be mentioned as examples. *Nouns*—grandjury, grandjuror, eulogist, consignee, consignor, mammoth, maltreatment, iceberg, parachute, malpractice, fracas, entailment, perfectibiliy, glacier, firewarden, safety-valve, savings-bank. *Adjectives*—gaseous, lithographic, peninsular, repealable, retaliatory, dyspeptic, missionary, nervine, meteoric, minerological, re-imbursable. *Verbs*—to quarantine, revolutionize, retort (v.i.) patent, explode (v.i.) electioneer, re-organize, oxydize, magnetize. Many hundred words of this kind, have been added.

Evidence like this can scarcely be ignored, and the fact is that Webster increased the best English word lists by some ten to twelve thousand words, perhaps twenty per cent, and mostly with words that, not like *chuk,* clearly belonged in any competent dictionary.

Webster also strengthened definitions. For example, Johnson had defined *mortgage* as "A dead pledge; a thing put into the hands of a creditor." This is pretty well meaningless. Webster gives the etymology, "Fr. *mort,* dead, and *gage,* pledge," and continues,

Literally, a dead pledge; the grant of an estate in fee as security for the payment of money, and on the condition that if the amount shall be paid according to the contract, the grant shall be void, and the mortgagee shall reconvey the estate to the mortgager.

The definition continues with an extensive quotation from Blackstone.

Thus Webster, if he was obnoxious—and he could be—may mark the turning point in the growth of the American language. His dictionary of

1828 probably provides the first considerable impact of American upon British English. The tide had not yet turned; a century was to elapse before we were to hear more than random shrieks of anguish that the purity of British English and Parisian French were being prostituted by vile words from across the Atlantic. But a beginning had been made.

Meanwhile, lexicography has become a minor specialty in the New World, growing more professional with the years. It even fomented a war—or what was playfully called a war—the War of the Dictionaries, which provides another bit of evidence that a frontier country was becoming adult enough to fight about language. The "war" centered on Webster, of course, who never welcomed a place on the periphery of things, but it centered, also, on a mild little man, a pedagogue turned editor, whose name, forgotten a century later, was once known in all literate households.

Joseph Emerson Worcester (1784–1865), a New Hampshire farm boy, worked his way through Yale, taught school, acquired a modest reputation as a geographer and hack editor turning out gazetteers and historical atlases along with geography textbooks, and was hired by Webster's publisher to edit "the dictionary" into a school text, which he did competently. In 1830 he brought out his own desk dictionary, which enjoyed a modest sale, and he spent much of the next thirty years revising and enlarging it, living quietly as a deacon, praying his God for life and light—he was plagued by cataracts, for which the ophthalmology of the day provided little relief—until he could finish his great work. Like Webster before him, he survived to see his labor into print, 1,786 pages of it,[27] and he had yet a few years in which to savor his achievement.

As the subject for a psychological study, Deacon Worcester would be no match for the fiery Webster, but I am not alone in believing he produced a better dictionary. He had, of course, the advantage of being able to learn from Webster, but for whatever reason, he relied remarkably little upon the older man, from whom, as a matter of course, he got his start. He was greatly embarrassed when his 1830 volume, pirated in London—it could happen on either side of the water—was billed as "Compiled from the materials of Noah Webster, LL.D., by Joseph E. Worcester." Perhaps for this reason, perhaps because of the rivalry of publishers, perhaps because of a singular lack of cordiality on Webster's part for his younger rival, perhaps because of his native conservatism, he tended to avoid Webster's works and his innovations. He treated

---

[27] *A Dictionary of the English Language* (Boston: Hickling, Swan, and Brewer, 1860).

Webster with great respect and praised "the dictionary" more cordially than Webster ever praised any book not his own, but Worcester tended to rely more on British lexicography than had the Sage of New Haven, who was at heart more reformer than "harmless drudge."

If we accept Worcester's statement—and presumably we may, for he was an honorable gentleman, and his volume seems to bear him out—he used Webster's work sparingly and acknowledged his borrowings. "With respect to a very few words of doubtful origin," he writes in his preface,

Dr. Webster's etymology is noted in connection with those of other etymologists; but in no case, so far as is known, without giving him credit. In other respects, the rule adopted and adhered to, as to Dr. Webster's dictionary, has been to take no word, no definition of a word, no citation, no name as an authority, from that work.

Worcester's eulogist was probably forming a judicious estimate when he declared,

The tendency of his mind was practical rather than speculative. As a lexicographer, he did not undertake to reform long-established anomalies in the English language; his aim was rather to preserve it from corruption. . . . In the mazy paths of etymology, if he cannot claim the merit of an original explorer, his good sense preserved him from the wild aberrations and extravagancies in which many have been misled.[28]

One might add, however, that if Worcester did not follow Webster in etymological "aberrations," he recognized Webster's virtues, and followed his predecessor in recording American pronunciation—albeit on his own authority—and in noting American additions to the English word stock.

Demonstrating the excellence of one dictionary over another is a wordy business, and I know no adequate study that can be summarized.[29] The only alternative is to offer a brief sample; obviously, this can be unjust, since entries from either dictionary could be quoted to the disadvantage of the other, and my only defense is that I have tried random sampling and that the following entry seems to me suggestive in many ways of the differences between the books. The first is Webster's:

DIPH′ THONG, *n.* [Gr. διφθογγος; δις and φθογγος, sound; L. *diphthongus.*]
A coalition or union of two vowels pronounced in one syllable. In uttering a

---

[28] Frequently printed, perhaps most conveniently in the Illustrated Subscription Edition of Worcester's dictionary (Boston: George V. Jones, 1882), p. viii.

[29] While the first edition of *Language in America* was in press, this need was largely filled through a detailed study by an excellent lexicographer; see Joseph Friend, *The Development of American Lexicography, 1798–1864,* Janua Linguariu, 37 (The Hague: Mouton & Co., 1967).

diphthong, both vowels are pronounced; the sound is not simple, but the two sounds are so blended as to be considered as forming one syllable, as in *joy, noise, bound, out.* [The pronunciation *dipthong* is vulgar.]

The second is Worcester's. Here the sequence of letters, beginning with *S.* and *W.,* for Sheridan and Walker, refers to dictionaries Worcester had consulted. *R* stands for rare, *Ch. Ob.* for *Christian Observer.*

DĬPH′ THŎNG (dĭp′ thŏng) [dĭp′ thŏng, *S. W. P. J. F. Sm. C.;* dĭf′ thŏng, *E. K. Scott;* dĭf′ thŏng *or* dĭp′ thŏng, *Ja.*], *n.* [Gr. δίφθογγος; δίς, double, and φθέγγομαι, to utter; L. *diphthongus;* Fr. *diphthongue.*] A union of two vowels in one syllable; as in v*ai*n, C*æ*sar, br*ow.*

☞ A diphthong is *proper* if both vowels are sounded, as in *boil; improper,* if only one of the vowels is sounded, as in *beat.*

☞ "In the English pronunciation of *diphthong, triphthong, aphthong,* and *ophthalmic,* dropping the *h,* which in our language is superfluous as a mark of aspiration with a consonant, we pronounce the remaining consonant *p* in the usual manner." *Smart.*

DĬPH′ THŎNG (dĭp′ thŏng), *v.a.* To form or pronounce as a diphthong. [R.]
Ch. Ob.

At a minimum, one can say that Worcester does not copy slavishly from Webster, and that he contributes considerable new matter. He includes the verb as an entry, which Webster does not. For pronunciation, he has checked at least eight dictionaries, excluding Webster, and he has been at some pains to determine the reasons for the sounds; he comes to conclusions different from Webster's. He includes citations not in Webster; elsewhere he lists numerous periodicals, British and American, which he had read for citations, along with standard writers. His definition differs somewhat in concept and notably in terminology from Webster's, and one might add that subsequent editors of Webster's dictionary changed the statement so that it is in some ways closer to Worcester's than to Webster's, in the etymology and in the distinction between a proper and an improper diphthong. Of course, Worcester was not working alone. If Webster had a son-in-law on the Yale faculty, Worcester had a father-in-law on the Harvard faculty, and editorially the battle between the dictionaries was, to a degree, a war between Yale and Harvard, a conflict in which Yale contended under some handicaps. Professor Goodrich, Webster's successor, felt free to add entries which could be thought of as new words developed since Webster's time, but he did not touch *diphthong* and thousands more that had already issued from the sacrosanct parental pen. Presumably, Worcester edited as he pleased.

Thus by 1860, the new country in the New World, as yet less than a century old and better known for its bumptiousness than its learning, had two of the best dictionaries that had ever been prepared anywhere. The volumes might have been left at that, quietly competing with each other, except for the exigencies of salesmanship. In that day most states adopted a dictionary by legislative act; these adoptions could be lucrative, in direct sales to schools and government offices, and in indirect impact upon individual purchasers. In many state capitals the adoption of an official dictionary became the occasion for spates of bad oratory and good whisky.

Here we must notice the rise of the G. & C. Merriam Company, Springfield, Massachusetts, merchants, who, by the time Webster's dictionary was reaching its second edition, were advertising "Books, Stationery, and Paper-Hangings." They acquired the rights to Webster's dictionaries, not then very remunerative, and promoted them vigorously; when Worcester's book invaded the market, the "war" was on, with editorials in newspapers, speeches, cartoons showing the dictionaries battling each other like pugilists, and a local passenger conductor who would call out, going to Worcester, Massachusetts, "Worcester! Worcester! All change from Webster." A good many users did not change from Webster, whose name now became a battle cry, and many swore by him dead who had sworn at him living.

Curiously enough, the Merriams descended from a rural printer who had been among those who tried to pirate the Blue-Backed Speller, although quite possibly innocently, it never having occurred to a printer that an author had any rights. The official account of this company[30] attributes success to the fact that George and Charles Merriam were "exceptional men," endowed with farsightedness, "a high sense of public responsibility," and "the sheer ability to make money by the careful management of operations." This estimate may be warranted, but contemporaries also praised the adequacy of the Merriam stocks of Monongahela whisky and the skill of the company's representatives in applying beverages shortly before votes were taken. Certain it is that some state legislatures voted drunk with other spirits than those of lexicography, and whereas the lists of testimonials collected by Worcester's publishers were notable for their college presidents, the Merriam supporters included most of the journalists and legislators.

Whatever the reason, the descendants of Webster's dictionaries so extensively outsold the descendants of Worcester's dictionaries that the

---

[30] Robert Keith Leavitt, *Noah's Ark, New England Yankees, and the Endless Quest,* cited earlier, pp. 46–52. This is repeated almost verbatim in *Word Study,* III (Feb., 1958), 8.

latter are now scarce and hard to come by, even the later printings. Webster may have been a less adequate lexicographer than Worcester, but his influence was incomparably greater, particularly since he was soon given credit for much that he did not do. Worcester's book must be included among those works that have suffered, through the anomalies of publishing, a neglect that their excellence did not deserve. Another is *The Century Dictonary and Cyclopedia,* a many-volumed work edited by the scholarly William Dwight Whitney and a distinguished staff, issued 1887–91 after fifteen years of labor. With it, American lexicography came of age, but the set never sold widely, and is now long out of print.

And so, *sic transit* lexicography. *Worcester* is now associated with an English shire, a meat sauce, and various communities, but no longer with word books. Only to a few users does the word *Century* suggest a dictionary, and Webster's great volume can no longer be recognized in its lineal descendant, the *New International.* The fate of such works can be instructive, but we might postpone the moral until we have considered the role of another student of language whose name was written in delible ink, Goold Brown.

Webster
Worcester
Horne Tooke

16

GOOLD BROWN, GRAMMAR, AND THE LITTLE RED SCHOOLHOUSE

With grammar, languages work. With language, minds work. With minds—we are not sure about minds and men, whether men are of them, above them or below them, cabined or freed by them. Much depends on how one delineates mind. Yet however we define these concepts, we can observe that men and mind and grammar interact. During the nineteenth century they stimulated a growth upon the North American continent that involved, also, the impact of the colonial temper of society and the American educational system as symbolized by the little red schoolhouse, all embodied in a complex of assumptions, beliefs, and mores which grew with the century, and which, variously muted and transmuted, are with us yet.

However we categorize this development, the notions involving grammar permeated men far more than did any works of lexicography, including Webster's great dictionary. Not many buyers could afford that two-volume folio work; copies of the early editions are scarce. Even the abridgments intended for what were called "primary schools" were expensively bound, and copies I have seen were not much worn.[1] Even these had to compete with pirated books from England, from which the devil of British origin had been exorcised by being "abridged for the use of schools, by an American citizen."[2] To be contrasted with the dictionaries are the spellers, the grammars, the books of readings, mainly

---

[1] My copy is *A Dictionary for Primary Schools* (New York: F. J. Huntington, 1839). The entry list includes more than thirty thousand words, but the definitions are most meager; even a complicated entry like *get* is treated in six words, as follows: "to gain, obtain, win, learn, reach." A competing abridgment of Walker's dictionary has fewer entries, but more nearly adequate definitions.

[2] I am citing John Walker, *A Critical Pronouncing Dictionary* (Philadelphia: Grigg & Elliot, 1838). As though identifying his most successful rival, Webster singled out Walker's books for an attack, in the volume cited above, p. vi.

292 AMERICAN ENGLISH IS BORN

bound in pieces of board or cardboard, pasted over with paper. Most of them must have been worn to pulp, and survivors are usually badly battered. Children trying to learn lived with these humble compilations, but not with dictionaries, not even with abridgments of the abridgments.

Why did grammar become the fetish of the schools? Supposedly, the schools taught the three R's, and rightly. In a pioneer society, reading, writing, and arithmetic were the minimal essentials of democratic communication. But why grammar? Most cultures, even relatively sophisticated cultures, have not much taught the grammar of the native language, except as an advanced subject. Obviously, a formal knowledge of grammar is not necessary to competent or even superb composition. We have no reason to suppose that Chaucer, Shakespeare, Milton, or their contemporaries studied English grammar; when Chaucer wrote a textbook for his young son, it concerned the handling of a scientific instrument, not the principles of grammar. The Egyptians based their educational system upon composition, but on the cultivation of epistolary style, not on grammar. The Romans studied oral composition as the basis of persuasive oratory, but when Virgil studied in Athens he pursued rhetoric, not grammar. Why did a backwoods people slave at the grammar of their native language?

I am not sure of the answer, but I suspect that it involves a sort of misguided unconscious pun, a sliding middle term. Generally, colonial institutions followed British institutions, and adopted their names. British elementary schools had been called "grammar schools" from the Middle Ages, but the grammar they taught was not the subject to which Webster was addressing himself when he wrote a grammar. They taught Latin, sometimes Greek, and the whole body of classical literature, science, and morals that the classical world had bequeathed. True, they started with the rules and paradigms of accidence, since the matter to be read was in Latin, and the student had first to learn to read a language whose grammatical principles he would not have learned when he learned English naturally. But that was only the introduction to grammar, the tools of the trade with which the student was to work. Grammar was the whole body of human knowledge, or at least an elementary approach to it. These old grammar schools were select, training only the children of the wealthy and only the more intellectual of them, along with lucky youngsters bright enough to become charity scholars. American elementary schools could attempt no such program as British "grammar schools" offered. Still, the schools were called "grammar schools," and what should a grammar school offer if not grammar? How much this dual use of a word had to do with the growth of the American school system may be hard to determine, but one may suspect that the logical fitness of teaching grammar in a grammar school may have had its influence during the decades. Whatever the cause, the fact is that the teaching of whatever was called "grammar" throve mightily.

If in the beginning was the word, the word in the new nation was *correctness*—and the unholy trinity was perhaps spelling, elocution, and parsing. Colonials are inherently self-conscious, fearful of doing something gauche, and English-speaking America had been rebuked so long and so roundly by the mother country that we need not marvel if natives of the colonies and then the young nation suffered from complexes. Clearly, they did. They were embarrassed about their clothes, their ignorance, their poverty, their lack of breeding, about everything that was better done in beaver-hatted Britain than it could possibly be done in the wild lands where beaver were sources of pelts. The colonials tried to improve themselves, and for improvement they turned to the schools and to lecturers who could, they trusted, tell them how to behave. They relied on education and manners, notably in language, but perhaps the best evidence that British contempt for American culture was well grounded may appear in the American response. The American school system was not calculated to sharpen either creative or critical minds; obsession with spelling and parsing does not suggest either philosophic insight or humane breadth. Correctness is a virtue, but a limited virtue, and colonial America was as yet too naive to understand how little it was asking when it yearned to be correct.

The pre-Revolutionary colonies were not, apparently, unduly perturbed about usage. The spelling is easiest to check; the following are spellings of two common words taken from lists collected by the late Professor Miles Laurence Hanley.[3]

lieutenant	leiftenant	lift	liuetenant	leftennent
left.	leut	lieuftenant	leiuetennant	leftenent
lieut	leftanant	leutenente	lifft	leiutenant
liften	lifetenant	leftannant	lieftenant	T. (abbr)
liut	leift	leivtenant	lefftenant	lefetenant
liftenant	levt	leivt	liuetants	leftentent
leftennant	leftent	leeftenent	leftenant	luit
lenienant	lefuntenant	liewt	lewtt	levetennant
leften	leftoenant	levet	leuitenant	lef.
leuten	leuet	leiftennant	liuetennt	leutenant

[3] So far as I know, these lists have not previously been printed. I have them from a mimeographed copy, undated and unidentified, except that it is entitled *A Partial List of Spellings Taken from 40 Diaries and 10 Sets of Town and Parish Records from the States of Massachusetts and Connecticut and from the Period Before the Revolutionary War.* I used a copy which the late Professor Arthur Garfield Kennedy bequeathed to the Stanford University Library.

receive	receeve	recevd	receaud	receveed
recieve	receyve	reseved	receaved	reseveing
reseve	reseave	received	receyued	receauing
recive	recives	receued	reecived	receaving
receve	receved	reced	reseaved	receavinge
reesaue	receivd	recieved	resed	recieveing
resaiev	recieued	recued	resued	
resaive	resaived	receaued	reseued	
reseive	recived	reciev'd	resseued	

One might notice here that for *lieutenant* we are dealing with two pronunciations, one based upon the British and one upon the French, and with supposed abbreviations of both of these. Even so, we can scarcely suppose that any single spelling could be called correct, or that any large percentage of the people had an urgent sense that standards in spelling were imperative.

Noah Webster has sometimes been blamed for the American devotion to spelling. He should be largely exonerated; his vision may have been wild-eyed, but it was not petty. He provided a useful elementary text-book, which included spelling, but that can scarcely be held against him. If he became better known for his speller than for his mature works, this is only to say that his countrymen applauded his lesser virtues, and were generally incapable of embracing his larger ideas—even when these were well founded, as of course they were not always. Webster contributed to spelling as a fetish, since he supplied the service book for spelling as a ritual, but if we wish to account for the American school system, for its role in language and the role of language in society, we shall need to probe the unschooled minds and the misunderstood needs of a backwoods people, a people that remained culturally colonial after it was no longer politically colonial. We cannot expect any very clear explanation, but we might try to observe part of the process, and for this observation grammar is likely to be more revealing than is spelling.

Grammar, as the word has been used in the American school system, is a curiously illegitimate offspring. Insofar as it relates to the form and structure of a language, it is the grammar of Latin, ingeniously warped to suggest English. As we have seen, Latin and English grammars are essentially, radically different; Latin relies extensively upon inflection, that is, upon the altering of the form of a word to reveal its use. English is largely analytic or distributive; that is, it relies upon the order of words in the sentence, upon particles like *of, in, by, but,* and the like, when order is not sufficiently revealing, and upon other less obvious devices—see Chapter 21. Thus we should not expect that a grammatical statement drawn from Latin would serve English very well.

Curiously, however, the grammatical description that developed in the eighteenth century and flourished in the nineteenth is even less applicable to English than it might have been. English and Latin are both Indo-European languages; if they cannot be linked through Universal Grammar, they can be linked through their common parent. Indo-European grammar was highly inflectional; it had elaborate paradigm systems for nouns, verbs, and modifiers, and devices of this grammar have decayed more or less in various languages. For example, the essentials of sentence structure survived in both Latin and English; both use subjects and verbs. On the other hand, the elaborate classifications of nouns were reduced from Indo-European to Latin and became almost extinct in Modern English. In Latin the classes of nouns had shrunk to about five, with various waifs and strays; Modern English retains, in effect, only one class, as represented in *boy* and *boys,* with a few remnants like *child* and *children, deer* and *deer.* Similarly, the elaborate case system of Indo-European, presumably reflected roughly in the fifteen or so cases of Lithuanian, had been combined into a half dozen in classical Latin, but has mostly disappeared from Modern English, where many genitives or possessives can still be recognized by form, as in *boy* and *boy's,* but all modifiers have lost indication of case, and most words functioning as subjects and complements cannot be identified by form. The parts of speech have similarly declined in English; Latin parts of speech can be identified with only minor overlapping, but the part of speech of most English words can be recognized only by function or structure, as in "We *fish* for *fish* in the *fish* pond." Inevitably, words have what is now called privilege of occurrence in English, and words like *mother, squawk,* and *photosynthesis,* which are mainly concerned with meaning, can usually be distinguished from words like *the, on,* and *who,* which are mainly concerned with grammar, but anything resembling a system of parts of speech in Modern English is so patchy that the term seems scarcely appropriate.

Thus, if early American grammarians had concentrated on the similarities between Latin and English grammar, they might have produced a grammatical description revealing within its limits. The essential functions are similar in the two languages; both grammars use subjects which combine with verbs to form predications, use complements to elaborate and refine these predications, make extensive use of a variety of modifiers, and employ coordination and subordination. Curiously, however, nineteenth-century grammarians tended not to study in much detail these areas of similarity in the two languages, but they studied with zeal and they fought with acrimony about anything which pertained to the supposed parts of speech. They would ask how many parts there are, and how they should be defined, while fighting wordily over the answers, but they did not ask how many kinds of complements there are.

That is, they seemed to have been concerned with determining the correct, or at least with condemning the incorrect. They were occupied with branding supposedly false constructions and uses, not much with understanding the working of language, and in this crusade for correctness their all-purpose weapon was an exercise known as parsing. This device was appropriate enough for anyone learning Latin as a second language. No doubt a native speaker of ancient Rome grasped the sense of a Latin sentence without deliberate consideration of the grammar, but Latin grammar was not native to Englishmen. They had to learn paradigms as exercises and use them to construe. That is, they had to parse each word, and, by its form, determine its part of speech and its occurrence in the appropriate paradigm. When words had been parsed, their functions could be determined—subjects could be distinguished from objects, verbs from verbals, and modifiers could be linked with words modified. In the end the sentence could be construed and its meaning revealed. Similarly, in Latin composition, parsing would determine correctness.

In a language like Modern English, however, parsing in this sense has not much use. The subject of a sentence is recognized not by form but by other grammatical devices, and the same is true of most other parts of the sentence. That the method was inappropriate, however, did not keep it from flourishing in the little red schoolhouse, where learning was not usually profound, rules were venerated, and pedants were kings.

The rise of parsing as a panacea for colonial ills can be traced in the textbooks of the day, through their content and their popularity. We have already mentioned Noah Webster's grammar, Part II of his *Grammatical Institute,* a modest work—the copy I have been citing contains a mere 136 pages and fewer than 50,000 words. Webster is philosophical enough to start by asking, "WHAT is grammar?" but he is succinct enough to answer in one short sentence. The book is divided into two main parts, the *Grammatical Institute* proper, about sixty pages, and an appendix, a curious jumble of paradigms not previously used, examples, discussions of what we would call usage, and "critical remarks," notably from Bishop Lowth and Joseph Priestley, again with the emphasis on usage.

In the *Institute* itself, Webster has a second sort of division, each page being divided roughly into two parts by a horizontal line, below which occur Webster's misetymologies of particles—*if* comes from *give, yet* from *get*—along with sage observation. Above the line appear a grammatical rule, examples, remarks, and finally, bits labeled FALSE CONSTRUCTION. At the end of the *Institute* appear some six pages called "AN EXERCISE," accompanied by an explanation: "The following examples will teach children to distinguish the parts of speech, and enable them to understand their connection by agreement and government, according to the foregoing rules." This carries a footnote, as follows: "This is called parsing. In this children may be much assisted by a Pocket Dictionary, which distinguishes the parts of speech. This method of parsing the English Language, which has been hitherto very little practised, is the only way to obtain a thorough knowledge of it." Webster then reprints a paragraph of prose, beginning, "A woman who has merit . . . " which he parses as follows:

A   The indefinite article.
woman A noun, in the singular number, nominative case to the verb *retains*.
who   A relative pronoun, referring to a woman, its antecedent, nominative case to the verb *has*. Rule 6.
has   A transitive verb in the indicative mode, present time, third person singular, agreeing with its nominative *who*. Rule 1
merit   A noun, in the singular number, objective case after *has*. Rule 9.

This continues for some five small pages and doubtless, within its limits, is a useful sort of game. One might ask how the children, even with a pocket dictionary, were to know that *woman* was here in the nominative case, unless they knew by some sort of grammatical sense not dealt with in Webster's book that *woman* was here the subject. Still, children could certainly play the game, with or without a pocket dictionary, and no doubt it did more good than harm. In any event, we might notice that Webster, although he apparently felt that he was to a degree an innovator in commending parsing, makes no great to-do about it.

Webster's book, as we have seen, was superannuated by Murray's. Lindley Murray (1745–1826), commonly but not very advisedly called "the father of English grammar," practiced law in Philadelphia until the Revolution, when, as a devout Quaker, he avoided hostilities, entered business, acquired a modest fortune, and after peace was signed, retired to England as a country gentleman. Nearby was a small girls' school which lacked books, and Murray, a charitable gentleman, condensed and simplified Bishop Lowth's grammar for them. The little girls liked it, and it was printed. It was revised and reprinted, reprinted everywhere, until it dominated the market both in England and in the United States, and Murray started on a second career, that of textbook writer, producing a collection of elocutionary readings and a speller, keeping his books revised, until he died a wealthy man, the author of books selling by the million.[4]

Webster's textbooks, if they were never conventional, were never orderly either—curious jumbles—but Murray's had all the Quaker virtues; they were well ordered, helpful, quietly firm, blending instinct with sweet reasonableness. Murray never calls names or shouts, and he explains carefully on whose authority and on what good sense he adjudicates. Selections in his reader have strong moral sense; all copies I have seen include a statement that the work is "designed to assist young persons to read with propriety and effect; to improve their language and sentiments, and to inculcate some of the most important principles of piety and virtue."[5] In his grammar he mentions "the learned Horne Tooke," but he does not make the mistake of using him much, and he includes as an appendix what Webster sorely lacked, what is, in effect, a rhetoric, "rules and observations for assisting young persons to write with perspicuity and accuracy. To be studied after they have acquired a competent knowledge of English grammar."

His reliance upon parsing is comparable to Webster's. When he has completed his discussion of syntax he continues:

As we have finished the explanation of the different parts of speech, and the rules for forming them into sentences, it is now proper to give some examples of the manner in which the learners should be exercised, in order to prove their knowledge, and to render it familiar to them. This is called parsing.

His method is similar to Webster's. For the sentence, "Strive to improve," he writes, "Strive is an irregular verb neuter, in the imperative mood, and

---

[4] Murray's *English Grammar, Adapted to the Different Classes of Learners*, was first published in 1795, but like Webster's book it was printed—and no doubt pirated—in all sorts of odd places. More than six hundred printings in English have been discovered, in points as remote as Calcutta, India, and Frankfort, Kentucky, and the work was translated into Dutch, Danish, Swedish, German, Russian, and Japanese; see R. C. Alston, "Bibliography and Historical Linguistics," *The Library*, 5th ser., XXI (1966), 189. The copy from which I shall quote is purportedly printed "from the last English Edition" (Exeter, N.H.: John J. Williams, 1822). The book served all purposes; it was, for example, abridged—and perhaps restolen—as a prefix to *Entick's New Spelling Dictionary* (New Haven, Conn.: Increase Cook & Co., 1807), and doubtless served other hack uses. Murray's speller (1804) seriously rivaled Webster's and *The English Reader* was so popular that it was stereotyped; my copy (New York: H. H. Wallis) is undated.

[5] The elaborate title page of one of my copies reads in part: *The English Reader, or, Pieces in Prose and Verse, Selected from the Best Writers . . . to Which Are Prefixed . . . Rules for Reading Verse with A KEY by M. R. Bartlett* (Utica, [N.Y.]: William Williams, 1830). An undated copy with a more subdued title page is identified as "Stereotyped by H. & H. Wallis, New-York."

of the second person singular. (Repeat the present tense, etc.)" These "specimens of parsing" occupy about eight pages out of more than three hundred.

Such restraint was not to continue. As the new nation moved into the nineteenth century, school use increased; the first quarter century saw the population more than double, although this was not a time of heavy immigration—Britons did not swarm to what had become a foreign country, and the flood from Ireland had not yet commenced. Children must have been scampering everywhere. With relative prosperity, schools were built, and the post-Revolutionary generation of young men had grown up enough to write books. The result was a flood of local grammars.

On the whole, they were not distinguished works. A teacher would write a little grammar book, perhaps no more than thirty or forty duodecimo pages, have it published by the local printer, and hope to use it in his own school and to sell it in neighboring communities. Some such ran through several editions and emigrated to Boston, New York, or Philadelphia, but most of them made their provincial ripples and vanished, carrying their "parsing tables" with them. Goold Brown, to whom I shall refer again, thought they deserved little more, and in his monumental bibliography labeled one of them "A sham." Another induced the splutter, "Fudge!" and concerning others he observed, "2d Edition, (altered to evade the charge of plagiarism)" and "(largely stolen from G. Brown.)" Regardless of who stole from whom, however, this new generation of grammars relied more and more upon parsing.

The most successful, apparently, were those penned by Samuel Kirkham, a schoolteacher turned phrenologist, with an eye for opportunities; he also wrote a book on *Remarkable Shipwrecks* (Harrisburg: J. S. Wiestling, 1824). In 1823 he published *A Compendium of English,* turned out by the local newspaper shop, "Printed at the Herald Press, by J. P. Thomson, for the author." It burgeoned; soon it was being printed in Harrisburg and Albany, and it achieved the crowning accolade, being stereotyped in New York. Kirkham asserted that he had received more than six hundred flattering letters concerning his book, although these apparently included polite responses acknowledging complimentary copies. To his original *Compendium* he added "Familiar Lectures" and a "System of Philosophical Grammar, in Notes"— largely adapted from Webster and Horne Tooke—and based his book on "A New Systematic Order of Parsing." He was soon able to boast that he had sold 40,000 copies, and for the 11th edition in 1829, that more than 22,000 copies had been "demanded" in the previous year. Later he raised his claim to 60,000 a year; the book achieved its 80th edition by 1840, and it was still being revised and stereotyped as late as 1857, long after his death.

He relied on definitions, rules, and parsing, especially on parsing. The following is typical, the beginning of the parsing of *John's hand trembles:*

John's is a noun, the name of a person—proper, the name of an individual—masculine gender, it denotes a male—third person, spoken of—singular number, it implies but one—and in the possessive case, it denotes possession—it is governed by the noun "hand," according to

RULE 12. *A noun or pronoun in the possessive case, is governed by the noun it possesses.*

Declined—sing. nom. John, poss. John's, obj. John. Plural—nom. Johns, poss. Johns', obj. Johns.

Students repeated this ritual with appropriate variations for every word, and there are dozens of these rules, with numbered notes, followed by exercises on "FALSE SYNTAX." All this must have been something between torture and a soporific rigmarole, but Kirkham recommends it as both pleasant and profitable for the students. As for the teacher, "By pursuing this system, he can, with less labor, advance a pupil farther in a practical knowledge of this abstruse science, in *two months,* than he could in *one year* when he taught in the 'old way.' " He points out that teachers will no longer have to listen to students repeating rules they have learned by rote, with no knowledge of what they mean. "This system," he declares, "obviates the necessity of pursuing such a stupid course of drudgery." The children would learn the rules by repeating them over and over in parsing, which Kirkham asserts they will find great fun. He admits that other writers have devised means of parsing, but he finds these rival methods inadequate. "Some writers have, indeed," he writes, "attempted plans somewhat similar; but in no instance have they reduced them to what the author considers a regular systematic order." In a way he was right; if his purpose was to produce little mimics, he had pushed the system about as far as it could be made to go.[6]

Kirkham prided himself upon his regularity, and indeed he deviated but little from his rules. For example, under Rule XVIII, Note 6, under

[6] I have been citing Samuel Kirkham, *English Grammar, in Familiar Lectures; accompanied by a Compendium, Embracing a New Systematic Order of Parsing,* new ed. (New York: Collins and Brother, n.d.). It was copyrighted 1857, and a note on the fly leaf indicates that one E. V. Weber had it in 1859. It is leather-bound, and apparently was a prized possession; Weber, at that time in Wisconsin, signed it again in 1865, and it was later signed three times by Edmond P. Weber.

"ADDITIONAL EXERCISES IN FALSE SYNTAX," the following sentence rests upon false syntax: "My cousin gave his fine pair of horses for a poor tract of land." This sentence is not condemned because it is dull, but because "Adjectives should be placed next to the nouns which they qualify," and accordingly the sentence should read *"his pair of fine horses,"* not *"his fine pair of horses."* For the same reason, *a new pair of shoes* and *an elegant piece of furniture* are considered false syntax. Of course, one of Kirkham's "young learners" might have objected that the writer may have meant a fine pair; after all, fine horses can be mismatched into an unbalanced pair, but if Kirkham was concerned with such matters his book does not suggest it. He was promoting a "regular systematic order," basing his order upon rules, which he smugly assures the reader have been taken from Lindley Murray, changed only in those rare instances in which the great man had been in error. He complains that some faddists have tampered with Murray. But not Samuel Kirkham. Apparently Murray's status as a grammarian rose as his sales declined, as had Lowth's before him. Relying on Murray, Kirkham asserted that his compendium alone "may be properly considered an 'Ocular Analysis of the English Language.' " Furthermore, for those who wished philosophical notes, he had added them; they were not intended as "a useless exhibition of pedantry," but were rather a concession to "a kind of *philosophical mania"* which had arisen of late.

If Kirkham ever attracted sixty thousand admirers in one year, they did not include Goold Brown. Like Noah Webster, Brown was a New England pedagogue, albeit a very successful one, and he was as learned, perceptive, devoted, devout, indefatigable, conceited, contentious, and cantankerous as Webster himself. And he hated Samuel Kirkham and all his works, especially his textbooks, which vastly outsold Brown's. Brown was never one to shun a good fight, if it could be carried on in print, though he was proud of the fact that he had been able to talk with Kirkham at a funeral without mentioning grammar or any other exacerbating subject. Brown beat him in the end. He outlived him and outlasted him, and he produced a colossal work that stood as a beacon in the study of language, even though it was a beacon that led to no port, an anachronism that was obsolete before it was finished.

Goold Brown (presumably pronounced to rhyme with *fooled,* since it was a family name, formerly spelled Gould) was born to a Quaker family in Providence, Rhode Island, March 7, 1791. His father, himself a schoolteacher and writer of essays, tutored his child in Latin and Greek, and sent him to a good school, but could not afford college. The son later asserted that he had taught four languages for many years—the fourth was probably Hebrew—and he occasionally quotes French. He says that for a time he had to indulge in "mercantile pursuits," which he found repugnant; as a teacher he rose rapidly until he headed his own academy in New York, which he says he conducted "for about twenty years." He was enough of a figure in the metropolis to read a eulogy before two literary groups, who ordered it printed. He published several textbooks, generally successful although they did not sell as did Kirkham's, and sometime after 1836 he left New York and eventually retired to Lynn, Massachusetts, to finish his monumental work, *The Grammar of English Grammars.*[7] He says that freedom from pecuniary worries had permitted him to escape the restrictions of his profession; whether he got money from his textbooks, from a bequest, or from some other source he does not explain. He died a fortnight after correcting proofs on the revised edition of 1857, leaving behind him the reputation of having been a good husband, father, and churchgoer.

Brown fought the good fight, against ignorance, change, and all other grammarians. As for ignorance, no doubt as a teacher he considered it his greatest enemy, but he managed to say very little about it. As to change, while professing an open mind he usually tried in his published works to preserve things as they were, or as he had decided they were, even in the face of his own evidence. For example, he says of the parts of speech, "We must count them ten, and preserve their ancient order as well as their ancient names," although the evidence he has just cited makes clear that there was no "ancient" agreement on any of these subjects.[8] As to grammarians, he is generous with the word *learned,* but he condemns them all.

According to Brown: Lowth was "extremely erroneous"; Priestley, mainly notable for his "haste and carelessness," was no grammarian at all; and Samuel Johnson's grammar was in many ways the best, but Brown further says that he could not open Johnson's works without "shedding a tear," for they are all "most truly contemptible performances," in short, "a reproach to the learning and industry of a nation which could receive them with the slightest approbation." The dictionary "of what he *calls* the English language" is, according to Brown, valuable only for its bulk, and nearly a third of it is

as much the language of the Hottentots as of the English; and it would be no difficult matter so to translate any one of the plainest and most popular numbers of the *Spectator* into the language of this dictionary, that

---

[7] (New York: Samuel & William Wood, 1851). Except as otherwise noted, I shall cite the first edition. Brown revised for the fourth edition (1857), but a rough check suggests that the changes were minor. After Brown's death other hands added an index, and the work survived at least its tenth edition (1880).

[8] P. 119.

no mere Englishman, though well read in his own language, would be able to comprehend one sentence of it.[9]

As for Lindley Murray, his books were "as *incomplete* as they are *inaccurate*." American grammarians fared no better:

> The history of *Dr. Webster,* as a grammarian, is singular. He is remarkable for his changeableness, yet always positive; for his inconsistency, yet very learned; for his zeal "to correct popular errors," yet often himself erroneous; for his fertility in resources, yet sometimes meagre; for his success as an author, yet never satisfied; for his boldness of innovation, yet fond of appealing to antiquity. His grammars are the least judicious, and at present the least popular of his works . . . it is impossible to place any reliance upon the authority of a man who contradicts himself so much. . . . How many different schemes of classification this author invented, I know not; but he might well have saved himself the trouble of inventing any. . . .[10]

In Brown's view all grammarians are obtuse and inaccurate—all except a few who wrote in Latin and on Latin—composing nothing but solecisms. He seeds his "Improprieties for Correction" with supposed "false syntax" from his rivals, and he never manages to remain long aloof from his favorite subject, the venality, stupidity, and literary inelegance of grammarians. No one can accuse him of being less than ample in excoriation, and his Ciceronianism rises with his wrath. His great work runs to more than a thousand folio pages in small print, more than a million words, and throughout it he is usually insulting somebody. The introduction, which alone would make a sizable book of perhaps 125,000 words, generally supports the thesis that the study of grammar as a profession has always been the habitat of a "various and worthless . . . set of quacks and plagiaries [*sic*]."[11] Success has come to those who had neither "learning nor talent." Murray floundered "in fallacy or absurdity . . . from necessity," and if, as Webster charged, he plagiarized, Webster's "passages in question were not worth copying," and Murray's books do not differ much anyhow, "except in quantity of paper." But here, as elsewhere, Kirkham leads all the rest—"The one who seems to be now taking the lead in fame and revenue, filled with glad wonder at his own popularity is SAMUEL KIRKHAM."

After the manner of the critics of the day, Brown professes benevolence. So inconsequential a writer as Kirkham does not warrant serious criticism, and Brown would wish to be no less than kind to anyone:

---

[9] Pp. 126–27.
[10] Pp. 118, 120.
[11] P. 15.

It is cruel in any man, to look narrowly into the faults of an author who peddles a school-book for bread. The starveling wretch whose defence and plea are poverty and sickness, demands, and must have, in the name of humanity, an immunity from criticism, if not the patronage of the public.[12]

But the fact is that, "he treats nothing well; for he is a bad writer. . . ." He can scarcely write a page of English, has patched up a grammar "by the help of Murray's text only" into a "paltry scheme" which has succeeded because, whom the author cannot intimidate, he bribes. "Have plagiarism and quackery become the only means of success in philology?" Brown asks. Apparently so, but "Is it not a pity, that 'more than one hundred thousand children and youth' should be daily poring over language and logic like this?" So it goes; Kirkham is attacked for pages, and subsequently excoriated in footnotes and held up to ridicule as the master of impropriety.

Actually, Kirkham, like Brown, writes rather well. Though perhaps a bit stiffspined, he is devoid of neither vigor nor rhetorical artifice. Why did Brown detest him so? Jealousy of a man whose books had run through more than a hundred editions may be involved, but it is also true that Kirkham had the temerity to fight back, at least a little. Brown had apparently accused him of writing books without merit, and Kirkham appealed,

What! a book have no *merit,* and yet be called for at the rate of sixty-thousand copies a year! What a slander is this upon the public taste! What an insult to the understanding and discrimination of the good people of these United States! According to this reasoning, all the inhabitants of our land must be fools, except one man, and that man is GOOLD BROWN![13]

But poor Kirkham was no match for Brown, who was more learned, more alert, more persistent, and much more voluminous.

Actually, Brown produced a more significant, more capable volume than all this acrimony would suggest. When he asserts that in other grammarians there are "a hundred gross solecisms for every tolerable definition," we can only shrug, and class it with his other ample generalizations. He also claims: "A majority of all the definitions and rules contained in the great multitude of English grammars which I have examined, are, in some respect or other, erroneous."[14] The fact is, however, that when he observes, "It is certain that we have hitherto had, of our language, no complete grammar," he is stating a simple fact, and

---

12 P. 28.
13 P. 31, n. Brown cites the *Knickerbocker,* October, 1837, p. 361.
14 P. 101.

when he implies that he has come closer than any other to filling that want, he is not exaggerating.

Within its definition, and on its assumptions, *The Grammar of English Grammars* is a remarkable book. It opens with a bibliography of some 548 items, not to mention various editions, mainly grammars, many of them obscure. I know nothing even remotely comparable. Brown must have known many of these works intimately, for he seeded his discussions with tens of thousands of quotations from them. Furthermore, the whole is keenly done; Brown had a penetrating and discriminating mind, and, granted his hidebound assumptions, he is often revealing, even brilliant.

Of course his many-storied pile of gingerbread could not endure as he trusted it would. It had no foundation. When he assumed that "grammar is essentially the same in all languages,"[15] he was providing no basis for an enduring work, and when he assumed that grammar had not changed since Aristotle, he was revealing the superficiality of his thinking and of his research. Some contemporary Americans did know better. Even Noah Webster, if he never read Jacob Grimm, Rasmuss Rask, and Franz Bopp, did know that something was happening in Europe, and Webster antedated Brown by a quarter century. Brown's contemporaries had been going to Tübingen, Heidelberg, Jena, and Berlin, and returning with a new world of insight, the foundations of philology. Even as Goold Brown was revising his monumental tome, Professor George P. Marsh was preparing his *Lectures on the English Language,*[16] which, delivered at Columbia College, announced the new study of language in the New World. William Dwight Whitney, distinguished professor of Sanskrit at Yale, was preparing for his *Language and the Study of Language.*[17] Inevitably, these books are now obsolete, for much has been learned since, but a modern student of language finds them essentially sound. To the same student Goold Brown's great tome is a platypus-like creature out of an antediluvian world. Culturally, Brown died, as he was born, in the eighteenth century; he never got much beyond the classical horizon that his father had shown him as a boy.

Thus it was that Goold Brown, an intelligent and learned, if acrimonious, scholar, a pious Quaker devoted to mankind, attempted Herculean labors but produced only a monumental anachronism. His was the last great voice of eighteenth-century misunderstanding of the nature of language. As a secondary school pedagogue, he was not much

---

[15] P. 6.
[16] (New York: Scribner, 1859).
[17] (New York: Scribner, 1867).

tumbled in the scholarly ferment of his day, and retired among the good folk of Lynn he would have been yet more sheltered. Even so, the evidence was before him; Professor William Chauncy Fowler of Amherst produced quite a respectable grammar, which Brown includes in his bibliography.[18] He could have learned from it, but it came out too late to be of much use in Brown's first edition, and one may doubt that he used it for the second. Brown was well into his sixties, apparently in declining health, and anyhow he thought he knew the answers. Thus we may hope that Brown died as he would have wished to, the author of *The Grammar of English Grammars,* the definitive study of the English language for all time.

It is less than that. One might plausibly guess that no man is now living, or ever will be again, who has read *The Grammar of English Grammars* attentively from beginning to end. It is deader than the dodo, in whom, after all, there is considerable interest. But at worst, Brown and his works are involved in a pleasant irony. Looked at in retrospect, Goold Brown is not the archenemy of Samuel Kirkham, but they become together the two notable laborers in the vineyard of obsolete English language teaching.

Kirkham popularized parsing. His textbooks were based upon it, and they were used in the schools as were no others. Furthermore, his were the textbooks to beat; any textbook writer in his day who wanted to sell books would be likely to try to outparse him. Goold Brown never managed to do this, though his texts, somewhat revised, were reprinted as recently as an anniversary edition in 1923. Brown's great contribution was that, while making Kirkham personally ridiculous, he provided the Kirkham textbooks with a philosophical reason for being, and Kirkham's method, parsing, with the authority of a calf-bound tome. Nobody ever managed to controvert Goold Brown in detail; there was too much of him.

Furthermore, Brown was admired. Pedagogues and editors who were no more scholars than he exalted him. The *Massachusetts Teacher* praised *The Grammar of English Grammars* for its "masterly discussion," and advised "every progressive teacher" to "do as we have done—buy it and use it constantly." The *Connecticut Common School Journal* called it a "work of unequalled excellence and worth," and the *Indiana School Journal* wrote, "This is among Grammars what 'Webster's Unabridged' is among dictionaries, and is undoubtedly the most complete and best grammatical treatise ever published." It was called "the great work of a

---

[18] Brown cites *English Grammar* (New York: Harper, 1850), 675 pp. It was later enlarged to *The English Language in Its Elements and Forms* (New York: Harper, 1855), 796 pp., but this does not appear in Brown's revision.

great workman," and was recommended as the means to "gain a thorough knowledge of the formation, rise and progress of our noble language, of its principles, powers, elements, and combinations, of its adaptedness to conversation, poetry, prose, the forum, pulpit, or halls of legislation. . . . ."[19] This went on and on; for nearly half a century the book was praised on all sides. Thus, between them, Samuel Kirkham and Goold Brown did much to fasten upon the minds of American youth the conviction that the first of the deadly sins is grammatical impropriety, and that salvation is to be sought through the repetition of rules. If prissiness and pedantry have dogged the use of language in the United States, part of the cause is apparently to be sought in the cult of parsing, where Samuel Kirkham and Goold Brown are among the patron saints.

Although their influence upon the course of language can readily be exaggerated, figures like Noah Webster and Goold Brown are highly symbolic. They wrote, and in the study of language we have tended to attach too much importance to the written word. The tradition has an honorable ancestry. Classical Latin, Greek, and Hebrew now exist only in written form, and these were long assumed to be better languages than any modern tongue, worthy not only of preservation but also of imitation. Furthermore, as the study of language grew in modern Europe, including England, many writers concerned with language resembled social workers and law enforcement officers more than they did scholars. They were concerned with controlling language, not with understanding it, with policing language for what they called its purity rather than studying language as life. And of course, if a writer believes that he can control language—as many eighteenth-century savants thought they could and many voluble contemporaries believe we should —he had best start with written language, and perhaps end with it, since written language is easier to convict of being wrong than is oral speech and easier to reform into what is called correct. It is there; it can be pinned down, and it is unalterable.

Thus eighteenth-century writers tended to think of language as written, to work with its written form, and to believe that written works could fix language and determine its course. As we have seen, even men like Webster and Johnson believed this until they learned better, and even when they learned to think on sounder principles, they never

---

[19] In several of the editions such encomiums were assembled at the end of the volume under the title "Brown's Grammars." The page seems to be an advertising flier bound into the book. The version in the fifth edition, for example, includes similar praise for abridgments of the major work, *The Institutes of English Grammar* and *The First Lines of English Grammar,* both stereotyped.

learned to work much on these principles. The concern for the written word continued; the great students of language in the late nineteenth and early twentieth centuries were philologists. They knew that speech was basically oral, but they tended to work with older languages or the history of modern languages, and hence they had to rely mainly on written materials. Naturally, if not inevitably, they tended to think in written forms, and would use spellings and words when they might better have used sounds and structural units which may be either greater or less than the words in a dictionary. Thus if, as Shelley thought, poets are the unacknowledged legislators, they are so in that they gave memorable form to ideas which thereby more readily insinuate themselves into many minds. They are not, however, extensively legislators of speech; we may quote Shelley's "Bird thou never wert" facetiously, but the phrase has not saved either *thou* or *wert* as words. Poets may be kings in Keats' "realms of gold," but language is democratic, not monarchic.

Noah Webster had great influence upon American lexicography, but he probably had less influence on American English than is normally assumed. In fact, he probably had less influence than had Goold Brown, and Brown had less influence than had his despised rival, Samuel Kirkham. Brown taught the teachers of oral language, but Kirkham and his multitudes of cheap little books taught the users of oral English. He told them what to do; they probably did not do it much, but no doubt they tried to. In language no man counts for much, but few have counted for as much as did Samuel Kirkham, although he is now so forgotten that he appears in but few reference works, and so far as I can recall, prominently in no histories or serious discussions of the language.[20]

---

[20] He probably lurks behind Mencken's Samuel Kirkman; see Mencken/McDavid, *The American Language,* cited earlier, p. 535.

17

LINGUISTIC GROWING PAINS—FROM WITHOUT

As the new nation grew, American English sprouted and spread. These changes had little observable impact upon grammar in the sense in which I am using the word in this book, the way a language works. Such changes there must have been. I shall try to survey them in retrospect, but changes in grammar are slow, and nineteenth-century American grammar, so far as we know now, is not demonstrably different from nineteenth-century British grammar. Grammar in the sense of usage does show differences in pattern, as we have seen in an earlier chapter, so that the American who said *et* and *ain't, seen* and *seed* for *saw,* although he was devising nothing new, was echoing a British ancestor who was preserving older English forms that were even then becoming unfashionable. For reasons we have observed, some of these forms became commoner in the New World than they had been in the Old. Inevitably, these forms spread west, developing their own patterns of occurrence as they migrated, but the Iowans and Chicagoans who say *ain't* are echoing the Easterners who had said *ain't,* as the colonials had echoed the contemporaries of Shakespeare and Milton.

Similarly, as we have noticed, various British pronunciations were somewhat jumbled in crossing the Atlantic and appear in new distributions in the New World, although they are the same old pronunciations imported from the mother country. Likewise, these pronunciations moved west, so that pronunciations arrived in Oklahoma after their long trips from Virginia, Georgia, and other points central and south, while immigrants to Oregon and Washington had earlier been at home in New Jersey, Pennsylvania, and points north. Some development in pronunciation there was; there always is, but Western dialects are in some ways more conservative than Eastern dialects, as Eastern dialects had been more conservative than British dialects. For example, take the distinction between the nasal /n/ and the nasal /ŋ/, commonly thought of in spellings like *goin'* and *going*. As we have seen, the /ŋ/ pronunciation partly replaced the /n/ pronunciation in England, but the change was late, and sophisticated, and hence *n*-speakers on the American seaboard probably exceeded those in Britain. For similar reasons, the *n*-speakers moved west in the New World and prospered, and accordingly there are relatively more *n*-speakers as against /ŋ/-speakers in the Middle West than in Boston.

Thus the most noticeable developments in what might be called Middle American—that is, American English from about the time of the beginning of the great western movement to the First World War—appear in vocabulary. The most obvious developments, although by no means the most important, involve words borrowed from other languages. This borrowing represents three different sorts of sources, each resulting in different patterns, as follows: borrowing from the native Amerindian languages, borrowing from other invading Indo-European languages, and borrowing from what might be called the camp followers, the languages that came in the wake of the languages that established and consolidated the beachheads.

As for Amerindian, we have already noticed that from their first contact with the natives the invaders began acquiring a few words, for local plants like *hickory, potato, tomato,* and *chocolate;* for strange animals like *raccoon, opossum, terrapin;* for strange creatures from the sea, *quahog, menhaden;* along with words involved in the family relationships and living customs of Amerindians: *squaw, papoose, manitou, tomahawk,* and *wampum.* More than half of these borrowings presumably date from the seventeenth century; the practice was never extensive, and it rapidly declined, since the nineteenth century saw the extinction of most Amerindian languages in what is often called the Continental United States, or the reduction of Amerindian speakers to remnants culturally and linguistically doomed. This destruction took place under conditions that did not much encourage borrowing from the native languages.

The settlement of the east coast does small credit to the humanitarian motives of the white men, but there were exceptions. The prospect of slaughter or starvation encouraged circumspection among early settlers, and many religious leaders, Penn and Roger Williams for example, tried to treat the natives as brothers. Furthermore, the seventeenth and eighteenth centuries saw the efflorescence in western Europe of the doctrine known as primitivism, a belief that man's native goodness survives best in a savage state. This idea was widespread; it not only engaged the philosophically minded like Montaigne, but it also promoted popular novels of lovers who escaped parental wrath by fleeing to the noble denizens of the forest, who would understand that love must triumph over the trammels of society. Thus to many an early American settler the Amerindians were "noble savages," nature's noblemen, not so distantly removed from Adam and Eve as are most of us. The Amerindians, on their part, often evinced a childish curiosity and friendliness.

These early honeymoons and truces did not last long. As the invaders pushed west, the Amerindians became more and more aware that they were being dispossessed, debauched, and slaughtered. They grew to hate the newcomers, and the outcome has demonstrated that they had good reason for their hate; they have been, except for remnants, exterminated. Meanwhile, the whites became less tolerant; the noble denizens of the forest were now looked upon as lying, murdering, treacherous, dirty heathen, probably unwelcome to God and certainly bad for business. Thus a sort of cold war existed between the races, a war that readily erupted into shooting. The dominant idea was succinctly put by General John Sullivan in a toast drunk by his officers celebrating a victory in the War of 1812, "Civilization or death to all American Savages."[1] Understandably, the Amerindians tended to avoid the newcomers, except when frontiersmen and pioneers were likely to be sources of hunting materials or firewater, or when the invaders had horses and other livestock that a clever marauder might hope to seize as a worthy prize. That was the Amerinidian attitude; the whites, of course, called the operation stealing.

Thus, linguistic exchange did not characterize the movement west. Language thrives on friendship and social intercourse, and both sides were hampered by fear and distrust. The Amerindians suffered most in numbers, the invaders having guns and stronger medicine. The invaders suffered most in cultural myopia; for example, they feared being scalped, but they suffered more from one another and from the rigors of the climate than they did from the aborigines. Barring a few battles in which Amerindians were aiding invaders who were fighting one another —in Braddock's defeat, for example, and in the campaigns led by Tecumseh—probably fewer white men were killed by Indians than were shot in the accidental discharge of the invaders' own weapons or by the blunders of trigger-happy compatriots. The number who were killed by gun or tomahawk were few when compared with the thousands who died from hunger, thirst, freezing, or disease induced by privation. For example, in western Nevada the old immigrant trail crosses the Sixty-

[1] Roy Harvey Pearce, *The Savages of America,* cited earlier, p. 55. Pearce surveys the changing attitudes of the white men; so far as I know, nobody has done the like for the Amerindians.

mile Desert, where the waters that flow west and those that flow east both vanish in sinks. This trail had only one virtue; after the first few crossings nobody lost it. Travelers had only to follow the bleaching bones of animals, the wrecked and abandoned wagons, the shallow graves of men, women, and children—not killed by Amerindians, who had the good sense to stay away and let the invaders die.

Accordingly, after some acquisition of native words along the eastern seaboard, few Amerindian words were borrowed for nearly two centuries, by which time the Indians were enforcedly peaceful. Since they were no longer a threat, the white men became more friendly, and other changes were permeating the white culture. Tolerance increased, and various whites developed a lively interest in the natives, studied them and their ways, tried to help them or to cultivate them as tourist attractions. Thus from the Southwest we get *kiva* for a religious room, *hogan* for a native hut, *yebuchi* for a deity, and *katchina* for another deity or the doll that represents it, although many such words have limited currency. From the Northwest we get *cayuse* for horse, *chinook* for a warm wind, *potlatch* for a feast, *hooch* for liquor, *skookum* meaning powerful, *pemmican* and *muckamuck* for food, the latter of which has been perverted into *high muckamuck*. Words like *wickiup, kinnikinnick, atlatl, kyak,* and *igloo* have been picked up scatteringly, but the total is not large, and most of the words are but little known.

Occasionally, an Amerindian word, often not so recognized, may be seized upon for special use. *Podunk,* the name of a band of Amerindians —the word apparently means neck or corner of land—became the name of a pond and a community, and finally a term for a remote or backward community. *Tularaemia* has an Amerindian root. Nahuatl *tullin* became Spanish *tule,* a name for a tall bullrush, which with the Spanish suffix *-ar,* meaning "place-where," became the name of a California county, *Tulare County.* This was the scene of the discovery that the disease which was decimating rabbits and ground squirrels was the so-called "rabbit disease" that was killing human beings also. With the Greek suffix, *-aemia,* the disease became *tularaemia.* For political purposes *mugwump* seems to have been picked up from Amerindian, and *caucus* may have been.

Once an Amerindian word gets into the stream of American English it can, of course, grow as words do. For example, *Tammany* has given rise to dozens of meanings and phrases. The word comes from a Delaware chief whose name has been variously spelled *Tammenund, Tamanen,* and the like. Social and political societies were named for him and were said to have a patron saint, *Saint Tammany,* along with a *King Tammany,* and various sorts of *Sons of Tammany.* In turn the clubs became the ancestor of the *Tammany Ring,* which gave rise to *Tammany Heelers, Tammany braves,* and *Tammany Hall,* which started as a building and became the name of a ruling clique, even a synonym for corrupt politics, and went on to become the *wigwam,* replete with *sachems,* and supported by *Tammanyites.* This sort of thing could happen to any Amerindian place or personal name, of course, as it did in limited ways with *Chautauqua, Mackinaw,* and *Mississippi,* but the total is relatively small. Some words purport to be translations of Amerindian words—*paleface, Great White Father, Black Hawk,* and the like, and these can have secondary lives, but even with such additions, the impact of Amerindian upon American speech is small aside from place names.

These conclusions are not unique; other peoples have been submerged, leaving behind them little linguistic evidence other than names on the land. We know relatively little of prehistory in Amerindia, but whatever destroying there was of one people by another seems to have displaced languages more than it mingled them. Likewise, when our Germanic ancestors overcame inhabitants of the British Isles, named for the Brythonic Celts, the natives were partly driven out, partly absorbed. but in the areas where English triumphed, little that was Celtic remained except in names for rivers, villages, and the like. The Celtic element in the language is still small, mostly borrowed in later times. Similarly, in Spain, the Iberians and Ligurians left a few names behind them but few working words in the language that was to grow from Latin into Spanish. Examples could be multiplied. If the invading language is spoken by only a relatively few of a new ruling class, it may decline, as Anglo-Norman did when it eventually succumbed to the native English, but where one people rolls over another, the submerged language is likely to leave few remnants but names. Thus, although hundreds of thousands of North American Indians gave permanent names to thousands of places, a mere handful of Amerindian words have found their way into the working parts of the language, and many of those were borrowed from Latin America, usually by way of Europe, or have been adopted in recent years.

So much for the borrowings into English from Amerindian; quite different patterns characterize the borrowings in the New World from languages of the Old. Here we must deal first with the other invading tongues, which for North America were restricted for all practical purposes to French, Dutch, and Spanish; Russian accounts for names like Russian River, but words like *borscht* and *sputnik* have come later by other channels. In this connection we should recall a distinction we made earlier, in Chapter 7, between dominant languages—in this instance, English—and the moribund languages. For North America, all these rival Indo-European languages have been moribund, except Spanish south of the Mexican border and in some adjacent islands, and possibly French in Canada. That is, we need not be much concerned with dialects in these languages, but mainly with their impact as languages.

Most spectacular was Dutch. Hollanders were so scarce that, by the end of Peter Stuyvesant's rule, New Amsterdam had perhaps 2,500 inhabitants, yet modern American speech preserves from these few Hollanders more words in common use than from the hundreds of thousands of northern Amerindians. We have already observed in Chapter 7 that the borrowed words were few, but these few include *boss, Santa Claus, waffle, cole slaw, sleigh, saw buck, dope, dumb* ("stupid"), *logy, snoop,* and *spook.* Few Amerindian words, except *tobacco, chocolate, potato,* and *tomato* from South America, have attained any such popularity. We may notice that the Dutch terms tend to be short and picturesque, and that New York became and has long been the financial, cultural, social, and literary capital of the country. Whatever the reason, more words per capita have been borrowed into American English from these early Hollanders than from any other sort of non-English speakers. Later Hollanders had mainly local impact.[2] Neither *andijvie* (endive) nor *snijboonen* (salted beans) has become popular; see, for example, *The Palimpsest,* XLV (1964), after p. 161.

Even *Yankee,* that much researched word, is probably from Dutch. The term was well enough known by 1758 so that General James Wolfe, the conqueror of Quebec, offered to lend "two companies of Yankees, and the more as they are better for ranging and scouting than for either

---

[2] I have already cited, in connection with Dutch, Marckwardt, *American English,* to which should be added as a general survey Thomas Pyles, *Words and Ways of American English* (New York: Random House, 1958). The great mine was of course H. L. Mencken, *The American Language,* also cited earlier. The most important early writings on American English are excerpted in Mitford McLeod Mathews, *Beginnings of American English* (Chicago: University of Chicago Press, 1931; in Phoenix Books, 1963). Older glossaries and dictionaries of American English, notably those by R. H. Thornton, John Russell Bartlett, and Alfred L. Elwyn, are now mainly superseded by two excellent sets, *A Dictionary of American English* (hereafter referred to as DAE) and *A Dictionary of Americanisms* (hereafter DA), both cited earlier. Remarkable for its day was M. Schele de Vere, *Americanisms; The English of the New World* (New York: Scribner, 1872). I shall make scattering use of it. For less conventional language, the following are useful: *The American Thesaurus of Slang,* ed. Lester V. Berrey and Melvin Van den Bark (New York: T. Y. Crowell, 1943), and *Dictionary of American Slang,* ed. Harold Wentworth and Stuart Berg Flexner (New York: T. Y. Crowell, 1960). Of historical interest is *The American Slang Dictionary,* ed. James Maitland (Chicago, 1891), published by the author.

work or vigilance." The term was used in contempt during various bickerings in New England, but gained respect with the report of a supposed Indian tribe, the Yankos, whose name was supposed to have meant "invincibles," who were conquered by the New Englanders, and to whom they bequeathed their title. This etymology was rejected by certain Virginians, who derived the word from Cherokee *eeanke,* meaning "coward" or "slave," which they asserted the New Englanders had earned by refusing to help the Virginians against the Cherokees. During the War Between the States, the word was applied by Confederates to all Union soldiers, usually in the form *damyankee.* During both world wars it was used in its clipped form *Yank,* by the British for all Americans, and it has been picked up, notably in communist propaganda, in various spellings like *yanqui.* No entirely convincing etymology has been discovered, but it is probably Dutch, *Jan Kaas* having been a Dutch West Indian pirate, whose name was common among freebooters, whence it may have been used for settlers in New Amsterdam. It became *Jan Kees,* "John Cheese," a general term perhaps more like Joe Doakes than John Doe or John Q. Public, and was applied in contempt to Connecticut traders, whose business ethics stirred something less than admiration among the Hollanders. Apparently *Yankees* was mistaken for a plural of *Yankee,* as *pease* had earlier been mistaken for a plural and had developed a singular, *pea.* Thus one of the terms for all citizens of the United States apparently stems from a slang term of a few emigrated Dutchmen.

Of the invading languages, French left the most widespread evidence, presumably because the French played so many roles in so many places. The French moved up the St. Lawrence River, along the Great Lakes, and on to the west, carrying words like *portage, pirogue, bateau, cache, toboggan, voyageur, caribou, parfleche,* and *lacrosse* with them. From New Orleans they worked north, bringing or concocting such words as *praline, picayune, parlay, lagniappe, bayou,* and *sazarac,* although some of these words had come from other languages, *parlay* from Italian *paroli,* a gambling term, *bayou* from Choctaw *bayuk,* and *lagniappe* probably from Quechua through Spanish *la napa. Crevasse!* was a shout of terror, for a break in the *levee*—another French word from *levée,* meaning raised—warned that unless the break was mended, water would be pouring out from the Mississippi River, raised above the surrounding low lands. From Nova Scotia, as we have seen, Arcadians brought a French dialect known as *Cajun* to what is now Texas and Louisiana. French appeared sporadically all along the east coast, notably toward the south, where the Huguenot immigration is as worthy of legend as is the Puritan settlement of New England. As early as 1628

Walloons who spoke French at New Rochelle would walk the eighteen miles to Petticoat Lane in New York to worship. Doubtless from such random groups grew *carryall* from *cariole,* and *charivari,* often spelled *shivaree,* from no one knows what. The international stature of the French language provided words; when the new Congress established a monetary system, it determined that the subdivisions of the dollar would be the *dime* (French *dime,* from old French *disme, tithe,* from Latin *decem* and *decemus* involving the idea "ten" and "tenth"), *cent* by the same route from Latin *centum,* hundred, and *mill,* the thousandth part of a dollar, from Latin *milia* through French *mille.* It was said that Americans were so enamored of Paris that they hoped, if they were good, they would go there when they died, and the pro-Gallic, anti-British sentiment led to the growth of French words in many areas.

One of the most fruitful terms was *prairie.* The word, from classical Latin *pratum* through Medieval Latin *pretarium,* meant a meadow in French, but it came to serve for all sorts of wild land in the New World, from plateaus to swamps. It often carried another syllable, suggested in spellings like *perarie, perairie,* and *parara.* Dickens said that "the word Prairie is variously pronounced *paraaer, parearer,* and *paroarer.* The latter mode of pronunciation is perhaps the most in favor." What he meant by these spellings is any man's guess.[3] There was the *prairillon,* a little prairie, the *level prairie,* the *rolling prairies, salt* or *soda prairies,* the *trembling prairie,* the *chocolate prairie,* which a writer in *Putnam's Magazine* described as "a few mud-lumps, a few, almost floating, islands, and a trembling prairie into which one would sink as into quicksand." The various sorts of prairies led to *prairie dog, prairie wolf, prairie hen, prairie chicken, prairie fire, prairie itch, prairie oyster*—a raw egg, salted and peppered and known also as a *prairie cocktail*—and *prairie bitters.* This was a tasty compound of water and buffalo gall, which was supposed to be good for all ills—apparently anybody who survived it was not likely to die soon of anything else.

French words were consistently subject to change in pronunciation since French abounded in sounds difficult for English or Amerindian tongues. Thus the Osage orange, which was used by the Indians for bows, was called *bois d'arc,* "bow tree," but this was simplified to *bodock.* Many of the changes involved a shift in accentuation. Latin words carried the emphasis on the next-to-the-last or second-to-the-last syllable; as endings fell off in French, stress tended to fall at the end, or

---

[3] See *American Notes,* frequently reprinted; the passage opens Chapter XIII, "A Jaunt to the Looking-Glass Prairie and Back." Most of the subsequent evidence appears in either the DA or the DAE where *prairie* and its compounds run for more than ten wide columns each.

near the end, of words. Thus Chaucer pronounced the French word *liquor* so that it would rhyme with our word *poor*, but the pattern of English is to stress the first syllable, and when the stress moved forward—as it did also in words like *labor, nature,* and *summoner*—the last syllable weakened. The same thing happened to French words in American English, so that we now pronounce *levée* as we do *levy, Depot, coulee, bureau,* and many others have developed similarly.

Numerically, the most extensive borrowings are from Spanish, partly because, in sweeping west, English was inundating Spanish as well as Amerindian, but partly also because a large body of Spanish speakers to the south have been a continuing source of linguistic immigrants and the highway for Spanish-Mexican culture. Not more than about thirty words from Dutch have become clearly part of modern American speech; the number can be doubled for French, and multiplied many times for Spanish, although a considerable number of these words are best known mainly in restricted areas in New York City, along the Mexican border, and in California. Various lists run into the hundreds, and by counting words like *playa,* a dry lake, and *borrasco,* a depression in mining, the words in genuine if limited circulation could probably be raised above a thousand. Furthermore, this tendency is continuing; *rumba*—from African through Latin American Spanish—is usually included in lists of Latin American borrowings, but names of more recent dances like the *samba* and *mambo* are not. Foods like *tacos, tortillas, enchiladas, frijoles refritos, tamales,* and *chili con carne* have long been acclimated from Mexican Spanish, but now they are being followed by *sopapillas, tostados,* and *tornados.*

The words fall into notable groups. As South American native words are likely to appear in Spanish dress, so the names of flora and fauna of the Southwest, along with fish from the gulf, are likely to acquire Spanish names: *barracuda, bonito, burro, chigger* or *jigger, cockroach, coyote, marijuana, mesquite, mustang, palomino, peyote, pompano, ocatilla,* and on through the alphabet to *vinegarroon,* a large scorpion with a vinegar-like smell, and *yucca,* with its *yucca moth.* Many of these words are basically Amerindian, of course; the coyote was only the prairie wolf with an Amerindian name. Some have come a long way. The agriculturally minded Moors brought with them *al-fachafacha,* "the good fodder," which the Spaniards brought to Mexico as *alfalfa,* which found its way into the Southwest, and has worked back through the Middle West carrying its name with it. Captain John Smith recorded the first known English use of *cockroach,* mentioning "a certain India Bug, called by the Spaniards a *Cacarootch,* the which creeping into chests they eat and defile with their ill-scented dung."[4] The *cucaracha* was presumably a wood louse; how the name became attached to the various sorts of long brown beetles that enjoy associating with human beings is unknown.

Since the handling of cattle in the Old West used practices developed on the *hacienda* and imported by Mexicans, ranch life abounded with terms more or less Hispanized; *alforja, appaloosa, buckaroo, chaps, chaparral, cinch, corral, cuarta, honda, lariat, lasso, latigo, mustang, peon, poncho, quirt, ranch, resta, remuda, rodeo, sombrero, stampede, wrangler,* and many more. Spanish terms, of course, were more or less twisted to new uses; the *rodeo* was a roundup, not an exhibition of stunts like bulldogging. Words were adapted by cowboys who were no specialists in international affairs: *mecate,* a twisted horsehair lead rope, became a *McCarty,* as though it had been invented by some eponymous Celt, and a *ten-gallon hat* involves a statement of its possible contents only through folk etymology; *galon* is Spanish for *lace,* and the term records the practice of winding lace around fashionable male headgear; *loco* meant crazy before it was applied to the pea-like plants which induce a sort of dementia in western cattle and sheep. On the other hand *vamoose* is not much changed from Spanish *vamos,* "let's go," and *hoosegow* is a roughly accurate spelling in English for the pronunciation, common in both Mexico and Spain, of *juzgado,* "convicted," since Spanish *j* is roughly equivalent to English *h,* and in the *se-seo* pronunciation a *z* sounds like English *s,* and in many Mexican dialects the *-ado* suffix of the past participle is frequently reduced to a diphthong /aʊ/ that rhymes roughly with *how.*

Spanish in the United States, in addition to being a fruitful source of borrowings, is remarkable also in the degree to which it is fragmented by dialects. But here we must recall the distinction drawn earlier between the effect of dialects of a dominant language and of moribund, occluded languages. In Latin America dialects of Spanish and Portuguese are important as dialects because those languages became dominant. In the United States the significance of Spanish dialects is minor because the language is occluded and moribund. We may expect that the dialectal aspects of Spanish will affect American English mainly in vocabulary, and not very extensively in that. Curiously, the Mexican Spanish of the Southwest provides a case that is about as near to an exception as one can hope to find. Many of the words borrowed from Mexican Spanish were in some way indigenous; they had come from Amerindian languages

---

[4] I owe the reference to Thomas Pyles, *Words and Ways of American English,* cited earlier. Mitford Mathews must consider the word no Americanism, since he omitted it from the DA; the DAE includes the entry but not the quotation.

(*mesquite, poncho*), or they were involved in the kind of ranching later taken up by English-speaking cattlemen (*lariat* from *la reata*). Thus words that exist in few Latin American dialects, and that have never found their way into European Spanish, are firmly established in American English. But in other mass movements from Spanish-speaking countries the impact of dialectal variations has been slight. So many people have moved from Puerto Rico to New York City that Manhattan and its environs now constitute the largest Puerto Rican community anywhere. These new arrivals present problems, both for themselves and for the urban community, and the problems involve language; but the complications arise from the fact that these people speak Spanish rather than English and that they are crowded into ghettos, not that they speak Antilles Spanish as contrasted with Mexican Spanish. Cubans have recently found their way to Miami, Florida, in such numbers that if one hears voluble language pouring from a telephone booth, the speech is almost as likely to be Spanish as English; but the important fact is that the language is Spanish, not that it is middle-class Antilles Spanish and hence different from the ghetto Puerto Rican speech heard in New York City.

Among what can be called camp-follower languages, those that joined the Indo-European stream after the conflict with Amerindian was mainly over, German has had the widest influence. Germans started coming early, mainly to Pennsylvania, and the flow of industrious folk seeking better opportunities continued throughout the nineteenth century, augmented by waves induced by religious or political persecution. Some cities, like Milwaukee, Chicago, and St. Louis, became heavily German, but the bulk of the Germans were farmers, scattered widely wherever good land was cheap. One can still encounter, almost anywhere in the Middle West, modest buildings that were kept in good repair until the automotive world left them isolated among their fields, on which the word *Turnverein* can still be distinguished. They commemorate the onetime network of physical culture clubs; *Saengerfests* have become traditional in some communities, and *hamburger* and *wiener* establishments are ubiquitous. Various Germanisms have become common, including *loafer, bum, ouch, nix, phooey, fresh* (impudent), *pinochle, stein, poker*—which may also be French—*spiel, bub, hex,* and *katzenjammer*.

Not unexpectedly, many words refer to food and drink, from *apfel* (apple) to *strudel* and *beer soup* to *zwieback*. Roughly half of the words that Professor Marckwardt has identified as German[5] refer to edibles

---

[5] *American English,* cited earlier, pp. 52–53.

and potables, and he could have greatly augmented this list if he had cared to add the bewildering varieties of *-burgers,* from *mooseburgers* to *Trumanburgers,* and the varieties of more specialized foods like *Braunschweiger, Thuringer, Hassenpfeffer,* and *Wienerschnitzel.* They include such common words as *bock* and *lager beer, delicatessen, dunk, noodle, pretzel, pumpernickel, sauerkraut,* and the various *wursts,* along with specialties like *ponhaws,* the Pennsylvania Dutch equivalent of Philadelphia scrapple, and *snits,* Pennsylvania Dutch for slices of fruit, especially dried slices. Even words for social phenomena like *beer garden* and *rathskeller* involve food and drink.

Other bodies of Germanic imports reflected the vigor of nineteenth-century German universities and German intellectual life, which throve in many fields, scientific, literary, critical, and scholarly. American students went to German universities and brought home the German university system along with scholarly and scientific terms, and German learned journals set a standard and a pattern. The result is a considerable number of learned terms, not much known to laymen, but current among specialists: *Festschrift* (a collection of papers celebrating a learned scholar), *Textkritik* (textual criticism), *Zeitgeist* (spirit of the times),·*Sturm und Drang* (storm and stress, an aspect of Romanticism), *Märchen* (folktales), *Sprachgefühl* (sense for language), *Volkswanderungzeit* (time of the wandering of peoples), and dozens more, along with already well-established words like *semester* and *seminar.* Similarly, German culture was ascendant during the formative years of the United States, and Germany managed to be the central figure in two world wars while losing both of them. Accordingly, American English borrowed words like *Zeppelin,* especially military terms like *Blitzkrieg, Blitz, Stuka,* and *Panzer,* many of them shortlived.

The most amusing body of German-American speech is unquestionably Pennsylvania Dutch, which was mentioned in Chapter 7, but its impact upon standard American English is hard to determine, although slight by any count. Presumably *dunk* and *hex* come from Pennsylvania Dutch, but how much that dialect was involved in *smearcase* is uncertain, and we do not know whether or not *rain worm* is only a translation of *Regenwurm.* Most Pennsylvania Dutch words have not travelled far; German *Pfannhase* became *ponhaws,* but even when folk-etymologized into *pondhorse*—along with *ponhorse, ponehoss,* and *ponhoss*—it has not spread far. A hen with her brood became a *klook* and her *peeps,* but these charming samples of onomatopoeia have remained local. Some influence upon local grammar there has been; "My vacation is over" has been rendered "My off is all," although the following sign for a doorbell out of order may be apocryphal: "Button don't bell. Bump."

GOOK YUSHT AMOHL DOH!

Monsleit un Weibsleit!!
Buwa un Maed—Yungy un Olty

ATTENTION!

DER EAGLE DRUG SHTORE

Der Besht un der Wholsealsht!

WM. S. SEAGER OBBADEAKER.

In der Dritt Shtrose, Sued Bethlehem.
Alsfort uf hond, olly sorta fun de beshty Drugs un Meditziena, un on de wholsealshty prices. Also, Paint, Oehl, Glaws, Varnish, &c. Mer hen aw an neier article dos gor net gebutta konn waerra; es is de bareemt

"SALTED SODA"

un waerd g'used for seaf kocha. Prowiers amohl—de directions we mers braucht geena mit. Om Eagle Drug Shtore is aw der plotz for

PATENT MEDITZIENA, BITTERS, &C., &C.

Fun olly ort, un on de wholsealshty prices.
Also, Coal-Oehl, Lompa, Waugha-Schmeer, &c., &c.
Now mind was mer sawya; mer hen olles uf hond was mer denka konn in unser line of bisness. We g'sawt, unser prices sin wholsealer dos in ennichem onnera Drug Shtore in County. Ferges't net der platz,

IN DER DRITT SHTROSE UNICH DER LOCUST
SUED BETHLEHEM

Now is de tseit; macht eich bei, un judg'd for eigh selwer; kummt in foor weasa, uf horseback, uf dem Railroad, odder tsu foos—mer sin gor net particular wie, yusht so dos ker kummt on

DER EAGLE OBBADEAK IN SUED BETHLEHEM

Un bringt eier greenbacks mit. Wholseal for cash—sell is unser style.

WILLIAM S. SEAGER

Obbadeaker[6]

This combination of Anglicized German and Pennsylvania Dutchified English has been the medium of some humor. The advertisement on page 321 is said to have been published in a Bethlehem, Pennsylvania, newspaper of August 28, 1969.

Anyone who knows a little German can have fun with this. "Monsleit un Weibsleit!! Buwa un Maed—Yungy un Olty" is clearly "men and women, boys and girls, young and old." "Obbadeaker" is presumably *apotheker,* the German equivalent of *apothecary.* "Der Eagle Obbadeak" is presumably the same thing as the "Drug Shtore," which seems to have been situated in Third Street, that is "Dritt Shtrose" (dritte Strasse). "Bareemt" is presumably *beruhmt,* "famous," and "g'used" must be English *used* with the remains of a German *ge-* employed to make a past participle out of what already is one. Among the articles suitable for "unser line of business" would seem to be "Waugha-Schmeer," which I am assuming is *axle grease,* based upon German *Wagon.* "Now is the time" (*tseit* for *Zeit*) we are told, "Come (*macht eich bei,* since *eich* is no doubt *euch,* for "you") . . . uf horseback, uf dem Railroad, odder tsu foos (*zu Fuss,* meaning "on foot"). It closes, "And bring your greenbacks with you. Wholesale for cash—that is our style." Earlier, *wholesale* has appeared as both a comparative adjective, *wholsealer,* and a superlative in two forms, *wholsealsht* and *wholsealshty.*

Thus, in one way or another, the Germans had extensive influence, in the days of their immigration and later. They were the most numerous; while immigration quotas were fixed on the basis of a percentage of the immigrants prior to 1920, the German quotas were second in size, following those for the United Kingdom. Within limits Germans resisted assimilation, being concentrated enough, especially in the cities, to maintain their own social groups, and the German newspapers throve as did no other foreign-language press. Furthermore, Germans were prosperous, and money talks in any language.

The pattern of German can be observed in most of the other camp-follower languages, except that they had less impact, a few terms for special foods, and not much more. After the Germans, the next largest quota is the Irish, but most of them talked some sort of English. They imported few words. The Italians have the next largest quota; they helped to popularize *macaroni, spaghetti, pizza,* and *pizzeria,* and to

---

6 Quoted in Frederic Klees, *The Pennsylvania Dutch,* cited earlier, p. 283; he acknowledges James O. Knauss, Jr. *Social Conditions among the Pennsylvania Germans in the Eighteenth Century as Revealed in the German Newspapers Published in America* (Lancaster, Pa., 1922), reprinted from *The Proceedings of the Pennsylvania German Society,* vol. 29 (1922).

introduce *ravioli, minestrone, spumoni, tortoni, asti spumante,* and probably *policy ticket* (now *numbers*), *black hand,* and *Mafia,* although these have some currency in Britain, also. Scandinavians contributed *smörgasbord, lingonberries,* and *lutfisk,* along with *ski* and some words associated with it. Chinese or Pidgin English provide *chow, chow mein, chow yuk, chop suey, won ton,* and other foods, along with *joss, fantan, tong,* and *tong war.* Japanese provides *sukiyaki, kimono,* and the word for second generation, *Nisei,* which has become a generic term for Americanized Japanese. Czech provides *kolachy* (*koláč*), a filled dough tart; Finnish gives us *sauna* (a steam bath), and Portuguese supplies *cuspidor,* formerly spelled *cuspidora,* apparently picked up in the East Indies from Dutch *kwispedoor,* for spit box. The number of Jews is obscured in their national origins—German, Austrian, Dutch, Polish, and Russian, especially—but they are numerous, and they often brought with them old and distinctive cultures. Furthermore, many of them were cultured and witty, so that along with *kosher* foods, *matzoth, blintzes,* and *gefilte fish,* the Jews have provided a considerable number of engaging words, *schnozzle* for a big nose, *kibitzer* (from a small bird that may peep and chatter over one's shoulder), *schmaltz* (meaning chicken fat) for something "corny," and *schmo,* a stupid person, derived from a word for the male organ. *Putz* has the same origin. In fact, several Yiddish slang words would scarcely have been admitted to polite Anglo-Saxon society had they appeared in their English equivalents.

One body of foreign speakers does not fit any of these groups, the Negroes, brought to the New World as slaves, and hence not immigrants in the sense that they came voluntarily or had any control as to whither they were migrating. They brought with them no Indo-European language, or any language that could hope to maintain itself; slaves spoke many languages, and they were deliberately scattered so as to discourage concerted action against their masters. None of their languages survived in any connected form, but Negroes were numerous, long comprising nearly ten per cent of the population, and their impact must have been considerable, partly because they were the largest and most persistently aberrant body of speakers that has ever been absorbed within the continental United States. They came knowing no English and speaking languages having grammars radically different from Indo-European grammars. Many Negroes were worked in gangs, and they lived in quarters remote from the white men, among other Africans whose languages they could not understand. To the whites they seemed so inept that they were assumed to have speech defects, even defects of hearing, since they could not detect many spoken sounds. They had no such defects; very few people, even highly educated people, can hear a sound they cannot themselves produce, and many Negroes have demonstrated that they can be highly literate, even eloquent, in handling English or any other language. Snatched from nonliterate societies, however, and denied most cultural opportunities, they were ignorant to a degree that is now difficult to imagine.

Negroes, slave and free, were scattered through all the colonies and early states. They were gradually absorbed into the population, but with the great growth of cotton and sugar plantations in the early nineteenth century, Negroes were imported in hordes into parts of the South. The result is described by M. Schele de Vere, professor at the University of Virginia; he was writing in about 1870, or a little before, and Frederick Law Olmsted, whom he quotes, had written shortly before 1860. He speaks of the "varieties and classes" of Negroes, and continues:

The Virginia slave, for generations accustomed to the nicer functions of a house servant, in daily contact with gentlewomen, and accustomed to hear at table and during long journeys on horseback or in private carriages, the conversation of intelligent men, was far above the average of the British laborer, to say nothing of the French peasant. He spoke fair English, infinitely better, at all events, than the Yorkshire yokel, or even the thorough-bred Cockney. The slave on a sugar or cotton plantation in the Southwest, on the other hand, was but a step removed from the African savage; his speech, largely intermixed with African terms, was well-nigh unintelligible. But even in the so-called Border States there was an immense gulf between the house-servant and the ruder *field-hand*. Some of the former possessed not only knowledge, but even refinement; body-servants, as they were called, taken abroad by their masters, astonished European gentlemen by their politeness of manner and their inbred courtesy, and the Ex-President of Liberia, long a slave in Virginia, never once lacked the dignity and self-possession required by his high office, when presented at foreign courts, or on the far more trying occasions when he returned to his native State and met his former masters. But the *field-hand* was, what Mr. Olmsted says of him: "on an average a very poor and very bad creature, much worse than I had supposed before I had seen him, and grown familiar with his stupendous ignorance, duplicity, and sensuality. He seems but an imperfect man, incapable of taking care of himself in a civilized manner. . . .[7]

Since field hands greatly outnumbered domestics, we need not be surprised that few Negro African words entered the common stream of American English speech. The word *goober,* formerly *goobapea,* from Congo *nguba* (kidney), became a name for a peanut, and Georgia became the *Goober State,* with back-country Georgians and some other Southerners called *Goober-Grabbers* and *Goober-Grubbers.* The *Dic-*

[7] Vere, cited earlier, is referring to Frederick Law Olmsted, *A Journey in the Back Country* (London, 1860), p. 432; first American edition (New York: Mason Brothers, 1860).

tionary of Americanisms quotes a rural Georgia paper of 1834, "But he so seam I frade of he, I guess he steal my goober." Apparently the Dahomey or Togo *vodu,* a word for some sort of spirit or its fetish, picked up a French spelling in New Orleans (*vaudoux, vandoo, voudou*) and was well established there in the early nineteenth century, perhaps by way of Santo Domingo, when a local paper reported that a suburban house was used "as a kind of temple for certain occult practices and the idolatrous worship of an African deity, called *Vandoo.*" The word has become even more popular in the form *hoodoo,* with derivatives like *hoodoo stick,* a "divining rod." The number of these common words is few, but more than a thousand such terms have been traced to African roots in recent studies; they now have sparse currency and are dying out, but they must be the remnants of tens of thousands of African words which had some currency among the illiterate slaves and their descendants.

Thus, although Negroes as a group never developed a distinctive dialect—a body of locutions used by Afro-American speakers and by no one else—and although few words have entered the American English wordstock through Negro streams, Negroes probably account for much more of southern speech than now appears. We have noticed in earlier chapters that the southern colonies drew their speech from the same areas as did the New England colonies, and that, particularly in earlier times, these speech areas participated in common sounds and common terminology. Yet today New England and southern speech differ, especially in tone and speech rhythm. Quite probably these differences have been encouraged by the presence of what amounted to a large and continuing body of foreign speakers, speakers who, in many communities, outnumbered the whites. Furthermore, Negro and white children regularly played together, and even the more cultured white children learned English by imitating the Negro mammy. If the Negro did not much influence American English by importing words, he probably did influence it considerably by constituting a body of imperfect speakers of the sort that promote linguistic change.

18

LINGUISTIC GROWING PAINS—FROM WITHIN

Consider the word *corn.* It could scarcely have a more honorable ancestry. It derives from Indo-European *-ger-,* "to ripen, to grow firm," and it appears also in *kernel,* meaning "a little corn," and Latin *granum,* which gives us *grain, granary,* and the like. It was common in Old English as a generic term for grain, and it has become the name for the staple British grain, known as wheat in the United States, but doubtless Captain John Smith used the word in the older generic sense when he wrote in 1608, "Shortly after it pleased God (in our extremity) to moue the Indians to bring vs Corne . . . to refresh vs."[1] In the New World, however, *corn* became the name of the particular kind of grain that God moved the Indians to bring, and the grain, sometimes called *maize* from Taino *mahiz* through Spanish, played a large part in the American economy. In woods areas it could be planted among the girdled trees before a pioneer had found time to clear his land, and when the fat prairies were opened to settlement, corn soon became a staple. It could be eaten green in the summer, and, hulled or ground into meal, it could be boiled, baked, or fried the remainder of the year. Being a tropical plant, it throve during the hot summer nights of the Middle West, and generally in the South. Europe has never raised much corn; the season in most areas is too short and the nights too cool, but in the United States it provided various foods, oil, and syrup as well as hominy, grits, and various sorts of breads, cakes, soups, and porridges with such names as *Johnny cake, corn pone,* and *Indian pudding.* The grain fattened the hogs and helped the hens to lay, and the stalks provided fodder to bring the cattle through the winter. As a result corn entered variously into American life and gave rise to more than two

---

[1] In both the DA and the DAE, cited earlier. Most of the unacknowledged evidence below can be found in one or both of these dictionaries.

hundred compounds and phrases based upon the American use of the word *corn—corn hill, cornfield, corn husking, corn shock,* even *corn specie* when grain was used for money, *cornstalk fiddle* with a *cornstalk bow* when the pioneer had a party, or a *Cornhusker State* when he became political.

Similar development can be observed in *railroad.* Strictly speaking, the word is not an Americanism in the sense of a road composed of rails running lengthwise, to hold flanged wheels; the word was used in England in that sense, although but little, and the word is now practically unknown there. British trains run on railways. The word is, however, native American as a way built across swampy ground, a road of the sort more often called *corduroy,* which, if we may believe James Russell Lowell, was made up partly of logs or rails laid crossways and partly of obliging alligators. It is also native American in the sense of railroading a bill, a project, or a person, and the compounds are American: *railroad grade, railroad cut, railroad conductor, railroad euchre, railroad senator,* and dozens more.

We might contrast this sort of thing with the life of borrowed words, which were few in the first place and have mainly produced few offspring. *Cruller baby,* a baby shaped like a cruller, is said to be rare as, fortunately, are such children. No derivatives at all have been recorded for *lagniappe, ponhaws, katzenjammer, chow mein,* and many others. Most such words develop a few compounds and derivatives; *portage* develops *portage road, portage summit,* and *portage rope. Kibitzer* leads to *kibitz* and *kibitzing*—or perhaps it is the other way around—but on the whole the activities vital enough to produce many words were familiar enough to be named out of the native language.

In the *Dictionary of Americanisms,* Mitford M. Mathews distinguishes three sorts of Americanisms: "outright coinages, as *appendicitis, hydrant, tularaemia;* such words as *adobe, campus, gorilla,* which first became English in the United States; and terms such as *faculty, fraternity, refrigerator,* when used in senses first given them in American usage."[2] Words of the first sort have been few until recently, when the

---

[2] See DA, Introduction. Some writers on usage, including the best known of the British commentators, H. W. Fowler, consider words like *stocky, storm,* and *stovepipe* Americanisms, because, although formerly in use in England, they are now unused or little used there. As Gilbert M. Tucker has pointed out, in *American English* (New York: Alfred A. Knopf, 1921), pp. 71–72, this can be a bit silly, since we should have to say that *sick* and *sickness,* used in the King James version of the Bible instead of *ill* and *illness,* are Americanisms, although no speakers of English had been born in America at the time of the King James translation. Fowler, noticing that *guess* was "a favorite word of Chaucer's," admitted that it must be "good old English," but added it "is not good English." It could not be, he implied, since it was an Americanism, for "we have it not from

great growth of the physical sciences, especially of chemistry and pharmacology, has led to the wholesale coining of words employing Greek and Latin roots to describe and name new inventions and discoveries, *barbiturate, methacrylic, sulfanilamide,* and the like. The second sort of Americanisms we have observed in the previous chapter; they, also, are few. Americans have grown the great bulk of Americanisms— and they are numerous enough so that *A Dictionary of American English* runs to more than 2,500 double-column pages—by using the English language differently than it was used in the Old World.

This is only another way of saying that Americans are human. All peoples are always devising new uses for their words; at the same time that Americans were devising Americanisms, Britons were devising Briticisms, but we may appropriately ask whether or not Americans have been uncommonly given to new uses of words, uncommonly productive of vocabulary. We need not be surprised if this is true; after all, the last two centuries have been fruitful in social evolution and revolution, and during that time the United States has gone from a backwoods world to automation, and in recent decades Americans have been among the leaders in new movements of many sorts.

Americanisms have grown in varied climates. Some few exotics have attracted wide attention, of which the most permeating has been *OK, O.K., okay, okeh, oke, oky-doky,* or however it is spelled or pronounced, it having varied at home and combined with local expression abroad, with *o-ke* of Liberian Djabo and Burmese *hoak-keh,* which happens to mean "is so." <u>The most</u> widespread American word, it is perhaps as near as any to being worldwide in its use. During World War II, American troops found the expression wherever they went; an American officer reported that all of the Japanese guards in the prison camp at Davao knew the word, and troops operating in North Africa found it among relatively isolated Arabs. It apparently filtered through both the iron and the bamboo curtains, and village children in Spain may say it instead of *salud* as greeting.

It has prompted etymological guesses, some intentionally humorous. Learned wags from the effete eastern seaboard liked to twit homespun politicians with their ignorance of spelling, and to concoct stories in which one president or another originated the expression when he

---

Chaucer, but from the Yankees." He has a point, of course, although some of us would assume that Americanisms can be good English even though not good British English.

    This concept is horrible to many Englishmen, but so far as discussions in this book are concerned, the essential requirement is that we understand our terms. I shall use the word *Americanism* with Professor Mathews' definition, but I shall not hesitate to notice words which have survived in American although not in British English, or have been reimported into England.

marked papers *O.K.,* for *Oll Kurrect*—General Andrew Jackson was a conspicuous victim, as was Ulysses S. Grant, although he was still in his teens when the expression became popular. It was also said to represent homey spellings of *Out of Kash, Out of Klothes,* and *Orful Kalamity.* It was attributed to French—you can take your choice between *O qu'oui* (Oh, but yes!) recorded by Laurence Sterne in 1768, or French sailors during the American Revolution making assignations with girls who were invited *aux quais* (to the quays). It was said to have come from Greek ὤχ ὤχ, an incantation against fleas; from German, where *O.K.* stood for *Oberst Kommandant* (commanding officer), presumably implying official approval; or from Finnish *oikea,* meaning "correct." President Woodrow Wilson and some others thought it came from Choctaw *hoke,* meaning "it is." It was said to have arisen from tinned biscuits during the War Between the States, these being good biscuits and marked *O.K.* for the initials of the manufacturers, the Orrins-Kendall Company. Or it could have come from Anglo-Saxon through Danish and Norwegian sailors who used *H.G.* (pronounced *hahgay*) for *hofgor,* meaning "ready to put to sea." Or it could come from British English; Sir Anthony Palmer remembered it from his childhood, and was sure it was not an Americanism—English gentlemen do not hear Americanisms in their childhood—deriving it instead from Cockney *orl korrec;* or if you wish something more official, it arose from approving bills in the House of Lords by Lord *O*nslow, Lord Chairman of Committees, and by his counsel, Lord *K*ilbracken.

The trouble with all these etymologies is that they smack too much of the methods we have already associated with Noah Webster, walking around his table looking for words in any language having the right letters and a plausible meaning. Once you have a likely word, you can always think of a story to explain what might have happened, which soon becomes what did happen. In the face of this continued confusion, one hesitates to assert that the ghost has finally been laid by patient research in place of ingenious guesses, but we now have a statement so well documented that it cannot be lightly ignored.[3]

Apparently the innovation stems from a fad for acronyms which swept

---

[3] Allen Walker Read, "The First Stage in the History of O.K.," *American Speech,* XXXVIII (1963), 5–27; "The Second Stage in the History of O.K.," *AS,* XXXVIII (1963), 83–102; "The Folklore of O.K.," *AS* XXXIX (1964), 5–25; "Later Stages in the History of O.K.," *AS,* XXXIX (1964), 83–101; "Successive Revisions in the Explanation of O.K.," *AS,* XXXIX (1964), 243–67. These studies are being followed with more details, for example, Richard Walser, "A Boston 'O.K.' Poem in 1840," *AS,* XL (1965), 120–26. This last provides further clear evidence that everybody knew and used the term; that is the point of the effusion, which cannot really be called a poem. It gives evidence, also, of the playing with initials; O.K., it seems, means that the editor is "Off for Kuba" for the winter.

Boston in the summer of 1838, a fashion which may have given us also
N.G. for *no good.* Letters were used for drinks, *M.J.* for *mint julep* and
G.C. for *Gin Cocktail.* On June 12 the Boston *Morning Post* reported
that the "Secretary of the Boston Young Men's Society for Meliorating
the Condition of the Indians, F.A.H. (fell at Hoboken) on Saturday last
at 4 o'clock in a duel W.O.O.O.F.C. (with one of our first citizens).
What measures will be taken by the Society R.T.B.S. (remains to be
seen)." Soon *O.W.* appeared for *Oll Wright,* since misspelling seems to
have been part of the fun. Part of the fun, also, were bogus societies,
and they are involved in the first discovered use of *OK;* it seems that the
A.B.R.S. (Anti-Bell-Ringing Society), which had as its purpose the
combatting of an ordinance of the Boston Common Council prohibiting
the ringing of dinner bells, was going to New York by way of Providence, where it was assumed that the Committee on Charity Lecture
Bells of Providence "would have the 'contribution box,' et ceteras, *o.k.,*
—all correct—and cause the corks to fly, like *sparks,* upward." The fad
spread to New York, where by the spring of 1839 you could read the
following: ". . . A.R., N.S.M.J., is the reply; and the parties bow and
separate. O.K., all correct; I.S.B.D., it shall be done; A.R, N.S.M.J., all
right, 'nough said 'mong gentlemen—and so forth."

The journalistic fad, however, would doubtless have died but for
politics. In the presidential campaign of 1840 the Whigs were promoting
the homespun character of their candidate, William Henry Harrison,
supposedly devoted to log cabins and hard cider; the Democrats, urging
a second term for Martin Van Buren, born in the village of Kinderhook
in the Hudson Valley, revived such titles as the *Sage of Kinderhook,* the
Magician or *Wizard of Kinderhook,* and led to the Democratic *O.K.
Club,* the Old Kinderhook Club, which first met in New York, March
24, 1840. These clubs, calling themselves such things as *Butt Enders*
and *Huge Paws,* could be rowdy, and among the projects of the O.K.
Club was breaking up a meeting of the New York Whigs at Masonic
Hall, March 27. The New York *Herald* reported the affair as follows:
"About 500 stout, strapping men marched three and three, noiselessly
and orderly. The word *O.K.* was passed from mouth to mouth. A cheer
was given, and they rushed into the hall upstairs like a torrent." Eventually they were ejected, which led rival newspapers to call the club the
K. O. Club, the "Kicked Out Club." The name ballooned. The National
Intelligencer reported "The Irish Locofocos (Democrats) of the 6th
Ward have been parading the streets with shillelahs, swearing 'O.K.'
etc." and the slogan became so popular that the Whigs picked it up, too,
and had their cider kegs "marked with large letters. 'O.K.'—oll korrect." A chant of triumph, apparently for either party, became "O.K.,

O.K., O.K.," and the fad spread west, for by the next January the New Orleans *Picayune* could print, "I'm O.K.—off for the calaboose," and a little later the St. Louis *Reveille* carried the following: "In settlin land as is kuvvered with water I got O.K. the wust possible name. I was out ove kabin out ove kredit out ove korn out ove kash out ove kumfort." Shortly afterward readers were assured that "a custom against which much absurd prejudice has hitherto prevailed, is all correct, or in common parlance, O.K., O.K. . . . The ladies have found out the true meaning of these mysterious capitals . . . is—Only Kissing." By November 6, 1840 the new expression was apparently familiar in the wilds of Iowa, for *The Iowa Standard* reprinted a supposed conversation with a bewildered Frenchman, who presumably reported in the *Baltimore Clipper*, "I read ze grand national affair, and ven I come to ze end I beheld O.K.! I glance my eye to ze report of ze election and he begin wiz O.K. Every ting has O.K.—and I never shall comprehend him." The piece contains "contradictory definitions," which the editor assures us "are highly amusing." They are *all korrect, orful katastrophe, oll for Kent, oll konfirmed, oll komplete, oll kentuck, orrid kalamity,* and *oll kompelled.*

The evidence for this account of the origin and growth of America's most popular coinage is so massive that one wonders how it could ever have been in doubt, and this wonder has provided the basis for engaging study of the ways of mankind with etymologies. Apparently the battle was that of objective scholarship against engaging folklore, with the folklore winning most of the time. It was more plentiful, more attractive, and, unless one examines the sources, quite plausible. Consider the supposed derivation as an English oral reproduction of French *aux quais,* which was supposed to have derived from sailors making assignations. This received popular support from analogous stories and is apparently still doing so. On December 9, 1953, the respected London *Daily Telegraph* printed the following on the authority of a Somerset gentleman:

American scholars have assured me that it [okay] derives from "Aux Quais," which in the 18th century was stencilled upon casks of Puerto Rico rum intended for export. Since this rum was considered the best the world produced, the letters O.K. came to stand for anything perfect or excellent.

The fact that no body of American scholars has ever believed that rum, Puerto Rico, or the eighteenth century had anything significant to do with *okay* did not deter the tale. Even more recently (January 21, 1963), the Chicago *Tribune* printed an account, attributed to a citizen of Rockford, Illinois, who, hearing a Paris airline official say that the ticket was okay, remarked upon the prevalence of American terms abroad. The account continues:

> He [the airline official] replied that O.K. is a French expression and that it originated in New Orleans before the Louisiana purchase. The city was French and its chief item of commerce was cotton. The cotton had to be checked for quality and weight before it was placed on the dock for loading.
>
> When the stevedores came before the inspectors with a bale of cotton which met the specifications, the latter said, "Au quai," which was pronounced "O.K." and meant "to the dock."
>
> This was before 1803, or 36 years before the earliest appearance which has been found in print.

What is happening here? Apparently some fact—often a fact unknown to some people, like the similarity of pronunciations in *OK* and *aux quais,* or a vaguely remembered fact, like the name of the president who was supposed not to be able to spell—generates a tale to account for the fact. Since the tale is generated, it fits the fact, and it is likely to be plausible unless closely examined. Of course the skeptic can ask how being an airline official in Paris makes one an authority on eighteenth-century New Orleans, but most people would have more fun telling the story than questioning it. After all, the tale offers an earlier explanation, and must not the earliest be right? It comes from far away, and if even foreigners know these things, must they not be true? The tale teller, noticing the similarity of the accounts, instead of assuming that since they are mutually contradictory, they are probably all fabrications, assumes that since they have details in common, they must be reliable. And the tale flatters the teller, particularly if he can feel that he would have known better than the ignorant stevedore; we all like to possess esoteric information. For some such reasons, apparently, the folklore of etymology can be extremely durable.[4] Anyone who wishes to query his acquaintances can discover that although the facts have been in print for years and have been several times surveyed, most Americans today believe either that the origin of *OK* has baffled the best scholars, or that it stems from some simple folkloristic bit, of which the most popular is presidential innocence of orthography.

After the manner of American English, the word has grown various grammatical uses. If anything is okay, one can okay it with an okay; within limits he can even "do it okay," although *okayly* seems not to have developed, and most speakers avoid *okay* adverbially. The word is generally respectable, although avoided in formal English; highway de-

---

[4] *AS,* XXXIX (1964), 22, in the sequence of articles cited earlier.

partments do not hesitate to erect signs saying "Right Turn OK On Red," but *okay* appears in few if any statutes or judicial opinions. College professors approve papers with *OK*, but hesitate to use *okay* in scholarly or scientific papers. Abroad, British telegraphers were using the symbol as early as 1873 to indicate that a message had been received without garbling, and before the end of the century it was popular enough to be used in a London music-hall song. Still later it was one of the words with which timid Britons feared that American moving pictures were undermining the British Empire, but recently even that furor has declined, and modern British dictionaries tend only to note that it has an American derivation. By 1935 the Judicial Committee of the Privy Council determined that *OK* on a legal document meant that "the details contained . . . were correctly given," and in the same year H. W. Horwill did not think it worth listing in his *Dictionary of Modern American Usage*. The word has almost completely replaced *righto,* which I heard regularly in England in 1930 but almost never thirty years later. Apparently the humorous *O.K.* of the Boston journalistic wits and the New York Locofocos has become standard English, if not as yet formal English. Meanwhile, in its native land it has sprouted *AOK,* which seems to mean more OK than OK, if that is possible.

Coinages that attain currency and permanence are rare in any language, and American English is no exception. A few more could be instanced—*jeep, telephone,* and *Kodak,* for example—and various marginal or dubious cases might be offered, words like *Yankee* and *blizzard,* which are under suspicion of being some sort of borrowing, but which have developed so much and from such uncertain sources that origins remain uncertain. Such random words, however, are few, if spectacular. The bulk of Americanisms have grown by the normal semantic processes, stimulated by something native.

Words associated with land transportation can be informative. When the colonies were settled, transportation depended upon domesticated animals, mainly horses and various sorts of bovines, in certain areas asses and mules. These beasts had been worked for years; they and all their anatomical parts were well named, along with their appurtenances. A horse, for example, along with familiar parts like *lips, teeth,* and *ears,* also had a *forelock, poll, withers, croup, cannon, fetlock, pastern, stifle, gaskin, coronet,* and the like. The saddle he wore, the harness with which he was fitted, the vehicles he drew were all elaborately named, and these words were imported with him. A few words like *buggy* and *surrey* are adapted to vehicles different from those known in England, but most Americanisms associated with horses grew out of new uses for the horse, notably herding cattle on open range. The *quarter-horse* was developed and was combined into a *string* and used in cattle drives serving *drag men, swing men,* and *tail riders.* He was trained to become a *cutting horse,* which was also a *whittler* or a *peg pony,* and he learned special techniques, such as *jumping to a set* so that he could take the shock of a lassoed animal, and if necessary he could be managed by *earing down,* subduing him by pulling down his ears.[5]

Cowboy terminology, however, was exotic; the basic vocabulary concerning horses was imported. With automotive power, however, the pattern shifts. Neither the steam locomotive nor the internal combustion motor used in automobiles was an American invention, but the great distances in the New World and the growing wealth of its inhabitants encouraged rapid transportation. The United States was ripe to grow with steam, and accordingly railroading grew independently in the New World, after its own pattern and partially with its own terminology.

Some railroading terms reflect the peculiarities of American transportation. Doubtless in the tightly hedged little island of Britain domesticated animals straying between the *metals* on the *permanent way* were no great problem, but when the American *railroads* pushed through the American *backwoods* and out into the unfenced *prairies,* a *cowcatcher* was a necessary, even a humanitarian, device. The early ones protruded in front of the locomotive and consisted of some sort of platform, basket, or sling arrangement, supported on a pair of wheels. Apparently the idea was that if Bossie was overtaken on the *tracks,* her feet would be gently knocked from under her, and she would be ridden along on the *cowcatcher* until the train could be stopped and she could be unloaded. Of course modern cowcatchers are intended to do no more than remove the carcass, and they are more likely to remove canines than bovines, but the term serves to suggest how American railroad terms grew out of American railroading. Similarly, the British *bogie* is not used in the United States; American roads carrying heavy equipment are not so twisty as to need an extra swivel truck to support an overhang.

Other railroading terms differ in the two countries for no apparent reason except that practices grew severally and brought their own terms into being as they did so. British railways have the phenomena, but they do not use the words; there are no *fast freights,* no *brakemen* to stop them, and no *depots* to stop at; they develop no *hot boxes* and make no *stopovers. Switch engines* do not *side-track gondolas, flat cars,* or *box cars.* There are no *flagmen, expressmen,* or *baggage masters,* no *track walkers* or *section hands,* no *Pullmans* or *Pullman porters.* Naturally,

---

[5] See Bruce Grant, *The Cowboy Encyclopedia* (Chicago: Rand McNally, 1951).

the American slang terms are even more numerous and characteristic; the brakeman becomes a *hind hook* or *shack,* a *groundhog* if he works a freight, a *dude wrangler* on a passenger train. A *yardmaster* is a *ringmaster* or *bull goose,* a station master is an *ornament*—epithets by the thousand.

With the advent of the automobile, all this was augmented, for if the American economy grew with steam, it matured with gasoline. Internal combustion engines are complex contrivances; even a rather simple carburetor may have more than two hundred named parts, many of them locally applied. Traction and suspension are elaborate; an *upper trunnion bushing* may sound like a British hamlet, but it is part of a front wheel *assembly,* another Americanism. Furthermore, the automobile has entered into daily lives, as it has not as yet in other countries, and as the railroad never did in any country. Only the Van Sweringens and the Jim Hills owned a collection of railroads, and even they did not park them in their homes. Americans live with *parking lots, stop lights, safety zones, speed cops, filling stations,* and *boulevard stops,* and automobiles enter so much into American thinking that phrases like *step on it* and *get a green light* grow naturally. We need not ask what kind of service is offered at a *service station,* and a young couple may have no plans to buy a home, but they could not conceive of life without a car. A small American child is likely to think of "the car" as part of the family.

Now another stage has arrived with jet propulsion and rockets. The United States has become the only great developer of rockets outside the communist bloc, and accordingly words involved in rocketry and for space concepts generally tend to appear in American English and from thence to be borrowed and translated into hundreds of other languages. Most new terms are old words used in a new sense; *orbits* were well known before any *space-age nose cone* was *orbited* into *orbit,* although these semantic uses are only beginning to appear in dictionaries. When we put a *Gemini* into *parking orbit* any child will know the words, even though he does not know that his grandfather recognized the *Gemini* as twin stars, named from the Latin term for twins, from the word for *double.* At this writing *parking orbit* is still rare enough to require explanation, but only because, the term is as yet theoretical. Once we have started sending up any sort of *space platform*—a term that no longer needs explanation—and this *space hardware* goes into orbit awaiting a rendezvous, the phrase *parking orbit,* unless it has been superseded by then, will start appearing in headlines and will be heard on radio and television. Within weeks people everywhere will have forgotten that it is a new locution, not to mention that it is an Americanism.

More than normally significant are American political terms. We should notice first that American democracy is American. Democracy, itself, of course is not; as a theory more or less practiced it is old, and it has developed variously in Switzerland, the Scandinavian countries, and elsewhere, but American democracy is not transplanted British democracy, although it has its roots in English political, social, and religious life. American democracy was not imported in the eighteenth century from English democracy for the obvious reason that England was not a democracy. Democracy was associated with the guillotine, with the bloodletting on the Seine, and the sons of English monarchy did not trust it; it was scrupulously avoided when the founding fathers, firm in the English tradition, set up the American government, as an outmoded electoral college has long attested.

English society rested upon medieval society, but the seeds of democracy were sowed with Protestantism. The Universal Church of the Middle Ages was authoritarian; Jehovah ruled by will, through His deputy Christ, through His deputy Peter, and through Peter's church. It was benevolent, and it did great good, but it was anything but democratic. Almost all Protestant movements tended toward democracy; even if Protestantism differed only in substituting conviction of sin for acceptance of sacraments as the basis of salvation, this sense of conviction had to come from the sinner, and thus the power to save was shifted at least in part to the individual. Not all Protestant churches were equal in their reliance on the individual, as their names indicate: *Episcopal,* from the word for bishop; *Presbyterian,* from *presbytery; Congregational,* from the *congregation* of worshipers being self-governing; *Methodist,* from the methodical study and worship of the founders; *Baptist,* from the importance attached to adult immersion; and the like. Even so, democracy and Protestantism were emotionally and philosophically related, and a plausible explanation of the differences between English and American democracy can be developed, at least in part, on the assumption that English democracy is the sort that could be expected to grow from the philosophy of the Anglican church, whereas American democracy is the sort that could have been expected from the theocratic and congregational principles popular in the New World.

American democracy as we know it is the product of the nineteenth and twentieth centuries. Not all aspects of American political history cause an American to swell with pride, but the result has certainly been good, and we can scarcely expect natural growth involving some very unhandsome human beings to be universally pretty. Democracy as a system and as a philosophy has grown in at least one of its manifestations in the United States, and even a random sketch of native political terms should reflect something of what man has done to language, and possibly, what language has done to man when these terms become the intellectual counters with which candidates get themselves elected. Terms in the following list were selected arbitrarily, but I hope that the whole may be roughly representative.[6]

admission (of the states into the Union). The *Journals of the Continental Congress* for 1777 provide that no further colony shall be admitted "unless such admission be agreed to by nine states." Subsequently, states were admitted by application to Congress on approval of their constitutions. Once admitted, a state enjoyed equal rights with all other states; a similarly liberal policy would probably have deterred the dissolution of the British Empire.

angel. A financial backer of a political candidate, apparently a borrowed theatrical term.

Australian ballot. A ballot containing the names of all candidates, with provisions for casting it secretly. First used in southern Australia, it was introduced into the United States after 1880, but as late as 1888 *The Nation* was suggesting that with the Australian secret ballot "bribery in the choice of Congressmen might be discouraged to some extent." Formerly, parties printed their own ballots, and Republican Negroes in the South were prevented from voting by being told there were no more Republican ballots.

big stick. "A policy of forcing through something one desires to achieve." The phrase is attributed to Theodore Roosevelt, who, when requesting a large navy, was quoted as recommending that the nation "tread softly, but carry a big stick."

carpetbagger. A carpet bag—the term occurring in England as early as 1840—was a cheap bag made by fastening a piece of carpet to a frame. *Carpetbagger* was used as a term of derision for indigent northern adventurers, who, when they went south after 1865 to profit from the confusion following war, could carry all their worldly possessions in a carpet bag. An English traveler in 1868 referred to "what the Southerners call 'carpet-baggers,' men travelling with little luggage and less character, making political capital out of the present state of affairs." The term has been revived to designate a candidate who has moved recently to a political area, presumably with the main purpose of running for office.

caucus. A meeting of party members or others of a group to agree upon a course of action, either candidates to be supported or principles to be

---

[6] Any exhaustive list would be prohibitively long, but I have endeavored to be relatively objective by abstracting terms mostly from Wilbur W. White, *White's Political Dictionary* (Cleveland and New York: World Publishing Company, 1947), selecting those that seem to be among the more common or the more revealing. I have probably been partial to the picturesque, but I have tried not to favor words that are either flattering or derogatory to American mental and moral processes. It can be assumed that direct quotations not otherwise acknowledged appear in the citations in DA or DAE, cited earlier, or in White. For other political dictionaries and articles on the subject see Mencken and McDavid, p. 168, n. 6.

espoused. The origin of the word is a bit obscure, but the best guess associates it with the Caucus Club—the name presumably comes from a Latin word for a drinking vessel—which by 1763 was meeting in Boston. By 1809 a traveler could write, "The meeting to which I allude is in use in all parts of the United States and is denominated a caucus." In British politics the word was used for a committee to direct party affairs, and by 1865 was sufficiently known for an Oxford mathematics lecturer, in *Alice in Wonderland,* to amuse children with a dodo that directs a *caucus race,* in which anybody runs whenever he pleases, everybody wins, and they all get prizes.

civil service. See *spoils system.*

collective bargaining. Strictly speaking, the term is not an Americanism, having been proposed by Beatrice Webb in London in 1891, but it had its own development in this country, particularly after the Wagner Act of 1935 guaranteed the right of Labor to organize. The system has promoted the orderly settlement of labor disputes.

Congress. A national or state legislative body, usually composed of a Senate and a House of Representatives, the latter comprising the Congressmen. Congress as a concept has entered so much into American thinking and Congress as a force has been so potent in American growth that *Congress* and *Congressional* have led to dozens of phrases and compounds. Not only do we have the *Congressional Record* and *Congressional Medals of Honor,* but women wore *Congress boots,* relatively relaxed footgear with elastic in the sides, and men bought land at the *Congress price* and managed to get through a *Congress Sunday,* a time of "humiliation, fasting, and prayer."

dark horse. A compromise candidate, previously not considered in the running. The analogy is from the race track, where a "dark" horse is one previously little known. The dark horse is, in effect, made possible by the convention system of nominating, since ballots are cast in primaries without bargaining. James K. Polk is generally considered the first dark horse elected to the presidency.

Democrat. The words *Democrat* and *Democratic* have been associated with a party that shows considerable continuity from Colonial days to contemporary times, a party composed generally of the lower income groups and their intellectual sympathizers. George Washington, a Federalist and a landed gentleman, disapproved of them, writing, "You could as soon scrub the blackamore white as change the principle of a profest Democrat." Today the landed gentleman has been largely replaced by representatives of big business, but roughly the party alignments have been maintained.

doubtful state. A state that does not regularly vote for either party, for example, at this writing, New York or Pennsylvania. The concept grows from the practice of voting by states in the Electoral College.

direct primary. A system by which party candidates are chosen by ballot of the voters, rather than by representatives in a convention. The system is intended to reduce the power of party bosses, since candidates cannot be nominated by bargaining for votes.

Electoral College. A group of electors chosen by the several states to cast ballots for the president and vice-president. The institution reflects eighteenth-century faith in enlightened individuals and distrust of democracy. Theoretically, the citizens of the various states would know their fellows well enough to choose the best men in the state. These representatives would become a college to deliberate and choose the best man as president and the next best as vice-president. Whoever originated this system knew very little of the way of an American politician with a caucus or an American voter with a ballot. Commonly, although not exclusively, voters have chosen electors pledged to vote for a given candidate.

fat cat. Resembles an "angel," a candidate who is nominated because he contributes handsomely to the party's campaign funds.

favorite son. Although George Washington was called Columbia's favorite son, the term is now used for a candidate having mainly local support. Delegates may be pledged to a favorite son as a courtesy, with the expectation that they will be released from their pledges after the first ballot.

federal. This and related words like *federated, federation,* and *"fed"* stem from Latin *foedus,* a league or treaty; in nearly two centuries of shifting political thought they have had various uses. When an inter-colonial government was being considered, some political leaders wanted no league at all, some wanted a strong union, and some wanted a federation of independent states. Thus *federalist* became an appropriate designation of attitude. The principle of States' rights was tested in the War Between the States and presumably discredited in its more extreme forms, but it is still an issue between and within political parties, and thus the term is still usable. Meanwhile, in many senses *federal* has become in effect a synonym of *national,* particularly in compounds like *federal aid, Federal Bureau of Investigation, Federal Communications Commission,* and so through the alphabet.

fence. Fences are something a legislator can mend when he returns to his constituents, soliciting votes for the next election, or they are places where a candidate can sit while pondering on which side to get off.

filibuster. Etymologically, this word results from borrowing, but its current use reflects simon-pure American democracy—or an obstruction of it, since it is intended to impede the majority from enacting its will. Dutch *vrijbuiter* became English *freebooter* and Spanish *filibustero,* one who gets free booty. Toward the middle of the nineteenth century a number of expeditions were mounted from New Orleans and points in Texas and aimed at various Latin American countries, for example, the attack led upon Cuba in 1850–51 by Narciso López. The participants were called *filibusters* and the activity *filibustering.* By 1853 a Congressman could be guilty of "filibustering against the United States," and soon the word was restricted in English to the practice of endeavoring to talk to death a bill otherwise sure of passage.

floor leader. One who directs legislative processes for his party. Practical floor leaders must have existed from the earliest sessions of legislatures, but the formal organization is recent. The *Dictionary of Americanisms* found no use of the term earlier than 1899.

full faith and credit. The phrase is from Article IV, Section 1, of the Constitution: "Full faith and credit shall be given in each state to the public acts, records, and judicial proceedings of every other state." This was a guaranty of equality before the law; colonies do not enjoy "full faith and credit."

general welfare clause. This is another of those terms that have provided the barricades at which the battles to define American democracy have been fought. Article I, Section 8, of the Constitution provides that "Congress shall have power to lay and collect taxes, duties, imports and excises, to pay the debts and provide for the common defense and general welfare of the United States." Those commentators who believe in a strong central government have pointed out that if Congress can provide for the general welfare, it can provide for anything. Those who believe in States' rights have insisted that the whole context makes clear that Section 8 refers to financial and military welfare, not social and moral welfare.

globaloney. A shortlived blend used by Clare Booth Luce in her maiden speech in Congress, February, 1943, intended to ridicule American international involvements.

grass roots. Basically, the phrase seems to come from mining; in 1876 a writer describing the Black Hills wrote: "Gold is found almost everywhere, in the bars, in the gravel and sand of the beds, even in the 'grass roots.'" Apparently it referred to the ground just under the surface, nothing so deep as the foundation of things, but the association of grass with country living and the figurative use of *roots* was too strong. It came to refer to anything fundamental, local, folksy, and independently democratic.

gerrymander. This is one of the few famous examples that lead laymen to assume that large numbers of words are coinages. During the political battling of 1812, under Governor Elbridge Gerry, precincts in northeastern Massachusetts were so juggled that the map of a voting district somewhat resembled a griffin-like creature, humorously called a Gerrymander, a blend of *Gerry* and sala*mander*. The term has since been generalized so that almost any electioneering skulduggery can be called *gerrymandering*.

greenback. Paper money, not supported by gold or silver, printed during the War Between the States, the back printed in green ink. Later the Greenbackers became a splinter, cheap-money party.

hat in the ring. To throw one's hat in the ring is to become a candidate; presumably the reference is to a boxing ring.

Homestead Act. *Homestead* as a word goes back to Old English *ham sted*, but the concept that a man could acquire a home legally from the nation by filing on land and living on it seems to be American.

Indian title. The rights of Indians to the land they inhabited. Indian titles have not always been respected, but as early as 1660 settlers were enjoined to clear their lands of Indian titles, and at this writing Indians are still being reimbursed in very large claims for infringement of their titles.

integration. Opposed to segregation, especially of the white and Negro races. Racial discrimination has been common from earliest times, and individual Americans have not been notably tolerant, but Americans through their governments have made signal efforts to legislate tolerance.

Jacksonian Democracy. Political parties have been shifting bodies of voters with varying alignments, but the folksy, farmer-labor character of the Democratic party presumably stems more from the backwoods Andrew Jackson than from any other source.

Jeffersonian Democracy. Thomas Jefferson can be called the first Democratic President, but as a son of eighteenth-century enlightenment, he was no believer in democracy in the modern sense. He deprecated cities and believed in a sort of oligarchy of gentleman farmers, but his name has become a refuge for dissident Democrats who would be horrified if they knew what their professed forbear espoused.

Jim Crow laws. Jim Crow was the name of a popular song and dance copyrighted by Thomas D. Rice in 1828, and a character in the song; the publication apparently led to the use of the term for a Negro singer or actor, especially a lively dancer. A Jim Crow car, a car exclusively for Negroes, was in use in Boston as early as 1841, but the Jim Crow laws, enforcing racial segregation, have been mainly Southern.

junket. The word comes from Latin *juncus,* "a reed," associated with sweet cream cheese brought into town for sale in a reed basket. Washington Irving used the term in something of its modern sense in 1809 when he referred to "Those snug junkettings and public gormandizings." By 1862, apparently, *junketing* referred more particularly to unwarranted travel at public expense; the New York *Tribune* asked, "On what principle . . . are these junketers . . . allowed the use of steamboats at an expense of from $300.00 to $500 a day?" With air travel and the participation of the United States in world affairs, the word "junket" has been even more closely associated with travel for pleasure obtained under pretense of official investigation.

kangaroo court. An illegally constituted court, presumably so named because its justice can be expected to proceed by leaps and bounds.

keynote speech. Presumably it provides the key note for the subsequent chorus of campaigners. The term but not the phenomenon is apparently recent, with the first noted citation in 1886.

Ku Klux Klan. A name used for various organizations, particularly in the South, most frequently to intimidate Negroes. The fact that the name derives from the Greek *kyklos,* circle (of the Confederate Knights of the Circle), recalls the notable pseudoclassical bent of southern aristocrats. When it was founded, it apparently included many responsible and respectable citizens, but its character changed, and when it was investigated in 1965, a remarkable number of its leaders were characterized as "morons," "bullies," "criminals," and "mental cases." The guess that *Ku Klux* is intended to echo the sound of cocking a rifle apparently has no foundation.

lame duck. A picturesque figure, probably on the analogy of a *sitting duck,* for a defeated politician still in office, especially a defeated congressman in the short session after an election. With the abrogation of the short session, *lame ducks* have become *dead ducks.*

landslide. Figurative term for an avalanche of votes that buries everything. Both the word and its application to politics seem to be American, the latter apparently in the late nineteenth century.

lobby. As a name for a foyer, *lobby* is no Americanism; it comes from Latin *lobium*, seen also in *lodge*. Nor is the idea of a paid representative who endeavors to influence official acts restricted to the New World; barons, dukes, and lords obtained part of their wealth and power through their supposed ability to influence royal acts, and many a medieval person looked upon his patron saint as a sort of lobbyist in the Court of Heaven. The application of the name for a lobby being attached to the person who lurks in the foyer to buttonhole legislators seems to be a native development.

locofoco. This word preserved echoes of some of the ruggeder aspects of American democracy. Presumably it stems from a blunder; the inventor of a self-lighting cigar and a match would have known the word *locomotive*, which had lately become popular. On this analogy he named his invention *locofoco*, assuming that the word would mean self-lighting. Actually, if it means anything it would be something like *fireplace*, since *locus* means *place*, not *self*, and *foco* presumably came from Italian *fuoco*, fire. On the night of October 29, 1835, the word acquired political significance. At a meeting in Tammany Hall the party wheels were prepared to roll through a slate of candidates, when an insurgent antimonopoly group, the Equal Rights Democrats, staged a well-planned uprising. The professionals had the answer to such nonsense; they turned off the gas, leaving the hall in darkness, but for once the amateurs had thought far enough ahead. They produced candles and locofocos, carried the meeting, and elected their slate. The Whigs were delighted at this evidence of a split within their opponents' ranks, and ridiculed the Equal Rights groups as "Rowdies," "Noisy Brawlers," "Revolution mongers," "Infidels," "The Guy Fawkes of Politics," and "Loco-focoes." The latter epithet stuck, and although the Equal Rights Democrats went the way of most splinter groups, the name was soon used derisively for all Democrats and was eventually adopted by the Democrats themselves as a sort of boast.

logrolling. A handsome figurative use. As early as the eighteenth century, a *logrolling* party was one in which neighbors helped a settler build a log cabin or clear his land of fallen trees. In politics the word refers to any kind of cooperative connivance, usually of the sort described in "You help me with my skulduggery, and I'll help you with yours."

manifest destiny. A handsome phrase calculated to sanctify any sort of imperialism or exclusive privileges, it being assumed that the manifest destiny of the Anglo-Saxon peoples was to absorb the North American continent.

Monroe Doctrine. Varying policies stemming from President James Monroe's statement to Congress, December 2, 1823, calculated to discourage further European adventures in the New World, mainly in Latin America, but including also the Russian penetration of the Northwest. It afforded Latin American nations some protection, but it has also irked southern neighbors when used as an excuse for intervention.

muckraker. Theodore Roosevelt, borrowing from *Pilgrim's Progress*, used the "Man with the Muckrake" to decry those who charged corruption. He was opposing indiscriminate and irresponsible slander, but devoted reformers, notably Lincoln Steffens in his exposés of corrupt city governments, accepted the epithet as a badge of honor.

mugwump. An inconsequential word with a consequential sound. From an Algonquian word meaning "chief," used derisively, it became a term for those who could not support James G. Blaine for President, and "mugwumped to Cleveland." It led to a cartoon of a lugubrious bird sitting on a fence, "with his mug on one side and his wump on the other." This was a welcome perversion, since Americans have always needed picturesque but delicate terms for indelicate subjects. The word provided related terms, *mugwumpian, mugwumpery, mugwumpcy, mugwumpism,* and the like.

platform. Another fine figure of speech, apparently popularized shortly before 1850, in which the candidate stands upon a platform made up of planks to represent the principles of his party.

pocket veto. A device by which an executive can veto a bill by not signing it, in effect, by keeping it in his pocket, thus avoiding the necessity of explaining his refusal.

pork barrel. The pork barrel was a pioneer device for preserving meat, but not until the current century were bills to render useless rivers navigable and to dredge unprofitable harbors called "pork." Filling the pork barrel may provide a congressman with votes from grateful constituents.

precinct. The precinct is the working unit for elections. It is a religious term, with the basic idea of surround; the *praecinctum* was the area surrounding a religious edifice. In theocratic New England the word became the name of an ecclesiastical, and eventually of a political, subdivision.

primary. Direct primary election, in effect an election within a party, by means of which voters cast ballots directly for candidates, not for representatives at a convention. Primaries have been developing during the past century, so that, at this writing, they are common as a means to choose state and local candidates and delegates to national conventions.

public school. In the United States, a free, publicly supported school. Surely significant is the fact that the most extensive experiment in universal, free education has been carried on in a country founded on belief in the inherent rights of man and nurtured in the conviction that democracy can function only with an informed electorate.

radical. The word stems from Latin *radix,* "root," and hence meant "basic" or "fundamental," but in politics it has been used to designate partisans of all persuasions: the most conservative in Yugoslavia, various middle-of-the-roaders in Europe, various reform groups, especially communists, in the United States. The word was long associated with the Radical Republican Party, which before and after the War Between the States recommended punitive measures against slaveholders and Southerners generally.

railroad. To put through with undue and presumably illegal speed; bills have been railroaded through legislatures, slates have been railroaded through conventions, and incumbents have been railroaded out of office. The more British term, railway, has not so developed.

rally. The word comes from French *re-* plus *allier,* that is, "go together again," and apparently enters politics from military terminology. In the days when battles were won by massed charges, the field was likely to become confused with noise, dust, and smoke. Scattered troops would endeavor to regroup by rallying, by converging on something conspicuous, as in "So we'll rally round the flag, Boys. We'll rally once again." The rallying was supposed to result in a charge, or at worst, in an orderly defense. In politics a rally became any popular assembling to promote anything.

rank and file. This phrase is both military and redundant. The ranks are soldiers counted laterally and the files are the same soldiers counted vertically, and whichever way you counted them they included everybody but the officers—the term was formerly used in the plural, the *ranks and files*. In politics the term includes everybody but the party leaders.

red tape. Official delay. Strictly speaking, the word is not an Americanism, since it stems from the red tapes used to tie up British legal documents, but with the great proliferation of American government it has become characteristic, and one of the first citations of the word in this sense comes from Washington Irving: "His brain was little better than red tape and parchment."[7]

Republican. Roughly a synonym of *democratic, republican* was long a word to conjure with, especially among liberal dissident groups. In the days during and immediately after the Revolutionary War the Republican party opposed the Constitutionalists, especially in Pennsylvania. The present Republican party gained its ascendancy through its antislavery program, and is now composed partly of moderates, partly of conservatives, including some very conservative conservatives, at this writing notably the John Birch Society and other "right-wingers."

segregation. See *integration.*

Senate. *Senate* is not an Americanism except in compounds like *State Senate* or in the idea that this use suggests, as a deliberative body for a political subdivision of a nation, but the United States Senate is a distinctly American institution which has provided a pattern for many lands. Most state legislatures include senates patterned upon it, and emergent democracies elsewhere, notably in Latin America but also in Asia and Africa, have been influenced by it. The word relates to Latin *senex*, meaning old, and reflects somewhat the nature of the Roman Senate, theoretically the functioning instrument of an oligarchy, but one which frequently became a debating society for the venerable. Alexander Hamilton was suspicious of the whole notion of a senate; he wrote, "In your time your New York Senate . . . will be liable to degenerate into a body purely aristocratical." He need not have worried; the Senate has tended to be somewhat more informed and literate, somewhat more generously financed than the lower house, but it has been no private club of the idle rich.

shirt-sleeve diplomacy. Professor White, referred to earlier, has a good definition, as follows: "Slang term for the handling of international relations with directness and without the usual polite observances of diplomacy. The term is used both in praise, as in the first sense above, and in criticism,

---

[7] In the Knickerbocker *History*. Being no Americanism, the word is not entered in the DA or DAE, but will be found in the *Oxford English Dictionary*. Apparently the word did not become popular in the sense of confusion and delay until recently. Webster never entered it, and his successors picked it up only late in the century. Worcester entered *red-tapist*, which he defined as a public employee "who binds parcels in red tape."

as in the latter sense." Lowell praised the procedure, writing, "In this brown-fisted rough, this shirt-sleeved Cid . . . My lungs draw braver air," but many dealers in international affairs have found "open covenants openly arrived at" an impossible ideal, and American diplomats through the decades have often been accused of being pathetically naive.

spellbinder. Emotional orators who hold their audiences as if bound by a spell are not restricted to American democracy, but relatively unsophisticated communities have provided ample fields for windy oratory. Spellbinders were common phenomena in frontier politics, and they are perhaps now more characteristic of rural southern communities than of most other parts of the United States.

spoils system. No doubt the practice of rewarding the faithful with jobs and emoluments is as old as politics, but the theory that public office is to be thought of as the spoils of war owes its origin to New York politics and its national development to the administration of Andrew Jackson. Senator William Learned Marcy, later head of the Hunkers, a splinter Democratic group party, defended the traffic in offices in his home state, saying that "They (New York politicians) see nothing wrong in the rule that to the victor belong the spoils of the enemy." However striking Marcy's analogy may have been, the system inevitably fostered abuses, and many decent people were outraged. The poet and good Quaker, John Greenleaf Whittier, resorted to theology to voice his wrath: "I should as soon think of worshiping the devil with the Manicheans as to fall down and do homage to Andrew Jackson with the adolatrous 'Spoils Party' of the day." Little relief came, however, until after the Pendleton Act of 1883 providing for civil service on a nonpartisan basis for many posts, with competitive examinations and the like.

squatter. The term appeared at least as early as 1788 designating people who settled upon public land without the formality of title. In the day of sparse surveying and inaccurate maps, of hordes of landseekers, many of them indigent and some of them lawless, in the day of inadequate land laws and few officers of the law—many of whom were or had been squatters themselves—squatting was widely condoned on the frontier and is probably not quite unknown today. In effect, the Homestead Acts made squatting obsolete, and incidentally made honest tenants of many a previously promiscuous squatter.

standpatter. A term out of poker for a player who stands on a pat hand, the word suggests that American politicians have included, along with idealistic reformers, some who stubbornly voted for vested interests, deaf to any arguments for the public good. The term was applied particularly to Republicans in the early twentieth century who stood pat on a high tariff.

stump. The stump as a rostrum in a pioneer country is recorded as early as 1716, and at least in the satire of the Tories even General Washington did not disdain stump speaking:

> When Congress sent great Washington
> All clothed in power and breeches,
> To meet old Britain's warlike sons
> And make some rebel speeches . . .

Upon a stump, he placed himself,
Great Washington, did he,
And through the nose of Lawyer Close
Proclaimed great liberty.[8]

In the early days, adequate halls were scarce, and political meetings often took place in the open. Beleaguered by squalling children and yapping dogs, the itinerant politician welcomed any way to mount something where he could be seen, and so did his audience. Sometimes a platform wagon served—there is the tale of the speaker, who, when his audience dwindled to one, discovered that the sole patient listener was the owner of the wagon— sometimes a rock or a porch, but in most pioneer communities stumps were abundant. If not, one could be provided by cutting down a tree. The term, however, survived the supply of stumps or the occasion for them, so that *to stump* is to electioneer.

town meeting. The supposed foundation of American democracy. As early as 1636, Salem, Massachusetts, held a "generall Court or towne meeting," and the institution in its purity was restricted to New England. In many of the colonies, mass meetings concerned local problems, but apparently only in New England could town meetings elect officers and legislate for the community.

unit rule. The rule by which a delegation is obligated to vote as a body. A device of machine politics, it is being gradually eliminated.

veto. As a word, *veto,* from Latin, "I forbid," is no Americanism, but it has developed as part of the American system of checks and balances among the branches of the government, permitting the chief executive, within prescribed limits, to nullify an action of a legislature.

ward heeler. A ward was a British municipal division, but in the United States the term is used mainly as the name of the voting division larger than a precinct. *Ward heelers, bummers,* and *bosses* have often provided the practical grass-roots politics, along with some of the corruption and political shenanigans.

Whig. *Whig* is another of the ancient political terms that in the United States have flown many colors. In England, the Whigs were a liberal party as opposed to the Tories, and the terms were transported to Colonial America, the Whigs being the revolutionary party, the Tories loyal to the crown. Later, the anti-Jackson party was called Whig, and it was presumably to this group that Lincoln was referring when he reminded his audience that if his opponent was right in saying that the Whigs were all dead, they were about to hear a speech by a dead man.

White House. The official residence of the President of the United States. The building was named the Palace by the designer, but was painted white after it was gutted by fire that darkened the gray Virginia limestone. The

---

[8] *Songs and Ballads of the American Revolution,* ed. Frank Moore (New York: Appleton, 1856), pp. 99–101. I owe the reference to Robert M. Estrich and Hans Sperber, *Three Keys to Language* (New York: Rinehart & Company, 1952), p. 192.

building became popularly known as the White House and Theodore Roosevelt made the title official by using it on his stationery. The word has become a synonym for the President, the Presidency, and the United States government and its policy.

zoning. Cities are no American phenomenon, but industrial development in the United States has stimulated the rapid growth of cities in previously sparsely populated areas and has encouraged municipal planning. Through restrictions upon buildings and their purposes—restrictions known as *zoning*—attempts to direct urban growth have proliferated in the United States and are spreading to other countries.

In summary, one notices at once that these words tend to fall into three groups: (1) a few coinages or picturesque borrowings, *Gerrymander, filibuster,* and *locofoco;* (2) a modest number of familiar words turned to a new use, *lobby, rally,* and *stump;* (3) a considerable number of new compounds, the newness of the idea revealed by putting common words together, *kangaroo court, spoils system, pocket veto, Homestead Act,* and *keynote speech.* The first two of these sorts are relatively few, the third relatively numerous. In fact, this may be the most conspicuous American contribution to the English language, that the New World has provided tens of thousands of new compounds, compounds which reflect the fact that something in the New World differed from something in the Old, and this difference is made most readily apparent by some sort of qualifier that entered into a new compound.[9] This characteristic of American English is likely to be so striking that even a thumbing of the pages of either of the great dictionaries of American English will suggest that a typical page of Americanisms includes mainly compounds, whereas any dictionary of the whole English language will present but few compounds per page.

For example, consider the word *red.* This is, of course, no Americanism as a word, and hence without local development would not appear in a dictionary of Americanisms at all, yet so numerous are the special uses, mainly compounds, that *red* in the *Dictionary of American English* runs for some twenty columns of small type. The *Dictionary of Americanisms* offers briefer citations but even more compounds. The following is a summary: Indians were *red men,* who could be *red brethren, red children,* or *red devils,* depending on the point of view, of whom *Red Paint Indians* were a Maine variety, with compounds growing out of this name. A *red cent* could get cut back down to *red*—"Many who came into Frisco had not a dad-blasted red left to their name." More than two dozen trees and shrubs include the word *red: red astrachan,* an apple;

---

[9] Marckwardt, *American English,* has a good survey; see especially pp. 83–92. See also Mencken/McDavid, pp. 205–06.

red bay, the so-called southern laurel; *red beech,* the American beech; *red berry,* any of several, including the American baneberry; *red birch,* the water or broom birch; *red buckeye,* the relatively small southern species; *redbud,* and many more, including the *red American larch,* the *red-flowering maple,* the *red osier dogwood,* and the *red russet apple.* *Red* appears in more than a dozen herbaceous plants, including the *red cohosh* and the *red trillium.* Some other dozens of words are of sufficiently local currency so that the *Dictionary of Americanisms* banishes them into a sort of subcategory, words like *red bark cypress, red heart hickory, red ink plant, red puccoon,* and *redtown pippin.* Similarly, there are some dozens of running and crawling things: *red copperhead, red-backed salamander, redbug,* a minute chigger, not to be confused with *red cotton bug,* which similarly should not be confused with *cotton red-bug.* There are *redlegged grasshoppers,* different from *redthighed locust, red bead snakes,* along with more imposing *red* creatures, *moose, fox, wolves, lynx, squirrels,* and even *sand rats.* Similarly, *red* is involved in the names of dozens of fish and crustaceans, often several fish per name, or several names per fish: *red bass* or *red drum; redbreast,* the *red-breasted bream; red dace,* the *shiner* or *redfin;* the *redfish,* any of several red-marked fish, along with several called *redmouth;* the *red horse* is several sorts of fish; and compounds readily mount to three words, *red-spotted trout* and *red-throat trout,* the cutthroat; the *red fallfish* and the *red-sided minnow.* Similarly, various birds incorporate the word red: *red-backed sandpiper, robin redbreast, red-cockaded woodpecker, red-poll warbler, red-shafted flicker, red-tailed hawk, red-napped sapsucker, red-vented thrush, redstart,* a warbler, and many more. Miscellaneous combinations employ red: *red brick* as a building material could also become the word for a building, and a British *red coat,* either the coat itself or the man who wore it, could lead to *redcoat-ism*—"I call it downright roguery—it is British aristocracy, Sir—real redcoatism."[10] Codfish boiled with beets and cubed pork, when chopped fine and "het up for breakfast" became *red flannel hash.* In the South, back-country people were *rednecks,* and in New Jersey they could be *Redstone farmers,* and freshets that brought down red loam were *red rises.* Children played *red lion* and *Red Rover,* and adults who drank too much *red liquor* might get the *red monkeys.* Not only *red dog* or *red pup banks* were guilty of *red tapey methods.* In a husking bee a boy might get a *red ear kiss,* which was not a kiss on a red ear but a kiss for finding an ear of red corn.

As phenomena, compounds are obvious as well as numerous. Not

---

[10] Quoted in DA from the Nashville, Tennessee, *Sothron* (1841).

that anyone has counted them, so far as I know, nor could anyone, exactly. Before the count could be completed the total would have changed, even if we could agree as to which associations of words are compounds and when a new association has become a compound, but in general the state and the trend of the vocabulary are clear without the obfuscation inherent in statistics.

Politics was not the only social phenomenon to affect language. Consider religion. New sects flowered in many lands during the nineteenth century, but they flourished especially in the New World, partly because it was a *new* world, and partly because it provided a haven from the Old. These sects tended to be aberrant, even bigoted, and to attract emotional and exotic adherents. Many were shortlived, but even fleeting faiths may enter deeply into beliefs and emotions of the communicants, and scatter the language with new terms, picturesque if fugitive. The Baptists gave rise to the *Pedobaptists,* to the *Anabaptists,* the *Antipedobaptists,* all divided more or less into *open-communionists* and *close-communionists,* including *Freewill Baptists, General Baptists* or *Dunkards, Old School Baptists, Anti-Mission* or *Hard-Shell Baptists, Seventh-Day Baptists, Sixth-Principle Baptists, Disciples of Christ Baptists,* also called *Campbellites, Winebrennarians* or *Church of God Baptists,* and the *Christian Connection of Unitarian Baptists.* Many of these terms came from the Old World, of course, but they were popularized and proliferated by fresh splinter sects in the New. Among the earlier American groups were the *Shakers,* headed by an *Elect Lady,* through whom blessings flowed, and the reception of these blessings was evidenced by *heavy dancing,* which requires its own definition:

heavy dancing . . . is performed by a perpetual springing from the house floor, about four inches up and down, both in the men's and women's apartments, moving about with extraordinary transport. . . . This elevation affects the nerves, so that they [the dancers] have intervals of shuddering, as if they were in a violent fit of the ague. . . . They sometimes clap their hands, and leap so high as to strike the joists above their heads. They throw off their outside garments in these exercises, and spend their strength very cheerfully in this way.[11]

Of the new American religions the *Latter-Day Saints* (also called *Latterday* and *Latter Day Saints*), popularly called *Mormons,* have provided an unusual body of terminology. In effect, all members in good standing in the Church are *saints,* so that "When the Saints Go

---

[11] *A Theological Dictionary,* ed. Charles Buck (Philadelphia: Joseph J. Woodward, 1826), under *Shakers;* this seems to be a slight enlargement of the London edition.

Marching In" is sung in Barcelona and in Salt Lake City with widely
different concepts. There are also saintesses, and most men are priests,
progressing from one priesthood to another, from the *Aaronic* to the
Melchizidech. Words like *prophet, revelator,* and *seer* are used with
special meanings, and a *witness* witnesses not to the truth of the Christian faith but to the reality of the Golden Tablets from which the Book
of Mormon was presumably translated. The *Church* is the organization,
edifices are likely to be *temples* or *chapels,* and very important is the
stake house, a building concerned with local secular activities. The
theory is that the lines of truth and authority extend from temples,
notably that at Salt Lake City, and at the other end of each of these lines
is a *stake,* or *Stake of Zion,* to hold up the *curtain of strength and faith*
outside of *Zion.*

On the other hand, what was perhaps the best show on the frontier,
the *camp meeting,* or revival, has provided only a spattering of terms
like the *jerks.* The camp meeting was at once exciting and respectable; it
could become an orgy, and it might save your soul. Strange things
happened; the wicked were overcome with a conviction of sin, and threw
away their cards and their whisky. Respectable matrons got the jerks
and cavorted in scandalous manners; powerful men fainted dead away.
Preachers shouted, so it was said, so that they could be heard for miles.
What they shouted has seldom been preserved, because all this was
spontaneous and unrecorded, and one guesses that their shouting was
neither very original nor very literate. It may not have introduced much
vocabulary, but it probably popularized old favorites of devotion. The
learned sermons of eighteenth-century British divines have been printed
ad nauseam, and doubtless these frontier shoutings would have been
even more wearisome in any quantity, but good samples are now hard to
come by.[12]

Changes not mainly social had their linguistic impacts, also. In the
West fresh terminology grew from new inventions, changed patterns of
life, and strange lands. Take steamboats. There were no steamboats
when the eastern colonies were settled, and when steamboats were
developed, eastern rivers had no great employment for them. Eastern
water systems are not broadly developed; they tend to tumble over
waterfalls and to be too short and shallow to encourage traffic. Even
rivers like the Hudson and the Delaware were few, and they presented

---

[12] Some circuit riders and other early preachers have left excellent reminiscences.
For example, the *Autobiography of Peter Cartwright,* ed. W. P. Strickland
(New York: Carlton & Porter, 1857) contains descriptions of the impact of his
sermons in Kentucky, Illinois, and elsewhere, but few samples of the sermons
themselves.

few problems; the same boats that scurried around Manhattan could ply the Hudson.

Western rivers were different, with different boats, different stream beds, different navigation, and different words. The rivers were gigantic, thousands of miles long, miles wide, and reaching into vast, wealthy areas, not otherwise readily traveled. The rivers were sources of great potential wealth, but they had their dangers; they tumbled over few rock ledges, but they were treacherous in their own way. They cut through great, wooded, alluvial plains; they diminished to a trickle in drouth, but they roared in flood, slicing new channels, undercutting banks, ripping up forests and tumbling them into the river. Thus the bars and shoals were ever shifting in these rivers, and worse, they were populated with a transient assortment of uprooted or inundated trees, well disposed to poke holes in the bottoms of steamboats.

Thus the problem of steamboating on what was known as the "western waters" was this: Can I make enough money at outrageous tolls and fares to pay for the boat before it is wrecked or blown up? The result, of course, was close study of dead trees in the river, with a resultant highly specialized terminology. The generic term for these arboreal hazards was *snag,* an old word, probably from Old Norse, for a sharp, projecting point, but the trade also required words for particular sorts of snags. Among them were *planters;* many water-loving trees will take root if thrust into wet ground; uprooted trees, or parts of them, acted as though they had been transplanted to the river bottom, and would grow there, more or less upright, but submerged at least part of the year. Even more dangerous were the *sawyers.* These were trees, floated down the river, root system and all; if one went aground in such a way that its roots were upstream—or if, carried by the current, the trunk swung downstream when the branching roots dragged it to a stop—the trunk would "saw" up and down, carried under by the rush of the current, only to rise slowly in rhythm. Thus a sawyer could be invisible to an oncoming steamer, only to rise to punch a hole in it. These words led also to compounds, *snagboat,* or *snagscow,* a boat built to remove snags; *snag chamber* or *snag room,* a watertight chamber to take the blow from a snag, and the like. *Snag* developed into a verb, "A Mississippi steamer, that snagged and went down on Yazoo Bend," and the verb could be used figuratively, "Feller citizens, jine me in snaggin' 'em." A mild oath developed, "I snaggers." Thus English flowed west, becoming more American with each wave.

19

CUSPIDORS, CRINOLINE, AND THE WAYWARDNESS OF LANGUAGE

Some tendencies in language are furtive, but they may be the more revealing for that. The more deeply they are obscured in the ways of men and of minds, of certain sorts of men with particular mental and emotional quirks, the more they may suggest the nature of language, of psychology, of social mores, and of subconscious interactions among whatever forces move deeply within us.

Tall talk is a case in point. This language existed, although it has not been sharply defined or located. It may have been native to the frontier; Marckwardt includes it in a chapter called "Yankee Ingenuity and the Frontier Spirit," explaining that "the frontiersman, ring-tailed roarer, half horse and half alligator, described himself as *kankarriferous* and *rambunctious,* his lady love as *angelliferous* and *splendiferous.* With consummate ease he could *teetotaciously exfluncticate* his opponent in a *conbobbenation,* that is to say a conflict or disturbance, or *ramsquaddle* him *bodaciously,* after which the luckless fellow would *absquatulate.*"[1]

Such terms have been few and mainly fugitive, but many students have found them significant as well as bizarre. Mencken treats tall talk *in extenso,* quotes Sir William Craigie for its importance, and asserts that "it decorated everyday speech, especially in the Jackson country and beyond the mountains."[2] Professor Thomas Pyles records the same belief, although with reservations;[3] he devotes a chapter to "Tall Talk, Turgidity, and Taboo," but his treatment indicates that he is uncertain who is pulling whose leg. "Rodomontade and turgidity," he writes, "born of a new expansiveness of spirit and nourished by backwoods braggadocio, were rampant in the American speech of the first half of

---

[1] *American English,* pp. 98–103.
[2] Mencken/McDavid, pp. 146–50.
[3] *Words and Ways of American English,* pp. 97–100.

the nineteenth century, particularly in what was then our west." This statement seems to identify the frontiersman as the putative father of tall talk, but Pyles makes clear that the ringtailed roarer may be more folkloristic than historic, observing that, "it [tall talk] remains a minor characteristic of American English to this day, and the leaping, shouting, boastingly rhapsodical backwoodsman, the self-styled 'half hoss, half alligator, and a touch of the airthquake,' the 'yaller flower of the forest,' who spoke it—or is supposed to have done so, for one suspects, despite ample evidence of his reality, that he was to some extent a literary convention—is still popularly regarded as having been a sort of beau ideal of American manhood." Pyles later declined to adjudicate among possible sources of tall talkers, whether they were pleasant legends or unpleasant people.

For our purposes, however, we cannot avoid the issue. The tall talk was there, on the printed page if not on the frontier, and we must ask how it appeared there and, if possible, why it appeared there. It may not be important as language, but it must be revealing for the way man makes language, or language makes man, or both.

Marckwardt offers the most intriguing explanation I know of. He suggests that this tall talk is a remote echo—remote in both time and place—of the folk talk of the rousing days of good Queen Bess. "It stems, I believe," he writes, "from the ornate diction of the Elizabethans. . . . To put it in another way, the Elizabethan tendency toward hyperbole or overstatement was, in this country, never submerged by the countermovement toward litotes, or understatement, which was a feature of the English classical revival of the late seventeenth and eighteenth centuries." Marckwardt supports his contention with Nathaniel Ward's *The Simple Cobbler of Aggawan* (1647), citing, among other exuberances, "a multimonstrous manfrey of heteroclytes and quicquidlibets." Marckwardt might have pointed out, also, that variants of old ballads have been found in the Appalachians, and that odd bits of terminology that have not survived generally in either England or the United States have been found in secluded mountain valleys, although the extant terms are homey rather than bizarre.

Marckwardt's thesis is so engaging that I would gladly support it, but I have difficulty doing so. Both time and place give me trouble. Tall talk appeared presumably about 1830; by this time writing, and even printing, were pretty common. If Mike Fink, Davy Crockett, and their fellow half-alligators were whooping out the transported speech of Shakespeare's "rude mechanicals," somebody must have been talking in like manner for more than two hundred years. Where were these people and why did nobody notice their outrageous diction and comment upon it?

They could have been hiding in the mountains. But if so, why did they not stay there? They were discovered in the highways of trade, broad-horning keel boats and running for office, and nobody suggests that the ringtailed roarers had recently roared down from the hills. No doubt the Finks and the Crocketts were the spiritual heirs of Jack Wilton and Bottom the Weaver, but if Elizabethan exuberance lingered unrecorded among Yankee backwoodsmen until it could rise as the Spirit of the West, the intervening spoor is suspiciously intermittent. Furthermore, as Pyles was apparently aware, words like *elegantiferously* suggest literate bad taste rather than illiterate efforts to talk like grandfather. Marckwardt appropriately observes that the majority of such terms "are built upon very few suffixes: *-acious, -iferous, -ticate,* and *-icute* are prominent among them." Granted this characteristic, one might plausibly assume that the tall talk comes from a restricted and rather recent tradition, not from random survival of an agglomeration of ancient dialects.

All this, however, involves too much argument and too little fact. We should examine the evidence more carefully than, so far as I know, it has previously been examined.

Earlier writers seem not to have been much impressed by tall talk. John Russell Bartlett,[4] who can probably be called the first serious student of American English, was aware of the trend, but treated it lightly. He said it was what was called in England *fine writing,* "but which with us is better known as 'highfalutin!' " He enters words such as *absquatulate,* and gives three citations: the New York *Herald* for 1847 recorded that a prisoner had been surrendered by his bail, "fearing he was about to absquatulate"; in an undated citation the New York *Tribune* noticed that a station master "has absquatulated with funds belonging to the railroad"; and before 1860 the word could be used in an ecclesiastical figure of speech, since a sermon included "Hope's brightest visions absquatulate with their golden promises." He quotes with apparent approval a correspondent who says, "The use of extravagant terms is very common," especially by "deficiently educated persons who edit newspapers, and more frequently by the same class of people

---

[4] *A Glossary of Words and Phrases Usually Regarded as Peculiar to the United States,* ran through four editions, 1848, 1859, 1860, and 1877 (the later editions Boston: Little, Brown). A Rhode Island bank clerk turned bibliographer and antiquary, Bartlett (1805–86) did not use the historical method carefully, although it was well known in his day. Consequently, his entries are often difficult to date and his sources sometimes hard to identify, but he provided a revealing volume, the nearest thing to a standard statement available until the twentieth century. He is not to be confused with John Bartlett (1820–1905), the Boston bookseller whose name is associated with *Bartlett's Quotations.*

when speaking in public." He adds that "In the South and West this custom prevails to a greater extent than at the North," by which he presumably meant the Northeast, and he gives a sample of this exaggerated style in the newspaper in Springfield, Illinois, a eulogy to a female singer, one Miss Wyatt, as follows:

Illumined by the lyric muse, she is magnificent. All nerve, all palpitation, her rounded form is the fittest setting for her diamond soul! She has grace which is more than beauty, and distinction which adorns still more than grace. She appears the incarnation of genius!—it struggles within her!—inspiration quivers down her snow-white arms, and trembles on her fingers' ends,—passion wrestles in her quivering frame, and shudders through her limbs. Her soul flickers in every accent, and looms up in every pantomime, while serene smiles play about her mouth. Her drapery follows her gestures,—her gestures, her passions. Every attitude is a model, every pose is a classic statue.

She sounds nauseating, but that was apparently not the intent, and Bartlett is inclined to treat the paragraph more as bad taste and cheap journalism than as evidence of a significant development in American English, although he also points out that this sort of thing was very much not in fashion in the England of his day. We should perhaps note, also, that Bartlett, although he was the soul of objectivity when compared with many of his contemporaries, was not above authoritarian pronouncements of right and wrong where a modern student would be content to record the social status of variants. For example, he compiled a considerable list of "words incorrectly pronounced," which include " 'offen' for 'often,' " which latter pronunciation he apparently considered correct, and " 'wunt' " for " 'won't.' " In this last he was probably preferring the pronunciation which rhymes with *don't,* which seems to have been a late importation into seaboard cities like Boston, as against the pronunciation which rhymes with *bunt,* which is closer to the Old English source of the word and which survives extensively in both British and American dialects.

In short, Bartlett was aware of verbal exaggeration in his day, but he was inclined to attribute it to the bad taste of relatively few parvenus, not to the American ethos in its frontier manifestation. He was succeeded by Richard H. Thornton (1845–1925), whose work put the study of Americanisms on a sound foundation.[5] Thornton took tall talk

---

[5] *An American Glossary: Being an Attempt to Illustrate Certain Americanisms upon Historical Principles,* 2 vols. (Philadelphia: Lippincott; London: Francis, 1912). Thornton was a Lancashireman, admitted to Oxford, but was too poor to attend. After working in London, he emigrated to Canada and in 1874 to the United States; eventually he attended law school, and practiced in Pennsylvania.

seriously. He not only enters *absquatulate,* but eschewing Bartlett's badly identified examples, he gives sixteen new ones, 1837–62. His citations notably suggest journalistic humor; he notes a heading over an accident reported in the Philadelphia *Spirit of the Times,* June 20, 1842, as *A Wharf Absquatulated,* along with the following from the St. Louis *Reveille,* August 18, 1845, " 'Money makes the mare go,' is thus refined: 'The circulating medium compels the female nag to absquatulate.' " Obviously, this is intended to be funny, saying something homey or obvious in pompous, flapdoodle words. Thornton adds tall talk that Bartlett had missed—for example, *bodaciously,* which he defines as "an absurd exaggeration of 'bodily' "—and cites, along with a half dozen others, the preface to *Sketches of David Crockett,* "[I cannot] regale you with the delicate repast of a constant repetition of the terms bodyaciously, teetotaciously, obfisticated, &c."

Furthermore, Thornton adds an appendix of picturesque passages, nearly half of which could be characterized as tall talk. Thornton so designates most of them, but a reader notices at once that they fall mainly into two categories, bombastic oratory emitted by presumably serious lawyers and politicians, and frontier braggadocio which may be no more than the vaporings of lively journalists who found filling columns with large words and wild tales easier than collecting the news. Included in the supposedly serious exaggeration is the following from a tribute by Congressman Albert G. Brown of Mississippi, delivered in the House of Representatives, April 17, 1840, and concerning John C. Calhoun, a highly successful practical politician to whom qualities properly associated with divinity have not usually been attributed:

And how,—how, sir, shall I speak of him—he who is justly esteemed the wonder of the world, the astonisher of mankind? Like the great Niagara, he goes dashing and sweeping on, bidding all created things give way, and bearing down, in his resistless course, all who have the temerity to oppose his onward career. He, sir, is indeed the cataract, the political Niagara of America; and, like that noblest work of nature and of nature's God, he will stand through all after time no less the wonder than the admiration of the world. His was the bright star of genius that in early life shot madly forth, and left the lesser satellites that may have dazzled in its blaze to that impenetrable darkness to which nature's stern decree has destined them; his the mighty magazine of mind, from which his country clothed herself in the armor of defence; his the broad expansive wing of genius, under which his country sought political protection; his the giant mind, the elevated spotless

---

In 1884 he became the first dean of the Law School of the University of Oregon, where he served for more than twenty years and, except for occasional trips to England, lived in Portland for the remainder of his life—he signed the preface to his great work from London.

mien, which nations might envy, but worlds could not emulate. Such an one needs no eulogium from me, no defence from human lips. He stands beneath a consecrated arch, defended by a lightning that will not slumber, but will leap forth to avenge a word, a thought, a look, that threatens him with insult. The story of his virtuous fame is written in the highest vault of your political canopy, far above the reach of grovelling speculation, where it can alone be sought upon an eagle's pinions and gazed at by an eagle's eye. His defence may be found in the hearts of his countrymen; his eulogium will be heard in the deep-toned murmurs of posterity, which, like the solemn artillery of heaven, shall go rolling along the shores of time until it is ingulfed in the mighty vortex of eternity. Little minds may affect to despise him; pigmy politicians may raise the war cry of proscription against him; be it so; insects buz around the lion's mane, but do not arouse him from his lair. Imprecations will add but other links to the mighty chain that binds him to his countrymen; and each blast of your trumpet will but awaken millions to his support.[6]

One may presumably assume that Congressman Brown was proud of his effusion, which probably represented at once flag-waving, electioneering, and shirttail-clinging, but one doubts that it is tall talk in any literal sense, although Thornton so labels it. We may well doubt that Congressman Brown talked that way.

Similarly, the frontier braggadocio, although it purported to be talk, was probably composed of journalistic gems of something less than the purest ray serene. The following is Thornton's Exhibit No. 1; it is said to come "from a Florida newspaper, about the year 1840":

As we were passing by the court-house, a real "screamer from the Nob," about six feet four in height, commenced the following tirade: "This is *me,* and no mistake! Billy Earthquake, Esq., commonly called Little Billy, all the way from the No'th Fork of Muddy Run! I'm a small specimen, as you see, a remote circumstance, a mere yearling; but cuss me if I ain't of the true imported breed, and can whip any man in this section of the country. Whoop! won't *nobody* come out and fight me? Come out, some of you, and die decently, for I'm spileing for a fight, I hain't had one for more than a week, and if you don't come out I'm flyblowed before sundown, to a certingty. So come up to taw!

"Maybe you don't know who little Billy is? I'll tell you. I'm a poor man, it's a fact, and smell like a wet dog; but I can't be run over. I'm the identical individual that grinned a whole menagerie out of countenance and made the ribbed-nose baboon hang down his head and blush. W-h-o-o-p! I'm the chap that towed the Broad-horn up Salt River, where the snags were so thick that the fish couldn't swim without rubbing their scales off! —fact, and if any denies it, just let 'em make their wills! Cock-a-doodle-doo!

"Maybe you never heard of the time the horse kicked me, and put both his hips out of jint—if it ain't true, cut me up for fish bait! W-h-o-o-p! I'm the

---

[6] Thornton, II, 983.

very infant that refused its milk before its eyes were open, and called out for a bottle of old Rye! W-h-o-o-p! I'm that little Cupid! Talk about grinning the bark off a tree—'tain't nothing; one squint of mine at a bull's heel would blister it. O, I'm one of your toughest sort,—live for ever, and then turn to a white oak post. I'm the ginewine article, a real double-acting engine, and I can out-run, out-swim, chaw more tobacco and spit less, and drink more whiskey and keep soberer than any man in these localities. If that don't make 'em fight (walking off in disgust) nothing will. I wish I may be kiln-dried, and split up into wooden shoe-pegs, if I believe there's a chap among 'em that's got courage enough to collar a hen!"

This does not much suggest a transcript of native of Muddy Run speech. It sounds much more like Scriblerius amusing himself. I doubt that Ye Editor was able to transcribe this rather long tirade exactly—shorthand was not a journalistic accomplishment of the day, and he was merely walking past, not sitting with trimmed quill poised. I note, also, that whoever composed this discourse has some sense of paragraph organization and says, "I'm the identical individual that grinned a whole menagerie out of countenance," terminology which I would not associate with Muddy Run, but which could have been penned by the admirer of the flickering-souled Miss Wyatt, provided he had inherited a sort of minor journalistic genre, the tall talk tirade.

Thornton's other specimens suggest the qualities of his leading example. The following is Number III, from the Cincinnati *Miscellany,* I (1845), 65:

Well, I will walk tall [sic; talk?] into varmint and Indian; it's a way I've got, and it comes as natural as grinning to a hyena. I'm a regular tornado, tough as a hickory, and long-winded as a nor'wester. I can strike a blow like a falling tree, and every lick makes a gap in the crowd that lets in an acre of sunshine.

The following is from the *Oregon Weekly Times,* June 19, 1858:

Fellow-citizens, you might as well try to dry up the Atlantic Ocean with a broomstraw, or draw this 'ere stump from under my feet with a harnessed gad-fly, as to convince me that I ain't gwine to be elected this heat. My opponent don't stand a chance; not a sniff. Why he ain't as intellectual as a common sized shad. Fellers, I'm a hull team with two bull-dogs under the wagon and a tar-bucket, I am. If thar's anybody this side of whar the sun begins to blister the yea'th that can wallop me, let him show himself,—I'm ready. Boys, I go in for the American Eagle, claws, stars, and stripes, and all; and may I bust my everlastin' button-holes ef I don't knock down, drag out, and gouge everybody as denies me!"

To me this passage, also, smells more of the copy desk and the handset font than it does of the election stump; the half-horse half-alligators that were presumed to initiate tall talk did not generally discuss intellectuality in Latinate terms. Even if it does reflect stump oratory it need not, therefore, reflect frontier talk. One should notice that frontier lawyers, also, became involved in this verbiage. Thornton cites an Illinois lawyer who defended a client addicted to burglary by admitting, "True, he was rude, so air our bars. True, he was rough, so air our buffaloes." Apparently he assumed that bestiality being the nature of his client, innocence was not at issue.

Perhaps the key figure is David Crockett (1786–1836), a born ham actor, a coon-hatted frontiersman who joked himself into Congress, posing as what he was, only more so. He asserted that he had been cradled in a snapping turtle's shell, twelve feet long, had killed wolves as an infant, and was weaned on rattlesnake eggs and whisky, using a spoon made of a buffalo hoof with an eagle's leg for a handle. Grown to maturity, he liked his bear steaks salted with hail, peppered with buckshot, and sizzled on lightning—after he had broken a cantankerous thunderbolt to the bit, of course—but he preferred wildcat steaks raw. He thrashed his weight in assorted beasts, squeezed the wind out of bears while being careful not to squeeze them too hard, leaped mighty rivers, dragged stalled steamboats, and for solid comfort slept with a crocodile skin stuffed with Indian scalps as pillow. He even "wrote" several books, reminiscences which vary widely in style; he says that a friend helped him "classify the matter," and students have noticed that none of the styles in his books suggest the much duller manner of writing observable in the few letters he is known to have penned with his own hand.[7] To the Whigs he was a godsend; having supported the Democrat, Jackson, he revolted and became the Whig evidence of their homespun appeal. They made him a hero, but even west Tennessee had to grow up sometime, and when the "Coonskin Congressman" lost an election he went off to Texas and was killed at the Alamo. That was 1836; Crockett's books were known everywhere in the West and South, and we may plausibly guess that they had something to do with the growth of Crockett-like tales in newspapers which began in the late thirties, became popular in the forties and fifties, and dwindled out in the Far West during the next decade or two. Thornton's last dated citation is 1862; he could have found later ones, from the Mark Twain–Dan De Quille school of hilarity on the Comstock Lode, for example, but the fad was obviously worn out by that time. The trick was too easy and too readily became repetitious.

---

[7] Details have been deftly excerpted in Van Wyck Brooks, *The World of Washington Irving* (New York: E. P. Dutton, 1944), pp. 380–82; see also, Pyles, pp. 98–100; Marckwardt, pp. 99–100, both cited earlier.

Besides, men simply did not fight and die that way. Even Mark Twain, when he described murders, handled them quite differently. He records that one Jack Williams, "an efficient city officer," robbed a man at gun point, and "was assassinated while sitting at a card table one night; a gun was thrust through the crack of the door and Williams dropped from his chair riddled with balls."[8] One Joe McGee, a desperado and special policeman, was rumored to have done the shooting, and was marked for revenge.

After twelve months of distress (for McGee saw a fancied assassin in every man that approached him), he made the last of many efforts to get out of the country unwatched. He went to Carson [City] and sat down in a saloon to wait for the stage—it would leave at four in the morning. But as the night waned and the crowd thinned, he grew uneasy, and told the bar-keep that assassins were on his track. The bar-keep told him to stay in the middle of the room, then, and not go near the door, or the window by the stove. But a fatal fascination seduced him to the neighborhood of the stove every now and then, and repeatedly the bar-keeper brought him back to the middle of the room and warned him to remain there. But he could not. At three in the morning he again returned to the stove and sat down by a stranger. Before the bar-keep could get to him with another warning whisper, some one outside fired through the window and riddled McGee's breast with slugs, killing him almost instantly.

McGee was presumably a tough fellow, but no ringtailed roarer in the Mike Fink tradition. One recalls, also, that although Twain wrote tall talk in Virginia City, Nevada, as a reporter, when he later composed a serious novel, he sent Huckleberry Finn rafting through the heart of the Mike Fink country and peopled the Mississippi River with a riotous assortment of alcoholics, thugs, murderers, quacks, and feuding families, but nobody gets ramsquaddled or exflunctified. Even Mark Twain, one suspects, did not believe that tall talkers were among the common backwoods fauna.

This raises the question of what dictionaries are and are not good for when we endeavor to reconstruct the history of a language. They are indispensable; they allow us to know certain useful things with surprising ease. When a dictionary sends us to the *Louisville Advertiser* of October 23, 1831, wherein a man refers to himself as "Clear meat-ax disposition; the best man, if I a'nt, I wish I may be teetotaciously exfluncted!" we can be moderately sure that somebody in Louisville by 1831 knew the word *exflunct* and thought others would recognize it. Similar citations reveal that the word could also appear as *exflunticate*

---

8 *Roughing It* (Hartford, Conn.: American, 1872), pp. 348–49.

and *exflunctify*. The following, from the Troy, New York, *Statesman* for July 3, 1832, assures us that the word was not restricted to the frontier:

My wife is a screamer; she can whip her weight in wild cats; dine on tenpenny nails; wash 'em down with aqua fortis; and row about up Niagara Falls with a crowbar for an oar; it's true, every word on't; if 'taint, I hope I may be teetotaciously exfluncted.

From a dictionary we may even have some evidence that *teetotaciously exfluncted* became a sort of cliché, when we observe that an Indiana congressman used it in the House, declaring that "the administration is bodaciously used up, teetotaciously exflunctified"—or if he did not say this, he was so quoted by an exuberant newsman (*Congressional Globe,* July 20, 1845, p. 545). We have evidence that this word was known, and we could acquire similar information about *obflisticate*—and its variant forms such as *obflusticate, obfusticate,* etc.—which by 1832 could be used to mean something like *eclipse;* Crockett wrote that he would be "te-to-tatiously obfusticated," rather than accept an office. By 1830 *ramsquaddle* meant something similar—"They ought to be ram-squaddled and chewed up by a ringtailed roarer." From dictionaries we can learn that these words existed on some sort of level, but were they used, except as a sort of fleeting journalistic fad? Were they used, except in limited circles and there mainly to be funny? Dictionaries make educated guesses possible, but their evidence is often far from conclusive.

Some collateral evidence suggests that tall talk was a fad and a more restricted fad than many observers have supposed. The words are used in restricted context; with rare exceptions tall talk evinces a sort of comic strip gregariousness. If you find one word in a sentence there are likely to be more, whereas most writing, instead of including an occasional such word, contains none. The words themselves do not show much variety or ingenuity; building *bodily* up into *bodyaciously*—with or without the first *y*—required no great wit, and the pattern appears to be followed roughly in *teetotaciously* and *monstropolous.* Anybody learned enough to know *obfuscate,* who would not be Little Billy Earthquake from Muddy Run, could easily blow it up into *obflusticate,* perhaps by making a blend of *obfuscate* and *fluster.* Most of these words are now dead; a few, like *hornswoggle,* sometimes included among them and apparently older, were not much associated with the ringtailed tradition, and did not die with it.

At least one foreign traveler encountered one of these inflated words, but he did not suggest that it was involved in Mike-Finkian talk. Captain Frederick Marryat, a naval officer turned novelist, was one of the more perceptive and objective observers of the American scene, and having traveled the western waterways in 1837–38 he should have encountered a ramsquaddler if there were many about. In the course of recording a number of conversations that have the ring of reality, and observing that most American English could be paralleled in British dialects, he inserts the following:

> But there is one word which we must surrender up to the Americans as their *very own,* as the children say. I will quote a passage from one of their papers:—
> "The editor of the *Philadelphia Gazette* is wrong in calling *absquatiated* a Kentucky *phrase* (he may well say phrase instead of *word.*) It may prevail there, but its origin was in South Carolina, where it was a few years since regularly derived from the Latin, as we can prove from undoubted authority. By the way, there is a little *corruption* in the word as the *Gazette* uses it, *absquatalized* is the true reading."
> Certainly a word worth quarrelling about![9]

One might notice here that South Carolina was by no means the frontier in the 1830's, that at least one editor recognized the word as a Latin coinage, and that the folklore was apparently already growing that this sort of thing was characteristic of Kentucky. Marryat's satirical comment suggests that he considered this a very small matter, and to me it suggests that he deprecated all this as journalistic persiflage. Certainly he did not add that he had heard any such talk in Kentucky.

At about the same time the diplomat Charles Augustus Murray incorporated a long description of Kentuckians in his *Travels in North America.*[10] He found them "brave, generous, proud, frank, and hospitable," but felt he had to give his "unqualified reprobation" to "the cowardly and almost universal practice of carrying a dirk-knife" and of using it in "rough and tumbles" where "they tear one another's hair, bite off noses and ears, gouge out eyes, and in short, endeavor to destroy or mutilate each other." He adds that he is "fully aware that the stories current respecting 'gouging' are exaggerated," but it is notable that he does not observe that these picturesque folk talked picturesque cant.

Random reading of contemporary newspaper files suggests that tall talk had nothing to do with ordinary living or talking, even on the frontier. I have lately tried such an experiment, reading doggedly

---

9 *Diary in America with Remarks on Its Institutions* (Philadelphia: Carey & Hart, 1839), II, 30–40; the material on language is conveniently reprinted in *Beginnings of American English,* ed. Mitford McLeod Mathews, cited earlier, pp. 131–38, and in Mencken/McDavid, cited earlier, Suppl. 1, pp. 49–55.

10 (London: Richard Bentley, 1839), I, 209–14; the passage is conveniently reprinted in *America Through Foreign Eyes,* ed. Ronald Bartel and Edwin R. Bingham (Boston: D. C. Heath and Co., 1956), pp. 100–102.

Cuspidors, Crinoline, and the Waywardness of Language   363

through nineteenth-century newspaper files of the pioneer Middle West. Adopting the editorial rather than Queen Victoria's regal *we,* I can say that we were not amused. Such files can be fascinating if one wants to know what kind of dress goods the women were buying or how bigoted local party politicians could be, but of wit, even of blatant braggadocio, there was almost none. The humor was mostly scissors-and-paste and generally gauche. As anything but evidence of a forgotten time, the files are mainly dull. As documents these files are priceless, of course, but they do not suggest a land burgeoning with linguistic ingenuity. They suggest a small businessman, usually neither very bright nor very learned, who is more interested in subscriptions to his paper and collections for his advertising than he is in the delights of a resilient language, and who either knows how to set type or can hire someone who does. Davy Crockett said he liked a book that would "jump out of the press like a new dollar from a mint-hopper," but the pioneer journalism I have read, with rare exceptions, suggests dog-eared paper currency, dragged from a billfold by reluctant fingers.

Nor do the accounts of frontiersmen lead one to suppose their conversation sparkled with bumptious vigor. The poet Bryant was charmed with the conversation of a gangling youth he met in Illinois, but the young man did not profess to stem from the miscegenation of a hyena and a rhinoceros, nursed on panther's milk. He was Abraham Lincoln, fresh from reading Blackstone and ancient history. Similarly, travelers from abroad were generally not impressed with the linguistic charm of backwoodsmen, whatever else might engage them. Charles Dickens, one of the more literate of the travelers, found much to admire. He declared that educated Americans were the most charming people he had ever met; he praised the treatment of factory workers in Lowell, Massachusetts, and contrasted it favorably with the treatment of similar people in his own country. He asserted, "Nor did I ever once, on any occasion, anywhere, during my rambles in America, see a woman exposed to the slightest act of rudeness, incivility, or even inattention."[11] When he had to travel on boats or in coaches in the then West, however, he was bored and disgusted. Practically the only interesting person he met from Harrisburg, Pennsylvania, to St. Louis was an Indian chief. The local white people spat everywhere and washed almost nowhere; they guzzled and hogged, but they seldom said anything interesting. He recorded their speech, perhaps not always accurately, noticing what he would have called bad grammar rather than sprightly vocabulary. Of course he may have been prejudiced, but he was too good a journalist to

---

[11] *American Notes* (1842), many times reprinted; this is early in Chapter X.

miss tall talk if he had heard much of it. If he had found himself surrounded by Mike Finks and Davy Crocketts jabbering folksy confabulations on their native broadhorns, he could scarcely have failed to notice them, and he saw enough of the Ohio and Mississippi valleys so that he would have encountered this sort of thing had it been prevalent. One should remember, also, that he was in the United States in 1842, just when tall talk should have been at its most raucous. He might have been horrified at Mike Fink's manners, but he would not have missed the supposed Finkian vocabulary.

Here is Dickens' account of dinner conversations, three days from Pittsburgh to Cincinnati, in what should have been the heart of the tall talk country:

Nobody says anything, at any meal, to anybody. All the passengers are very dismal, and seem to have tremendous secrets weighing on their minds. There is no conversation, no laughter, no cheerfulness, no sociality, except in spitting; and that is done in silent fellowship around the stove, when the meal is over. Every man sits down, dull and languid; swallows his fare as if breakfasts, dinners, and suppers, were necessities of nature never to be coupled with recreation or enjoyment; and having bolted his food in a gloomy silence bolts himself, in the same state. But for these animal observances, you might suppose the whole male portion of the company to be the melancholy ghosts of departed book-keepers, who had fallen dead at the desk: such is their weary air of business and calculation. Undertakers on duty would be sprightly beside them; and a collation of funeral-baked meats, in comparison with these meals, would be a sparkling activity.

These social deaf-mutes do not suggest Mark Twain's rivermen, "Iron-jawed, brass-mounted, copper-bellied corpse-makers—half brother to the cholera, nearly related to the small-pox on the mother's side." Nor are Dickens' stagecoach people any better, and stagecoach drivers were supposed to be picturesque fellows, dodging arrows and emitting tall talk. Here are the coachmen from Cincinnati to Columbus:

The frequent change of coachmen works no change or variety in the coachman's character. He is always dirty, sullen, and taciturn. If he be capable of smartness of any kind, moral or physical, he has a faculty of concealing it which is truly marvelous. He never speaks to you as you sit beside him, on the box, and if you speak to him, he answers (if at all) in monosyllables. He points out nothing on the road, and seldom looks at anything: being, to all appearance, thoroughly weary of it, and of existence generally.

So it was, apparently, wherever Dickens went in the West. He changed to a livelier boat, but found little livelier companionship.

I never in my life did see such listless, heavy dullness as brooded over these meals: the very recollection of it weights me down, and makes me, for the moment, wretched. Reading and writing on my knee, in our little cabin [Mrs. Dickens was with him] I really dreaded the coming of the hour that summoned us to table: and was glad to escape from it again as if it had been a penance or a punishment.

The captain's wife was aboard, with a few women friends, and this helped some, since she was "disposed to be lively and agreeable" but

Nothing could have made head against the depressing influence of the general body. There was a magnetism of dullness in them which would have beaten down the most facetious companion that the earth ever knew. A jest would have been a crime, and a smile would have faded into a grinning horror.

Even a Kentucky giant was no more voluble; one of them was so tall that he "went bobbing down the cabin, among men of six feet high and upwards, like a lighthouse walking among lamp-posts," but his ambition was to drive a hackney coach, and mostly he just whittled. Dickens dismisses Kentucky giants as follows:

There never was a race of people who so completely gave the lie to history as these giants, or whom all the chroniclers have so libelled. Instead of roaring and ravaging about the world, constantly catering for their cannibal larders, and perpetually going to market in an unlawful manner, they are the meekest people in any man's acquaintance: rather inclining to milk and vegetable diet, and bearing anything for a quiet life.

Most travelers were less detailed than Dickens, but in part they support him. Mrs. Frances Trollope, mother of the novelist, was not amused either. The following is her description of diners in Memphis:

They ate in perfect silence, and with such astonishing rapidity that their dinner was over literally before ours was begun; the instant they ceased to eat, they darted from the table in the same moody silence which they had preserved since they entered the room, and a second set took their places, who performed their silent parts in the same manner.[12]

De Tocqueville thought the Americans, whom he treated with great consideration, were solemn and far from picturesque in speech; "I thought that the English constituted the most serious nation on the face of the earth," he records, "but I have since seen the Americans and I

---

[12] *Domestic Manners of the Americans* (1832), the original not much available in this country, but several times reprinted; the passage is in Chapter III.

have changed my opinion." He attributed American gravity to democratic politics, explaining that "Neither the coarse oaths of the populace
nor the elegant and choice expressions of the nobility, are to be heard
there."[13] Not everyone would have agreed with him that the New
World was free of profanity, but he apparently was not impressed by
any tall talk. Charles Augustus Murray discusses the Kentuckians; he
deprecated their brawls, their caving in one another's chests, their carrying dirks with which to slash their relatives; he concedes that "the stories
current respecting 'gouging' are exaggerated, and mostly invented," but
records nothing that could be called tall talk. Apparently he found what
he called the "western yeoman" rather surly and without much sense of
humor.[14]

Local reminiscences of hunters and desperadoes, insofar as I have
sampled them, seemed to confirm, in a negative way, these reports of
foreign observers. Most famous toughs were illiterate or nearly so; they
were involved in amazing doings, but they seldom emitted picturesque
talk except at second hand. Of course there were the Davy Crocketts,
but Davy was less half-horse, half-alligator than he was half-ham, half-
poet, who happened to be born the son of a frontier tavern keeper.
Farther west, Jim Bridger, reported the obsidian mountain so clear that
it served as a natural telescope, and the canyon in the "peetrified"
forest, which he could leap because gravity had been petrified, too, but
there was not much elongated vocabulary with these tall tales, and
anyhow, as Bernard DeVoto has pointed out, "Jim knew the right
journalists."[15]

Most of these pioneer reminiscences, except those by educated
people, have been doctored by somebody, and one does not know,
except by guessing on internal evidence, whether the editor has spiced or
blanched the vocabulary. For example, consider Meshack Browning,
whose adventures, "roughly written down by himself," were "revised and
illustrated by E[dward Stabler]," who asserts, "My task though a 'labor
of love,' is comparatively a very humble one, and has been mainly confined to the correction of grammatical errors." I have heard this work attacked as a forgery, but if so, it is a very clever forgery; it is too dull to
be the work of a lively mind, a string of monotonously triumphant
hunting expeditions, interspersed with a few other incidents, apparently
told because a garrulous old man could remember them, but even a tale
with a Davy Crockett plot has no Davy Crockett vocabulary. The follow-

---

[13] Alexis de Tocqueville, *Democracy in America,* trans. Henry Reeve (New York·
    Adlard, 1838), II, 232–34.
[14] *T avels in North America,* cited earlier, I, 211–15.
[15] *cross the Wide Missouri* (Boston: Houghton Mifflin, 1947), p. 169.

ing is from Browning's account of his boxing match with a bear—not a big one. It seems he had caught a medium-sized bear by mistake in a wolf trap, and he suggested to a companion named Knox that a grown man ought to be able to "fight that bear with his naked hands." The idea appealed to Browning, and deciding to try it, he freed the bear. The account continues:

> As I knew that he would want to go down the hill, I waited until he found he was free from the trap, and attempted to go off, when I made at him. He rushed at me with a snort that made Knox shriek like a woman; but as he came toward me, I ran down the hill into the bottom. As he did not seem disposed to try to catch me, I again faced about to receive him; Knox all the while screaming at me to leave. But being determined to give him a crack or two, at all hazards, I stood till he came within reach, when I struck him in the ear as hard as I could, and turned his head around. He then became mad, and rose on his hind-feet to make for my face or neck; but I struck him in the pit of his stomach, which seemed to double him up. He made another sudden attempt to run under my legs, when, seeing that he would get hold of me if I stood still, I made a leap, and as he came on, landed in his rear.[16]

By this time Knox could stand the strain no longer, and let the dogs loose on the bear; accordingly, Browning killed it with his knife. The account is clear and orderly, but it gives us no reason to suppose that this veteran hunter was a ringtailed roarer.

This is not, of course, to suggest there were no tough fellows in the West, that picturesque words did not come from the frontier, and that violence had nothing to do with them. Mike Fink presumably lived and was presumably shot through the heart at Natchez-under-the-Hill. According to the story, he was shooting a small object off a fellow roisterer's head, when he decided to have a bit of fun, and crease the roisterer's scalp a bit, too. The concussion knocked out the roisterer, who was supposed dead, but he revived and evidenced the dormancy of his sense of humor by shooting Mike. This sort of thing doubtless happened; keelboaters did get drunk and shoot up Natchez before shooting up one another. Boasting and brawling must have been part of an ebullient brew on the American frontier that had unexpected impacts upon language, but insofar as this impact included pseudo-Latinisms like *slantindicular* and *blustiferous,* we can suspect a scribbler in the woodpile.

Van Wyck Brooks and Thomas Pyles have suggested, I assume independently, the analogy between western tall talk and the manner

---

[16] *Forty-four Years of the Life of a Hunter; Being Reminiscences of Meshack Browning, a Maryland Hunter* (Philadelphia: J. B. Lippincott & Co., 1869), p. 233.

and vocabulary of Gargantua and Pantagruel. Brooks asks if tall tales "were not . . . the natural growths of a world that had burst its bonds, a young mind that had cast the skin of ancestral conventions and social forms and exulted in a freedom that knew no limit? In this sense the frontier had something in common with Rabelais, who spoke for a lusty France that was trying its strength after the long constriction of the Middle Ages."[17] He notices the gigantic proportions of mountain, river, desert, and prairie, and mentions exaggeration in the Hindu epics, which had come from a people who had burst into a new world. These analogies, if they are not evidence and not very specific, must have some validity. Marckwardt points out that there must be something here; exuberance and exaggeration were not characteristic of Massachusetts Bay.

My own guess is that the efficient cause, if we can talk about causes, is to be sought in democracy as a political, social, and educational force. The colonies had not been democratic, in politics or in spirit, nor was the new West, but it was growing that way. Back Bay Boston could probably not have produced Davy Crockett or Andrew Jackson, but if it had, theocratic New England would not have taken them seriously. On the frontier, hopeless people acquired hope; tethered people lost their restrictions; limited people found themselves in an unlimited world. Of course, many of the results were bad; crude people may prosper financially and socially in a crude world, and a raw, untamed world is crude. How could culture become a pattern where ignorance and crudity were kings? The aspects of western life which shocked and disgusted Dickens were merely the accidents of a raw democracy become the approved formalities of life. The little people, the untutored people, who would have been kept in their place in well-regulated Britain, had here become their own place. The frontier, and the West generally, was absorbing democracy too fast for its own good, and the result could be something between exuberance and license. One notices, for example, that although exuberance, exaggeration, and lack of balance were common concomitants of the frontier, the combination is apparently most observable in politics. Presumably this sort of thing can be expected wherever heady stimulants like freedom and democracy come quickly. As I write, turbulence is sweeping over Africa even more devastatingly than it swept over the American West; the American backwoodsman did not understand the responsibilities of democracy, and could not be expected to understand them, any more than a recently liberated black man from the jungle can be expected to distinguish between *uhuru* and license.

---

[17] *The World of Washington Irving,* cited earlier, pp. 382–83.

The frontier was new, and it was raw; and its rawness and its lawlessness were accentuated by a growing democracy which seemed to sanction a world without heritage. All this had its impact upon manners, as visiting Europeans, not to mention cultured natives, were aware, and we may plausibly assume that it affected language, too, although the details are difficult to isolate. The frontier must have influenced habits of language along with practices in expectoration.

What did this western tall talk amount to? Obviously some of it smelled of the winter evening, if not much of the campfire. It was at least a fad in journalism. It must have had genuine substance in politics; rabble rousing is neither new nor old, and was certainly common in stump oratory, and was even carried to the highest legislative halls, at least when legislators were talking "for buncombe," for the folks back home. Apparently this sort of thing permeated the courts, as well; in a drab frontier society a lawing was one of the few good shows; no doubt many a frontier shyster played more to the courtroom than he did to the court, more to the jury than to the bench. Even if he lost a case, he became a hero if his harangue was hilarious or bombastic enough. Highfalutin language may have been mostly a journalistic fad so far as the keelboat roarers were concerned, but it was a movement in politics and at least a tendency in law, and it surely pervaded mores, including language.

All this leads to the question: What was frontier journalism like? What did frontiersmen read, if they read anything? On the whole, frontier newspapers were pallid, moral, conventional, conservative, and dull, put together with paste and scissors by printers or small businessmen more interested in advertising and paid circulation than in language. For example, I have before me a reprint of the *Territorial Enterprise,* volume I, number 3 (January 1, 1859), the newspaper later made famous by Mark Twain, published in what was then Carson Valley, Utah Territory. The page-one news is as follows: a poem, presumably by a youth of sixteen, advising young people not to marry too young; an editorial pointing out that friends in prosperity do not necessarily continue friends in adversity; a piece called "CURE FOR LOVE," which prescribes a home remedy composed of such ingredients as prudence, patience, and common sense; an editorial clipped from the Philadelphia *North American* called "defects of American Society," which identifies the leading defect as "pretension"; a quotation from "M. Guizot's Memoirs" concerning Lafayette; a longish piece from the Springfield *Republican* called "A Boy's Trials"—it seems that one of them was being forced to sit with girls in school; an editorial called "You Will Be

Wanted"—it urges young men to work hard and prepare themselves for better jobs; two clipped squibs called "EDITING A PAPER," and "HE is ONLY a Printer"; a dramatic sketch called "She is Dying," which ends with the guardian angel looking down from heaven and saying "Hush!"; a few squibs to fill columns, presumably clipped, and apparently intended to be humorous or edifying. The page contains no local news, little that could be called news of any sort, and nothing even remotely suggestive of tall talk. If the readers expected tall talk, they did not get it, and yet if longevity is an evidence of success, this was one of the most successful frontier periodicals.

All this leads to a larger problem—how do languages change? Specifically, does language well up from the masses or trickle down from the literate and the fashionable? Both theses have been advanced, and the case of the tall talk, if it cannot be final, is pertinent. If, as many writers have believed, tall talk is indigenous talk, the spontaneous overflow of frontier feelings, then we have here a case in which language has been made, however impermanently, by the minds, emotions, and inclinations of the folk. If, as I have endeavored to argue, tall talk stems mainly from literate if not very discriminating professionals, then this language manifestation suggests that vocabulary can seep down. Of course, the fact that in one instance language flowed from the journalist's desk and the political podium to the keelboat—if it ever got there—does not prove that language cannot flow the other way, also, but at least the example is instructive. If a love of tall talk started as a journalistic fad, rather like the Boston clubman's fad for initials which became involved in *O.K.,* we can account for the transience of exuberant terminology by assuming that it never had any broad base, the kind of base that the Mike Finks of the world could have given it if they had ever talked this stuff.

Tall talk throve on the frontier, if it was not indigenous to it. Another penchant, we may suppose, stems from the eastern seaboard and from middle-class prudery—not to say prissiness—which spread westward in the wake of the frontier. It must have been in part a reaction to the crudity of a new country, and if tall talk was the prerogative of the men, elegance was the glory of the women, elegance in words as in skirts. In its milder forms it preferred *lady* and *better half* to *woman* and *wife,* both of which savor of biology. E. Douglas Branch thought he could isolate a cult of sentimentality that existed in its pantalooned purity after about 1835.[18] Corrupted by various sorts of prudery, it was preserved

---

[18] *The Sentimental Years* (New York and London: Appleton-Century, 1934), *passim,* e.g., pp. 11–12.

for decades in the chaste pages of publications like *Godey's Lady's Book*. Seemingly the American counterpart of British Victorianism, the cult was probably accentuated by colonialism and by an understandable revulsion against the sort of frontier gaucherie that made expectorating a masculine national pastime. By this terminology, females were all ladies, and had no legs, but got on as they could with *limbs*, a rather vulgar term for *lower extremities*, which were concealed past the toes if possible. A lady had no organs at all, and almost nothing but various sorts of embroidery, beading, and impermeable goods between the toes and the neck. *Godey's* describes how all these female encasements were to be made, with such terminology as *tarletan, Bismarck crepe, Cluny edgings, peau de soie,* and hundreds more. Mothers were greatly admired, but Godey, who advised females on almost everything, did not instruct a lady as to how to become one. Everything was chaste as well as elegant; a modern reader observes that even the *coquette headdress* is composed of "a wreath of small roses" with green leaves, and "from these leaves depend pearl or crystal drops." Ladies, apparently composed of about equal parts of faith, patience, beauty, morality, and skill in needlework—which included making tissue-paper hyacinths—could be distinguished from their husbands by the difference "between *obedience* that yields from fear of hell, and *submission* that flows from faith in heaven." The ladies, of course, had the faith. These beings did not live anywhere; they *resided,* preferably in four-story monstrosities composed of *parlors, boudoirs, sculleries, nurseries, foyers, verandahs,* and *chambers,* and they produced *infants,* not babies. If one of these blessings happened outside matrimony it was a *Sunday child, base-born, come-by-chance, stolen colt, ketch colt, old-field colt, woods colt;* and such terms were common among the elegantly disposed but socially underprivileged folk, along with ladies having social pretensions. *Cock* was avoided either for a pile of hay or a rooster—roosting was a nocturnal occupation in which any bird could respectably indulge. We have already noticed what squeamish Americans did to terms for the uncastrated male bovine; they presumably did not know that *bull* is related to *phallus,* from an Indo-European root meaning "to swell up," but they acted as though they did, denominating the creature a *gentleman cow.*

The growing prominence of ladies required new terms for them. Louis Antoine Godey, along with his editor, Mrs. Sarah Josepha Hale, who was the arbiter here, if anybody was, rejoiced for nearly two small-type columns that the growing female world had revived old terms for women and engendered new ones.[19] Mrs. Hale sometimes called her sisters

---

[19] "Editor's Table," *Godey's Lady's Book and Magazine,* LXXV (1867), 79.

women, but Godey apparently avoided such frankness. The editor points out that

We have learned that a vital connection exists between the language of a nation and its mode of thought; that change in the latter results from and reacts upon the former . . . and that when a new thing or new combination of things emerges from the tumult of affairs, it cannot long remain without a fitting appelation.

"Feminine termination" had been declining since the days of Chaucer, we are told,

But with modern movement for the enlargement of the sphere of women came a necessity for distinction before unfelt . . . In such cases the word *female* has been prefixed; but such a collocation is both cumbrous and weak, and savors often of vulgarity. The unpleasant effect of calling a lioness a *female* lion, or an actress a *female* actor is obvious.

Accordingly, replacing *female doctor* with "doctress will be a wonderful gain to our language alike in strength and sweetness." The editor—or *editress,* as she no doubt would have preferred—admitted that this sort of thing could be carried too far, pointing out that "Such words as *soldieresses* and *builderesses,* or *childresses* have very properly fallen out of our language." Still,

The poetry of women is distinctive and peculiar; their acting is of wholly different parts; their manner of teaching has influences which men cannot reach; their medical practice is required for human preservation; and the language gains greatly in beauty, force, propriety, and power by conveying these differences in a single word.

Accordingly, the following are recommended as endings in -*ess,* preferred because it came from "Saxon," for "Professions, Pursuits, Epithets," and we are assured that these words "are now used by the best English writers."

Actress	Instructress	Preceptress	Teacheress
Adventuress	Monitress	Professoress	Tormentress
Arbitress	Murderess	Sculptress	Traitress
Authoress	Negress	Shepherdess	Victress
Citizeness	Paintress	Songstress	Waitress
Doctress	Poetess	Sorceress	
Governess	Portress	Stewardess	
Huntress	Postmistress	Tailoress	

One doubts that some of these words, for example *victress* and *professoress,* were very popular anywhere, but Godey's approval would have helped. Recommended also are female "Titles of Office, Rank and Respect," including the following: Ambassadress, Ancestress, Britoness, Chieftainess, Educatress, Inheritress, Jewess, Managress (from Manager), and Pythoness.

All this rests upon a mild sort of taboo that restricted certain subjects, notably sex and bodily excretion, and was directed particularly toward common words. Curiously, the taboo seems to represent not only a sort of quarantine for the young, but also a conspiracy against the ignorant, for the taboo could be somewhat lifted by arcane terms, which in effect meant latinate terms. Four- and five-letter words were deplored, but *penis* and *rectum* are more acceptable than synonyms no shorter. Perhaps they are privileged as medical necessities, but they are part of a system of taboos that has operated with varying force at various times and social levels during our immediate past. Of such were the contrasts, from cuspidors to crinoline, of a relatively uncultured people blundering from the backwoods toward something approximating European civilization.

PART FOUR

AMERICAN ENGLISH COMES OF AGE

20

MAN'S ESTATE IN LANGUAGE

Puberty may be father to the man, but a period of maturation follows. Only after becoming physically adult does a young person become emotionally and intellectually adult, and so with language. Usually, language is so integrated with the users of it that maturity in language is likely to be closely associated with maturity in society. During the twenties of this century a clearheaded Frenchman, André Siegfried, in a book entitled *America Comes of Age,* observed that the United States could now take its place as an adult among nations. At about the same time a similar observation could have been made about American English.

Coming of age is not one thing. A young person may be legally unable to vote one day and legally adult the next but the change is not so sudden, and usually a birthday is no more than a symbol. Still, looking back, a young adult can perceive that subtly something has happened, and he can usually know roughly when, and more or less clearly how. With 'American society and American English the change can perhaps best be associated with the first World War. The United States was not heavily involved for a protracted period, nor can even a great war mature a people unless they are about ready to mature of themselves, but the incident at Sarajevo did spark revolutions throughout the world which probably hastened American maturity and illuminated American maturation.

Until about the time of the 1914–18 war, the United States, well supplied with raw materials, imported almost everything else—human beings, religions, customs, education, science and technology, ideas, manufactured goods, books—in fact, most things that could bring language with them. The few terms Americans developed, like names for the phenomena of the New World, they largely kept to themselves be-

377

cause nobody else needed them much. Early in the new century, however, exporting began; baseball terms drifted south of the border and into the Orient. Soon American moving pictures were carrying Americanisms with them, and by the second World War, American military power and American technical competence were ferrying American ways into the far corners of the world, and American English went with them. Furthermore, the United States had become the native land of automation, the world symbol for the machine age, and as we have seen, the world's leading exporter of all sorts of space-age terminology. The United States had grown to a competence in which she could lend approximately as much as she borrowed, and she could lend to the most culturally advanced peoples, those of western Europe. What was more important, she had grown sufficiently self-reliant so that she no longer needed to be self-conscious about borrowing. She had learned, after three centuries of juvenility, to treat language equals as equals.

Inevitably this new maturity affected American English both at home and abroad. At home the changes were not spectacular. To a degree, the same old tendencies notable in the nineteenth century continued into the twentieth, although with some shift in direction. Americans have gone on making new words they need, especially new compounds, but the trends are different. The old geographical frontier faded away, while new frontiers developed in science, technology, industry, and even in scholarship, social sciences, and the arts. The continent was by now well scattered with understandable names; except as new cities were built, new industries devised, and new ways of living developed, no new names were needed. Similarly, most birds, beasts, fish, and even insects had been discovered and named; no more terms were needed except for rare species, and their names were so technical as to fall within a specialized area, the terminology of the new learning. Living patterns changed so rapidly with automotive travel, municipal living, and mass means of communication, that vocabulary concerned with private and public life has continued to grow, but on the whole the growing part of the language is no longer the part with which people live.

The new vocabulary grows from the way men have learned to think, particularly with the new ways in which man is still learning to think. Here new terminology tends to be international; physical science, social science, scholarship, music, art, philosophy, all the specialized ways in which man is learning to labor in the mind are more or less international. A technique that appears anywhere soon spreads throughout the cultured world; a new idea leaps political, social, and linguistic barriers. Much of the new vocabulary, pillaged from the ancient storehouses of language, Greek and Latin, reflects the common resources for many of the most productive cultures. Thus the America that has come of age is not so much exporting new Americanisms that are names for indigenous objects; the new terminology is to a degree an international vocabulary in which American English is assuming an adult role.

Consider television. It is not an 'American invention, nor is it the exclusive invention of any nationally identifiable body of people. Television as we know it is the result of hundreds of inventions, hundreds of evidences of rethinking, hundreds and thousands of refinements. Many of these are recorded in terms that embody old Latin and Greek, words and semantic fragments which have long been the universal quarry of inventors and technicians in search of terms, but since much of the research and development has been done by Americans, the Latin and Greek is disseminated in American guise. *Television* itself relies on a Greek root plus an Anglicized Latin word; thousands of other words like *iconoscope* and *kinoscope* incorporate developments from Latin and Greek, especially from Greek. On the whole, the biological sciences having pre-empted Latin after the Linnaeus classification, the physical sciences turned most frequently to Greek. Once these words with their classical echoes have become attached to the object, they are exported all over the world; the Spanish word *television* is the American word pronounced in a Spanish manner. I found that the Erse words which I could guess most readily appeared in television shops. Which of this Anglicized Graeco-Latin stems from British and which from American English and which from both might be difficult to determine in many instances, but that much of it comes from American use not the most rabid Yankeephobe could deny. Meanwhile, American slang and cant terms for electronic equipment, like *tweeter* and *woofer* for high- and low-pitched speakers, are less broadcast, but even they enjoy some dissemination.

At the other end of the spectrum from the learned terms are the local slang and argot. Doubtless all times and peoples have had their equivalent, and we probably need not take seriously chauvinistic assumptions that Americans have been distinctively ingenious in refurbishing old terminology; we have already observed that Elizabethan England had its thieves' cant, and not without the cooperation of the Parisian underworld has *argot* itself been borrowed from French. Some neologisms are notably apt; *gangbang* for a *lineup,* or sequential rape, provides a memorable term for infamous conduct, but it could doubtless be paralleled in many languages. Manufacturers coin words; at this writing teenage shoes called *Grubbies* are said to be "carefully ripped and messed-up before being sold so as to give them that casual, lived-in look." Some peculiarities of the American scene, however, have provided remarkable bodies of words, most of them ephemeral.

Fads have had their impacts, most of them temporary. *Sputnik,*

Russian for satellite, within a few years sired more than two hundred *nik* coinages; *lunik* and *dognik* (variants *pupnik* and *mutnik*) were natural names for a moon shot and a rocket with a dog, respectively. American failures to launch a satellite became *goofniks, flopniks, pfftniks,* and *sputterniks.* This new familiarity with *-nik* in the context of space exploration also helped reinforce the general acceptance of the related Yiddish suffix *-nik,* which can be used "to convert a word into a label for an ardent practitioner or devotee of something," so that a *nudnik*—from *nudzheh,* to bore or pester—is a confirmed pest, one whose "purpose in life is to bore the rest of humanity." Accordingly, *-nik* coinages have enjoyed wider currency than have most Yiddish terms: *beatnik,* a devotee of the "beat" generation; *phoodnik,* a nudnik with a Ph.D. degree; *sicknik,* a malingerer; *straightnik,* one who is not homosexual. *Hoaxnik, alrightnik, no-goodnik, kaputnik,* and *bottlenik* should require no explanation beyond the Jewish love of wit and language.[1]

Sports and amusements contributed their share. Baseball was an American invention; it has carried new uses of words like *pitch, strike, foul,* and *base* into far languages and strange tongues. Horse racing was by no means an American invention, but American cultures, both Anglo-Saxon and Latin American, have been horse-based as have few other extensive societies, with a corresponding efflorescence of horse-racing slang. By way of random sample, the following is an extract from one page of racing terms:[2]

drop down: to run with cheaper horses, especially in claiming races.

drugstore handicap: any race in which drugs are used to stimulate horses, or in some cases to deaden the pain in bad feet.

dump: to bet heavily on a horse, at the last minute before starting time, to keep the odds up.

dust a horse: to give a horse a narcotic or drug before a race, especially cocaine. See *boat race, hophead.*

dutch a book: purposely to force a bookie out of business by betting so that the book inevitably loses.

dwell: of a horse, to get away slowly at the start.

dynamiter: a bookie who bets with another bookie to cover bets he does not wish to keep.

eagle bird: a horse with a better chance of getting into the money than his odds indicate.

Available lists suggest that more than a thousand such terms have considerable currency.

---

[1] *Names,* VIII (1960), 188–89; Leo Rosten, *The Joys of Yiddish* (New York: McGraw-Hill, 1968), pp. xiv-xv, and under such entries as *-nik* and *nudnik.*

[2] David W. Maurer, "The Argot of the Racetrack," *PADS,* Nov., 1951, p. 25.

Dramatic and other formal spectacles have sired picturesque terms. In the day when every hamlet had its opera house—which offered almost every sort of cheap entertainment, but no opera, which has never been cheap—the United States supported an unbelievable number of *hoofers, end men, leg ladies,* and various sorts of *hams.* Such folksy performers were rendered obsolete by the movies, which brought a new set of amusement terms and exported them to the world—*cream puffs, funny-boners, white meaters, pantie peelers, shredded wheat, shakers, hamateurs, draw names, hoof-and-mouth artists, heavenly bodies,* and *lefty mugs.* These are now dodo-dead, and as the public moving picture is superseded by the private moving picture, called television, the new devices have attained a popularity in the United States not approached elsewhere, and have encouraged new locutions, *good guys and bad guys, horse opera,* and *show* in the sense *Ed Sullivan Show.* Whether this sequence of new and exportable terms results from the broad base of American wealth, the American love of fads, the immensity of the American market, or all three and more too, the result for language is obvious.

The breadth of American acres, the relative plenitude of food, and the prevalence of American transportation have led to other sources of ephemeral vocabulary. Among the more genial were the hoboes. Itinerant ne'er-do-wells are no American monopoly, but within limits the hobo seems to have been an American institution. Europe had its gypsies; these itinerants had, as they still have, shady reputations, but the New World never acquired many gypsies. No doubt most of them could not afford passage, and if they came they arrived as deported criminals; liberated they tended to become prosperous and sedentary. The American equivalents of the Elizabethan Uprightman with his doxie did not need to take to the road in the New World. Law enforcement was sufficiently lax so that they throve in the cities. The hobo might be a small criminal, but he could be a somewhat more genial character, one who was merely averse to work if it threatened to become a habit and averse to surroundings when they became too familiar.

Itinerants came in several grades: *hoboes* proper, much respected in *Hobohemia* if not outside it; *tramps,* a cut above *dingoes, scenery bums, mopers* and *moochers;* and *yeggs,* "too mean to be bums and too lazy to be good tramps,"[3] who lived by *rolling dead ones,* that is, by robbing drunks, along with specialized itinerants like *mushfakers,* who pretended to mend umbrellas and the like, and *jockers,* who kept *road punks,* boys

---

[3] Dean Stiff, *The Milk and Honey Route* (New York: Vanguard, 1931), has a glossary; the particular quotation, p. 217. I suspect that *Dean Stiff* may be a *nom de plume* for Nels Anderson.

who served various purposes, including the homosexual—a development which may reflect an old use of the word *punk* as *prostitute*. They traveled in *side-door Pullmans*, more commonly known as boxcars, or would scuttle into the *possum belly* under passenger cars, and if they were *trapeze artists*, rode the *rods, guts,* or *gunnels,* the trusses that were slung under the older boxcars—that is, they did if they could avoid the *yard dicks*, company police, and endure being *underslung*, when *shacks*, railroad men, pelted them with rocks or dragged a piece of iron under the car so that it would bounce up and batter them. They could *panhandle* on the streets, or *toot the ringer* at back doors, hoping to get a *sitin* or at worst a *handout*, especially if circumstances could be so arranged that the lady of the house saw a hobo eating grass on the lawn. With luck, vagrants might get an occasional *tin roof*, a free drink supposedly so called because it was *on the house*.

They normally resided in the *jungle*, some sort of vacant area from which they would presumably not be driven, although they might aspire to a *bridal chamber*, a *flophouse*, providing floor space, or a *boodle jail*, where, for a mild misdemeanor they might hibernate, or they might get a hospital bed if they could *chuck a dummy*, fainting or throwing a fit. In the autumn they could *follow the birds*, go south, even using their *tie pass* if necessary, although walking the railroad was both unpleasant and unprofessional. If they *ate a snowball*, wintering in the north, they might *go on a hummer*, be on the bum but not down and out, and progress to *being on their uppers*, almost down and out. They might even get so low as to go to the *Y.M.C.A.*, which letters were expanded into *You Must Come Across*, or stage a conversion for the benefit of a *mission stiff* who was *working for Jesus* in one of the *fisheries*, institutions intended to salvage human derelicts along *skid row*, known as the *main stem*. They were not necessarily averse to work, sporadically, and would become *wheat willies, harvest stiffs, bridge stiffs*—those working with rough lumber would become *splinter bellies*—even *jerries* working with other *gandy dancers* on the railroad right-of-way, particularly if a pretense to work would avoid *getting a fanner*, attention by the police, or residence in either the *little school* or the *big school*, a local reformatory and the state penitentiary respectively.[4]

In recent decades the hobo has declined, and his terminology with him. Possibly the reduction of railroad traffic and the increase of the police and of welfare agencies have deprived him of his natural prerogatives. Doubtless the increase in cheap cars, free employment bureaus,

---

[4] Most of this material is from Stiff, either the glossary or *passim* throughout the text.

and bored or lonesome truck drivers have cut into the fraternity. With the development of mechanized and socialized living the need for unskilled and odd-job labor has declined, and as an itinerant farm laborer the hobo has found his manhood insulted by swarms of little Mexican children, the families of migratory workers, who pick beans faster than he can. Whatever the reason, the true hobo appears to be going the way of the dodo, the passenger pigeon, and the whooping crane. Not that there are now no skid rows wobbling with winos, but Hobohemia seems to be approaching its last seacoast.

The itchy-footed, light-fingered vagrant who in a more pastoral society became the hobo now tends to become the urban confidence man, sophisticated in his own way and master of a vocabulary even more picturesque than that attributed to his predecessor.[5] He is the ne'er-do-well turned professional, where he has been joined by a remarkable collection of small thieves and big gamblers, associated with the *grift,* notably in mobs involved in some sort of *big* or *short con.* These *grifters,* to be distinguished from *heavy rackets men* who rely on muscular or ballistic persuasion, expect mainly to swindle by their wits, their skill, and their elaborate techniques.

A grifter's dream is the *big store,* which in such variations as the *wire,* the *pay-off,* and the *rag* provides a tribute to American ingenuity and know-how, if not to American Sunday school atmosphere. In operating the *wire,* for example, a *steerer* or *roper* identifies a *mark,* and plays gently upon his greed, eventually bringing him to what appears to be a Western Union station, a busy place with messages being received and sent, telephones ringing, and respectably dressed people accepting what look like large sums of money. Gradually the mark learns how this comes about; by being a little slow in reporting the results of races a telegraph official can make it possible for a few chosen persons to bet on the race after it is run, a sure thing. The mark bets a little, then more, and wins phenomenally, but as soon as he bets a sufficient sum, there is a mistake, and he loses. The employee who made the mistake is fired for

---

[5] David W. Maurer, *The Big Con,* rev. ed. (New York: Bobbs-Merrill, 1963; reprinted, New American Library, as *Whiz Mob*). Professor Maurer, a student of linguistics who specializes in underworld jargon, has himself become a minor folkloristic figure. Men who flick the fringes of the law are notably suspicious of anyone interested in them, perhaps particularly those who endeavor to pry into the implications of their deliberately arcane terminology. They have apparently come to trust Maurer, however, and a whole body of tales is growing up of how they show their loyalty to one of the fraternity by trying to apply the works to any deans or trustees who they fear may be trying to push "the Prof" around. Maurer, understandably, does not feel that displays of mobster muscle would enhance either his scholarly or his academic standing.

his incompetence, but the only way to recoup losses is to bet heavier the next time, which bets lead to still larger losses.

During the process of being roped, the mark has met various people, including an *inside man;* surrounded by evidences of wealth and affluence, this person can be very potent in encouraging large bets and in *cooling the mark* when he has been fleeced. If the mark becomes troublesome, he can be *blown off,* for example, with the *cackle-bladder.* By this device either the *roper* or the *inside man,* seemingly furious that his friend has lost his money, starts a fight with his accomplice, draws a gun and apparently shoots him. Blood spurts over the mark, and the bloodstained weapon is thrust into his hand; uniformed police rush in. The mark may be given *the button,* allowed to talk his way out of arrest, or he may be hustled out a side door, provided with clean clothes, and put aboard a plane or train for another city. He will gradually be moved from city to city to avoid threatened police investigation, until finally he arrives at no address with no clues. What he does not know, of course, is that the cartridge in the supposed murder weapon was a blank, that the blood that squirted on him was chicken blood from a bladder concealed in the accomplice's mouth, and that within minutes after the supposed police raid, conducted by members of the mob, the Western Union office had been stored away for the next victim. No doubt, with the decline of the telegraph, the particular operation that Maurer is here describing has vanished, but it will have retired only to slough its skin and appear in fresh colors.

With suitable variations in costuming, personalities, and decor, the *big store* may become any sort of apparently legitimate business establishment, for example an investment brokerage house, wherein the mark can be bilked of tens of thousands for bogus stock or for stock that somehow vanishes. Inevitably, the minds which devise and direct these devices are lively enough to indulge in language. "Of all criminals," Maurer writes, "confidence men probably have the most extensive and colorful argot." Many cons are extremely intelligent, but Maurer believes, also, that they include a high proportion of "remarkably original minds," minds which "derive a pleasure which is genuinely creative from toying with language," minds which are uncommonly agile "and which see and express rather grotesque relationships in terms of the flickering, vastly connotative metaphor which characterizes their argot." For example, an *addict* is a mark who is *knocked* again and again. In the *big mit,* to use Maurer's words, the mark "is enticed into the store, drawn into a crooked poker game and cold-decked on his own deal." Variations are the *tear-up* and the *huge duke.* When a grifter has to leave in a hurry, he *cops a heel* or *lights a rag,* avoiding *paying his fare* if possible; that is, "A kinky kayducer will always cop the short." On the way he may *count and read,* steal from the mark's wad while pretending to examine it for counterfeit bills. *Coarse ones* are bills of large denomination intended to trick the mark, and dollars are *push notes, bumblebees, case notes, seed,* and *fish.* The etymology of such terms may be uncertain; to *sew a man up* is obvious enough, since the pickpocket warns the mark against pickpockets, and obligingly sews his wallet— already lightened of its currency and plumped out with worthless paper—into his pocket. Often, however, the origin is likely to remain obscure to a mere law-abiding citizen. *Prat-out* is not what a lover of slapstick comedy might imagine; it is an elaborate device in the *pay-off* to induce the mark to pay zealously, a variant of the *shut-out,* but none of these words mean what they seem to.

This sort of thing continues. Recently a Senate investigating committee was told, "I had the bug in, the block-out work done and the shiner on, but the other guy turned up with luminous readers." This seems to mean that the gambler had a clip under the table to hold cards slipped out of the deck, had marked cards by blocking out parts of the design on the back, and was wearing a ring with a small mirror that permitted him to see the underside of cards as they were dealt. His intended victim, however, arrived wearing tinted glasses that enabled him to detect colored markings not otherwise visible.

Slang terms appear in patterns of time, place, and occupation. Street cable cars operate only in San Francisco these days, and accordingly, only there does one find *gripmen,* husky fellows who *work the platform,* operating the device to grip the cables. Oil drillers are said to favor food tropes; *appetizers* are TNT; *apple butter,* engine belt dressing; *beans,* valves; *biscuits,* rocks; *cabbage,* bearings; *catsup,* red acid; *donuts,* tubing; *macaroni,* big pipe; *spaghetti,* little pipe; and so on through the buffet. During the early 1960's, when all were worrying about supposed Russian hegemony, the *missile gap* was formed; it led to all kinds of gaps, *deterrent gap, missile-deterrent gap, tax gap, guidance gap,* even a *truth gap,* the whole presumably leading to a *gap gap.* At about the same time a dance craze called the *twist* produced various offspring known as the *wobble,* the *mashed potato,* the *hully gully,* the *pony,* the *Watusi,* the *slop,* the *waddle,* the *locomotion* and the *shag;* most of them became victims of infant mortality, having lasted only a few months or years. Campus slang varies highly; "Let's check the bods in the fishbowl" (Let's see what girls are in the library) works only on campuses having a glassed-in reading room. Examinations could be *Flunkenstein monsters* anywhere, genuine *flunkasauruses,* although the term appears to be southern.

Negroes are said to have a body of terminology restricted to Harlem and some other colored communities; a *bag* is a point of view or pattern of behavior; *blow,* a party, or as a verb, to do something; *boss,* good; *busted,* arrested; *cents,* dollars; *cop,* to take part in ("He couldn't cop because he was in slam"); *fox,* pretty girl; *gig,* a job or to work; *grit,* food or to eat; *ice,* very good; *jump salty,* become angry; *member,* a Negro; *mickey mouse,* pompous or important person ("She put him down because he was a mickey mouse cat"); *ralph bunche,* talk oneself out of trouble; *run,* a purpose; *saying something,* excellent; *slam,* prison; *taste,* liquor; *tore down,* drunk; *vines,* clothes; *woke,* conversant; *woof,* to boast.[6]

Perhaps the most interesting questions to be asked here are psychological and philosophical: Who makes slang? Why do they make it? What are the subjects of slang? These matters have been too little studied. No doubt some slang provides a defense for the otherwise defenseless; Berrey and Van den Bark list more slang terms for stupid, boring, gauche, and deceitful persons than for important, admired, congenial people, but even these latter epithets tend to ridicule the subject.[7] Terms for admired people range from *aceroo* to *wonder-for-hogs.* Slang is promoted, perhaps notably among teenagers, by the love of being in fashion, and by indolence; devising slang may require a mind, but using it does not. More than anything else, perhaps, it stems from a love of play. Why an unwelcome person is a *big beezack* I do not know, but one senses that the term is somehow funny.

Something can probably be inferred from the subjects of slang. In the United States far more people are involved in golf, as participants and spectators, than in horse racing, yet Berrey and Van den Bark give fifteen pages of terms from the turf for two pages from the links. The baseball diamond provides fifteen pages for the basketball court's one. Trades, occupations, professions, and industry occupy much of the time of most men and many woman, yet these subjects provide only 72 pages of terms as against 130 for sports and games. We might readily guess that women would attract more slang terms than men, young and old women more than middle-aged women, gay women more than conventional ones, but not always is the picturesque, the unusual, or the disapproved the most fertile subject of slang. Courtesy seems to have

---

6 William Melvin Kelly, "If You're Woke You Dig It," *The New York Times Magazine,* May 20, 1962, p. 45.
7 We have no adequate dictionary of American slang. The best is Harold Wentworth and Stuart Berg Flexner, *Dictionary of American Slang* (New York: Thomas Y. Crowell, 1960); but I am relying mainly on Lester V. Berrey and Melvin Van den Bark, *The American Thesaurus of Slang* (New York: Thomas Y. Crowell, 1943), which serves my present purpose because of its organization.

attracted more slang than discourtesy, kindness more epithets than malevolence. One might expect that divorce would attract more slang than marriage, and that the contrary is true may reflect the fact that more people are engaged in matrimony more of the time than they are in divorce. Similarly, slang terms for Irishmen and Jews exceed those for Amerindians, possibly because few modern Americans deal with aborigines. Of course, we are at the mercy here of the available evidence, and the editors of many slang dictionaries and thesauruses have been at the mercy of the material they could collect, but the body of printed data seemingly raises as many questions as it answers.

A special sort of slang, the blatant use of language in advertising, stimulates the hackles of most policemen of usage, particularly the self-appointed ones, and is imitated somewhat by almost everybody else. *Like,* long used and disapproved as a synonym for *as, as though, as if* (like I said; he looked like he was pooped), is now even more used and more disapproved. *Terrific* has lost its etymological sense associated with terror and means acceptable, above average. *Colossal* no longer suggests anything associated with the Colossus of Rhodes, and means rather large, unusual, very good. A *galaxy of stars* is now a number of relatively mediocre performers, especially female, probably cheap and dull. Thus a few locutions associated with vulgate speech have been popularized and a few standard words with knowable meanings have been debased. To offset these real though limited losses to the language, some not very original minds have been mildly stimulated to use a word they accept as fashionable and new. The result of all this can probably not be labeled good, but it scarcely warrants the frenzy it sometimes releases.

American geographical dialects have tended in the twentieth century to become somewhat less pronounced in the United States, what with mass media of communication, extensive shifting of populations, and the great growth of the public school system. Meanwhile, however, some social dialects have grown, especially those associated with the new American ghettos—*ghetto,* itself, is a new American word in this sense, since until recently in the United States it referred to an area inhabited by Jews, as it still does in England. The Negro ghettos have attracted the most attention because they are the largest and are associated with eastern cities; following is part of an account in a Negro ghetto dialect of "Operation Jappin," harassing a schoolteacher:

The tomcat [the sly and ruthless student leading the operation] begins with a stinging hit [first attack] and the sandbaggin' starts—things are thrown, strange noises come out of nowhere, children are unresponsive. The tomcat tells the tadpoles [classmates] that it is now time for the chicken to become an eagle [for more aggressive action] and they had better trilly along [join the group] because the sun has fallen on its belly [it's too late to back out].

The first step is to unzip the teacher [make her back down], so the tomcat takes the long dive [openly defies her], hoping she puts him in cold storage [punishes him] so he can then dress her in red dresses [insult her]. He and his friends get bolder, and outflap [outwit] and scramble [gang up on] her daily. All morning they shoot her down with grease [play dirty tricks on her] until finally she is ready for the big sleep [gives in]. They continue the heart-deep kicks [fun] until they are sure she is frozen on the needle [does not know what to do].[8]

A sort of dialect characteristic of some of the Negro ghetto areas in northern cities is essentially more damaging than it would otherwise be, and much more durable, because it is rooted in the sociology and the speech habits of centuries. For a hundred years or so after the anti-slavery activities of the mid-nineteenth century, Negroes found their way north in considerable numbers. They tended to include the more edu-cated of their race—former domestic servants, skilled artisans, and the like—and being somewhat distributed through white communities, their children grew up speaking the social and geographical dialects of their areas. After the second World War, however, the poorest Negroes from the back country came, and in great numbers, crowding into the decay-ing inner cities of communities like Washington and Baltimore. They were the descendants of ante-bellum field hands, who had been kept in ignorance and squalor, learning to talk only various sorts of pidgins or pidgin-like jargons. Liberated, they tended to stay on as sharecroppers on marginal lands, obscure but kept "in their place." Now they are increasing mightily, and their concentration—albeit induced by poverty —gives them cohesion. The following is a sample of what their children speak:

Din teacher start checkin' de boys, see which one had i'. An' one boy named Bill Bailey had a whole pocketful of i'. An' teach say I'm teach. Say I'ma tell dis to de princiba, too, dat chu go 'roun' stealin' school prope'ty. My muvver pay for dis whin she paid for de tax. She say, you muvah ain' pay for dis. Dis b'long to de school. An' she start talkin' all lot ov' ol' junk an' waste half de peri'd. Din we start talkin' 'bout light, how speed o' light an' na speed o' soun' an' all 'a' kinna stuff.[9]

---

[8] John M. Brewer, "Ghetto Children Know What They're Talking About," *The New York Times Magazine*, Dec. 25, 1966, p. 33.

[9] The quotation is from an article written by Peggy Thomson for the Washington *Post* and variously reprinted; I am quoting from the *Los Angeles Times*, June 11, 1967, sec. F, p. 3.

This sort of thing presents problems, because these youngsters need to learn to use the standard language of the world outside their ghetto communities if they are to acquire a good education and hold good jobs. Standard English is a subject of instruction in the schools, but it is also the medium of instruction, so that the troubles of ghetto children are at least doubled.

Some of their speech habits are predictable. In reducing terminal consonants and simplifying the declensional system in the verb, they are doing only what speakers of English, especially the less tutored speakers, have been doing for hundreds of years, except that the process has been accelerated—we have noticed earlier that languages at war tend to change rapidly and to simplify. Likewise in vocabulary, the ghetto-dwellers have produced fabulous if somewhat evanescent riches, and we can draw parallels with pioneers everywhere—even though the area being pioneered is a decaying inner city—and with peoples living a somewhat secret life, for the American Negro like the European Jew has often had reason not to love the police. But in one area the ghetto dialects may be exceptional. Usually the grammar of one language does not much affect the grammar of another, but ghetto speech may preserve, at least scatteringly, the grammar of African languages brought by slaves centuries ago. Yoruba, for example, makes little use of verbs, and thus when a Black boy in Harlem says, "You my girl," he may only be echoing the speech of his ancestors. I say *may* because certainty is impossible; we know too little of which slaves brought what speech from where, but we may plausibly guess that scraps of African grammar and usage have survived enough to further complicate the troubles of ghetto speakers. How can such children be taught to use the standard language, especially when they continue to live in communities that reinforce their speech habits? Currently one of the most promising approaches is that being furthered by the Center for Applied Linguistics, which is endeavoring to develop courses and to train instructors who can teach acceptable English to these ghetto children as though the prestige dialect were a second language. The experiment sounds as though it might work, given enough support.

Thus Negro ghetto speech has wide implications; but even more interesting linguistically and socially—although as yet less devastating politically—is Calo (called Pachuco in some areas), the argot of the Mexican-American ghettos. Here, vividly, is evidence of the impact of man upon language and of language upon man.[10] The speech has grown from the

---

[10] I know no general study, but there is a careful monograph with emphasis on phonology—Lurline Coltharp, *The Tongue of the Tirilones*, Alabama Linguistic and Philological Series, 7 (1965)—restricted to El Paso; a briefer monograph

turbulent mingling of cultures, from the clash of languages, and from the smuggling that is rife all along the Mexican border from Matamoros to Tijuana, where *sneakers* (smugglers) run everything from *perdidas* (prostitutes) to *milk ropes* (pearl necklaces), and especially narcotics. The argot apparently centers in the narcotics trade, and several investigators have reported that narcotic gangs will not admit a *choir boy* (an apprentice) unless he knows Calo. Presumably knowledge of the argot is some assurance that he is not an *eel* (a spy) or a *finger louse* (a government informer), and without a knowledge of Calo the Pachucos, the established practitioners of the cult, could not converse safely with a recruit.

The argot relies more upon Spanish than upon English in both grammar and vocabulary and is not intelligible to uninitiated speakers of either tongue. Apparently it originated in El Paso, which is and always has been the most important point of entry from Mexico into the United States. The town, on the north bank of the Rio Grande River, was little more than a suburb of the Mexican Juarez on the south bank until the railroads came through, when a community of Norteamericanos grew up around the old Mexican village. The modern business district still still clusters along the railroad, somewhat north of the river, and the residential areas for what are locally called Anglos have spread north, west, and east. To the south live the descendants of the old Mexican families, along with subsequent immigrants who have crossed the border more or less legally, some thirty thousand in all, crowded into the lower lands between the business district and the river. They live in poverty, ignorance, and squalor that rival conditions in the worst Negro ghettos of the northern cities. Of course some escape; a good school system and Texas Western College are open to them, and many are bilingual—trilingual if one counts Calo—but those who become wealthy enough to leave are replaced by fresh immigrants, many of whom are underprivileged even by Mexican standards. The ghetto goes on.

Communications with Anglos are limited. Tourists and shoppers pass through to Juarez without stopping, and workers employed in local factories are often taken to and from work in buses supplied by the

concerning Tucson—George Carpenter Barker, *Pachuco: An American-Spanish Argot and Its Social Functions in Tucson, Arizona,* University of Arizona Bulletin Series, 21, no. 1 (Jan. 1950); and a number of good articles including the following: Haldeen Braddy, "Narcotic Argot along the Mexican Border," *American Speech,* XXX (1955), 84–90; "Smugglers' Argot in the Southwest," *American Speech,* XXXI (1956), 96–101; "The Pachucos and their Argot," *Southern Folklore Quarterly,* XXIV (1960), 255–71. I have used also a mimeographed paper by George R. Alvarez, which treats Calo in southern California. For my copy, I am indebted to Professor P. G. Patel.

employer. As one research worker, Professor Lurline Coltharp, observed, "there are casual meetings in stores" and some other contacts; the federal government "affects individuals through the draft boards, the Border Patrol and the FBI, particularly the narcotics division." Various agencies have tried to uplift the district, but the investigator concluded that contact with local governments is mainly "with the agents of law enforcement," although "There is also contact with the individuals who visit prostitutes in the area."[11] All this scarcely adds up to much community between the Anglos and the non-Anglos, who may include Negroes, Chinese, and other nonwhites. One need not be surprised that intoxication is induced by sniffing glue and even gasoline and through weird combinations of barbiturates and narcotics, that various sexual aberrations are commonplace, and that about half of the adolescents in the district are " 'actively in a gang or on the periphery of a gang,' although only 10 or 15 per cent are 'hoods.' "[12] Nor need we be surprised that the cant of smugglers has grown into a regional and class dialect, one of the possessions that help to unite a people who have fewer possessions than do most of their neighbors.

How old Calo may be, we do not know. Growing in the underworld as a secret means of confounding *los chotos* (*suckling lambs,* that is, the police), it did not advertise itself; and natives knew that unexplained curiosity could lead to gang beatings or being ripped up the belly. Only lately has it attracted learned attention, and investigators have had to work with great circumspection and, sometimes, with armed help. From El Paso, the argot seemingly spread both east and west, notably to Tucson and to Los Angeles. It has developed local dialects based on local circumstances and on changes in the trade; for a time *Chinese needle work* (opium smuggling) was common, but more recently, marijuana going north and munitions going south have brought new vocabulary. Even *marijuana,* from the Spanish for *Mary Jane,* may be a Calo coinage.

In its native ghetto, Calo seems to be strictly male speech; for although many females young and old know it, no decent ghetto girl will acknowledge acquaintance with a word of it. In many areas, for a woman to do so is tantamount to admitting that she is a gang moll. In other sections, however, where Calo is more involved with the peddling and use of narcotics than with smuggling, words out of the argot circulate freely; and in some areas, perhaps particularly in southern Cali-

---

11 See Coltharp, cited earlier, pp. 1–56, especially pp. 10–11, 16–17.
12 Again I am quoting Coltharp, p. 16, who is here quoting Harold S. Rahm, *Office in the Alley* (Austin, Texas: Hogg Foundation for Mental Health, 1958), p. 4.

fornia, Calo has so filtered through teenage gang speech that it has become an "in" accomplishment carrying only secondary criminal overtones. In some sections, a relatively young Mexican who has grown up in the States can be expected to use Spanish to his parents and other older relatives, along with native Mexicans. He will use English in school, at work, and for public purposes generally; but he may use Calo with relatives his own age, with any gang in which he moves, and with others who are united in part by their knowledge of Calo. Within such groups in Calo terminology a human being is either an *escuadra,* a law-abiding person, or he is a *vato loco,* one who spends a reasonable amount of time in jail for stealing and handling dope. The first word is obviously a translation of English *square;* the second means something like *crazy guy* and is here a term of approbation. A *vato loco* can do little wrong unless he becomes a *relaje* (Spanish *relajar,* to relax, weaken), one who in any way sides with an *escuadra,* in which case he can never again do anything right. Individual words may develop more or less extensively, and on matters outside smuggling, albeit more than normally associated with fighting and sex. Coltharp has noticed the varied uses of the Spanish word for *mother, madre,* as follows:

It has a negative meaning in the phrase *ni madre,* "nothing"; *puro madre,* defined as "heck no"; and *vale madre,* "not worth anything." However, it has a meaning in the general range of severe pummeling in other phrases. *Desmadrar* was given as "to beat someone bad" and *dar por la madre* "to beat up." However, the shortening of this into *por la madre* elicited the description "hit him all over his mother. Hit the daylights out of him."[13]

Calo has even become the medium of some folk literature. The late Professor George Carpenter Barker collected two variants of a popular ballad that in one version starts as follows:

Me astaba sonondo un frajo
Cuando la jura llegó.
Miguel quedó destendido
Pero mi cuate terció.[14]

Barker translates this as follows: "I was getting doped up with a torch / When the cops arrived. / Miguel they let go / But he turned in my pal." The poem continues to recount that the pal was such a hophead that he died and went to glory, where St. Andrew attempted to send him to hell, but the pal bribed all the saints with marijuana.

---

[13] Coltharp, p. 84.
[14] *Pachuco,* cited earlier, pp. 35–36.

At many times and in many places something approaching dialect has sprung up as an outgrowth of having fun with language. Some coherent group has developed arcane terms which have spread, but usually the fad has too little social or geographical foundation to endure. Consider Boont-link, or Boontling, of which the following is said to be a sample:

The hob started with the apple-heads all nettied, and the seekers active. But the high-heeler got teetlipped when he decked that raggin was going on, and harped to the raggers to either shy or pike. Then came the midnight chiggrel. Two of the kimneys, Punk and Spring Knee, got into a fister and knocked the chiggrel on the floor. Punk was high-heeled and kept in branding irons until his apple-head, Em, could get the higs for bail.

This has been interpreted as follows:

The dance started with the women all fancy-dressed and the ladies' men active. But the man in charge got angry when he noticed that indecent dancing was going on, and ordered the dancers to either quit or leave. Then came the midnight supper. Two of the men, Punk and Spring Knee, got into a fight and knocked all the food onto the floor. Punk was arrested and kept in handcuffs until his wife, Em, could get the money for bail.[15]

This manner of speaking developed in an isolated mountain valley in northern California, apparently starting about 1880 as a joke among the school children and spreading eventually to the adults until the inhabitants of Boonville and the surrounding ranches were unintelligible to people outside the valley, or at least they could be if they chose. During the 1920's, however, modern roads brought hundreds of new people into the valley; Boont-link declined and is now a curiosity among some of the older speakers.

Even a cursory examination of the speech reveals that it does not have the characteristics of a genuine dialect. The grammar and pronunciation are those of conventional English; only a relatively few words are different, and they are concoctions, often suggestive of slang, used to replace words in a conventional English sentence. Women are *apple-heads,* handcuffs are *branding irons,* and candy is *dulcy,* the last being probably no more than the local pronunciation of Spanish *dulce,* sweet, or it might be Italian, since many Italians settled in northern California. A modest number of substitutions of this sort, accompanied

---

15 Lynwood Carranco and Wilma Rawles Simmons, "The Boonville Language of Northern California," *American Speech,* XXXIX (1964), 283–84. See also several articles by Myrtle Read Rawles in *Western Folklore,* especially " 'Boont-ling'—Esoteric Speech of Boonville, California," *WF,* XXV (1966), 93–103, which also contains passages and glossary.

by no basic differences in language, is not enough to support a dialect, and we need not be surprised that the speech broke down quickly. Of course, if the isolation had continued, the answer might have been different; if the white community had remained isolated for the centuries or millennia that Amerindians may have lived in the same valley, a distinct dialect or even a language might have grown, and the drift might have been accelerated by the rapid changes induced by teenage play, but genuine dialects, apparently, must have solid bases.

Another tendency in modern American speech, although also not a true dialect, is more pervasive and will probably prove more enduring. I refer to the solemn turgidity characteristic of much learned, professional, and official prose. A popular news magazine despairs as follows: "The English language ain't well. Abused and confused by Americans, it is turning into No-English, a flabby hodgepodge of slang and jargon that don't mean much to nobody. . . . Linguistic chaos exists everywhere . . . throughout the great oral wastes of the nation."[16] By way of evidence, the periodical provides attacks upon most users of the language except journalists, who alone, apparently, remain comprehensible in a degenerate nation devoted to ruining its native tongue. For example, "No verbalizers are more vain about their precision with words than American lawyers and judges. And no group is more guilty of convoluted clauses and hackneyed diction."

The catastrophe is neither so imminent nor so overwhelming as jeremiads like this suggest. In a language so debilitated the magazine in question never could have been edited, and in the subsequent years, English has not become "sheer babble" nor has the nation collapsed. The fact probably is that more good prose is printed in the United States these days than has ever before been published in any country anywhere. Anyone who shouts that the English language is on the verge of disintegration should be condemned to read the unselected prose of earlier generations. Few journalists have done this, and they would find it a painful assignment.

Part of the explanation stems from the fact that prose is not one thing. Good journalistic prose is not good legal prose, good scientific prose, or good scholarly prose. Just as journalists object to legal writing, lawyers object to journalistic writing. Journalists say that scientific writing has no charm or vigor, and scientists become even more furious with journalists, whom they accuse of inaccuracy and blatant untruth. The fact seems to be that any body of good writing requires various sorts of rhetorical skills, and that few writers, if they master one of these, ever manage to command another.

---

[16] "The English How She Is Spoke," *Newsweek,* Feb. 13, 1961, pp. 87–88.

Admittedly, much American writing is needlessly clumsy; the proportion of such writing to the whole has increased and probably will continue increasing. Our society being what it is, we must expect this. Obviously, English can be better taught and better practiced than it is today, but a society which puts a premium upon complexity, which endeavors to educate all sorts of people who are incapable of supporting much education, and which then elevates these half-educated mediocrities into positions where they must speak publicly, can expect a relatively large percentage of mediocre prose. The choice seems to be this: You can have a simple, unsophisticated society with a few Thomas Jeffersons writing literate prose for all the people, or you can have all the people writing their own muddle-headed prose, which will exist side by side with the literate writing of the new generation of Thomas Jeffersons. Our country is committed, voluntarily or not, to a society built upon broadly based education and broadly based responsibility, and accordingly we must expect a flood of undistinguished prose. We could study language and rhetoric more than we have, and if we do, we may expect within limits to improve American writing and speaking, but a society such as ours can scarcely hope to eliminate the linguistically underprivileged and the rhetorically indisposed. Incidentally, other countries moving into socialized, specialized societies complain of a similar debasement of their languages. The movement is worldwide, and we who are leading the march toward specialization can expect to be in the van, also, of the jargon producers.

Characteristically, the severest criticisms have been leveled at those parts of our society that have been most hospitable to half-trained, middling sorts of minds. Government, especially government by bureaus and agencies, has ballooned; on the whole, governmental offices have been staffed competently from the only source of people who could be hired and who could do the job at all, but when these incumbents, who had never labored in their rhetoric till now, had to speak or write, the results have frequently been ludicrous. The pronouncements of prosaic minds become official, and no doubt they influence the minds and the language of others, including young imitators who aspire to administrative positions—every teacher of composition has groaned to see students eliminating homely, vigorous words in favor of Latinate, generalized terms, seemingly, on the theory that the longer the word the greater the respectability.

The following tale may be apocryphal, but it has analogues. A government bureau received a telegram inquiring if hydrochloric acid could safely be used to clean a boiler tube. The bureau replied "Uncertainties of reactive processes make use of hydrochloric acid undesirable where alkalinity is involved." The bureau then received a letter of thanks, which added that the writer would now clean his boiler with the acid. The bureau wired back, "Regrettable decision involves uncertainties. Hydrochloric will produce submuriate invalidating reactions." Again the recipient thanked the bureau for assuring him that the acid was a safe cleanser. At that the bureau abandoned jargon, and wired, "Hydrochloric acid will eat hell out of your tube." Less amusing but equally terrifying evidence could be multiplied; the following, from a military officer, was submitted by Representative James A. Quigley of Pennsylvania as creeping federalese:

The Board of Commissioners took the position that as the Secretary of the Army necessarily would consider the board's recommendation against the legislation and the board's reasons for its action, in connection with both references, the advising you of the board's views and recommendations should be delayed until final action by the Secretary of the Army on your reference to the Department of Defense.

Meanwhile, a representative of the Pentagon offered the following definition: "Overkill equals total nonsurviveability plus." The president of a large corporation, reporting a bad year, pointed to "the slowdown in order activity," in part because of a "dollar factor increase," and in part because of "the inertia of reactivating" programs which had never been activated. Nonetheless, he was optimistic, asserting: "With relatively limited exposure to date, our superior performance capabilities and adaptability to a wide range of portable, mobile, and airborne environments have generated rapid and far-reaching customer acceptance," with which "we expect to steadily increase our penetration in this market."

Doubtless this endemic jargonitis flourishes in our nouveau riche country more than in most societies, but anyone who supposes that the same virus is not spreading should read Sir Ernest Gowers' *Plain Words: Their ABC*,[17] an attempt "to help officials in their use of written English." Gowers wisely observes, "I suspect that this project may be received by many of them [the officials] without any marked enthusiasm or gratitude." He notes that the following were "all written for plain men," and wonders what plain men made of them:

Prices are basis prices per ton for the representative-basis-pricing specification and size and quantity.

---

[17] (New York: Alfred A. Knopf, 1955); originally published as *The Complete Plain Words* (London: The Controller of Her Britannic Majesty's Stationery Office, 1954).

Where particulars of a partnership are disclosed to the Executive Council the remuneration of the individual partner for superannuation purposes will be deemed to be such proportions of the total remuneration of such practitioners as the proportion of his share in partnership profits bears to the total proportions of the shares of such practitioner in those profits.

The treatment of this loan interest from the date of the first payment has been correct—i.e. tax charged at full standard rate on Mr. X and treated in your hands as liability satisfied before receipt.

Gowers, like observers on the western side of the Atlantic, finds that scientists resemble bureaucrats in their addiction to involuted prose:

Reserves that are occupied in continuous uni-directional adjustment of a disorder are no longer available for use in the ever-varying interplay of organism and environment in the spontaneity of mutual synthesis.

Jargon breeds jargon, apparently, on both sides of the Atlantic; in the following British exchange, the first comes from departmental regulations:

Every woman by whom . . . a claim for maternity benefit is made shall furnish evidence that she has been, or that it is expected that she will be, confined by means of a certificate given in accordance with the rules. . . .

One woman replied as follows:

In accordance with your instructions I have given birth to twins in the enclosed envelope.

Similarly, on both sides of the Atlantic, jargon has sprung from the use of old figures of speech when metaphorical language has become so familiar as to be used without awareness of its figurative quality. Gowers, intrigued by the implications of *breakdown* when it implies classification, collected the following.

Care should be taken that the breakdown of patients by the department under whose care they were immediately before discharge is strictly followed.

Unfortunately a complete breakdown of British trade is not possible.

Statistics have been issued of the population of the United States, broken down by age and sex.

A Mr. Henry Strauss, writing in the London *Times,* has noticed that the jargonic development of *bottleneck* provides "the biggest bottleneck in housing," "bottlenecks must be ironed out," "bottlenecks ahead," "bot-

tleneck in bottles," "the most drastic bottleneck," "bottleneck . . .
which is particularly far-reaching and decisive," "the overriding bottleneck," and "what is planned is actually a series of bottlenecks." The
word reaches its inevitable development in the "worldwide bottleneck"
and the "vicious circle of interdependent bottlenecks." Contemplating
such marvels, Gowers understandably wonders, "What barnacular song
do the puddering sirens sing to lure the writer into the land of Jar-
gantua?"

The speech of small-time American politicians is not more literate,
but it is sometimes more picturesque. The following were heard on the
floor of the Wisconsin State Senate, and could doubtless be paralleled in
other legislatures:[18]

The banker's pockets are bulging with the sweat of honest workingmen.

My integrity was imposed upon.

I know there is a beautiful maximum behind the scenes that I'll never
catch up with.

This is a bill for accountants, figureheads, and whatnots.

This is enough to make your head stand on end.

Milwaukee is the golden egg that the rest of the state wants to milk.

I will defend anyone's right to agree with me.

He was absolutely right to a certain extent.

When we get to the bridge we'll jump.

None of them facts are factual facts.

We put out no false misinformation.

You've got to consider egress and degress from the building.

This guy was down in Illinois under a consumed name.

This program is absolutely essential. What's more, it's necessary.

In this connection we might note that a collection of set phrases has
developed among politicians without which many public figures would
be left speechless. They send up *trial balloons,* and they fear *boomer-
angs that may backfire.* They deprecate *changing horses in midstream,
rocking the boat,* and *killing the goose that laid the golden egg,* while
accusing their opponents of being *ostriches that hide their heads in the
sand,* of *dragging red herrings,* of getting on *band wagons,* of *being out
of step,* of *emitting half truths,* and of *straining at a gnat but swallowing
a camel.* They fear *hot potatoes* and deplore *political footballs.* As one
of them put it, "I didn't want to jump the gun and be left on a limb."

---

[18] *The New Yorker,* XXXVIII (Oct. 14, 1961), p. 184.

They like to *get off the hook,* to be sure *the door is open,* and that *cards are laid on the table.* Back home, they *mend their fences,* particularly *at the grass roots,* while *keeping an ear to the ground.* The more literate jargonists are now beginning to speak of *throwing the baby out with the bath.* Whatever the reason for the popularity of such phrases, one can scarcely fail to notice that they embody simple figures of the sort beloved of the more conventional cartoonists. That ostriches do not hide their heads in sand does not deter a politician from using *ostrich* as a verb, and people who could not distinguish a red herring from any other sort, who would not know why it should or should not be dragged, delight in commanding such eloquence.

We are probably in the presence here of something subtle and pervading in man's mind and in his use of language. We love these phrases and we do not wish to lose them. More than a quarter of a century ago a research worker discovered and published the fact that Voltaire did not say, "I disapprove of what you say but I will defend to the death your right to say it." In my youthful innocence I confidently expected that this discovery would attract wide attention and lead to the correction of the error. The report has remained undisturbed in a scholarly journal, and probably no day passes without some American quoting Voltaire for what he did not say. The misquotation is too good to lose.

Samples of the resultant sorts of prose were written into the *Congressional Record* by the Honorable Morris K. Udall of Arizona, under suspicion of harboring a sense of humor. He professes to have written the following letter to a constituent:

DEAR FRIEND: You have expressed alarm at the rate of Federal spending, and asked me as your Congressman where I stand. I had not intended to discuss this controversial question at this particular time. However, I want you to know that I do not shun a controversy. On the contrary I will take a stand on any issue at any time no matter how fraught with controversy it may be. Here is exactly how I stand.

If, when you say "Federal spending" you mean the billions of dollars wasted on out-moded naval shipyards and surplus airbases in Georgia, Texas, and New York; if you mean the billions of dollars lavished at Cape Kennedy and Houston on a "moondoggle" our Nation cannot afford; if sir, you mean the $2 billion wasted each year in wheat and corn price supports which rob midwestern farmers of their freedoms and saddle taxpayers with outrageous costs of storage in already bulging warehouses; if you mean the $4 billion spent every year to operate veterans hospitals in other states in order to provide 20 million able-bodied veterans with care for civilian illness; if you mean such socialistic and pork-barrel projects as urban renewal, public housing and TVA which cynically seek votes while robbing our taxpayers and weakening the moral fiber of millions of citizens in our

Eastern States; if you mean the bloated Federal aid to education schemes calculated to press Federal educational controls down upon every student in the nation; if you mean the $2 billion misused annually by our Public Health Service and National Institutes of Health on activities designed to prostitute the medical profession and foist socialized medicine on every American; if, sir, you mean all these ill-advised, unnecessary Federal activities which have destroyed States rights, created a vast, ever-growing, empire-building bureaucracy regimenting a once-free people by the illusory bait of cradle-to-grave security, and which indeed have taken us so far down the road to socialism that it may be, even at this hour, too late to retreat—then I am unyielding, bitter and foursquare in my opposition, regardless of the personal or political consequences.

But, on the other hand, if when you say "Federal spending" you mean those funds which maintain Davis-Monthan Air Force Base, Fort Huachuca, and other Arizona defense installations so vital to our Nation's security, and which every year pour hundreds of millions of dollars into our State's economy; if you mean the Truman-Eisenhower-Kennedy-Johnson mutual security program which bolsters our allies along the periphery of the Iron Curtain, enabling them to resist the diabolical onslaught of a godless communism and maintain their independence; if you mean those funds to send our brave astronauts voyaging, even as Columbus, into the unknown, in order to guarantee that no aggressor will ever threaten these great United States by nuclear blackmail from outer space; if you mean those sound farm programs which insure our hardy Arizona cotton farmers a fair price for their fiber, protect the sanctity of the family farm, insure reasonable prices for consumers, and put to work for all the people of the world the miracle of American agricultural abundance; if you mean those VA programs which pay pensions to our brave soldiers crippled in mortal combat and discharge our debt of honor to their widows and orphans and which provide employment for thousands of Arizonans in our fine VA hospitals in Tucson, Phoenix, and Prescott; if, sir, you refer to such Federal programs as the central Arizona reclamation project which will, while repaying 95 percent of its cost with interest, provide our resourceful people with water to insure the growth and prosperity of our State; if you mean the Federal educational funds which build desperately needed college classrooms and dormitories for our local universities, provide little children in our Arizona schools with hot lunches (often their only decent meal of the day), furnish vocational training for our high school youth, and pay $10 million in impact funds to relieve the hard-pressed Arizona school property taxpayers from the impossible demands created by the presence of large Federal installations; if you mean the Federal medical and health programs which have eradicated the curse of malaria, smallpox, scarlet fever, and polio from our country and which even now enable dedicated teams of scientists to close in mercilessly on man's age-old enemies of cancer, heart disease, muscular dystrophy, multiple sclerosis, and mental retardation that afflict our little children, senior citizens, and men and women in the prime years of life; if you mean all these Federal activities by which a free people in the spirit of Jefferson, Lincoln, Teddy Roosevelt, Wilson, and F.D.R. through a fair and progressive income tax, preserve domestic tranquillity and promote the general welfare while preserving all our cherished freedoms and our self-reliant national character, then I shall support them with all the vigor at my command.

This is my stand and I will not compromise.

Sincerely,

Morris K. Udall
Member of Congress.

Among the learned professions and the academic disciplines the newer activities, especially those requiring relatively little liberal arts training, have been the most roundly criticized for their jargon. Speech teachers have been more reprimanded than philologists, chiropractors more than surgeons. Many students of writing have noted that mathematicians, practicing an ancient and honorable discipline which promotes clear, logical thinking, include many abstruse individuals who nevertheless write well. Physicists and astronomers generally write better than do educationists, sociologists, and psychologists. The following was penned by a social scientist of national reputation:

It is clear, then, that the optimum total situation implied in the baby's readiness to get what is given is his mutual regulation with a mother who will permit him to develop and co-ordinate his means of getting as she develops and co-ordinates her means of giving. There is a high premium of libidinal pleasure in this co-ordination—a libidinal pleasure which one feels is only insufficiently formulated by the term "oral."

Some of the most conspicuous practitioners of what has been called "dehumanized language" appear among the ranks of the newer professions, the guidance counselors and psychological testers. Such offenders are not necessarily American; a professor at Leeds observed that many such people write "a Martian discourse, lethargic with passives and numb with the impersonal, periphrastic and as musical as the shutting of a filing cabinet."[19] One Wall Street analyst quotes another Wall Street analyst as follows: "Penetration of the recent intermediate upside resistance point on some volume would augur well unless followed, or perhaps preceded, by a move on volume to a support level," which the second analyst interprets to mean, "It'll go up if it doesn't go down." Some of this obscurantism, of course, is deliberate; I have not seen a sign in any commercial airplane advising passengers what to do in case of a crash, but I have seen many that provide instructions in case of "damage to the airplane structure." One assumes that *crashes* deter

---

[19] William Walsh, "Our Marshmallow Society," *The Nation*, Sept. 5, 1959, p. 112.

more ticket sales and encourage more panic than does *damage to the airplane structure.*

In fact, the airplane seems to have promoted a pervasive movement toward jargon, of which a recent naval disaster provides an example. While the USS *Forrestal,* on duty in the Gulf of Tonkin, was preparing to launch planes, an accidental fire ignited fuel, which in turn detonated ammunition. Before the fires were quenched, thirty planes were wrecked and hundreds of men severely wounded or killed, some roasted in their cockpits. A few pilots escaped, dodging fireballs and fighting through walls of flame. I heard two of them interviewed on television, and I was so intrigued with their pilotese that I recorded some of what they said. In a way I knew these young men; hundreds like them have passed through my classes. I know how they would have talked a few years before, but since that time something has happened to them, and they no longer use English as they used to. One man was strapped into his cockpit, ready for takeoff, when the explosions started and flames billowed around him. The boys that I knew, recounting the event, would have said something like, "Man, I tore my harness off and got the hell out of there." But not this young man. In process of becoming a pilot something had been so deeply instilled that not even the prospect of fiery death made him talk colloquial English. He said, "I determined that it was time to abandon the aircraft. I proceeded to the catwalk area." One should perhaps add that he had been badly burned, and that this was not his official report. He was just talking to a newsman.

If aeronautic English is startling, what has been called "spacespeak" is fantastic, as though language becomes more remote from man as it rises farther from earth.[20] Space people do not put rockets or missiles in orbit; rather, *launch vehicles* may *achieve orbital insertion* when *systems* no longer *experience malfunction,* when *go–no-go decisions* have all become *affirmative.* Meanwhile, homey terms like *countdown* and *blastoff* have become suspect. Once the vehicle has achieved orbital insertion, the occupants, after a period of IVAR (incremental velocity adjustment routine), may indulge in *life support,* that is, an *eat period,* and relying upon the ELSS (environmental life support system) and the AMU (astronaut maneuvering unit), may proceed to EVA (extra vehicular activity) in process of employing ATDA (augmented target docking adapter). And so on. Inevitably, such terminology has led timid souls to predict the dessication of human speech, but one might recall

---

[20] I know of no comprehensive study here, but there are many journalistic reports. I am relying in part on Russell Baker, "Observer," *The New York Times,* Western Edition, May 21, 1963, p. 8, and a piece signed from Washington by Rudy Abramson, June 19, 1966, which appeared in the *Los Angeles Times* for that date, sec. F, p. 6.

that no small body of specialists, whether new scientists or new sports-casters, has been able to harm a language much.

An inept yearning for elegance, which inspires much turgid prose, has gone so far as to corrupt even the honest cop, who is developing what has been aptly termed "the constabulary style."[21] The modern officer, whether because of the dignity of the law he enforces or the echoes of the police school he attended, can now adorn a police blotter with rhetoric like the following: "The car had backed into the house siding, leaving somewhat a state of collapse." "The complainant talked in riddles constantly and this officer's opinion is that everything she said was made up of quite a few fabrications." "Upon entering the establish-ment, found the suspect in a heated argument with the bartender using profane language as punctuation." "The suspect beat a hasty but lawful retreat." "Mrs. J—— stated that she wished to commit herself to the state hospital for alcoholism. She was advised that she could do so after she sobered up. She agreed to this. Mr. J—— declined to sober up at this time." "The undersigned contacted the complainant who had been drinking to excess. She stated that the subject started the argument and told her that he was leaving the apartment and was taking the fifth of whisky, which both had been drinking out of, with him. He ended up getting struck over the head with the bottle, which broke." "While con-ferring in reference to the situation, it was soon discovered that the subject had departed his state of detention, along with the evidence, running from the establishment." "Upon arrival observed the subject being held to his feet by a passing male citizen to refrain him from falling down. Subject was cooperative, polite and denounced himself for drinking too much. Due to subject's attitude, he was transported home to the waiting arms of his wife." "The subjects were contacted at the above address and it was learned that Mr. and Mrs. L—— were having a disagreement and it seemed that they had traded blows to each other's eyes." "By the suspect's own admission to drinking during the prior hours, the smell of intoxication on his breath and his bloodshot eyes all to subordinate the state of drunkenness. The suspect was warned by this officer on their first meeting what consequences might be if he were to violate the ordinances spoken about."

Officers are apparently developing their own narrative styles. One wrote as follows:

Mr. Y—— was observed by reporting officer attempting to get into his car. After several attempts, which extended from the hood to the trunk, Mr. Y—— finally found the door and fell into the front seat. Such actions

---

21 Carleton Williams, "The Constabulary Style," *Esquire*, Nov., 1964, pp. 106–07, 166.

necessitated investigative action by this officer, and Mr. Y—— was approached, and upon being properly identified, he greeted the officer with, "Here, my friend, take the keys to my car," thus handing the officer his house keys. Such cleverness and display of good sense was rewarded by officer taking Mr. Y—— to his residence and depositing him therein.

Another officer, with an experimental flair, is developing economy in reporting conversation, as follows:

At the above location, this officer observed G—— slumped over the wheel of his vehicle. The officer asked G—— what seemed to be his problem. G—— stated that he was waiting, oh. He was then asked what he was waiting for. G—— then stated that he was just waiting, oh. He was then taken to the office to be booked. While at the booking desk, G—— became very belligerent and used profane language toward the arresting officers, etc. The "etc." was meant to be the matron.

Along with expanding vocabulary that patently falls within some determinably changing pattern of life are words whose growth is less explicable. On the analogy of astronomy we might call them "nova" words, since they flare into sudden prominence, and if not inexplicably, seemingly outside the main patterns of linguistic change. Sometimes they are revivals; I should estimate that the word *presently* is presently used most frequently in the United States—although probably not in England —as I have just used it in this sentence. Some hundreds of years ago this was the common use, but this meaning declined so much that dictionaries edited a few decades ago labeled it "obsolete or dialectal." Other expanding words involve recently developed uses of old terms or sudden expansions of uses that had previously enjoyed only moderate currency. Consider *state* as a verb; the *Century* dictionary, edited shortly before 1900, recognized four uses as follows: to establish, to bestow upon, "to express the particulars of," and to allege. Most professional writers still use this word with restraint, but the great body of amateurs, if those who have passed through my classes are exemplary, use this word as some of us still employ the word *say*. Some apparent nova are new coinages; *brainwashed* was probably popularized through defectors in the Korean police action, but it has grown so rapidly that recently a prospective presidential candidate found himself much embarrassed at having asserted he had been brainwashed. Apparently he meant to say in vigorous language that he had been misinformed, but this particular nova seems not to have generalized as fast as he had assumed. Similarly, *critical* is growing, and in other senses than those concerned with criticism, as in the headline INJURED WOMAN / SAID NOT CRITICAL. Some

century, if old sounds have fallen out of the language or any new ones
have appeared, we do not have clear evidence. On the other hand, we do
have evidence that shifts in population are changing the relative importance of dialects, and perhaps altering the dialects themselves.

American society has grown more informed and more subtle; so has
American English, and no doubt they interact upon each other. The
sophisticated humor of *The New Yorker* would have been unthinkable a
half century ago in a periodical of wide circulation, as the files of *Judge*
and the old *Life* testify, and these periodicals were lambent wit when
compared with the humor of the nineteenth century. Even the comic
strips use linguistic humor; *Pogo* is instinct with the play of language,
with a pedantic bigot talking in Gothic script and Miggle's grocery signs
squirming with puns. In a recent *Archie* comic strip some teenagers are
visiting a patient; the conversation is as follows: "How do you feel?"
"With my hands!" "How do you sleep?" "With my eyes closed!" "What
did the doctor say it was?" "His day off!" If puns do not embody the
most profound humor, they may be contrasted with the horseplay on
which my generation was nourished; we were encouraged to believe that
humor was the Captain using his gouty foot to kick a hat with a brick in
it and Maude planting her mule-shoes on some departing rump. Especially popular is the grammar joke, as in "Husbands think their wives
should wear their dresses longer—at least a couple of years."

Thus far in the twentieth century—and the trend will probably continue—population has moved to the cities and toward the West and
South. For some areas, these trends have tended to offset each other.
States like Illinois, Michigan, Pennsylvania, and New York, composed
partly of relatively static rural communities, have profited also from
great cities, and have doubled or trebled in population. Similarly,
southern and western states without great cities, like Tennessee and
Wyoming, have shown moderate growth. States outside the South and
Far West with no great cities, like Vermont and Iowa, have shown little
or no increase. Meanwhile states like Texas, Florida, and California,
which have profited both from their geographical positions and their
growing cities, have multiplied in population by from five to ten times.
An obvious result of these shifts is that the influences of urban living
and of Western and Southern dialects have grown. Usage is becoming
more standardized; children are more policed, at least so far as speech is
concerned, in cities than on farms, and urban adults are under more
pressure to act like white-collar people than are farmers and ranchers.
The second clear trend is that Western speech has grown, Southern
somewhat less. We should here recall what we learned in connection
with the Colonial American dialects; once a dialect is fairly well estab-

lished in an area, subsequent immigration tends to be absorbed with only minor influences upon the native dialect. Thus the three East Coast dialects that developed during the seventeenth and eighteenth centuries tended to continue through the nineteenth and into the twentieth century in spite of the millions of immigrants that moved into and through these areas. Similarly, the dialects of the Far West (Rocky Mountain, Intermountain, and West Coast) were all established during the nineteenth century; by 1900 all readily habitable land was at least sparsely settled. The twentieth century saw great immigration into this area and little emigration from it, so that a population of the ten far-western states in 1900 of slightly more than three million ballooned in little more than a half century to more than twenty-five million, an average growth of more than eight times. The western migration was absorbed, however, as the east coast migration had been; the earlier migration to the West had come from the Middle West, and thus Western dialects represent mainly a translation and muddling of Middle-Western speech. Twentieth-century Hoosiers and Hawkeyes went to California and Oregon for the same reason that their ancestors had come to Indiana and Iowa; they were looking for new land. Few great dialectal pockets developed; thus Far Western speech is even more clearly a development of Midwestern speech than Midwestern is of East Midland. Among the partial exceptions, in that they approach dialect islands, are the speech of the Latter-day Saints centering on Salt Lake City and that of the Mexican-Spanish areas in the Southwest, but these are not closely related to either Northern or Southern American, and are dissipating.

Thus four great dialectal areas seem to have developed in the United States—Northeastern, Southern, Midland-Midwestern, and Far Western, of which the last is the most nearly uniform and will probably eventually be the largest. It is closely related to Midland-Midwestern, which is at present so much the largest that it is sometimes called Standard or General American. These two dialects are likely to account for considerably more than two-thirds of American speakers, with the remaining scant third divided perhaps about equally between Northeastern and Southeastern. Thus the twentieth century has continued, although for different reasons, what the nineteenth century began, the great efflorescence to the west of the Midland dialects at the expense of those which developed at either end of the East Coast.

Other tendencies are not so clear. The Southern states have experienced both immigration and emigration. Will enough Northerners move into Florida to shift the dialect away from Southeastern, and if so, will it move toward Northeastern or Midwestern? Certainly some cities like Miami are no longer clearly Southern, nor are the communities of "senior citizens." Will Texas become a Western rather than a Southern state? Thus far the Texas dialects seem to be holding fairly firm in the face of extensive Northern infiltration. Greater New York is in part a linguistic law unto itself, in part a border city between Northeastern and Midland, and a great mecca for overflow Middle Westerners. What will triumph there, Washington Square, the Bronx, or the backlash from Kalamazoo?

By whatever channels, some non-Midland forms seem to be permeating Western speech. A relatively high diphthong in words like *house* and *out,* characteristic of much Southern speech, seems to be making headway against the standard lower sound; that is, /æʊ/ is tending to replace /aʊ/ among many younger speakers. Does this result from extensive emigration from the rural South to the West, from the migration of Negroes north, or from some subtler drift in the language? Any answer would be no more than a guess. Similarly, the Southern tendency to make two syllables of words like *seed, road,* and *same*—a variant strong in certain parts of Britain—seems to be spreading in vulgate in many areas. But at best these changes are not well documented; if they exist as anything more than the impressions of random observers, they are probably the minor results of population shifts rather than linguistic changes growing from language itself.

Some local dialects have resisted leveling and continue to grow. Consider, for example, the speech of what is locally known as "Baulamer" or "Baulmer /bɔlmər/," still spelled *Baltimore.* Following are the entries for the letter *p* as they appear in one glossary:[23]

Padder—powder	Pearl—peril
Pall—pile	Peril—pearl
Pancake—pound cake	Pixture—picture
Paramour—power mower	Poeleece—police (one man)
Parrots—pirates	Poplar—popular
Patapsico—Patapsco	Popular—poplar
Paul burier—pall bearer	Precint—precinct
Pawn off—palm off	Prolly—probably
Payment—pavement (sidewalk)	Pruin—prune

Even a cursory examination of this list will reveal relationship to several dialects, and the apparently continued working of well-known linguistic principles like those involved in syncopation, the simplification of diphthongs and consonant clusters, and folk etymology. Meanwhile, local conditions are breeding local uses; a great exodus of the more

[23] John Goodspeed, *A Fairly Compleat Lexicon of Baltimorese,* 3d ed. (Baltimore: Sunpapers, n.d.).

affluent whites to the suburbs has led to the abandonment or cheapening of many of the older parts of the city, with a corresponding deterioration of the schools in those areas, which now serve mainly Negroes. Accordingly, at least among the school population, "inner city" has become a derogatory as well as a geographical term, meaning poor, inadequate, underprivileged.

Grammar, also, is subtle and for short terms its shifts are difficult to identify and evaluate. Quantitative statistics of the use of individual grammatical structures are impossible to attain, and linguistic geography, which may eventually provide estimates, is in its infancy. Meanwhile engaging guesses are possible.

For example, I have already quoted a critic of modern English who was objecting to the overuse of the passive voice, the construction in which the actor is not the subject of the sentence, as in *Jonah was swallowed by a whale,* and as Chaucer put it, later *was spouted up.* That is, the actor, the whale, either does not appear at all, or he is in the predicate. This construction can be very useful. It permits a newspaper to report that Gangster A was shot and killed, and this without printing the libelous statement that Gangster B murdered him. It permits a scientist or scholar to describe what has happened without having to identify the cause, and the identifying of causes can be an uncertain business that careful writers may wish to avoid. It promotes clarity by permitting the writer to move a word into a position where it can be readily modified.

Many flabby writers, however, emit one passive sentence after another, apparently without recognizing that they do so from no reason except habit, or that Latinate longings corrupt various sorts of styles, not excluding the learned or the constabulary. Why is this? One of the causes seems to be rooted in the nature of modern English grammar. The sentence is the basis of English communication, and the grammar of these sentences is extensively embodied in the order of the words, in the position of words within the sentence. The result is that once a word is committed to paper, it starts a pattern that must be continued, unless the writer starts over again. To take a simple example, if a user of English writes *the,* he has started a pattern which must result in something like *the lecturer* or *the muddle-headed, interminable, badly informed lecturer.* Once he has written *the* he must come inevitably to a word like *lecturer,* no matter how many words like *interminable* may intervene. Furthermore, these words must be like *interminable.* Except in very unusual constructions they cannot be units like *as soon as* or *oxydize,* and if these modifiers become relatively complicated, they cause trouble, as in the following: "He is the woman who found our lost cat's husband," and "I'm the one who doesn't listen and that's the reason he doesn't understand's wife."

This simple pattern of article-modifier-noun causes few native speakers any trouble, but the pattern of the core of the sentence is more complicated. The basic sentence pattern is subject-verb-complement, and hence any word that can be a subject, once it is committed to paper as the beginning of a sentence, without warning that it is not a subject, becomes the subject of the sentence. In the following beginnings, we know that *candidate* is not the subject of the main part of the sentence: *Despite the candidate . . ., If the candidate . . ., As for the candidate. . . .* Other words warn us that, although *candidate* is a possible subject, in this sentence it is not the subject of the main predication. If, however, the sentence starts *The candidate . . .,* the writer must accept *candidate* as the subject or start over. Thus he can write *The candidate lost because he lied.* Suppose, however, that the writer, instead of using his actual subject, *candidate,* as the grammatical subject, wrote down the words *The reason.* He is now committed to a sentence something like the following: *The reason the candidate was defeated was because of being caught lying.* The careless use of the wrong subject has led to the enforced use of the passive voice, with a resultant clumsy sentence; and many a careless writer becomes a weak writer because he acquires the habit of choosing inappropriate subjects and either does not know how to revise sentences or does not bother to do so. Furthermore, as we have seen above, the passive voice can be very useful in scientific, scholarly, and professional prose. White-collar Americans have increased mightily in our day, and their writing has ballooned proportionately. No doubt these passive structures become so familiar to many writers, the passive orders develop so much into mental as well as linguistic patterns, that writers think as well as write in the passive. Thus we probably have here a fairly clear example of the influence of language upon the use of the mind, in this instance not a very happy use of it.

Something similar develops from expletive constructions, that is, from constructions which start with *it* or *there* when these words have no clear antecedent. These structures have their use; they are handy if the writer has no need of a subject or verb, but feels he should fill the usual sentence pattern. *There is no answer* is an expletive construction, and if that is all the writer or speaker has to say, it may be a good sentence, better than *No answer exists at this time.* The construction can be useful, also, if the predicate is so complicated that the writer has little use for a subject and verb, as in the following: *There may be several reasons for the candidate's having lost the election, not excluding his native stupidity, his habit of lying about his record during his frequent appearances on television, and his referring adversely to motherhood while addressing the DAR.* Such sentences are unusual, however, and writers addicted to expletives seldom compose them. *It* and *there* say nothing; they fill part of the sentence pattern. Usually they must be followed by a word like *is, was,* or *were,* words which usually say little. The result is that when a writer pens *there was,* he has thrown away the subject and verb, often the strongest parts of the sentence, and if he does this consistently, his prose will suffer. Starting with expletives is easy, however; the writer can put down *there was* and not have to activate so much as one brain cell while doing it. Of course, he will pay in the end; he will find himself trying to flounder his way out of a needlessly convoluted sentence, but he will probably never know that he has only himself and his indolence to blame. Or, more likely, he has his habits to blame. Expletive thinking can become a habit of mind, as can passive thinking, and thus we are probably once more in the presence of an influence of grammar upon the mind.

All grammars are baffling, but they may become more understandable if viewed in perspective. Do we know anything about the nature of language and the past of the English language that will illuminate the present? Specifically, we know that once a pervading tendency has developed in language, it tends to continue. For example, tense English vowels started moving forward and upward in the mouth. This drift may have begun in Old English times; it was broadly apparent more than five hundred years ago, and was continuing until recently, perhaps is still continuing in some dialects. Can such long trends tell us anything about the effects of English in the twentieth century?

Fortunately, we know a great deal about the past of English grammar. English comes from Proto-Indo-European, an ancient language that was extensively synthetic; it had many and elaborate inflectional paradigms of grammatical forms. By Old English times, something more than a thousand years ago, these inflectional devices had shrunk to about half their former plenty, so that classes of verbs and nouns had been reduced to something more than a half dozen apiece; cases were being lumped together, verb forms simplified, and only remnants of inflection survived among modifiers. Furthermore, this older grammar had probably decayed much more extensively than might be inferred from a poem like *Beowulf,* which can be somewhat uncertainly dated as after A.D. 700. Verse remained conservative through an elaborate rhetorical system, but the earliest surviving prose can be understood mostly by the order and use of words, and the inflections can be largely ignored. Most inflections surviving in Old English were lost in Middle English, so that today we have only a scattering, and even these are in some trouble. Few modern speakers can command *who* and *whom* with any confidence, and children labor to distinguish *girls, girl's* and *girls'*. Obviously, we have lost most of our sense for inflection as a grammatical device. We now lose inflections slowly, partly because we have few to lose.

Thus, if we think of the change from synthesis to analysis as loss of inflectional devices, the change is so nearly complete that inflection cannot be considered very important in twentieth-century American English grammar. Assuming that inflection was not declining in the Indo-European of 3000 B.C., a graph of inflectional loss as it affects modern English would look something like Figure 1.

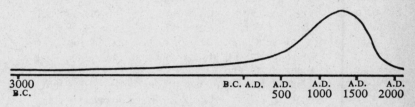

| 3000 B.C. | | B.C. A.D. | A.D. 500 | A.D. 1000 | A.D. 1500 | A.D. 2000 |

Fig. 1. Loss of Inflection in English.

Loss of inflection, however, is not the only evidence of grammatical change. If English had done nothing but lose inflections, so little grammar would remain that nobody could use the language. Obviously, grammar must have been growing as well as decaying, and some of these new growths are obvious. More rigid word orders developed, phrasal verbs replaced conjugated verbs, and words formerly used for their meaning were so converted that they acquired grammatical use. Doubtless there were other changes; different patterns of tone and stress would have been inevitable, but these are hard to study. In any event, we probably do not yet well understand the nature of analysis in grammar nor recognize all of its devices, but even one of these, that of converting meaningful words to grammatical uses, should reveal something.

The process had begun early. A word that we write *have* had been converted into an auxiliary. This came from an Indo-European base, something like **-gap-*, meaning to seize or hold, seen in Latin *capere* and in English derivatives of it, like *captive* and *capture*. By devising verb combinations of two or more words, different verbal uses could be distinguished without declining the meaningful part of the verb, as in *has been, have been,* and *had been*. This process of converting words to auxiliaries continued in Old English. For example, Proto-English had no distinctive future; it used one declined form for both present and future. Old English did, however, have a verb *sceolan* from an Indo-European base meaning to owe, and *willan,* meaning to wish or desire. These words developed as auxiliaries, the forms that we now know as *shall* and *will;* but duties and desires are all concerned with the future, and hence forms with *shall* and *will* became simple futures.

This conversion of words continued. A sheriff could say, "I am going to Canterbury to arrest a murderer," or more simply, "I am going to arrest a murderer." Either sentence would be conceived as description of motion to a point at which a future action would take place. Perhaps because the action is usually more important than the going, however, such descriptions of present action have become simple futures; when junior says, "I am going to do my homework," and if this statement can be taken at face value, he does not expect to go. He expects to sit.

The process is still continuing, and for a staid activity like grammar, in a lively manner. The future is always uncertain, and, as we have seen in Chapter 4, many sorts and degrees of expressed uncertainty are drifting toward simple futures. *We expect Aunt Susan Sunday* may mean that the family will spend the rest of the week expecting, and *Aunt Susan expects to arrive Sunday* may describe the aunt's state of mind, but usually such statements are simple futures and not much else. *Get* has already become an auxiliary, at least in American speech—so far as my observation goes, it is still mainly a meaningful verb in British usage—and words like *plan, hope,* and *expect* are developing as auxiliaries, although they retain more or less use as meaningful symbols. In Southern speech, *calculate* and *figure*—and in some folk speech, *reckon* —are undergoing similar development. This process of building phrasal verbs has now gone so far that we can concoct patterns like *I should have liked to be able to leave.* This verb requires a number of words, but it cannot be called wordy because it says a great deal, and all with the verb. It implies that the speaker, at some past time, was in such a state that he would willingly have left at a future time, but that for other reasons he had eventually to recognize that his expected departure would have to be canceled. Such a verb is a notable linguistic creation; we have been making such verbs very industriously during the last century or two, and we are probably still devising them.

Now let us look at another parallel development. In Old English, a reader was fairly certain what the verb was and what the complement was, but in contemporary English this distinction is becoming obscured. In the sentence, "Little Sharon took a tramp in the woods," whether Sharon is the athletic type or is becoming a juvenile delinquent depends upon the subtle interacting of the verb and the object. In the more respectable denotation, *tramp* becomes almost part of a verb, *to take a tramp* being the rough equivalent of *to tramp*.

We might notice what has happened to *on*. It comes from an Indo-European base meaning slanting or obliquely toward, a meaning and use that it still roughly retains in *The travelers press on*. As the inflections of nouns declined in English, *on* was one of the words, often called prepositions, that developed to show the relationships of objects in constructions like *on a hill, on the wall, on hand, on a certain day, on sale, on strike, on account of his stubbornness,* a line of development revealed in a use like that of Samuel Purchase, "There lyeth nine little Ilands *on* a row," although the word has become little more than a connective in *on tap, on time*. Thus the word has moved out of the modifier and into the verb, and to be precise it often must be part of the verb but separated from it by the object. *The cook turned the stove on* is not ambiguous, and this in spite of familiar copybook rules against ending sentences with prepositions, whereas *The cook turned on the stove,* if it means anything, suggests that the lady was swiveling on the range. Of course *on* is not here a preposition, but it is one of the words that purists try to keep out of a terminal position, although obviously it belongs there, since the complement here serves best within the verb, not after it.

Constructions like this abound in modern English. Consider an ordinary sentence like *You better do something about getting production up*. Is the verb *better,* which occupies the usual verb position? Obviously not, although it is essential to the verb, which cannot work without it. Historically it was an adjective or an adverb, or perhaps a noun, being cut down from *You had better, You'd better. You do something* is a different sentence, and *You had do something* no sentence at all. One could say that the verb is *better do* and that *something about getting production up* is the complement. On the other hand, one could just as well say that *better do something about getting* is the verb and that *production* is the complement. Of course *up* has to be part of either the verb or the complement; *getting production* is not the same as *getting production up*. Curiously, if *production* is the complement, it controls the verb, since *You better do something about getting up* is a different sentence. Furthermore, two words here are of the sort which we normally associate with complements, *something* and *production,* but they must occur within the verb and separated from each other. The verb makes no sense without them, and they must be in these particular positions.

The typical English sentence is supposed to be something like *Johnny loves Lucy,* in which each of the sentence parts, *Johnny, loves,* and *Lucy,* has its own integrity. Now notice what happens if we assort the verb-like words and the complement-like words according to this pattern, using the sentences above:

Subject	Verb	Complement
Johnny	loves	Lucy
You	better do about getting up	something production

Thus, not only do we have words like *better* behaving in new ways in modern English, but the whole complex of verb and complement has become so fluid that the parts blend in a complicated order and are so interreliant that one may have no meaning without the other. As a meaningful verb *better do about getting* is nonsense, as is the complement *something production* unless its parts are properly disposed within a verb. And this is a very simple sentence, nothing like the following, in which the intermingling of verb and complement is still more confounded: *He did not fancy finding himself tricked into needing money to take a plane for Washington to investigate the rumor of his having been arrested for entertaining call-girls.*

Now, we might observe that the increase in what have been called *merged verbs, verbal word sets, verb-adverb combinations, verbs with separable suffixes,* and whatnot, verbs like *turn in, turn on, turn off, turn up, turn down, turn into,* represent a recent trend in English. A few appeared in Old English, but not many, and a few more in Middle English. By Shakespeare's time they are not yet common in formal or polite speech, but they must have been growing popularly; Shakespeare's clowns apparently use them more than do his kings. For example, in *A Midsummer Night's Dream* Theseus and Hippolyta use few such structures, but verbal combinations abound in the talk of Bottom and the other rude mechanicals. Starveling reports that Bottom *cannot be heard of,* and when he is found he promises, "I will tell you everything, right as *it fell out.*" *To hear of* is not the same as *to hear,* and *to fall out* is not the same as *to fall.*

One of the distinguishing characteristics of these structures is that, *in toto,* they mean something other than the words mean when not in combination, as will appear in the following variants:

> That will make him turn in his grave.
> That will make him turn in his suit.
> That will make him turn in.
> The tadpole turned into a frog.
> The driver turned into a blind alley.
> The river ran into the sea.

The husband ran into his wife on the parking lot.
The reds in the print dress ran into the yellows.
His losses on the market ran into the millions.

We might notice, however, that not all of these examples have clear implications. The first set provides a sharp distinction; in *turn in his grave,* the word *in* is a preposition and not part of the verb. That is, it shows how *grave* relates to the word *turn,* or modifies it; or, to use conventional terminology, it introduces the prepositional phrase *in his grave,* which modifies the verb *turn.* In the second sentence, however, *in his suit* does not tell where the recruit revolved, and in the third sentence *turn in,* means *to go to bed,* not *to turn,* and not necessarily *in.* But other examples are not so clear; I believe I could devise a moderately good defense of either case for the last two sentences, that is, that *into* either is or is not part of the verb *ran into.* This blending of structures I find very common in modern American sentences, that they contain complicated predicates, and that within these predicates the distinctions among verbs, complements, and adverbial modifiers are by no means sharp. That is, our grammar seems to be becoming more fluid; this change has been taking place rapidly during the last century or two, and I suspect it is continuing rapidly right now—rapidly, that is, as changes go in grammar, where all changes dawdle.

How has this come about? The answer cannot be certain, since the history of these verbs with separable suffixes has never been written, and less attention has been given to the development of fluidity in the complement than the question deserves, but I have a theory which I offer for what it may be worth. Constructions of this sort grew slowly during the Middle Ages, but more widely in folk speech than in formal English; in the late Middle Ages and early Renaissance they increased rapidly, possibly because of the rapid decline of inflection. By the seventeenth and eighteenth centuries they were becoming standard speech. For example, Sir John Borlase Warren, Baronet and Knight of the Bath, reporting officially from Dublin Castle, October 18, 1798, wrote: "The *Melampus* had arrived off Lough Swilly with another Frigate in Tow, which she had been sent in pursuit of."[24] Such constructions increased rapidly in the nineteenth century and to date in the twentieth. They grew rather more—and this is the least provable portion of my thesis—in the colonies and in the United States than they did in the mother country because they had been more characteristic of vulgate and middle-class speech than of upper-class speech, which tends toward the formal English. Thus, when lower-class and middle-class people became the basis

---

[24] MS, Trinity College, Dublin, not, so far as I know, published.

of American society, these relatively fluid distributive structures grew more rapidly in the New World than in the Old.

The latter part of this theory can as yet be labeled nothing more than an interesting guess. When I try to prove to myself that British speakers use fewer verbs with separable suffixes than do the Americans, and turn to an English novel for evidence, I find so many fluid structures that I must concede that the case is not clear. If I start looking at the folksier evidences of British usage, I encounter bits like the following comic cartoon: a couple are sitting on a sofa, she is smugly pleased with herself, he has two black eyes, and the room is a shambles. Two guests are observing the wreckage furtively, while the man of the house says, "Well, Ethel and I finally had it out last night." That the humor here is neither very original nor very subtle probably assures us that the cartoon was not intended for a sophisticated audience, and that *to have it out* must be common in British usage. Whether or not fluid predicates have grown more rapidly on the west side of the Atlantic than on the east, and however much verbs with suffixes at the ends of the sentences may have been imported as what purists call "corruptions" from the United States, fluid verb patterns have such indigenous life in Britain that we must attribute the popularity of constructions like *have it out* and *do him in* to independent growths in both major branches of Modern English.

Similarly, if it is true that American English is moving toward analysis more rapidly than is British English, we can probably assume that fluidity in the use of words is relatively more common in the New World. That is, words tend to have a broader grammatical spread, to be subject to wider privilege of occurrence. Looked at in a restricted way, this tendency in language is what is often called "conversion," the change of one part of speech to another part of speech, but if we think of this fluidity as a natural quality of analysis in language, then the concept of conversion as something reprehensible has lost its validity. Certainly, this sort of thing is growing on both sides of the Atlantic, and no adequate studies have compared the two bodies of speech in this regard, but at least American English abounds in such structures. In the headline CREW QUITS SINKING SHIP, the meaning changes depending upon whether *quits* is a main verb or an auxiliary, and the use of *quits* determines the grammar of *sinking*. Likewise, in *Would you hit a woman with a baby?* the meaning and the grammar change depending upon whether *with* goes with *hit* or *woman*.

Now we must ask ourselves what sense all this makes, big sense or little sense. Are we observing one big shift in grammar, two or three shifts in grammar, or lots of little shifts? Of course we can detect small shifts, including many that I have not attempted to label here, but the evidence permits us to ask whether one central many-faceted grammatical movement is still active, a movement which started thousands of years ago and is likely to continue well into the future. Earlier we noticed that English grammar has been jettisoning inflection, that this movement reached a peak between 1400 and 1500 and declined thereafter for want of inflections to get rid of. We have since noticed that this discarding of grammar presumed also the growing of grammar, and that among these new growths were verbs with separable suffixes. A graph might look something like Figure 2. Now let us superimpose our diagrams for these two developments, remembering meanwhile that as these graphs approach modern times they also approach guesswork. A guess, however, might look like Figure 3.

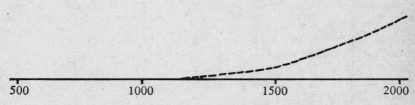

Fig. 2. Development of Verbs with Separable Suffixes.

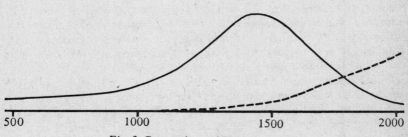

Fig. 3. Comparison of Figures 1 and 2.

Now let us assume that the shift from inflection toward distribution is a much more complex movement than these two suggest—that it includes, for example, a growing fluidity in the predicate, which develops late. And let us assume that there are other important shifts, such as the change in tonal patterns, the growth of variety in subordinational devices, and the like. If we were to plot a half dozen grammatical trends we might

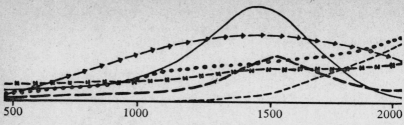

Fig. 4. The Shift from Inflection toward Distribution. This diagram is intended to be suggestive only; in the present state of our knowledge it cannot be accurate. The solid line represents loss of inflection; – – – – – – represents increase in verbs with separable suffixs; —• —• —•represents increase in phrasal verbs; •••••••••represents growth of fluidity in the predicate; — ıı— ıı— represents the conversion of words to grammatical uses; and — — — — represents the increase in subordinating devices. We know so little about changes in stress and tone that I have not attempted even a guess. If I were to hazard one, I should draw a long, rather flat regular bell curve, which would approximate a composite of all the other curves.

get something like Figure 4. That is, if we were to chart all the aspects of a shift from inflection toward distribution, we would draw a composite curve very different from the graph for the loss of inflection only, which began to rise somewhat later than the year 500 and declined sharply after about a thousand years. We would have, instead, a series of overlapping foothills, which, when reduced to a composite, would give us a curve that started some thousands of years ago, and has never suffered any sharp decline. If we have passed the peak at all, we may still be rather high on a long descent that represents the shift from one basic sort of grammar toward another basic sort of grammar. English can still be very much more distributive than it is now, and if we look at the whole trend broadly enough, we may still guess that we are involved in a movement which is likely to continue, perhaps quite actively, for some hundreds or thousands of years more.

Now, inevitably, we must ask another question, even though we get no certain answer to it: which is hen and which is egg? That is, did the new grammar grow because the old grammar died from some internal weakness of its own, or some unsuitability of its new environment? Or did the old grammar die because the new grammar was growing and the old no longer had much use? Specifically, did inflections fall out because they were no longer needed, or did they fall out from causes within the language—from changes in the degree of stress accent, for example—and thus occasion the growth of other devices like word order? We have no final answer, and the readiest guess is that the inflections fell out and upset the language enough to trigger other changes. This has been the common guess, or at least it used to be the common guess; after all, the dropping of inflectional endings is readily observable in Middle English, and since classical Latin and Greek had endings, we tended to feel that endings were good things which language would preserve if it could.

The opposite, however, is plausible also, and has some evidence to support it. For example, we have seen that Old English was developing a relatively rigid word order while it yet retained enough endings so that they could have been used for an adequate working grammar. Quite possibly, English may have developed its grammar because it was shifting toward something, not merely recovering from a disaster.

Thus we may plausibly assume that a broad drift has been moving through the English language, a drift away from inflection and toward distribution, that this drift is not complete and is continuing in our time. This drift no doubt accounts for numerous minor eddies in current grammatical usage that obscure the main movement while contributing to it. We may logically guess that American speech has shifted more rapidly than has British speech, and that this leadership among the newer English dialects may be continuing. Of course we would be foolhardy to assume that American speech is here in the van; one would be inclined to guess that South African English, in conflict with Afrikaans and various African languages, might change more rapidly than any American speech, and nobody knows what to expect in India and Australia, but we have no reason to doubt that English grammar, perhaps notably American English grammar, is growing with such glacial deliberateness as can be expected of broad movements in language.[25]

---

[25] Since an earlier edition of this book went to press, we have what seems to be clear evidence that for the first time a nonhuman creature has learned to use a "language." Starting in June 1966, Drs. Beatrice T. Gardner and R. Allen Gardner, psychologists at the University of Nevada, endeavored to teach an infant chimpanzee American Sign Language. Within the forty-four months that the attempt continued, the young chimpanzee, named Washoe, learned nearly a hundred signs so well that she became fluent with them and could generate sentences. That is, she had acquired an elementary vocabulary, had learned to use a simple grammar, and had come to understand what language is. The Gardners are themselves careful not to claim that Washoe learned to use a language; see "Two-Way Communication with an Infant Chimpanzee," in Allan M. Schrier et al., eds., *Behavior of Nonhuman Primates* (New York: Academic Press, 1971), pp. 117–82. I salute their humility, but I am sure the significance of their achievement is being underestimated, and with the help of the extensive moving pictures they have taken of Washoe, I have reexamined the evidence in an article scheduled to appear in the October 1972 issue of *College Composition and Communication*. The evidence does not permit us to assume that nonhuman beings can devise a language, but it does allow us to believe that at least some nonhuman creatures can learn to use a language.

21

AMERICAN ENGLISH AT HOME: THE LEARNED AND THE LETTERED

On the whole, mass movements seem to have made language in America, as elsewhere, but what of the poet and the scholar, the learned and the literate? Does not an Einstein influence language more than does an ignoramus? Obviously, he must. In the past, the role of belletristic and other self-consciously artistic writing has inspired a good bit of learned nonsense, but that is no reason to belittle the subject.

For example, Chaucer used to be called the "well of English unde-filed," and reputable works have asserted that Modern English comes from the English of London because Chaucer wrote in it, that Chaucer became the model on which the English language was patterned, that Chaucer is responsible for the refining of a barbarous tongue, and the like. Presumably no one person ever had that much impact upon language, and certainly not a poet who was admired but was never popular. For example, in Chaucer's day inflections were falling off rather rapidly. Chaucer used them, at least some of them. Did he stem the flood of departing endings? By no means; they fell off faster in the century after his death than they had in the century before his birth. In his day the Old English third person plural pronouns *hie, hierre, hiem* were being replaced by new Scandinavian words from which we get *they, their, them.* Chaucer used a mixture of these, retaining the old form for the accusative (*hiem, hem*), but using the new form in the nominative (*thei, they*). Thus he writes concerning Thomas à Becket and his presumably miraculous cures. "That hem hath holpen whan that they were seke" (Who has helped them when they were sick). Did Chaucer arrest this change from Old English to Scandinavian pronouns? Again the change continued so rapidly that soon *hem* for *them* existed only in vulgate use and in some remote dialects.

Or consider Shakespeare. If any poet who appeals to sophisticated people could change the language, Shakespeare would be that poet. Within limits he has been popular. He is so nearly unique that he is known as "the bard," is translated into all civilized languages, is studied in all schools where English is taught, and is universally admired. Certainly some phrases and sentences are more widely used than they would have been but for him, bits like "The play's the thing," "To be or not to be," and "The lady doth protest too much." But he did not direct the course of the language; the grammar of Shakespeare is now so little understood that it has become the subject of learned dissertations and of courses in graduate school.

Thus, although the impact of literature upon language is easy to overestimate, few would doubt that it has influence, even though the impact is diffuse, indirect, and difficult to describe. Endeavoring to identify and measure the impact of genius and of trained minds, we probably cannot hope to be exact. We can notice, as we have already implied, that without nuclear physics the word *fission* would not have its modern currency and connotative power, but how can we estimate the impact of modern physics directly upon language and indirectly upon the users of language? We are told that most of the important physicists are still living and active; these creative scientists, thinking differently, working differently, and expressing themselves differently than did their forbears, must have some impact on language.

Furthermore, however permeating science and technology are in our lives, the study of language and the practice of literature probably exert more direct bearing upon linguistic use than we can expect from most sciences. Here, curiously, we have had latter-day revolutions. Previous chapters have implied that new insights—glottochronology and linguistic geography, for example—have enlarged and refined our concepts of language, but these scattering references have no more than suggested the fructifying ideas that have bloomed in language studies. Similarly with literature, and surprisingly. Literature we have had with us from the earliest days, apparently; at least it appears among the most primitive folk we know, and one might suppose that all ways of writing had been developed and adequately described, that all genres would be known to all peoples. But not so. Innovation has characterized almost every sort of writing in recent time, and Americans have been among the innovators. How has all this new writing and thinking affected language? The answer is not obvious, but we must begin somewhere, and we may as well start with something familiar, prose.

Much prose is not artistic, of course, and much that is artistic in fact makes no artistic pretensions, but the mere bulk of production and consumption cannot be ignored. We readily forget how little immediate popular impact the written word has had until recent times. We speak of the "invention" of printing in the West, and mention such dates as that of the Gutenberg Bible (1456) as though the printed word immediately assumed the role to which we now assign it. This idea is unsound. Early printed books were imitations of handwritten books; they were even deliberately made somewhat irregular so that they would look like the genuine article, as wormholes are deliberately drilled into modern antique furniture. Printings were small and for the wealthy; they were supposed to be "just as good" as handwritten copies, and they were somewhat cheaper, but they were so few and so little cheaper that their social impact must have been almost nil.

They had even less to do with literary creativity than their number would suggest. The following, mostly brief pamphlets, are the known publishings of William Caxton, the first English printer, during the early years of his press, first at Bruges and later at Westminster:[1]

1475—*The Recuyell of the Historyes of Troye* (translation of a medievalized version of the Troy story)
1475—*The Game and Playe of Chesse* (how to play chess)
1476—*Les Quatre derrenieres choses* (popularized morality and theology; what the layman should know about death, doom, hell, and heaven)
1477—*Dictes or Sayengis of the Philosophres* (translated proverbs)
    Book of Courtesy (good manners)
    Advertisement of Sarum Pica (feast days of the church)
    Cato, Parvus et Magnus, 2 eds. (elementary textbook)
    Queen Anelida and the False Arcyte (brief pieces from Chaucer)
    The Temple of Brass (more Chaucer, now called *Parliament of Birds*)
    Infancia Salvatoris (in Latin; elementary material for priests)
    The History of Jason (familiar classical tale of Jason)
    The Churl and the Bird, 2 eds. (popular fables)
    The Horse, the Sheep, and the Goose, 2 eds. (fables)
    Stans Puer and Mensam (conduct book by John Lydgate, the so-called "drivelling monk" of Bury St. Edmunds)
    The Temple of Glass (popular medieval dream allegory)
    Ordinale Secundum Usum Sarum (ecclesiastical handbook)
1478—*Moral Proverbs of Cristyne*
    Boethius de Consolatione Philosophiae (Chaucer's translation of a Roman classic)
    The Canterbury Tales
    Horae ad Usum Sarum (canonical hours in the Salisbury use)
    Propositio Johannis Russell (Latin: brief address on relations with the Low Countries)
1479—*Cordyale* (translation of *Les Quatre derrenieres choses*)

---

[1] Nellie Slayton Aurner, *Caxton: Mirour of Fifteenth-Century Letters* (Boston and New York: Houghton Mifflin, 1926), pp. 212–14. A few dates are conjectural.

Dictes or Sayengis (proverbs; reprint; see 1477)
Nova Rhetorica (Latin: also called *Margarita Eloquentiae;* detailed rhetoric especially adapted to ecclesiastical use)

The flavor revealed in these five years continues; there are *Chronicles of England,* various saints' lives, more elementary textbooks, and well-known classical and medieval works. Chaucer's verse was *belle lettres,* of course, but he was long dead, and even his last great work, the *Canterbury Tales,* could no more be considered contemporary literature than *Leaves of Grass* and *Evangeline* are today contemporary literature. The only possible exception is Malory's *Morte D'Arthur,* but that was apparently printed as the whole truth about King Arthur and his knights, not for any literary merit.

The fact is that during the first century of English printing, few people could, or apparently did, write anything literary with the expectation of its being published. Exceptions would have been too few to set a pattern. By Shakespeare's time a few people could pick up a few extra shillings in hack writing; the London printers had to combine to force one ne'er-do-well to promise not to write any more works on the diseases of the horse. With minor revisions, he had sold the same pamphlet to half the printers in town. Plays were occasionally pirated, or when they had outlived their popularity and were supposed worthless as theatrical attractions, they were sometimes sold outright to a printer as a sort of by-product of the theater business. By Milton's time people printed political and theological pamphlets, to small audiences and probably with little effect. Not until the late seventeenth century was there a daily news-paper, and that was a trivial sheet—the word is to be taken literally, since it was one sheet—with a circulation of a few hundred. Periodicals grew in the eighteenth century, but actual copies were few, small, and fugitive; a circulation of five hundred represented a booming success. Usually a writer of sorts would associate with a printer, the writer penning all the copy himself, and the printer setting up an issue of a few pages. That was a publishing house; usually the printer dictated the terms, so much so that one hack sold a printer at one time the prospective products of his pen for the remainder of his life. Most periodicals survived for only a few issues, or at best a few years. Not until the nineteenth century did printed books become very common, and not until the twentieth did publishing develop to the extent that an average man in the United States lives in a perpetual shower of printed wood-pulp.

Most of this printing, of course, has nothing to do with artistic ex-pression, but even the artistic portion of it is mainly prose. This is part of a worldwide trend; primitive peoples tend to express themselves artistically in verse, and as they become more sophisticated they turn to prose, although with occasional revivals of verse, usually revivals of limited breadth and appeal. Early American literature developed under the influence of such a revival, known as the Romantic movement, and thus we need not be surprised to find that the nineteenth century in the United States tended to admire Longfellow, Lowell, Bryant, and their fellow poets, writers who are now considered rather thin and sentimental and are little read, along with poets like Emily Dickinson and Walt Whitman, who are still admired but never were popular. Similar trends can be observed in Latin America.

The native American artistic tradition has been a prose tradition. For a time, it was derivative. Irving imitated various romantics, from Southey to the German collectors of *Märchen;* Cooper followed Scott's pattern, but with Natty Bumppo and Chingachgook replacing Gurth the Swineherd and Meg Merrillies. Even Hawthorne and Melville, though they sometimes spoke with a native idiom, were derivative as well—after all, a colonial culture must inevitably be mainly derivative. The most notable exceptions stem from Samuel L. Clemens, known as Mark Twain.

Hemingway says he learned to write in part from studying and imitating Twain's *Huckleberry Finn,* and while he contracted debts to such people as Gertrude Stein and Sherwood Anderson, one can see what he means by comparing sample passages. The following is from Melville's *White-Jacket:*

> But by far the most striking object to be seen behind the ensign was a human skeleton, whose every joint articulated with wires. By a rivet at the apex of the skull, it hung dangling from a hammock hook fixed in a beam above. Why this object was here will presently be seen; but why it was placed immediately at the foot of the amputation-table only Surgeon Cuticle can tell.

This is clear, telling writing, but it has about it a remoteness, a genteel reserve that can be observed in many British writers of the nineteenth century, along with their American imitators. The following is from Hemingway's *To Have and Have Not:*

> I always liked him all right and I'd gone in a boat with him plenty of times in the old days, but he was changed now since he lost his arm and that fellow down visiting from Washington made an affidavit that he saw the boat unloading liquor that time, and the customs seized her. When he was in a boat he always felt good and without his boat he felt plenty bad. I think he was glad of an excuse to steal her. He knew he couldn't keep her but maybe he could make a piece of money while he had her. I needed money bad

enough but I didn't want to get in any trouble. I said to him, "You know I don't want to get in any real trouble, Harry."

"What worse trouble you going to get in than you're in now?" he said. "What the hell worse trouble is there than starving?"

Here is something notably different. The drama is played low; no skeletons dangle about, and the talk of crime that will inevitably lead to violence and various amounts of manslaughter appears casually with a humdrum iteration. Hemingway speaks through the minds of his rather simpleminded characters with a simplicity that saves the folk banalities of these people from sentimentality: "When he was in a boat he always felt good and without his boat he felt plenty bad." Part of his secret, of course, is linguistic fidelity; if Hemingway learned from Mark Twain, he was not tricked into learning Twain's fatal love of showmanship. What he did learn was to listen acutely to the native idiom, to the rhythms of speech, to the twist of homey words, to the folk syntax. This he could have learned from Twain; the following is from the *Huckleberry Finn* that Hemingway says he studied:

Col. Grangerford was a gentleman, you see. He was a gentleman all over; and so was his family. He was well born, as the saying is, and that's worth as much in a man as it is in a horse, so the Widow Douglas said, and nobody ever denied that she was of the first aristocracy in our town; and pap he always said it, too, though he warn't no more quality than a mudcat himself. Col. Grangerford was very tall and very slim, and had a darkish-paly complexion, not a sign of red in it anywheres; he was clean shaved every morning all over his thin face, and he had the thinnest kind of lips, and the thinnest kind of nostrils, and a high nose, and heavy eyebrows, and the blackest kind of eyes, sunk so deep back that they seemed like they was looking out of caverns at you, as you may say. His forehead was high, and his hair was black and straight and hung to his shoulders. His hands was long and thin, and every day of his life he put on a clean shirt and a full suit from head to foot made out of linen so white it hurt your eyes to look at it; and on Sundays he wore a blue tail-coat with brass buttons on it. He carried a mahogany cane with a silver head on it. There warn't no frivolishness about him, not a bit, and he warn't never loud. He was as kind as he could be—you could feel that, you know, and so had confidence. Sometimes he smiled, and it was good to see; but when he straightened himself up like a liberty-pole, and the lightning begun to flicker out from under his eyebrows, you wanted to climb a tree first, and find out what the matter was afterwards. He didn't ever have to tell anybody to mind their manners—everybody was always good-mannered where he was.

This passage borders on a staginess that Hemingway outgrew, if he ever had it—"the lightning begun to flicker out from under his eyebrows"— but Twain had learned, long before Hemingway tried it, to make homely sentiment sound real by bringing it out from relatively dumb mouths. They both knew the power of a word like *good* when it is used by a practical fellow mainly concerned with what he can see, hear, or get his hands on.

The impact of fictional talk upon the use of language cannot be accurately measured, nor can the impact of Hemingway's sense of language be gauged among a generation of young novelists who endeavored to imitate him, but some influence can surely be assumed. Even less impact should be presumed for poetry, since even a widely admired poet like Robert Frost was not widely read—he usually had to farm, teach, or lecture to make a living. Curiously, however—and this is curious, because poetry is such an ancient art that revolutions in it are less to be expected than in a young genre like the novel—we have seen within the last half century a whole revolution in verse, with one variety of New Poetry following upon another variety of New Poetry, and all of them stimulated by revived attention to language.

First came free verse. Poets like HD (Hilda Doolittle) and Hart Crane tried to use more varied and subtle rhythms of language based upon contemporary speech, abandoning the older and more formal patterns made up of relatively regular repetition of iambic, trochaic, dactylic, and anapestic feet, somewhat varied by spondees and the like. That is, the writers of free verse were trying to do with words what the new composers like Schoenberg and Bartók were trying to do with notes, and one of the purposes and one of the effects was to permit freer, fresher, more vigorous use of vocabulary. Soon the free-verse poets were all mixed up with the imagists, people like Harriet Monroe and Elinor Wylie, who made use of French nineteenth-century artistic theory, but in poetry, reliance upon images requires the image-making power of words. This can be seen in a poem like Amy Lowell's familiar *Patterns,* in which the patterns in the woman's brocaded dress, the patterns in the garden, the patterns in a young woman's life, become involved in "a pattern called a war," which fits into the patterns of life and death.

All this seems to have reached a climax—although one never knows —with the New Poetry that centered upon T. S. Eliot and his associates and followers, who have attempted to make words work harder than they ever worked before. Eliot's *The Waste Land* was perhaps the basic document here, and Eliot, later a British citizen, was an American when he wrote it. Words work on various levels and with various connotations, and whatever the reader may think of deliberate ambiguities so obscure that they rest upon the poet's personal experiences—Eliot has been forced, or at least impelled, to provide extensive notes to the poem—few would deny that the work is impressive and none could deny that its influence has been widespread, in and out of poetry. It has become a sort of testament for the disillusionment of modern society.

A glance at some of Eliot's language should be revealing. The central symbol in *The Waste Land* is apparently the Fisher King, a figure in Arthurian romance with Christlike overtones, whose loss of virility is reflected in the loss of fertility in the land itself. The fact that Eliot was here relying upon a monograph by Jessie L. Weston, a work only partially accepted by scholars, is beside the point; the point is that Eliot accepted these symbols and that they have become real in his poem if a bit dubious in some of Miss Weston's sources. This concatenation of sex, faith, and society is worked out in the linking of many symbols and many-leveled words and wide-ranging references. For example, a few words of description of a sumptuous ceiling are supposed to suggest through echo the sumptuous ceiling which hung over Aeneas and Dido when their child was conceived, and thus a few words through a reference to Virgil's *Aeneid* are supposed to suggest sex and suicide, duty and desertion, and several other things that only Eliot would know. Or perhaps not even he would know; one school of criticism would insist that a poem is greater than the poet, that it "should not mean, but be," that the poet was only the poet, and that the poem has its reality only in the readers, who collectively may make more of it than Eliot could. However that may be, the multiple use of imagery by a many-leveled use of words is implicit in the concept of poetry here embodied. One could list examples by the thousand. The mention of a game of chess in *The Waste Land,* for instance, is intended to recall a game of chess in a Renaissance play; the mother is domestically employed on the stage, carrying on a conversation with her daughter in the next room, describing the moves in a game of chess that the daughter is presumably playing with her suitor. Actually, the daughter is being seduced, and the details are revealed to the audience in the *double entendres* of the chess moves. This sort of quadruple-decked use of language has driven poetry lovers of the older persuasions to distraction, but it is indisputably interesting as language, and its influence within narrow circles has been profound.

We should note, of course, that these changes are not American monopolies. Literature is still lively and interesting in Britain, and literary figures are beginning to appear in other portions of the English-speaking world; endeavoring to determine whether or not American writers are now leading English in its role as part of world literature would be contentious and not very profitable, but the main fact is obvious. American writers now speak without hesitation in their own idiom; when they borrow from French, or German, or Russian, or

Chinese, they can do so directly without going first through England, as most American literary and linguistic importers did during the eighteenth and nineteenth centuries. Literary American English has its own impact upon literature and language; it is part of the whole process of coming of age.

Developments in the novel and in poetry are only the most notable of many growths in modern literature. We have had a new drama, in which Eugene O'Neill and others have played with language. Meanwhile, the paragraph, with its reliance upon certain key words, has been developed in the United States as never before; one reason that modern students have trouble with Milton's prose, apparently, is that he did not write paragraphs in the modern sense. Particularly important, perhaps, is the development of modern nonfictional prose in the New World. The growth of science and scholarship, the serious interest in earthly phenomena, have led to an efflorescence of clear, vigorous, American nonfictional prose. One might notice the following from Rachel Carson's *Under the Sea Wind:*

> Sight of the young mackerel roused the cod from the semi-torpor in which he had lain since the last feeding time and kindled his hunger. He swung his heavy body out from the ledge and climbed steeply to the shoal. Scomber fled before him. As the young mackerel rejoined his fellows who had been lying in an updraught of current from the face of the cliff, the whole school quickened to a sense of alarm and fled away across the shoal as the dark form of the cod loomed into sight at the brink of the rock wall.

I cite this passage, not because it is unusually good writing, either from an absolute point of view or in comparison with Miss Carson's other work. It is more typical than distinctive. Clear, sharp, vigorous; full of concrete detail embodied in sturdy, simple words, it is representative of a very large body of prose published in the United States in recent decades and still being published, prose that subtly strengthens the use of the English language. This whole subject has been neglected in American writing; indisputably, much American professional prose is dull and turgid, as we have observed, but growing, also, in the United States, is a sense of scholarly, scientific, historical, critical, and other sorts of rhetoric which are perhaps not new in the world but are indigenous, and taken as a movement they become extremely impressive. I am thinking of the writings of people like Rachel Carson in marine biology, Earnest A. Hooton in anthropology, Bernard De Voto in history, Van Wyck Brooks, Joseph Wood Krutch, Lionel Trilling, and Edmund Wilson in criticism, Carl Sandburg in biography, and many more.

Even rhetoric itself can be included among the areas of revolution, or perhaps of incipient revolution. To appreciate what is now beginning, we need to recall a bit of history. Rhetoric is presumably the art of using language well, and it has been revered since before Aristotle, we have generally assumed, put it in order. Roman rhetoric grew from Greek rhetoric, and when writing became a subject for serious study in England in the eighteenth century, English rhetoric became classical rhetoric applied to contemporary English.[2] Similarly, as the movement has grown to make the teaching of composition in the United States a more serious activity, many pedagogical thinkers have assumed that we need only revive classical rhetoric. Lately, however, skeptics have arisen.

Any examination of classical rhetoric will reveal room for skepticism —in fact, the skepticism often came from thoughtful teachers of rhetoric who found that the classical statement did not seem to fit modern writing very well. That it should not fit is plausible enough when one balances classical rhetoric against the modern use of English in America.

First we should disabuse ourselves of a misleading assumption based upon a false analogy. The Greeks could write; they even had the alphabet from which ours descends, and we have Greek manuscripts, surviving from works that were written down. We also write, and all our important works are either issued in written—that is, printed—form or they are soon committed to writing. Ergo, we assume that the Greeks used writing very much as we do. Not at all. With them, language was mainly oral. Homer probably could not write, and whether or not he could, his works were presumably intended for oral recitation. The Greek plays were by definition intended for oral production, and presumably so few plays have survived because few copies were made. Plato's dialogues profess to have been oral, and whereas they may have been composed in writing, or parts of them may have been, they reflect an oral tradition. Aristotle's "works" are presumably his lecture notes, more or less augmented from notes taken by his students. As for Greek fiction, it is all late.

Thus Greek *rhetorike techne* was a much more restricted term than is modern English rhetoric. Almost any composition book can now be called a rhetoric, but the Greek word is related to *rhetor,* an orator, and rhetoric was the art of public speaking. Furthermore, public speaking was a specialized thing, highly formalized, including formal addresses in cases at law, and especially in its Roman developments, speeches of statesmen in the Forum. It included, also, artistic performances in imitation of these legal or political addresses. A rhetor would prepare

---

[2] Perhaps the standard work was Hugh Blair, *Lectures on Rhetoric and Belles Lettres,* 2 vols. (London: W. Strahan and T. Cadell, 1783, and frequently reprinted), within its assumptions a sensible and penetrating book.

and deliver an oration, using classic models for form and style, which would be listened to and applauded as a virtuoso performance. Music had not as yet developed sufficiently to thrive much as a performing art, but rhetoric had, and rhetors used oral compositions for public entertainments as a cellist will use the compositions of Bach. Classical speeches, intended to free or convict a prisoner, to sway votes or to move audiences, were persuasive in intent, but these artistic rhetorical exhibitions were not intended to persuade anybody. They were shows built on the patterns of an art calculated to persuade.

When Aristotle enunciated the principles of rhetoric, then, he did not mean to tell people how to write. He meant to tell them how to prepare a formal address designed to sway audiences and lead to action. Of course, such speeches are still employed; defense and prosecuting attorneys still address juries, but many cases at law now rely on briefs and most of the oral cases do not hinge on legal histrionics. We hear political oratory during election years, and most people become bored after very little of it, but even addresses ostensibly composed for delivery in Congress are actually prepared to be printed in the *Congressional Record* for written dissemination.

One need not labor the point; most modern American serious or artistic use of language is not intended to persuade. I am not sure what the percentages of various sorts of modern writing are. I am not even sure of the categories of modern writing, although I am quite sure that the classical four—narration, description, exposition, and argumentation—are not now the most revealing. What has been called exposition would certainly subdivide into explaining and informing, and probably into exploring, with each category larger than arguing. As for description, it usually appears within one of the other three, and the techniques of fictional and nonfictional prose are so various that these sorts of writing scarcely belong in only one category. And so on.

So far as my case at the moment is concerned, however, the answer is obvious: formal oral persuasion is not the whole of nonpoetic use of the language in the United States today. It does not comprise even a relatively large segment. Anyone who doubts this need only start counting the columns in a newspaper which are mainly argumentative, or walk through the stacks of a library counting the volumes devoted mainly to persuasion. Probably the largest body of oral suasive modern English now takes the form of advertising over radio and television, and the form of that prose does not readily suggest 'Aristotle.

The classical rhetorical statement persisted after classical times and manners had gone. It had the weight of names like Aristotle, Cato, and Cicero behind it, and thus for centuries western rhetoricians have been notably traditional. The notion seems to have been, although it was so much assumed that it was not much argued, that rhetoric was universal as language was supposed to be universal, and even when Universal Grammar fell into disrepute, the universality of rhetoric was not much questioned. The study had begun early, was extensively developed by the later Greeks and the Romans, was taken up by the Church fathers, and persisted through the Middle Ages, when rhetoric became one of the subjects taught in the universities, partly because it was encouraged by the church, which prized it as the basis of sermonizing, and partly because it was an international necessity. The flowers of rhetoric were required when, as Chaucer put it, "men to Kings write." Rhetoric bloomed all over sixteenth-century France, was imported thence into such backward lands as England, and found its way to the New World, where Washington, Jefferson, and the Adams family wrote as well as they did partly because they had studied classical rhetoric and had imitated orators like Burke, who also had imitated classical models. Even recently, when the improvement of the native tongue has become a matter for lively concern, many of the more serious teachers have turned to rhetoric to provide depth and authority for their instruction.

Of course, some of what Aristotle said is still pertinent; many well-constructed works have beginnings, middles, and ends. Aristotle's remarks on figures of speech have their relevance, although a modern critic would not get far with T. S. Eliot if he restricted himself to Aristotle, even though he added the *Poetics* to the *Rhetoric*. In fact the most obvious limitation arises from the fact that modern English occurs in such varied genres that it cannot be adequately described in one sort of rhetorical statement. The writing of a novel like *The Sound and the Fury* does not much suggest the narrative record of a cyclone. The rhetoric of a scientific article differs from the rhetoric of an account of the same subject in a popular news magazine.

Similar differences appear in the details of composition. Any serious modern writer knows that he lives among uncertainties, and usually, the more learned he is, the more he becomes aware how inexplicable is the world. If he is writing expository or informational prose, he must constantly make clear to his reader the degree of his uncertainty. He must distinguish what he asserts because the evidence is overwhelming, what he accepts because his conclusion is at least plausible, and what he offers, shrouded in all its uncertainties and partial contradictions, because, after all, something must be said, and a likely guess is better than no guess at all. He must also distinguish many variations upon these. For this subtlety in evaluating degrees of so-called truth, modern English offers the writer a multitude of tools and techniques, but I know from sad experience as a teacher who has tried to teach such subjects that most incipient writers cannot control these devices. Only the experts can, but this is a rhetorical problem, subject to rhetorical solution. On the other hand, it is not a question that strongly attracted the older rhetoricians; they were writing for orators concerned with persuading, and an oratorical persuader is not likely to be much bothered with degrees of truth. He assumes that truth is one, and that he has it.

Reasons for differences between ancient and modern rhetoric are not far to seek. If style is the man, the modern American rhetoric should differ from classical Greek rhetoric; whether for better or for worse, modern Americans differ sharply from ancient Greeks—how sharply we readily forget, since names like Socrates, Plato, and Aristotle are familiar words everywhere. In spite of the brilliance of its art, literature, and philosophy, Athens could not be called a city by modern standards; it was the center of a largely agrarian, slaveholding society. Combats in the *Iliad* could be settled by one hero bashing another with a rock, and when Ulysses comes home to discover, as an absentee king, that affairs of state are in confusion, he slips around to the back of the palace and bunks with the swineherd, who proves to be an old acquaintance of his. Later, he introduces governmental reform by shooting down the culprits with his bow and arrow. This makes a good story, but it does not reflect a complex, highly socialized way of life.

So much for the broad approach; what about composition in smaller elements, in sentences and words? Here we must deal with grammar and the nature of vocabulary, and as we have seen, the grammars of classical Greek and Latin differ from the grammar of Modern English. Since the classical tongues made little use of word order as a grammatical device, they could use word order as a rhetorical device, distributing words for their form, balancing them against one another, building them into sequences of sound—devices that are particularly telling for oral delivery. Accordingly, the older rhetoricians made elaborate studies of figures of speech, including figures that relied upon sound. English, on the other hand, can use word order but sparingly for rhetoric since word sequence is extensively involved in grammar; hence balance is less important in modern English than in Latin and Greek. Modern English, on the other hand, is unusually rich in devices for modification and subordination, which give English great variety and subtlety. A rhetoric of modern American English should probably give as careful study to subordinational devices as earlier rhetoricians gave to figures of speech.

The periodic sentence provided the foundation for classical structure; for example, the following is from Jonathan Edwards, an American minister writing in the classical tradition:

When the great and angry God hath risen up and executed His awful vengeance on the poor sinner, and the wretch is actually suffering the infinite weight and power of indignation, then will God call upon the whole universe to behold that awful majesty and mighty power that is to be seen in it.

Periodic sentences can become much more involved, thundering, more instinct with climax than this, but even a moderately periodic sentence like this one moves with majesty. It must, indeed, have sounded rather like the wrathful Jehovah of the Hebrew prophets when thundered over a God-fearing Puritan congregation, but most modern writers of American English do not want to sound like any sort of Jehovah, and the best of them avoid oratorical sentences.

Similarly, classical rhetoric recommended balanced sentences, such as the following from Thomas Babington Macaulay:

Thus the Puritan was made up of two different men: the one all self-abasement, penitence, gratitude, passion; the other proud, calm, inflexible, sagacious. He prostrated himself in the dust before his Maker, but he set his foot on the neck of his king.

Indubitably, this is effective writing; it is orderly, incisive, terse. It hits like a series of blows. It is neat; almost everything is balanced against something else so that, if one kind of Puritan has four qualities, the other sort of Puritan must have four. If a given pattern dominates one half of a compound sentence, it must dominate the other, but it is the prose of a man who has simplified all questions and who knows all answers.

Modern writers, however, are commonly not so sure of themselves as writers used to be; they find themselves in a world whose complexities do not respond to simple questions, and where good questions lead not to answers, but to harder questions. They make more use of what is coming to be called the cumulative sentence, in which, for clarity, the subject and verb usually appear early, but these lead into a cumulative, complex predicate as in the following:

But the Acropolis of Athens is the clearest illustration of the deceptive magic of time. Time has purified it, sweeping away the gaudy confusion, leaving only the stainless marble; the Parthenon stands alone in majestic simplicity, in the perfection of its skeletal outlines. And so we forget that these temples were once painted in lively colors and decorated with gold leaf, in something like Oriental luxuriance. We forget the huge statues of gods that were crowded into them, and about them, in utter disregard of harmony and proportion. We forget the astonishing clutter of slabs, statues, and monuments that filled the Acropolis—a hodge-podge that makes Radio City seem a model of architectural restraint.

This is from Herbert J. Muller's *The Uses of the Past.* In a way, Muller's subject is the same as Macaulay's; each is endeavoring to interpret a past time, but Muller is less oratorical than Macaulay, and more prepared to give evidence, thinking more in paragraphs than in sentences. He constructs few resounding periods; he is inclined to give the reader the subject and verb at once ("We forget . . . ,") and to use this supposed grammatical core of the sentence as the leader of a parade of details that are to follow. He builds sentences that work but do not strut. They move easily in a flexible, relaxed informality, but they carry with them a load of detail which would have broken the backs of stiffer, less yielding structures.

Such sentences used to be called "loose," and theoreticians disapproved them however much professional writers practiced them—after all, no one should write loose prose. Now, however, since we are able to call them "cumulative"—accumulation is a good thing, especially in an affluent society—we can recognize the virtues of such style, and even surmise that the cumulative style of writing is natural in an analytic grammar and adaptable to the needs of a highly sophisticated, technological society suffering from the knowledge explosion but not from the need of oratorical grandeur. The cumulative sentences seem to be native in the English-speaking tradition, to be at home there. *Beowulf,* although it is formal in style and somewhat oratorical, includes about an equal proportion of periodic and cumulative sentences; obviously Chaucer cultivated cumulative sentences, and so did Shakespeare, and this in the face of an academic tradition based upon Latin. That is, a typical pattern for a Muller sentence, if there could be such a thing, would differ from a typical pattern for a Macaulay sentence, and within limits this is a difference between times as well as men. The differences no doubt reflect many influences, but among them, apparently, are the tempers of contrasting times and the impact of contrasting grammars.

Modern artistic prose, moreover, reveals subdivisions not much delineated in classical rhetoric. It is varied, but even if we ignore prose fiction, which was not consciously a classical art form, it includes at least three sorts, the prose of popularized knowledge, the prose of specialized knowledge, and the prose of mass media. The first we have already sampled in a paragraph by Rachel Carson, the writing of a person at once learned and literate, and addressed to readers less learned but willing to become more so. Such writing has rhetorical principles, although these have not been well described in our tradition. In another sort of rhetoric a learned person addresses his colleagues; I should say that the following is a fair sample:

Probably the last person able to give an accurate account of Tahitian legend and history from the native point of view, Arii Taimai had proved to be informatively loquacious and had graciously co-operated with Adams's design, conceived when it became plain that his stay must lengthen, to put her memoirs in writing. The son and daughter, Tati and Marau, had translated her discourse while Adams took notes. *Tahiti* is thus in essence the old matriarch's narrative, organized and composed by Henry Adams. It has had little chance for attention, since it has only recently become easily accessible. Of the first edition, somewhat inaccurately entitled *Memoirs of Marau Taaroa, Last Queen of Tahiti* and privately printed in Washington, 1893, two copies are in the Adams collection in the Massachusetts Historical Society.* Copies of the second edition are to be found in the same collection and also in a number of university libraries; more accurately named *Memoirs of Arii Taimai,* it was privately printed in Paris, 1901, with revisions, rearrangements, and additions. The latest readily available edition, with the convenient main title simply of *Tahiti,* was edited in 1947 for the Scholars' Facsimile and Reprints by Robert E. Spiller, who contributed a helpful introduction. The map drawn according to the 1769 survey by Captain James Cook forms a frontispiece, as in the second edition, and the seven genealogical tables prepared by Adams intersperse the text. Unfortunately, however, an index has not been supplied.

This is from Robert A. Hume's *Runaway Star,* a critical study of Henry Adams; the quoted paragraph does not represent the author's most attractive prose, but of its sort it is good writing, clear, orderly, economical, and in restrained good taste. It is not good popular writing, but it is not intended to be. Most literate readers have never heard of *Tahiti,* and would not willingly expose themselves to a description of differences among its editions, but the material is presented as devotees of Adams would be likely to want it. That is, this sort of writing has its own rhetorical principles, so that it differs from what Rachel Carson addressed to a wide audience, but probably does not differ essentially from what she addressed to her fellow marine biologists. For example, a rhetorical statement describing popular, informative writing would be likely to suggest that the author do something to attract and stimulate the reader's attention. The rhetoric of scholarly and scientific writing must recognize that specialists do not require titillation, and that they are repelled and irked by such a suggestion; they are angered by this waste of their time. In their view, anyone who tries to interest a scientist or scholar in his own field is guilty of bad taste and is probably incapable of close study.

Quite different, of course, is prose prepared for dissemination by mass media. It differs in audience and usually in purpose, and hence it differs also in vocabulary, sentence structure, development, and organization. Even when it uses the medium of speech, in radio or television, it is not

---

* Professor Robert E. Spiller informs me that other copies of this first edition, of which probably about ten were printed, are now in private hands. [Hume's note.]

spoken English in the sense that an address in the Roman Forum was spoken Latin. It is addressed to no known persons. The speaker may not know the age, sex, social status, race, or even the nationality of those to whom his words are to come, and the rhetorical statement of good writing, as the words must be defined for these purposes, will differ widely from the rhetoric worked out by our classic forebears and even from the rhetoric of written prose as it was known a few centuries ago.

We might now consider two areas in which the simple fact of man's influence on language and language's influence on man is quite certain, but where the degree or amount of influence is bafflingly vague. I refer to what is often called general semantics and to medicine, especially to psychiatry and psychoanalysis. In each of these the impacts are presumably not peculiar to the Americas, but they do occur. Nor are they the results of learned influence, but they are revealed by learned studies, so that we may as well consider them here.

First to general semantics. The word *semantics,* unmodified, has a long and honorable ancestry; it is a general term for the study of meaning. General Semantics—with the *general* and sometimes capitalized—is more recent, more dramatic, and more limited. It recognizes that in any strict sense a word cannot "mean," and that a meaning cannot be defined. Words will have referents, objects to which they refer, that will be common to all users of the language—the referent for *airplane* is not confused with the referent for *woodpecker*—but most of what a word can do is not inherent in the word itself but grows from the users of the word, from their natures and experiences, from both their emotions and their intellects. The impact of *airplane* is likely to change with a person's first plane ride, and *woodpecker* can alter sharply if a worker on a night shift is kept awake by a bird drumming on the roof overhead.

Many general semanticists, however, and notably in the United States, are not mainly concerned with meaning, not even with meaning as it is assumed to reside in the users of the word. They are concerned with what this "meaning," this using of words, does to human beings as individuals and *en masse.* They will point out, for example, that the fear of Communism and Communists in the United States does not stem exclusively from Communist activity. Practicing Communists are few in the United States, and never have been many, yet people were so terrorized by the word that McCarthyism became possible. Similarly, Communist countries have called themselves democratic in order to appeal to believers in democracy, and at this writing Red China discredits benevolent American actions by calling all Americans imperialists and aggressors. Similarly, the debauching of natural resources can be made popular by calling it progress, and the population explosion can be combated, if at all, only when birth control is called planned parenthood. Rather curiously, although general semantics grew almost simultaneously on both sides of the Atlantic Ocean, it has attracted but little attention in Great Britain while becoming popular in the New World—in Canada as well as in the United States—siring a scholarly journal entitled *ETC.*, a book club, and many organizations. The reasons for this efflorescence must be both sociological and linguistic, and, whatever they are, undeniably significant.

Here is clear evidence that words made by man have become influences upon man himself. This phenomenon is not peculiar to American English; in fact, as a governmental device it is probably declining in the United States. It is fundamental in the foreign and domestic policy of many countries—especially, today, of Communist countries—but it is relatively well understood by the American electorate, and since it is essentially inimical to the principles of democracy, it is formally disapproved. On the other hand, individual politicians employ it, more or less consciously; *motherhood, God, liberty, justice,* and other noble words have been used to deprive Afro-Americans and other minority groups of the most elementary human rights, including life itself. Meanwhile, since Americans lead the world in the amount of advertising they emit and absorb and in the use they make of mass media like television, denizens of the American mass market are perhaps more nearly under the domination of the loaded words of business than members of any other group.

If the nature of the evidence is clear, however, the amount is not. How much does this sort of thing affect or even determine thinking and acting? Words so heavily loaded as *Christianity* and *Communism* are not numerous; on the other hand, semanticists point out that all words are more or less loaded for somebody, and that our emotions are not much understood and that their powers are usually underestimated. Some semanticists write as though they believe that rational processes are all but unknown and that all human beings are victims of their vocabularies. Obviously, this sort of thing can be carried too far, but quite as obviously most observers do not carry it far enough. Words are potent weapons, even for self-destruction.

This last fact brings us to mental illness and the means by which we know about it—psychology, psychiatry, and psychoanalysis. Here, indeed, we are moving among mysteries, vague truths of which most people are but dimly aware, where the experts, by their own admission, are confused. This last is no adverse criticism; rather, it is praise of scientific and professional men who face frankly the limits of their knowledge in a realm where knowing anything is extremely difficult. Practitioners in mental illness now possess a set of techniques that seem to work and that sometimes work miracles, but often these techniques rest upon the flimsiest sorts of theses and philosophies. Students of the mind are the first to admit that they do not understand the conscious mind, let alone the subconscious or unconscious mind, whatever that is.

Most students of mental and emotional problems agree, however, that language is somehow involved in the subconscious, although how is not obvious. Language provides the conscious mind with one of its readiest ways of working, and language may also structure and culture the mind, but does language culture unconscious as well as conscious mental and emotional patterns? The question has been but little asked, and the answer is most obscure, but that language provides the unconscious with a tool is quite clear. The fact is written all over the literature of mental illness.

For some such reasons, apparently, free association works as well as it does. The patient, responding quickly to words, may draw from his unconscious as well as his conscious mind. Or, to put it in another way, presumably the subconscious portion of ourselves finds a means of expressing what it has not been able to free in any other way.

Often what are called "insights" take the form of words. Take, for example, the famous case reported by Karen Horney,[3] in which a patient called Clare had a devastating attachment to a man with whom she was having an affair. She suspected that he was tired of her and was trying to get rid of her, but she was so dependent upon him that she could not face this fact, and it was ruining her life. One night she dreamed that she saw a large, beautiful bird, having uncommonly graceful movements, but it flew away, becoming smaller and smaller until it vanished. She was disturbed when she woke up, but did not understand why until the words came to her, "the bird has flown." Then she realized that someone had once characterized her lover as "a bird that never settled down," and that, his name being Peter, she had associated him with a Sunday School song about Jesus taking children under his wing. Once she had the conscious clue from her unconscious self, she could relate the flying bird to other men on whom she had relied and who had failed her—her father, a former husband, a childhood idol.

Clare had more such experiences; she awoke with a name on her lips, the name of a woman she had known long ago. She recalled a conversation with the woman, a conversation which meant little to her at the time, although now she could see that it applied to her own troubles.

---

[3] *Self-Analysis* (New York: Norton, 1942), *passim,* but especially Chapter 8.

The phrase "two on an island" came to her, permitting her to understand a dream in which she had been sitting on a tower in a swamp, and helped her to understand that her reliance upon Peter was not love but a morbid dependency. Of course, Clare was not cured at once by these insights, but the methods of treatment employ language since it seems to provide one means with which the subconscious endeavors to express itself.

Some insights through words involve puns and various uses of a term. A woman who numbered among her symptoms a complex of neurotic aberrations obtained some help when she thought of the word *fall*. She had wondered why she was so terrorized by heights that she could not endure being in an airplane, but once the word had occurred to her she knew it was associated with the fact that, when she had first bobbed her hair, her somewhat bigoted father had called her a "fallen woman." The associations go much deeper than the words, of course, but apparently the word serves as a sort of key or trigger to unleash what had been dammed up beyond conscious awareness.

Now to linguistics. We have noticed that in earlier centuries, study of language in America, even when it was relatively original, as it was with Webster, still moved mainly among ideas and techniques conceived and developed in Europe. Language study in the New World was derivative and usually less competent than in the better established, better educated societies. Webster and Worcester made use, in their own ways, of what Bailey and Johnson had learned to do in England. In the nineteenth century, the philology developed by British and Continental scholars found its way to the New World, where it was practiced by a few students.

With the twentieth century, however, the United States became mature, as in other areas, in the study of language. Americans like George Lyman Kittredge and John Matthews Manly were as good as the best European scholars, and of those who work in the English language, more reside on the west side of the Atlantic than on the east side. The great *Oxford English Dictionary* relied upon Britons with some help from Americans, but this work, monumental as it is, led to a half dozen more detailed dictionaries, of which only the Scottish are being done in the Old World. Formerly, all important editions of literary works were done in England or on the Continent; about the only exception was Francis James Child's *Ballads.* Now many standard editions are American: Klaeber's *Beowulf,* Robinson's *Chaucer,* the Manly and Rickert *Canterbury Tales,* the Johns Hopkins *Spenser,* the Boswell papers, the Walpole letters, and on through the list. It is scarcely surprising that the *Annals of the New York Stage* were prepared in New York, but it is surprising to find the *Annals of the London Stage* edited in the Middle West.

In language study, two streams are conspicuous. Beginning mainly after the first World War, Henry L. Mencken, a journalist, critic, and editor, began berating Britons for their condescension to American speech, and bethwacking his fellow countrymen for their neglect of the native idiom, which he preferred to call the American language. His attacks were spirited, verging at times on the tantrumic, but he was also witty, devoted, and indefatigable, so that as he revised, he reformed both his irascibility and his wayward linguistics until *The American Language* grew into a monument of scholarship, indispensable to any study of American English. Insofar as it was intended to arouse his fellow Americans, it has been so successful that the study of American dialects, once neglected, has become almost a fad, with collegiate courses offered everywhere, doctoral candidates preparing dissertations, and books on American English assured of at least a modest sale.

Among Mencken's less audible contemporaries were a number of the professors whom he was fond of twitting, including Leonard Bloomfield of the University of Chicago, Edward Sapir of Yale, and Franz Boas of Columbia.[4] They all had intimate connection with scholarship in Europe, although they worked independently; with help from some others they imported the best European thinking of the day, George Wenker's dialect or linguistic geography, Ferdinand de Saussure's structural analysis, and the like.

The explosive ideas, however, came in grammar. Here, as we have seen, the central concept was the phoneme, still an arcane term, something to juggle and conjure with, since it has given American students the opening for which they were longing, to be more nearly scientific. Earlier students had no concern with science; they wanted to be philosophic, to think about language, and to be traditional, to tap the ancient reservoirs of learning. The results, as we have seen, were not always good, and when etymology developed with the new knowledge about language families, writers on language liked to refer to themselves as "scientific." As early as about 1860, George P. Marsh was regretting that "the modern science of linguistics was so little practiced in the New World,"[5] and Whitney's *The Life and Growth of Language* was printed in the

---

[4] If the American linguistic school had a founder, it was Leonard Bloomfield, whose *Language* (New York: Henry Holt, 1933) is still standard. Sapir died relatively young, but his *Language*, cited earlier, now available in paperback, Harvest Books HB7, promises to endure. Boas long dominated the more linguistic aspects of anthropology in this country.

[5] *The Origin and History of the English Language* (New York: Scribner, 1861), p. 25.

International Scientific Series, and carried the half title, *An Outline of Linguistic Science*. These works were scientific, or relatively so, when compared with the speculations of Voltaire, which were mainly subjective. They were scientific, also, in that they attempted to derive their conclusions from observed linguistic facts, and to order these facts by what some philologists called "laws." But they were not scientific in the sense that their conclusions rested upon exact units of measurement, repeatable experiments, or principles readily reducible to mathematical formulae.

The twentieth century brought changes. Advances in physics permitted laboratory study of language, which is uttered as sound—whatever it may be as mental process—and spectrographic analysis permitted breaking the recorded waves of human speech into their components, so that differences in sound can be seen, plotted, and studied. In the laboratory, such analysis led to amazing results. Machines were built which can talk audibly, if not very loquaciously, and what is called communications theory has facilitated telephonic traffic. Formerly, to carry a conversation by wire, the sound had to move as a complete wave; now we know that the entire wave can be reconstructed from a cross section of it. Thus modern long-distance communication does not require carrying sound waves; an electronic device reduces the waves to cross sections, the cross sections are transmitted, and upon reception are reconstituted by another electronic device. Thus one wire can carry many messages simultaneously, because it is carrying cross sections of wave lengths, which do not interfere with one another, instead of waves, which would interfere. Thus, the results of scientific, phonetic study of language have been invaluable, but for most purposes the machinery is too expensive and cumbersome and the results too elaborate. We have found no economical way to teach elementary composition with a team of computers and spectrographs, and as yet grammar has baffled the machines.

But what machines could not do to simplify grammatical study, an idea did. The *phoneme* provided no new knowledge, but it did promote a more practical way of looking at the old knowledge. A phoneme is a working unit of sound in a given language, and to see how it functions we might contrast it with a phonetic unit. We have already had occasion to make use of phonetic and phonemic transcriptions, but not to discuss them. The relation between sounds and symbols for language, commonly called letters, has long been understood, and ideally, an alphabet is a collection of symbols which represent the sounds of the language. Most alphabets are traditional, however, and do not equate well with the working units of any language. For example, *a* represents different sounds in *hat, stalk, hate, park, abide, father, marry,* and the like, not to mention that it suggests different sounds for different speakers in words like *aunt* and *ask* and has no sound at all in *meat, broad,* and *road.* Obviously, an ideal alphabet would provide one symbol for each sound and each sound would be represented by a single symbol, but for various reasons actual alphabets are mostly far from ideal. Something like standard American English could be written with between forty and fifty symbols, and even American English is not standard; if one adds all the British dialects, the symbols might reach a hundred. Furthermore, in a rapidly socializing world, language is not exclusively provincial. Accordingly, an attempt was made to produce a world alphabet, one that would incorporate all sounds made by man and would provide a unique symbol for each. The result, the International Phonetic Alphabet (known as IPA), has greatly promoted the recording of languages and has provided a means of thinking more accurately about language than had formerly been possible, but it is not simple. Hundreds of symbols had to be devised, described, and standardized, until IPA was a complex and beautiful instrument, and a useful one as well, but the more it proliferated the more cumbersome it became.

Furthermore, IPA, detailed though it is, is not entirely adequate. It identifies isolated sounds, but it does not reveal how these sounds are put together. Speech is not made up solely of isolated sounds; it includes patterns of pitch, stress, and pause, and perhaps some other things not yet well understood. These needs are inadequately supplied by IPA; it includes some symbols for tone, but they work mainly in units, as in Chinese, where the same sound uttered with different tones has different grammatical or semantic value. Some symbols vary in stress; for example, [ə] is roughly the unstressed equivalent of [ʌ], as in *above* [əbʌv], but even such rough equivalents are few, and to provide three or four different pitches and as many different stresses for each IPA symbol would run the total into the thousands, which is clearly impractical. Diacritical marks would help, but are at best clumsy.

The phoneme provided the solution. A phoneme is a working spread of sound in a given language; it is whatever the users of the language recognize as a unit. For example, the initial and medial sounds of *titter* differ from the terminal sound of *flit,* but since all these sounds associated with the spelling *t* are treated by most speakers of American English as one sound, /t/ is a phoneme of Modern American English speech. In American English /t/ and /d/ are two phonemes, since *dead* /dɛd/, and *debt* /dɛt/, have distinct meanings, but they are not necessarily two phonemes in certain American Indian languages where the distinction between the voiced /d/ and the voiceless /t/ is not always maintained. Thus it is not scientific in any rigid sense; it is not exactly measurable; it is not universal; it is not permanent. Phonemes cannot be measured in the laboratory; they are not the same for French and English, and they are not the same for Middle English and Modern English. But they do provide a practical working tool which simplifies grammatical study and permits it to become relatively objective. Perhaps it works as well as it does for just this reason, that instead of being part of objective reality it comes out of human understanding; after all so, in part, does language.

Although this idea is simple, it inevitably becomes complex in its application; language is itself complex, and we should probably not expect even simple ideas to remain simple in their ramifications. For example, the phoneme /t/ can be readily described as it appears in any language, but the pitch, stress, and junctures with which phonemes like /t/ are pronounced are also working spreads of sound and can also be called phonemes. (These terms may require definition. Roughly, *pitch* refers to the highness or lowness of the speaking tone, *stress* refers to the vigor or tenseness of pronunciation, and *juncture* refers to pauses between linguistic units, though the word *juncture* implies something more than *pause* since it implies also the other changes that accompany the pause.) These phonemes, however, work in conjunction with one another, and thus an uttered body of speech will consist of what are called segmental phonemes like /t/ and suprasegmental phonemes or suprasegmentals, those which cannot be broken up, which are the stresses, pitches, and junctures as these combine in spoken utterance.

A book like this one is not the place to pursue phonemic analysis, but we can note that the phoneme has given great new impetus to language study, and that this study is prosecuted in the United States as in few other parts of the world. It was the basis of teaching little-known languages for military purposes during World War II. It is the basis on which English is being taught, by the Peace Corps, by Fulbright scholars, and by many others in odd places throughout the world. Most well-trained missionaries now know how to practice structural linguistics, as structural language study is often called. All people who work with primitive languages use it. For English, however, the great development came in our understanding and our teaching of the native language, particularly of its grammar.

Here we should note that if the phoneme is not rigidly scientific, it is precision itself when compared with flabby concepts like "A noun is the name of a person, place, or thing," or "A sentence is a complete thought." There is no such thing as a complete thought, and all sorts of persons, places, and things (*red, singing, rain*) function in ways that preclude their being what we think of as nouns. Thus the phoneme provided a long step toward objectivity in grammatical analysis. It permitted grammarians to say, in effect, let us be as scientific as we can. Let us start with the most objective things we have, be objective when we can, and go wherever such data lead us. What are the most objective aspects of language? They are sound, which in its workable form is the phoneme, and structure, which often appears as the order of linguistic units. Let us, the structuralists said, use these to the exclusion, if possible, of loose concepts like meaning and function.

The result was what is called structural analysis, structural linguistics, linguistic analysis, and the like. It swept through modern language studies, especially in the United States, and was widely exported, in systems worked out by people like George L. Trager, Charles C. Fries, Henry Lee Smith, Bernard Bloch, Harold Whitehall, and others. It was no more than thriving as an applied approach, however, before it submerged in two even more startling approaches, both somewhat associated with the seminal thinking of Professor Zellig Harris of the University of Pennsylvania.

In 1957, one of Harris' students, Noam Chomsky of the Massachusetts Institute of Technology, published a slim, paperbound volume[6] that has probably had more influence on the writing and teaching of English grammar than any other 116 pages printed before or since. It provided the foundation, since much built upon by Chomsky and others, of a radically different grammatical statement. All previous grammatical descriptions had been based upon language in existence, upon linguistic cadavers as it were, language written, or printed, or spoken and recorded, language already fixed. Chomsky endeavored to write the grammatical description of a language coming to be, by formulating the rules by which sentences not in existence could be generated. That is, Chomsky tried to describe the grammatical sense that exists in the users of the language, whereby they can bring into being sentences which they and their audiences may never have heard, but which are immediately intelligible to anyone conversant with the language.

Such grammatical descriptions are now called *generative* grammars. Theoretically, various grammatical statements should be possible, depending upon the assumptions with which the grammarian starts, but to date only one has attracted much attention, called *transform* or *transformational grammar,* because of the prominence in the grammatical analysis of what are called *transforms.* Transformational grammarians start with what they call *kernel sentences,* usually identifying four or five of these, basic sorts of simple sentences like *John loves Lucy, Lucy is an*

---

6 *Syntactic Structures,* Janua Linguarum, 4 ('s-Gravenhage: Mouton, 1957).

imbecile, Lucy is kittenish. By keeping the meaningful portions of these sentences but transforming the structure, the grammarian can produce what are called *transforms.* Thus *John loves Lucy* will transform into *Does John love Lucy?* and *Lucy is loved by John.* Similarly, *Lucy is kittenish* will transform into *kittenish Lucy.* Transformationalists believe that by systematizing the transforms of their kernel sentences they can account for all possible structures in the English language. The grammatical statement thus becomes very simple, at least in its elements, and transformationalists make all this graphic by using formulas from mathematics. Everything stems from S——→ NP + VP, which means, "a sentence can be written as a noun phrase plus a verb phrase," which is roughly equivalent in the older terminology to saying that a sentence is composed of a subject and predicate. So stated, the transformational position seems not to amount to much, but it does possess an order, logic, and simplicity that seem to be very teachable. At least for the teaching of grammar in the grade schools, it promises to sweep the country.

Chomsky's grammatical approach owed much to mathematics; the other contemporary development, known as *tagmemics* and pursued especially by students of Professor Kenneth L. Pike of the University of Michigan, relies upon physics. The name uses a rejuvenated Greek word, *tagmeme,* which presumably means a chunk of something, in this instance a chunk of language. Since *chunk* is a highly adaptable concept, tagmemics had from the start a fluidity that does not characterize either structural linguistics or transformational grammar, and tagmemists have tried to study bodies of language that other grammars exclude. Structural linguists and transformational grammarians—in this they resemble the older philologists—limit themselves mainly to what is called *phrase structure;* in effect, they are principally concerned as yet with no larger units than the sentence. Tagmemists, however, have adopted from physics the terms *particle, wave,* and *field,* and they use these to start with small linguistic units, particles, like phonemes and morphemes (morphemes are working units of language, somewhat similar to what are commonly called words), and go on to the larger problems of sentences and paragraphs working together, that is, to wave and field. Here they conceive that "Language is trimodally structured into semiautonomous but interlocking modes—phonology, grammar, and lexicon."[7] Thus the tagmemists are concerned with the problems that grammarians have always faced, but they attack, also, most of the larger problems which have hitherto been the province of rhetoric, except that the tag-

[7] Robert E. Longacre, "Some Fundamental Insights of Tagmemics," *Language,* XLI (1965), 65–76; Kenneth L. Pike, "Language as Particle, Wave, and Field," *The Texas Quarterly,* II (1959), 37–54.

memists try to study rhetorical problems with the objectivity that is claimed for the new grammars. Longacre writes, "The goal of tagmemic analysis is not simply to isolate constituents but to reveal relationships." As yet the nontagmemists do not concede that the tagmemists have discovered much that leads to an understanding of language, but theirs is at least a striking approach.

Nor have we heard the last of these proposed grammars. As this book goes to press the linguistic fraternity is recoiling from a slim volume by Prof. Sydney M. Lamb of Yale University, which reads like the manifesto of the next phase of the grammatical revolution, stratificational grammar.[8] Obviously, this is a book to be fought over, and the battle is joined. Lamb is appropriately cautious in his claims; he insists that his statement is tentative, requiring both testing and elaboration, and if he is tentative I must be even more so. The broad outlines, however, seem clear. Lamb is concerned with precise grammatical description, which the older grammars could not provide, but even more he is searching "the structural relationships which underlie the linguistic data," and he seems to be combining at once greater simplicity in his grammatical elements and broader grasp of the role of grammar in language than have most of his predecessors—one is tempted to guess, than any of his predecessors. He recognizes what he calls stratal systems in language, which rely upon dichotomies of *and* as against *or* (that is, choice or no choice), *upward* as against *downward* (that is, toward meaning as against toward phonology), and *ordered* as against *unordered*. These can combine among themselves, so that one gets *unordered downward and* and the like, eight possibilities, and Lamb uses what he calls *tactical analysis* and *realization analysis,* and there you have the basis of grammar. This may sound confusing, presumably because the terms are new and the concepts strange, but it is simple in its outlines, and it seems to point at the essentials of linguistic generation and communication, not at its periphery—some of us have been unhappy because transformations, for example, however useful they may be in some grammatical approaches, certainly do not reflect the working of the human mind. The result is that some grammarians believe that Lamb has gone as far beyond Chomsky as Chomsky went beyond Saussure. If his statement seems a long way from Goold Brown, one can say only that it is. And Lamb will not be the last to reassess grammar.

---

[8] *Outline of Stratificational Grammar* (Washington, D.C.: Georgetown University Press, 1966). As Lamb points out, he is elaborating Louis Hjelmslev's glossematics, but he has extended the approach more than he in his modesty admits. The book contains an appendix by Leonard E. Newell providing samples of stratificational analysis.

This book is no place to evaluate these grammatical statements, to prognosticate their probable futures, or to guess what successors or descendants may appear. It is, however, the place to notice that American students of language, by developing concepts like transformation, tagmemics, and linguistic stratification, are helping to make that supposedly dusty subject, grammar, one of the liveliest fields for study and controversy.

Meanwhile, we should notice the rise of a new sort of persons, whom we might call humanistic engineers. On the whole they do not devise new theories of grammar or develop new ways of using language. Mainly, they have not initiated the revolutions, but they make them work. They simplify the new ideas into generally comprehensible order, and they dramatize them in teachable form. They write; they edit; they lecture. They are the consultants who develop curricula, who teach the graduate students, who upgrade the teachers and bring them the new word, who write the textbooks, who devise new teaching media, who urge on the well-meaning and stimulate the bureaucrats of learning. Concerned with the future, they are able to turn dreams into the future. Of course, this work has always been done, more or less, but any survey of earlier textbook writing will reveal that it was done most haphazardly and usually badly. Now America has a loosely organized but recognized and highly professional body of people who are bound together by their common knowledge and their common purpose. In an area like language and literature they are numbered in the thousands.

They are not much sung. Universities do not name buildings after them, or grant them honorary degrees, or even pay them as much money as the pure scientists and scholars usually command, but they often influence more human beings for more good than do those whose pictures appear in the paper. They are seldom reviewed; they do not appear on the best-seller list; but they may write books that are sold in the thousands and millions, and not books that are skimmed and tossed aside, either—books that are read in labor and anguish, resold and restudied again. Here, indeed, is man affecting language, and language affecting man, but most Americans do not know that these people exist, to say nothing of knowing that they are a sort of freemasonry of learning, a secret society so secret it has no constitution and no officers, though it has, through a natural collusion of publishers and professional groups, its annual meetings, its recognized leaders, its conclaves, its own permeating way of working, a way that in the end does much to channel the interplay of language and minds.

Numerous areas of modern language study and use might attract us, but at least one has such international implications and such widespread concern that we can scarcely ignore it. The subject, of course, is spelling, and here we can record mainly what we have not done. To promote world peace and understanding we have sent billions of dollars, hundreds of thousands of fighting men, tens of thousands of devoted teachers and workers. Meanwhile, all sorts of individuals are concerned about English spelling: I get many letters from individuals asking what they can do. We all know that the world needs a world language, that English shows the greatest promise of becoming a world language, and that its greatest weakness lies in its chaotic spelling. But nothing much is done.

Gestures there have been. There was a Simplified Spelling Board that talked a great deal of sense. The Swedish philanthropist Wenner-Gren set up a foundation, but not much has come of it. Our British cousins are doing a bit better; of George Bernard Shaw's estate, dedicated to spelling reform, some survived the courts; Sir James Pitman has been expending profits from Pitman shorthand to experiment with ITA (Initial Teaching Alphabet) as a better means of teaching youngsters to read, but all the while the fantastic English spelling has grown more fantastic, and Americans must bear more than a limited share of the blame, although Pitman's ITA has been tried in some American schools. Spelling is a vested interest, but it was less vested in the New World than in the Old, and as Jefferson and Franklin saw, something could have been done about it. Nothing was done by the government, however, and private attempts like that of Noah Webster came to little. Spelling reform continued to be a subject for learned discussion and philanthropic generosity throughout the nineteenth century, which resulted in one way or another in random reforms; *catalogue* is now becoming *catalog* and *aesthetic* is commonly *esthetic*.[9] No broad programs, however, are now being pursued or even seriously contemplated. Americans have been notable importers of new words, including many with new spellings, but the NAM and Chambers of Commerce do not promote economy by subsidizing or practicing simpler spelling. The American Legion and the DAR do not discourage future wars by promoting world spelling; candidates do not stand for office on simplified spelling planks. Meanwhile, every time we borrow a *sputnik,* a *czardas,* or a *Phyllostomatidae* the concatenated structure worsens.

Spelling reform, of course, is not easy. It is not a matter of knowledge; we know enough to reform spelling, and have known for a long time. It is a social problem. It can be achieved only if government, industry, education, publication, and large bodies of important people

---

[9] The Mencken/McDavid abridgment of *The American Language,* pp. 483–502, contains a good summary of the movement, and concludes that spelling reform would be less beneficial than is commonly supposed.

believe in it and will sacrifice for it, but at least a start would not be difficult. We could, for example, keep the spelling from growing worse. Rather easily we could set up a board of review which could make recommendations for the spelling of new words, which spellings would be incorporated into dictionaries and become standard usage. Once we had made that start we might do something toward simplifying existing spelling, perhaps along the lines that Pitman has been employing, with apparent success. But as yet the United States, presumably the land of promise, of hospitality to new ideas, of social betterment, of mass movement, has here made no mass move. Attempts like that of the Chicago *Tribune* to spell *night* as *nite* are too few, too scattered, and too poorly planned to have much effect.

Perhaps we can do little more here than to record one abortive attempt, an attempt that has been so little noticed that it may warrant relatively extended treatment. Theodore Roosevelt, a man of many virtues and ingenious vices, was notable for his strong and sometimes precipitate enthusiasms. He was so impressed by new spelling rules promulgated in 1906 by the American Simplified Spelling Board that he ordered the Public Printer to follow these rules and to adopt a list of three hundred simplified spellings in all future government publications. The horror that shuddered through the Government Printing Office spread to Congress, where Democrats and Republicans forgot their differences and rallied *en masse* to denounce this travesty upon Americanism. President Roosevelt countermanded the order, and the nation settled back into the comfortable ways of peace and cumbersome spelling, although one can scarcely refrain from observing that had the President gone on a long vacation at that point, leaving the order behind him, he might have started a spelling reform that could have grown into a significant movement. True, the Spelling Board's improvement could have been improved, but it would not have been difficult to implement, and it is certainly better than what we have now.

The new spelling rules were as follows:[10]

1. When a word begins with or includes *ae* or *oe,* substitute *e:* esthetic, medieval, subpena. But retain the diphthong at the end of a word: alumnæ.[11]
2. When *bt* is pronounced *t,* drop the silent *b:* det, dettor, dout.
3. When -ceed is final, spell it -cede: excede, procede, succede.
4. When *ch* is pronounced like hard *c,* drop the silent *h* except before *e,*

---

[10] Simplified Spelling Board, *Simplified Spelling List* (Washington, D.C.: Government Printing Office, 1906).

[11] For *diphthong,* which concerns sound, not spelling, one should presumably read *digraph* or *ligature,* since the *æ* in *alumnæ* would normally be called a ligature. For clarity the style has been somewhat modernized.

i, and *y:* caracter, corus, eco, mecanic, stomac, tecnical. But retain architect, chemist, monarchy.

5. When a double consonant appears before a final silent *e,* drop the last two letters: bizar, cigaret, gavot, gazet, giraf, program.

6. When a word ends with a double consonant, substitute a single consonant: ad, bil, bluf, clas, dol, dul, eg, glas, les, los, mes, mis.

7. Drop the final silent *e* after a consonant preceded by a short stressed vowel: giv, hav, liv.

8. Drop the final silent *e* in the common words: are, gone, were.

9. Drop the final silent *e* in the unstressed final short syllables: ide, ile, ise, ite, ive (activ, bromid, definit, determin, practis).

10. Drop the silent *e* after *lv* and *rv:* involv, twelv, carv, deserv.

11. Drop the silent *e* after *v* or *z* when preceded by a digraph representing a long vowel or a diphthong: achiev, freez, gauz, sneez.

12. Drop the *e* in final *oe* when it is pronounced *o:* fo, ho, ro, to, wo.

13. When one of the letters in *ea* is silent, drop it: bred, hed, hart.

14. When final *ed* is pronounced *d,* drop the *e:* cald, carrid, employd. But not when a wrong pronunciation will be suggested: bribd, cand.

15. When final *ed* is pronounced *t,* substitute *t:* addrest, shipt, helpt, but not when wrong pronunciation will be suggested: bakt.

16. When *ei* is pronounced like *ie* in brief, substitute *ie:* conciet, deciev, wierd.

17. When a final *ey* is pronounced *y,* drop the *e:* barly, chimny, donky.

18. When final *gh* is pronounced *f,* substitute *f* and drop the silent letter of the preceding digraph: enuf, laf, ruf, tuf.

19. When *gh* is pronounced *g,* drop the silent *h:* agast, gost, goul.

20. When *gm* is final, drop the silent *g:* apothem, diafram, flem.

21. When *gue* is final after a consonant, a short vowel or a digraph representing a long vowel or a diphthong, drop the silent *ue:* tung, catalog, harang, leag, sinagog. But not when a wrong pronunciation would be suggested: rog (rogue), vag (vague).

22. When a final *ise* is pronounced *ize,* substitute *ize:* advertize, advize, rize, wize.

23. When *mb* is final after a short vowel, drop *b:* bom, crum, dum, lim.

24. When *ou* before *l* is pronounced *o,* drop *u:* mold, sholder, but not sol (for soul).

25. When *ough* is final spell *o, u, ock,* or *up,* according to the pronunciation: altho, boro, donut, furlo, tho, thoro, hock, hiccup.

26. When *our* is final and *ou* is pronounced as a short vowel, drop *u:* color, honor, labor.

27. When *ph* is pronounced *f,* substitute *f:* alfabet, emfasis, fotograf.

28. When *re* is final after any consonant save *c,* substitute *er:* center.

29. When *rh* is initial and the *h* is silent, drop it: retoric, rithm.

30. When *sc* is initial and the *c* is silent, drop it: senery, sience.

31. When *u* is silent before a vowel, drop it: bild, garantee, gard, ges.

32. When *y* is between consonants, substitute *i:* analisis, fisix, gipsy, paralize, rime, silvan, tipe.

The resulting three hundred sample words are not very terrifying; the following are those beginning with *a:*

New Form	Old Form	New Form	Old Form
abridgment	abridgement	antipirin	antipyrine
accouter	accoutre	antitoxin	antitoxine
accurst	accursed	apothem	apothegm
acknowledgment	acknowledgement	apprize	apprise
addrest	addressed	arbor	arbour
adz	adze	archeology	archaeology
affixt	affixed	ardor	ardour
altho	although	armor	armour
anapest	anapaest	artizan	artisan
anemia	anaemia	assize	assise
anesthesia	anaesthesia	ax	axe
anesthetic	anaesthetic		

The following are samples throughout the remainder of the alphabet:

New Form	Old Form	New Form	Old Form
bark	barque	hock	hough
blest	blessed	humor	humour
behavior	behaviour	jail	gaol
brazier	brasier	judgment	judgement
bun	bunn	kist	kissed
caliper	calliper	lacrimal	lachrymal
center	centre	licorice	liquorice
cue	queue	mama	mamma
cyclopedia	cyclopaedia	mold	mould
defense	defence	odor	odour
deposit	deposite	pedagog	pedagogue
dike	dyke	phenix	phoenix
dram	drachm	phenomenon	phaenomenon
dulness	dullness	pigmy	pygmy
Eolian	Aeolian	plow	plough
eon	aeon	polip	polype
epaulet	epaulette	primeval	primaeval
era	aera	program	programme
esophagus	aesophagus	prolog	prologue
esthetic	aesthetic	propt	propped
ether	aether	pur	purr
exercize	exercise	quartet	quartette
fagot	faggot	rancor	rancour
fantasm	phantasm	raze	rase
fantasy	phantasy	reconnoiter	reconnoitre
fantom	phantom	rime	rhyme
favorite	favourite	rumor	rumour
fiber	fibre	saber	sabre
gage	gauge	silvan	sylvan
gild	guild	simitar	scimitar
gipsy	gypsy	sipt	sipped
good-by	good-bye	sithe	scythe
hiccup	hiccough	skilful	skillful

New Form	Old Form	New Form	Old Form
smolder	smoulder	thoro	thorough
somber	sombre	thru	through
stedfast	steadfast	vigor	vigour
subpena	subpoena	wagon	waggon
succor	succour	whipt	whipped
sulfate	sulphate	whisky	whiskey
sulfur	sulphur	wilful	willful
sumac	sumach	wo	woe
synonim	synonyme	wrapt	wrapped
tho	though		

Many of these words, like *center* for *centre, jail* for *gaol,* and *era* for *aera* have already found their way into common use, but many more have not, and they would simplify the learning process. No one is likely to be able to figure how many millions of dollars worth of schoolroom space, how many teacher-months and student-years of time are wasted teaching and learning a junk-pile accumulation of spellings, but the total must be large. So far as spelling is concerned, Yankee rock-ribbed conservatism has triumphed over Yankee ingenuity.

Humor is characteristic of maturity, especially intellectual maturity. Children display little sense of humor, and as awareness develops, humor is usually crude, tending to horseplay and cruelty. Hence, if Americans are approaching maturity in their sense for language, we should expect them to use language increasingly for humorous purposes; although using statistics on such a subject would in itself be humorous, one can easily find evidence of sophisticated playing with language. One evidence appears in what seems to be a growing body of linguistic folklore. For example, we are told that an electronic translator produced "The meat is rotten, but the whisky is all right," this purporting to represent the original, "The spirit is willing but the flesh is weak." No doubt machine translators produce howlers; at least human translators do, but whether this particular gem reflects the dark unfathomed caves of mechanical process, or the equally unfathomed processes of human wit, can probably not be known. I have heard the tale in at least a half dozen forms, factually attributed to at least a dozen different sources, including persons as widely diffused as Pierre Salinger and Nikita Khrushchev. Folklore has been at work, also, with "a blind idiot" as the supposed translation of "out of sight, out of mind," and many others. The following fun with American English redundancy has been amusing linguists of late; actually, languages work only by a degree of redundancy, and a sober theory suggests that the redundance of the language determines its flexibility, but the following results from no serious study:

LADLE RAT ROTTEN HUT

Wants pawn term, dare worsted ladle gull hoe lift wetter murder inner ladle cordage honor itch offer lodge dock florish. Disc ladle gull orphan worry ladle cluck wetter putty ladle rat hut, end fur disc raisin pimple caulder ladle rat rotten hut. Wan moaning rat rotten hut's murder colder inset: "Ladle rat rotten hut, heresy ladle basking winsome burden barter and shirker cockles. Tick disc ladle basking tudor cordage offer groin murder hoe lifts honor udder site offer florist. Shaker lake, dun stopper laundry wrote, end yonder nor sorghum stenches dun stopper torque wet strainers."

"Hoe-cake, murder," resplendent ladle rat rotten hut, end tickle ladle basking an stuttered oft. Honor wrote tudor cordage offer groin murder, ladle rat rotten hut mitten anomalous woof.

"Wail, wail, wail," set disc wicket woof, "evanescent ladle rat rotten hut! Wares or putty ladle gull goring wizard ladle basking?"

"Armor goring tumor groin murder's," reprisal ladle gull. "Grammars seeking bet. Armor ticking arson burden barter end shirker cockles."

"O hoe! Heifer blessing woke," setter wicket woof, butter taught tomb shelf, "Oil tickle shirt court tudor cordage offer groin murder. Oil ketchup wetter letter, an den—O bore!"

Soda wicket woof tucker shirt court, end whinney retched a cordage offer groin murder, picket inner widow an sore debtor pore oil worming worse lion inner bet. Inner flesh disc abdominal woof lipped honor betting adder rope. Zany pool dawn a groin murder's nut cup an gnat gun, any curdle dope inner bet.

Inner ladle wile ladle rat rotten hut a raft attar cordage an ranker dough bell. "Comb ink, sweat hard," setter wicket woof, disgracing is verse. Ladle rat rotten hut entity bet rum end stud buyer groin murder's bet. "Oh grammer," crater ladle gull, "Wart bag icer gut! A nervous sausage bag ice!" "Buttered lucky chew whiff, doling," whiskered disc ratchet woof, wetter wicket small. "Oh grammar, water bag noise! A nervous sore suture anomalous prognosis!" "Buttered small your whiff," inserter woof, ants mouse worse waddling. "Oh grammar, water bag mousey gut! A nervous sore suture bag mouse!"

Daze worry on forger nut gull's lest warts. Oil offer sodden throne offer carvers an sprinkling otter bet, disc curl an bloat Thursday woof ceased pore ladle rat rotten hut an garbled erupt.

Mural: Yonder nor sorghum stenches shut ladle gulls stopper torque wet strainers.[12]

All in all, the intelligentsia do help steer the language, although probably more indirectly than directly, and perhaps mainly in ways of which they are themselves unaware.

---

[12] This tale exists in many forms because many people have had fun contributing to it, so that it has become a bit of folklore, a communal folk production of the literate mind, if that is not a contradiction in terms. I quote it from *Word Study*, XXVIII, no. 5 (May, 1953), 4. The editor pronounced it anonymous; it has been associated especially with the name of Professor H. C. Chace.

22

AMERICAN ENGLISH ABROAD

British Mother Tongue has never liked to admit that her American offspring was legitimate. Conceived in whatever kind of transoceanic, backwoods doings, the foundling was unwanted and her existence ignored. As American speech grew and tended to take on character, it was first ridiculed and then dismissed in condescending pity. So far as we know, one Francis Moore, a companion of Oglethorpe, writing sometime before 1744, recorded the first Americanism, barring Indian words which subsequently became Americanisms, by describing the site of Savannah as follows: "It stands upon the flat of a Hill; the Bank of the River (which they in barbarous English call a *bluff*) is steep, and about forty-five foot perpendicular." What is barbaric about the word *bluff* he does not explain, nor does he notice that he requires a number of conventionally acceptable words to do what the single American word *bluff* accomplishes, but the method of ridicule by calling names is relatively easy, and in the centuries ahead it was to become familiar.

British reviewers were perhaps the worst. Their greatest charity was damnation with faint praise, but the anti-American anathemas of Gifford, Jeffrey, Southey, Sydney Smith, and their associates are somewhat blunted by the fact that they treated Keats, Byron, Wordsworth, Leigh Hunt, and Coleridge little better. No man with liberal persuasions could expect justice from conservative reviewers, Whig or Tory, and the sons of the American Revolution were inevitably looked upon as dangerous radicals to be put down with any weapon at hand. Even travelers, however, who were generally appreciative of American hosts and considerate of the hosts' feelings, condemned American speech. Contempt was so common and so acrimonious that it bothered even some sojourning Britons: Captain Frederick Marryat complained of Dickens that "it is largely due to his influence that there is still today in

Europe such a prejudice against things American. He constantly exaggerated the worst characteristics of Americanisms, and could write, for instance, a whole passage ridiculing the abuse of the verb 'to fix.' "[1] Emerson, a man not easily stirred to retort, condemned Dickens' reporting (*Journal*, Nov. 25, 1842), saying that the author of *American Notes* had "picked up and noted with eagerness each local phrase" and had then so concocted them that "no such conversations ever occur in this country in real life."

Some critics tempered their derision with pity. Captain Thomas Hamilton complained in *Men and Manners in America* that "The amount of bad grammar in circulation is very great; that of barbarisms enormous." He objected that *"missionary* had become *missionairy,"* apparently unaware that the American pronunciation merely preserves the Latin accent and an earlier British pronunciation, and that the British usage placing the accent on the first syllable was in his time a relatively recent development. He complained that *angel* and *danger* have become in the New World *ângel* and *dânger,* and whatever he may mean by this circumflex, possibly that in American speech the initial sound is likely to be a pure vowel instead of the British diphthong, he clinches the matter by adding "etc." He derides the development of new uses of *clever,* apparently unaware that *clever* had been used in England at least as early as 1732 to mean *genial,* and that Goldsmith had written, "Let us be merry and clever." He continued,

The privilege of barbarizing the King's English is assumed by all ranks and conditions of men. Such words as *slick, kedge,* and *boss,* it is true, are rarely used by the better orders; but they assume unlimited liberty in the use of *expect, reckon, guess,* and *calculate,* and perpetrate other conversational anomalies with remorseless impunity.

Of these words, *boss* can be considered an Americanism since it had no standing in England and had grown in the New World under the influence of Dutch, but the others are all old, although some like *kedge* (1627), which meant "to warp a ship," *guess* and *slick* (both used by Chaucer), had fallen out of fashion. Even *reckon,* which goes back to Old English, had been used as early as 1603 in the sense which probably disturbed Hamilton, that of *believe, assume,* or *understand* in their more general uses. He was probably objecting to the development of *expect* (1520) and *calculate* (1750) as auxiliaries; they were common in England as main verbs.

---

[1] Marryat, cited earlier, also objected to the American use of *fix,* although less extensively; see also Florence Marryat, *The Life and Letters of Captain Marryat,* 2 vols. (London: R. Bentley & Son, 1872).

Hamilton, however, does not differ much from Captain Basil Hall, Mrs. Frances Trollope, and many others in his horror of the "remorseless impunity" of American speakers, but he is notable for his prediction of impending disaster, as in the following:

> Unless the present progress of change be arrested by an increase of taste and judgment in the more educated classes, there can be no doubt that, in another century, the dialect of the Americans will become utterly unintelligible to an Englishman, and that nation will be cut off from the advantages arising from their participation in British literature.

Presumably Hamilton, who seems to have been a generally genial guest, regretted this imminent doom of the New World, but he need not have worried; the century that he allotted to witness the confounding of American speech elapsed more than thirty years ago.

Toward the end of the nineteenth century, however, and on into the twentieth, this pity for backwoodsmen changed to rage and insult that have not always stopped short of bad manners. While the supposed American barbarisms stayed safely on the western side of the Atlantic, where they could be expected to corrupt only the native barbarians, Englishmen could scoff or pity or even send an occasional missionary, from whom the benighted might hear a bit of good English. All this changed, however, when Americanisms began to return across the water to corrupt the homeland.

The reaction was long, loud, and emotional—to avoid any unkind terms like *bigoted*.[2] For example, the following is from the London *Saturday Review,* December 13, 1913:

> When the American Ambassador tells us, in some degree at least seriously, that better English is spoken in America than in England, it is really too much. . . . The Americans are . . . rich. They are, or seem to be, confident of themselves. They excel at the business of games. They make things "hum." But it is absurd to pretend they speak good English. Their English, and their spelling of English, which we are sorry to say is imitated by English writers who should know better, are most unpleasant. Their twang is sometimes so.

To use the writer's own terminology, a statement like this is becoming more "absurd" every year, notably because the writer is here doing no more than embody his own self-righteousness. A word like *twang* has

---

[2] Mencken has been the most assiduous collector of this material. It appears *passim* in his work, but notably pp. 31–88 of the McDavid revision. Many of my quotations will be lifted from him without further notice. Engaging, also, is Gilbert M. Tucker, *American English* (New York: Alfred A. Knopf, 1921), from whose work I shall borrow occasionally.

no linguistic meaning; it is a way of being unkind. A "twang" is nothing that a student of language can identify; it is a way the other fellow speaks, and this sort of condemnation of anybody who does not speak the local British dialects has been going on in England, as elsewhere, for a long time. For example, John of Trevisa, a contemporary of Chaucer's, complained that because of the "commyxstion and medling" (two words which mean "mingling") in parts of the country "longage ys apeyred" (language is damaged), "and some vseþ strange wlaffyng, chytering, harrying, and garryng grisbittyng." This is not easy to modernize accurately, but it means something like the following: "Some use outlandish mumbling, chattering, rasping, and grating, chomping up their words." We cannot, of course, describe any Middle English dialect on the basis of these epithets; we cannot from Trevisa's description reconstruct the language that irked him. We can know only that he did not like it. Being a southerner, he attacked the northern dialects as a matter of course, saying, "Al þe longage of þe Norþumbreas, and specialych at ʒork, is so scharp, slytting, and frotyng, and vnschape, þat we Souþron men may þat longage vneþe vndurstonde" (All the language of the Northumbrians, and especially of York, is so harsh, piercing, grating, and formless that we southerners can scarcely understand that language). As is to be expected, students of Middle English do not find northern speech any more formless than southern speech, nor Trevisa's charge of "piercing and grating" any more revealing than the *Saturday Review*'s "twang."

The explanation, presumably, is to be sought in what sociologists call ethnocentrism, the very widespread prejudice that leads all groups to think they are better than other groups, that leads primitive societies all over the world to call themselves "The People," and to assume that all other groups are somehow subhuman. This attitude on the part of British speakers toward the English language is perhaps best expressed by a writer in the *New Statesman,* June 25, 1927. The revelation came in connection with a meeting in London of the International Conference on English, which had as its purpose reconciling differences between British and American usage. The *Statesman* was not interested in reconciliation. "Why should we offer to discuss the subject at all with America?" the periodical asked. . . . "For all serious lovers of the English language it is America that is the only dangerous enemy." At this point the mild-mannered and scholarly editor of the American *Saturday Review* used the word *Anglicism* alongside the word *Americanism.* For the *New Statesman* this was to add outrage to inanity; the writer explained: "What Dr. Canby meant by it, presumably, was some usage which his own country had not adopted," and went on to insist, "He claimed for America a right equal to our own to decide what is English and what is not! That is a claim which we cannot too emphatically repudiate. . . . The English language is our own."

This sort of attitude is understandable but not very defensible. Many Britons consider the English language their private possession and become furious if they see themselves as losing their autocratic power. Momism is probably as common in language as in family relations. Of course, many cultured Englishmen know better, but attitudes like that embodied in the following news dispatch are by no means restricted to the uneducated:

> LONDON (Reuters)—A purist today took issue with British use of "meaningless prepositions, in the American manner."
> F. E. Bailey, in a letter to the Daily Telegraph, complained about a story headed "Facing up to the heat."
> He declared that since World War II British newspapers had been spattered with such phrases, and the result "is murder for an English child learning its own language."
> Mr. Bailey, the purist, declared:
> "One does not meet up with one's girl friend, one meets her.
> "One does not sit in on a committee, one sits on it.
> "One does not test out a car, one tests it.
> "Nor does one try out a horse, or a recipe, one tries them."[3]

No speaker of American English would wish to have the blood of murdered British innocents on his hands, but one doubts that the impact of American usage is so lethal among British youth as Mr. Bailey implies. In the first place, the use of words like *up* and *in* as parts of modern complex verbs—they are, I take it, what Mr. Bailey means by *meaningless prepositions*—is not restricted in Great Britain to postwar journalists. Such locutions occur as early as Old English and in most recent writers, but just to provide a prewar nonjournalistic sample I opened Richard Hughes' *The Innocent Voyage* (published in the United States as *High Wind in Jamaica*) and noticed the following:

> . . . if it was a weekday, the meat was put to cool on the cabin shelf, ready to warm *up* in tomorrow's soup, and the crew and children ate the liquor with biscuit; but if it was Sunday, the captain took the lump of meat and with a benevolent air cut it *up* in small pieces, as if indeed for a nursery, and mixed it *up* with the vegetables. [The italics do not appear in the original.]

One should note that Mr. Hughes is here speaking in his own voice, not through the mouth of an American, and that his standing at Oxford

---

3 Reprinted here from *The New York Times,* August 15, 1959. I owe the reference to Mr. David Keightley.

University and his reputation as one of the leading novelists of our day should assure even a British purist that he writes the English language.

That this sample is not exceptional would seem to be confirmed by scholarly studies in England. A rough check of the entries in Frederick T. Wood's *English Verbal Idioms*[4] reveals that most of the verbal phrases he records are not recent and are used on both sides of the water—one should note that for Wood "English" apparently refers to the language as it is used in England, not to the English language as distinct from other languages, but I have checked his entries against American publications that are avowedly local. That is, most of the phrases recorded by Wood and utilizing "prepositions in the American manner" are not recently borrowed Americanisms. Some are clearly Briticisms; the entries under *do,* for example, include *do down* in the sense of cheat (He would do down his best friend) and *do out* in the sense of clean or make tidy (While you do out the dining room, I'll tidy up the study), neither of which I have heard in this country. Certainly they are not common enough so that they could have found their subversive way into British English through the treachery of the flicks. On the other hand, some *do*-phrases common in the United States do not appear in Wood, for example, *do time for* in the sense of serve a sentence in jail.

Nor are Mr. Bailey's prepositions equally meaningless. He says that "One does not meet up with one's girl friend." *To meet up with* is presumably an Americanism; at least it is so accepted by the *Dictionary of Americanisms,* and one can say only that it is redundant, that redundancy can be expected from careless speakers everywhere, but that this particular locution is not used by careful speakers on either side of the Atlantic. Thus the difficulty is not that British speakers are adopting Americanisms but that they adopt inept Americanisms. They need only borrow more wisely.

Mr. Bailey is on even less certain ground in some of his other animadversions. He includes the phrase "sit in on a committee." This construction may have developed in Britain, but I do not recall having heard it in the United States, and I doubt that it is common here. I suspect that Mr. Bailey is here unconsciously falling into Dickens' old trick of misquoting the locution before ridiculing it. The construction he probably means to attack is "to sit in on the meeting of a committee." Here the little word *in* is far from meaningless; *to sit on a committee* and *to sit in on the meeting of a committee* are quite different. The construction with *in on* implies that the person in question is not a member of the committee but that he attends a meeting of the committee as an observer, and if a language can make that distinction with

---

4 (London: The Macmillan Co.; New York: St. Martin's Press, 1964).

one two-letter word, it is not doing badly so far as economy is concerned. If the British have not as yet developed the locution *to sit in on,* they will do well to borrow it.

Mr. Bailey's other examples are more complicated linguistically, and I shall attempt to do little with them here, although they could be defended; in American English, at least, *to try* and *to try out* reveal relatively sharp and useful distinctions. Apparently, the British and American dialects have drifted somewhat apart in their use of verbs like *test* and *try* and in the employment of particles like *out,* but this is not to say that the American uses do not have meaning, that all changes in Britain are *prima facie* good, and that all changes in the United States inevitably bad. The changes, whether we like them or not, are part of the broad drift of English in modern times; that question I shall endeavor to discuss in the next chapter.

Here, as elsewhere, the more inconsequential the points at issue, the angrier people become about them. The following is from "Speaking of Books," edited by Donald P. Adams, who could never have been accused of latitudinarianism in usage; this particular column was signed by J. D. Furnas:[5]

An anonymous writer in the august London Times Literary Supplement is unhappy about the British edition of a recent American translation from the French of "Portrait of a Man Unknown" by Nathalie Sarraute. The sore point is not the quality of the novel or the faithfulness of the rendering but the "Americanisms" in the text, including "even the spelling." Surmising that the book was reproduced "by some sort of photo-lithographic process from the American edition," this cultivated reviewer-with-alarm goes on:

"By the reason of relative costs we are likely to see more of this. It is the kind of thing about which people get cross. Indeed the occasion might well be thought to have arisen for an Anglo-American agreement on spelling (as well, perhaps, as some agreement on idiomatic usages in the written, if not the spoken, language)."

Presumably we need have no doubt as to what sort of "agreement" the gentleman has in mind; unless Americans agree to use British spelling in anything that might conceivably be printed abroad, how can British readers be protected from getting cross? I do not recall hearing any American complain about getting cross because he has to read continental classics in British spelling and idiom, nor do many American publishers respell standard British writers, but a British publisher has no qualms at all about asking an American writer to have his work respelled to palliate local custom. I have long wondered whether Sinclair

[5] *The New York Times Book Review,* Feb. 28, 1960, p. 2.

Lewis approved the travesty of *Babbitt* that was printed in London,[6] or whether the British publisher just quietly altered the original. It seems highly unlikely that Lewis could have approved.

Babbitt may not be a great novel, or even Lewis' best work, but it is Americana, a revealing portrait, perhaps a satire, of an aspect of American life. It is a document of importance, and is so recognized the world over. No doubt it has contributed greatly to the European concept of Americans as gross money-grubbers, and thus it may have done, inadvertently, a disservice to international understanding, but if it is to be reprinted at all, it should be reproduced as a document, as accurately as may be. It is not, in England. In the British editions Babbitt protests that he is not a "labour agitator," envies graduates of "Princetown," drinks at "public houses" where he occasionally downs martinis that have lost their "vigour," wears a "derby" and a "waistcoat," has friends who address him as "old dear," patronizes "news-stalls" or gets his paper from the "paper-carrier," listens to "gramophones," has "neighbours" and in front of his house "turf" where robins "clamour," suffers from "malaise," drives a "good motor," which consumes "petrol," uses "tyres," "tyre cases," and "sparking plugs"; he races "trams" and "tram cars" past "chemist shops" and "hoardings" advertising "cinema films" in "picture theatres," while observing "lorries" and "goods vans," driven by "lorry drivers" making their way to "goods stations." And so on to the "business centre."

How any scholar can consider this perversion of a text less than outrageous I do not know, but I am concerned, not with editorial misdemeanors for themselves, but rather for the light they cast on the impact of language and language customs upon man. Americans tend to be modest about their language, probably because they are inured to being looked down upon. A similar becoming modesty is harder to find in England, however; the English are a polite people, and although they tend to consider their American cousins more boorish than they, they are usually polite enough not to express this opinion in the presence of an American, at least on most subjects. When the native language is under discussion, however, Britons who would never make fun of American political institutions feel no compunctions about ridiculing American speech, apparently assuming that insults in language are to be applauded, since they are part of the war that all right-thinking speakers of English should wage against the corruptions of the mother tongue.

I recall a dinner party given by an English gentleman who had lived

---

[6] Published in Britain, Jonathan Cape, 1932, and variously reprinted, Traveller's Library, Florin Books, New Small Crown, and in 1959, Panther Books. The version was called to my attention by John Mershon, Groton, Conn.

abroad enough to have lost whatever insularity he may have been born to. The guests were mostly English, but they included two or three Americans, and the conversation turned to British and American speech. One woman was unusually obnoxious; Americans, she said, were debasing English. They talked with a nauseating nasal twang, used bad grammar, spoke in such a slovenly manner that anyone who knew English had difficulty understanding them, and were now corrupting British youth by filling English theaters with their disgusting cinema films. I gather the Americans did not mind; they had all lived in England long enough to have become accustomed to this sort of thing, but the host was perturbed. He tried to change the subject; he tried to divert the lady by admiring her dress. He did everything that politeness and his position as host would permit, and he was abetted by other Englishmen, but the lady was not to be stopped. She seemed to feel that truth augments through iteration.

At length one of the young Americans spoke up, praising British speech, as he supposed, at its best. He had been invited to attend a meeting of the Oxford Union, where he had delighted in the addresses by Philip Guedalla, Lord David Cecil, and other masters of English diction. They were witty and urbane. "But do you know," he continued, using his best imitation of cultured British speech, "if I hadn't been passably conversant with the dialect of the American Negro, I couldn't have understood those chaps."

There was a gasp, followed by general laughter. Later, the young man apologized to me, not for having put the lady in her place—that, he thought, he owed to his host—but he did not want to appear guilty of racial prejudice. He knew, however, that the lady was enough of a snob so that she would be horrified, which apparently she was. At least we heard no more from her that evening about the crudities of American linguistic practices.

As a matter of fact, as my young friend well knew, there was enough truth beneath his remark to give color to his seeming naïveté. There is, of course, no such thing as the "dialect of the American Negro." Cultured black Americans cannot be distinguished in their speech from cultured white Americans, and ignorant black residents speak very much as do their ignorant white neighbors, from whom, during the generations, they have mainly learned their speech. Of course, locutions from Africa have affected American dialects, as I observed earlier; a modest number of imported words have been recorded, and some descendants of Africans may preserve remnants of African grammars. In the ghettos, dialects are developing rapidly today, some of them intended to deceive the police and other representatives of the "establishment." To date, at least two such dialects have been identified, and doubtless there are more, but these developments stem from social conditions; blackness or whiteness as such does not determine speech. In reality, many Americans with African ancestry use language beautifully, and if there is any difference in linguistic ability based on race, the evidence suggests that descendants from at least some African groups—and Afro-Americans, again, are not one thing—have special aptitude for language. However that may be, southern American vowels, as we have observed in an earlier chapter, show many remarkable similarities to the vowels of British Received Standard, and thus speakers from the northern United States may find that they understand British English more easily if they have had a Negro servant from the South, or have had some continued association with uneducated black speakers.

No doubt some British lifting of the eyebrow in the presence of American usage stems from an association of cultured American speech with certain sorts of uncultured British speech. We have seen in an earlier chapter that this similarity has an honorable ancestry, but most speakers of English, either British or American, know little of linguistic ancestry. Of course, the modern Briton might remind himself that the process which gave American speech its character did much to give the whole English language its vigor. After the Norman invasion, English ceased to be an official language in England, and was preserved by the little people, the poor people, the middle and lower classes. The result is that the bulk of the Modern English words of daily living are English, not French or Latin, and the language is the more terse and vigorous for the presence of these short, generally explosive words. I should be very far from saying that as English is more vigorous speech for relying upon the talk of common people, American English is more vigorous than British English because it grew from the speech of common men and escaped the elegancies of the court in London. If this is true, it is scarcely certain and obvious, but at least the analogy is there, and it provides no basis for Anglomania in language.

If the British are a bit provincial in their reception of English dialects not native to the British Isles, they are the spirit of latitudinarianism in foreign borrowing when compared to their neighbors across the English Channel, the French. So far as their native language is concerned, custodians of *l'esprit gallois* seem to have lost at once their sense of balance and their sense of humor; presumably the current French isolationism in language is a passing fad, but it provides a revealing example of the hysteria that can develop when language change becomes involved with pride and affronted nationalism. We may marvel that a great nation and people like the French, with a universally admired tradition of wit, learning, and culture, should become perturbed and even frightened at the borrowing of a few thousand words—mainly technical words known only to specialists. The spectacle may suggest the becurled spinster of the cartoons who trembles at the sight of a mouse, but it reveals in dramatic form the vagaries of man with his language, and in this instance evidence of the impact of English, especially American English, abroad. All this becomes the more ironical when one remembers that extensive borrowings from French have helped English become the great language it is, and that French itself grew from a Celtic base, overrun by Frankish German, which in turn was so inundated by Latin that French is now called a Romance language. But hysteria is no promoter of a sense of irony.

A sentence like the following disturbs modern Frenchmen: "Jean Dupont, un business-man très up-to-date, a donné une surprise party dans son bungalow ce dernier week-end."[7] Apparently the consciousness of this sort of thing grew after the second World War, when French lunch habits were upset by American *milk bars* and *snack bars* where *hot dogs* and *sandwiches* were available, and where winebibbing Frenchmen could drink milk. French butcher shops were invaded by *viande hachée,* sometimes frankly labeled *hamburger* and pronounced *om-bourzhay.* This sort of thing got worse, especially in *le sport,* where *un prize fighter* in *le ring* could be *knockouté* in the *first round. Un lob* became popular with *tennis men,* and at the racetrack a lucky bettor might pick an *outsider* (pronounced *ootseedair*). Horrified purists remarked the naturalization of *ice creme, gangster, groggy, best-seller, pin-up, cover girl, black out, fair-play, goal, hold-up, living room, shoot, sportsman, pull-over, bleu jeans, footballer, manager, pipe-line, sex-appeal,* and *strip-tease,* although *jazz, cowboy, movie,* and *Hollywood* (pronounced *ollyvoot*) were naturalized before Americanisms became a menace and hence are causing little concern. Similarly, *okay* and *camping* pass, apparently sterilized by their acceptance as international words.

The trouble mounted. Polls called *Gallups* (pronounced *ga-loop*) were conducted to determine the threat of these new words to the French language and to French culture; the *Académie Française* moved to expunge inappropriate borrowings from its forthcoming dictionary of universal French, and *L'Office du Vocabulaire Français* mobilized its

---

[7] The sentence, probably concocted for exemplary purposes, appeared in "Too Much English Impassions French," *The New York Times,* March 29, 1959, p. 1. For other accounts in the *Times,* which I shall cite without further acknowledgment, see Aug. 5, 1964, and *The New York Times Magazine,* Nov. 29, 1959, p. 52; and June 28, 1959, pp. 11, 44. I am indebted to Mr. George Rathmell for collecting material which was readily available only in Paris.

3500 members and offered a prize to the newspaper that would show the greatest respect for the French language by eschewing foreignisms. The Office of French Vocabulary designated November 30, 1959, as "a day without accidence of vocabulary," and recruited five hundred volunteers to scan the press on that day, while editors and writers were warned "to be on guard against misuse of French words and letting English words slip in." Everyone hoped, of course, that some newspaper would remain pure; none did. *Parisien Libéré* received a loving cup for publishing with a mere half dozen misdemeanors, but, as the Paris *Herald Tribune* put it, "Other newspapers got dirty looks for making as many as 60 [mistakes]."

Meanwhile, *Le Figaro,* popular Parisian daily, conducted a weekly feature to determine which of the new Anglicisms were fit to find a place in French; was a word like *mixer,* the word for a culinary electrical device for combining foods, really necessary? Could not a Gallicism, or something approaching a Gallicism, be found? Could not the new word *parking* be abandoned for something more French, *parcage* for example, since people apparently would not tolerate *stationnement?* Can a French *demarreur* properly be called a *starter?* What would happen if the popular translation *homme d'affaires* for a businessman should lead also to *femme d'affaires?* And was not French culture itself in danger, threatened with becoming *la civilisation cocalcoolique?*

Perhaps the most amazing evidence revealing this to-do is provided by a book titled *Parlez-vous Franglais?* by a professor at the Sorbonne, René Etiemble, a volume of 376 pages, which is said to have sold widely.[8] Etiemble has lived in both England and the United States, and he professes to love both the American and the British people, but he professes, also, to believe that speakers of English are in league, probably deliberately so, to destroy the French language, and with it the French spirit, French culture, anything French. He left his post at the University of Chicago, he says, partly because he could no longer endure the "air-conditioned nightmare" of American life, and partly to awaken his countrymen, who, he says, when they are bereft of their language, can face only "decadence and servitude." He objects to American slang, but he fears even more the words of "American merchants," words like *tee-shirt, sweater, hitchhiking, handshake, welcome, toilette* (borrowed, of course, from French, although in a different sense), *jeep, surprise party,* and *cheeseburger steak.* Even French scientific language, he asserts, is being "sabotaged." In fact, one would be tempted to surmise that the learned author is pulling our leg, and that the whole is an

---

[8] (Paris: Gallimard, 1964). I have seen no translation as yet.

elaborate satire upon the French purists, except that the book is too long, too vituperative, and too repetitious to be very funny. Personally, since I respect Etiemble's scholarship, I hope that *Parlez-vous Franglais?* was a jovial hoax turned with such skill that it was taken seriously by the people it was intended to satirize, but whatever the author's intent, the international comment is the same. Jest or jeremiad, it has been taken seriously by many Frenchmen, and in the face of that fact one can only marvel.

If the witty Etiemble was pulling our leg, we may be quite sure that Charles de Gaulle, acting as the elected embodiment of the French people, was no leg-puller. He spoke with military firmness and dispatch against the national "enemy," English. Apparently the declaration of war was prompted by two French-Canadians, M. Paul Gerin-Lajoie, Quebec Minister of Education, and Pierre Laporte, Quebec Minister of Culture, who emerged from a meeting of the French cabinet, December 2, 1965, jubilating that "France and Quebec are going to fight franglais together," and promising that "a congress would be held next year to promote French scientific vocabulary, which, until now . . . has been heavily infiltrated by English."[9] Meanwhile, President de Gaulle announced formation of a High Commission for the Defense and Expansion of the French Language, under the personal chairmanship of Premier Georges Pompidou. A distinguished body was assembled, and by the time Lent was over,[10] Pompidou was ready to address the committee at his official residence, l'Hôtel Matignon. He reminded his audience that at the founding of the United Nations, Russian, Chinese, Spanish, and English had been recognized as official languages along with French; this, he said, had been "a blow difficult to endure," but French had continued to evidence its "vitality and utility" in the subsequent fight against these assaults from without. Meanwhile, "The most insidious attacks have come from within. Writers, professors, ordinary citizens who love our language have never ceased to manifest their indignation at the infamous abuse (*le brassage abusif*) of our language at the hands of that other foreign language." M. Pompidou used the singular, and that the offending tongue is not Spanish, Russian, or Chinese, becomes apparent when he goes on to explain that French is suffering in this unequal combat, and is the more in need of help, because the foreign attacker has at its disposal not only the traditional means of diffusion (presumably printing), but also songs, which can be disseminated *par le*

---

[9] See the Paris *Herald Tribune* for the date; United Press International disseminated a long account widely published in the United States and elsewhere under dates December 4 and 5.
[10] I quote from *Le Figaro,* March 26, 1966.

disque ou par l'image, that is, by records, moving pictures, and television.

Possibly the proper reaction to this speech would have been: Just wait till he finds out about tapes! More seriously one might recall that language is the helpmeet of man, that she has never been unfaithful to him, and that there is no likelihood she ever will be, that she has always given him anything he wanted if he wanted it badly enough. France has declined as a world power in the last half century and is likely to decline more, but not from any infidelity of the French language, which will continue to provide the French people with a means of achieving anything of which they are capable, and this in spite of some hospitality to guests from abroad. She reminds one of Desdemona; she deserves more trust from her insanely jealous Othello than some of her well-wishers seem ready to accord her. Meanwhile, one might observe that the campaign seems not to be going well. President de Gaulle warned French scientists, especially those subsidized by the government, to avoid Anglicization, but I notice in a current journal *le grammaire transformationelle dite Chomskienne* ("the so-called Chomskyite transformational grammar"), which would seem to be a clear case of corruption from the United States.

Something similar was attempted in Spain, although little has come of it. In the spring of 1964 the Royal Spanish Academy at Madrid launched a campaign to protect the Spanish language from Anglo-American corruptions, notably those that have come via Hollywood, but the movement did not amount to much. Adults continued to patronize the Cow Boy Bar and the adults' offspring increasingly sported 'American sweat shirts emblazoned with COACH in large letters. In Barcelona, the second Spanish city, the Instituto des Estudios Norteamericanos, a goodwill gesture associated with the United States Information Service, has burgeoned into a full-fledged college, rapidly becoming self-supporting, and many an ambitious Spaniard who has long been kept out of the modern world to which he aspires, believes that English provides the passport to a better life.

Italy has been enduring somewhat similar devastation from American borrowings. For centuries the conviction has been that a locution not found in Dante's *Commedia,* or stemming from such a word, can have no official existence. Now, however, some terms are too raucously obvious to be ignored. There is *spyders,* for example, a term for sports cars; sports cars did not exist in the *Paradiso,* not even in the *Inferno,* and the word is obviously a phonetic spelling of British or American *speeders.* And what is one to do about *strip tease, baby doll, Latin lover,* and *jet set?* Not to mention *topless* when used to describe female bathing apparel, which is felt to be offensive both linguistically and morally.

Faced with inroads of American words, Vienna is maintaining her traditional sophistication rather better than is Paris. Apparently terms like *gimmick, layout, good-will mission,* and *do-it-yourself,* have become common and occasion no more than a shrug. Of the dozens of different hair sprays, it is said that not one carries the German word for *spray;* manufacturers explain that "the English word has more sales appeal to the Austrian customer." American music is provided by *combos* that play *rock and roll* and give themselves English names in the American manner, *Rockets* and *Hurricanes.*

Outside Europe the reception of American English has been mixed. In general, words flow from one of the Americas to the other without attracting much notice, with the Latin Americans borrowing especially words associated with the dynamic machines and concepts of modern society. *Bulldozer, jeep,* and *robot* are picked up entire, however they are pronounced; *astronautas* is not changed much, and one might notice that it is the American *astronaut* not the Russian *cosmonaut* that is borrowed. Meanwhile, each *brecha* (breakthrough) furthers the *exportation de cerebros* (brain drain), terms which are attempts to translate the English into Spanish, although the Spanish word did not previously have just that meaning. Other terms represent more or less translation, more or less adoption: *cabinas espaciales* (space capsules), *la programa espacial* (the space program), *estación interplanetaria* (space platform), and *computadores* (computers). In Africa and much of Asia, Americanisms move freely and inconspicuously, but considering the rampant nationalism of Communist China one need not be surprised to learn that English of any persuasion is faring badly, or to read the following in the Hong Kong *Far Eastern Economic Review:*

A century of association with Europeans "tainted" the Chinese language with alien words. To purge such evil influences the main state-operated provision store in Shanghai was served by the Red Guards with a list of commodity names which should be used henceforth. Thus cocoa (*ke ke*) becomes *hong se fen* (red colored powder); coffee beans (*ka fei dou*) becomes *he se dou* (brown colored beans); ground coffee (*ka fei fen*) becomes *huang la fen* (yellow bitter powder); chocolate bar (*chiao ke li*) becomes *hsiang tsao kuan* (fragrant grass—or vanilla—bar); beer (*bi jiu*) becomes *mi mai chi jiu* (rice and wheat gaseous wine).[11]

We might ask ourselves what sorts of words have been borrowed into European languages and compare this movement with other streams of borrowing. We have a ready and curiously ironical parallel in the borrowings from French into English. Beginning more than a thousand

---

[11] I have silently corrected what seem to be a few typos; I have the passage from *Atlas,* Jan. 13, 1967, p. 53.

years ago, the British Isles, then backward offshore islands, began absorbing Continental culture, the flow coming mainly through France. This flow of culture brought Greek-Latin-French terminology, and the resulting English language moved to various parts of the New World, including what is now the United States. Now the flow is returning to France, and it will be instructive to follow the earliest and the latest of these language movements.

The English borrowing from the Continent began as soon as Roman traders and soldiers moved north, increased during the thirteenth century, and maintained a high plateau ca. 1250–1650, during which time English was borrowing thousands of words every century. After the isolation induced by the Cromwellian wars a decline set in, but the borrowing continued and is still continuing at a moderate rate. The words brought by this flood were mainly concerned with the kinds of living, thinking, and working that stemmed from Mediterranean culture but were not so common in the barbaric northland. Some were relatively common terms associated with new things; the Christian church brought words like *faith, temple, minister, mass,* and *church* itself. Education and learning brought words like *study, education, manuscript, scholar,* and *science.* The courts and justice, music and the other arts, the amenities of cultured living, dressing, and eating brought their words, but the bulk of the new terms were highly specialized. When war became the activities of knights, words like *aventail, ailette, cubitiere, cuisse, genouillere,* and *soleret* appeared, words now so strange that most American readers would be unable to define one of them. The same thing happened in other areas, for example, in astronomy, where the astrolabe required its Latinate battery of technical names. Almost all the specialized terms of literary criticism—even *literature* and *criticism*—came in from Greek, Latin, Italian, and French; only words like *song* and *tale* are native.

Now for the recent French borrowings from English. As to their origin, some few are British, *karting,* for example, which is rare in the United States; in England it is associated with the sportive use of automotive vehicles, notably motorcycles. Some words could have come in from any sort of English, *suspense* for example, although one suspects that American advertising, much more sensational than British promotional copy, popularized the word. Similarly, technical terms may be difficult to trace; *penicillin,* the name for a substance developed in England from penicilliums, could have spread either across the English Channel or the Atlantic Ocean, and probably did spread across both. Something similar would be true of words associated with atomic fission, like *fallout.*

The great bulk of the identifiable words, however, were borrowed into

France from the United States, and one observes at once that they fall into the same categories as those words borrowed into England from France hundreds of years earliér. They comprise two groups, words of daily living not necessarily common in the United States but native there, and specialized terms, mostly from science and technology. For the former, they are perhaps not the words that Americans associate with their daily lives, but they are words involved in the daily lives of Americans and the sort of things that are indigenous enough so that, when they are borrowed, they are characteristic: *boogie-woogie, teen-ager, supermarket,* and *missile-gap.* They are words like *drugstore,* which Etiemble found repugnant—and one should recall that although a drugstore dispenses drugs, as does a British chemist shop, the institutions differ. They include an unusual number of words associated with sports or with teenage antics; Etiemble cites the following, which an American can guess at, even if he does not know French: *La balle quitta le fairway, rebondit sur le green, tomba dans le bunker. Le putting devenait impossible. Il prit son fer 4 et la balle s'égara dans le rough.* Since golf is a Scottish game, not all of these words need be attributed to what Etiemble calls *l'impérialisme yanqui,* but Etiemble makes clear that above all he fears *yanquisation,* the *idiotisme americain,* that the bulk of the words that *martyrisent notre langue* come from the *idiots outre-Atlantique.* Etiemble says he counted more than 3500 such words, borrowed into French, most of which would have come from the United States. He thought he identified more than 25,000 technical and scientific words, and considering the present relative states of British and American science and technology we may reasonably guess that the bulk of these words, too, originated in the United States, although many of them will have been borrowed from Latin or Greek, and they are probably current in Britain, where some of them will have been developed.

So much for the borrowing of Americanisms in Europe. It is taking place more or less everywhere, as American specialties are imported, and is received with more or less hospitality, more or less resentment. It probably will not have deep impact in Europe; most of us outside France have more faith in the vigor and resilience of the French language than have some of its users. Similarly, Latin America has borrowed some English, notably modern American borrowings, but Spanish and Portuguese are too well established for any other language to play more than a secondary or tertiary role, at least in the immediate future, and this in spite of grumblings against Portuguese in Brazil, which can scarcely have much future outside that country. In the smaller emergent nations of Africa and Asia, however, the function of English, notably American English, may be very different.

To understand this difference we must consider the manners in which the roles of language shift, in a complex social world, with the social and political importance of the users of the language, and with the extent of the language itself. In a tribal society, a language can function normally even for a small group; the Havasupai, living deep in the Grand Canyon of the Colorado, probably never numbered more than a few hundred, or at best a few thousand. A tribe mainly self-sufficient needs little inter-tribal communication; the needs of barter can be satisfied by a few bilinguals or by some simple set of signs such as those used by the Amerindians. The linguistic needs of a complex nation with a great language are not essentially different; international relations tend to be minor when compared with national and local affairs, for which the local language is adequate. In actuality, the international affairs may be considerable, as were those of the native speakers of Spanish, French, and English—say in the eighteenth century—but great states can afford the expense in men and goods required for international communication, travel, translation, education, mass media, and the like.

Small states in a complex society, however, find themselves under-privileged. Even the Scandinavian countries, highly cultured though they are, sense handicaps. They know that the world will not learn Icelandic, and broadcasting in an obscure language, or translating into it, can never be a well-rewarded venture. Accordingly, sophisticated countries like Sweden and the Netherlands have deliberately cultivated second, third, and fourth languages, and they have been helped in this because their native tongues are closely related to German and English. Belgium has escaped by turning to French, albeit not without riots in the streets when language becomes involved with racial minorities; on October 14, 1962, nineteen persons were injured and forty-one arrested in Brussels when rival linguistic groups used fists, rotten eggs, empty jars, and homemade bombs on one another.[12] For many of the emergent nations of Africa and Asia, however, few palliatives are available.

Consider India. Anything but a minor country, it has great advantages over Ghana or Nepal, but no universal language.[13] In 1950, the Central Government, partly as a means of emphasizing Indian independence from the British Commonwealth of Nations, both political and social, declared that the national language would be Hindi. India has a

---

[12] *The New York Times,* Western Edition, Oct. 15, 1962, pp. 1, 3.
[13] The problem of language in the emergent nations has been subject to no adequate study. R. B. LePage, *The National Language Question* (London: Oxford University Press, 1964), provides a beginning, including a survey of the situation in India. Political aspects of the problem are well surveyed in Ram Gopal, *Linguistic Affairs of India* (Bombay: Asia Publishing House, 1966), but the linguistic discussion leaves much to be desired.

population approaching half a billion, of which some 150 million speak Hindi, but Hindi is not one thing, being composed of Hindustani, Urdu, and Punjabi, with various dialects, and while this decision made the northern Indians moderately happy, it made the speakers of nearly a thousand other dialects quite unhappy—statistics differ with the definitions of "language" and "dialect," but the total 845 has a degree of authority. The country was given fifteen years, until 1965, to make the change, but the change was obviously impossible, and Nehru had to announce an indefinite extension. Furthermore, he had to make the announcement in English so that at least some people in all communities could tell others what it meant, for although only three per cent of the population speak English, this is the educated three per cent, well dispersed throughout the country.

Schoolchildren may suffer even more than do their parents. If they are lucky, they are born into a community where they need learn only two languages for minimal purposes, Hindi and English, but in any except certain populous northern areas they may expect to learn four languages before they have the equivalent of a high school education. They cannot at first be instructed in either English or Hindi, because these would not have been spoken in their family. They must start with the local speech, progress to the state speech, and eventually learn English and Hindi, without which national and international affairs would be denied them. If they have scientific, scholarly, or other learned pretensions, they may still need French, German, Russian, Chinese, and Arabic, and need them rather more than would a European or an American. Furthermore, their theoretically "native" languages may vary highly in grammar and vocabulary, since one may be Indo-European, another Dravidian, and a third Negrito, which reveal no discernible relationships. It is as though an American child had to learn two or three languages other than English and not related to it, Chinese, Arabic, and Choctaw, for example. The child may have to learn several scripts, also; a Tamil child may have to learn three.

All this is for India, one of the populous nations of the earth, and custodian of an ancient civilization. It has the advantage of an extensive school system where English has been compulsory ever since Thomas Babington Macaulay recommended it in 1835. Beside India, most of the emergent nations are poor and confused. Little formal instruction has ever been given in any language, and the local speech may never have been reduced to an alphabet. Even if the native tongue can be written, translators are not obtainable to turn the learning of the world into an obscure dialect, publishing houses are not available to print in the local medium, and no cultured body of readers has been built to buy published material and thus to support publishing. What can such a young state do?

No one has found a sensible solution, even if a new people is prepared to be sensible—a rash of riots and revolutions attests that emergent peoples may not be prepared to practice sane thinking or accept sound research. Theoretically, several courses are possible. The new country can teach its own language and try to insulate itself from the world. Actually, this is not possible; barbarism cannot endure, faced with culture. A deliberately backward state becomes an easy victim, and even the "have-not" citizens of such a state will follow their own interests and imitate their "have" neighbors. The state can go to the other extreme, adopt a widely spoken language, provide compulsory education, and require that all instruction be given in the official language. This will work—at this writing it is working in Ghana, for example—but it can be hard to implement and it causes trouble. The school system is expensive, teachers difficult to obtain; furthermore, by creating an elite of those who know the new official language, it foments prejudice and sets children against their parents, the generations against one another. As an alternative, the state can compromise; for example, it can encourage the study of a foreign language by offering it in the schools, while recognizing also some sort of pidgin, a blend of the native with the foreign language. This combination will work and may provide the best system where a developed pidgin is available, but it, too, causes trouble. Instead of creating an elite of government employees, educators, priests, and the cultured wealthy, alongside an uneducated commonality, this system creates a still more select elite which knows a widely spoken language, a middle class which can use the pidgin, and an uneducated class that cannot use even pidgin.

Thus the problem remains, and emergent nations must recognize it, unofficially if not officially. Most of them try to make some use of a language having worldwide currency; most of these states choose English, and most of them rely upon some combination of governmental and popular approval. For example, in Teheran more than a hundred schools give instruction in English to thousands of adults, and the Iranian government supports the movement with the slogan, "If you don't know English, you know nothing."[14] In Kabul, when English courses were announced, Afghans queued up in a blizzard for the privilege of registering. Even the Russian and Chinese Communists have found that, if they

---

[14] A good survey of the recent rapid spread of English will be found in Lincoln Barnett, *The Treasure of Our Tongue* (New York: Alfred A. Knopf, 1964), especially pp. 1–22 from which I take this example. I shall use it occasionally hereafter without further citation.

are to have audiences, they must broadcast and print much of their propaganda in English.

Since the purpose of this book is mainly to study American English, and in this instance its impact abroad, we have next to ask ourselves whether we have here to deal with British English, American English, or some other kind of English. The answer is, all of them. The answer suggests, also, that influences from the United States are increasing.

The basis of the world role of English is British. The native language of the British Isles was exported to Canada, Australia, India, South Africa, and hundreds of islands, big and little, as part of the same movement that brought English to what is now the United States. The explorers, settlers, and traders were followed by missionaries, teachers, and government servants, and since such people tend in the United Kingdom to be relatively cultured, the English thus disseminated throughout the world was notably literate, considering that the dissemination was but little directed and that the recipients were often innocent of formal instruction. The imperial flag upon which, for a time, the sun never set, carried English to far and strange places, and in varying degrees established it in them. For these reasons, presumably, when a Pakistani banker today has to correspond with a banker in Tokyo, Manila, Malaya, or even neighboring India, he writes English. Such an Oriental may not write good English; a recent Pakistani newspaper carried the following account: "The thief, apprehended by the cop, disgorged twelve bicycles." But the author means to write English, not Russian or Chinese.

With the emergence of Hollywood, and of the United States as a world power after the First World War, a new trend appeared, which after the Second World War became dominant. The British, Dutch, and French empires collapsed. Official schools closed; official representatives went home; missionary or other private schools received less support and declined, while British and European businessmen lost their monopolies and enjoyed ever-narrowing slices of the market. Meanwhile, new English-speaking nations like Australia, sprung from the dominions in the former British Commonwealth, were becoming dissemination centers in their own right, but the great change stemmed from American economic hegemony and from a new vigorous international policy.

The United States had been remarkably isolationist. It had had room to grow, having lately been a colony itself, and an ingrown fear— healthy or morbid, depending upon your point of view—of "foreign entanglements" and European wars. Now, rightly or wrongly, it conceived that its true enemy was communism, that communism could be fought with prosperity, and that consequently aiding backward countries—provided they would oppose or at least resist communism—was at once good politics and good business, along with being humanitarian. Billions were poured into the emergent nations.

Ostensibly, this aid took the form of arms, economic and political know-how, educational and medical assistance, and the like, but the whole movement became much more involved with language than anyone had anticipated. Partly this trend grew from giving the recipients what they wanted; natives wanted the English language, and within limits were capable of absorbing it, whereas they mostly did not want American democracy and could not understand it when it was forced upon them. Many Peace Corps representatives, recruited to teach agriculture or to show poverty-stricken blacks that white Americans are not afraid to work with their hands, found themselves teachers of English, whether or not they had either the inclination or the special training for the job.

Curiously, however, just at this time Americans had become peculiarly fitted to disseminate the English language. Books are cheaper than bombers, and the knowledge of English more broadly based than the knowledge of electronics. The American system of universal education has seen to that; most young Americans are literate, so that the pool of prospective teachers is numberless. Recently, linguists have multiplied in the United States as nowhere else in the world. We have discovered that structural analysis permits the study and teaching of any language, in any language, with relative ease, and we have produced more such scholars and teachers conversant with these techniques than are available elsewhere. Furthermore, the American system of higher education, which for a job of this sort is obviously without a peer, is becoming more and more geared to produce modern pure and applied linguists. The result is that with the world crying for English as it has never begged for any single language before, the United States possesses, in teachers and in technique, the greatest body of potential disseminators of a language that has ever been available to a learning-starved world.

Accordingly, world usage is shifting from British toward American English. Not always is this change welcomed by British teachers abroad or by native teachers trained in British schools. One of my former students told me that she had had some delay coming to the United States to study; she had had the money to come, and the American university had been ready to admit her, but the officials of the British missionary school she had attended refused to release her credentials except to a British institution. Since her father was a general, she had no serious difficulty getting her credentials, but she might have had more had her father been a sergeant.

Most of this shift is not formally associated with any Anglo-American rivalry. For example, the National Council of Teachers of English, an American organization, is preparing a sequence of volumes to be used teaching English in backward parts of the world, and is taking every precaution to produce books which will be usable by teachers, whether their preparation is 'American, British, or anything else, but in spite of the best official efforts these books will be American books. They are being written and edited by Americans, who know American English; the authors could not write the books in British English if they wanted to. Similarly American teachers, of necessity, teach American speech. Consider the girl from American Falls, Idaho, who takes a post teaching in Manila. She is not anti-British; she is just doing something interesting abroad, and following her profession, but she will teach American English, even Snake River Valley English, because that is all she knows. Or consider the Peace Corps boy from Keokuk, Iowa; he is probably unconscious what kind of English he is teaching, but it will not be British Received Standard.

Perhaps the shifting state of English abroad can be observed as well as anywhere in the local newspapers springing up in the South Pacific, printed in pidgin, for example in the *Nu Gini Toktok* (*New Guinea News*) disseminated from Port Moresby.[15] Obviously, the pidgin is based upon British English; *council* is spelled *kaunsil, delegate* is *deleget, something* is *samting, belong* is *bilong* (when it is not reduced to *long*), *officer* is *ofisa, doctor* is *dokta,* and *mister* is *mista.* These spellings all suggest British vowels. 'Alongside this basic British terminology are American imports so little changed that they need no explanation; *radio program, basketbal, besbal, Amerika, hit parade, listeners choice, women's hour, pikinini, king size.* The two comic strips are American, *Mickey Mouse* and *Henry;* the rodent seems to be universal, but the activities of the taciturn Henry are sufficiently foreign that running comment in pidgin is provided to explain why the pictures are funny. This is the sort of thing happening in an area where British influence has been strong, in a land now mandated to Australia.

Even in Cairo, long a bastion of the British Empire, the *Egyptian Gazette,* declaring that English is the property "of all the world," bolstered the argument by insisting it "is not the property of capitalist Americans." In portions of Africa which the British never much penetrated, English would inevitably be American English; that would be available through the Peace Corps, through the United States Office of Information, through moving pictures and radio tapes, but British Eng-

---

[15] All the terms below appear in No. 46 (August 15, 1963).

lish would be heard mainly through the survival of adventurers or globe-trotting businessmen, relatives of Conrad's Heyst and Lord Jim, who are now a declining breed. In a part of the world torn with dissension almost every upheaval brings American English to bear, even though the upheaval may be directed at the United States. When Russian machinery is shipped to Africa it arrives with instructions in English and labeled "Made In U.S.S.R." Even "Yankee go home" is apt to be scrawled in English.

Thus the role of American English abroad is demonstrating once more the ancient principle that language follows power, influence, and social exchange. No doubt the reasons for anything so extensive as the current English language explosion are complex. Many observers have suggested that English has grown because it is an easy language; its vocabulary has much in common with French and Spanish, some with German and Italian, and it has jettisoned most of the inflections and ablauts that complicate many languages. Thus it has the simplest grammar, and the grammar most readily adapted to pidgins, of all the great languages, except possibly Chinese, which has complicated tone patterns and has never been reduced to an alphabet having general currency. It is written in the Latin alphabet, the only expanding means of written communication, the lack of which is handicapping Russian, Chinese, and Arabic. The common words in English are mostly short words, having sufficient variety in form—both written and oral form—so that they are readily learned and easily distinguished.

These arguments must be admitted, but so far as we know, no language anywhere or at any time has ever triumphed solely or even mainly because of its virtues as a language. Francophiles sometimes suggested that French became the international language of culture and diplomacy because it was the most fluid and beautiful tongue; one might notice, however, that it grew to power when Paris was the cultural capital of the world and when French arms were triumphing on four continents. With the decline of France, however, French declined, so that delegates to the United Nations request more than twice as many transcripts in English as in French. Currently, many Latin Americans are resisting the spread of English into Latin America lest it supersede Spanish, which they believe should be preserved because it is the most beautiful language in the world. We may be inclined to sympathize with this attitude, but we shall have to predict that beauty alone is not likely to save Spanish or any other language. Lincoln Barnett has suggested that French pilots use English because the exigencies of flying require terse speech, and *jet* and *flaps* are more practical than *avion à reaction* and *volets de flexion;* doubtless he has a point, but one recalls that

American English took to the air when American planes dominated the skies during the recent war, and that American planes have been ubiquitous ever since.

Thus although we may assume that the English language is spreading through the world partly because it is a good language with a simple grammar and a vast and highly flexible vocabulary, and because it is aided by the Latin alphabet and modern linguistic study, we must observe that it is triumphing because American culture is advancing on a broad front. American sports and amusements have intrigued people all over the world, and accordingly *baseball* and *basketball* are worldwide terms; even the name for a hideous instrument like the *juke box* appears in almost infinite spellings and pronunciations. American science and technology blend with the world movement, but they carry words like *jet* and *antibiotic* with them. The United States has led the free world, even when some of those who were fed and protected have resented having to receive, and language has gone with leadership. American loans and American bulldozers have spoken in American idioms, sometimes consciously, always unconsciously, and the impact is inevitable. The United States has the highest standard of living ever enjoyed by any large body of people anywhere; the analogy may be fallacious, but inevitably many underprivileged peoples accept it—if you want a higher standard of living, learn American.

The result is that American English, for better or for worse, is becoming more and more a world language, is being spread by American culture and is spreading American culture much more rapidly than even the specialists were predicting a decade ago.

23

THE FUTURE OF AMERICAN ENGLISH

So, we have come to the present, some three and a half centuries after the first English was spoken on the North 'American continent. During that time American English was born, shaping itself from the various speech of displaced Englishmen, Welshmen, Irish, and Scots, until it is obviously the most rapidly burgeoning dialect of the most rapidly expanding language.

What of the future? Can one project the future of American English? On the whole, man so delights in extrapolating himself that he might well be defined as the autoprophetic animal, but for whatever reason, he has not been much given to predicting the future of his language, except to predict its ruin if it should change. These predictions, as we have seen, have been uncommonly fallacious, perhaps because they rested on uncommonly false premises. On the whole, men have assumed that change was bad for language, and have become furious when they found it changing. Anger does not promote speculative thought, and many a virtuous but irate user of the language, who might have studied speech to his profit, gave his devotion to the hopeless project of preventing change. Now we believe we know better, a great deal better. We know that languages always change, and whether or not change is good for language, it is inevitable. Furthermore, these changes seem to be amenable to rule, or at least they respect discernible principles.

That man has so sparingly prophesied the future of language may reflect his ignorance of the nature of change; if he knew that language was changing, he detected only the minor aberrations, not the broad significant movements. In fact we might promulgate a sort of Law of Popular Linguistic Awareness, somewhat as follows: The greater the individual ignorance of language and the more infinitesimal the linguistic observation, the higher the linguodynamic temperature index. Or to put the matter informally, the less people know, the madder they get. Most people, however, maintain their equilibrium by ignoring the whole subject.

For example, about a third of the present inhabitants of the globe speak languages descended from Indo-European, which, as we have seen, flourished in Europe five thousand or more years ago. In the subsequent millennia it died or, rather, was so transformed that it survived only through daughter languages; in the same sense, all immediate descendants died, and dozens of languages sprang up in their places. Yet we may probably assume that few speakers of these languages were aware that their speech was changing much, to say nothing of charting the lives and deaths of the languages.

For several reasons previous peoples did not know enough to deal with language change. Partly they did not understand how language works, and partly they did not know what their ancestors had done to language. On both these counts we are now much better informed than any body of people has been in the past. Even so, detecting drifts in language is difficult. Changes take place over hundreds of years, or thousands, and tend to pass undetected until long after they are part of the language. Languages are usually anatomized after they are dead, or at best when something suggestive of rigor mortis has overtaken the portion of language under study.

Consider the Great English Vowel Shift, by which the stressed Old English vowels moved forward and upward in the mouth, so that a word formerly pronounced like the modern word *hay* is our word *he*. Changes of this sort worked through the language for centuries, but apparently nobody noticed them. Chaucer remarked that words did not mean what they used to, that the terms for love-making had changed. Caxton, the English printer, complained that he did not know which words to use when he translated, that some people said *eggs* and some *eier*. But nobody observed that changes in meaning and sound fall into patterns, and that the future of these patterns might be predictable from the past.

All this raises an interesting question: Have we turned the corner in our study of language? Earlier generations could not predict the future of language, could not have done so had they tried. They had no fundamentally sound understanding of language, and they had accumulated no large body of objective fact concerning it. We now believe we can formulate fundamentally sound postulates, and we have accumulated mountainous bodies of fact that seem to be reliable and revealing. Can we now turn our autoprophetic proclivities to man's great invention? Specifically, can we now plot the future of a language and say with some confidence what English will become in America?

We might try. First we might notice a few principles, which we suppose are firmly established:

1. Languages always change; at least they always have and we must assume they always will.
2. They change in many ways at the same time, but mostly slowly and over long periods.
3. The change is mainly unconscious; the evidences of change that come to public attention are usually scattered, few, and relatively insignificant.
4. Something can be done to direct change consciously, but probably not much.
5. Once a broad change has started—often called "drift" in language—it is likely to continue until it has worked itself out in all parts of the language or dialect affected, or at least for a long time.

Of course we could add more principles, but these should carry us some distance, even though we limit our observation to five prominent areas: vocabulary, grammar, pronunciation, usage, and the relationships between language and society.

Vocabulary is relatively easy, for here we can speak with great confidence and in some detail. Throughout the history of the English language we have been borrowing words from other languages, devising new words by juggling those we already have, and killing off a few. Consistently, we have borrowed and invented more than we destroyed, so that from a vocabulary of a few thousand recorded Old English words, and presumably a few thousand that went unrecorded, we now have many more than a half-million Modern English words. With minor variations, this trend will continue.

We may always expect what might be called *novae* in the language, words or groups of words which will undergo a sort of meaning-explosion. In an earlier chapter we observed the impact of locomotion upon vocabulary. Gentlemen kept their deer in parks, but after people got used to parking cars, they found they could park almost anything else, including their offspring, and the offspring could park his gum. The same thing is happening and will continue to happen in other areas of enlivened interest, in connection with airplanes, rockets, outer space, plumbing, microscopy, atomic fission, automation, medicine, television, city planning, social welfare, and skiing. Ski bums have names for their *Geländesprünge* and the ski bunnies for their sitzmarks. At this writing, musical groups with popular aspirations are adopting gruesome and uncomplimentary names for themselves; the *Beatles* apparently started the fad, and were imitated by *The Animals, The Neanderthals,* and *The Piltdown Men.* A women's auxiliary calls itself *Cooties* and names its officers after various *pediculosi,* Head Louse, The Noble Gray-back, and the like; such fancies are usually short-lived, but fresh examples can be expected. One cannot predict such movements in detail—in the early 1960's one could not have anticipated that *acid-head, pot, tea, horse,* and *high* would become common college slang—but one can predict that such efflorescences will be felt in the language in various minor ways, that fads we shall have always with us. Individual cultured fad words at the moment include *serendipity, mystique, charisma, establishment,* and *euphoria.*

Words like *communist* and *communism* are not so frightening as they were; an American on the mainland cannot—as apparently he can in some island dialects—call his son "a real communist" and mean only that the three-year-old is a mischievous little rascal, but such words are changing and will continue to weaken, especially if communism declines as a world threat. We may expect many similar evidences of semantic change, some falling into minor patterns, some random. We may expect every new war to produce its own slang; the *doughboys* of one war became the *dogfaces* of the next, and are now the *grunts* and *ground pounders* in Vietnam. If these *grunts* are killed, they no longer "go west"; they are *zapped* or *waxed,* they *get schnitzled* or *get their plows cleaned.* Being conversant with modern military terminology, they call water *potable,* and dealing with modern equipment a plane prone to disaster becomes a *thud* and a two-seated plane a *double thud.* Such terms will continue to sprout if military actions continue, and will change with tactics and equipment.

Our patterns of borrowing have changed, but not much recently, and are continuing; we borrow from Latin and Greek for scientific purposes, and we shall borrow more from new cultures as they gain greater international prominence. Borrowings from French will continue, but somewhat decline. We have lately revamped *satellite* under the influence of East Europeans and *common market* through West Europeans, and we shall borrow more from Russian, Chinese, Arabic, Latin American, and African languages, as users of these tongues develop. We are doing this now as we have done it in the past, when we borrowed *kasbah* and *casaba* from Arabic, *canasta* and *tortilla* from Mexican Spanish. We have already borrowed *ombudsman* from Swedish, but the word will not be widely used unless this officer, an official representative of the people, becomes common in American government.

In an earlier chapter we observed some trends in groups of words. In transportation, words like *lariat* and *cutting horse* are American because they reflect an American use of horses, and *a kick in the pants* for a sure winner is American horse-racing slang, but on the whole, words associated with horse transportation are British because the horse was an important object in Great Britain. Two sets of automotive terms grew on the two sides of the Atlantic, meanwhile, because automotive vehicles developed somewhat independently in England and the United States. With space travel, however, we have returned to a pattern of borrowing, but with the direction reversed; since rocketry has developed in the United States, rocket terms are now moving abroad in the form of American speech, moving even into British speech. This tendency may be expected to continue, and to be paralleled in atomic fission, automation, computers, municipal planning, urban renewal, and wherever American thought and technology lead a large portion of the world.

Of course, these activities may themselves change, and as they do their vocabulary will shift. For example, wars always produce vocabulary, more or less permanent. In the recent past, wars have tended to be total, with one body of people fighting another body with all its resources, with all citizens concerned about the progress of the battles and dealing with the words that grew out of the fighting. English acquired words like *stuka* and *blitzkrieg*. The Vietnam affair, on the other hand, insofar as it affected most Americans, involved policy and humanitarian convictions, so that at least some of the war words grew out of discussions at home. *Escalation* developed a whole new meaning and fathered *de-escalation*. *Hawk* and *dove* found new uses both capital and lower case. Thus a new kind of conflict bred a different set of words, and considering the probable future of the United States in world affairs, we may see more such half-wars.

The growth of non-English speech from within our borders is likely to decline as the native bilingual speakers grow fewer. At this writing, borrowing from Yiddish is ballooning, partly because of the great increase in the importance of Jews, especially in literature and the mass media, but partly also because of the charm of Jewish wit and Yiddish speech. Leo Rosten points out that a word like *paskudnyak* carries "a nasality of scorn" that "adds cadence to contempt."[1] Such borrowings will decline, however, as fewer young Jews learn Yiddish.

Other tendencies, also, will continue to affect our vocabulary; some slang and colloquial expressions will become standard speech, although guessing the individual locutions might be hazardous. In the past we have been uncommonly prolific in terms for young women, but most of them have not lasted, and at this writing *tomato* seems to be going to the same oblivion which has been pioneered by *skirt, babe, muggess,* and *hank-of-hair*. Perhaps the most enduring slang will grow from new areas

[1] *The Joys of Yiddish,* cited earlier, p. 282

like space travel, where terminology is in demand, or in activities becoming highly characteristic of a growing portion of our culture, for example, *to give the brushoff* or *the runaround*. No doubt these phenomena have been always with us, but the runaround becomes more labyrinthine as business and government diversify and interweave. As the practice becomes systematized with the development of the secretary and the receptionist, the results of the runaround are both more numerous and more baffling in modern Washington than they would have been among the troglodytes. Slang of this sort, in all probability, built into the business and political life of the nation, is the most likely to endure.

Slang, we must assume, is universal; only the sorts and the terms are local, but some of our fadlike developments produce locutions too solid to be termed slang. Presumably they are congenial to our sort of society. Prompted by our scientific and technological efflorescence, by our bureaucratic proliferation, we have engendered an amazing brood of words composed of initials or opening syllables, and this trend, if we may trust the projection of a plotted curve, is only beginning. Our ancestors were content with an occasional *Nabisco* (National Biscuit Company) or *GOP* (Grand Old Party), but concoctions of this sort have so ballooned in recent decades that the most recent dictionary of such terms includes more than 45,000, from *AUDREY* (Automatic Digit Recognizer) to *ZANC* (Zambia National Congress), and new ones appear every day.[2] Some of even recent origin have become so common that they are seldom thought of as acronyms or initialisms, *noncoms* for noncommissioned officers, *radar* from Radio Detection and Ranging. At this writing others like *ZIP Code* (Zone Improvement Plan) are rapidly outgrowing their origin. Most of them are brief and very handy—*HEW* (Health, Education, and Welfare), *GI* (General Issue or Gastrointestinal), but a few are monstrosities, *ADCOMSUBORDCOM-PHIBSPAC* (Administrative Command, Amphibious Forces, Pacific Fleet, Subordinate Command). It is all growing so rapidly that an acronymic coinage has been devised to describe it by its rapid growth, *FASGROLIA* (Fast-Growing Language of Initialisms and Acronyms). Furthermore, the fad has now become reversed, so that organizations are named to provide an attractive acronym. The idea was apparently popularized when the Navy outsmarted the Army with the meaningful *WAVES* as against the meaningless *WAC;* now any action group can get itself called *REACH* (Revitalizing Education for All Children),

---

[2] Frederick G. Ruffner, Jr., *Acronyms and Initialisms Dictionary,* 2nd ed. (Detroit: Ruffner, 1966).

VISTA (Volunteers in Service to America), *PATH* (Plan of Action for Tomorrow's Housing), *FIGHT* (Foundation for the Improvement—you fill in the remainder), *SHAME, HELP, AIDS,* or whatever may produce money or members.

Other specialties of ours are developing at a less lively rate. We are building new involved technical terms, mainly by combining Greek and Latin roots and affixes; hundreds of words involving smallness are being built on *micro-,* words like *microseismometrograph, microlepidopterous,* and *microcolorimetrically.* At the same time we are shortening words, words like *polio* for *poliomyelitis,* which may appear first as slang or cant terms but may eventually acquire common currency. We are fond of blends or portmanteau words, not only because they are handy— *motelodge* is shorter than *motor hotel and lodge*—but also because they can be engaging, terms like *jargantuan, imagineering, Renovated, bureaucrazy, the cremains,* and *sexpert.* A *philanthropoid* is said to be one who officially gives other people's money away. We have fads, usually rather short-lived, although they leave remnants behind them, of doing things with affixes like *super-, -wise, -eria,* and *-rama.* An occasional inexplicable term will appear or become popular; at this writing *trod* is developing to mean what *tread* used to. A national magazine carries the subhead "This is the time of year when a man numbs himself with cold while trodding marsh and thicket." Similarly, *money* increasingly appears as *moneys* when it refers to public funds. Most of these tendencies will probably continue, and they will involve varying elements—the fad of adding *-like* seems to have passed, and the fad of adding *-wise* seems to be passing, whereas prefixing *in-* is now in. Such changes are spectacular, but they usually involve but few of the terms in the total word stock. More extensively we shall create the bulk of our new words by adapting old terms to new purposes; we had orbits and satellites long before any man-made satellites were thrust into orbit. Of most of these changes we are unconscious; few people, and even few dictionaries, have noticed that the plural of *plan* has developed a meaning distinct from the singular, as in the sentence *Since our plan has been accepted we can now start making plans.*

We are also abandoning words. We have silently interred hundreds of terms in denominational theology, words like *Passalorynchites,* which means a finger to the nostril, devised for a sect which believed in buttoning the lip. As the automobile replaced the horse it obliterated much terminology related to horses; few Americans can distinguish a horse's *pastern* or identify the *billet* on his harness. If now the hovering craft replaces the automobile, or even if electrically driven motors replace internal combustion engines, many terms will fade away. With the passing of the hand press, much of the picturesque terminology of the old printing trade is vanishing; *summer, winter,* and *trisket* no longer appear in dictionaries as parts of presses, and with photographic and electronic methods of setting type, the terminology associated with handset and molten type will mostly become obsolete.

Next, to grammar. Here details are much more obscure, but we should be able to extrapolate in even this slippery subject. As earlier chapters have made clear, we know something of what has been happening in English; it has been losing inflectional changes and developing other sorts of grammatical devices. On the other hand, to take the place of inflections we have been developing a rigid word order in the sentence. *He is lying still* does not mean *he is still lying. I made out as much of it as I could* means something different from *I made as much out of it as I could. The high cost of living* means something quite different from *the cost of living high,* and *cost high living the of* means nothing at all. We have moved modifiers or prepositions into the verb, and thus have developed complex verb forms, especially to express the future and ideas that are relatively timeless. If a businessman writes *We have been considering your proposal,* he almost certainly is not using a perfect. That is, the action is not finished; he does not mean that they have considered the proposal and have now stopped considering; he probably means that the proposition has been under consideration—a fine phrasal verb, that—that it is at present still being considered, and that his company may do something about it in the future. Whether this proliferation of verb forms is now slowing down might be difficult to determine, but it is continuing and, one suspects, in a lively manner.

Meanwhile, phrasal developments seem to have been moving all through the language, into adjectives, into adverbs, into sentence modifiers, into complements, which become imbedded within verbs. In *dozens of ducks* do the *dozens* modify the *ducks* or the *ducks* the *dozens?* Where does the verb end and the complement begin in the sentence *Why don't you get the man to change your tire?* We observed in Chapter 21 that this sort of fluidity has been growing recently in English sentences, and we have no clear evidence that it has stopped.

We might pause at this point to see what kind of sense we can make of these changes, bigger sense or smaller sense, one kind of sense or many kinds of sense, and here we must consider some broad questions about the nature of language. Scholars have no sure and simple way of classifying languages, and partly for this reason students of what is called linguistic science have trouble being scientists. Mathematicians can presumably distinguish positive from negative numbers; paleontologists know molluscs from vertebrates; biologists may have a bit of bother distinguishing plants from animals, although the confusions do not trouble them much. But as yet we have no way of saying with any exactitude what kind of language any given language is. Having admitted so much, I can add that we have observable tendencies in languages, even though no one language, apparently, ever works by using only one of these tendencies. As we have noticed in earlier chapters, grammar can work through a change in form of grammatical units, that is, by inflection, by sticking words and syllables together, and by incorporating the subject or the complement or both, within the verb, but the sort we are interested in works by leaving words unchanged, while developing elaborate and relatively fixed orders and positions for these words. This grammatical tendency, called analysis, isolation, or distribution, is characteristic of Chinese and of a few primitive languages, including some Amerindian, but it is notable also in Modern English.

In fact, much of the history of English grammar can be succinctly comprised in the statement that it is the grammar of a language moving from synthesis and toward analysis. The loss of inflection and the growth of phrasal verbs, for example, are thus not two tendencies but two aspects of one tendency. Superficially they may appear as two or more because this whole broad movement probably works through various phases, and the loss of inflection was characteristic of an early phase. That is, if we are to assume that the loss of inflection, the development of rigid order, and the conversion of words to new grammatical uses are three parts of the same movement, and if we were to chart them superimposed—as we endeavored to do in an earlier chapter—we should have a rise and decline of inflection and fixed order overlapped by but mainly followed in time by a rise in conversion as the whole development toward analysis moves through various phases of drift operative over thousands of years. The decline in the loss of inflection may not mean at all the decline of the rate of a trend toward analysis. It may indicate only movement into another phase of that trend. Similarly, if we assume that our development of phrasal verbs has now gone so far that we are somewhere near the apex of that development, and that it must now be expected to decline, we cannot be sure that some other distributive device may not be increasing, that the line between the verb and the complement, for example, may not be in process of obscuring. Furthermore, we should recall that broad movements in language, once well begun, do not stop quickly. If the many movements in Modern English grammar constitute aspects of one drift that has been continuing for thousands of years, and if at least some manifestations of this drift still work vigorously, we shall have to guess that this whole tendency may go on for centuries or longer.

Now another question arises, one of those that are probably un-answerable but that nonetheless thrust up their inscrutable heads. Why has English been changing this way? We do not know why. In fact, rather usually in language we do not know why changes come about, even small changes; we can discover that the language changed, where it changed, and when it changed, but we can only guess why it changed. If I am to attempt a guess, then, I must preface it with clear warning that it is a guess and no more, that I have no controlled evidence for my answer, and that many good students of language would say that the very question is impertinent, since it is not by its nature subject to conclusive demonstration.

With this apology then, I shall offer a guess on the assumption that the theory is interesting, even though it is not conclusive and some students would say it is improbable. It is this: there must be in man a felt need for the quality of language, as there is a felt need for language itself. This need will no doubt work by many laws and even by accident, but it probably has a tendency, as language does, to work toward its own satisfaction. The nature of this need may not be the same at all times. For example, very primitive people may be satisfied with ap-petites, with goods, and with grammars that are inadequate for highly sophisticated peoples, for highly trained and subtle minds. I suspect that this is true, and if it is, we may expect that a people's sense of language may shift subtly and slowly as the culture changes.

Now one might observe that a mature inflectional grammar is rela-tively rigid. We have had no opportunity to observe such a language during its early stages, but we assume that it develops as classifiers become inflectional affixes. For example, let us suppose that a given language, like English, includes subjects and complements, that the sub-ject is the actor and that action is associated with the syllable *do,* whereas the complement is passive, and that passivity is associated with the syllable *pa.* Suppose we now wish to say that the man spanked the boy, we have only to indicate the idea of spanking and add *man-do boy-pa* and we know who spanked whom. Similarly, any other name for an object can become an actor and hence a subject by adding *-do,* whether the concept is *woman-do, duck-do, rain-do,* or whatever, and the same process can be continued to distinguish the animate from the inanimate, the male from the female, and these symbols, which were once meaning-ful words, even names for things, may become so formalized as clas-sifiers that they lose their meaningful use and become only symbols of grammatical function. Furthermore, these syllables may erode, as un-accented parts of complex words tend to, so that *man-do* becomes *mano* and *man-pa* becomes *mana,* and the words that have become suffixes and finally inflectional endings are no longer recognizable as the words from which they developed. During its period of elaboration, such a system would be highly adaptable; it could rest upon any concepts and could incorporate any forms, but once it has developed and the paradigms are recognized and enshrined in the language as "correct," it tends to be immune to certain sorts of change. It does not readily admit of additions; it can decay, if old forms no longer serve a function, and old forms may develop new uses, but both changes tend to be slow, so that at least relatively speaking an inflectional system is a rigid system. On the contrary, a distributive system is flexible. It has no paradigms in the conventional sense, and its forms are potentially infinite. It can make and shift these forms with relative rapidity and ease, and it is flexible in large ways as well as in small, with one area of grammar ballooning while others change more slowly. That is, an analytic grammar is well suited to a rapidly growing language, and to a people that is growing rapidly in culture, in vocabulary, and in the range and subtlety of the ideas that the grammar must express.

Phrased more bluntly, then, my guess is this: that an analytic grammar is highly appropriate for a sophisticated people, and that the growth of analysis in English is in part a natural response to a desire for a more flexible grammar. If this is an answer at all, it is only a partial answer. Most European languages have been becoming more distributive and less inflectional for centuries. If English has moved toward distribution more rapidly than have German and Russian, presumably this growth was accelerated by many influences, including the long fight for English against French.

Fortunately, for our purposes, we need not settle such questions. We need only observe that if English grammar changed in response to a felt need for more flexibility in a rapidly growing language, the medium of a people moving relatively rapidly into sophisticated life, then both of these reasons would lead us to assume that the changes would continue. If a flexible grammar is suited to a complicated and sophisticated society, then we must observe that our society shows little signs of returning to simplicity. If an analytic grammar is suited to a growing language, then we must observe that the rapid growth of English is not likely to lessen in the near future. That is, if our kind of grammar results from need, then the need is still there, and English can go a good bit farther in employing analysis as a grammatical principle. The likely guess is that it will do so.

Now, before we leave grammar and take up sound as a subject in itself, we might observe sound as a grammatical device, and notice that speakers of English have probably changed their pitch and stress since

Old English times, and that these changes doubtless reflect growth in grammar. Here our knowledge is inadequate because sound as a grammatical device has been studied seriously only recently, and we do not understand it well. *Soups on honey* may suggest a gruesome gastronomic experience, but *"Soup's on, Honey,"* may be a welcome invitation. Orally, the differences in the use of the voice reveal the grammar; in writing, punctuation approximates the vocal intonations. Similarly, the play of pitch, stress, and juncture in speaking reveals the difference between *"The heat's on low, Joe,"* and *"The heat's on Low Joe."* One suspects that these oral grammatical devices may still be developing, paralleling our phrasal developments, but we are not yet able to describe these accurately.

Noting changes in sound is not easy; sounds are much more durable than meanings, and usually more durable than grammar. In the last thousand years English has lost one consonant, a continuing k sound, $/\chi/$, somewhat like the German hackle, and probably a corresponding voiced velar fricative $/\gamma/$; it has moved the plosive $/k/$ so that it is now spelled *ch*—in phonemics $/t\int/$ or $/\check{c}/$—and a word that used to be spelled *fisc* is now *fish;* it has seen some shifting among vowels and diphthongs, and has undergone the Great English Vowel Shift referred to above. The unstressed vowels and most of the consonants have shifted very little. That does not give us much to work on except to say that any changes in sound in our time are likely to be slight.

Individual words will alter somewhat; two pronunciations of *neither* and *either* have been battling it out, along with two of *greasy.* Such broad changes as we are experiencing probably reflect the spread of local dialectal pronunciations into wider areas; for instance, Midwestern fathers who say *cows* /kaʊz/ and *house* /haʊs/ *may* have sons who have picked up a Southern pronunciation, *ca-ows* /kæʊz/ and *ha-ouse* /hæʊs/. Whether the growing population of the Middle West and Far West is increasing the pronunciation of the retroflex in words spelled *-er, -or,* and the like, or whether the prestige pronunciation of the eastern seaboard is encouraging reduction of these sounds to simple vowels, might be hard to guess. There is some tendency to voice consonants usually voiceless; *school* can become *sgool, south* can rhyme with *mouth* used as a verb, and *mizzes* for either *Mrs.* or *misses* has a considerable ancestry. Any exact information must wait upon the further development of linguistic geography; meanwhile, we can say that pronunciation is changing only scatteringly.

We might notice one deep-seated trend. In the past, languages have always changed so much in sound that a language would fracture into dialects and eventually into separate languages with pronunciations as different as those of French and Spanish. But some forces work to standardize language, and it is possible that influences like the movies, radio, television, and American tendencies to migrate are now so much impeding linguistic change that pronunciation in English may be becoming more standard than less so. If so, the degree of rapidity in change will not be the same for all speakers. For example, I should guess—and it can be no more than a guess—that at this time the trend has reversed and that within the borders of the continental United States, pronunciation of English is becoming more nearly standard, but that the United States, Australia, and Britain are still tending to drift apart in pronunciations.

And now for usage. By usage I mean the social approval or lack of it involved in any locution. Should one say *tomayto* /təmetə/ or *tomahto* /təmɑtə/? May we say *Everybody took their hats* and *She invited my wife and I?* Such problems reduce conscientious parents to despair and send mild men into paroxysms, shudders which will decline with the years, or rather, will be replaced by a different set of paroxysms. This is not to say, of course, that a child's saying *He don't* and *I ain't* makes no difference. Socially, and even financially, it may make a great deal of difference. People who have been taught to say *I am very much pleased* shudder when they hear a cultured person say *I am very pleased,* as almost everybody does now. Half a century ago purists insisted that the past participle should never be preceded by *very* unless it was protected with an insulating *much,* and some of us were so imbued with this supposedly eternal truth that we still wince if we hear that anyone is *very pleased.*

Of course, linguistically it makes little difference which locution triumphs; the next generation will like it, if an older generation did not. And few of these locutions ever come to popular attention. We may detest the cigarette companies for what they are doing to *like* and fight for underdog *as,* but meanwhile most of the changes in language are taking place without notice. For every change in usage that arouses embattled zeal in the handbooks, the letters-to-the-editor columns, and the grade schools, hundreds are passing quietly and unrebuked into the language of tomorrow. Few purists now upbraid *The New York Times* when it uses *providing that* instead of *provided that,* although not so long ago, *providing that* was clearly bad usage.

As for generalizations, we can predict that in a few instances usage will change rather rapidly; in most others it is changing slowly, even imperceptibly. Some few changes will be fought stubbornly; for a few usages the purists will probably win. For most usages they will lose, partly because they usually do, but mainly because they will never become aware that changes are afoot.

Now we must raise another question difficult to deal with: What changes in society are occasioning changes in language? Language lives on the tongues of men, more particularly on the tongues of women, who for biological and social reasons transmit language to children. Here our time has seen no great change, at least not in the United States. Women still have babies, and while the family continues to be the basic social unit, we may expect that these babies will, in due course, learn the native language in the family and the neighborhood, mainly from their mothers and from other children who have learned from their mothers. But society has changed. If people still come into the world in the same way they always have, in America they no longer make a living as they used to, or characteristically live as they used to.

We all know what has happened here. A century ago more than half the population of the United States subsisted by farming and lived relatively isolated lives. Today fewer than ten per cent are farmers, and the percentage continues to decline. Perhaps half the population lives in great cities; most people live in or near large communities, and their communal life is enhanced by the great growth of mass media. Men used to put their hand to the plow, but now they put it to the ballpoint pen; instead of punching cows, they punch typewriters. Formerly, the Psalmist tells us, the voice of the turtle was heard in the land, but now it is the voice of the announcer, and his well-policed diction is supplemented by jargonic memos in quintuplicate. That is, the average man has become the white-collar man, and he has become a great emitter of words, although he is not usually very fluent in them. The results of all this, of course, are legion, too numerous to be analyzed here; we can notice only samples. One will certainly be that as colleges expand and as more students go to college, the impact of college slang in the language will increase. Many would call this a bad thing, although I am not one of them. Another impact will certainly be that as government grows, as business grows, as the number of people grow who have relatively pedestrian minds and limited educations, but who must by the nature of their jobs make solemn pronouncements, we can expect jargon to grow. Many would call that a bad thing, and I certainly am among them, although I doubt that we shall be able to do much about it. At least, many of the students who have passed through my courses in composition were busily preparing themselves to become automatic jargon-producing machines, and I fear I did little to stem the flow of this product.

Perhaps the significant observations here might spring from the relative numbers of people who use language informedly and seriously. Roughly speaking, we might distinguish the lettered in a community, those who use language with skill and training; the literate but unlettered, those who can read and write readily enough but do not much do so and do not much study the use of language; and the relatively illiterate, those who cannot read and write or who have only a rudimentary command of these skills. The oral use of language is likely to be roughly commensurate. The first group, the lettered, has always been small, is still small, but has grown somewhat. The last group, the relatively illiterate, was formerly very large, so large that it either dominated speech or played a leading role in it. The middle group, the unlettered literate, was formerly relatively small, but it now comprises a large group, perhaps the largest of the three. It exists as a great new force in our language use and hence in our language making. Formerly language sprang noticeably from the illiterate folk, or it filtered down from the lettered few; these tendencies continue, of course, but more and more we shall have locutions developed and popularized by the rapidly growing linguistic middle class.

Now we should ask ourselves a provocative but difficult question. Are new sorts of language developing? Once there was only oral language; nobody knew how to write. Then written language brought with it the possibility of civilization. Is any new sort of language promoting another revolution in human life? Possibly. Computers now work by means of what are called languages. That is, the programmer, the man who is trying to give instructions to the machine, speaks, let us say, English, but the computer cannot understand this language. The machine has a sort of language of its own, a language built into it by its designer, but this language the programmer is not likely to know. Accordingly, a limited means of communication is devised which both the programmer and the machine can understand, and it is in this so-called language that the human being addresses the machine and receives his answer.

This means of communication is not a language in the sense in which I have been using the word. Little IBM machines do not learn Resselrig or Fortran from their mothers. More significantly, a symbol system like Fortran probably has no adequate means of growing to satisfy the unconscious needs of its users. It is rather like what is called a pidgin. The pidgins we have known in the past have grown up for business reasons, and in fact the word *pidgin* is presumed to be the south-sea corruption of the word *business—pidgin English* is merely *business English*.

These pidgins are not languages in the sense that they are adequate means of communication on any subject. They are languages, however, in the sense that they permit limited communication on certain subjects, and within these limits they are precise and accurate. This, I take it, is what systems like Fortran are; they provide adequate and accurate means of communication within prescribed limits between two individuals, neither of whom can understand the other's normal means of communication. That is, Fortran is what one might call a computer pidgin—perhaps we should coin the blend, *compidgin*. Such signal systems may change the future world as much as written language has changed the world we know. Instead of giving courses in Freshman English Composition we may have to give Elementary, Intermediate, and Advanced Compidgin. And all this may come more rapidly than we can now imagine.

Computer languages will change, of course. They are in their infancy, and they may become oral as well as printed. I am told that even now machines are being designed which can be addressed in English and will reply in kind—Africans may be forced to learn English in order to use their computers!—but even so computer English is not likely to be like other English in the foreseeable future. Data processing machines cannot think, and since thinking is essential in language as we know it, compidgin is likely to differ from the English of human beings so long as a processing machine is at one end of the communicating.

Meanwhile, we might notice that the linguistic limitations of computers seem to be appearing. For a time they were expected to solve or greatly simplify the growing need for translation, but the anticipated breakthrough has not come. Language seems to be associated with minds, and computers have no minds. Recently, a distinguished committee pointed out that "To date there has been no satisfactory machine translation of scientific texts, and none is expected soon." The committee concluded that human translators are still a "bargain," being both cheaper and more accurate than machines.[3]

As language moves into machines, it is moving also into the outer universe. We have already seen that the preliminary gestures, involving mainly orbiting vehicles, have led to startling changes in some American English. American colonies in space, on the moon, or on other planets would doubtless trigger even broader changes in language. We cannot predict much, however, until we know who is going where and how, although we might remind ourselves that language has always been tough, resilient, and adaptable.

What, then, are we doing to our language? Various things, but mainly we are continuing to do what we have been doing for the past few hundred years. We are still building the vocabulary rapidly, partly by borrowing new words and pursuing new fads, but mainly by finding new

---

[3] The Automatic Language Processing Advisory Committee reported to the National Science Foundation, the Central Intelligence Agency, and the Department of Defense; it included many of the most distinguished American linguists. I have seen only news dispatches, dated about November 27, 1966.

uses for old words, applying them to new things and new activities. Our usage is changing rapidly within very narrow limits, but otherwise rather slowly. Sound and grammar are probably working together, the sound changing partly with the grammar and the grammar changing relatively rapidly toward more analytic constructions. But "relatively" rapidly is still very slow. Deep movements in linguistic change are for the ages. Mainly the fluff, like the bickering over *like* and *as,* the juggling of *like* and *dig,* appears on the surface. Meanwhile, we are devising a new electronic pidgin which may do as much to the minds and the manners of tomorrow as the written word did to the uncivilized hordes of yesterday, for Mother Tongue can be a surreptitious, effective female, and in the end, what she wants, she gets.

So much for the unconscious future of American English. What are we likely to do about it consciously? This is one of those auto-expansive questions, explosive because the United States seems to be moving into a new era. The age of the frontier gave way to the age of technology and harnessed energy. Now, apparently, the age of technology and the machine is merging into the age of education and knowledge, when men will give more of their time to thinking and experimenting and to learning these skills than they will to what is commonly called work. The machine can outwork man's hands and out-recall his memory; it can outdo man in classifying details and calculating probabilities, but it cannot think creatively. That, apparently, is to be man's job, and the more complicated and technical the job becomes, the more men's lives must be given to learning and education. But how does man think? He thinks best and most with language—even mathematics is becoming more and more a language, because mathematicians need language, specialized language to think with. Inevitably, we shall have more study and teaching of language, especially the native language, American English. People are demanding it, foundations recognize it, and at long last the federal government is joining local governments in supporting it.

Fortunately, just at this time teachers of English are learning to do their job better. Many an English teacher, many a well-trained teacher who was confident that she was a credit to her profession, taught little but punctuation, spelling, some supposed grammar that had never been the working grammar of English or any other known language, along with various bits of usage, some of them, like the prohibition against the preposition at the end of the sentence, erroneous. Some of these teachers, told that they were not teaching their students about writing by making them identify the supposed parts of speech, were desperate. "If I don't teach them grammar, how can I use up the class time?" Now these same teachers are beginning to see that, although they certainly must teach spelling, punctuation, and usage, they can also teach students how to read and write, and that writing has much more to do with organization, development, clear and vigorous predication, accurate and subtle use of subordination, than with distinctions between the gerund and the gerundive. They are learning that teaching the use of the native language means teaching the use of the mind and of the basic tool for civilization, and that teaching English can be much more exciting than they had ever supposed.

The result is that teaching the native language is profiting from new emphases and will continue to do so. More understanding of language will be taught. So will more listening. Many school systems pay lip service to a fourfold approach to the native language—reading, writing, speaking, and listening—but as yet this approach is often more words than action, at least so far as listening is concerned. Some colleges and universities attempted what was called Communications, an integrated approach to language, but the courses were often based upon inadequate philosophy and plagued by poorly prepared teachers. The movement appears dead. Most secondary schools still profess what they call the Language Arts, but teach them indifferently. The result is that courses in keeping one's mouth shut intelligently are few and are badly needed. In a world that relies more and more upon communication, and on communication at the local level in committees and service groups, the ability to listen intelligently and sympathetically is essential. This is one of the better points made by the general semanticists; as yet they have not been much heard on this subject, however widely they may have been heard on some others, but they will be. Listening is an art, and it can be taught; in the future it will be taught more. Similarly, as one aspect of teaching English, discussion of rhetoric will increase. As I endeavored to indicate in Chapter 20, we are now moving into a revolution in our concept of the artistic use of prose, both fiction and nonfiction, and these developments will continue.

Apparently we shall have new methods of working with the English language and new tools. I have mentioned linguistic geography, structural linguistics, generative grammar, and the like. Nonlinguistic machinery like the paperback book industry will have its effect; I am told that manufacturers of blue jeans have had to redesign their product, an essential to teenage wardrobes in this country and abroad, so that the hip pockets will accommodate paperback books. Blue jeans as worn by cowpunchers helped conquer the last physical frontier in the United States; equipped with a holster for paperbacks they may be involved in conquering new frontiers in mental competence. Similarly, language command may be promoted by new techniques in the pre-preschool, by which children learn to read before they learn to speak. They should be able to do this; learning to speak is impeded by the complicated job of training muscles in the tongue, but a child can recognize its own toes at a very early age, and can learn to associate the printed word *toes* with the objects. In fact, children might even acquire the concept of the variety of languages; they could learn that *Zehe, doigt, dedo del pie,* and *digitus* all refer to the same wriggling object.

One of the most interesting developments, attended by the most violent reactions, concerns that veteran audio-visual aid, the dictionary. In modern language study, the dictionary was one of the first tools to be well understood, well conceived, and well built. For western Europe— including England—grammar suffered from the infirm foundation of classical grammars; since classical grammars were assumed to reveal Universal Grammar, western European thinkers were not spurred to develop their own grammatical statements on the basis of their own observations of their own grammars. Lexicographers did not so suffer, however, since classical tongues had no dictionaries, presumably in part because the classical languages were used mainly for oral purposes. With fewer languages and with fewer international documents involved, translation was not a very important function among early Mediterranean peoples, and thus bilingual and polylingual glossaries were not much in demand.

In western Europe, however, where all learned works were in Latin or Greek, tongues not always well understood, interlinear glosses became common; glosses were collected into glossaries, and glossaries evolved into dictionaries. By the late seventeenth century, as we have seen, lexicography was becoming established, and what are called historical principles of making dictionaries had been discovered. Conversant lexicographers, including Bailey, Johnson, and others in England, understood that meaning can be revealed through citations; they built their dictionaries by collecting uses of words and by deriving meanings by the uses to which native speakers of the language put these words. With such procedures lexicographers assumed that the principles of their study had been discovered and that these principles needed only more adequate development and more perceptive application.

Now we seem to be on the brink of another development. To understand it we should recall an American institution, the *New International Dictionary.* In an earlier chapter we have seen that Noah Webster's dictionary passed into the hands of George and Charles Merriam, obscure printers and bookbinders in Springfield, Massachusetts, and that during the latter half of the nineteenth century, the book was repeatedly improved. It prospered, and through it the Merriams, until the company greeted at once the new century and the new horizons of an emergent country by issuing the *New International*. It became standard; every school and college of any account either had or hoped to get copies. Citizens bolstered their egos and their social stations by acquiring it; newspapers, magazines, publishing houses, and governments wrote the *New International* into their style sheets; it became a national, if not an international, institution, a symbol and a product of the new culture of the New World. Webster had referred to his book as "the dictionary," as if there had been no other; his contemporaries did not so think of it, but many users of the *New International* did. It was *Webster,* and it was "the dictionary."

But dictionaries are not immortal. The *Oxford* was begun a century or so ago, and in its completed form is now approaching a half century of use; there is no active program to revise it, and there probably will not be for some time. A desk dictionary, on the other hand, faces charges of obsolescence after about ten years; the middle sort of dictionary like the *New International* cannot be expected to last much more than a quarter of a century. By 1925 the Merriam people were beefing up their editorial staff for a revision, and when the new edition came from the press, it was hailed as an even greater triumph than the first edition. After another quarter of a century, in the 1950's, the Merriams prepared for another happy rebirth, but the resulting offspring was scorned from coast to coast as a monster, even before many people outside the Merriam coterie had seen it, and this condemnation was confirmed before anybody had had time to study it carefully or test it with extensive use.

One must ask the occasion of such reversal and of such unproportioned violence—dictionaries are useful tools, which usually inspire more loyalty than pyrotechnics. First we might notice that the reactions were more nearly wails of sadness and disillusionment than bellows of wrath. The grief suggested a leader lost, a ruler abdicated, an idol overthrown, a savior exposed as a charlatan, and the violence of the reaction reminds one that the *New International* and all works associated with it long enjoyed a veneration that partook of the religious. People who felt themselves allied with Light believed in good dictionaries, and to oppose good dictionaries was to declare oneself a servant of the Powers of Darkness. All this was associated with the word *Webster,* which in turn was associated with the *New International,* and to derogate that dictionary or any of its relatives was like invoking Mohammed in the First Baptist Church.

Apparently, this is what happened. The new edition was announced for September 28, 1961. To prepare for the event, the Merriam promotional department issued a press release for September 7, which was picked up as the basis of a wire story, which in turn was printed from coast to coast. The Merriam promotional people were good publicists who knew what newspapers would want to print, and they were probably relying on the widely held thesis that any publicity is good publicity. Whatever the cause, the result was that the new edition was ridiculed almost everywhere, mainly on the basis of *ain't*. The forthcoming dictionary was greeted with leads like "The word 'ain't' ain't a grammatical mistake any more," and heads like "It Ain't Good," "Saying Ain't Ain't Wrong: See Webster," and "The Death of Meaning."[4] Perhaps half of all this condemnation concerned *ain't*, one in 450,000 entries and not a very important one at that, about one two-millionth of the book. Some papers wrote their own notices, apparently using the publicity statement, although they pretended that the pronouncement represented acquaintance with the volume. This is unlikely, since the volume was not due off the presses for three weeks, and nobody could study such a book with care in less than several months of undisturbed time, which few busy journalists can spare.

For example, someone wrote in the *Washington Sunday Star,* under date of September 10,

. . . perhaps the most shocking thing in the whole book is that it takes a rather respectful view of "ain't" as a word that is now "used orally in the U.S. by cultivated speakers." This is certainly a far cry from the dictionary's 1934 edition, which bluntly—and correctly, in our view—brands "ain't" as a "dialectical" and "illiterate" expression employed by people on the fringes of polite society.

One might notice several matters here; the author refers to "the whole book," but he certainly had not studied it, and he probably had not seen it. He uses the autoprotective, irrefutable "perhaps." This saves him, but means nothing. It is "perhaps" true that the sun will not rise tomorrow and that the current President of the United States has forty-seven illegitimate children, but both statements, which are perhaps true, are extremely unlikely. Furthermore, the writer mishandles the quotation from the third edition of the *New International* and is apparently unaware of the contents of the edition he praises. If the *Star* writer had been citing the dictionary and not the publicity sheet, he probably would have provided a more extensive quotation—at least he' should have—which does

---

[4] A good sampling of the notices and reviews, including all that I refer to below, is printed in *Dictionaries and THAT Dictionary,* ed. James Sledd and Wilma R. Ebbitt (Chicago: Scott, Foresman & Co., 1962).

much to change the color of the whole, as follows: "Though disapproved by many and more common in less educated speech, used orally in most parts of the U.S. by many cultivated speakers esp. in the phrase 'ain't I.' " This may be too latitudinarian; I doubt that anyone can successfully deny that it is literally true, although I personally should estimate that it leaves the impression that the word is more widely accepted than it is. Curiously, however, the second edition was rather less condemnatory—the *Star* writer to the contrary. The second edition did not say that *ain't* is " 'dialectical' and 'illiterate' "; it said the word is *"Dial. or Illit.,"* which means that it is sometimes illiterate and sometimes dialectal. Now, being dialectal is no condemnation at all, at least if one relies upon the definition in the same second edition that the *Star* writer was praising. The definition of *dialectal* is that it refers to *dialect* or *dialects;* the definitions of *dialect* include the following: "4. a. The customary speech of a rank or social class; as a peasant *dialect;* rural *dialect;* negro *dialect;* the *dialect* of the educated class. . . . 5. The cant or jargon of a class, profession, trade, or the like, as, the lawyer's *dialect."* Thus, if one reads the definition in the second edition literally, *ain't* can be characteristic of the use of either "the *dialect* of the educated class," or "the lawyer's *dialect."* That is, taken literally, the statement in the second edition of the *New International* is somewhat more permissive than that in the third edition; I doubt that the editors of the second meant exactly what they said, but the upshot of the whole is that the editors of both the second and the third edition were saying about the same thing, except that the editors of the third were saying this so clearly that the users of the dictionary knew what they meant, whereas even the admiring users of the second did not understand it.

The chorus, varying from the jocund to the superior-contemptuous, did not end with the prepublication notices; journalists who professed to have studied the third edition, and who had an opportunity to do so, were more inclusive, but they were also more abusive. Roy H. Copperud in *Editor & Publisher* has characterized the whole as "a flurry of nitwitted commentary." Not all the reviewers had nits in their wits, but many were writing the sheerest nonsense, and some were seemingly striving to see how sheer they could get. The new edition was "cheap and corrupt," a "scandal and a disaster," it was "shocking," "sabotage," "a serious blow to good English." Two reviewers, Wilson Follett in the *Atlantic* and Dwight Macdonald in *The New Yorker,* were widely quoted in other reviews by other reviewers who obviously did not take time to study the book. Follett concludes that "we have seen a century and a third of illustrious history largely jettisoned." Anyone who agrees with him should be condemned to reading Noah Webster's 1828 dictionary until he discovers how bad American lexicography used to be.

Although Follett wrote one of the better reviews, he gives no great understanding of what a dictionary should do and how it should do this. "Think—if you can—" he writes, "of an unabridged dictionary from which you cannot learn who Mark Twain was (though *mark twain* is entered as a leadsman's cry), or what were the names of the apostles, or that the Virgin was Mary the mother of Jesus of Nazareth, or what and where the District of Columbia is!" He puts an exclamation mark after this as though nobody could think such a thought, although many can, and Mr. Follett could have, had he first asked himself what a dictionary is and what it is not. He would very soon have found the answer that it is not an encyclopedia, that the editors of a dictionary are inevitably pressed for space trying to make their book a good dictionary, and that accordingly they should not waste space doing the jobs of encyclopedists, geographers, and the Bureau of Census. Lower-case *mark twain* gets in because it is part of the English language; upper case Mark Twain does not because he was part of the human race, American literature, the history of journalism, or what not. The Virgin Mary and the District of Columbia do not belong in a dictionary just because they are well known; so are the multiplication table and the poem inscribed on the Statue of Liberty, but they very properly are found no place in the third edition. Some dictionaries appropriately contain a jumble of almost everything; if a man has only one reference work he may like to have all sorts of useful bits in it, but people who buy the *New International* do not rely on only one reference work. Objecting to the exclusion of routine encyclopedic material from an extensive dictionary is like objecting to the *Atlantic* because it does not reprint the zodiac and contain a recipe for making soap. A century ago, *Fisher's Improved Housekeeper's Almanac* contained both, doubtless because the editor assumed that his publication was the unique reference work in many households, and he put in anything that might be handy. But the *Atlantic* is not a farmer's almanac, and the *New International* should not be a general reference work for those who do not have access even to a one-volume encyclopedia.

Macdonald did rather better. He started with much the same prejudices as those who restricted their comments to *ain't,* but he did study the book, and he made an effort to be fair; he even found a few virtues in the book and duly records them. Unfortunately, he never seriously considers whether this work does or does not provide a revealing description of modern American English. He does not like it as a tool for desk editors. Having been an editor, I know that one of the hazards of the occupation is that the sense of a blue pencil in the hand tends to make the wielder weigh everything by its use on the copy desk. Macdonald suffers, as most other reviewers suffered, because he thinks of the *New*

International mainly as a usage book. A writer in the *Chicago Daily News* (October 20, 1961) puts it this way: "What's the point in any writer's trying to compose clear and graceful prose, to avoid solecisms, to maintain a sense of decorum, if that peerless authority, Webster's Unabridged, surrenders abjectly to the permissive school of speech."

One might assume that a writer—any writer—could find reasons for cultivating "clear and graceful prose" regardless of what any dictionary does or does not do, but even so I suspect that we are here at the core of the matter, and it is a much more significant matter than the discrediting of a great book by testy and imperceptive reviewers.[5] The fact is that most Americans, even most cultured Americans, do not know what a great dictionary is good for; they buy such dictionaries for the wrong reasons and use them for the wrong purposes. A great dictionary is intended to describe the language, and being permissive or nonpermissive about usage is none of its business. This mainly is what great dictionaries have been, ever since there have been great dictionaries; this is what all makers of great dictionaries thought they were trying to do when they edited their volumes. To use them for any other purpose is to misuse a highly specialized tool. No book can be a "peerless authority" in language, but if it is to be an authority, a great dictionary should be admired for its description of the language, not for the pejorative it attaches to *ain't*.

The American public, however, should not be much blamed. It has been misled, and in high places. Nowhere in the long introduction to the second edition of the *New International* did the editors say that the volume was the authority on usage or should so be used. The publishers, however, said this at length and repeatedly; *Word Study,* the official organ of the Merriam Company, long carried a department headed WEBSTER DECIDES. Questions concerning usage were solicited, and they were answered largely, if not entirely, by quoting the *New International.* The volume itself was regularly, and extensively, advertised as "the Supreme Authority." The intent, apparently, was to create the assumption that no one could be sure he was speaking or writing properly unless he consulted the single "supreme authority," and this

---

[5] There are exceptions. A few understanding, although rather brief, reviews appeared in England. I have mentioned Copperud's above, and Millicent Taylor wrote a capable review for the *Christian Science Monitor.* A few college professors, including Margaret Bryant, Karl W. Dykema, Albert Marckwardt, Priscilla Tyler, and James Sledd, wrote good reviews, but they appeared mostly in professional journals like *College English,* where they were quarantined from the general public. For a summary of the entries excised from the second edition and the reasons for the excisions, see Philip B. Gove, "The Nonlexical and the Encyclopedic," *Names,* XIII (1965), 103–15.

'was often the result. Of course, we should have known better; we might have suspected that nobody can brand a word and have his brand valid for all times and places. How can a few editors decide, for all times, all societies, and all parts of the English-speaking world, whether *teenage* is slang, a colloquialism, a dialectal form, standard usage, or what? Editors will not agree, and are the editors whom the Merriam people happen to hire always right, and those editors whom other publishers hire always wrong if they differ from the *New International* editors? As a matter of fact, *teenage* does not appear in the second edition, the only word so spelled which is entered there being a dialectal Briticism meaning "brushwood used for fences and hedges." The obvious moral is that no book can be an authority for everything for all time. We should have been more skeptical of the Merriam advertising, but the American people had grown accustomed to accepting the *New International* with something approaching religious faith. Skepticism simply was not in good taste if it concerned the Deity or the Dictionary.

Naturally, people want usage books, and they have every right to them. People who are uncertain about accepted usage want to be told, by somebody they can trust, and in a way they can understand. Those who believe they know want their convictions confirmed. But the fact is that a great dictionary is not a good tool for this purpose; it is too cumbersome, too expensive, too resistant to change. Usage is but a minor aspect of language study. Pedagogically the *ain't* problem is extremely difficult, although linguistically it is simple. Teaching Johnny not to say *ain't* may be exasperating, boring, even impossible, but knowing when to use *ain't* and when not to use it is easy, even for Johnny. Furthermore, usage changes too fast to be amenable to treatment by a book like the *New International*. Using a great dictionary to settle usage problems is like using an elephant gun to shoot sparrows.

The answer, presumably, is that we should use usage books for usage and great dictionaries for what they are meant for. A desk usage book would not need to be large; 15,000 entries—not 450,000—would easily cover all usage problems commonly at issue. Such a book could be revised frequently enough that it would contain words like *teenage*—or is it *teen-age?*—and once linguistic geography is developed, such books could be remarkably accurate, not just one editor's guess. Such books would be under no obligation to be what some reviewers have called "permissive"; their business would be to describe usage in such a way that description becomes prescription, and thus the *Chicago Daily News* writer, if he needs encouragement in avoiding solecisms, will have it, and ordinary folk, if they are in doubt, can be told quite simply that for most purposes they should avoid *ain't*.

The difficulty has been that most people have not been willing to pay almost fifty dollars for an elaborate description of American English. They are not that much interested in the state and nature of any language, including their own. Accordingly, to sell the *New International* as a commercial venture, the Merriam people had to convince the public that nobody could write or speak correctly unless he owned a so-called "unabridged" dictionary—of course there is no such thing as an unabridged dictionary, since all dictionaries are reduced from what they might be, but a usage book should be heavily abridged. The result was that books were misused, and that in part they were jumbled to encourage misuse.

I suspect that this will not continue. Long before another quarter century elapses, and a fourth *New International* is called for, we are likely to have numerous cheap, reliable usage books, published at popular prices and widely disseminated. Even journalists will discover that they can continue as honorable professional people without consulting "the unabridged" for most spellings, for hyphenation, and to discover that *consensus of opinion* is redundant and *this present-day world of ours* can be called quite a few derogatory names.

Thus, there may never be a fourth *New International* in the sense that there was a first and a second. Apparently, a great dictionary of a great language cannot be successfully published as a commercial venture. This is not to say that great dictionaries are done, that in lexicography there will "be no more cakes and ale." It probably does mean, however, that the next great dictionary of American English—quite possibly to be edited at Springfield and published by the Merriam people—will have to be subsidized by the government or by some foundation. It should be; the standard dictionary of a language is the need of the people, from which the people will profit; they should be expected to pay for it, and if it is to be done well they probably will have to pay for it, directly or indirectly. That is the real tragedy of the *New International,* third edition; its editors faced an impossible assignment. Cramped for space, crippled by inconsistencies between printing costs of an adequate dictionary and sales receipts for a commercially feasible dictionary, they tried to produce the dictionary of American English, a volume which the purchasers wanted mainly to treat as a usage handbook. In another quarter of a century, no doubt, all these matters will be more widely understood; we shall have better dictionaries, even though they are subsidized and are not publishing gold mines, and we shall have more usable usage books as well.

Meanwhile, we might notice that not only has the third edition of the *New International* been condemned for not being what it should not have been, it has not been praised for what it is. It is probably an epochal work whose significance will eventually be recognized. Very much as the *Accademia della Crusca* defined meaning through citations, Dr. Philip B. Gove and his associates on the third edition have endeavored to reveal usage by citation. They have recognized, as do all lexicographers, that nobody can use usage labels like *dialectal* and *slang* in any objective, satisfactory way. Instead, they have tried to reveal usage by judiciously selected examples; they cite careful users of the language, but along with them they quote Art Linkletter saying "like I do," and an obscure Florida weekly printing "like he was." They also cite a pugilist and a professional baseball player. Presumably, if one wants to sound like Art Linkletter, an obscure Florida weekly, a pugilist, or a professional baseball player, he knows how to do it, and if he does not want to, he knows what to avoid. That is, the editors of the third edition have tried to apply the same principles in revealing usage that have become standard practice in revealing meaning. If they have not been entirely successful in this pioneering work, we can condemn them only for not having done superbly what nobody else has attempted, for most of the language, to do at all.

One further prophecy must detain us: American English is not about to slump into a sodden slough of jumbled jargon. One ought not need to say this, since the notion of the decay of language as against the growth of language is little more than an echo of the Garden of Eden myth, but the notion persists and today inspires both vehemence and despair, even among highly literate people. For example, Lincoln Barnett, whose book I quoted earlier, writes as follows:

To almost everyone who cherishes the English language for its grace and beauty, its combination of precision and flexibility, the social philosophy of the Structural Linguists seems past comprehension—epitomizing indeed the "anti-intellectualism of the intellectual." Among all the forces of cultural vandalism at work in the country, their influence has been, perhaps, the most insidious.[6]

Elsewhere Barnett explains that "The precepts of Structural Linguists condone slovenly speech and slovenly writing," that "Structural Linguists . . . deny the importance of writing and the written word," that they recoil from "what they consider the 'socio-ethnic snobbery' of graceful speech." As a result Barnett fears that English may "degenerate

---

[6] *The Treasure of Our Tongue*, pp. 285–86; there is more in the same vein. I cite him because at this writing his book is the most recent, and because, being engagingly presented and issued by a good publisher, it will probably have wide impact.

into a babel of regional dialects, social stratifications, vulgarities, jargon, and juvenile slang," which he very rightly feels would be unfortunate.

This is the sort of thing that is likely to make structural linguists— lower case since structuralists are neither a corporate body nor a political party—laugh out loud, because they cannot conceive how well-meaning, harmless, devoted, and learned people can be doing so much damage, or how anyone can believe that they do, but apparently people do believe this. Macdonald and Follett, quoted above, also blame the Structural Linguists—also upper-case, as though they were the Communist International—for the rape of the *New International,* assuming that Dr. Gove is a structural linguist. It so happens that Gove is not a structural linguist, although doubtless he would be flattered to have it supposed that he had mastered this technique along with his others.[7] Thus whatever their crimes, the structural linguists did not destroy the *New International Dictionary;* in fact, as anyone who has canvassed the earlier chapters of this book will know, structural linguistics has little to do with lexicography, or with anything that seems to be bothering the prophets of linguistic doom.

Of course, some structuralists may be interested, also, in usage, as some Republicans are also Episcopalians, but being permissive or not permissive is not any of a structuralist's business, as a structuralist. He is concerned with analyzing language by structure. Similarly, practicing literary art is not, professionally, his business. It so happens, however, that a number of structuralists have written rather well; Edward Sapir is one of the founders of structural study and a very capable poet. Harold Whitehall, a practicing structuralist, has written good verse and very telling literary criticism, along with some superb translations, but literary craftsmanship is not the business of a structuralist any more than it is the business of Wernher von Braun. On the other hand, when Barnett says that structural linguists "deny the importance of writing and the written word," he is flatly mistaken. Structuralists start with oral language, partly because it is the basic form of any language, and partly because it is easier to work with and they feel that their study is as yet in its infancy. They profess, however, to make all forms of language their province, and curiously, they specialize in studying written poetry, and believe that they are revolutionizing our understanding of prosody.[8]

---

[7] In the hope of avoiding the charge of special pleading, let me say that I am no structural linguist, either, although I admire what the structuralists have done and respect what they are trying to do, as I am convinced any fair-minded person must who will investigate their work. It is surely no condemnation of them or of any scientists that they work in "rarefied realms," for which Barnett ridicules them; see p. 281. Where else can a specialist do most of his work?

[8] See, for example, Samuel R. Levin, *Linguistic Structures in Poetry* (The Hague: Mouton, 1962) and Seymour Chatman, *The Theory of Meter* (the same, 1966).

Thus most of the adverse critics of the structural linguists quite literally do not know what they are talking about. Of course they are
talking about something, and to take them seriously we must ask why
they predict the collapse of the English language, even though, in fixing
on structuralists, and especially on upper-case Structural Linguists, they
are misusing words. These critics vary in their use of terms, and if we
cannot define their terms we labor under difficulties; but apparently by
Structural Linguists they mean almost any student of language who uses
a recently developed technique, and particularly those who are believed
to preach that in language "anything goes." They apparently believe that
such people comprise most of those who today write, think, study,
teach, or do research in modern English, and that these people dominate
the school system at all levels.

If this were true it would be unfortunate, perhaps not so devastating
as some of these prophets suggest, but in crying need of reform. The
fact, however, is that it is not true, although we could find some color
for the belief. All modern students of language recognize that, whether
we like it or not, in the end, use determines language, and that this
fundamental principle must be taken into account when we think about
language or work with it. No doubt using this thesis, the educators who
conceive of the school system as primarily a device for adjusting young
people to their environments have recommended permissiveness in
usage. They are the same people who recommend social promotion, no
homework for students, and the reduction of the study of the native
language to talking on the telephone. I take it that such educators are
now going out of fashion in the secondary schools; they never have been
in fashion in the colleges and universities outside colleges of education,
and they have been viewed with horror by all modern students of language, including the structural linguists. I believe I have known most of
the students of modern language in this country who have gained any
reputation in recent years; I do not know one who would subscribe to
the formula, "anything goes," which has disturbed Barnett, J. Donald
Adams, Jacques Barzun, and a number of others. Linguists all believe in
the delineation and application of standards, which is apparently what
the embattled defenders of prescription believe they are fighting for.
Even teachers who believe in permissiveness in usage are relatively rare;
I speak at a modest number of institutes for English teachers, and I
cannot at the moment recall one who believed that "anything goes,"
although plenty of them had come to the institute to get information
with which to battle a principal or superintendent who did. Thus the
curious fact is that people like Barnett are bloodying the heads of their
allies, teachers and scholars who believe as much as the journalists do in
promoting the clear and vigorous use of the native language, although as

specialists they do not usually speak in the broad terms of popularized writing.

Thus the fact is that although some permissivists have not always shown discretion in the extent of their permissivity, either in usage or in spankings, there is not now, and so far as I know never has been, a body of students of language who preached that "anything goes," or any body of English teachers who were inculcating such notions. True, linguists have often advised teachers not to spend all their time on minor matters of usage, urging them to teach sentence structure, adequate development, grace and precision of predication along with spelling, punctuation, and grammatical form. Quoted out of context, their advice can be made to sound latitudinarian; Robert A. Hall of Cornell University, John B. Carroll of Harvard, and Charles Carpenter Fries of Michigan have been so attacked, but how anyone can read their works *in extenso* and believe anything of the sort about them passes my understanding.[9] Furthermore, even if the theory and practice of teaching usage were as bad as the lachrymose prophets seem to suppose, there would still be no reason to predict that English is likely to "degenerate into a babel" of any sort. The fact is that we have no record of any language anywhere at any time which "degenerated into a babel" for any reason, and certainly not because it lacked a dictionary to excoriate certain common locutions or a vociferous prescriptive grammar. Most languages have grown and have lived most of their lives entirely without writing and without works, written or oral, to police the language. How did they manage to grow? What kept them from babel?

One of Barnett's own examples may be instructive. Barnett much admires the writings of Shakespeare and the translators of the King James version of the Bible, and understandably; most students of language would agree with him. But what was the *New International Dictionary* that, as yet uncorrupted by structural linguists, provided Shakespeare with his vocabulary? There was none; there was no dictionary of any kind.[10] What was the grammar that purified Shakespeare's style by expunging his "vulgarities"? Again, there was none. Ben Jonson, Shake-

---

[9] For what seems to be a fairly clear case, in which Barzun attacks Fries without understanding him, see Charles C. Fries, *Linguistics: The Study of Language* (New York: Holt, Rinehart and Winston, 1964), p. 92, note 1. The volume is a partial reprint of Fries' *Linguistics and Reading*.

[10] John Florio published an Italian-English dictionary, *A World of Words*, in 1598, but no one can say that the author of *Romeo and Juliet*, first Quarto, 1597, still had to learn how to write. Shortly after this time small dictionaries of English began to appear, lists of supposed "hard words," with brief definitions. Shakespeare, if he ever saw such a work, would have considered it beneath his notice.

speare's younger contemporary, wrote a grammar, apparently intended to help beginners learn Latin; it could have had no influence on Shakespeare or the learned translators of the King James, who were no longer schoolboys. What was the handbook that policed Shakespeare's usage? Again there was none. Apparently the first prescriptive injunction was that of George Fox in 1660; he thought anybody was an "Ideot and a Fool" if he used *you* as a singular pronoun. Schoolteachers like Roger Ascham were beginning to raise the question of propriety in usage, but they could scarcely have influenced Shakespeare. Ascham considers the value of the English letters and raises questions of appropriate spelling; Shakespeare, like most of his contemporaries, was so little concerned with spelling that he had no standard way of spelling his own name.

That is, so far as we can discover, policing usage in language is not necessary to the health of language or to good writing. This is not to say, of course, that dictionaries, grammars, spellers, thesauruses, and handbooks of usage have no value; they are extremely useful, and publishers are zealously improving them, but languages do not "degenerate into babel" without them. Nor is this discussion to suggest that the use of language should not be studied and practiced; the Elizabethans, though they had no grammars or dictionaries, studied language. They studied the rhetoric of Latin and Greek, and they practiced translation,[11] one of the best disciplines to promote acuity and fluidity in the use of language. In fact one might notice a strong correlation between the great cultures and those that have placed a premium on the study and practice of the native language, including the Chinese, Egyptian, Hebrew, classical Greek and Roman, and the Western European.

The teaching of the native language in the United States suffers mainly because taxpayers have not wanted to pay for better teaching. This is not the only reason, but it is basic. Many a good teacher, who knows how to teach and wants to teach, cannot do so because she is asked to do the job of two teachers, and the taxpayers, through the legislatures, the schoolboards, or whatnot, will not provide the money that would hire a second teacher. Learning to use the native language well is a hard job; it necessitates hard teaching, but it can be taught, granted enough well-trained teachers are provided for the job. As a matter of fact, getting the money for such teachers is not made easier by

---

[11] See, for example, F. O. Matthiessen, *Translation, an Elizabethan Art* (Cambridge, Mass.: Harvard University Press, 1931). For introductions to the Western tradition in the study of rhetoric, see Charles Sears Baldwin, *Medieval Rhetoric and Poetic* [to 1400] (New York: The Macmillan Co., 1928); William Garrett Crane, *Wit and Rhetoric in the Renaissance: The Formal Basis of Elizabethan Prose Style,* Columbia University Studies in English and Comparative Literature, 129 (Gloucester, Mass.: P. Smith, 1964).

critics who imply that, since all modern students of the native language are either knaves or fools, money given to them is money wasted. At best, closefisted, stiffnosed people find it difficult to believe that literacy, especially highly cultivated literacy, is a social good worth paying for, but of late there is some change, and more understanding from the Barnetts and the Folletts would be welcome. Meanwhile, we might parody a remark on the state of the nation by observing that those who now declare that the language is going to the devil are not likely to see it get there.

Perhaps we should add a guess as to the future of American English abroad. Here we must deal with social, political, military, and other forces, along with linguistic trends, and we must remind ourselves that in many developments—in military actions, for example—changes are likely to be much more rapid than in language. Still, within limits, tendencies now operative can be expected to continue.

If English is to become a world language, what kind of English will it be? Formerly, the answer would have been easy; English was either native British English or exported British English. This is no longer true; as we have seen, although exported British English is still common, especially in Africa, Asia, and the Pacific islands, American English is growing rapidly, and if the choice were between British and American, the choice for the future would not be British. But this is not the choice. Australia is developing its own brand of English, which will dominate the continent and be in much better position to influence Asia and the Pacific islands than will either British or American speech. Or consider India; its population is approaching a half billion, and English may become its basic language. It is the only common language and is growing rapidly; if India ever puts its political, social, economic, and linguistic house in order and speaks English even as a second tongue, it may become the great base for that language in the greatest of continents. Thus if English becomes a world language, it will not be British Received Standard, the class and regional dialect of a few million speakers; it will be the result of the interplay of various dialects of English, a reconciliation in which British English will play a part, but probably not a leading one.

This prospect will disturb some sensitive Britons. No doubt Colonel Blimp would like English to be the possession of his London club, but it will not be. Language works in accordance with its own nature; we can try to understand this nature, and talk sense, or we can ignore it and talk nonsense; these are among the facts of life with which Colonel Blimp must live, whether he likes them or not. No people—at least no people in recorded time—ever created a language; no speakers of a language have title to it.[12] Language came either from the Deity, as some people trust, or it was developed by mankind, as most students now believe, but in any event it is not the property of any part of the human race.

All members of the human race have inherited it from their unknown and uncountable ancestors, and all users of language have equal rights in all of it or any part of it. The so-called English language is a form of Indo-European—which Colonel Blimp did not invent—which stems from languages as yet unknown. That it underwent extensive enlargement and refinement in the island of Britain—more by borrowing from other languages than by the preservation of any supposed purity—all speakers of English must be grateful, but that contributions to the language come from any particular body of users of the language does not make it their possession nor the preserve of any favored few of their descendants. It is no more the property of the Anglo-Saxons who moved to England than it is the property of the Saxons who did not move from Saxony. It is no more the property of the Cockney whose parents stayed in London than it is of the children of the Cockney who promoted the expansion of English by taking it to Australia. It is as much the property of an Indian who has chosen to learn English because he wanted it as it is the property of the Yorkshireman who had it thrust upon him. Actually, in spite of Colonel Blimp's preferences, this seems to be right and just, but just or not, this in language is the way of the world.

We should consider the role of this English in the world to come. English has been increasing; it accelerated when speakers of English were the most numerous among the victors in World War I; it accelerated further when speakers of English were the most widely spread of victors in World War II, and it accelerated still more when speakers of English became leaders of the free world. Furthermore, this acceleration has been greater in the second decade after the war than it was in the first. We may reasonably predict that, barring military or other sociopolitical catastrophes, English will continue to expand more than will any other language outside the communist areas, and this expansion will continue to accelerate. How English will fare in competition with com-

---

12 Many Esperantists will of course not agree with me, but I can only say that in the sense in which I am using the word, Esperanto or any other devised code of communication is not a language. It is not and never has been the unique linguistic means of communication of a body of people. Very properly, devisers of languages have started with the idea of language; they borrowed grammatical devices, sound systems, alphabets, and vocabularies. This is not to belittle their work, but only to distinguish between natural languages and a devised system of communication. The labor and devotion of Esperantists and others who have tried to devise world languages is admirable, but results to date do not permit us to predict that much will come of their efforts.

munist languages, notably Russian and Chinese, will hinge on military and political developments that are hazardous to predict, but at the moment the conflict between Communism and Democracy-Capitalism seems not to be going badly for the free world, and, as we have seen in the recent chapter, even Russia and China are tending to use English more and more, and even in propaganda directed at English.

The phrase "world language" can be used in at least two ways. It can refer to a widely known language; in this sense English is a world language now. In all populous parts of the world people speak it and write it, and can understand it if it is written or spoken. This is not true of Bantu or Albanian, which are not world languages in any sense. In another sense a world language would be a language used as the primary means of communication by all human beings, or at least, a language that all literate people everywhere could be expected to know. In this second sense English is not a world language, but it is moving in that direction more rapidly than is any other. Whether it becomes a world language is beyond anyone's power to determine—for language relies upon society and works mainly in accordance with its own nature, but not exclusively. If man has not been able to determine the course of language, men have been able to influence it. Is English the best of all possible world languages? If not, can it be made so? And what should we do about it, if anything?

We need compare English as a potential world language with very few others. German as a potential world tongue did not survive the First World War and the later Nazi butcherings, and French did not much survive the Second War, although this estimate will not be much accepted in the Fifth Republic, where desperate efforts are intended to "maintain" French as the international language. For 1966 the budget to promote the French language and culture abroad was increased twenty-five per cent to more than a million dollars, and 32,000 teachers of French were being supported in former French colonies. Meanwhile, although French had been the international language, in sessions of the General Assembly of the United Nations speakers who use English are likely to outnumber those who use French by about two to one, and scientists who write English in learned journals are likely to outnumber those who write French by much larger proportions, in many areas eight or ten to one.

Spanish has great potentialities in Latin America, but South and Central America have too many revolutions, too few schools, and too little continental unity; Spanish is a world language in one sense, but it cannot become a world language in the other sense in the foreseeable future. Specifically, nothing like a standard Latin American Spanish seems to be developing, and Castilian Spanish is no more likely to become a controlling standard in the former Spanish colonies than British Received Standard has become a controlling dialect in the former British colonies. For a time Cuban speech was admired as the "best" Latin American Spanish, but Cuba is now pretty much isolated, politically, socially, and economically. The potentially great central power is Brazil, where Portuguese, not Spanish is the native tongue. The two other leading countries, Mexico and Argentina, are not large enough nor sufficiently advanced in culture to dominate the whole area, and they suffer from their extreme positions at the northern and southerly ends of the Spanish-speaking block. The smaller central countries have not attained eminence. Bolivia was well started but has suffered of late from instability, as has Peru. At the moment, Venezuela is promising but has a long way to go. Other countries are even less likely. Some intellectuals and many teachers are laboring to establish European Spanish as a standard, but they have had little success, and they probably will not have much. Peninsular Spanish would seem to be too much divorced from Latin American Spanish, too far removed in space, and too foreign politically and socially ever to become a dominant Latin American dialect. But if Spanish is ever to become the major intercultural language it must do so on the basis of Latin American Spanish, for Spain, however glorious its past, is too restricted in space and potential population to be taken seriously as the home of a world language. Thus the prospects for Spanish are poorer than one might at first suppose, since apparently a world language must have a standard form, or relatively few closely related forms, whereas Latin America seems to be producing no standard dialect; and if Castilian can be considered a received standard for the mother country—which is doubtful—it is so situated, geographically and socially, that it can have only a limited future.

Other western European languages, including Italian, have long been outdistanced. Arabic is not possible; many Arabic speakers have been culturally backward and are now politically incompatible. Since no African tongues and few Asiatic bodies of speech have more than local currency, the only comparison of importance is that among English, Russian, and Chinese. Actually, a minor language like Basque, which would not occasion jingoistic jealousy, might be best, but introducing such a language into the schools for a generation throughout the world would require international cooperation on a scale that cannot at this time be seriously considered. Similarly, a language like Armenian might serve, since it is already a *lingua franca* in the Middle East and has the advantage of being an Indo-European tongue, but it has too little base in commerce, culture, and politics.

The first virtue, perhaps, that a world language should have is uniformity. Are all users of the language using the same sort of language? Obviously not, but clearly English is far in the lead; English dialects are numerous but not highly divergent. Almost all speakers of English can understand almost all other speakers of English; *honor* and *center* confuse no one by being spelled *honour* and *centre*. This is not true of Russian, where Muscovites do not do well in Uzbeck, Georgian, or Byelorussian, to say nothing of the various Uralic dialects. It is still less true of Chinese, where some so-called dialects are so divergent that in many parts of the world they would be called separate languages. Thus if either Russian or Chinese is to become a world language, some time and considerable standardization will be imperative, but of course in autocratic countries standardization is easier than it is in democracies. In China, Northern Mandarin has been standardized and is said to be spreading very rapidly through required teaching in the schools.

Distribution is important, and here again, thanks to the British Empire, to British exploration and colonization, to British maritime industry, English is far in the lead, being spread over the world as is no other tongue, in both written and oral forms. Chinese would be second, of course, but is not widely spread outside the Orient. Russian is mainly local, and while it is spreading as a learned language with the growth of Russian science and scholarship, it has little overseas currency except as a learned language. Prestige also is important, and here again English ranks far above Russian or Chinese. The prestige of French is still high, but prestige alone will not support a language, and French must be ruled out on other considerations.

Of great importance is the alphabet. The written form of a language is almost always secondary, of course, but it can be significant, particularly for the learned and official functions of language. Here again English is far in the van. It uses the Latin alphabet, the only alphabet that with its descendants is expanding much. Chinese has no alphabet at all, and hence is at a great disadvantage, although the Chinese government is endeavoring to move toward an adapted Latin alphabet and may succeed in doing so. Most of the alphabets of the world stem from the Latin alphabet and preserve their source in their resemblances; most unwritten languages are adopting the Latin alphabet when they are written; many languages that have been written in an alphabet other than Latin are adopting the Latin alphabet; few if any languages that use Latin letters are abandoning them. Thus, if we are not to have a world language, it would seem clear that we are to have a world alphabet, and of the three potential world languages, English is the only one that now uses it.

In some ways, the Russian alphabet is better. It was more or less consciously devised by adapting the Greek alphabet to the Russian language.[13] Devising alphabets works much better than devising languages; for example, an adequate writing system was devised by a moderately educated Cherokee. Cyrillic was presumably devised in the ninth century and has undergone revision extending into present times. It has more than thirty characters, depending upon which symbols are counted as letters, as compared with twenty-six for English. Thus the Russian alphabet comes closer than does the English to the ideal of one symbol for each sound and one sound for each symbol. On the other hand, Cyrillic uses some badly made letters. The Latin alphabet underwent centuries of simplifications; most of the forms are relatively simple, neat, and not much subject to confusion. Russian letters, on the other hand, tend to be messy; they have too many strokes, too many curlicues, too many diacritical marks, and too many letters readily confused with other letters. For example, е is not the same as ё, и not the same as й; ь is not the same as ъ, and neither is what much of the world means by *b*. The symbols ш and щ represent quite different sounds and letters. Furthermore, the printed and the script forms of the letters differ considerably. Thus Russian presents an initial rebuff for a user of any other language; actually, learning a new alphabet is not difficult, but it looks hard and it discourages dabbling in the language. Any reader of a language that uses a Latin alphabet can make something of a guess at the pronunciation of any other language using that alphabet, but to a reader of Latin letters, Russian looks like strange insects scattered over the page.

What can we say of the internal competence of these languages? Here we should consider at least spelling, grammar, and vocabulary. As for spelling, all the world knows that English spelling is chaotic and that little is being done about it. Chinese, in effect, has no spelling at all, and the worst spelling could not be so complex and confused as is the Chinese use of ideographs, complicated as they are by tone. Russian is clearly the best in this, if not entirely phonetic. Russian is not so phonetic as Spanish, but Spanish is ruled out on other grounds.

Simplifying spelling is not easy, for, as we have seen, it is a social and political problem, not mainly a language problem. If the United States were to adopt a simplified spelling system, would the British accept it? Probably not; they will not accept even *labor* as against *labour*. If the Indians were to adopt a simplified spelling system, would the apartheid South Africans accept it? Certainly not. A start is being made with what are called the Initial Teaching Alphabet and the Augmented Roman

---

[13] It is called Cyrillic for the Saint Cyril who is presumed to have devised it, but how much credence should be granted this legend is a matter of dispute.

Alphabet, both of which attempt to provide a phonemic alphabet by restricting the use of the symbols at present recognized and adding a few more. These alphabets seem to increase learning rates, both for small children and non-native speakers, but as yet they have been used at only the most elementary levels. Something might be done, however, for adults. Personally, I believe that a spelling commission, adequately constituted, could standardize the words coming into the language, and thus keep English spelling from growing worse, which it is at present, but if we must prophesy the future on the basis of present conduct, not much spelling reform can be expected in English for some time. And the more English becomes a world language, the more complicated the reform will be.

What of grammar? Although all grammars inherit strange and unnecessary quirks, so far as we know, all are adequate. They apparently serve to express whatever their users are able to think, and although they tend to be conservative and not to change rapidly, they can grow when they need to. Thus we have no reason to believe that any of these great languages would be inadequate grammatically for anything that could be required of a world language, but presumably a simple grammar is easier to learn than a complicated one. Here, again, English does not do badly; English and Russian spring from the same grammar, that of Indo-European, but English has sprung farther, jettisoning, as we have seen, most of its inflections and developing analytic devices in their stead. Russian has been doing the same thing, but much less of it, so that Russian has now moved about as far toward distribution as English had gone a thousand years ago. It seems not to be simplifying very rapidly just now. As for Chinese, it is said to be even more analytic— and hence presumably easier in this respect—than English, getting on without inflections for number, articles for the noun, a conjugated verb, and the like.

In vocabulary Chinese is weakest, since until recently it had borrowed few words from any of the other great languages, and it is particularly weak in words for science and technology. The result is that these words must now be borrowed from abroad, in which case they are difficult for natives, or they must be concocted from native roots and remain difficult for non-natives. Since Chinese does not have an accepted alphabet, arranging words in sequence becomes extremely complicated; only an accomplished student of the language can use a Chinese dictionary.

Russian is intermediate. Since it is an Indo-European language, it has cognates with all western European languages—except oddments like Basque—and with Sanskrit and Hindi in India. It has borrowed heavily, and by very interesting patterns. Russian culture stemmed from Greek, and hence Greek words flowed into it as Latin words flowed into western European languages, although less extensively. When, in the seventeenth and eighteenth centuries, Russian nobility and intellectuals admired French culture, French words came in, for fashionable things, for education, for government, for learning, for the arts. With the ascendancy of German science and technology in the nineteenth century, German words arrived, followed by English words, first in British forms, now mainly in American. Parts of tractors, airplanes, refrigerating equipment, moving pictures, and the like are usually represented in Russian by American borrowings. Furthermore, Russian vocabulary is growing rapidly, especially in the key areas of science and technology. Thus, so far as vocabulary goes, Russian would not do badly as a world language.

English vocabulary is superb. It presumably constitutes the largest body of words ever brought together in one language, and it is growing at an astonishing rate. Of course bigness is not necessarily a virtue, but bigness in vocabulary usually is. The more words are available, the more precise each word can be. A language will be only as precise as the users of the language make it, and we have already heard some gloomy prophets who fear that English is becoming more slovenly; I know of no reliable evidence that would justify these fears, and although the question of improvement or decline in the precision of modern English is probably not subject to certain solution, we may plausibly assume that with more and better education, with more and better linguistic tools, with more complex cultural and intellectual life, precision in language is not likely to decline.

English vocabulary has other advantages. It profits, as Russian does, from having cognates with all other Indo-European tongues, and it has profited even more than has Russian from its borrowings. The borrowings are more extensive than are those of Russian and come from a greater variety of languages, and English relies more upon the Latin tradition, which has become the ancestor of more language and of more important languages than has Greek—French, Spanish, Italian, Portuguese. Wherever these languages are known, reading English is much easier than reading Russian or Chinese, and learning English is easier.[14] English profits, also, from the variety of its vocabulary; as we have seen, it is rich in tough, terse native words, and in complex and mellifluous growths from Latin or Greek, and the latter provide still greater variety

---

[14] To appreciate the usefulness, for the learning of languages, of participation in the Indo-European language family, see Lancelot Hogben, *The Mother Tongue* (London: Secker & Warburg, 1964; New York: Norton, 1965).

through Romance channels like French, Italian, and Spanish. Furthermore, English participates in—is quite probably the leader in—the international growth of science and technology that accounts for the greatest body of new words, one of the most active bodies of specialized words. These terms, mainly derived from Latin and Greek in accordance with practices long familiar to speakers of English, are of unusual importance for emergent countries. Thus if the English vocabulary is not the best of all possible vocabularies for world use, it would seem to be, without a close second, the best that has ever been developed to serve the needs of emergent peoples.

Should users of English do anything to further their speech as a world language? From what we know of language we must conclude that English-speakers cannot do much about it, even if they want to. If English were not potentially a world language, no amount of tinkering, doctoring, and promoting would make it one. But it does have that potential, and if we cannot control its growth, we may be able to direct it a bit. At least two things we might do. First, we could try to do something about spelling. Tinkering with spelling can be dangerous, and reforming it is not easy, but it can be reformed; it is, after all, a formal system, man-made, in part deliberately made, and it is much easier to alter than more basic aspects of language—grammar and pronunciation, for example. Second, we should encourage the learning of English as a second language. This we are doing rather well, and better every year; partly this was deliberate, promoted by all sorts of individuals and agencies, but partly we blundered into it. We should not blunder out; whatever economy axes may do to other parts of foreign aid programs, the program to help people learn English should be expanded rather than curtailed. In the end, we may do more good for world peace, for the well-being of a free, democratic world, with our precious heritage of the English language than with any other tool we have been given or have devised.

We may probably assume that we shall not deliberately debase our language. Languages suffer from abuse, not from use, and I am not here referring to anything so restricted as usage, the supposed correctness of language and the deliberate attempt to be "incorrect." We have recently, I take it, at the deliberate instance of an advertiser, reduced the functioning use of *as* and have vested this use in *like*. Sensitive ears are affronted by the change, but the language will probably not suffer. During the last two thousand years hundreds of means of expressing relationships have grown, thrived, and been replaced. Old English used *hwa hwæt swa* (who what so), *ða hwil ðe* (though while the), and many more that are now so strange that they cannot be reduced accurately to modern equivalents. Most of them have vanished or have changed, but the language has not become incoherent. Advertisers have deliberately made *cozy corner* into *kozee korner, slow* into *slo,* and *easy* into *EZ,* but spelling has not become less authoritarian, and these are not the words that learners mainly misspell. In fact, distortions of language can apparently be tortuous without notable damage, very much as a contortionist can twist the body out of shape and do no more to it than make it supple.

Some distortion of language probably is abuse, however, since it uses language to twist mental processes and warp minds—and in turn the minds warp the language. This sort of thing was apparently done as national policy in Hitler Germany, and it is still practiced in some Communist countries. Lately, East Germany, in what was described as a reform move, banned calling Western peoples *carrion vultures, imperialist bloodsuckers, dehumanized bandits, scum and dregs of humanity,* and *moneybag hyenas,* and forbade calling a specific Western statesman a *delirious subhuman being* or a *despoiler of corpses.*[15] We are not likely to have to enforce any such recantation for either British or American English, for although we may have indulged during war in such terms as *Hun*—which certainly harmed us more than they did the enemy—we have not deliberately subverted the language to the supposed needs of the state, and we probably shall not do so.

So much for English as a world language. What of English and world society? Here we must observe a curious concatenation, a working together of politics, geography, the knowledge explosion, democracy, the mass media, and education, along with language. In one sense the United States is the new British Empire, though an empire based on commercial and technological colonies, not on political colonies, so that the centers of world power are the U.S.S.R., which holds the center of the Eurasian heartland, the great land mass, and the United States, which more than any other nation directs sea and air power. From its relatively safe base in the New World—safe at least for the present and presumably for the near future—it is the center of flexible, far-ranging power, as the U.S.S.R. is the center of relatively fixed, land-based power. In all this it is helped by the English language, and it helps English.

Still more permeating is the interreliance of language with cultural forces. Here the name *Nieuw Amsterdam* was curiously prophetic, for the old Amsterdam played a fructifying role in Europe and the world. In population it has never been the greatest of cities; it spoke a language

---

[15] I have used a summary in *Inside the ACD,* VII (1954), no. 1.

but little known, and it was the center of what was never more than a secondary power, usually not even that. But it sat at the crossroads of Europe, it had maritime sinews, it was wealthy, and it was tolerant. Almost anyone could go there, and many did, especially those who were in bad trouble for good reasons. If the Bible could not be translated in England, it could be translated in Holland, printed there, and exported. If a freethinker was not free to think in Spain or Italy or Germany or France, he was likely to be able to think, write, and publish in Amsterdam, even though he was a heretic. Thus for centuries the Netherlands was the center of intellectual ferment, the home more than any other of those who live with ideas and grow them. All this was made possible by the essential democracy of the Netherlands and the availability of French, and especially of Latin, as world languages.

Now all this is changed. Latin is no longer a world language, and if French still is a world language it is, as we have seen, giving way to English. Refugees no longer go mainly to Amsterdam, for mainly refugees no longer flee—they are drawn. True, some thinkers still flee; as an example, within recent years in the same week a violinist fled from persecution in China and a daughter of Stalin fled restraints in the U.S.S.R. Both came to the United States. They will enjoy personal freedom, and they will profit from the American thirst for art and knowledge, but they are the exceptions. Most of the surge of brains and culture to the New World answers to a pull, not a push.

This is not to say that London and Paris are no longer intellectual, as well as political, capitals. They are, as are many other cities, including Moscow and Peking, but the great fact here is the combination of the English language with American wealth, American industry, American mass media of communication, and the American system of research and higher education. The resulting drift, called the "brain drain," is pulling brains from all over the world, but the surge does not rest solely upon this bringing together of elite. In almost any American research institute, on almost any faculty, on almost any publisher's list, even in any musical organization, the bulk of the individuals will be natives, so that the results seem to come not only from the importation of brains, but also through the cross-fertilization of brains. Notably, also, the knowledge explosion is not restricted to a single center. True, in the mass media New York and Hollywood occupy unique positions, but more important probably is the system of research, technology, and higher education, and this is spread throughout the nation. The center, if there is a center, is not a geographical place but a system, the great complex of higher education, and this no longer relies upon a Harvard or a Yale. The land is now dotted with dozens and hundreds of capable universities and research institutes, any of which will welcome any man from anywhere, so long as he brings with him a brain, sound training, and an idea. The American educational and research system, which has no close competitor anywhere in the extent and breadth of its interest, is thus in a way the new Amsterdam, and we are apparently now only in its early stages. The United States, with the English language and its educational resources, is leading the world into whatever the new era offers, and although this new world is most apparent in science and industry, it is rooted deeply in a new hospitality to the wise, the radical, the alert of all persuasions. After the racial and national melting pot in the New World we have the intellectual melting pot, a ferment that in the end is likely to be much more significant for the world.

One more prophecy must detain us: as the United States has moved toward an urban-centered society, the pattern of dialectal growth has shifted. The drift will continue. Formerly, on this continent as in many places, languages and dialects have moved toward land that was unused or underused; for North America, migration toward land meant colonization west across the Atlantic and then infiltration west across the continent. Recently, American dialects have moved toward industry and culture, toward cities. A new body of speech has appeared in Miami Beach, with a Northern-Midland enclave growing in a Southern area, and in Houston with a new Texan subdialect, but most dramatically new bodies of speech now flourish with the transplanting of blacks to northern ghettos. The dialects of these newcomers are not submerged as the language of migrants usually has been; the blacks occupy inner cities in process of being abandoned, and crowded together they maintain their speech. The result is a whole new scattering of language communities, reflecting Southern-speaking areas of origin and the impact of new urban concentrations. Although these dialectal groups are not as yet well defined, some patterns are emerging. Harlem speech is old enough to be distinctive. It differs from black speech in the Washington-Baltimore area, which was influenced first from the Piedmont and later from the plantation culture of the southern coastal plain. Middle Western cities like Chicago, Detroit, and Cleveland have ghettos harboring Gulf dialects, including those of New Orleans and Memphis, along with Highland Southern speech from south of the Ohio River. Watts reflects Texas and doubtless other areas. To plot these burgeoning dialects will require more use of linguistic geography, but meanwhile we can notice that black speech has developed dramatically in the past fifty years and that it promises to continue spawning urban-centered speech communities.

Thus in many areas, both in language itself and in its relations with men, the future of American English can, within limits, be extrapolated.

24

MAN AND LANGUAGE: LANGUAGE AND MAN

This is the end of the line.

In all voyages, some travelers will look forward to the destination. Others may enjoy the ride or the view out the window. These last should be told, what they have doubtless concluded, that this exploration has come to nothing so final as a depot. They can stop now without missing much. For those interested in destinations, however, we should ask ourselves where we are.

First we should recall that, in planning this book, I proposed examining two usual states of language, the one peaceful and sedentary, the other aggressive and in motion. For the first we used the Amerindian tongues, for the second the Indo-European, especially Spanish and English. We can now observe that the similarities between these groups are greater than the differences. Apparently language lives so much by its own lights and its own laws that, within limits, it goes its own way, regardless of circumstances. If its speakers all die, it too may disappear, but while it lives, it follows in a broad way its own laws—for example, it continues to change, but grammar and sound change slowly and mainly from within, while specialized vocabulary changes rapidly and is subject to borrowing.

Differences can be observed, however, and they may be significant. Our sample is too restricted to be reliable, and no samples are entirely representative—many of the most important Amerindian cultures did not survive to be studied, the Inca and the Aztec, for example, and no great widespread Amerindian tongue worked side by side with an invading language for a long period, nothing like the conflict of French and English in Canada, or between the same languages in England during the Middle Ages. Similarly, American English is not the most typical of examples; once it had triumphed and had become the accepted means of communication for a great body of people, once it had become what I have called "mature," it had little time in which to indulge this maturing in tranquility. Two world wars heavily damaged all other great powers, and during the same period a new technology, centered to a considerable degree in the United States, forced the new nation into a role that it had never much coveted. From having been a colonial, importing nation, the United States became an exporter of culture and language, with only the briefest of transitions. That is, American English has never much lived, as have most languages, as the nearly unique means of communication for a relatively stable people. And here we should remind ourselves that peace and stability must be natural to language, which could have started only with such surroundings. Furthermore, most languages must have done much of their growing in relative peace and stability, not much intruding and not much intruded upon. American English, on the other hand, developed in conflict, and once it had become established it moved rapidly into international world turmoil that has no parallel in the past, and it seems now to be spreading into limitless space.

Still, the sample provides basis for informed guessing. First we might notice that our evidence gives us no reason to believe that war stimulates language, except in spectacular ways and usually for transient phenomena. Of the peoples we have studied, the great innovators, the great producers of language and languages, were the Amerindians. They developed thousands of dialects having distinctive qualities, but running through this welter of forms and devices we can observe widespread principles, principles sufficiently common to encourage a conviction that much of this linguistic wealth grows from the elaboration of relatively few parent tongues. Of course, we do not know that the somewhat sedentary lives of most Amerindians in recent times caused their linguistic fertility; there must have been a time when the Amerindians were moving into an unoccupied continent, when languages were fragmenting. Perhaps fragmentation, not peace, encouraged the growth of languages among the aborigines, but social stability seems not to have inhibited language in any dominant way. Perhaps we may assume that both space and peace encourage linguistic fertility.

On the other hand, languages in motion and in conflict reveal their own patterns of change—and here we should notice that languages are almost never in lively conflict unless at least one of them is in motion or has recently been so. All languages we observed changed with motion and conflict, but the changes seemed to come from within, and to be conservative rather than inventive, as though the languages had closed ranks in the presence of danger. The notably invading languages, English and Spanish, have both become more nearly standardized in the New World than in the old; curiously, they seem also to have standardized in similar ways, and insofar as we have evidence from the Amerindian languages in motion or in conflict, these tongues seem to confirm the evidence of the Indo-European languages. They did not noticeably balloon when they encountered a new and hostile culture, or if they did, the change was set in motion through new industry or social change. The coming of the horse culture to the plains brought unprecedented prosperity to the Amerindians and apparently stimulated some dialectal development, but the slaughtering of the Six Nations brought no similar efflorescence. War may promote trade, and the trade may promote language, but apparently war, at least for those who lose, induces the culture to draw in upon itself, to inhibit all sorts of cultural interchange, including language.

Something can be observed about the dialects of languages in motion. Not only are the new dialects less diverse than the old, but they have identifiable qualities, since emigrants are selected at the source, partly by accident, but partly by what we might call natural tendency. The geographical source may be accidental; the early emigrants from both England and Spain came from the southern portions of those countries, but this is surely a coincidence growing from other circumstances. On the other hand, the exported dialects were mainly middle-class and lower middle-class, and selection of this sort would seem to be inherent in the nature of popular movements, since the poorest people cannot move in great numbers and since the wealthiest do not want to. Thus the movement of an aggressive language leads to an efflorescence of certain dialects, these dialects somewhat blended with one another, but coming from intermediate social classes, however they may be distributed geographically. Of course, other sorts of migration are possible, but they are probably rare.

A word might be added on the role of dialect in migration. Among sedentary peoples dialect is secondary; Amerindians of the Great Basin have preserved many dialects, and they are themselves aware of these, but one does not observe that any group of these peoples has fared better or worse because of his dialect. Now that the United States has become the user of a sedentary language, the importance of dialect has declined; that Senator John F. Kennedy came from Massachusetts and Senator Lyndon B. Johnson from Texas, and that both spoke distinctive dialects, did not prevent either from being elected President. Similarly, among languages in motion, dialect did not much matter, provided these tongues were not to survive; that is, if they were what I have called moribund colonial languages, dialect mattered little, except that it might somewhat increase the generally disruptive power of any second speech.

In the dominant languages, on the other hand, the role of dialect is quite different; here the dialects of the immigrants did much to determine the speech of the newly occupied area. What was dialectal in the area of emigration became standard usage in the language of the land of immigration, and presumably this influence could go so far as to determine the character of a new language, as the dialect of Cuba, for example, may become a new language, if that island continues much isolated from the remainder of South America. Here, of course, social and political factors may enter to supplement the impact of dialect; the flight of the intellectual and cultured classes from Cuba will enhance the importance of the rural and laboring classes and will further speed linguistic change on a dialectal basis. Conversely, dialectal shifts induced by migration may have social and political consequences; presumably part of the dislike that many Britons harbor for all things American stems from the association of American speech with other than prestige dialects in England.

Our evidence seems to suggest further that a disturbance in language like that brought about by the incursion of the Indo-European tongues in the Americas sets up a sequence of about three periods. Before the advent of the language in motion, the native language thrives through natural growth, borrowing by social and economic contact and expanding to meet the needs of the users of the language. When a linguistic invasion begins, both languages tend to become conservative, although each may pick up a few terms from the other or from their conflict—for example, *tomahawk* and *Great White Father*—all more or less altered and mistranslated. After the initial shock, both bodies of languages start developing in special ways; the defeated language borrows terms from the conquering language, and the conquering language indulges in various unusual growths, in name-giving, in new compounds, in bodies of terms such as those reflecting life on river steamboats or the open range. After a time, the third period sets in; the conquering language becomes sedentary, and develops again a balanced, healthy growth—for example, although the nineteenth century in the United States produced picturesque terms like *cayuse* and *gerrymander,* the great increase in American English vocabulary, and most American exportations, are products of the mature period after World War I. By now the new dialect can be expected to have developed new patterns, but it will have returned, also, to some old ones. Some of these are likely to be accelerated: the development of an analytic grammar may have been accelerated in the New World, but it was not started there, and the practice of pillaging the classical tongues for new scientific terms was brought from the Old World, however it may have flourished in its new home.

During all this, polyglotism has played some role, and so far as our

AMERICAN ENGLISH COMES OF AGE

evidence suggests, the cause of this polyglotism does not matter much, although the mingling of languages must usually stem from the movement of peoples. Mingling encourages some borrowing of terminology, whether the language picks up *boss* from Dutch speakers in New York or *rodeo* from Spanish speakers in the Southwest, but these impacts are minor, more picturesque than permeating. On the other hand, polyglotism seems to encourage the breakdown of languages from within; apparently sounds change more readily, the grammar simplifies, and growths already in process may be accelerated. This would seem to be true among the Amerindians saying "Me go now," among the African slaves saying "Dey ben" as an inclusive predication, and in ghettos everywhere. For limited times and groups the influence is clear; for larger groups and longer periods, such impacts, if they exist, are harder to detect, but they may be sufficiently broad and permeating to have great eventual impact. For example, we have some reasons to postulate that American English grammar is simpler than the grammar of British English, and that it has moved more rapidly toward analysis than has the more sedentary British speech. If polyglotism has had any such impact as this—although as we have seen, such a generalization would be difficult to demonstrate in the present state of our knowledge—its importance is considerable, whether good or bad. Many students of language would consider such simplifications and developments mainly to the good, although many laymen, who tend to resent change of any sort, would assume they are bad. Recalling our earlier observation as to what war between the whites and the Amerindians did to their speech, we might suggest a curious contrast: that war between peoples may inhibit change in language, but that war between languages, as evidenced in polyglotism, may accelerate it.

With so much by way of introduction we may raise once more our fundamental questions, and if we now inquire whether man has influenced language and language has influenced man, the answer is a clear and emphatic yes. If, however, we then ask how much man has influenced language and how much language has influenced man, we shall have to reply as certainly that we do not know. Thus, the question should be phrased something like this: In what ways and to what degrees have man and language reacted upon each other? Here the answers are likely to be hazier and less reliable than we could wish, but the questions can be broached.

First we must notice that if man and language are interreliant, they are also self-reliant. Man has made language; or at least he is responsible for much of its present state. Languages about which we know a great deal seem to have been changing during the past two or three thousand years in accordance with the same fundamental principles. Man obviously is making language now, and thus if it was not originally his conscious creation, we must still assume that he made all of it or much of it, and that it must stem from what, in a very broad sense, he "wanted." On the other hand, although it is his creature, it is also independent of him. It works in ways he never consciously intended, and it has done in some particulars what he did not want it to do. Even when he understands language, he often can do nothing about it; for example, we believe that the word *houses* was once pronounced so that it would rhyme with *you Sis,* that is, /husɪs/. This change came about through the working of linguistic principles, through the voicing of a voiced consonant—/s/ became /z/—when it appeared between vowels or terminally after vowels, since vowels are voiced. If man were now to resent this change, and endeavor to change /z/ back to /s/ he would find himself impotent in the face of the powers of language, with the working of a law that operates within language and without the will of man. Examples like this could be multiplied infinitely.

Of the two sorts of interreliance, the impact of man upon language is the more apparent. After all, made made language, or much of it, and that is influence with a vengeance. It is perhaps most apparent in vocabulary, where we can observe that man's activities influenced language extensively and directly, sometimes even self-consciously. Modern scientists deliberately make words, and technological developments result in new words, in space and automation for example, even though the promoters of these activities are absorbed in the subjects themselves and the growth of vocabulary is only incidental. Similarly, men kill words, although usually not deliberately; an occasional word may suffer from a taboo, but most of those that disappear famish from neglect. The terms for medieval armor have mostly vanished because the armor became scrap or museum pieces.

Man has had less impact upon other aspects of language. He has influenced usage a little; we teach children not to say *ain't* and to avoid other discredited four-letter and five-letter words, but linguistically we are here engaged in much ado about very little, and often with little effect. Among modern American speakers, the few deplore obscuring the distinction between *like* and *as,* but the many continue to obscure it. Most usages go happily about their business of becoming popular or unpopular without rising to man's awareness. Similarly, man consciously changes sounds, although not many sounds and not much. There is some effort to replace the /n/ phoneme with the /ŋ/ phoneme in terminal positions—that is, to discourage what is called "dropping g's"—some effort to use the so-called broad *a*—/a/ rather than /æ/—but mainly sounds do not change much, and when they do, they mostly change by linguistic principles and drifts of which the users of language are unaware.

Similarly, English grammar has changed without much of man's conscious help. During the last thousand years or so revolutionary changes have swept through English, perhaps particularly American English, but the users of the language have been largely unaware of these changes. Had they known, linguistic policemen might have tried to stop them; had anyone been able to say, in a nationally audible way, "We are losing our precious heritage of an inflectional system, and being invaded by a new, radical, untried, analytic principle boring from within," the Watch and Ward Society, the Committee on Un-American Activities, or some medieval equivalent of the John Birch Society might have aroused the English-speaking peoples to save our dying grammar. No one made such protests, however, partly because nobody knew what was happening. Even if purists had campaigned to save English inflections and to suppress the rise of word order, their efforts probably would not have come to much; changes in grammar are glacier-like in their movements, hard to detect and hard to stop.

Of course, unconsciously man must have been changing grammar; English grammar has changed broadly and persistently. It is probably still changing, and man must be the instrument if not the inspiration of this change, but what lies back of these changes we do not know. Is it pure accident? shifts in society? some felt need, felt if unexpressed? We do not understand grammar very well. This much can be observed, however; apparently languages always rise to any demand placed upon them; in one way or another the grammar will become sufficiently complex and subtle so that the users of a language always find that the grammar is adequate to anything they are able to think and say. Thus as man grows, he inevitably makes the language grow; the society he evolves makes the language evolve, if any evolution is needed.

Now to the more slippery but more intriguing question, "How has language changed man?" Here again the vocabulary is easiest, for the case is clearest. Most people cannot think much without language, and they cannot think precisely without precise language. As a vocabulary grows and sharpens, it permits broader, sharper use of the mind. Similarly, human interest in an area—whether the area be South American potatoes as food or North American microtechnology as a basis for rocketry—the interest provides terms, and the new terms presumably promote new interest. How pervasive is this impact of words upon mind? We cannot at this time say with any precision, but the impact is obviously there, and it is considerable. In some areas it is startling, as in psychiatry and psychoanalysis.

Biologically or psychologically, usage probably has very little impact upon man. How does it change a person, whether he says *ain't I* or *am I not?* Socially, however, the impact may be tremendous. To a large measure a person is known by the language he keeps, and as society becomes more complex, as everybody knows more people but knows them less, the casual impressions based upon usage become more and more important. Most usages, once firmly acquired, stay with the user for life, and thus usages influence men's lives in multitudinous ways, of which the speakers are variously conscious.

Sound is rather similar. Phonetically, all sounds are good, and most languages have a handsome range of them, but for an individual speaker, one should be as beneficial as another. We do not use glottal clicks, but we should probably be neither better nor worse off if we did. Of course, pronunciation becomes involved in usage; one pronunciation is thought of as right and another as wrong, and thus pronunciations are shibboleths. The sound of language can provide an art form, and thus a means of art, even for those persons who cannot afford pianos or have not been born into an affluent society. And art is clearly very deep in man, very much one of his needs.

What of grammar and man? The pattern of grammar is rooted in patterns of thinking; rationally one would assume that it must do something to pattern the minds that use the language. If so, the evidence is hard to come by. All grammars are different, but all grammars seem to be adequate to their users, and so quantitatively we have no evidence at all. Qualitatively the evidence is difficult to sift; should not a grammar based upon change of form affect minds differently from a grammar based upon change of position and grouping of units? One should suppose so, but we do not know how. Should not a grammar that requires its users to decide how far away is every object, how apprehensible it may be to the speaker, whether it is stationary or moving, encourage a sense of space in users of the language? One would expect so, and some Amerindians who have such grammars seem to possess a notable consciousness of space, as white speakers who use a language which involves tense in the verb seem to be remarkably aware of time, but for the present such assumptions must remain assumptions. Would not a language that requires the user, every time he makes an assertion, to decide on what authority he makes it promote an awareness of evidence, and of the importance of its validity? One might assume so, and Whorf apparently believed he had evidence that such a grammar had that effect, but here, once more, the conclusions have been contested.

What about the whole sense of reality that is embodied in language, what does it do to man? Must not languages as wholes affect men as wholes, so that man and the world he inhabits are only in part realities, and are in part reflections of the language he has inherited? Within limits this must be true, and scholars like Whorf have guessed that those limits are very large, but if they are large, they are as yet hazy.

Consider, for example, the possible role of language in the evolution of man. It is man's great virtue that he can use language, and his great limitation apparently that he must, for if man has supersensory powers we know little of them. When man forsook his arboreal habitat for the solid earth, when he moved from *homo haerens* to *homo ambiens,* he brought several abilities and possibilities with him, or he soon acquired them. He had an opposable thumb, which permitted him to use tools dexterously; he has been developing that ability ever since, has developed such tools that he can now live in ease and comfort and has even devised tools which permit him to live in the air and to travel in space. He either was a carnivore or he became one, and thus was able to devour the stored energy of fauna and not have to spend much of his time chewing and digesting the relatively non-nourishing flora. And he possessed a brain of such complexity that he could use it to reason and to devise and use language.

Now we should notice that biological evolution had apparently provided man with these abilities, but if man is still evolving biologically, scientists are not as yet able to demonstrate the fact. Possibly man has stopped developing as an organism; more likely he is changing so slowly that the alterations are imperceptible during the brief period that scientists have been capable of observing, or he is not now in one of those periods that organisms may occasionally experience, when change greatly accelerates. Obviously, however, human change has accelerated in recent decades, and these changes must be included in "evolution," insofar as this term is definable. We cannot say that man is now more moral, or more pious, or more gentle than he was; but on the other hand we cannot say that Cro-Magnon man was more moral than Peking or Neanderthal man, although we must assume that Cro-Magnon man was more "advanced." Using anything like objective measurements, then, man has advanced greatly in the last few decades; man now has more goods, more know-how, more security, more highly developed skills, a more complex society, and more ability to use his mind rationally than any body of men has ever possessed before. That is, we must assume that whether or not biological evolution has ceased, social evolution has accelerated, that social evolution is much more rapid than biological evolution, and that in our present state it promises to carry man farther and faster than did any earlier sort of evolution. Ptolemy may have been nearer to being right than we have supposed; if man's earth is not the center of the universe, his mind may be.

To spell this out, one might note some theories of modern biology as embodied, for example, in Pierre Teilhard de Chardin's *Le Phénomène Humain.*[1] Teilhard reviews the growth of world and the growths of life, which he thinks of as layers in expanded being. Recently, we entered a new layer, not a layer of anything physical except that man is physical and his concept must be a physical reality, space-time, an insight that already has pushed man farther into evolution. And now, Teilhard believes, we are entering the next great stage in evolution; as he puts it, "Under our modern disquiet, what is forming and growing is nothing less than an organic crisis in evolution," an evolution that springs from "the terrible gift of foresight," in a new layer of earth where the next "great game" is being played, in which "we are the players as well as . . . the cards and the stakes." That is, we are entering a layer of earth which is mind, and mind thinks with language, expresses by means of language, and receives through language. If Teilhard is right—and many scientists agree with him—man is entering the great age of his evolution, when growth comes from mind, and to a marked degree, so far as we know, language is the means of mind.

And now we have returned to language. Language and the ability to use language apparently provided man with the tools he needed to become human; certainly they permitted him to develop and preserve civilization. As society developed, communication with language and the promotion of thought through language have become ever more crucial, and apparently as man continues to acquire understandings and competences, language will be even more important. Man could not have gone to the moon merely with an opposable thumb, not even with an opposable thumb and a new outer brain, but with a thumb and a brain and language he can go, and so far as we can now foresee, his evolution may be unlimited. He may be able even to evolve beyond language, but if he does, language will have been one of the tools with which he developed that power.

Thus, although the influence of man upon language is relatively apparent, the influence of language upon man may, in the end, prove to have been the more potent.

What of the more mysterious aspects of man, those parts of his nature of which we know little? Is language there also? Clearly, it is. The probing of psychoanalysis reveals that somewhere below or above or beyond man's conscious knowledge of himself are forces very strange and frighteningly powerful. And there, too, are hints of language. Terms

---

[1] *The Phenomenon of Man,* rev. ed., trans. Bernard Wall (New York and Evanston: Harper & Row, 1965); original, 1955. See perhaps especially pp. 214–15, 224, 229–30.

are tossed up in dreams and in psychiatric insights, but of what storms these are the flotsam we often do not know, nor do we understand the strange craft of which this flotsam may be the wreckage. Even in the innermost parts of man we find language, but often we know little of what language is doing there.

INDEX